First Published 2024

FiNGERPRINT! CLASSICS
Prakash Books

Fingerprint Publishing
@FingerprintP
@fingerprintpublishingbooks
www.fingerprintpublishing.com

ISBN: 978 93 6214 606 9

"But nothing is lasting in this world. Even joy begins to fade after only one minute. Two minutes later, and it is weaker still, until finally it is swallowed up in our everyday, prosaic state of mind, just as a ripple made by a pebble gradually merges with the smooth surface of the water."

Nikolai Vasilyevich Gogol (1809–1852) stands as one of the most enigmatic and influential figures in Russian literature. Born in the small Ukrainian village of Sorochyntsi, Gogol was the third of 12 children. His early life in the rural heartland of the Russian Empire profoundly influenced his literary works, which often feature vivid depictions of Ukrainian folklore, landscapes, and provincial life.

Gogol's father, a minor landowner and an amateur playwright, instilled in him a love for literature and storytelling. This early exposure to theatrical works and folklore shaped his unique narrative style, characterized by a blend of realism and fantasy. After completing his education at the Nizhyn Gymnasium of Higher Sciences, Gogol moved to Saint Petersburg in 1828, hoping to make a name for himself as a writer and public servant.

Gogol's early years in Saint Petersburg were marked by hardship and disappointment. His first published work, a romantic poem, was a failure, and his attempts to secure a stable government position were thwarted by bureaucratic indifference. However, his fortunes changed in 1831 with the publication of Evenings on a Farm Near Dikanka, a collection of short stories that drew heavily on Ukrainian folklore and culture. The collection was well-received, earning Gogol critical acclaim and establishing him as a rising star in Russian literature.

Gogol's most celebrated work, Dead Souls, was published in 1842. This novel, which he described as an "epic poem in prose," offers a satirical yet poignant exploration of Russian society. Through the misadventures of its anti-hero, Chichikov, Gogol presents a vivid tableau of the moral and spiritual decay afflicting the Russian aristocracy and bureaucracy. Dead Souls is widely regarded as one of the greatest works of Russian literature and a precursor to the great Russian novels of the 19th century.

In addition to his prose, Gogol made significant contributions to Russian drama. His most famous play, The Inspector General (also known as The Government Inspector), premiered in 1836. This biting satire of bureaucratic corruption and human folly was met with both acclaim and controversy, as it exposed the widespread inefficiency and moral decay within Russian officialdom. The play's enduring popularity lies in its timeless themes and Gogol's sharp wit, making it a staple of Russian theater.

In addition to this, his short story, "The Overcoat" is often regarded as a masterpiece of Russian literature, celebrated for its deep empathy for the marginalized, its incisive social critique, and its haunting, surreal atmosphere. The story's impact on Russian literature is profound, with many later writers, including Fyodor Dostoevsky and Leo Tolstoy, acknowledging Gogol's influence. As Dostoevsky famously remarked, "We all came out from Gogol's 'Overcoat'," underscoring the story's seminal role in shaping the literary landscape of 19th-century Russia.

Despite his literary success, Gogol's life was marked by personal turmoil and spiritual crisis. Deeply religious, he became increasingly preoccupied with matters of faith and morality. This inner conflict culminated in the dramatic burning of the second volume of Dead Souls in 1852, an act that symbolized Gogol's struggle with his creative and spiritual demons.

Gogol's health deteriorated rapidly, and he died on March 4, 1852, in Moscow. He was only 42 years old. Gogol's unique narrative voice and his exploration of the absurdities of provincial life resonated with readers, cementing his reputation as a master storyteller.

Contents

Dead Souls   **9**

   Introduction By John Cournos   11
   Preparer's Note   13
   Author's Preface to the First Portion of This Work   15
   Dead Souls   19

Play   **359**

   The Inspector-General   361

Short Stories   **483**

   The Overcoat   485
   The Nose   513
   Memoirs of a Madman   537

DEAD SOULS

Translated by D. J. Hogarth

Introduction By John Cournos

Nikolai Vasilievich Gogol, born at Sorochintsky, Russia, on 31st March 1809. Obtained government post at St. Petersburg and later an appointment at the university. Lived in Rome from 1836 to 1848. Died on 21st February 1852.

Preparer's Note

The book this was typed from contains a complete Part I, and a partial Part II, as it seems only part of Part II survived the adventures described in the introduction. Where the text notes that pages are missing from the "original", this refers to the Russian original, not the translation.

All the foreign words were italicised in the original, a style not preserved here. Accents and diphthongs have also been left out.

Author's Preface to the First Portion of This Work

Second Edition published in 1846
From the Author to the Reader

Reader, whosoever or wheresoever you be, and whatsoever be your station—whether that of a member of the higher ranks of society or that of a member of the plainer walks of life—I beg of you, if God shall have given you any skill in letters, and my book shall fall into your hands, to extend to me your assistance.

For in the book which lies before you, and which, probably, you have read in its first edition, there is portrayed a man who is a type taken from our Russian Empire. This man travels about the Russian land and meets with folk of every condition—from the nobly-born to the humble toiler. Him I have taken as a type to show forth the vices and the failings, rather than the merits and the virtues, of the commonplace Russian individual;

and the characters which revolve around him have also been selected for the purpose of demonstrating our national weaknesses and shortcomings. As for men and women of the better sort, I propose to portray them in subsequent volumes. Probably much of what I have described is improbable and does not happen as things customarily happen in Russia; and the reason for that is that for me to learn all that I have wished to do has been impossible, in that human life is not sufficiently long to become acquainted with even a hundredth part of what takes place within the borders of the Russian Empire. Also, carelessness, inexperience, and lack of time have led to my perpetrating numerous errors and inaccuracies of detail; with the result that in every line of the book there is something which calls for correction. For these reasons I beg of you, my reader, to act also as my corrector. Do not despise the task, for, however superior be your education, and however lofty your station, and however insignificant, in your eyes, my book, and however trifling the apparent labour of correcting and commenting upon that book, I implore you to do as I have said. And you too, O reader of lowly education and simple status, I beseech you not to look upon yourself as too ignorant to be able in some fashion, however small, to help me. Every man who has lived in the world and mixed with his fellow men will have remarked something which has remained hidden from the eyes of others; and therefore I beg of you not to deprive me of your comments, seeing that it cannot be that, should you read my book with attention, you will have NOTHING to say at some point therein.

For example, how excellent it would be if some reader who is sufficiently rich in experience and the knowledge of life to be acquainted with the sort of characters which I have described herein would annotate in detail the book, without missing a single page, and undertake to read it precisely as though, laying pen and paper before him, he were first to peruse a few pages of the work, and then to recall his own life, and the lives of folk with whom he has come in contact, and everything which he has seen with his own eyes or has heard of from others, and to proceed to annotate, in so far as may tally with his own experience or otherwise, what is set forth in the book, and to jot down the whole exactly as it stands pictured to his memory, and, lastly, to send me the jottings as they may issue from his pen, and to continue doing so until he has covered the entire work! Yes, he would indeed do me a vital service! Of style or beauty of expression he would need to take no account, for the value of a book lies in its truth and its actuality rather than in its wording. Nor would he need to consider my feelings if at any point he should feel minded to blame or to upbraid me, or to demonstrate the harm rather than the good which has been done through any lack of thought or verisimilitude of which I have been guilty. In short, for anything and for everything in the way of criticism I should be thankful.

Also, it would be an excellent thing if some reader in the higher walks of life, some person who stands remote, both by life and by education, from the circle of folk which I have pictured in my book, but who knows the life of the circle in which he himself revolves, would undertake to read my work in similar fashion, and methodically to recall to his mind any members of superior social classes whom he has met, and carefully to observe whether there exists any resemblance between one such class and another, and whether, at times, there may not be repeated in a higher sphere what is done in a lower, and likewise to note any additional fact in the same connection which may occur to him (that is to say, any fact pertaining to the higher ranks of society which would seem to confirm or to disprove his conclusions), and, lastly, to record that fact as it may have occurred within his own experience, while giving full details of persons (of individual manners, tendencies, and customs) and also of inanimate surroundings (of dress, furniture, fittings of houses, and so forth). For I need knowledge of the classes in question, which are the flower of our people. In fact, this very reason—the reason that I do not yet know Russian life in all its aspects, and in the degree to which it is necessary for me to know it in order to become a successful author—is what has, until now, prevented me from publishing any subsequent volumes of this story.

Again, it would be an excellent thing if some one who is endowed with the faculty of imagining and vividly picturing to himself the various situations wherein a character may be placed, and of mentally following up a character's career in one field and another—by this I mean some one who possesses the power of entering into and developing the ideas of the author whose work he may be reading—would scan each character herein portrayed, and tell me how each character ought to have acted at a given juncture, and what, to judge from the beginnings of each character, ought to have become of that character later, and what new circumstances might be devised in connection therewith, and what new details might advantageously be added to those already described. Honestly can I say that to consider these points against the time when a new edition of my book may be published in a different and a better form would give me the greatest possible pleasure.

One thing in particular would I ask of any reader who may be willing to give me the benefit of his advice. That is to say, I would beg of him to suppose, while recording his remarks, that it is for the benefit of a man in no way his equal in education, or similar to him in tastes and ideas, or capable of apprehending criticisms without full explanation appended, that he is doing so. Rather would I ask such a reader to suppose that before him there stands a man of incomparably inferior enlightenment and schooling—a rude country bumpkin whose life, throughout, has been passed in retirement—a bumpkin to whom it is necessary to explain each circumstance in detail, while never forgetting to be as simple of speech as though he were a child, and at every step there were a danger of employing terms beyond his understanding. Should these precautions be kept constantly in view by any reader undertaking to annotate my book, that reader's remarks will exceed in weight and interest even his own expectations, and will bring me very real advantage.

Thus, provided that my earnest request be heeded by my readers, and that among them there be found a few kind spirits to do as I desire, the following is the manner in which I would request them to transmit their notes for my consideration. Inscribing the package with my name, let them then enclose that package in a second one addressed either to the Rector of the University of St. Petersburg or to Professor Shevirev of the University of Moscow, according as the one or the other of those two cities may be the nearer to the sender.

Lastly, while thanking all journalists and litterateurs for their previously published criticisms of my book—criticisms which, in spite of a spice of that intemperance and prejudice which is common to all humanity, have proved of the greatest use both to my head and to my heart—I beg of such writers again to favour me with their reviews. For in all sincerity I can assure them that whatsoever they may be pleased to say for my improvement and my instruction will be received by me with naught but gratitude.

PART ONE

PART ONE

CHAPTER I

To the door of an inn in the provincial town of N. there drew up a smart britchka—a light spring-carriage of the sort affected by bachelors, retired lieutenant-colonels, staff-captains, land-owners possessed of about a hundred souls, and, in short, all persons who rank as gentlemen of the intermediate category. In the britchka was seated such a gentleman—a man who, though not handsome, was not ill-favoured, not over-fat, and not over-thin. Also, though not over-elderly, he was not over-young. His arrival produced no stir in the town, and was accompanied by no particular incident, beyond that a couple of peasants who happened to be standing at the door of a dramshop exchanged a few comments with reference to the equipage rather than to the individual who was seated in it. "Look at that carriage," one of them said to the other. "Think you it will be going as far as Moscow?" "I think it will," replied his companion. "But not as far as Kazan, eh?" "No, not as far as Kazan." With that the conversation ended.

Presently, as the britchka was approaching the inn, it was met by a young man in a pair of very short, very tight breeches of white dimity, a quasi-fashionable frockcoat, and a dickey fastened with a pistol-shaped bronze tie-pin. The young man turned his head as he passed the britchka and eyed it attentively; after which he clapped his hand to his cap (which was in danger of being removed by the wind) and resumed his way. On the vehicle reaching the inn door, its occupant found standing there to welcome him the polevoi, or waiter, of the establishment—an individual of such nimble and brisk movement that even to distinguish the character of his face was impossible. Running out with a napkin in one hand and his lanky form clad in a tailcoat, reaching almost to the nape of his neck, he tossed back his locks, and escorted the gentleman upstairs, along a wooden gallery, and so to the bedchamber which God had prepared for the gentleman's reception. The said bedchamber was of quite ordinary appearance, since the inn belonged to the species to be found in all provincial towns—the species wherein, for two roubles a day, travellers may obtain a room swarming with black-beetles, and communicating by a doorway with the apartment adjoining. True, the doorway may be blocked up with a wardrobe; yet behind it, in all probability, there will be standing a silent, motionless neighbour whose ears are burning to learn every possible detail concerning the latest arrival. The inn's exterior corresponded with its interior. Long, and consisting only of two storeys, the building had its lower half destitute of stucco; with the result that the dark-red bricks, originally more or less dingy, had grown yet dingier under the influence of atmospheric changes. As for the upper half of the building, it was, of course, painted the usual tint of unfading yellow. Within, on the ground floor, there stood a number of benches heaped with horse-collars, rope, and sheepskins; while the window-seat accommodated a sbitentshik 4, cheek by jowl with a samovar 5—the latter so closely resembling the former in appearance that, but for the fact of the samovar possessing a pitch-black lip, the samovar and the sbitentshik might have been two of a pair.

During the traveller's inspection of his room his luggage was brought into the apartment. First came a portmanteau of white leather whose raggedness indicated that the receptacle had made several previous journeys. The bearers of the same were the gentleman's coachman, Selifan (a little man in a large overcoat), and the gentleman's valet, Petrushka—the latter a fellow of about thirty, clad in a worn, over-ample jacket which formerly had graced his master's shoulders, and possessed of a nose and a pair of lips whose coarseness communicated to his face rather a sullen expression. Behind the portmanteau came a small dispatch-box of redwood, lined with birch bark, a boot-case, and (wrapped in blue paper) a roast fowl; all of which having been deposited, the coachman departed to look after his horses, and the valet to establish himself in the little dark anteroom or kennel where already he had stored a cloak, a bagful of livery, and his own peculiar smell. Pressing the narrow bedstead back against the wall, he covered it with the tiny remnant of mattress—a remnant as thin and flat (perhaps also as greasy) as a pancake—which he had managed to beg of the landlord of the establishment.

While the attendants had been thus setting things straight the gentleman had repaired to the common parlour. The appearance of common parlours of the kind is known to every one who travels. Always they have varnished walls which, grown black in their upper portions with tobacco smoke, are, in their lower, grown shiny with the friction of customers' backs—more especially with that of the backs of such local tradesmen as, on market-days, make it their regular practice to resort to the local hostelry for a glass of tea. Also, parlours of this kind invariably contain smutty ceilings, an equally smutty chandelier, a number of pendent shades which jump and rattle whenever the waiter scurries across the shabby oilcloth with a trayful of glasses (the glasses looking like a flock of birds roosting by the seashore), and a selection of oil paintings. In short, there are certain objects which one sees in every inn. In the present case the only outstanding feature of the room was the fact that in one of the paintings a nymph was portrayed as possessing breasts of a size such as the reader can never in his life have beheld. A similar caricaturing of nature is to be noted in the historical pictures (of unknown origin, period, and creation) which reach us—sometimes through the instrumentality of Russian magnates who profess to be connoisseurs of art—from Italy; owing to the said magnates having made such purchases solely on the advice of the couriers who have escorted them.

To resume, however—our traveller removed his cap, and divested his neck of a parti-coloured woollen scarf of the kind which a wife makes for her husband with her own hands, while accompanying the gift with interminable injunctions as to how best such a garment ought to be folded. True, bachelors also wear similar gauds, but, in their case, God alone knows who may have manufactured the articles! For my part, I cannot endure them. Having unfolded the scarf, the gentleman ordered dinner, and whilst the various dishes were being got ready—cabbage soup, a pie several weeks old, a dish of marrow and peas, a dish of sausages and cabbage, a roast fowl, some salted cucumber, and the sweet tart which stands perpetually ready for use in such establishments; whilst, I say, these things were either being warmed up or brought in cold, the gentleman induced the waiter to retail certain fragments of tittle-tattle concerning the late landlord of the hostelry, the amount of income which the hostelry produced, and the character of its present proprietor. To the last-mentioned inquiry the waiter returned the answer invariably given in such cases—namely, "My master is a terribly hard man, sir." Curious that in enlightened Russia so many people cannot even take a meal at an inn without chattering to the attendant and making free with him! Nevertheless not ALL the questions which the gentleman asked were aimless ones, for he inquired who was Governor of the town, who President of the Local Council, and who Public Prosecutor. In short, he omitted no single official of note, while asking also (though with an air of detachment) the most exact particulars concerning the landowners of the neighbourhood. Which of them, he inquired, possessed serfs, and how many of them? How far from the town did those landowners reside? What was the character of each landowner, and was he in the habit of paying frequent visits to the town? The gentleman also made searching inquiries concerning the hygienic condition of the countryside. Was there, he asked, much sickness about—whether sporadic fever, fatal forms of ague, smallpox, or what not? Yet, though his solicitude concerning these matters showed more than ordinary curiosity, his bearing retained its gravity unimpaired, and from time to time he blew his nose with portentous fervour. Indeed, the manner in which he accomplished this latter feat was marvellous in the extreme, for, though that member emitted sounds equal to those of a trumpet in intensity, he could yet, with his accompanying air of guileless dignity, evoke the waiter's undivided respect—so much so that, whenever the sounds of the nose reached that menial's ears, he would shake back his locks, straighten himself into a posture of marked solicitude, and inquire afresh, with head slightly inclined, whether the gentleman happened to require anything further. After dinner the guest consumed a cup of coffee, and then, seating himself upon the sofa, with, behind him, one of those wool-covered cushions which, in Russian taverns, resemble nothing so much as a cobblestone or a brick, fell to snoring; whereafter, returning with a start to consciousness, he ordered himself to be conducted to his room, flung himself at full length upon the bed, and once more slept soundly for a couple of hours. Aroused, eventually, by the waiter, he, at the latter's request, inscribed a fragment of paper with his name, his surname, and his rank (for communication, in accordance with the law, to the police): and on that paper the waiter, leaning forward from the corridor, read, syllable by syllable: "Paul Ivanovitch Chichikov, Collegiate Councillor—Landowner—Travelling on Private Affairs." The waiter had just time to accomplish this feat before Paul Ivanovitch Chichikov set forth to inspect the town. Apparently the place succeeded in satisfying him, and, to tell the truth, it was at least up to the usual standard of our provincial capitals. Where the staring yellow of stone edifices did not greet his eye he found himself confronted with the more modest grey of wooden ones; which, consisting, for the most part, of one or two storeys (added to the range of attics which provincial architects love so well), looked almost lost amid the expanses of street and intervening medleys of broken or half-finished partition-walls. At other points evidence of more life and movement was to be seen, and here the houses stood crowded together and displayed dilapidated, rain-blurred signboards whereon boots or cakes or pairs of blue breeches inscribed "Arshavski, Tailor," and so forth, were depicted. Over a shop containing hats and caps was written "Vassili Thedorov, Foreigner"; while, at another spot, a signboard portrayed a billiard table and two players—the latter clad in frockcoats of the kind usually affected by actors whose part it is to enter the stage during the closing act of a piece, even though, with arms sharply crooked and legs slightly bent, the said billiard players were taking the most careful aim, but succeeding only in making abortive strokes in the air. Each emporium of the sort had written over it: "This is the best establishment of its kind in the town." Also, al fresco in the streets there stood tables heaped with nuts, soap, and gingerbread (the latter but little distinguishable from the soap), and at an eating-house there was displayed the sign of a plump fish transfixed with a gaff. But the sign most frequently to be discerned was the insignia of the State, the double-headed eagle (now replaced, in this connection, with the laconic inscription "Dramshop"). As for the paving of the town, it was uniformly bad.

The gentleman peered also into the municipal gardens, which contained only a few sorry trees that were poorly selected, requiring to be propped with oil-painted, triangular green supports, and able to boast of a height no greater than that of an ordinary walking-stick. Yet recently the local paper had said (apropos of a gala) that, "Thanks to the efforts of our Civil Governor, the town has become enriched with a pleasaunce full of umbrageous, spaciously-branching trees. Even on the most sultry day they afford agreeable shade, and indeed gratifying was it to see the hearts of our citizens panting with an impulse of gratitude as their eyes shed tears in recognition of all that their Governor has done for them!"

Next, after inquiring of a gendarme as to the best ways and means of finding the local council, the local law-courts, and the local Governor, should he (Chichikov) have need of them, the gentleman went on to inspect the river which ran through the town. En route he tore off a notice affixed to a post, in order that he might the more conveniently read it after his return to the inn. Also, he bestowed upon a lady of pleasant exterior who, escorted by a footman laden with a bundle, happened to be passing along a wooden sidewalk a prolonged stare. Lastly, he threw around him a comprehensive glance (as though to fix in his mind the general topography of the place) and betook himself home. There, gently aided by the waiter, he ascended the stairs to his bedroom, drank a glass of tea, and, seating himself at the table, called for a candle; which having been brought him, he produced from his pocket the notice, held it close to the flame, and conned its tenour—slightly contracting his right eye as he did so. Yet there was little in the notice to call for remark. All that it said was that shortly one of Kotzebue's 6 plays would be given, and that one of the parts in the play was to be taken by a certain Monsieur Poplevin, and another by a certain Mademoiselle Ziablova, while the remaining parts were to be filled by a number of less important personages. Nevertheless the gentleman perused the notice with careful attention, and even jotted down the prices to be asked for seats for the performance. Also, he remarked that the bill had been printed in the press of the Provincial Government. Next, he turned over the paper, in order to see if anything further was to be read on the reverse side; but, finding nothing there, he refolded the document, placed it in the box which served him as a receptacle for odds and ends, and brought the day to a close with a portion of cold veal, a bottle of pickles, and a sound sleep.

The following day he devoted to paying calls upon the various municipal officials—a first, and a very respectful, visit being paid to the Governor. This personage turned out to resemble Chichikov himself in that he was neither fat nor thin. Also, he wore the riband of the order of Saint Anna about his neck, and was reported to have been recommended also for the star. For the rest, he was large and good-natured, and had a habit of amusing himself with occasional spells of knitting. Next, Chichikov repaired to the Vice-Governor's, and thence to the house of the Public Prosecutor, to that of the President of the Local Council, to that of the Chief of Police, to that of the Commissioner of Taxes, and to that of the local Director of State Factories. True, the task of remembering every big-wig in this world of ours is not a very easy one; but at least our visitor displayed the greatest activity in his work of paying calls, seeing that he went so far as to pay his respects also to the Inspector of the Municipal Department of Medicine and to the City Architect. Thereafter he sat thoughtfully in his britchka—plunged in meditation on the subject of whom else it might be well to visit. However, not a single magnate had been neglected, and in conversation with his hosts he had contrived to flatter each separate one. For instance to the Governor he had hinted that a stranger, on arriving in his, the Governor's province, would conceive that he had reached Paradise, so velvety were the roads. "Governors who appoint capable subordinates," had said Chichikov, "are deserving of the most ample meed of praise." Again, to the Chief of Police our hero had passed a most gratifying remark on the subject of the local gendarmery; while in his conversation with the Vice-Governor and the President of the Local Council (neither of whom had, as yet, risen above the rank of State Councillor) he had twice been guilty of the gaucherie of addressing his interlocutors with the title of "Your Excellency"—a blunder which had not failed to delight them. In the result the Governor had invited him to a reception the same evening, and certain other officials had followed suit by inviting him, one of them to dinner, a second to a tea-party, and so forth, and so forth.

Of himself, however, the traveller had spoken little; or, if he had spoken at any length, he had done so in a general sort of way and with marked modesty. Indeed, at moments of the kind his discourse had assumed something of a literary vein, in that invariably he had stated that, being a worm of no account in the world, he was deserving of no consideration at the hands of his fellows; that in his time he had undergone many strange experiences; that subsequently he had suffered much in the cause of Truth; that he had many enemies seeking his life; and that, being desirous of rest, he was now engaged in searching for a spot wherein to dwell—wherefore, having stumbled upon the town in which he now found himself, he had considered it his bounden duty to evince his respect for the chief authorities of the place. This, and no more, was all that, for the moment, the town succeeded in learning about the new arrival. Naturally he lost no time in presenting himself at the Governor's evening party. First, however, his preparations for that function occupied a space of over two hours, and necessitated an attention to his toilet of a kind not commonly seen. That is to say, after a brief post-prandial nap he called for soap and water, and spent a considerable period in the task of scrubbing his cheeks (which, for the purpose, he supported from within with his tongue) and then of drying his full, round face, from the ears downwards, with a towel which he took from the waiter's shoulder. Twice he snorted into the waiter's countenance as he did this, and then he posted himself in front of the mirror, donned a false shirt-front, plucked out a couple of hairs which were protruding from his nose, and appeared vested in a frockcoat of bilberry-coloured check. Thereafter driving through broad streets sparsely lighted with lanterns, he arrived at the Governor's residence to find it illuminated as for a ball. Barouches with gleaming lamps, a couple of gendarmes posted before the doors, a babel of postillions' cries—nothing of a kind likely to be impressive was wanting; and, on reaching the salon, the visitor actually found himself obliged to close his eyes for a moment, so strong was the mingled sheen of lamps, candles, and feminine apparel. Everything seemed suffused with light, and everywhere, flitting and flashing, were to be seen black coats—even as on a hot summer's day flies revolve around a sugar loaf while the old housekeeper is cutting it into cubes before the open window, and the children of the house crowd around her to watch the movements of her rugged hands as those members ply the smoking pestle; and airy squadrons of flies, borne on the breeze, enter boldly, as though free of the house, and, taking advantage of the fact that the glare of the sunshine is troubling the old lady's sight, disperse themselves over broken and unbroken fragments alike, even though the lethargy induced by the opulence of summer and the rich shower of dainties to be encountered at every step has induced them to enter less for the purpose of eating than for that of showing themselves in public, of parading up and down the sugar loaf, of rubbing both their hindquarters and their fore against one another, of cleaning their bodies under the wings, of extending their forelegs over their heads and grooming themselves, and of flying out of the window again to return with other predatory squadrons. Indeed, so dazed was Chichikov that scarcely did he realise that the Governor was taking him by the arm and presenting him to his (the Governor's) lady. Yet the newly-arrived guest kept his head sufficiently to contrive to murmur some such compliment as might fittingly come from a middle-aged individual of a rank neither excessively high nor excessively low. Next, when couples had been formed for dancing and the remainder of the company found itself pressed back against the walls, Chichikov folded his arms, and carefully scrutinised the dancers. Some of the ladies were dressed well and in the fashion, while the remainder were clad in such garments as God usually bestows upon a provincial town. Also here, as elsewhere, the men belonged to two separate and distinct categories; one of which comprised slender individuals who, flitting around the ladies, were scarcely to be distinguished from denizens of the metropolis, so carefully, so artistically, groomed were their whiskers, so presentable their oval, clean-shaven faces, so easy the manner of their dancing attendance upon their womenfolk, so glib their French conversation as they quizzed their female companions. As for the other category, it comprised individuals who, stout, or of the same build as Chichikov (that is to say, neither very portly nor very lean), backed and sidled away from the ladies, and kept peering hither and thither to see whether the Governor's footmen had set out green tables for whist. Their features were full and plump, some of them had beards, and in no case was their hair curled or waved or arranged in what the French call "the devil-may-care" style. On the contrary, their heads were either close-cropped or brushed very smooth, and their faces were round and firm. This category represented the more respectable officials of the town. In passing, I may say that in business matters fat men always prove superior to their leaner brethren; which is probably the reason why the latter are mostly to be found in the Political Police, or acting as mere ciphers whose existence is a purely hopeless, airy, trivial one. Again, stout individuals never take a back seat, but always a front one, and, wheresoever it be, they sit firmly, and with confidence, and decline to budge even though the seat crack and bend with their weight. For comeliness of exterior they care not a rap, and therefore a dress coat sits less easily on their figures than is the case with figures of leaner individuals. Yet invariably fat men amass the greater wealth. In three years' time a thin man will not have a single serf whom he has left unpledged; whereas—well, pray look at a fat man's fortunes, and what will you see? First of all a suburban villa, and then a larger suburban villa, and then a villa close to a town, and lastly a country estate which comprises every amenity! That is to say, having served both God and the State, the stout individual has won universal respect, and will end by retiring from business, reordering his mode of life, and becoming a Russian landowner—in other words, a fine gentleman who dispenses hospitality, lives in comfort and luxury, and is destined to leave his property to heirs who are purposing to squander the same on foreign travel.

That the foregoing represents pretty much the gist of Chichikov's reflections as he stood watching the company I will not attempt to deny. And of those reflections the upshot was that he decided to join himself to the stouter section of the guests, among whom he had already recognised several familiar faces—namely, those of the Public Prosecutor (a man with beetling brows over eyes which seemed to be saying with a wink, "Come into the next room, my friend, for I have something to say to you"—though, in the main, their owner was a man of grave and taciturn habit), of the Postmaster (an insignificant-looking individual, yet a would-be wit and a philosopher), and of the President of the Local Council (a man of much amiability and good sense). These three personages greeted Chichikov as an old acquaintance, and to their salutations he responded with a sidelong, yet a sufficiently civil, bow. Also, he became acquainted with an extremely unctuous and approachable landowner named Manilov, and with a landowner of more uncouth exterior named Sobakevitch—the latter of whom began the acquaintance by treading heavily upon Chichikov's toes, and then begging his pardon. Next, Chichikov received an offer of a "cut in" at whist, and accepted the same with his usual courteous inclination of the head. Seating themselves at a green table, the party did not rise therefrom till supper time; and during that period all conversation between the players became hushed, as is the custom when men have given themselves up to a really serious pursuit. Even the Postmaster—a talkative man by nature—had no sooner taken the cards into his hands than he assumed an expression of profound thought, pursed his lips, and retained this attitude unchanged throughout the game. Only when playing a court card was it his custom to strike the table with his fist, and to exclaim (if the card happened to be a queen), "Now, old popadia 7!" and (if the card happened to be a king), "Now, peasant of Tambov!" To which ejaculations invariably the President of the Local Council retorted, "Ah, I have him by the ears, I have him by the ears!" And from the neighbourhood of the table other strong ejaculations relative to the play would arise, interposed with one or another of those nicknames which participants in a game are apt to apply to members of the various suits. I need hardly add that, the game over, the players fell to quarrelling, and that in the dispute our friend joined, though so artfully as to let every one see that, in spite of the fact that he was wrangling, he was doing so only in the most amicable fashion possible. Never did he say outright, "You played the wrong card at such and such a point." No, he always employed some such phrase as, "You permitted yourself to make a slip, and thus afforded me the honour of covering your deuce." Indeed, the better to keep in accord with his antagonists, he kept offering them his silver-enamelled snuff-box (at the bottom of which lay a couple of violets, placed there for the sake of their scent). In particular did the newcomer pay attention to landowners Manilov and Sobakevitch; so much so that his haste to arrive on good terms with them led to his leaving the President and the Postmaster rather in the shade. At the same time, certain questions which he put to those two landowners evinced not only curiosity, but also a certain amount of sound intelligence; for he began by asking how many peasant souls each of them possessed, and how their affairs happened at present to be situated, and then proceeded to enlighten himself also as their standing and their families. Indeed, it was not long before he had succeeded in fairly enchanting his new friends. In particular did Manilov—a man still in his prime, and possessed of a pair of eyes which, sweet as sugar, blinked whenever he laughed—find himself unable to make enough of his enchanter. Clasping Chichikov long and fervently by the hand, he besought him to do him, Manilov, the honour of visiting his country house (which he declared to lie at a distance of not more than fifteen versts from the boundaries of the town); and in return Chichikov averred (with an exceedingly affable bow and a most sincere handshake) that he was prepared not only to fulfil his friend's behest, but also to look upon the fulfilling of it as a sacred duty. In the same way Sobakevitch said to him laconically: "And do you pay ME a visit," and then proceeded to shuffle a pair of boots of such dimensions that to find a pair to correspond with them would have been indeed difficult—more especially at the present day, when the race of epic heroes is beginning to die out in Russia.

Next day Chichikov dined and spent the evening at the house of the Chief of Police—a residence where, three hours after dinner, every one sat down to whist, and remained so seated until two o'clock in the morning. On this occasion Chichikov made the acquaintance of, among others, a landowner named Nozdrev—a dissipated little fellow of thirty who had no sooner exchanged three or four words with his new acquaintance than he began to address him in the second person singular. Yet although he did the same to the Chief of Police and the Public Prosecutor, the company had no sooner seated themselves at the card-table than both the one and the other of these functionaries started to keep a careful eye upon Nozdrev's tricks, and to watch practically every card which he played. The following evening Chichikov spent with the President of the Local Council, who received his guests—even though the latter included two ladies—in a greasy dressing-gown. Upon that followed an evening at the Vice-Governor's, a large dinner party at the house of the Commissioner of Taxes, a smaller dinner-party at the house of the Public Prosecutor (a very wealthy man), and a subsequent reception given by the Mayor. In short, not an hour of the day did Chichikov find himself forced to spend at home, and his return to the inn became necessary only for the purposes of sleeping. Somehow or other he had landed on his feet, and everywhere he figured as an experienced man of the world. No matter what the conversation chanced to be about, he always contrived to maintain his part in the same. Did the discourse turn upon horse-breeding, upon horse-breeding he happened to be peculiarly well-qualified to speak. Did the company fall to discussing well-bred dogs, at once he had remarks of the most pertinent kind possible to offer. Did the company touch upon a prosecution which had recently been carried out by the Excise Department, instantly he showed that he too was not wholly unacquainted with legal affairs. Did an opinion chance to be expressed concerning billiards, on that subject too he was at least able to avoid committing a blunder. Did a reference occur to virtue, concerning virtue he hastened to deliver himself in a way which brought tears to every eye. Did the subject in hand happen to be the distilling of brandy—well, that was a matter concerning which he had the soundest of knowledge. Did any one happen to mention Customs officials and inspectors, from that moment he expatiated as though he too had been both a minor functionary and a major. Yet a remarkable fact was the circumstance that he always contrived to temper his omniscience with a certain readiness to give way, a certain ability so to keep a rein upon himself that never did his utterances become too loud or too soft, or transcend what was perfectly befitting. In a word, he was always a gentleman of excellent manners, and every official in the place felt pleased when he saw him enter the door. Thus the Governor gave it as his opinion that Chichikov was a man of excellent intentions; the Public Prosecutor, that he was a good man of business; the Chief of Gendarmery, that he was a man of education; the President of the Local Council, that he was a man of breeding and refinement; and the wife of the Chief of Gendarmery, that his politeness of behaviour was equalled only by his affability of bearing. Nay, even Sobakevitch—who as a rule never spoke well of ANY ONE—said to his lanky wife when, on returning late from the town, he undressed and betook himself to bed by her side: "My dear, this evening, after dining with the Chief of Police, I went on to the Governor's, and met there, among others, a certain Paul Ivanovitch Chichikov, who is a Collegiate Councillor and a very pleasant fellow." To this his spouse replied "Hm!" and then dealt him a hearty kick in the ribs.

Such were the flattering opinions earned by the newcomer to the town; and these opinions he retained until the time when a certain speciality of his, a certain scheme of his (the reader will learn presently what it was), plunged the majority of the townsfolk into a sea of perplexity.

CHAPTER

II

For more than two weeks the visitor lived amid a round of evening parties and dinners; wherefore he spent (as the saying goes) a very pleasant time. Finally he decided to extend his visits beyond the urban boundaries by going and calling upon landowners Manilov and Sobakevitch, seeing that he had promised on his honour to do so. Yet what really incited him to this may have been a more essential cause, a matter of greater gravity, a purpose which stood nearer to his heart, than the motive which I have just given; and of that purpose the reader will learn if only he will have the patience to read this prefatory narrative (which, lengthy though it be, may yet develop and expand in proportion as we approach the denouement with which the present work is destined to be crowned).

One evening, therefore, Selifan the coachman received orders to have the horses harnessed in good time next morning; while Petrushka received orders to remain behind, for the purpose of looking after the portmanteau and the room. In passing, the reader may care to become more fully acquainted with the two serving-men of whom I have spoken. Naturally, they were not persons of much note, but merely what folk call characters of secondary, or even of tertiary, importance. Yet, despite the fact that the springs and the thread of this romance will not DEPEND upon them, but only touch upon them, and occasionally include them, the author has a passion for circumstantiality, and, like the average Russian, such a desire for accuracy as even a German could not rival. To what the reader already knows concerning the personages in hand it is therefore necessary to add that Petrushka usually wore a cast-off brown jacket of a size too large for him, as also that he had (according to the custom of individuals of his calling) a pair of thick lips and a very prominent nose. In temperament he was taciturn rather than loquacious, and he cherished a yearning for self-education. That is to say, he loved to read books, even though their contents came alike to him whether they were books of heroic adventure or mere grammars or liturgical compendia. As I say, he perused every book with an equal amount of attention, and, had he been offered a work on chemistry, would have accepted that also. Not the words which he read, but the mere solace derived from the act of reading, was what especially pleased his mind; even though at any moment there might launch itself from the page some devil-sent word whereof he could make neither head nor tail. For the most part, his task of reading was performed in a recumbent position in the anteroom; which circumstance ended by causing his mattress to become as ragged and as thin as a wafer. In addition to his love of poring over books, he could boast of two habits which constituted two other essential features of his character—namely, a habit of retiring to rest in his clothes (that is to say, in the brown jacket above-mentioned) and a habit of everywhere bearing with him his own peculiar atmosphere, his own peculiar smell—a smell which filled any lodging with such subtlety that he needed but to make up his bed anywhere, even in a room hitherto untenanted, and to drag thither his greatcoat and other impedimenta, for that room at once to assume an air of having been lived in during the past ten years. Nevertheless, though a fastidious, and even an irritable, man, Chichikov would merely frown when his nose caught this smell amid the freshness of the morning, and exclaim with a toss of his head: "The devil only knows what is up with you! Surely you sweat a good deal, do you not? The best thing you can do is to go and take a bath." To this Petrushka would make no reply, but, approaching, brush in hand, the spot where his master's coat would be pendent, or starting to arrange one and another article in order, would strive to seem wholly immersed in his work. Yet of what was he thinking as he remained thus silent? Perhaps he was saying to himself: "My master is a good fellow, but for him to keep on saying the same thing forty times over is a little wearisome." Only God knows and sees all things; wherefore for a mere human being to know what is in the mind of a servant while his master is scolding him is wholly impossible. However, no more need be said about Petrushka. On the other hand, Coachman Selifan—

But here let me remark that I do not like engaging the reader's attention in connection with persons of a lower class than himself; for experience has taught me that we do not willingly familiarise ourselves with the lower orders—that it is the custom of the average Russian to yearn exclusively for information concerning persons on the higher rungs of the social ladder. In fact, even a bowing acquaintance with a prince or a lord counts, in his eyes, for more than do the most intimate of relations with ordinary folk. For the same reason the author feels apprehensive on his hero's account, seeing that he has made that hero a mere Collegiate Councillor—a mere person with whom Aulic Councillors might consort, but upon whom persons of the grade of full General 8 would probably bestow one of those glances proper to a man who is cringing at their august feet. Worse still, such persons of the grade of General are likely to treat Chichikov with studied negligence—and to an author studied negligence spells death.

However, in spite of the distressfulness of the foregoing possibilities, it is time that I returned to my hero. After issuing, overnight, the necessary orders, he awoke early, washed himself, rubbed himself from head to foot with a wet sponge (a performance executed only on Sundays—and the day in question happened to be a Sunday), shaved his face with such care that his cheeks issued of absolutely satin-like smoothness and polish, donned first his bilberry-coloured, spotted frockcoat, and then his bearskin overcoat, descended the staircase (attended, throughout, by the waiter) and entered his britchka. With a loud rattle the vehicle left the inn-yard, and issued into the street. A passing priest doffed his cap, and a few urchins in grimy shirts shouted, "Gentleman, please give a poor orphan a trifle!" Presently the driver noticed that a sturdy young rascal was on the point of climbing onto the splashboard; wherefore he cracked his whip and the britchka leapt forward with increased speed over the cobblestones. At last, with a feeling of relief, the travellers caught sight of macadam ahead, which promised an end both to the cobblestones and to sundry other annoyances. And, sure enough, after his head had been bumped a few more times against the boot of the conveyance, Chichikov found himself bowling over softer ground. On the town receding into the distance, the sides of the road began to be varied with the usual hillocks, fir trees, clumps of young pine, trees with old, scarred trunks, bushes of wild juniper, and so forth. Presently there came into view also strings of country villas which, with their carved supports and grey roofs (the latter looking like pendent, embroidered tablecloths), resembled, rather, bundles of old faggots. Likewise the customary peasants, dressed in sheepskin jackets, could be seen yawning on benches before their huts, while their womenfolk, fat of feature and swathed of bosom, gazed out of upper windows, and the windows below displayed, here a peering calf, and there the unsightly jaws of a pig. In short, the view was one of the familiar type. After passing the fifteenth verst-stone Chichikov suddenly recollected that, according to Manilov, fifteen versts was the exact distance between his country house and the town; but the sixteenth verst stone flew by, and the said country house was still nowhere to be seen. In fact, but for the circumstance that the travellers happened to encounter a couple of peasants, they would have come on their errand in vain. To a query as to whether the country house known as Zamanilovka was anywhere in the neighbourhood the peasants replied by doffing their caps; after which one of them who seemed to boast of a little more intelligence than his companion, and who wore a wedge-shaped beard, made answer:

"Perhaps you mean Manilovka—not ZAmanilovka?"

"Yes, yes—Manilovka."

"Manilovka, eh? Well, you must continue for another verst, and then you will see it straight before you, on the right."

"On the right?" re-echoed the coachman.

"Yes, on the right," affirmed the peasant. "You are on the proper road for Manilovka, but ZAmanilovka—well, there is no such place. The house you mean is called Manilovka because Manilovka is its name; but no house at all is called ZAmanilovka. The house you mean stands there, on that hill, and is a stone house in which a gentleman lives, and its name is Manilovka; but ZAmanilovka does not stand hereabouts, nor ever has stood."

So the travellers proceeded in search of Manilovka, and, after driving an additional two versts, arrived at a spot whence there branched off a by-road. Yet two, three, or four versts of the by-road had been covered before they saw the least sign of a two-storied stone mansion. Then it was that Chichikov suddenly recollected that, when a friend has invited one to visit his country house, and has said that the distance thereto is fifteen versts, the distance is sure to turn out to be at least thirty.

Not many people would have admired the situation of Manilov's abode, for it stood on an isolated rise and was open to every wind that blew. On the slope of the rise lay closely-mown turf, while, disposed here and there, after the English fashion, were flower-beds containing clumps of lilac and yellow acacia. Also, there were a few insignificant groups of slender-leaved, pointed-tipped birch trees, with, under two of the latter, an arbour having a shabby green cupola, some blue-painted wooden supports, and the inscription "This is the Temple of Solitary Thought." Lower down the slope lay a green-coated pond—green-coated ponds constitute a frequent spectacle in the gardens of Russian landowners; and, lastly, from the foot of the declivity there stretched a line of mouldy, log-built huts which, for some obscure reason or another, our hero set himself to count. Up to two hundred or more did he count, but nowhere could he perceive a single leaf of vegetation or a single stick of timber. The only thing to greet the eye was the logs of which the huts were constructed. Nevertheless the scene was to a certain extent enlivened by the spectacle of two peasant women who, with clothes picturesquely tucked up, were wading knee-deep in the pond and dragging behind them, with wooden handles, a ragged fishing-net, in the meshes of which two crawfish and a roach with glistening scales were entangled. The women appeared to have cause of dispute between themselves—to be rating one another about something. In the background, and to one side of the house, showed a faint, dusky blur of pinewood, and even the weather was in keeping with the surroundings, since the day was neither clear nor dull, but of the grey tint which may be noted in uniforms of garrison soldiers which have seen long service. To complete the picture, a cock, the recognised harbinger of atmospheric mutations, was present; and, in spite of the fact that a certain connection with affairs of gallantry had led to his having had his head pecked bare by other cocks, he flapped a pair of wings—appendages as bare as two pieces of bast—and crowed loudly.

As Chichikov approached the courtyard of the mansion he caught sight of his host (clad in a green frock coat) standing on the verandah and pressing one hand to his eyes to shield them from the sun and so get a better view of the approaching carriage. In proportion as the britchka drew nearer and nearer to the verandah, the host's eyes assumed a more and more delighted expression, and his smile a broader and broader sweep.

"Paul Ivanovitch!" he exclaimed when at length Chichikov leapt from the vehicle. "Never should I have believed that you would have remembered us!"

The two friends exchanged hearty embraces, and Manilov then conducted his guest to the drawing-room. During the brief time that they are traversing the hall, the anteroom, and the dining-room, let me try to say something concerning the master of the house. But such an undertaking bristles with difficulties—it promises to be a far less easy task than the depicting of some outstanding personality which calls but for a wholesale dashing of colours upon the canvas—the colours of a pair of dark, burning eyes, a pair of dark, beetling brows, a forehead seamed with wrinkles, a black, or a fiery-red, cloak thrown backwards over the shoulder, and so forth, and so forth. Yet, so numerous are Russian serf owners that, though careful scrutiny reveals to one's sight a quantity of outre peculiarities, they are, as a class, exceedingly difficult to portray, and one needs to strain one's faculties to the utmost before it becomes possible to pick out their variously subtle, their almost invisible, features. In short, one needs, before doing this, to carry out a prolonged probing with the aid of an insight sharpened in the acute school of research.

Only God can say what Manilov's real character was. A class of men exists whom the proverb has described as "men unto themselves, neither this nor that—neither Bogdan of the city nor Selifan of the village." And to that class we had better assign also Manilov. Outwardly he was presentable enough, for his features were not wanting in amiability, but that amiability was a quality into which there entered too much of the sugary element, so that his every gesture, his every attitude, seemed to connote an excess of eagerness to curry favour and cultivate a closer acquaintance. On first speaking to the man, his ingratiating smile, his flaxen hair, and his blue eyes would lead one to say, "What a pleasant, good-tempered fellow he seems!" yet during the next moment or two one would feel inclined to say nothing at all, and, during the third moment, only to say, "The devil alone knows what he is!" And should, thereafter, one not hasten to depart, one would inevitably become overpowered with the deadly sense of ennui which comes of the intuition that nothing in the least interesting is to be looked for, but only a series of wearisome utterances of the kind which are apt to fall from the lips of a man whose hobby has once been touched upon. For every man HAS his hobby. One man's may be sporting dogs; another man's may be that of believing himself to be a lover of music, and able to sound the art to its inmost depths; another's may be that of posing as a connoisseur of recherche cookery; another's may be that of aspiring to play roles of a kind higher than nature has assigned him; another's (though this is a more limited ambition) may be that of getting drunk, and of dreaming that he is edifying both his friends, his acquaintances, and people with whom he has no connection at all by walking arm-in-arm with an Imperial aide-de-camp; another's may be that of possessing a hand able to chip corners off aces and deuces of diamonds; another's may be that of yearning to set things straight—in other words, to approximate his personality to that of a stationmaster or a director of posts. In short, almost every man has his hobby or his leaning; yet Manilov had none such, for at home he spoke little, and spent the greater part of his time in meditation—though God only knows what that meditation comprised! Nor can it be said that he took much interest in the management of his estate, for he never rode into the country, and the estate practically managed itself. Whenever the bailiff said to him, "It might be well to have such-and-such a thing done," he would reply, "Yes, that is not a bad idea," and then go on smoking his pipe—a habit which he had acquired during his service in the army, where he had been looked upon as an officer of modesty, delicacy, and refinement. "Yes, it is NOT a bad idea," he would repeat. Again, whenever a peasant approached him and, rubbing the back of his neck, said "Barin, may I have leave to go and work for myself, in order that I may earn my obrok 9?" he would snap out, with pipe in mouth as usual, "Yes, go!" and never trouble his head as to whether the peasant's real object might not be to go and get drunk. True, at intervals he would say, while gazing from the verandah to the courtyard, and from the courtyard to the pond, that it would be indeed splendid if a carriage drive could suddenly materialise, and the pond as suddenly become spanned with a stone bridge, and little shops as suddenly arise whence pedlars could dispense the petty merchandise of the kind which peasantry most need. And at such moments his eyes would grow winning, and his features assume an expression of intense satisfaction. Yet never did these projects pass beyond the stage of debate. Likewise there lay in his study a book with the fourteenth page permanently turned down. It was a book which he had been reading for the past two years! In general, something seemed to be wanting in the establishment. For instance, although the drawing-room was filled with beautiful furniture, and upholstered in some fine silken material which clearly had cost no inconsiderable sum, two of the chairs lacked any covering but bast, and for some years past the master had been accustomed to warn his guests with the words, "Do not sit upon these chairs; they are not yet ready for use." Another room contained no furniture at all, although, a few days after the marriage, it had been said: "My dear, to-morrow let us set about procuring at least some TEMPORARY furniture for this room." Also, every evening would see placed upon the drawing-room table a fine bronze candelabrum, a statuette representative of the Three Graces, a tray inlaid with mother-of-pearl, and a rickety, lop-sided copper invalide. Yet of the fact that all four articles were thickly coated with grease neither the master of the house nor the mistress nor the servants seemed to entertain the least suspicion. At the same time, Manilov and his wife were quite satisfied with each other. More than eight years had elapsed since their marriage, yet one of them was for ever offering his or her partner a piece of apple or a bonbon or a nut, while murmuring some tender something which voiced a whole-hearted affection. "Open your mouth, dearest"—thus ran the formula—"and let me pop into it this titbit." You may be sure that on such occasions the "dearest mouth" parted its lips most graciously! For their mutual birthdays the pair always contrived some "surprise present" in the shape of a glass receptacle for tooth-powder, or what not; and as they sat together on the sofa he would suddenly, and for some unknown reason, lay aside his pipe, and she her work (if at the moment she happened to be holding it in her hands) and husband and wife would imprint upon one another's cheeks such a prolonged and languishing kiss that during its continuance you could have smoked a small cigar. In short, they were what is known as "a very happy couple." Yet it may be remarked that a household requires other pursuits to be engaged in than lengthy embracings and the preparing of cunning "surprises." Yes, many a function calls for fulfilment. For instance, why should it be thought foolish or low to superintend the kitchen? Why should care not be taken that the storeroom never lacks supplies? Why should a housekeeper be allowed to thieve? Why should slovenly and drunken servants exist? Why should a domestic staff be suffered in indulge in bouts of unconscionable debauchery during its leisure time? Yet none of these things were thought worthy of consideration by Manilov's wife, for she had been gently brought up, and gentle nurture, as we all know, is to be acquired only in boarding schools, and boarding schools, as we know, hold the three principal subjects which constitute the basis of human virtue to be the French language (a thing indispensable to the happiness of married life), piano-playing (a thing wherewith to beguile a husband's leisure moments), and that particular department of housewifery which is comprised in the knitting of purses and other "surprises." Nevertheless changes and improvements have begun to take place, since things now are governed more by the personal inclinations and idiosyncracies of the keepers of such establishments. For instance, in some seminaries the regimen places piano-playing first, and the French language second, and then the above department of housewifery; while in other seminaries the knitting of "surprises" heads the list, and then the French language, and then the playing of pianos—so diverse are the systems in force! None the less, I may remark that Madame Manilov—

But let me confess that I always shrink from saying too much about ladies. Moreover, it is time that we returned to our heroes, who, during the past few minutes, have been standing in front of the drawing-room door, and engaged in urging one another to enter first.

"Pray be so good as not to inconvenience yourself on my account," said Chichikov. "*I* will follow YOU."

"No, Paul Ivanovitch—no! You are my guest." And Manilov pointed towards the doorway.

"Make no difficulty about it, I pray," urged Chichikov. "I beg of you to make no difficulty about it, but to pass into the room."

"Pardon me, I will not. Never could I allow so distinguished and so welcome a guest as yourself to take second place."

"Why call me 'distinguished,' my dear sir? I beg of you to proceed."

"Nay; be YOU pleased to do so."

"And why?"

"For the reason which I have stated." And Manilov smiled his very pleasantest smile.

Finally the pair entered simultaneously and sideways; with the result that they jostled one another not a little in the process.

"Allow me to present to you my wife," continued Manilov. "My dear—Paul Ivanovitch."

Upon that Chichikov caught sight of a lady whom hitherto he had overlooked, but who, with Manilov, was now bowing to him in the doorway. Not wholly of unpleasing exterior, she was dressed in a well-fitting, high-necked morning dress of pale-coloured silk; and as the visitor entered the room her small white hands threw something upon the table and clutched her embroidered skirt before rising from the sofa where she had been seated. Not without a sense of pleasure did Chichikov take her hand as, lisping a little, she declared that she and her husband were equally gratified by his coming, and that, of late, not a day had passed without her husband recalling him to mind.

"Yes," affirmed Manilov; "and every day SHE has said to ME: 'Why does not your friend put in an appearance?' 'Wait a little dearest,' I have always replied. ''Twill not be long now before he comes.' And you HAVE come, you HAVE honoured us with a visit, you HAVE bestowed upon us a treat—a treat destined to convert this day into a gala day, a true birthday of the heart."

The intimation that matters had reached the point of the occasion being destined to constitute a "true birthday of the heart" caused Chichikov to become a little confused; wherefore he made modest reply that, as a matter of fact, he was neither of distinguished origin nor distinguished rank.

"Ah, you ARE so," interrupted Manilov with his fixed and engaging smile. "You are all that, and more."

"How like you our town?" queried Madame. "Have you spent an agreeable time in it?"

"Very," replied Chichikov. "The town is an exceedingly nice one, and I have greatly enjoyed its hospitable society."

"And what do you think of our Governor?"

"Yes; IS he not a most engaging and dignified personage?" added Manilov.

"He is all that," assented Chichikov. "Indeed, he is a man worthy of the greatest respect. And how thoroughly he performs his duty according to his lights! Would that we had more like him!"

"And the tactfulness with which he greets every one!" added Manilov, smiling, and half-closing his eyes, like a cat which is being tickled behind the ears.

"Quite so," assented Chichikov. "He is a man of the most eminent civility and approachableness. And what an artist! Never should I have thought he could have worked the marvellous household samplers which he has done! Some specimens of his needlework which he showed me could not well have been surpassed by any lady in the land!"

"And the Vice-Governor, too—he is a nice man, is he not?" inquired Manilov with renewed blinkings of the eyes.

"Who? The Vice-Governor? Yes, a most worthy fellow!" replied Chichikov.

"And what of the Chief of Police? Is it not a fact that he too is in the highest degree agreeable?"

"Very agreeable indeed. And what a clever, well-read individual! With him and the Public Prosecutor and the President of the Local Council I played whist until the cocks uttered their last morning crow. He is a most excellent fellow."

"And what of his wife?" queried Madame Manilov. "Is she not a most gracious personality?"

"One of the best among my limited acquaintance," agreed Chichikov.

Nor were the President of the Local Council and the Postmaster overlooked; until the company had run through the whole list of urban officials. And in every case those officials appeared to be persons of the highest possible merit.

"Do you devote your time entirely to your estate?" asked Chichikov, in his turn.

"Well, most of it," replied Manilov; "though also we pay occasional visits to the town, in order that we may mingle with a little well-bred society. One grows a trifle rusty if one lives for ever in retirement."

"Quite so," agreed Chichikov.

"Yes, quite so," capped Manilov. "At the same time, it would be a different matter if the neighbourhood were a GOOD one—if, for example, one had a friend with whom one could discuss manners and polite deportment, or engage in some branch of science, and so stimulate one's wits. For that sort of thing gives one's intellect an airing. It, it—" At a loss for further words, he ended by remarking that his feelings were apt to carry him away; after which he continued with a gesture: "What I mean is that, were that sort of thing possible, I, for one, could find the country and an isolated life possessed of great attractions. But, as matters stand, such a thing is NOT possible. All that I can manage to do is, occasionally, to read a little of A Son of the Fatherland."

With these sentiments Chichikov expressed entire agreement: adding that nothing could be more delightful than to lead a solitary life in which there should be comprised only the sweet contemplation of nature and the intermittent perusal of a book.

"Nay, but even THAT were worth nothing had not one a friend with whom to share one's life," remarked Manilov.

"True, true," agreed Chichikov. "Without a friend, what are all the treasures in the world? 'Possess not money,' a wise man has said, 'but rather good friends to whom to turn in case of need.'"

"Yes, Paul Ivanovitch," said Manilov with a glance not merely sweet, but positively luscious—a glance akin to the mixture which even clever physicians have to render palatable before they can induce a hesitant patient to take it. "Consequently you may imagine what happiness—what PERFECT happiness, so to speak—the present occasion has brought me, seeing that I am permitted to converse with you and to enjoy your conversation."

"But WHAT of my conversation?" replied Chichikov. "I am an insignificant individual, and, beyond that, nothing."

"Oh, Paul Ivanovitch!" cried the other. "Permit me to be frank, and to say that I would give half my property to possess even a PORTION of the talents which you possess."

"On the contrary, I should consider it the highest honour in the world if—"

The lengths to which this mutual outpouring of soul would have proceeded had not a servant entered to announce luncheon must remain a mystery.

"I humbly invite you to join us at table," said Manilov. "Also, you will pardon us for the fact that we cannot provide a banquet such as is to be obtained in our metropolitan cities? We partake of simple fare, according to Russian custom—we confine ourselves to shtchi 10, but we do so with a single heart. Come, I humbly beg of you."

After another contest for the honour of yielding precedence, Chichikov succeeded in making his way (in zigzag fashion) to the dining-room, where they found awaiting them a couple of youngsters. These were Manilov's sons, and boys of the age which admits of their presence at table, but necessitates the continued use of high chairs. Beside them was their tutor, who bowed politely and smiled; after which the hostess took her seat before her soup plate, and the guest of honour found himself esconsed between her and the master of the house, while the servant tied up the boys' necks in bibs.

"What charming children!" said Chichikov as he gazed at the pair. "And how old are they?"

"The eldest is eight," replied Manilov, "and the younger one attained the age of six yesterday."

"Themistocleus," went on the father, turning to his first-born, who was engaged in striving to free his chin from the bib with which the footman had encircled it. On hearing this distinctly Greek name (to which, for some unknown reason, Manilov always appended the termination "eus"), Chichikov raised his eyebrows a little, but hastened, the next moment, to restore his face to a more befitting expression.

"Themistocleus," repeated the father, "tell me which is the finest city in France."

Upon this the tutor concentrated his attention upon Themistocleus, and appeared to be trying hard to catch his eye. Only when Themistocleus had muttered "Paris" did the preceptor grow calmer, and nod his head.

"And which is the finest city in Russia?" continued Manilov.

Again the tutor's attitude became wholly one of concentration.

"St. Petersburg," replied Themistocleus.

"And what other city?"

"Moscow," responded the boy.

"Clever little dear!" burst out Chichikov, turning with an air of surprise to the father. "Indeed, I feel bound to say that the child evinces the greatest possible potentialities."

"You do not know him fully," replied the delighted Manilov. "The amount of sharpness which he possesses is extraordinary. Our younger one, Alkid, is not so quick; whereas his brother—well, no matter what he may happen upon (whether upon a cowbug or upon a water-beetle or upon anything else), his little eyes begin jumping out of his head, and he runs to catch the thing, and to inspect it. For HIM I am reserving a diplomatic post. Themistocleus," added the father, again turning to his son, "do you wish to become an ambassador?"

"Yes, I do," replied Themistocleus, chewing a piece of bread and wagging his head from side to side.

At this moment the lacquey who had been standing behind the future ambassador wiped the latter's nose; and well it was that he did so, since otherwise an inelegant and superfluous drop would have been added to the soup. After that the conversation turned upon the joys of a quiet life—though occasionally it was interrupted by remarks from the hostess on the subject of acting and actors. Meanwhile the tutor kept his eyes fixed upon the speakers' faces; and whenever he noticed that they were on the point of laughing he at once opened his mouth, and laughed with enthusiasm. Probably he was a man of grateful heart who wished to repay his employers for the good treatment which he had received. Once, however, his features assumed a look of grimness as, fixing his eyes upon his vis-a-vis, the boys, he tapped sternly upon the table. This happened at a juncture when Themistocleus had bitten Alkid on the ear, and the said Alkid, with frowning eyes and open mouth, was preparing himself to sob in piteous fashion; until, recognising that for such a proceeding he might possibly be deprived of his plate, he hastened to restore his mouth to its original expression, and fell tearfully to gnawing a mutton bone—the grease from which had soon covered his cheeks.

Every now and again the hostess would turn to Chichikov with the words, "You are eating nothing—you have indeed taken little;" but invariably her guest replied: "Thank you, I have had more than enough. A pleasant conversation is worth all the dishes in the world."

At length the company rose from table. Manilov was in high spirits, and, laying his hand upon his guest's shoulder, was on the point of conducting him to the drawing-room, when suddenly Chichikov intimated to him, with a meaning look, that he wished to speak to him on a very important matter.

"That being so," said Manilov, "allow me to invite you into my study." And he led the way to a small room which faced the blue of the forest. "This is my sanctum," he added.

"What a pleasant apartment!" remarked Chichikov as he eyed it carefully. And, indeed, the room did not lack a certain attractiveness. The walls were painted a sort of blueish-grey colour, and the furniture consisted of four chairs, a settee, and a table—the latter of which bore a few sheets of writing-paper and the book of which I have before had occasion to speak. But the most prominent feature of the room was tobacco, which appeared in many different guises—in packets, in a tobacco jar, and in a loose heap strewn about the table. Likewise, both window sills were studded with little heaps of ash, arranged, not without artifice, in rows of more or less tidiness. Clearly smoking afforded the master of the house a frequent means of passing the time.

"Permit me to offer you a seat on this settee," said Manilov. "Here you will be quieter than you would be in the drawing-room."

"But I should prefer to sit upon this chair."

"I cannot allow that," objected the smiling Manilov. "The settee is specially reserved for my guests. Whether you choose or no, upon it you MUST sit."

Accordingly Chichikov obeyed.

"And also let me hand you a pipe."

"No, I never smoke," answered Chichikov civilly, and with an assumed air of regret.

"And why?" inquired Manilov—equally civilly, but with a regret that was wholly genuine.

"Because I fear that I have never quite formed the habit, owing to my having heard that a pipe exercises a desiccating effect upon the system."

"Then allow me to tell you that that is mere prejudice. Nay, I would even go so far as to say that to smoke a pipe is a healthier practice than to take snuff. Among its members our regiment numbered a lieutenant—a most excellent, well-educated fellow—who was simply INCAPABLE of removing his pipe from his mouth, whether at table or (pardon me) in other places. He is now forty, yet no man could enjoy better health than he has always done."

Chichikov replied that such cases were common, since nature comprised many things which even the finest intellect could not compass.

"But allow me to put to you a question," he went on in a tone in which there was a strange—or, at all events, RATHER a strange—note. For some unknown reason, also, he glanced over his shoulder. For some equally unknown reason, Manilov glanced over HIS.

"How long is it," inquired the guest, "since you last rendered a census return?"

"Oh, a long, long time. In fact, I cannot remember when it was."

"And since then have many of your serfs died?"

"I do not know. To ascertain that I should need to ask my bailiff. Footman, go and call the bailiff. I think he will be at home to-day."

Before long the bailiff made his appearance. He was a man of under forty, clean-shaven, clad in a smock, and evidently used to a quiet life, seeing that his face was of that puffy fullness, and the skin encircling his slit-like eyes was of that sallow tint, which shows that the owner of those features is well acquainted with a feather bed. In a trice it could be seen that he had played his part in life as all such bailiffs do—that, originally a young serf of elementary education, he had married some Agashka of a housekeeper or a mistress's favourite, and then himself become housekeeper, and, subsequently, bailiff; after which he had proceeded according to the rules of his tribe—that is to say, he had consorted with and stood in with the more well-to-do serfs on the estate, and added the poorer ones to the list of forced payers of obrok, while himself leaving his bed at nine o'clock in the morning, and, when the samovar had been brought, drinking his tea at leisure.

"Look here, my good man," said Manilov. "How many of our serfs have died since the last census revision?"

"How many of them have died? Why, a great many." The bailiff hiccoughed, and slapped his mouth lightly after doing so.

"Yes, I imagined that to be the case," corroborated Manilov. "In fact, a VERY great many serfs have died." He turned to Chichikov and repeated the words.

"How many, for instance?" asked Chichikov.

"Yes; how many?" re-echoed Manilov.

"HOW many?" re-echoed the bailiff. "Well, no one knows the exact number, for no one has kept any account."

"Quite so," remarked Manilov. "I supposed the death-rate to have been high, but was ignorant of its precise extent."

"Then would you be so good as to have it computed for me?" said Chichikov. "And also to have a detailed list of the deaths made out?"

"Yes, I will—a detailed list," agreed Manilov.

"Very well."

The bailiff departed.

"For what purpose do you want it?" inquired Manilov when the bailiff had gone.

The question seemed to embarrass the guest, for in Chichikov's face there dawned a sort of tense expression, and it reddened as though its owner were striving to express something not easy to put into words. True enough, Manilov was now destined to hear such strange and unexpected things as never before had greeted human ears.

"You ask me," said Chichikov, "for what purpose I want the list. Well, my purpose in wanting it is this—that I desire to purchase a few peasants." And he broke off in a gulp.

"But may I ask HOW you desire to purchase those peasants?" asked Manilov. "With land, or merely as souls for transferment—that is to say, by themselves, and without any land?"

"I want the peasants themselves only," replied Chichikov. "And I want dead ones at that."

"What?—Excuse me, but I am a trifle deaf. Really, your words sound most strange!"

"All that I am proposing to do," replied Chichikov, "is to purchase the dead peasants who, at the last census, were returned by you as alive."

Manilov dropped his pipe on the floor, and sat gaping. Yes, the two friends who had just been discussing the joys of camaraderie sat staring at one another like the portraits which, of old, used to hang on opposite sides of a mirror. At length Manilov picked up his pipe, and, while doing so, glanced covertly at Chichikov to see whether there was any trace of a smile to be detected on his lips—whether, in short, he was joking. But nothing of the sort could be discerned. On the contrary, Chichikov's face looked graver than usual. Next, Manilov wondered whether, for some unknown reason, his guest had lost his wits; wherefore he spent some time in gazing at him with anxious intentness. But the guest's eyes seemed clear—they contained no spark of the wild, restless fire which is apt to wander in the eyes of madmen. All was as it should be. Consequently, in spite of Manilov's cogitations, he could think of nothing better to do than to sit letting a stream of tobacco smoke escape from his mouth.

"So," continued Chichikov, "what I desire to know is whether you are willing to hand over to me—to resign—these actually non-living, but legally living, peasants; or whether you have any better proposal to make?"

Manilov felt too confused and confounded to do aught but continue staring at his interlocutor.

"I think that you are disturbing yourself unnecessarily," was Chichikov's next remark.

"I? Oh no! Not at all!" stammered Manilov. "Only—pardon me—I do not quite comprehend you. You see, never has it fallen to my lot to acquire the brilliant polish which is, so to speak, manifest in your every movement. Nor have I ever been able to attain the art of expressing myself well. Consequently, although there is a possibility that in the—er—utterances which have just fallen from your lips there may lie something else concealed, it may equally be that—er—you have been pleased so to express yourself for the sake of the beauty of the terms wherein that expression found shape?"

"Oh, no," asserted Chichikov. "I mean what I say and no more. My reference to such of your pleasant souls as are dead was intended to be taken literally."

Manilov still felt at a loss—though he was conscious that he MUST do something, he MUST propound some question. But what question? The devil alone knew! In the end he merely expelled some more tobacco smoke—this time from his nostrils as well as from his mouth.

"So," went on Chichikov, "if no obstacle stands in the way, we might as well proceed to the completion of the purchase."

"What? Of the purchase of the dead souls?"

"Of the 'dead' souls? Oh dear no! Let us write them down as LIVING ones, seeing that that is how they figure in the census returns. Never do I permit myself to step outside the civil law, great though has been the harm which that rule has wrought me in my career. In my eyes an obligation is a sacred thing. In the presence of the law I am dumb."

These last words reassured Manilov not a little: yet still the meaning of the affair remained to him a mystery. By way of answer, he fell to sucking at his pipe with such vehemence that at length the pipe began to gurgle like a bassoon. It was as though he had been seeking of it inspiration in the present unheard-of juncture. But the pipe only gurgled, et praeterea nihil.

"Perhaps you feel doubtful about the proposal?" said Chichikov.

"Not at all," replied Manilov. "But you will, I know, excuse me if I say (and I say it out of no spirit of prejudice, nor yet as criticising yourself in any way)—you will, I know, excuse me if I say that possibly this—er—this, er, SCHEME of yours, this—er—TRANSACTION of yours, may fail altogether to accord with the Civil Statutes and Provisions of the Realm?"

And Manilov, with a slight gesture of the head, looked meaningly into Chichikov's face, while displaying in his every feature, including his closely-compressed lips, such an expression of profundity as never before was seen on any human countenance—unless on that of some particularly sapient Minister of State who is debating some particularly abstruse problem.

Nevertheless Chichikov rejoined that the kind of scheme or transaction which he had adumbrated in no way clashed with the Civil Statutes and Provisions of Russia; to which he added that the Treasury would even BENEFIT by the enterprise, seeing it would draw therefrom the usual legal percentage.

"What, then, do you propose?" asked Manilov.

"I propose only what is above-board, and nothing else."

"Then, that being so, it is another matter, and I have nothing to urge against it," said Manilov, apparently reassured to the full.

"Very well," remarked Chichikov. "Then we need only to agree as to the price."

"As to the price?" began Manilov, and then stopped. Presently he went on: "Surely you cannot suppose me capable of taking money for souls which, in one sense at least, have completed their existence? Seeing that this fantastic whim of yours (if I may so call it?) has seized upon you to the extent that it has, I, on my side, shall be ready to surrender to you those souls UNCONDITIONALLY, and to charge myself with the whole expenses of the sale."

I should be greatly to blame if I were to omit that, as soon as Manilov had pronounced these words, the face of his guest became replete with satisfaction. Indeed, grave and prudent a man though Chichikov was, he had much ado to refrain from executing a leap that would have done credit to a goat (an animal which, as we all know, finds itself moved to such exertions only during moments of the most ecstatic joy). Nevertheless the guest did at least execute such a convulsive shuffle that the material with which the cushions of the chair were covered came apart, and Manilov gazed at him with some misgiving. Finally Chichikov's gratitude led him to plunge into a stream of acknowledgement of a vehemence which caused his host to grow confused, to blush, to shake his head in deprecation, and to end by declaring that the concession was nothing, and that, his one desire being to manifest the dictates of his heart and the psychic magnetism which his friend exercised, he, in short, looked upon the dead souls as so much worthless rubbish.

"Not at all," replied Chichikov, pressing his hand; after which he heaved a profound sigh. Indeed, he seemed in the right mood for outpourings of the heart, for he continued—not without a ring of emotion in his tone: "If you but knew the service which you have rendered to an apparently insignificant individual who is devoid both of family and kindred! For what have I not suffered in my time—I, a drifting barque amid the tempestuous billows of life? What harryings, what persecutions, have I not known? Of what grief have I not tasted? And why? Simply because I have ever kept the truth in view, because ever I have preserved inviolate an unsullied conscience, because ever I have stretched out a helping hand to the defenceless widow and the hapless orphan!" After which outpouring Chichikov pulled out his handkerchief, and wiped away a brimming tear.

Manilov's heart was moved to the core. Again and again did the two friends press one another's hands in silence as they gazed into one another's tear-filled eyes. Indeed, Manilov COULD not let go our hero's hand, but clasped it with such warmth that the hero in question began to feel himself at a loss how best to wrench it free: until, quietly withdrawing it, he observed that to have the purchase completed as speedily as possible would not be a bad thing; wherefore he himself would at once return to the town to arrange matters. Taking up his hat, therefore, he rose to make his adieus.

"What? Are you departing already?" said Manilov, suddenly recovering himself, and experiencing a sense of misgiving. At that moment his wife sailed into the room.

"Is Paul Ivanovitch leaving us so soon, dearest Lizanka?" she said with an air of regret.

"Yes. Surely it must be that we have wearied him?" her spouse replied.

"By no means," asserted Chichikov, pressing his hand to his heart. "In this breast, madam, will abide for ever the pleasant memory of the time which I have spent with you. Believe me, I could conceive of no greater blessing than to reside, if not under the same roof as yourselves, at all events in your immediate neighbourhood."

"Indeed?" exclaimed Manilov, greatly pleased with the idea. "How splendid it would be if you DID come to reside under our roof, so that we could recline under an elm tree together, and talk philosophy, and delve to the very root of things!"

"Yes, it WOULD be a paradisaical existence!" agreed Chichikov with a sigh. Nevertheless he shook hands with Madame. "Farewell, sudarina," he said. "And farewell to YOU, my esteemed host. Do not forget what I have requested you to do."

"Rest assured that I will not," responded Manilov. "Only for a couple of days will you and I be parted from one another."

With that the party moved into the drawing-room.

"Farewell, dearest children," Chichikov went on as he caught sight of Alkid and Themistocleus, who were playing with a wooden hussar which lacked both a nose and one arm. "Farewell, dearest pets. Pardon me for having brought you no presents, but, to tell you the truth, I was not, until my visit, aware of your existence. However, now that I shall be coming again, I will not fail to bring you gifts. Themistocleus, to you I will bring a sword. You would like that, would you not?"

"I should," replied Themistocleus.

"And to you, Alkid, I will bring a drum. That would suit you, would it not?" And he bowed in Alkid's direction.

"Zeth—a drum," lisped the boy, hanging his head.

"Good! Then a drum it shall be—SUCH a beautiful drum! What a tur-r-r-ru-ing and a tra-ta-ta-ta-ing you will be able to kick up! Farewell, my darling." And, kissing the boy's head, he turned to Manilov and Madame with the slight smile which one assumes before assuring parents of the guileless merits of their offspring.

"But you had better stay, Paul Ivanovitch," said the father as the trio stepped out on to the verandah. "See how the clouds are gathering!"

"They are only small ones," replied Chichikov.

"And you know your way to Sobakevitch's?"

"No, I do not, and should be glad if you would direct me."

"If you like I will tell your coachman." And in very civil fashion Manilov did so, even going so far as to address the man in the second person plural. On hearing that he was to pass two turnings, and then to take a third, Selifan remarked, "We shall get there all right, sir," and Chichikov departed amid a profound salvo of salutations and wavings of handkerchiefs on the part of his host and hostess, who raised themselves on tiptoe in their enthusiasm.

For a long while Manilov stood following the departing britchka with his eyes. In fact, he continued to smoke his pipe and gaze after the vehicle even when it had become lost to view. Then he re-entered the drawing-room, seated himself upon a chair, and surrendered his mind to the thought that he had shown his guest most excellent entertainment. Next, his mind passed imperceptibly to other matters, until at last it lost itself God only knows where. He thought of the amenities of a life, of friendship, and of how nice it would be to live with a comrade on, say, the bank of some river, and to span the river with a bridge of his own, and to build an enormous mansion with a facade lofty enough even to afford a view to Moscow. On that facade he and his wife and friend would drink afternoon tea in the open air, and discuss interesting subjects; after which, in a fine carriage, they would drive to some reunion or other, where with their pleasant manners they would so charm the company that the Imperial Government, on learning of their merits, would raise the pair to the grade of General or God knows what—that is to say, to heights whereof even Manilov himself could form no idea. Then suddenly Chichikov's extraordinary request interrupted the dreamer's reflections, and he found his brain powerless to digest it, seeing that, turn and turn the matter about as he might, he could not properly explain its bearing. Smoking his pipe, he sat where he was until supper time.

CHAPTER

III

Meanwhile, Chichikov, seated in his britchka and bowling along the turnpike, was feeling greatly pleased with himself. From the preceding chapter the reader will have gathered the principal subject of his bent and inclinations: wherefore it is no matter for wonder that his body and his soul had ended by becoming wholly immersed therein. To all appearances the thoughts, the calculations, and the projects which were now reflected in his face partook of a pleasant nature, since momentarily they kept leaving behind them a satisfied smile. Indeed, so engrossed was he that he never noticed that his coachman, elated with the hospitality of Manilov's domestics, was making remarks of a didactic nature to the off horse of the troika 11, a skewbald. This skewbald was a knowing animal, and made only a show of pulling; whereas its comrades, the middle horse (a bay, and known as the Assessor, owing to his having been acquired from a gentleman of that rank) and the near horse (a roan), would do their work gallantly, and even evince in their eyes the pleasure which they derived from their exertions.

"Ah, you rascal, you rascal! I'll get the better of you!" ejaculated Selifan as he sat up and gave the lazy one a cut with his whip. "YOU know your business all right, you German pantaloon! The bay is a good fellow, and does his duty, and I will give him a bit over his feed, for he is a horse to be respected; and the Assessor too is a good horse. But what are YOU shaking your ears for? You are a fool, so just mind when you're spoken to. 'Tis good advice I'm giving you, you blockhead. Ah! You CAN travel when you like." And he gave the animal another cut, and then shouted to the trio, "Gee up, my beauties!" and drew his whip gently across the backs of the skewbald's comrades—not as a punishment, but as a sign of his approval. That done, he addressed himself to the skewbald again.

"Do you think," he cried, "that I don't see what you are doing? You can behave quite decently when you like, and make a man respect you."

With that he fell to recalling certain reminiscences.

"They were NICE folk, those folk at the gentleman's yonder," he mused. "I DO love a chat with a man when he is a good sort. With a man of that kind I am always hail-fellow-well-met, and glad to drink a glass of tea with him, or to eat a biscuit. One CAN'T help respecting a decent fellow. For instance, this gentleman of mine—why, every one looks up to him, for he has been in the Government's service, and is a Collegiate Councillor."

Thus soliloquising, he passed to more remote abstractions; until, had Chichikov been listening, he would have learnt a number of interesting details concerning himself. However, his thoughts were wholly occupied with his own subject, so much so that not until a loud clap of thunder awoke him from his reverie did he glance around him. The sky was completely covered with clouds, and the dusty turnpike beginning to be sprinkled with drops of rain. At length a second and a nearer and a louder peal resounded, and the rain descended as from a bucket. Falling slantwise, it beat upon one side of the basketwork of the tilt until the splashings began to spurt into his face, and he found himself forced to draw the curtains (fitted with circular openings through which to obtain a glimpse of the wayside view), and to shout to Selifan to quicken his pace. Upon that the coachman, interrupted in the middle of his harangue, bethought him that no time was to be lost; wherefore, extracting from under the box-seat a piece of old blanket, he covered over his sleeves, resumed the reins, and cheered on his threefold team (which, it may be said, had so completely succumbed to the influence of the pleasant lassitude induced by Selifan's discourse that it had taken to scarcely placing one leg before the other). Unfortunately, Selifan could not clearly remember whether two turnings had been passed or three. Indeed, on collecting his faculties, and dimly recalling the lie of the road, he became filled with a shrewd suspicion that A VERY LARGE NUMBER of turnings had been passed. But since, at moments which call for a hasty decision, a Russian is quick to discover what may conceivably be the best course to take, our coachman put away from him all ulterior reasoning, and, turning to the right at the next cross-road, shouted, "Hi, my beauties!" and set off at a gallop. Never for a moment did he stop to think whither the road might lead him!

It was long before the clouds had discharged their burden, and, meanwhile, the dust on the road became kneaded into mire, and the horses' task of pulling the britchka heavier and heavier. Also, Chichikov had taken alarm at his continued failure to catch sight of Sobakevitch's country house. According to his calculations, it ought to have been reached long ago. He gazed about him on every side, but the darkness was too dense for the eye to pierce.

"Selifan!" he exclaimed, leaning forward in the britchka.

"What is it, barin?" replied the coachman.

"Can you see the country house anywhere?"

"No, barin." After which, with a flourish of the whip, the man broke into a sort of endless, drawling song. In that song everything had a place. By "everything" I mean both the various encouraging and stimulating cries with which Russian folk urge on their horses, and a random, unpremeditated selection of adjectives.

Meanwhile Chichikov began to notice that the britchka was swaying violently, and dealing him occasional bumps. Consequently he suspected that it had left the road and was being dragged over a ploughed field. Upon Selifan's mind there appeared to have dawned a similar inkling, for he had ceased to hold forth.

"You rascal, what road are you following?" inquired Chichikov.

"I don't know," retorted the coachman. "What can a man do at a time of night when the darkness won't let him even see his whip?" And as Selifan spoke the vehicle tilted to an angle which left Chichikov no choice but to hang on with hands and teeth. At length he realised the fact that Selifan was drunk.

"Stop, stop, or you will upset us!" he shouted to the fellow.

"No, no, barin," replied Selifan. "HOW could I upset you? To upset people is wrong. I know that very well, and should never dream of such conduct."

Here he started to turn the vehicle round a little—and kept on doing so until the britchka capsized on to its side, and Chichikov landed in the mud on his hands and knees. Fortunately Selifan succeeded in stopping the horses, although they would have stopped of themselves, seeing that they were utterly worn out. This unforeseen catastrophe evidently astonished their driver. Slipping from the box, he stood resting his hands against the side of the britchka, while Chichikov tumbled and floundered about in the mud, in a vain endeavour to wriggle clear of the stuff.

"Ah, you!" said Selifan meditatively to the britchka. "To think of upsetting us like this!"

"You are as drunk as a lord!" exclaimed Chichikov.

"No, no, barin. Drunk, indeed? Why, I know my manners too well. A word or two with a friend—that is all that I have taken. Any one may talk with a decent man when he meets him. There is nothing wrong in that. Also, we had a snack together. There is nothing wrong in a snack—especially a snack with a decent man."

"What did I say to you when last you got drunk?" asked Chichikov. "Have you forgotten what I said then?"

"No, no, barin. HOW could I forget it? I know what is what, and know that it is not right to get drunk. All that I have been having is a word or two with a decent man, for the reason that—"

"Well, if I lay the whip about you, you'll know then how to talk to a decent fellow, I'll warrant!"

"As you please, barin," replied the complacent Selifan. "Should you whip me, you will whip me, and I shall have nothing to complain of. Why should you not whip me if I deserve it? 'Tis for you to do as you like. Whippings are necessary sometimes, for a peasant often plays the fool, and discipline ought to be maintained. If I have deserved it, beat me. Why should you not?"

This reasoning seemed, at the moment, irrefutable, and Chichikov said nothing more. Fortunately fate had decided to take pity on the pair, for from afar their ears caught the barking of a dog. Plucking up courage, Chichikov gave orders for the britchka to be righted, and the horses to be urged forward; and since a Russian driver has at least this merit, that, owing to a keen sense of smell being able to take the place of eyesight, he can, if necessary, drive at random and yet reach a destination of some sort, Selifan succeeded, though powerless to discern a single object, in directing his steeds to a country house near by, and that with such a certainty of instinct that it was not until the shafts had collided with a garden wall, and thereby made it clear that to proceed another pace was impossible, that he stopped. All that Chichikov could discern through the thick veil of pouring rain was something which resembled a verandah. So he dispatched Selifan to search for the entrance gates, and that process would have lasted indefinitely had it not been shortened by the circumstance that, in Russia, the place of a Swiss footman is frequently taken by watchdogs; of which animals a number now proclaimed the travellers' presence so loudly that Chichikov found himself forced to stop his ears. Next, a light gleamed in one of the windows, and filtered in a thin stream to the garden wall—thus revealing the whereabouts of the entrance gates; whereupon Selifan fell to knocking at the gates until the bolts of the house door were withdrawn and there issued therefrom a figure clad in a rough cloak.

"Who is that knocking? What have you come for?" shouted the hoarse voice of an elderly woman.

"We are travellers, good mother," said Chichikov. "Pray allow us to spend the night here."

"Out upon you for a pair of gadabouts!" retorted the old woman. "A fine time of night to be arriving! We don't keep an hotel, mind you. This is a lady's residence."

"But what are we to do, mother? We have lost our way, and cannot spend the night out of doors in such weather."

"No, we cannot. The night is dark and cold," added Selifan.

"Hold your tongue, you fool!" exclaimed Chichikov.

"Who ARE you, then?" inquired the old woman.

"A dvorianin 12, good mother."

Somehow the word dvorianin seemed to give the old woman food for thought.

"Wait a moment," she said, "and I will tell the mistress."

Two minutes later she returned with a lantern in her hand, the gates were opened, and a light glimmered in a second window. Entering the courtyard, the britchka halted before a moderate-sized mansion. The darkness did not permit of very accurate observation being made, but, apparently, the windows only of one-half of the building were illuminated, while a quagmire in front of the door reflected the beams from the same. Meanwhile the rain continued to beat sonorously down upon the wooden roof, and could be heard trickling into a water butt; nor for a single moment did the dogs cease to bark with all the strength of their lungs. One of them, throwing up its head, kept venting a howl of such energy and duration that the animal seemed to be howling for a handsome wager; while another, cutting in between the yelpings of the first animal, kept restlessly reiterating, like a postman's bell, the notes of a very young puppy. Finally, an old hound which appeared to be gifted with a peculiarly robust temperament kept supplying the part of contrabasso, so that his growls resembled the rumbling of a bass singer when a chorus is in full cry, and the tenors are rising on tiptoe in their efforts to compass a particularly high note, and the whole body of choristers are wagging their heads before approaching a climax, and this contrabasso alone is tucking his bearded chin into his collar, and sinking almost to a squatting posture on the floor, in order to produce a note which shall cause the windows to shiver and their panes to crack. Naturally, from a canine chorus of such executants it might reasonably be inferred that the establishment was one of the utmost respectability. To that, however, our damp, cold hero gave not a thought, for all his mind was fixed upon bed. Indeed, the britchka had hardly come to a standstill before he leapt out upon the doorstep, missed his footing, and came within an ace of falling. To meet him there issued a female younger than the first, but very closely resembling her; and on his being conducted to the parlour, a couple of glances showed him that the room was hung with old striped curtains, and ornamented with pictures of birds and small, antique mirrors—the latter set in dark frames which were carved to resemble scrolls of foliage. Behind each mirror was stuck either a letter or an old pack of cards or a stocking, while on the wall hung a clock with a flowered dial. More, however, Chichikov could not discern, for his eyelids were as heavy as though smeared with treacle. Presently the lady of the house herself entered—an elderly woman in a sort of nightcap (hastily put on) and a flannel neck wrap. She belonged to that class of lady landowners who are for ever lamenting failures of the harvest and their losses thereby; to the class who, drooping their heads despondently, are all the while stuffing money into striped purses, which they keep hoarded in the drawers of cupboards. Into one purse they will stuff rouble pieces, into another half roubles, and into a third tchetvertachki 13, although from their mien you would suppose that the cupboard contained only linen and nightshirts and skeins of wool and the piece of shabby material which is destined—should the old gown become scorched during the baking of holiday cakes and other dainties, or should it fall into pieces of itself—to become converted into a new dress. But the gown never does get burnt or wear out, for the reason that the lady is too careful; wherefore the piece of shabby material reposes in its unmade-up condition until the priest advises that it be given to the niece of some widowed sister, together with a quantity of other such rubbish.

Chichikov apologised for having disturbed the household with his unexpected arrival.

"Not at all, not at all," replied the lady. "But in what dreadful weather God has brought you hither! What wind and what rain! You could not help losing your way. Pray excuse us for being unable to make better preparations for you at this time of night."

Suddenly there broke in upon the hostess' words the sound of a strange hissing, a sound so loud that the guest started in alarm, and the more so seeing that it increased until the room seemed filled with adders. On glancing upwards, however, he recovered his composure, for he perceived the sound to be emanating from the clock, which appeared to be in a mind to strike. To the hissing sound there succeeded a wheezing one, until, putting forth its best efforts, the thing struck two with as much clatter as though some one had been hitting an iron pot with a cudgel. That done, the pendulum returned to its right-left, right-left oscillation.

Chichikov thanked his hostess kindly, and said that he needed nothing, and she must not put herself about: only for rest was he longing—though also he should like to know whither he had arrived, and whether the distance to the country house of land-owner Sobakevitch was anything very great. To this the lady replied that she had never so much as heard the name, since no gentleman of the name resided in the locality.

"But at least you are acquainted with landowner Manilov?" continued Chichikov.

"No. Who is he?"

"Another landed proprietor, madam."

"Well, neither have I heard of him. No such landowner lives hereabouts."

"Then who ARE your local landowners?"

"Bobrov, Svinin, Kanapatiev, Khapakin, Trepakin, and Plieshakov."

"Are they rich men?"

"No, none of them. One of them may own twenty souls, and another thirty, but of gentry who own a hundred there are none."

Chichikov reflected that he had indeed fallen into an aristocratic wilderness!

"At all events, is the town far away?" he inquired.

"About sixty versts. How sorry I am that I have nothing for you to eat! Should you care to drink some tea?"

"I thank you, good mother, but I require nothing beyond a bed."

"Well, after such a journey you must indeed be needing rest, so you shall lie upon this sofa. Fetinia, bring a quilt and some pillows and sheets. What weather God has sent us! And what dreadful thunder! Ever since sunset I have had a candle burning before the ikon in my bedroom. My God! Why, your back and sides are as muddy as a boar's! However have you managed to get into such a state?"

"That I am nothing worse than muddy is indeed fortunate, since, but for the Almighty, I should have had my ribs broken."

"Dear, dear! To think of all that you must have been through. Had I not better wipe your back?"

"I thank you, I thank you, but you need not trouble. Merely be so good as to tell your maid to dry my clothes."

"Do you hear that, Fetinia?" said the hostess, turning to a woman who was engaged in dragging in a feather bed and deluging the room with feathers. "Take this coat and this vest, and, after drying them before the fire—just as we used to do for your late master—give them a good rub, and fold them up neatly."

"Very well, mistress," said Fetinia, spreading some sheets over the bed, and arranging the pillows.

"Now your bed is ready for you," said the hostess to Chichikov. "Good-night, dear sir. I wish you good-night. Is there anything else that you require? Perhaps you would like to have your heels tickled before retiring to rest? Never could my late husband get to sleep without that having been done."

But the guest declined the proffered heel-tickling, and, on his hostess taking her departure, hastened to divest himself of his clothing, both upper and under, and to hand the garments to Fetinia. She wished him good-night, and removed the wet trappings; after which he found himself alone. Not without satisfaction did he eye his bed, which reached almost to the ceiling. Clearly Fetinia was a past mistress in the art of beating up such a couch, and, as the result, he had no sooner mounted it with the aid of a chair than it sank well-nigh to the floor, and the feathers, squeezed out of their proper confines, flew hither and thither into every corner of the apartment. Nevertheless he extinguished the candle, covered himself over with the chintz quilt, snuggled down beneath it, and instantly fell asleep. Next day it was late in the morning before he awoke. Through the window the sun was shining into his eyes, and the flies which, overnight, had been roosting quietly on the walls and ceiling now turned their attention to the visitor. One settled on his lip, another on his ear, a third hovered as though intending to lodge in his very eye, and a fourth had the temerity to alight just under his nostrils. In his drowsy condition he inhaled the latter insect, sneezed violently, and so returned to consciousness. He glanced around the room, and perceived that not all the pictures were representative of birds, since among them hung also a portrait of Kutuzov 14 and an oil painting of an old man in a uniform with red facings such as were worn in the days of the Emperor Paul 15. At this moment the clock uttered its usual hissing sound, and struck ten, while a woman's face peered in at the door, but at once withdrew, for the reason that, with the object of sleeping as well as possible, Chichikov had removed every stitch of his clothing. Somehow the face seemed to him familiar, and he set himself to recall whose it could be. At length he recollected that it was the face of his hostess. His clothes he found lying, clean and dry, beside him; so he dressed and approached the mirror, meanwhile sneezing again with such vehemence that a cock which happened at the moment to be near the window (which was situated at no great distance from the ground) chuckled a short, sharp phrase. Probably it meant, in the bird's alien tongue, "Good morning to you!" Chichikov retorted by calling the bird a fool, and then himself approached the window to look at the view. It appeared to comprise a poulterer's premises. At all events, the narrow yard in front of the window was full of poultry and other domestic creatures—of game fowls and barn door fowls, with, among them, a cock which strutted with measured gait, and kept shaking its comb, and tilting its head as though it were trying to listen to something. Also, a sow and her family were helping to grace the scene. First, she rooted among a heap of litter; then, in passing, she ate up a young pullet; lastly, she proceeded carelessly to munch some pieces of melon rind. To this small yard or poultry-run a length of planking served as a fence, while beyond it lay a kitchen garden containing cabbages, onions, potatoes, beetroots, and other household vegetables. Also, the garden contained a few stray fruit trees that were covered with netting to protect them from the magpies and sparrows; flocks of which were even then wheeling and darting from one spot to another. For the same reason a number of scarecrows with outstretched arms stood reared on long poles, with, surmounting one of the figures, a cast-off cap of the hostess's. Beyond the garden again there stood a number of peasants' huts. Though scattered, instead of being arranged in regular rows, these appeared to Chichikov's eye to comprise well-to-do inhabitants, since all rotten planks in their roofing had been replaced with new ones, and none of their doors were askew, and such of their tiltsheds as faced him evinced evidence of a presence of a spare waggon—in some cases almost a new one.

"This lady owns by no means a poor village," said Chichikov to himself; wherefore he decided then and there to have a talk with his hostess, and to cultivate her closer acquaintance. Accordingly he peeped through the chink of the door whence her head had recently protruded, and, on seeing her seated at a tea table, entered and greeted her with a cheerful, kindly smile.

"Good morning, dear sir," she responded as she rose. "How have you slept?" She was dressed in better style than she had been on the previous evening. That is to say, she was now wearing a gown of some dark colour, and lacked her nightcap, and had swathed her neck in something stiff.

"I have slept exceedingly well," replied Chichikov, seating himself upon a chair. "And how are YOU, good madam?"

"But poorly, my dear sir."

"And why so?"

"Because I cannot sleep. A pain has taken me in my middle, and my legs, from the ankles upwards, are aching as though they were broken."

"That will pass, that will pass, good mother. You must pay no attention to it."

"God grant that it MAY pass. However, I have been rubbing myself with lard and turpentine. What sort of tea will you take? In this jar I have some of the scented kind."

"Excellent, good mother! Then I will take that."

Probably the reader will have noticed that, for all his expressions of solicitude, Chichikov's tone towards his hostess partook of a freer, a more unceremonious, nature than that which he had adopted towards Madam Manilov. And here I should like to assert that, howsoever much, in certain respects, we Russians may be surpassed by foreigners, at least we surpass them in adroitness of manner. In fact the various shades and subtleties of our social intercourse defy enumeration. A Frenchman or a German would be incapable of envisaging and understanding all its peculiarities and differences, for his tone in speaking to a millionaire differs but little from that which he employs towards a small tobacconist—and that in spite of the circumstance that he is accustomed to cringe before the former. With us, however, things are different. In Russian society there exist clever folk who can speak in one manner to a landowner possessed of two hundred peasant souls, and in another to a landowner possessed of three hundred, and in another to a landowner possessed of five hundred. In short, up to the number of a million souls the Russian will have ready for each landowner a suitable mode of address. For example, suppose that somewhere there exists a government office, and that in that office there exists a director. I would beg of you to contemplate him as he sits among his myrmidons. Sheer nervousness will prevent you from uttering a word in his presence, so great are the pride and superiority depicted on his countenance. Also, were you to sketch him, you would be sketching a veritable Prometheus, for his glance is as that of an eagle, and he walks with measured, stately stride. Yet no sooner will the eagle have left the room to seek the study of his superior officer than he will go scurrying along (papers held close to his nose) like any partridge. But in society, and at the evening party (should the rest of those present be of lesser rank than himself) the Prometheus will once more become Prometheus, and the man who stands a step below him will treat him in a way never dreamt of by Ovid, seeing that each fly is of lesser account than its superior fly, and becomes, in the presence of the latter, even as a grain of sand. "Surely that is not Ivan Petrovitch?" you will say of such and such a man as you regard him. "Ivan Petrovitch is tall, whereas this man is small and spare. Ivan Petrovitch has a loud, deep voice, and never smiles, whereas this man (whoever he may be) is twittering like a sparrow, and smiling all the time." Yet approach and take a good look at the fellow and you will see that is IS Ivan Petrovitch. "Alack, alack!" will be the only remark you can make.

Let us return to our characters in real life. We have seen that, on this occasion, Chichikov decided to dispense with ceremony; wherefore, taking up the teapot, he went on as follows:

"You have a nice little village here, madam. How many souls does it contain?"

"A little less than eighty, dear sir. But the times are hard, and I have lost a great deal through last year's harvest having proved a failure."

"But your peasants look fine, strong fellows. May I enquire your name? Through arriving so late at night I have quite lost my wits."

"Korobotchka, the widow of a Collegiate Secretary."

"I humbly thank you. And your Christian name and patronymic?"

"Nastasia Petrovna."

"Nastasia Petrovna! Those are excellent names. I have a maternal aunt named like yourself."

"And YOUR name?" queried the lady. "May I take it that you are a Government Assessor?"

"No, madam," replied Chichikov with a smile. "I am not an Assessor, but a traveller on private business."

"Then you must be a buyer of produce? How I regret that I have sold my honey so cheaply to other buyers! Otherwise YOU might have bought it, dear sir."

"I never buy honey."

"Then WHAT do you buy, pray? Hemp? I have a little of that by me, but not more than half a pood 16 or so."

"No, madam. It is in other wares that I deal. Tell me, have you, of late years, lost many of your peasants by death?"

"Yes; no fewer than eighteen," responded the old lady with a sigh. "Such a fine lot, too—all good workers! True, others have since grown up, but of what use are THEY? Mere striplings. When the Assessor last called upon me I could have wept; for, though those workmen of mine are dead, I have to keep on paying for them as though they were still alive! And only last week my blacksmith got burnt to death! Such a clever hand at his trade he was!"

"What? A fire occurred at your place?"

"No, no, God preserve us all! It was not so bad as that. You must understand that the blacksmith SET HIMSELF on fire—he got set on fire in his bowels through overdrinking. Yes, all of a sudden there burst from him a blue flame, and he smouldered and smouldered until he had turned as black as a piece of charcoal! Yet what a clever blacksmith he was! And now I have no horses to drive out with, for there is no one to shoe them."

"In everything the will of God, madam," said Chichikov with a sigh. "Against the divine wisdom it is not for us to rebel. Pray hand them over to me, Nastasia Petrovna."

"Hand over whom?"

"The dead peasants."

"But how could I do that?"

"Quite simply. Sell them to me, and I will give you some money in exchange."

"But how am I to sell them to you? I scarcely understand what you mean. Am I to dig them up again from the ground?"

Chichikov perceived that the old lady was altogether at sea, and that he must explain the matter; wherefore in a few words he informed her that the transfer or purchase of the souls in question would take place merely on paper—that the said souls would be listed as still alive.

"And what good would they be to you?" asked his hostess, staring at him with her eyes distended.

"That is MY affair."

"But they are DEAD souls."

"Who said they were not? The mere fact of their being dead entails upon you a loss as dead as the souls, for you have to continue paying tax upon them, whereas MY plan is to relieve you both of the tax and of the resultant trouble. NOW do you understand? And I will not only do as I say, but also hand you over fifteen roubles per soul. Is that clear enough?"

"Yes—but I do not know," said his hostess diffidently. "You see, never before have I sold dead souls."

"Quite so. It would be a surprising thing if you had. But surely you do not think that these dead souls are in the least worth keeping?"

"Oh, no, indeed! Why should they be worth keeping? I am sure they are not so. The only thing which troubles me is the fact that they are DEAD."

"She seems a truly obstinate old woman!" was Chichikov's inward comment. "Look here, madam," he added aloud. "You reason well, but you are simply ruining yourself by continuing to pay the tax upon dead souls as though they were still alive."

"Oh, good sir, do not speak of it!" the lady exclaimed. "Three weeks ago I took a hundred and fifty roubles to that Assessor, and buttered him up, and—"

"Then you see how it is, do you not? Remember that, according to my plan, you will never again have to butter up the Assessor, seeing that it will be I who will be paying for those peasants—*I*, not YOU, for I shall have taken over the dues upon them, and have transferred them to myself as so many bona fide serfs. Do you understand AT LAST?"

However, the old lady still communed with herself. She could see that the transaction would be to her advantage, yet it was one of such a novel and unprecedented nature that she was beginning to fear lest this purchaser of souls intended to cheat her. Certainly he had come from God only knew where, and at the dead of night, too!

"But, sir, I have never in my life sold dead folk—only living ones. Three years ago I transferred two wenches to Protopopov for a hundred roubles apiece, and he thanked me kindly, for they turned out splendid workers—able to make napkins or anything else."

"Yes, but with the living we have nothing to do, damn it! I am asking you only about DEAD folk."

"Yes, yes, of course. But at first sight I felt afraid lest I should be incurring a loss—lest you should be wishing to outwit me, good sir. You see, the dead souls are worth rather more than you have offered for them."

"See here, madam. (What a woman it is!) HOW could they be worth more? Think for yourself. They are so much loss to you—so much loss, do you understand? Take any worthless, rubbishy article you like—a piece of old rag, for example. That rag will yet fetch its price, for it can be bought for paper-making. But these dead souls are good for NOTHING AT ALL. Can you name anything that they ARE good for?"

"True, true—they ARE good for nothing. But what troubles me is the fact that they are dead."

"What a blockhead of a creature!" said Chichikov to himself, for he was beginning to lose patience. "Bless her heart, I may as well be going. She has thrown me into a perfect sweat, the cursed old shrew!"

He took a handkerchief from his pocket, and wiped the perspiration from his brow. Yet he need not have flown into such a passion. More than one respected statesman reveals himself, when confronted with a business matter, to be just such another as Madam Korobotchka, in that, once he has got an idea into his head, there is no getting it out of him—you may ply him with daylight-clear arguments, yet they will rebound from his brain as an india-rubber ball rebounds from a flagstone. Nevertheless, wiping away the perspiration, Chichikov resolved to try whether he could not bring her back to the road by another path.

"Madam," he said, "either you are declining to understand what I say or you are talking for the mere sake of talking. If I hand you over some money—fifteen roubles for each soul, do you understand?—it is MONEY, not something which can be picked up haphazard on the street. For instance, tell me how much you sold your honey for?"

"For twelve roubles per pood."

"Ah! Then by those words, madam, you have laid a trifling sin upon your soul; for you did NOT sell the honey for twelve roubles."

"By the Lord God I did!"

"Well, well! Never mind. Honey is only honey. Now, you had collected that stuff, it may be, for a year, and with infinite care and labour. You had fussed after it, you had trotted to and fro, you had duly frozen out the bees, and you had fed them in the cellar throughout the winter. But these dead souls of which I speak are quite another matter, for in this case you have put forth no exertions—it was merely God's will that they should leave the world, and thus decrease the personnel of your establishment. In the former case you received (so you allege) twelve roubles per pood for your labour; but in this case you will receive money for having done nothing at all. Nor will you receive twelve roubles per item, but FIFTEEN—and roubles not in silver, but roubles in good paper currency."

That these powerful inducements would certainly cause the old woman to yield Chichikov had not a doubt.

"True," his hostess replied. "But how strangely business comes to me as a widow! Perhaps I had better wait a little longer, seeing that other buyers might come along, and I might be able to compare prices."

"For shame, madam! For shame! Think what you are saying. Who else, I would ask, would care to buy those souls? What use could they be to any one?"

"If that is so, they might come in useful to ME," mused the old woman aloud; after which she sat staring at Chichikov with her mouth open and a face of nervous expectancy as to his possible rejoinder.

"Dead folk useful in a household!" he exclaimed. "Why, what could you do with them? Set them up on poles to frighten away the sparrows from your garden?"

"The Lord save us, but what things you say!" she ejaculated, crossing herself.

"Well, WHAT could you do with them? By this time they are so much bones and earth. That is all there is left of them. Their transfer to myself would be ON PAPER only. Come, come! At least give me an answer."

Again the old woman communed with herself.

"What are you thinking of, Nastasia Petrovna?" inquired Chichikov.

"I am thinking that I scarcely know what to do. Perhaps I had better sell you some hemp?"

"What do I want with hemp? Pardon me, but just when I have made to you a different proposal altogether you begin fussing about hemp! Hemp is hemp, and though I may want some when I NEXT visit you, I should like to know what you have to say to the suggestion under discussion."

"Well, I think it a very queer bargain. Never have I heard of such a thing."

Upon this Chichikov lost all patience, upset his chair, and bid her go to the devil; of which personage even the mere mention terrified her extremely.

"Do not speak of him, I beg of you!" she cried, turning pale. "May God, rather, bless him! Last night was the third night that he has appeared to me in a dream. You see, after saying my prayers, I bethought me of telling my fortune by the cards; and God must have sent him as a punishment. He looked so horrible, and had horns longer than a bull's!"

"I wonder you don't see SCORES of devils in your dreams! Merely out of Christian charity he had come to you to say, 'I perceive a poor widow going to rack and ruin, and likely soon to stand in danger of want.' Well, go to rack and ruin—yes, you and all your village together!"

"The insults!" exclaimed the old woman, glancing at her visitor in terror.

"I should think so!" continued Chichikov. "Indeed, I cannot find words to describe you. To say no more about it, you are like a dog in a manger. You don't want to eat the hay yourself, yet you won't let anyone else touch it. All that I am seeking to do is to purchase certain domestic products of yours, for the reason that I have certain Government contracts to fulfil." This last he added in passing, and without any ulterior motive, save that it came to him as a happy thought. Nevertheless the mention of Government contracts exercised a powerful influence upon Nastasia Petrovna, and she hastened to say in a tone that was almost supplicatory:

"Why should you be so angry with me? Had I known that you were going to lose your temper in this way, I should never have discussed the matter."

"No wonder that I lose my temper! An egg too many is no great matter, yet it may prove exceedingly annoying."

"Well, well, I will let you have the souls for fifteen roubles each. Also, with regard to those contracts, do not forget me if at any time you should find yourself in need of rye-meal or buckwheat or groats or dead meat."

"No, I shall NEVER forget you, madam!" he said, wiping his forehead, where three separate streams of perspiration were trickling down his face. Then he asked her whether in the town she had any acquaintance or agent whom she could empower to complete the transference of the serfs, and to carry out whatsoever else might be necessary.

"Certainly," replied Madame Korobotchka. "The son of our archpriest, Father Cyril, himself is a lawyer."

Upon that Chichikov begged her to accord the gentleman in question a power of attorney, while, to save extra trouble, he himself would then and there compose the requisite letter.

"It would be a fine thing if he were to buy up all my meal and stock for the Government," thought Madame to herself. "I must encourage him a little. There has been some dough standing ready since last night, so I will go and tell Fetinia to try a few pancakes. Also, it might be well to try him with an egg pie. We make then nicely here, and they do not take long in the making."

So she departed to translate her thoughts into action, as well as to supplement the pie with other products of the domestic cuisine; while, for his part, Chichikov returned to the drawing-room where he had spent the night, in order to procure from his dispatch-box the necessary writing-paper. The room had now been set in order, the sumptuous feather bed removed, and a table set before the sofa. Depositing his dispatch-box upon the table, he heaved a gentle sigh on becoming aware that he was so soaked with perspiration that he might almost have been dipped in a river. Everything, from his shirt to his socks, was dripping. "May she starve to death, the cursed old harridan!" he ejaculated after a moment's rest. Then he opened his dispatch-box. In passing, I may say that I feel certain that at least SOME of my readers will be curious to know the contents and the internal arrangements of that receptacle. Why should I not gratify their curiosity? To begin with, the centre of the box contained a soap-dish, with, disposed around it, six or seven compartments for razors. Next came square partitions for a sand-box 17 and an inkstand, as well as (scooped out in their midst) a hollow of pens, sealing-wax, and anything else that required more room. Lastly there were all sorts of little divisions, both with and without lids, for articles of a smaller nature, such as visiting cards, memorial cards, theatre tickets, and things which Chichikov had laid by as souvenirs. This portion of the box could be taken out, and below it were both a space for manuscripts and a secret money-box—the latter made to draw out from the side of the receptacle.

Chichikov set to work to clean a pen, and then to write. Presently his hostess entered the room.

"What a beautiful box you have got, my dear sir!" she exclaimed as she took a seat beside him. "Probably you bought it in Moscow?"

"Yes—in Moscow," replied Chichikov without interrupting his writing.

"I thought so. One CAN get good things there. Three years ago my sister brought me a few pairs of warm shoes for my sons, and they were such excellent articles! To this day my boys wear them. And what nice stamped paper you have!" (she had peered into the dispatch-box, where, sure enough, there lay a further store of the paper in question). "Would you mind letting me have a sheet of it? I am without any at all, although I shall soon have to be presenting a plea to the land court, and possess not a morsel of paper to write it on."

Upon this Chichikov explained that the paper was not the sort proper for the purpose—that it was meant for serf-indenturing, and not for the framing of pleas. Nevertheless, to quiet her, he gave her a sheet stamped to the value of a rouble. Next, he handed her the letter to sign, and requested, in return, a list of her peasants. Unfortunately, such a list had never been compiled, let alone any copies of it, and the only way in which she knew the peasants' names was by heart. However, he told her to dictate them. Some of the names greatly astonished our hero, so, still more, did the surnames. Indeed, frequently, on hearing the latter, he had to pause before writing them down. Especially did he halt before a certain "Peter Saveliev Neuvazhai Korito." "What a string of titles!" involuntarily he ejaculated. To the Christian name of another serf was appended "Korovi Kirpitch," and to that of a third "Koleso Ivan." However, at length the list was compiled, and he caught a deep breath; which latter proceeding caused him to catch also the attractive odour of something fried in fat.

"I beseech you to have a morsel," murmured his hostess. Chichikov looked up, and saw that the table was spread with mushrooms, pies, and other viands.

"Try this freshly-made pie and an egg," continued Madame.

Chichikov did so, and having eaten more than half of what she offered him, praised the pie highly. Indeed, it was a toothsome dish, and, after his difficulties and exertions with his hostess, it tasted even better than it might otherwise have done.

"And also a few pancakes?" suggested Madame.

For answer Chichikov folded three together, and, having dipped them in melted butter, consigned the lot to his mouth, and then wiped his mouth with a napkin. Twice more was the process repeated, and then he requested his hostess to order the britchka to be got ready. In dispatching Fetinia with the necessary instructions, she ordered her to return with a second batch of hot pancakes.

"Your pancakes are indeed splendid," said Chichikov, applying himself to the second consignment of fried dainties when they had arrived.

"Yes, we make them well here," replied Madame. "Yet how unfortunate it is that the harvest should have proved so poor as to have prevented me from earning anything on my—But why should you be in such a hurry to depart, good sir?" She broke off on seeing Chichikov reach for his cap. "The britchka is not yet ready."

"Then it is being got so, madam, it is being got so, and I shall need a moment or two to pack my things."

"As you please, dear sir; but do not forget me in connection with those Government contracts."

"No, I have said that NEVER shall I forget you," replied Chichikov as he hurried into the hall.

"And would you like to buy some lard?" continued his hostess, pursuing him.

"Lard? Oh certainly. Why not? Only, only—I will do so ANOTHER time."

"I shall have some ready at about Christmas."

"Quite so, madam. THEN I will buy anything and everything—the lard included."

"And perhaps you will be wanting also some feathers? I shall be having some for sale about St. Philip's Day."

"Very well, very well, madam."

"There you see!" she remarked as they stepped out on to the verandah. "The britchka is NOT yet ready."

"But it soon will be, it soon will be. Only direct me to the main road."

"How am I to do that?" said Madame. "'Twould puzzle a wise man to do so, for in these parts there are so many turnings. However, I will send a girl to guide you. You could find room for her on the box-seat, could you not?"

"Yes, of course."

"Then I will send her. She knows the way thoroughly. Only do not carry her off for good. Already some traders have deprived me of one of my girls."

Chichikov reassured his hostess on the point, and Madame plucked up courage enough to scan, first of all, the housekeeper, who happened to be issuing from the storehouse with a bowl of honey, and, next, a young peasant who happened to be standing at the gates; and, while thus engaged, she became wholly absorbed in her domestic pursuits. But why pay her so much attention? The Widow Korobotchka, Madame Manilov, domestic life, non-domestic life—away with them all! How strangely are things compounded! In a trice may joy turn to sorrow, should one halt long enough over it: in a trice only God can say what ideas may strike one. You may fall even to thinking: "After all, did Madame Korobotchka stand so very low in the scale of human perfection? Was there really such a very great gulf between her and Madame Manilov—between her and the Madame Manilov whom we have seen entrenched behind the walls of a genteel mansion in which there were a fine staircase of wrought metal and a number of rich carpets; the Madame Manilov who spent most of her time in yawning behind half-read books, and in hoping for a visit from some socially distinguished person in order that she might display her wit and carefully rehearsed thoughts—thoughts which had been de rigueur in town for a week past, yet which referred, not to what was going on in her household or on her estate—both of which properties were at odds and ends, owing to her ignorance of the art of managing them—but to the coming political revolution in France and the direction in which fashionable Catholicism was supposed to be moving? But away with such things! Why need we speak of them? Yet how comes it that suddenly into the midst of our careless, frivolous, unthinking moments there may enter another, and a very different, tendency?—that the smile may not have left a human face before its owner will have radically changed his or her nature (though not his or her environment) with the result that the face will suddenly become lit with a radiance never before seen there? . . .

"Here is the britchka, here is the britchka!" exclaimed Chichikov on perceiving that vehicle slowly advancing. "Ah, you blockhead!" he went on to Selifan. "Why have you been loitering about? I suppose last night's fumes have not yet left your brain?"

To this Selifan returned no reply.

"Good-bye, madam," added the speaker. "But where is the girl whom you promised me?"

"Here, Pelagea!" called the hostess to a wench of about eleven who was dressed in home-dyed garments and could boast of a pair of bare feet which, from a distance, might almost have been mistaken for boots, so encrusted were they with fresh mire. "Here, Pelagea! Come and show this gentleman the way."

Selifan helped the girl to ascend to the box-seat. Placing one foot upon the step by which the gentry mounted, she covered the said step with mud, and then, ascending higher, attained the desired position beside the coachman. Chichikov followed in her wake (causing the britchka to heel over with his weight as he did so), and then settled himself back into his place with an "All right! Good-bye, madam!" as the horses moved away at a trot.

Selifan looked gloomy as he drove, but also very attentive to his business. This was invariably his custom when he had committed the fault of getting drunk. Also, the horses looked unusually well-groomed. In particular, the collar on one of them had been neatly mended, although hitherto its state of dilapidation had been such as perennially to allow the stuffing to protrude through the leather. The silence preserved was well-nigh complete. Merely flourishing his whip, Selifan spoke to the team no word of instruction, although the skewbald was as ready as usual to listen to conversation of a didactic nature, seeing that at such times the reins hung loosely in the hands of the loquacious driver, and the whip wandered merely as a matter of form over the backs of the troika. This time, however, there could be heard issuing from Selifan's sullen lips only the uniformly unpleasant exclamation, "Now then, you brutes! Get on with you, get on with you!" The bay and the Assessor too felt put out at not hearing themselves called "my pets" or "good lads"; while, in addition, the skewbald came in for some nasty cuts across his sleek and ample quarters. "What has put master out like this?" thought the animal as it shook its head. "Heaven knows where he does not keep beating me—across the back, and even where I am tenderer still. Yes, he keeps catching the whip in my ears, and lashing me under the belly."

"To the right, eh?" snapped Selifan to the girl beside him as he pointed to a rain-soaked road which trended away through fresh green fields.

"No, no," she replied. "I will show you the road when the time comes."

"Which way, then?" he asked again when they had proceeded a little further.

"This way." And she pointed to the road just mentioned.

"Get along with you!" retorted the coachman. "That DOES go to the right. You don't know your right hand from your left."

The weather was fine, but the ground so excessively sodden that the wheels of the britchka collected mire until they had become caked as with a layer of felt, a circumstance which greatly increased the weight of the vehicle, and prevented it from clearing the neighbouring parishes before the afternoon was arrived. Also, without the girl's help the finding of the way would have been impossible, since roads wiggled away in every direction, like crabs released from a net, and, but for the assistance mentioned, Selifan would have found himself left to his own devices. Presently she pointed to a building ahead, with the words, "THERE is the main road."

"And what is the building?" asked Selifan.

"A tavern," she said.

"Then we can get along by ourselves," he observed. "Do you get down, and be off home."

With that he stopped, and helped her to alight—muttering as he did so: "Ah, you blackfooted creature!"

Chichikov added a copper groat, and she departed well pleased with her ride in the gentleman's carriage.

CHAPTER IV

On reaching the tavern, Chichikov called a halt. His reasons for this were twofold—namely, that he wanted to rest the horses, and that he himself desired some refreshment. In this connection the author feels bound to confess that the appetite and the capacity of such men are greatly to be envied. Of those well-to-do folk of St. Petersburg and Moscow who spend their time in considering what they shall eat on the morrow, and in composing a dinner for the day following, and who never sit down to a meal without first of all injecting a pill and then swallowing oysters and crabs and a quantity of other monsters, while eternally departing for Karlsbad or the Caucasus, the author has but a small opinion. Yes, THEY are not the persons to inspire envy. Rather, it is the folk of the middle classes—folk who at one posthouse call for bacon, and at another for a sucking pig, and at a third for a steak of sturgeon or a baked pudding with onions, and who can sit down to table at any hour, as though they had never had a meal in their lives, and can devour fish of all sorts, and guzzle and chew it with a view to provoking further appetite—these, I say, are the folk who enjoy heaven's most favoured gift. To attain such a celestial condition the great folk of whom I have spoken would sacrifice half their serfs and half their mortgaged and non-mortgaged property, with the foreign and domestic improvements thereon, if thereby they could compass such a stomach as is possessed by the folk of the middle class. But, unfortunately, neither money nor real estate, whether improved or non-improved, can purchase such a stomach.

The little wooden tavern, with its narrow, but hospitable, curtain suspended from a pair of rough-hewn doorposts like old church candlesticks, seemed to invite Chichikov to enter. True, the establishment was only a Russian hut of the ordinary type, but it was a hut of larger dimensions than usual, and had around its windows and gables carved and patterned cornices of bright-coloured wood which threw into relief the darker hue of the walls, and consorted well with the flowered pitchers painted on the shutters.

Ascending the narrow wooden staircase to the upper floor, and arriving upon a broad landing, Chichikov found himself confronted with a creaking door and a stout old woman in a striped print gown. "This way, if you please," she said. Within the apartment designated Chichikov encountered the old friends which one invariably finds in such roadside hostelries—to wit, a heavy samovar, four smooth, bescratched walls of white pine, a three-cornered press with cups and teapots, egg-cups of gilded china standing in front of ikons suspended by blue and red ribands, a cat lately delivered of a family, a mirror which gives one four eyes instead of two and a pancake for a face, and, beside the ikons, some bunches of herbs and carnations of such faded dustiness that, should one attempt to smell them, one is bound to burst out sneezing.

"Have you a sucking-pig?" Chichikov inquired of the landlady as she stood expectantly before him.

"Yes."

"And some horse-radish and sour cream?"

"Yes."

"Then serve them."

The landlady departed for the purpose, and returned with a plate, a napkin (the latter starched to the consistency of dried bark), a knife with a bone handle beginning to turn yellow, a two-pronged fork as thin as a wafer, and a salt-cellar incapable of being made to stand upright.

Following the accepted custom, our hero entered into conversation with the woman, and inquired whether she herself or a landlord kept the tavern; how much income the tavern brought in; whether her sons lived with her; whether the oldest was a bachelor or married; whom the eldest had taken to wife; whether the dowry had been large; whether the father-in-law had been satisfied, and whether the said father-in-law had not complained of receiving too small a present at the wedding. In short, Chichikov touched on every conceivable point. Likewise (of course) he displayed some curiosity as to the landowners of the neighbourhood. Their names, he ascertained, were Blochin, Potchitaev, Minoi, Cheprakov, and Sobakevitch.

"Then you are acquainted with Sobakevitch?" he said; whereupon the old woman informed him that she knew not only Sobakevitch, but also Manilov, and that the latter was the more delicate eater of the two, since, whereas Manilov always ordered a roast fowl and some veal and mutton, and then tasted merely a morsel of each, Sobakevitch would order one dish only, but consume the whole of it, and then demand more at the same price.

Whilst Chichikov was thus conversing and partaking of the sucking pig until only a fragment of it seemed likely to remain, the sound of an approaching vehicle made itself heard. Peering through the window, he saw draw up to the tavern door a light britchka drawn by three fine horses. From it there descended two men—one flaxen-haired and tall, and the other dark-haired and of slighter build. While the flaxen-haired man was clad in a dark-blue coat, the other one was wrapped in a coat of striped pattern. Behind the britchka stood a second, but an empty, turn-out, drawn by four long-coated steeds in ragged collars and rope harnesses. The flaxen-haired man lost no time in ascending the staircase, while his darker friend remained below to fumble at something in the britchka, talking, as he did so, to the driver of the vehicle which stood hitched behind. Somehow, the dark-haired man's voice struck Chichikov as familiar; and as he was taking another look at him the flaxen-haired gentleman entered the room. The newcomer was a man of lofty stature, with a small red moustache and a lean, hard-bitten face whose redness made it evident that its acquaintance, if not with the smoke of gunpowder, at all events with that of tobacco, was intimate and extensive. Nevertheless he greeted Chichikov civilly, and the latter returned his bow. Indeed, the pair would have entered into conversation, and have made one another's acquaintance (since a beginning was made with their simultaneously expressing satisfaction at the circumstance that the previous night's rain had laid the dust on the roads, and thereby made driving cool and pleasant) when the gentleman's darker-favoured friend also entered the room, and, throwing his cap upon the table, pushed back a mass of dishevelled black locks from his brow. The latest arrival was a man of medium height, but well put together, and possessed of a pair of full red cheeks, a set of teeth as white as snow, and coal-black whiskers. Indeed, so fresh was his complexion that it seemed to have been compounded of blood and milk, while health danced in his every feature.

"Ha, ha, ha!" he cried with a gesture of astonishment at the sight of Chichikov. "What chance brings YOU here?"

Upon that Chichikov recognised Nozdrev—the man whom he had met at dinner at the Public Prosecutor's, and who, within a minute or two of the introduction, had become so intimate with his fellow guest as to address him in the second person singular, in spite of the fact that Chichikov had given him no opportunity for doing so.

"Where have you been to-day?" Nozdrev inquired, and, without waiting for an answer, went on: "For myself, I am just from the fair, and completely cleaned out. Actually, I have had to do the journey back with stage horses! Look out of the window, and see them for yourself." And he turned Chichikov's head so sharply in the desired direction that he came very near to bumping it against the window frame. "Did you ever see such a bag of tricks? The cursed things have only just managed to get here. In fact, on the way I had to transfer myself to this fellow's britchka." He indicated his companion with a finger. "By the way, don't you know one another? He is Mizhuev, my brother-in-law. He and I were talking of you only this morning. 'Just you see,' said I to him, 'if we do not fall in with Chichikov before we have done.' Heavens, how completely cleaned out I am! Not only have I lost four good horses, but also my watch and chain." Chichikov perceived that in very truth his interlocutor was minus the articles named, as well as that one of Nozdrev's whiskers was less bushy in appearance than the other one. "Had I had another twenty roubles in my pocket," went on Nozdrev, "I should have won back all that I have lost, as well as have pouched a further thirty thousand. Yes, I give you my word of honour on that."

"But you were saying the same thing when last I met you," put in the flaxen-haired man. "Yet, even though I lent you fifty roubles, you lost them all."

"But I should not have lost them THIS time. Don't try to make me out a fool. I should NOT have lost them, I tell you. Had I only played the right card, I should have broken the bank."

"But you did NOT break the bank," remarked the flaxen-haired man.

"No. That was because I did not play my cards right. But what about your precious major's play? Is THAT good?"

"Good or not, at least he beat you."

"Splendid of him! Nevertheless I will get my own back. Let him play me at doubles, and we shall soon see what sort of a player he is! Friend Chichikov, at first we had a glorious time, for the fair was a tremendous success. Indeed, the tradesmen said that never yet had there been such a gathering. I myself managed to sell everything from my estate at a good price. In fact, we had a magnificent time. I can't help thinking of it, devil take me! But what a pity YOU were not there! Three versts from the town there is quartered a regiment of dragoons, and you would scarcely believe what a lot of officers it has. Forty at least there are, and they do a fine lot of knocking about the town and drinking. In particular, Staff-Captain Potsieluev is a SPLENDID fellow! You should just see his moustache! Why, he calls good claret 'trash'! 'Bring me some of the usual trash,' is his way of ordering it. And Lieutenant Kuvshinnikov, too! He is as delightful as the other man. In fact, I may say that every one of the lot is a rake. I spent my whole time with them, and you can imagine that Ponomarev, the wine merchant, did a fine trade indeed! All the same, he is a rascal, you know, and ought not to be dealt with, for he puts all sorts of rubbish into his liquor—Indian wood and burnt cork and elderberry juice, the villain! Nevertheless, get him to produce a bottle from what he calls his 'special cellar,' and you will fancy yourself in the seventh heaven of delight. And what quantities of champagne we drank! Compared with it, provincial stuff is kvass 18. Try to imagine not merely Clicquot, but a sort of blend of Clicquot and Matradura—Clicquot of double strength. Also Ponomarev produced a bottle of French stuff which he calls 'Bonbon.' Had it a bouquet, ask you?

Why, it had the bouquet of a rose garden, of anything else you like. What times we had, to be sure! Just after we had left Pnomarev's place, some prince or another arrived in the town, and sent out for some champagne; but not a bottle was there left, for the officers had drunk every one! Why, I myself got through seventeen bottles at a sitting."

"Come, come! You CAN'T have got through seventeen," remarked the flaxen-haired man.

"But I did, I give my word of honour," retorted Nozdrev.

"Imagine what you like, but you didn't drink even TEN bottles at a sitting."

"Will you bet that I did not?"

"No; for what would be the use of betting about it?"

"Then at least wager the gun which you have bought."

"No, I am not going to do anything of the kind."

"Just as an experiment?"

"No."

"It is as well for you that you don't, since, otherwise, you would have found yourself minus both gun and cap. However, friend Chichikov, it is a pity you were not there. Had you been there, I feel sure you would have found yourself unable to part with Lieutenant Kuvshinnikov. You and he would have hit it off splendidly. You know, he is quite a different sort from the Public Prosecutor and our other provincial skinflints—fellows who shiver in their shoes before they will spend a single kopeck. HE will play faro, or anything else, and at any time. Why did you not come with us, instead of wasting your time on cattle breeding or something of the sort? But never mind. Embrace me. I like you immensely. Mizhuev, see how curiously things have turned out. Chichikov has nothing to do with me, or I with him, yet here is he come from God knows where, and landed in the very spot where I happen to be living! I may tell you that, no matter how many carriages I possessed, I should gamble the lot away. Recently I went in for a turn at billiards, and lost two jars of pomade, a china teapot, and a guitar. Then I staked some more things, and, like a fool, lost them all, and six roubles in addition. What a dog is that Kuvshinnikov! He and I attended nearly every ball in the place. In particular, there was a woman—decolletee, and such a swell! I merely thought to myself, 'The devil take her!' but Kuvshinnikov is such a wag that he sat down beside her, and began paying her strings of compliments in French. However, I did not neglect the damsels altogether—although HE calls that sort of thing 'going in for strawberries.' By the way, I have a splendid piece of fish and some caviare with me. 'Tis all I HAVE brought back! In fact it is a lucky chance that I happened to buy the stuff before my money was gone. Where are you for?"

"I am about to call on a friend."

"On what friend? Let him go to the devil, and come to my place instead."

"I cannot, I cannot. I have business to do."

"Oh, business again! I thought so!"

"But I HAVE business to do—and pressing business at that."

"I wager that you're lying. If not, tell me whom you're going to call upon."

"Upon Sobakevitch."

Instantly Nozdrev burst into a laugh compassable only by a healthy man in whose head every tooth still remains as white as sugar. By this I mean the laugh of quivering cheeks, the laugh which causes a neighbour who is sleeping behind double doors three rooms away to leap from his bed and exclaim with distended eyes, "Hullo! Something HAS upset him!"

"What is there to laugh at?" asked Chichikov, a trifle nettled; but Nozdrev laughed more unrestrainedly than ever, ejaculating: "Oh, spare us all! The thing is so amusing that I shall die of it!"

"I say that there is nothing to laugh at," repeated Chichikov. "It is in fulfilment of a promise that I am on my way to Sobakevitch's."

"Then you will scarcely be glad to be alive when you've got there, for he is the veriest miser in the countryside. Oh, *I* know you. However, if you think to find there either faro or a bottle of 'Bonbon' you are mistaken. Look here, my good friend. Let Sobakevitch go to the devil, and come to MY place, where at least I shall have a piece of sturgeon to offer you for dinner. Ponomarev said to me on parting: 'This piece is just the thing for you. Even if you were to search the whole market, you would never find a better one.' But of course he is a terrible rogue. I said to him outright: 'You and the Collector of Taxes are the two greatest skinflints in the town.' But he only stroked his beard and smiled. Every day I used to breakfast with Kuvshinnikov in his restaurant. Well, what I was nearly forgetting is this: that, though I am aware that you can't forgo your engagement, I am not going to give you up—no, not for ten thousand roubles of money. I tell you that in advance."

Here he broke off to run to the window and shout to his servant (who was holding a knife in one hand and a crust of bread and a piece of sturgeon in the other—he had contrived to filch the latter while fumbling in the britchka for something else):

"Hi, Porphyri! Bring here that puppy, you rascal! What a puppy it is! Unfortunately that thief of a landlord has given it nothing to eat, even though I have promised him the roan filly which, as you may remember, I swopped from Khvostirev." As a matter of fact, Chichikov had never in his life seen either Khvostirev or the roan filly.

"Barin, do you wish for anything to eat?" inquired the landlady as she entered.

"No, nothing at all. Ah, friend Chichikov, what times we had! Yes, give me a glass of vodka, old woman. What sort do you keep?"

"Aniseed."

"Then bring me a glass of it," repeated Nozdrev.

"And one for me as well," added the flaxen-haired man.

"At the theatre," went on Nozdrev, "there was an actress who sang like a canary. Kuvshinnikov, who happened to be sitting with me, said: 'My boy, you had better go and gather that strawberry.' As for the booths at the fair, they numbered, I should say, fifty." At this point he broke off to take the glass of vodka from the landlady, who bowed low in acknowledgement of his doing so. At the same moment Porphyri—a fellow dressed like his master (that is to say, in a greasy, wadded overcoat)—entered with the puppy.

"Put the brute down here," commanded Nozdrev, "and then fasten it up."

Porphyri deposited the animal upon the floor; whereupon it proceeded to act after the manner of dogs.

"THERE'S a puppy for you!" cried Nozdrev, catching hold of it by the back, and lifting it up. The puppy uttered a piteous yelp.

"I can see that you haven't done what I told you to do," he continued to Porphyri after an inspection of the animal's belly. "You have quite forgotten to brush him."

"I DID brush him," protested Porphyri.

"Then where did these fleas come from?"

"I cannot think. Perhaps they have leapt into his coat out of the britchka."

"You liar! As a matter of fact, you have forgotten to brush him. Nevertheless, look at these ears, Chichikov. Just feel them."

"Why should I? Without doing that, I can see that he is well-bred."

"Nevertheless, catch hold of his ears and feel them."

To humour the fellow Chichikov did as he had requested, remarking: "Yes, he seems likely to turn out well."

"And feel the coldness of his nose! Just take it in your hand."

Not wishing to offend his interlocutor, Chichikov felt the puppy's nose, saying: "Some day he will have an excellent scent."

"Yes, will he not? 'Tis the right sort of muzzle for that. I must say that I have long been wanting such a puppy. Porphyri, take him away again."

Porphyri lifted up the puppy, and bore it downstairs.

"Look here, Chichikov," resumed Nozdrev. "You MUST come to my place. It lies only five versts away, and we can go there like the wind, and you can visit Sobakevitch afterwards."

"Shall I, or shall I not, go to Nozdrev's?" reflected Chichikov. "Is he likely to prove any more useful than the rest? Well, at least he is as promising, even though he has lost so much at play. But he has a head on his shoulders, and therefore I must go carefully if I am to tackle him concerning my scheme."

With that he added aloud: "Very well, I WILL come with you, but do not let us be long, for my time is very precious."

"That's right, that's right!" cried Nozdrev. "Splendid, splendid! Let me embrace you!" And he fell upon Chichikov's neck. "All three of us will go."

"No, no," put in the flaxen-haired man. "You must excuse me, for I must be off home."

"Rubbish, rubbish! I am NOT going to excuse you."

"But my wife will be furious with me. You and Monsieur Chichikov must change into the other britchka."

"Come, come! The thing is not to be thought of."

The flaxen-haired man was one of those people in whose character, at first sight, there seems to lurk a certain grain of stubbornness—so much so that, almost before one has begun to speak, they are ready to dispute one's words, and to disagree with anything that may be opposed to their peculiar form of opinion. For instance, they will decline to have folly called wisdom, or any tune danced to but their own. Always, however, will there become manifest in their character a soft spot, and in the end they will accept what hitherto they have denied, and call what is foolish sensible, and even dance—yes, better than any one else will do—to a tune set by some one else. In short, they generally begin well, but always end badly.

"Rubbish!" said Nozdrev in answer to a further objection on his brother-in-law's part. And, sure enough, no sooner had Nozdrev clapped his cap upon his head than the flaxen-haired man started to follow him and his companion.

"But the gentleman has not paid for the vodka?" put in the old woman.

"All right, all right, good mother. Look here, brother-in-law. Pay her, will you, for I have not a kopeck left."

"How much?" inquired the brother-in-law.

"What, sir? Eighty kopecks, if you please," replied the old woman.

"A lie! Give her half a rouble. That will be quite enough."

"No, it will NOT, barin," protested the old woman. However, she took the money gratefully, and even ran to the door to open it for the gentlemen. As a matter of fact, she had lost nothing by the transaction, since she had demanded fully a quarter more than the vodka was worth.

The travellers then took their seats, and since Chichikov's britchka kept alongside the britchka wherein Nozdrev and his brother-in-law were seated, it was possible for all three men to converse together as they proceeded. Behind them came Nozdrev's smaller buggy, with its team of lean stage horses and Porphyri and the puppy. But inasmuch as the conversation which the travellers maintained was not of a kind likely to interest the reader, I might do worse than say something concerning Nozdrev himself, seeing that he is destined to play no small role in our story.

Nozdrev's face will be familiar to the reader, seeing that every one must have encountered many such. Fellows of the kind are known as "gay young sparks," and, even in their boyhood and school days, earn a reputation for being bons camarades (though with it all they come in for some hard knocks) for the reason that their faces evince an element of frankness, directness, and enterprise which enables them soon to make friends, and, almost before you have had time to look around, to start addressing you in the second person singular. Yet, while cementing such friendships for all eternity, almost always they begin quarrelling the same evening, since, throughout, they are a loquacious, dissipated, high-spirited, over-showy tribe. Indeed, at thirty-five Nozdrev was just what he had been an eighteen and twenty—he was just such a lover of fast living. Nor had his marriage in any way changed him, and the less so since his wife had soon departed to another world, and left behind her two children, whom he did not want, and who were therefore placed in the charge of a good-looking nursemaid. Never at any time could he remain at home for more than a single day, for his keen scent could range over scores and scores of versts, and detect any fair which promised balls and crowds. Consequently in a trice he would be there—quarrelling, and creating disturbances over the gaming-table (like all men of his type, he had a perfect passion for cards) yet playing neither a faultless nor an over-clean game, since he was both a blunderer and able to indulge in a large number of illicit cuts and other devices. The result was that the game often ended in another kind of sport altogether. That is to say, either he received a good kicking, or he had his thick and very handsome whiskers pulled; with the result that on certain occasions he returned home with one of those appendages looking decidedly ragged. Yet his plump, healthy-looking cheeks were so robustly constituted, and contained such an abundance of recreative vigour, that a new whisker soon sprouted in place of the old one, and even surpassed its predecessor. Again (and the following is a phenomenon peculiar to Russia) a very short time would have elapsed before once more he would be consorting with the very cronies who had recently cuffed him—and consorting with them as though nothing whatsoever had happened—no reference to the subject being made by him, and they too holding their tongues.

In short, Nozdrev was, as it were, a man of incident. Never was he present at any gathering without some sort of a fracas occurring thereat. Either he would require to be expelled from the room by gendarmes, or his friends would have to kick him out into the street. At all events, should neither of those occurrences take place, at least he did something of a nature which would not otherwise have been witnessed. That is to say, should he not play the fool in a buffet to such an extent as to make every one smile, you may be sure that he was engaged in lying to a degree which at times abashed even himself. Moreover, the man lied without reason.

For instance, he would begin telling a story to the effect that he possessed a blue-coated or a red-coated horse; until, in the end, his listeners would be forced to leave him with the remark, "You are giving us some fine stuff, old fellow!" Also, men like Nozdrev have a passion for insulting their neighbours without the least excuse afforded. (For that matter, even a man of good standing and of respectable exterior—a man with a star on his breast—may unexpectedly press your hand one day, and begin talking to you on subjects of a nature to give food for serious thought. Yet just as unexpectedly may that man start abusing you to your face—and do so in a manner worthy of a collegiate registrar rather than of a man who wears a star on his breast and aspires to converse on subjects which merit reflection. All that one can do in such a case is to stand shrugging one's shoulders in amazement.) Well, Nozdrev had just such a weakness. The more he became friendly with a man, the sooner would he insult him, and be ready to spread calumnies as to his reputation. Yet all the while he would consider himself the insulted one's friend, and, should he meet him again, would greet him in the most amicable style possible, and say, "You rascal, why have you given up coming to see me." Thus, taken all round, Nozdrev was a person of many aspects and numerous potentialities. In one and the same breath would he propose to go with you whithersoever you might choose (even to the very ends of the world should you so require) or to enter upon any sort of an enterprise with you, or to exchange any commodity for any other commodity which you might care to name. Guns, horses, dogs, all were subjects for barter—though not for profit so far as YOU were concerned. Such traits are mostly the outcome of a boisterous temperament, as is additionally exemplified by the fact that if at a fair he chanced to fall in with a simpleton and to fleece him, he would then proceed to buy a quantity of the very first articles which came to hand— horse-collars, cigar-lighters, dresses for his nursemaid, foals, raisins, silver ewers, lengths of holland, wheatmeal, tobacco, revolvers, dried herrings, pictures, whetstones, crockery, boots, and so forth, until every atom of his money was exhausted. Yet seldom were these articles conveyed home, since, as a rule, the same day saw them lost to some more skilful gambler, in addition to his pipe, his tobacco-pouch, his mouthpiece, his four-horsed turn-out, and his coachman: with the result that, stripped to his very shirt, he would be forced to beg the loan of a vehicle from a friend.

Such was Nozdrev. Some may say that characters of his type have become extinct, that Nozdrevs no longer exist. Alas! such as say this will be wrong; for many a day must pass before the Nozdrevs will have disappeared from our ken. Everywhere they are to be seen in our midst—the only difference between the new and the old being a difference of garments. Persons of superficial observation are apt to consider that a man clad in a different coat is quite a different person from what he used to be.

To continue. The three vehicles bowled up to the steps of Nozdrev's house, and their occupants alighted. But no preparations whatsoever had been made for the guest's reception, for on some wooden trestles in the centre of the dining-room a couple of peasants were engaged in whitewashing the ceiling and drawling out an endless song as they splashed their stuff about the floor. Hastily bidding peasants and trestles to be gone, Nozdrev departed to another room with further instructions. Indeed, so audible was the sound of his voice as he ordered dinner that Chichikov—who was beginning to feel hungry once more—was enabled to gather that it would be at least five o'clock before a meal of any kind would be available. On his return, Nozdrev invited his companions to inspect his establishment—even though as early as two o'clock he had to announce that nothing more was to be seen.

The tour began with a view of the stables, where the party saw two mares (the one a grey, and the other a roan) and a colt; which latter animal, though far from showy, Nozdrev declared to have cost him ten thousand roubles.

"You NEVER paid ten thousand roubles for the brute!" exclaimed the brother-in-law. "He isn't worth even a thousand."

"By God, I DID pay ten thousand!" asserted Nozdrev.

"You can swear that as much as you like," retorted the other.

"Will you bet that I did not?" asked Nozdrev, but the brother-in-law declined the offer.

Next, Nozdrev showed his guests some empty stalls where a number of equally fine animals (so he alleged) had lately stood. Also there was on view the goat which an old belief still considers to be an indispensable adjunct to such places, even though its apparent use is to pace up and down beneath the noses of the horses as though the place belonged to it. Thereafter the host took his guests to look at a young wolf which he had got tied to a chain. "He is fed on nothing but raw meat," he explained, "for I want him to grow up as fierce as possible." Then the party inspected a pond in which there were "fish of such a size that it would take two men all their time to lift one of them out."

This piece of information was received with renewed incredulity on the part of the brother-in-law.

"Now, Chichikov," went on Nozdrev, "let me show you a truly magnificent brace of dogs. The hardness of their muscles will surprise you, and they have jowls as sharp as needles."

So saying, he led the way to a small, but neatly-built, shed surrounded on every side with a fenced-in run. Entering this run, the visitors beheld a number of dogs of all sorts and sizes and colours. In their midst Nozdrev looked like a father lording it over his family circle. Erecting their tails—their "stems," as dog fanciers call those members—the animals came bounding to greet the party, and fully a score of them laid their paws upon Chichikov's shoulders. Indeed, one dog was moved with such friendliness that, standing on its hind legs, it licked him on the lips, and so forced him to spit. That done, the visitors duly inspected the couple already mentioned, and expressed astonishment at their muscles. True enough, they were fine animals. Next, the party looked at a Crimean bitch which, though blind and fast nearing her end, had, two years ago, been a truly magnificent dog. At all events, so said Nozdrev. Next came another bitch—also blind; then an inspection of the water-mill, which lacked the spindle-socket wherein the upper stone ought to have been revolving—"fluttering," to use the Russian peasant's quaint expression. "But never mind," said Nozdrev. "Let us proceed to the blacksmith's shop." So to the blacksmith's shop the party proceeded, and when the said shop had been viewed, Nozdrev said as he pointed to a field:

"In this field I have seen such numbers of hares as to render the ground quite invisible. Indeed, on one occasion I, with my own hands, caught a hare by the hind legs."

"You never caught a hare by the hind legs with your hands!" remarked the brother-in-law.

"But I DID" reiterated Nozdrev. "However, let me show you the boundary where my lands come to an end."

So saying, he started to conduct his guests across a field which consisted mostly of moleheaps, and in which the party had to pick their way between strips of ploughed land and of harrowed. Soon Chichikov began to feel weary, for the terrain was so low-lying that in many spots water could be heard squelching underfoot, and though for a while the visitors watched their feet, and stepped carefully, they soon perceived that such a course availed them nothing, and took to following their noses, without either selecting or avoiding the spots where the mire happened to be deeper or the reverse. At length, when a considerable distance had been covered, they caught sight of a boundary-post and a narrow ditch.

"That is the boundary," said Nozdrev. "Everything that you see on this side of the post is mine, as well as the forest on the other side of it, and what lies beyond the forest."

"WHEN did that forest become yours?" asked the brother-in-law. "It cannot be long since you purchased it, for it never USED to be yours."

"Yes, it isn't long since I purchased it," said Nozdrev.

"How long?"

"How long? Why, I purchased it three days ago, and gave a pretty sum for it, as the devil knows!"

"Indeed? Why, three days ago you were at the fair?"

"Wiseacre! Cannot one be at a fair and buy land at the same time? Yes, I WAS at the fair, and my steward bought the land in my absence."

"Oh, your STEWARD bought it." The brother-in-law seemed doubtful, and shook his head.

The guests returned by the same route as that by which they had come; whereafter, on reaching the house, Nozdrev conducted them to his study, which contained not a trace of the things usually to be found in such apartments—such things as books and papers. On the contrary, the only articles to be seen were a sword and a brace of guns—the one "of them worth three hundred roubles," and the other "about eight hundred." The brother-in-law inspected the articles in question, and then shook his head as before. Next, the visitors were shown some "real Turkish" daggers, of which one bore the inadvertent inscription, "Saveli Sibiriakov 19, Master Cutler." Then came a barrel-organ, on which Nozdrev started to play some tune or another. For a while the sounds were not wholly unpleasing, but suddenly something seemed to go wrong, for a mazurka started, to be followed by "Marlborough has gone to the war," and to this, again, there succeeded an antiquated waltz. Also, long after Nozdrev had ceased to turn the handle, one particularly shrill-pitched pipe which had, throughout, refused to harmonise with the rest kept up a protracted whistling on its own account. Then followed an exhibition of tobacco pipes—pipes of clay, of wood, of meerschaum, pipes smoked and non-smoked; pipes wrapped in chamois leather and not so wrapped; an amber-mounted hookah (a stake won at cards) and a tobacco pouch (worked, it was alleged, by some countess who had fallen in love with Nozdrev at a posthouse, and whose handiwork Nozdrev averred to constitute the "sublimity of superfluity"—a term which, in the Nozdrevian vocabulary, purported to signify the acme of perfection).

Finally, after some hors-d'oeuvres of sturgeon's back, they sat down to table—the time being then nearly five o'clock. But the meal did not constitute by any means the best of which Chichikov had ever partaken, seeing that some of the dishes were overcooked, and others were scarcely cooked at all. Evidently their compounder had trusted chiefly to inspiration—she had laid hold of the first thing which had happened to come to hand. For instance, had pepper represented the nearest article within reach, she had added pepper wholesale. Had a cabbage chanced to be so encountered, she had pressed it also into the service. And the same with milk, bacon, and peas. In short, her rule seemed to have been "Make a hot dish of some sort, and some sort of taste will result." For the rest, Nozdrev drew heavily upon the wine. Even before the soup had been served, he had poured out for each guest a bumper of port and another of "haut" sauterne. (Never in provincial towns is ordinary, vulgar sauterne even procurable.) Next, he called for a bottle of madeira—"as fine a tipple as ever a field-marshall drank"; but the madeira only burnt the mouth, since the dealers, familiar with the taste of our landed gentry (who love "good" madeira) invariably doctor the stuff with copious dashes of rum and Imperial vodka, in the hope that Russian stomachs will thus be enabled to carry off the lot. After this bottle Nozdrev called for another and "a very special" brand—a brand which he declared to consist of a blend of burgundy and champagne, and of which he poured generous measures into the glasses of Chichikov and the brother-in-law as they sat to right and left of him. But since Chichikov noticed that, after doing so, he added only a scanty modicum of the mixture to his own tumbler, our hero determined to be cautious, and therefore took advantage of a moment when Nozdrev had again plunged into conversation and was yet a third time engaged in refilling his brother-in-law's glass, to contrive to upset his (Chichikov's) glass over his plate. In time there came also to table a tart of mountain-ashberries—berries which the host declared to equal, in taste, ripe plums, but which, curiously enough, smacked more of corn brandy. Next, the company consumed a sort of pasty of which the precise name has escaped me, but which the host rendered differently even on the second occasion of its being mentioned. The meal over, and the whole tale of wines tried, the guests still retained their seats—a circumstance which embarrassed Chichikov, seeing that he had no mind to propound his pet scheme in the presence of Nozdrev's brother-in-law, who was a complete stranger to him. No, that subject called for amicable and PRIVATE conversation. Nevertheless, the brother-in-law appeared to bode little danger, seeing that he had taken on board a full cargo, and was now engaged in doing nothing of a more menacing nature than picking his nose. At length he himself noticed that he was not altogether in a responsible condition; wherefore he rose and began to make excuses for departing homewards, though in a tone so drowsy and lethargic that, to quote the Russian proverb, he might almost have been "pulling a collar on to a horse by the clasps."

"No, no!" cried Nozdrev. "I am NOT going to let you go."

"But I MUST go," replied the brother-in-law. "Don't try to hinder me. You are annoying me greatly."

"Rubbish! We are going to play a game of banker."

"No, no. You must play it without me, my friend. My wife is expecting me at home, and I must go and tell her all about the fair. Yes, I MUST go if I am to please her. Do not try to detain me."

"Your wife be—! But have you REALLY an important piece of business with her?"

"No, no, my friend. The real reason is that she is a good and trustful woman, and that she does a great deal for me. The tears spring to my eyes as I think of it. Do not detain me. As an honourable man I say that I must go. Of that I do assure you in all sincerity."

"Oh, let him go," put in Chichikov under his breath. "What use will he be here?"

"Very well," said Nozdrev, "though, damn it, I do not like fellows who lose their heads." Then he added to his brother-in-law: "All right,

Thetuk 20. Off you go to your wife and your woman's talk and may the devil go with you!"

"Do not insult me with the term Thetuk," retorted the brother-in-law. "To her I owe my life, and she is a dear, good woman, and has shown me much affection. At the very thought of it I could weep. You see, she will be asking me what I have seen at the fair, and tell her about it I must, for she is such a dear, good woman."

"Then off you go to her with your pack of lies. Here is your cap."

"No, good friend, you are not to speak of her like that. By so doing you offend me greatly—I say that she is a dear, good woman."

"Then run along home to her."

"Yes, I am just going. Excuse me for having been unable to stay. Gladly would I have stayed, but really I cannot."

The brother-in-law repeated his excuses again and again without noticing that he had entered the britchka, that it had passed through the gates, and that he was now in the open country. Permissibly we may suppose that his wife succeeded in gleaning from him few details of the fair.

"What a fool!" said Nozdrev as, standing by the window, he watched the departing vehicle. "Yet his off-horse is not such a bad one. For a long time past I have been wanting to get hold of it. A man like that is simply impossible. Yes, he is a Thetuk, a regular Thetuk."

With that they repaired to the parlour, where, on Porphyri bringing candles, Chichikov perceived that his host had produced a pack of cards.

"I tell you what," said Nozdrev, pressing the sides of the pack together, and then slightly bending them, so that the pack cracked and a card flew out. "How would it be if, to pass the time, I were to make a bank of three hundred?"

Chichikov pretended not to have heard him, but remarked with an air of having just recollected a forgotten point:

"By the way, I had omitted to say that I have a request to make of you."

"What request?"

"First give me your word that you will grant it."

"What is the request, I say?"

"Then you give me your word, do you?"

"Certainly."

"Your word of honour?"

"My word of honour."

"This, then, is my request. I presume that you have a large number of dead serfs whose names have not yet been removed from the revision list?"

"I have. But why do you ask?"

"Because I want you to make them over to me."

"Of what use would they be to you?"

"Never mind. I have a purpose in wanting them."

"What purpose?"

"A purpose which is strictly my own affair. In short, I need them."

"You seem to have hatched a very fine scheme. Out with it, now! What is in the wind?"

"How could I have hatched such a scheme as you say? One could not very well hatch a scheme out of such a trifle as this."

"Then for what purpose do you want the serfs?"

"Oh, the curiosity of the man! He wants to poke his fingers into and smell over every detail!"

"Why do you decline to say what is in your mind? At all events, until you DO say I shall not move in the matter."

"But how would it benefit you to know what my plans are? A whim has seized me. That is all. Nor are you playing fair. You have given me your word of honour, yet now you are trying to back out of it."

"No matter what you desire me to do, I decline to do it until you have told me your purpose."

"What am I to say to the fellow?" thought Chichikov. He reflected for a moment, and then explained that he wanted the dead souls in order to acquire a better standing in society, since at present he possessed little landed property, and only a handful of serfs.

"You are lying," said Nozdrev without even letting him finish. "Yes, you are lying my good friend."

Chichikov himself perceived that his device had been a clumsy one, and his pretext weak. "I must tell him straight out," he said to himself as he pulled his wits together.

"Should I tell you the truth," he added aloud, "I must beg of you not to repeat it. The truth is that I am thinking of getting married. But, unfortunately, my betrothed's father and mother are very ambitious people, and do not want me to marry her, since they desire the bridegroom to own not less than three hundred souls, whereas I own but a hundred and fifty, and that number is not sufficient."

"Again you are lying," said Nozdrev.

"Then look here; I have been lying only to this extent." And Chichikov marked off upon his little finger a minute portion.

"Nevertheless I will bet my head that you have been lying throughout."

"Come, come! That is not very civil of you. Why should I have been lying?"

"Because I know you, and know that you are a regular skinflint. I say that in all friendship. If I possessed any power over you I should hang you to the nearest tree."

This remark hurt Chichikov, for at any time he disliked expressions gross or offensive to decency, and never allowed any one—no, not even persons of the highest rank—to behave towards him with an undue measure of familiarity. Consequently his sense of umbrage on the present occasion was unbounded.

"By God, I WOULD hang you!" repeated Nozdrev. "I say this frankly, and not for the purpose of offending you, but simply to communicate to you my friendly opinion."

"To everything there are limits," retorted Chichikov stiffly. "If you want to indulge in speeches of that sort you had better return to the barracks."

However, after a pause he added:

"If you do not care to give me the serfs, why not SELL them?"

"SELL them? *I* know you, you rascal! You wouldn't give me very much for them, WOULD you?"

"A nice fellow! Look here. What are they to you? So many diamonds, eh?"

"I thought so! *I* know you!"

"Pardon me, but I could wish that you were a member of the Jewish persuasion. You would give them to me fast enough then."

"On the contrary, to show you that I am not a usurer, I will decline to ask of you a single kopeck for the serfs. All that you need do is to buy that colt of mine, and then I will throw in the serfs in addition."

"But what should *I* want with your colt?" said Chichikov, genuinely astonished at the proposal.

"What should YOU want with him? Why, I have bought him for ten thousand roubles, and am ready to let you have him for four."

"I ask you again: of what use could the colt possibly be to me? I am not the keeper of a breeding establishment."

"Ah! I see that you fail to understand me. Let me suggest that you pay down at once three thousand roubles of the purchase money, and leave the other thousand until later."

"But I do not mean to buy the colt, damn him!"

"Then buy the roan mare."

"No, nor the roan mare."

"Then you shall have both the mare and the grey horse which you have seen in my stables for two thousand roubles."

"I require no horses at all."

"But you would be able to sell them again. You would be able to get thrice their purchase price at the very first fair that was held."

"Then sell them at that fair yourself, seeing that you are so certain of making a triple profit."

"Oh, I should make it fast enough, only I want YOU to benefit by the transaction."

Chichikov duly thanked his interlocutor, but continued to decline either the grey horse or the roan mare.

"Then buy a few dogs," said Nozdrev. "I can sell you a couple of hides a-quiver, ears well pricked, coats like quills, ribs barrel-shaped, and paws so tucked up as scarcely to graze the ground when they run."

"Of what use would those dogs be to me? I am not a sportsman."

"But I WANT you to have the dogs. Listen. If you won't have the dogs, then buy my barrel-organ. 'Tis a splendid instrument. As a man of honour I can tell you that, when new, it cost me fifteen hundred roubles. Well, you shall have it for nine hundred."

"Come, come! What should I want with a barrel-organ? I am not a German, to go hauling it about the roads and begging for coppers."

"But this is quite a different kind of organ from the one which Germans take about with them. You see, it is a REAL organ. Look at it for yourself. It is made of the best wood. I will take you to have another view of it."

And seizing Chichikov by the hand, Nozdrev drew him towards the other room, where, in spite of the fact that Chichikov, with his feet planted firmly on the floor, assured his host, again and again, that he knew exactly what the organ was like, he was forced once more to hear how Marlborough went to the war.

"Then, since you don't care to give me any money for it," persisted Nozdrev, "listen to the following proposal. I will give you the barrel-organ and all the dead souls which I possess, and in return you shall give me your britchka, and another three hundred roubles into the bargain."

"Listen to the man! In that case, what should I have left to drive in?"

"Oh, I would stand you another britchka. Come to the coach-house, and I will show you the one I mean. It only needs repainting to look a perfectly splendid britchka."

"The ramping, incorrigible devil!" thought Chichikov to himself as at all hazards he resolved to escape from britchkas, organs, and every species of dog, however marvellously barrel-ribbed and tucked up of paw.

"And in exchange, you shall have the britchka, the barrel-organ, and the dead souls," repeated Nozdrev.

"I must decline the offer," said Chichikov.

"And why?"

"Because I don't WANT the things—I am full up already."

"I can see that you don't know how things should be done between good friends and comrades. Plainly you are a man of two faces."

"What do you mean, you fool? Think for yourself. Why should I acquire articles which I don't want?"

"Say no more about it, if you please. I have quite taken your measure. But see here. Should you care to play a game of banker? I am ready to stake both the dead souls and the barrel-organ at cards."

"No; to leave an issue to cards means to submit oneself to the unknown," said Chichikov, covertly glancing at the pack which Nozdrev had got in his hands. Somehow the way in which his companion had cut that pack seemed to him suspicious.

"Why 'to the unknown'?" asked Nozdrev. "There is no such thing as 'the unknown.' Should luck be on your side, you may win the devil knows what a haul. Oh, luck, luck!" he went on, beginning to deal, in the hope of raising a quarrel. "Here is the cursed nine upon which, the other night, I lost everything. All along I knew that I should lose my money. Said I to myself: 'The devil take you, you false, accursed card!'"

Just as Nozdrev uttered the words Porphyri entered with a fresh bottle of liquor; but Chichikov declined either to play or to drink.

"Why do you refuse to play?" asked Nozdrev.

"Because I feel indisposed to do so. Moreover, I must confess that I am no great hand at cards."

"WHY are you no great hand at them?"

Chichikov shrugged his shoulders. "Because I am not," he replied.

"You are no great hand at ANYTHING, I think."

"What does that matter? God has made me so."

"The truth is that you are a Thetuk, and nothing else. Once upon a time I believed you to be a good fellow, but now I see that you don't understand civility. One cannot speak to you as one would to an intimate, for there is no frankness or sincerity about you. You are a regular Sobakevitch—just such another as he."

"For what reason are you abusing me? Am I in any way at fault for declining to play cards? Sell me those souls if you are the man to hesitate over such rubbish."

"The foul fiend take you! I was about to have given them to you for nothing, but now you shan't have them at all—not if you offer me three kingdoms in exchange. Henceforth I will have nothing to do with you, you cobbler, you dirty blacksmith! Porphyri, go and tell the ostler to give the gentleman's horses no oats, but only hay."

This development Chichikov had hardly expected.

"And do you," added Nozdrev to his guest, "get out of my sight."

Yet in spite of this, host and guest took supper together—even though on this occasion the table was adorned with no wines of fictitious nomenclature, but only with a bottle which reared its solitary head beside a jug of what is usually known as vin ordinaire. When supper was over Nozdrev said to Chichikov as he conducted him to a side room where a bed had been made up:

"This is where you are to sleep. I cannot very well wish you good-night."

Left to himself on Nozdrev's departure, Chichikov felt in a most unenviable frame of mind. Full of inward vexation, he blamed himself bitterly for having come to see this man and so wasted valuable time; but even more did he blame himself for having told him of his scheme—for having acted as carelessly as a child or a madman. Of a surety the scheme was not one which ought to have been confided to a man like Nozdrev, for he was a worthless fellow who might lie about it, and append additions to it, and spread such stories as would give rise to God knows what scandals. "This is indeed bad!" Chichikov said to himself. "I have been an absolute fool." Consequently he spent an uneasy night—this uneasiness being increased by the fact that a number of small, but vigorous, insects so feasted upon him that he could do nothing but scratch the spots and exclaim, "The devil take you and Nozdrev alike!" Only when morning was approaching did he fall asleep. On rising, he made it his first business (after donning dressing-gown and slippers) to cross the courtyard to the stable, for the purpose of ordering Selifan to harness the britchka. Just as he was returning from his errand he encountered Nozdrev, clad in a dressing-gown, and holding a pipe between his teeth.

Host and guest greeted one another in friendly fashion, and Nozdrev inquired how Chichikov had slept.

"Fairly well," replied Chichikov, but with a touch of dryness in his tone.

"The same with myself," said Nozdrev. "The truth is that such a lot of nasty brutes kept crawling over me that even to speak of it gives me the shudders. Likewise, as the effect of last night's doings, a whole squadron of soldiers seemed to be camping on my chest, and giving me a flogging. Ugh! And whom also do you think I saw in a dream? You would never guess. Why, it was Staff-Captain Potsieluev and Lieutenant Kuvshinnikov!"

"Yes," though Chichikov to himself, "and I wish that they too would give you a public thrashing!"

"I felt so ill!" went on Nozdrev. "And just after I had fallen asleep something DID come and sting me. Probably it was a party of hag fleas. Now, dress yourself, and I will be with you presently. First of all I must give that scoundrel of a bailiff a wigging."

Chichikov departed to his own room to wash and dress; which process completed, he entered the dining-room to find the table laid with tea-things and a bottle of rum. Clearly no broom had yet touched the place, for there remained traces of the previous night's dinner and supper in the shape of crumbs thrown over the floor and tobacco ash on the tablecloth. The host himself, when he entered, was still clad in a dressing-gown exposing a hairy chest; and as he sat holding his pipe in his hand, and drinking tea from a cup, he would have made a model for the sort of painter who prefers to portray gentlemen of the less curled and scented order.

"What think you?" he asked of Chichikov after a short silence. "Are you willing NOW to play me for those souls?"

"I have told you that I never play cards. If the souls are for sale, I will buy them."

"I decline to sell them. Such would not be the course proper between friends. But a game of banker would be quite another matter. Let us deal the cards."

"I have told you that I decline to play."

"And you will not agree to an exchange?"

"No."

"Then look here. Suppose we play a game of chess. If you win, the souls shall be yours. There are lots which I should like to see crossed off the revision list. Hi, Porphyri! Bring me the chessboard."

"You are wasting your time. I will play neither chess nor cards."

"But chess is different from playing with a bank. In chess there can be neither luck nor cheating, for everything depends upon skill. In fact, I warn you that I cannot possibly play with you unless you allow me a move or two in advance."

"The same with me," thought Chichikov. "Shall I, or shall I not, play this fellow? I used not to be a bad chess-player, and it is a sport in which he would find it more difficult to be up to his tricks."

"Very well," he added aloud. "I WILL play you at chess."

"And stake the souls for a hundred roubles?" asked Nozdrev.

"No. Why for a hundred? Would it not be sufficient to stake them for fifty?"

"No. What would be the use of fifty? Nevertheless, for the hundred roubles I will throw in a moderately old puppy, or else a gold seal and watch-chain."

"Very well," assented Chichikov.

"Then how many moves are you going to allow me?"

"Is THAT to be part of the bargain? Why, none, of course."

"At least allow me two."

"No, none. I myself am only a poor player."

"*I* know you and your poor play," said Nozdrev, moving a chessman.

"In fact, it is a long time since last I had a chessman in my hand," replied Chichikov, also moving a piece.

"Ah! *I* know you and your poor play," repeated Nozdrev, moving a second chessman.

"I say again that it is a long time since last I had a chessman in my hand." And Chichikov, in his turn, moved.

"Ah! *I* know you and your poor play," repeated Nozdrev, for the third time as he made a third move. At the same moment the cuff of one of his sleeves happened to dislodge another chessman from its position.

"Again, I say," said Chichikov, "that 'tis a long time since last—But hi! look here! Put that piece back in its place!"

"What piece?"

"This one." And almost as Chichikov spoke he saw a third chessman coming into view between the queens. God only knows whence that chessman had materialised.

"No, no!" shouted Chichikov as he rose from the table. "It is impossible to play with a man like you. People don't move three pieces at once."

"How 'three pieces'? All that I have done is to make a mistake—to move one of my pieces by accident. If you like, I will forfeit it to you."

"And whence has the third piece come?"

"What third piece?"

"The one now standing between the queens?"

"'Tis one of your own pieces. Surely you are forgetting?"

"No, no, my friend. I have counted every move, and can remember each one. That piece has only just become added to the board. Put it back in its place, I say."

"Its place? Which IS its place?" But Nozdrev had reddened a good deal. "I perceive you to be a strategist at the game."

"No, no, good friend. YOU are the strategist—though an unsuccessful one, as it happens."

"Then of what are you supposing me capable? Of cheating you?"

"I am not supposing you capable of anything. All that I say is that I will not play with you any more."

"But you can't refuse to," said Nozdrev, growing heated. "You see, the game has begun."

"Nevertheless, I have a right not to continue it, seeing that you are not playing as an honest man should do."

"You are lying—you cannot truthfully say that."

"'Tis you who are lying."

"But I have NOT cheated. Consequently you cannot refuse to play, but must continue the game to a finish."

"You cannot force me to play," retorted Chichikov coldly as, turning to the chessboard, he swept the pieces into confusion.

Nozdrev approached Chichikov with a manner so threatening that the other fell back a couple of paces.

"I WILL force you to play," said Nozdrev. "It is no use you making a mess of the chessboard, for I can remember every move. We will replace the chessmen exactly as they were."

"No, no, my friend. The game is over, and I play you no more."

"You say that you will not?"

"Yes. Surely you can see for yourself that such a thing is impossible?"

"That cock won't fight. Say at once that you refuse to play with me." And Nozdrev approached a step nearer.

"Very well; I DO say that," replied Chichikov, and at the same moment raised his hands towards his face, for the dispute was growing heated. Nor was the act of caution altogether unwarranted, for Nozdrev also raised his fist, and it may be that one of our hero's plump, pleasant-looking cheeks would have sustained an indelible insult had not he (Chichikov) parried the blow and, seizing Nozdrev by his whirling arms, held them fast.

"Porphyri! Pavlushka!" shouted Nozdrev as madly he strove to free himself.

On hearing the words, Chichikov, both because he wished to avoid rendering the servants witnesses of the unedifying scene and because he felt that it would be of no avail to hold Nozdrev any longer, let go of the latter's arms; but at the same moment Porphyri and Pavlushka entered the room—a pair of stout rascals with whom it would be unwise to meddle.

"Do you, or do you not, intend to finish the game?" said Nozdrev. "Give me a direct answer."

"No; it will not be possible to finish the game," replied Chichikov, glancing out of the window. He could see his britchka standing ready for him, and Selifan evidently awaiting orders to draw up to the entrance steps. But from the room there was no escape, since in the doorway was posted the couple of well-built serving-men.

"Then it is as I say? You refuse to finish the game?" repeated Nozdrev, his face as red as fire.

"I would have finished it had you played like a man of honour. But, as it is, I cannot."

"You cannot, eh, you villain? You find that you cannot as soon as you find that you are not winning? Thrash him, you fellows!" And as he spoke Nozdrev grasped the cherrywood shank of his pipe. Chichikov turned as white as a sheet. He tried to say something, but his quivering lips emitted no sound. "Thrash him!" again shouted Nozdrev as he rushed forward in a state of heat and perspiration more proper to a warrior who is attacking an impregnable fortress. "Thrash him!" again he shouted in a voice like that of some half-demented lieutenant whose desperate bravery has acquired such a reputation that orders have had to be issued that his hands shall be held lest he attempt deeds of over-presumptuous daring. Seized with the military spirit, however, the lieutenant's head begins to whirl, and before his eye there flits the image of Suvorov 21. He advances to the great encounter, and impulsively cries, "Forward, my sons!"—cries it without reflecting that he may be spoiling the plan of the general attack, that millions of rifles may be protruding their muzzles through the embrasures of the impregnable, towering walls of the fortress, that his own impotent assault may be destined to be dissipated like dust before the wind, and that already there may have been launched on its whistling career the bullet which is to close for ever his vociferous throat. However, if Nozdrev resembled the headstrong, desperate lieutenant whom we have just pictured as advancing upon a fortress, at least the fortress itself in no way resembled the impregnable stronghold which I have described. As a matter of fact, the fortress became seized with a panic which drove its spirit into its boots. First of all, the chair with which Chichikov (the fortress in question) sought to defend himself was wrested from his grasp by the serfs, and then—blinking and neither alive nor dead—he turned to parry the Circassian pipe-stem of his host. In fact, God only knows what would have happened had not the fates been pleased by a miracle to deliver Chichikov's elegant back and shoulders from the onslaught. Suddenly, and as unexpectedly as though the sound had come from the clouds, there made itself heard the tinkling notes of a collar-bell, and then the rumble of wheels approaching the entrance steps, and, lastly, the snorting and hard breathing of a team of horses as a vehicle came to a standstill. Involuntarily all present glanced through the window, and saw a man clad in a semi-military greatcoat leap from a buggy. After making an inquiry or two in the hall, he entered the dining-room just at the juncture when Chichikov, almost swooning with terror, had found himself placed in about as awkward a situation as could well befall a mortal man.

"Kindly tell me which of you is Monsieur Nozdrev?" said the unknown with a glance of perplexity both at the person named (who was still standing with pipe-shank upraised) and at Chichikov (who was just beginning to recover from his unpleasant predicament).

"Kindly tell ME whom I have the honour of addressing?" retorted Nozdrev as he approached the official.

"I am the Superintendent of Rural Police."

"And what do you want?"

"I have come to fulfil a commission imposed upon me. That is to say, I have come to place you under arrest until your case shall have been decided."

"Rubbish! What case, pray?"

"The case in which you involved yourself when, in a drunken condition, and through the instrumentality of a walking-stick, you offered grave offence to the person of Landowner Maksimov."

"You lie! To your face I tell you that never in my life have I set eyes upon Landowner Maksimov."

"Good sir, allow me to represent to you that I am a Government officer. Speeches like that you may address to your servants, but not to me."

At this point Chichikov, without waiting for Nozdrev's reply, seized his cap, slipped behind the Superintendent's back, rushed out on to the verandah, sprang into his britchka, and ordered Selifan to drive like the wind.

CHAPTER V

Certainly Chichikov was a thorough coward, for, although the britchka pursued its headlong course until Nozdrev's establishment had disappeared behind hillocks and hedgerows, our hero continued to glance nervously behind him, as though every moment expecting to see a stern chase begin. His breath came with difficulty, and when he tried his heart with his hands he could feel it fluttering like a quail caught in a net.

"What a sweat the fellow has thrown me into!" he thought to himself, while many a dire and forceful aspiration passed through his mind. Indeed, the expressions to which he gave vent were most inelegant in their nature. But what was to be done next? He was a Russian and thoroughly aroused. The affair had been no joke. "But for the Superintendent," he reflected, "I might never again have looked upon God's daylight—I might have vanished like a bubble on a pool, and left neither trace nor posterity nor property nor an honourable name for my future offspring to inherit!" (it seemed that our hero was particularly anxious with regard to his possible issue).

"What a scurvy barin!" mused Selifan as he drove along. "Never have I seen such a barin. I should like to spit in his face. 'Tis better to allow a man nothing to eat than to refuse to feed a horse properly. A horse needs his oats—they are his proper fare. Even if you make a man procure a meal at his own expense, don't deny a horse his oats, for he ought always to have them."

An equally poor opinion of Nozdrev seemed to be cherished also by the steeds, for not only were the bay and the Assessor clearly out of spirits, but even the skewbald was wearing a dejected air. True, at home the skewbald got none but the poorer sorts of oats to eat, and Selifan never filled his trough without having first called him a villain; but at least they WERE oats, and not hay—they were stuff which could be chewed with a certain amount of relish. Also, there was the fact that at intervals he could intrude his long nose into his companions' troughs (especially when Selifan happened to be absent from the stable) and ascertain what THEIR provender was like. But at Nozdrev's there had been nothing but hay! That was not right. All three horses felt greatly discontented.

But presently the malcontents had their reflections cut short in a very rude and unexpected manner. That is to say, they were brought back to practicalities by coming into violent collision with a six-horsed vehicle, while upon their heads descended both a babel of cries from the ladies inside and a storm of curses and abuse from the coachman. "Ah, you damned fool!" he vociferated. "I shouted to you loud enough! Draw out, you old raven, and keep to the right! Are you drunk?" Selifan himself felt conscious that he had been careless, but since a Russian does not care to admit a fault in the presence of strangers, he retorted with dignity: "Why have you run into US? Did you leave your eyes behind you at the last tavern that you stopped at?" With that he started to back the britchka, in the hope that it might get clear of the other's harness; but this would not do, for the pair were too hopelessly intertwined. Meanwhile the skewbald snuffed curiously at his new acquaintances as they stood planted on either side of him; while the ladies in the vehicle regarded the scene with an expression of terror. One of them was an old woman, and the other a damsel of about sixteen. A mass of golden hair fell daintily from a small head, and the oval of her comely face was as shapely as an egg, and white with the transparent whiteness seen when the hands of a housewife hold a new-laid egg to the light to let the sun's rays filter through its shell. The same tint marked the maiden's ears where they glowed in the sunshine, and, in short, what with the tears in her wide-open, arresting eyes, she presented so attractive a picture that our hero bestowed upon it more than a passing glance before he turned his attention to the hubbub which was being raised among the horses and the coachmen.

"Back out, you rook of Nizhni Novgorod!" the strangers' coachman shouted. Selifan tightened his reins, and the other driver did the same. The horses stepped back a little, and then came together again—this time getting a leg or two over the traces. In fact, so pleased did the skewbald seem with his new friends that he refused to stir from the melee into which an unforeseen chance had plunged him. Laying his muzzle lovingly upon the neck of one of his recently-acquired acquaintances, he seemed to be whispering something in that acquaintance's ear—and whispering pretty nonsense, too, to judge from the way in which that confidant kept shaking his ears.

At length peasants from a village which happened to be near the scene of the accident tackled the mess; and since a spectacle of that kind is to the Russian muzhik what a newspaper or a club-meeting is to the German, the vehicles soon became the centre of a crowd, and the village denuded even of its old women and children. The traces were disentangled, and a few slaps on the nose forced the skewbald to draw back a little; after which the teams were straightened out and separated. Nevertheless, either sheer obstinacy or vexation at being parted from their new friends caused the strange team absolutely to refuse to move a leg. Their driver laid the whip about them, but still they stood as though rooted to the spot. At length the participatory efforts of the peasants rose to an unprecedented degree of enthusiasm, and they shouted in an intermittent chorus the advice, "Do you, Andrusha, take the head of the trace horse on the right, while Uncle Mitai mounts the shaft horse. Get up, Uncle Mitai." Upon that the lean, long, and red-bearded Uncle Mitai mounted the shaft horse; in which position he looked like a village steeple or the winder which is used to raise water from wells. The coachman whipped up his steeds afresh, but nothing came of it, and Uncle Mitai had proved useless. "Hold on, hold on!" shouted the peasants again. "Do you, Uncle Mitai, mount the trace horse, while Uncle Minai mounts the shaft horse." Whereupon Uncle Minai—a peasant with a pair of broad shoulders, a beard as black as charcoal, and a belly like the huge samovar in which sbiten is brewed for all attending a local market—hastened to seat himself upon the shaft horse, which almost sank to the ground beneath his weight. "NOW they will go all right!" the muzhiks exclaimed. "Lay it on hot, lay it on hot! Give that sorrel horse the whip, and make him squirm like a koramora 22." Nevertheless, the affair in no way progressed; wherefore, seeing that flogging was of no use, Uncles Mitai and Minai BOTH mounted the sorrel, while Andrusha seated himself upon the trace horse. Then the coachman himself lost patience, and sent the two Uncles about their business—and not before it was time, seeing that the horses were steaming in a way that made it clear that, unless they were first winded, they would never reach the next posthouse. So they were given a moment's rest. That done, they moved off of their own accord!

Throughout, Chichikov had been gazing at the young unknown with great attention, and had even made one or two attempts to enter into conversation with her: but without success. Indeed, when the ladies departed, it was as in a dream that he saw the girl's comely presence, the delicate features of her face, and the slender outline of her form vanish from his sight; it was as in a dream that once more he saw only the road, the britchka, the three horses, Selifan, and the bare, empty fields. Everywhere in life—yes, even in the plainest, the dingiest ranks of society, as much as in those which are uniformly bright and presentable—a man may happen upon some phenomenon which is so entirely different from those which have hitherto fallen to his lot. Everywhere through the web of sorrow of which our lives are woven there may suddenly break a clear, radiant thread of joy; even as suddenly along the street of some poor, poverty-stricken village which, ordinarily, sees nought but a farm waggon there may came bowling a gorgeous coach with plated harness, picturesque horses, and a glitter of glass, so that the peasants stand gaping, and do not resume their caps until long after the strange equipage has become lost to sight. Thus the golden-haired maiden makes a sudden, unexpected appearance in our story, and as suddenly, as unexpectedly, disappears. Indeed, had it not been that the person concerned was Chichikov, and not some youth of twenty summers—a hussar or a student or, in general, a man standing on the threshold of life—what thoughts would not have sprung to birth, and stirred and spoken, within him; for what a length of time would he not have stood entranced as he stared into the distance and forgot alike his journey, the business still to be done, the possibility of incurring loss through lingering—himself, his vocation, the world, and everything else that the world contains!

But in the present case the hero was a man of middle-age, and of cautious and frigid temperament. True, he pondered over the incident, but in more deliberate fashion than a younger man would have done. That is to say, his reflections were not so irresponsible and unsteady. "She was a comely damsel," he said to himself as he opened his snuff-box and took a pinch. "But the important point is: Is she also a NICE DAMSEL? One thing she has in her favour—and that is that she appears only just to have left school, and not to have had time to become womanly in the worser sense. At present, therefore, she is like a child. Everything in her is simple, and she says just what she thinks, and laughs merely when she feels inclined. Such a damsel might be made into anything—or she might be turned into worthless rubbish. The latter, I surmise, for trudging after her she will have a fond mother and a bevy of aunts, and so forth—persons who, within a year, will have filled her with womanishness to the point where her own father wouldn't know her. And to that there will be added pride and affectation, and she will begin to observe established rules, and to rack her brains as to how, and how much, she ought to talk, and to whom, and where, and so forth. Every moment will see her growing timorous and confused lest she be saying too much. Finally, she will develop into a confirmed prevaricator, and end by marrying the devil knows whom!" Chichikov paused awhile. Then he went on: "Yet I should like to know who she is, and who her father is, and whether he is a rich landowner of good standing, or merely a respectable man who has acquired a fortune in the service of the Government. Should he allow her, on marriage, a dowry of, say, two hundred thousand roubles, she will be a very nice catch indeed. She might even, so to speak, make a man of good breeding happy."

Indeed, so attractively did the idea of the two hundred thousand roubles begin to dance before his imagination that he felt a twinge of self-reproach because, during the hubbub, he had not inquired of the postillion or the coachman who the travellers might be. But soon the sight of Sobakevitch's country house dissipated his thoughts, and forced him to return to his stock subject of reflection.

Sobakevitch's country house and estate were of very fair size, and on each side of the mansion were expanses of birch and pine forest in two shades of green. The wooden edifice itself had dark-grey walls and a red-gabled roof, for it was a mansion of the kind which Russia builds for her military settlers and for German colonists. A noticeable circumstance was the fact that the taste of the architect had differed from that of the proprietor—the former having manifestly been a pedant and desirous of symmetry, and the latter having wished only for comfort. Consequently he (the proprietor) had dispensed with all windows on one side of the mansion, and had caused to be inserted, in their place, only a small aperture which, doubtless, was intended to light an otherwise dark lumber-room. Likewise, the architect's best efforts had failed to cause the pediment to stand in the centre of the building, since the proprietor had had one of its four original columns removed. Evidently durability had been considered throughout, for the courtyard was enclosed by a strong and very high wooden fence, and both the stables, the coach-house, and the culinary premises were partially constructed of beams warranted to last for centuries. Nay, even the wooden huts of the peasantry were wonderful in the solidity of their construction, and not a clay wall or a carved pattern or other device was to be seen. Everything fitted exactly into its right place, and even the draw-well of the mansion was fashioned of the oakwood usually thought suitable only for mills or ships. In short, wherever Chichikov's eye turned he saw nothing that was not free from shoddy make and well and skilfully arranged. As he approached the entrance steps he caught sight of two faces peering from a window. One of them was that of a woman in a mobcap with features as long and as narrow as a cucumber, and the other that of a man with features as broad and as short as the Moldavian pumpkins (known as *gorlianki*) whereof *balallaiki*—the species of light, two-stringed instrument which constitutes the pride and the joy of the gay young fellow of twenty as he sits winking and smiling at the white-necked, white-bosomed maidens who have gathered to listen to his low-pitched tinkling—are fashioned. This scrutiny made, both faces withdrew, and there came out on to the entrance steps a lacquey clad in a grey jacket and a stiff blue collar. This functionary conducted Chichikov into the hall, where he was met by the master of the house himself, who requested his guest to enter, and then led him into the inner part of the mansion.

A covert glance at Sobakevitch showed our hero that his host exactly resembled a moderate-sized bear. To complete the resemblance, Sobakevitch's long frockcoat and baggy trousers were of the precise colour of a bear's hide, while, when shuffling across the floor, he made a criss-cross motion of the legs, and had, in addition, a constant habit of treading upon his companion's toes. As for his face, it was of the warm, ardent tint of a piatok 23. Persons of this kind—persons to whose designing nature has devoted not much thought, and in the fashioning of whose frames she has used no instruments so delicate as a file or a gimlet and so forth—are not uncommon. Such persons she merely roughhews. One cut with a hatchet, and there results a nose; another such cut with a hatchet, and there materialises a pair of lips; two thrusts with a drill, and there issues a pair of eyes. Lastly, scorning to plane down the roughness, she sends out that person into the world, saying: "There is another live creature." Sobakevitch was just such a ragged, curiously put together figure—though the above model would seem to have been followed more in his upper portion than in his lower. One result was that he seldom turned his head to look at the person with whom he was speaking, but, rather, directed his eyes towards, say, the stove corner or the doorway. As host and guest crossed the dining-room Chichikov directed a second glance at his companion. "He is a bear, and nothing but a bear," he thought to himself. And, indeed, the strange comparison was inevitable. Incidentally, Sobakevitch's Christian name and patronymic were Michael Semenovitch. Of his habit of treading upon other people's toes Chichikov had become fully aware; wherefore he stepped cautiously, and, throughout, allowed his host to take the lead. As a matter of fact, Sobakevitch himself seemed conscious of his failing, for at intervals he would inquire: "I hope I have not hurt you?" and Chichikov, with a word of thanks, would reply that as yet he had sustained no injury.

At length they reached the drawing-room, where Sobakevitch pointed to an armchair, and invited his guest to be seated. Chichikov gazed with interest at the walls and the pictures. In every such picture there were portrayed either young men or Greek generals of the type of Movrogordato (clad in a red uniform and breaches), Kanaris, and others;

and all these heroes were depicted with a solidity of thigh and a wealth of moustache which made the beholder simply shudder with awe. Among them there were placed also, according to some unknown system, and for some unknown reason, firstly, Bagration 24—tall and thin, and with a cluster of small flags and cannon beneath him, and the whole set in the narrowest of frames—and, secondly, the Greek heroine, Bobelina, whose legs looked larger than do the whole bodies of the drawing-room dandies of the present day. Apparently the master of the house was himself a man of health and strength, and therefore liked to have his apartments adorned with none but folk of equal vigour and robustness. Lastly, in the window, and suspended cheek by jowl with Bobelina, there hung a cage whence at intervals there peered forth a white-spotted blackbird. Like everything else in the apartment, it bore a strong resemblance to Sobakevitch. When host and guest had been conversing for two minutes or so the door opened, and there entered the hostess—a tall lady in a cap adorned with ribands of domestic colouring and manufacture. She entered deliberately, and held her head as erect as a palm.

"This is my wife, Theodulia Ivanovna," said Sobakevitch.

Chichikov approached and took her hand. The fact that she raised it nearly to the level of his lips apprised him of the circumstance that it had just been rinsed in cucumber oil.

"My dear, allow me to introduce Paul Ivanovitch Chichikov," added Sobakevitch. "He has the honour of being acquainted both with our Governor and with our Postmaster."

Upon this Theodulia Ivanovna requested her guest to be seated, and accompanied the invitation with the kind of bow usually employed only by actresses who are playing the role of queens. Next, she took a seat upon the sofa, drew around her her merino gown, and sat thereafter without moving an eyelid or an eyebrow. As for Chichikov, he glanced upwards, and once more caught sight of Kanaris with his fat thighs and interminable moustache, and of Bobelina and the blackbird. For fully five minutes all present preserved a complete silence—the only sound audible being that of the blackbird's beak against the wooden floor of the cage as the creature fished for grains of corn. Meanwhile Chichikov again surveyed the room, and saw that everything in it was massive and clumsy in the highest degree; as also that everything was curiously in keeping with the master of the house. For example, in one corner of the apartment there stood a hazelwood bureau with a bulging body on four grotesque legs—the perfect image of a bear. Also, the tables and the chairs were of the same ponderous, unrestful order, and every single article in the room appeared to be saying either, "I, too, am a Sobakevitch," or "I am exactly like Sobakevitch."

"I heard speak of you one day when I was visiting the President of the Council," said Chichikov, on perceiving that no one else had a mind to begin a conversation. "That was on Thursday last. We had a very pleasant evening."

"Yes, on that occasion I was not there," replied Sobakevitch.

"What a nice man he is!"

"Who is?" inquired Sobakevitch, gazing into the corner by the stove.

"The President of the Local Council."

"Did he seem so to you? True, he is a mason, but he is also the greatest fool that the world ever saw."

Chichikov started a little at this mordant criticism, but soon pulled himself together again, and continued:

"Of course, every man has his weakness. Yet the President seems to be an excellent fellow."

"And do you think the same of the Governor?"

"Yes. Why not?"

"Because there exists no greater rogue than he."

"What? The Governor a rogue?" ejaculated Chichikov, at a loss to understand how the official in question could come to be numbered with thieves. "Let me say that I should never have guessed it. Permit me also to remark that his conduct would hardly seem to bear out your opinion—he seems so gentle a man." And in proof of this Chichikov cited the purses which the Governor knitted, and also expatiated on the mildness of his features.

"He has the face of a robber," said Sobakevitch. "Were you to give him a knife, and to turn him loose on a turnpike, he would cut your throat for two kopecks. And the same with the Vice-Governor. The pair are just Gog and Magog."

"Evidently he is not on good terms with them," thought Chichikov to himself. "I had better pass to the Chief of Police, which whom he DOES seem to be friendly." Accordingly he added aloud: "For my own part, I should give the preference to the Head of the Gendarmery. What a frank, outspoken nature he has! And what an element of simplicity does his expression contain!"

"He is mean to the core," remarked Sobakevitch coldly. "He will sell you and cheat you, and then dine at your table. Yes, I know them all, and every one of them is a swindler, and the town a nest of rascals engaged in robbing one another. Not a man of the lot is there but would sell Christ. Yet stay: ONE decent fellow there is—the Public Prosecutor; though even HE, if the truth be told, is little better than a pig."

After these eulogia Chichikov saw that it would be useless to continue running through the list of officials—more especially since suddenly he had remembered that Sobakevitch was not at any time given to commending his fellow man.

"Let us go to luncheon, my dear," put in Theodulia Ivanovna to her spouse.

"Yes; pray come to table," said Sobakevitch to his guest; whereupon they consumed the customary glass of vodka (accompanied by sundry snacks of salted cucumber and other dainties) with which Russians, both in town and country, preface a meal. Then they filed into the dining-room in the wake of the hostess, who sailed on ahead like a goose swimming across a pond. The small dining-table was found to be laid for four persons—the fourth place being occupied by a lady or a young girl (it would have been difficult to say which exactly) who might have been either a relative, the housekeeper, or a casual visitor. Certain persons in the world exist, not as personalities in themselves, but as spots or specks on the personalities of others. Always they are to be seen sitting in the same place, and holding their heads at exactly the same angle, so that one comes within an ace of mistaking them for furniture, and thinks to oneself that never since the day of their birth can they have spoken a single word.

"My dear," said Sobakevitch, "the cabbage soup is excellent." With that he finished his portion, and helped himself to a generous measure of niania 25—the dish which follows shtchi and consists of a sheep's stomach stuffed with black porridge, brains, and other things. "What niania this is!" he added to Chichikov. "Never would you get such stuff in a town, where one is given the devil knows what."

"Nevertheless the Governor keeps a fair table," said Chichikov.

"Yes, but do you know what all the stuff is MADE OF?" retorted Sobakevitch. "If you DID know you would never touch it."

"Of course I am not in a position to say how it is prepared, but at least the pork cutlets and the boiled fish seemed excellent."

"Ah, it might have been thought so; yet I know the way in which such things are bought in the market-place. They are bought by some rascal of a cook whom a Frenchman has taught how to skin a tomcat and then serve it up as hare."

"Ugh! What horrible things you say!" put in Madame.

"Well, my dear, that is how things are done, and it is no fault of mine that it is so. Moreover, everything that is left over—everything that WE (pardon me for mentioning it) cast into the slop-pail—is used by such folk for making soup."

"Always at table you begin talking like this!" objected his helpmeet.

"And why not?" said Sobakevitch. "I tell you straight that I would not eat such nastiness, even had I made it myself. Sugar a frog as much as you like, but never shall it pass MY lips. Nor would I swallow an oyster, for I know only too well what an oyster may resemble. But have some mutton, friend Chichikov. It is shoulder of mutton, and very different stuff from the mutton which they cook in noble kitchens—mutton which has been kicking about the market-place four days or more. All that sort of cookery has been invented by French and German doctors, and I should like to hang them for having done so. They go and prescribe diets and a hunger cure as though what suits their flaccid German systems will agree with a Russian stomach! Such devices are no good at all." Sobakevitch shook his head wrathfully. "Fellows like those are for ever talking of civilisation. As if THAT sort of thing was civilisation! Phew!" (Perhaps the speaker's concluding exclamation would have been even stronger had he not been seated at table.) "For myself, I will have none of it. When I eat pork at a meal, give me the WHOLE pig; when mutton, the WHOLE sheep; when goose, the WHOLE of the bird. Two dishes are better than a thousand, provided that one can eat of them as much as one wants."

And he proceeded to put precept into practice by taking half the shoulder of mutton on to his plate, and then devouring it down to the last morsel of gristle and bone.

"My word!" reflected Chichikov. "The fellow has a pretty good holding capacity!"

"None of it for me," repeated Sobakevitch as he wiped his hands on his napkin. "I don't intend to be like a fellow named Plushkin, who owns eight hundred souls, yet dines worse than does my shepherd."

"Who is Plushkin?" asked Chichikov.

"A miser," replied Sobakevitch. "Such a miser as never you could imagine. Even convicts in prison live better than he does. And he starves his servants as well."

"Really?" ejaculated Chichikov, greatly interested. "Should you, then, say that he has lost many peasants by death?"

"Certainly. They keep dying like flies."

"Then how far from here does he reside?"

"About five versts."

"Only five versts?" exclaimed Chichikov, feeling his heart beating joyously. "Ought one, when leaving your gates, to turn to the right or to the left?"

"I should be sorry to tell you the way to the house of such a cur," said Sobakevitch. "A man had far better go to hell than to Plushkin's."

"Quite so," responded Chichikov. "My only reason for asking you is that it interests me to become acquainted with any and every sort of locality."

To the shoulder of mutton there succeeded, in turn, cutlets (each one larger than a plate), a turkey of about the size of a calf, eggs, rice, pastry, and every conceivable thing which could possibly be put into a stomach. There the meal ended. When he rose from table Chichikov felt as though a pood's weight were inside him. In the drawing-room the company found dessert awaiting them in the shape of pears, plums, and apples; but since neither host nor guest could tackle these particular dainties the hostess removed them to another room. Taking advantage of her absence, Chichikov turned to Sobakevitch (who, prone in an armchair, seemed, after his ponderous meal, to be capable of doing little beyond belching and grunting—each such grunt or belch necessitating a subsequent signing of the cross over the mouth), and intimated to him a desire to have a little private conversation concerning a certain matter. At this moment the hostess returned.

"Here is more dessert," she said. "Pray have a few radishes stewed in honey."

"Later, later," replied Sobakevitch. "Do you go to your room, and Paul Ivanovitch and I will take off our coats and have a nap."

Upon this the good lady expressed her readiness to send for feather beds and cushions, but her husband expressed a preference for slumbering in an armchair, and she therefore departed. When she had gone Sobakevitch inclined his head in an attitude of willingness to listen to Chichikov's business. Our hero began in a sort of detached manner—touching lightly upon the subject of the Russian Empire, and expatiating upon the immensity of the same, and saying that even the Empire of Ancient Rome had been of considerably smaller dimensions. Meanwhile Sobakevitch sat with his head drooping.

From that Chichikov went on to remark that, according to the statutes of the said Russian Empire (which yielded to none in glory—so much so that foreigners marvelled at it), peasants on the census lists who had ended their earthly careers were nevertheless, on the rendering of new lists, returned equally with the living, to the end that the courts might be relieved of a multitude of trifling, useless emendations which might complicate the already sufficiently complex mechanism of the State. Nevertheless, said Chichikov, the general equity of this measure did not obviate a certain amount of annoyance to landowners, since it forced them to pay upon a non-living article the tax due upon a living. Hence (our hero concluded) he (Chichikov) was prepared, owing to the personal respect which he felt for Sobakevitch, to relieve him, in part, of the irksome obligation referred to (in passing, it may be said that Chichikov referred to his principal point only guardedly, for he called the souls which he was seeking not "dead," but "non-existent").

Meanwhile Sobakevitch listened with bent head; though something like a trace of expression dawned in his face as he did so. Ordinarily his body lacked a soul—or, if he did possess a soul, he seemed to keep it elsewhere than where it ought to have been; so that, buried beneath mountains (as it were) or enclosed within a massive shell, its movements produced no sort of agitation on the surface.

"Well?" said Chichikov—though not without a certain tremor of diffidence as to the possible response.

"You are after dead souls?" were Sobakevitch's perfectly simple words.

He spoke without the least surprise in his tone, and much as though the conversation had been turning on grain.

"Yes," replied Chichikov, and then, as before, softened down the expression "dead souls."

"They are to be found," said Sobakevitch. "Why should they not be?"

"Then of course you will be glad to get rid of any that you may chance to have?"

"Yes, I shall have no objection to SELLING them." At this point the speaker raised his head a little, for it had struck him that surely the would-be buyer must have some advantage in view.

"The devil!" thought Chichikov to himself. "Here is he selling the goods before I have even had time to utter a word!"

"And what about the price?" he added aloud. "Of course, the articles are not of a kind very easy to appraise."

"I should be sorry to ask too much," said Sobakevitch. "How would a hundred roubles per head suit you?"

"What, a hundred roubles per head?" Chichikov stared open-mouthed at his host—doubting whether he had heard aright, or whether his host's slow-moving tongue might not have inadvertently substituted one word for another.

"Yes. Is that too much for you?" said Sobakevitch. Then he added: "What is your own price?"

"My own price? I think that we cannot properly have understood one another—that you must have forgotten of what the goods consist. With my hand on my heart do I submit that eight grivni per soul would be a handsome, a VERY handsome, offer."

"What? Eight grivni?"

"In my opinion, a higher offer would be impossible."

"But I am not a seller of boots."

"No; yet you, for your part, will agree that these souls are not live human beings?"

"I suppose you hope to find fools ready to sell you souls on the census list for a couple of groats apiece?"

"Pardon me, but why do you use the term 'on the census list'? The souls themselves have long since passed away, and have left behind them only their names. Not to trouble you with any further discussion of the subject, I can offer you a rouble and a half per head, but no more."

"You should be ashamed even to mention such a sum! Since you deal in articles of this kind, quote me a genuine price."

"I cannot, Michael Semenovitch. Believe me, I cannot. What a man cannot do, that he cannot do." The speaker ended by advancing another half-rouble per head.

"But why hang back with your money?" said Sobakevitch. "Of a truth I am not asking much of you. Any other rascal than myself would have cheated you by selling you old rubbish instead of good, genuine souls, whereas I should be ready to give you of my best, even were you buying only nut-kernels. For instance, look at wheelwright Michiev. Never was there such a one to build spring carts! And his handiwork was not like your Moscow handiwork—good only for an hour. No, he did it all himself, even down to the varnishing."

Chichikov opened his mouth to remark that, nevertheless, the said Michiev had long since departed this world; but Sobakevitch's eloquence had got too thoroughly into its stride to admit of any interruption.

"And look, too, at Probka Stepan, the carpenter," his host went on. "I will wager my head that nowhere else would you find such a workman. What a strong fellow he was! He had served in the Guards, and the Lord only knows what they had given for him, seeing that he was over three arshins in height."

Again Chichikov tried to remark that Probka was dead, but Sobakevitch's tongue was borne on the torrent of its own verbiage, and the only thing to be done was to listen.

"And Milushkin, the bricklayer! He could build a stove in any house you liked! And Maksim Teliatnikov, the bootmaker! Anything that he drove his awl into became a pair of boots—and boots for which you would be thankful, although he WAS a bit foul of the mouth. And Eremi Sorokoplechin, too! He was the best of the lot, and used to work at his trade in Moscow, where he paid a tax of five hundred roubles. Well, THERE'S an assortment of serfs for you!—a very different assortment from what Plushkin would sell you!"

"But permit me," at length put in Chichikov, astounded at this flood of eloquence to which there appeared to be no end. "Permit me, I say, to inquire why you enumerate the talents of the deceased, seeing that they are all of them dead, and that therefore there can be no sense in doing so. 'A dead body is only good to prop a fence with,' says the proverb."

"Of course they are dead," replied Sobakevitch, but rather as though the idea had only just occurred to him, and was giving him food for thought. "But tell me, now: what is the use of listing them as still alive? And what is the use of them themselves? They are flies, not human beings."

"Well," said Chichikov, "they exist, though only in idea."

"But no—NOT only in idea. I tell you that nowhere else would you find such a fellow for working heavy tools as was Michiev. He had the strength of a horse in his shoulders." And, with the words, Sobakevitch turned, as though for corroboration, to the portrait of Bagration, as is frequently done by one of the parties in a dispute when he purports to appeal to an extraneous individual who is not only unknown to him, but wholly unconnected with the subject in hand; with the result that the individual is left in doubt whether to make a reply, or whether to betake himself elsewhere.

"Nevertheless, I CANNOT give you more than two roubles per head," said Chichikov.

"Well, as I don't want you to swear that I have asked too much of you and won't meet you halfway, suppose, for friendship's sake, that you pay me seventy-five roubles in assignats?"

"Good heavens!" thought Chichikov to himself. "Does the man take me for a fool?" Then he added aloud: "The situation seems to me a strange one, for it is as though we were performing a stage comedy. No other explanation would meet the case. Yet you appear to be a man of sense, and possessed of some education. The matter is a very simple one. The question is: what is a dead soul worth, and is it of any use to any one?"

"It is of use to YOU, or you would not be buying such articles."

Chichikov bit his lip, and stood at a loss for a retort. He tried to saying something about "family and domestic circumstances," but Sobakevitch cut him short with:

"I don't want to know your private affairs, for I never poke my nose into such things. You need the souls, and I am ready to sell them. Should you not buy them, I think you will repent it."

"Two roubles is my price," repeated Chichikov.

"Come, come! As you have named that sum, I can understand your not liking to go back upon it; but quote me a bona fide figure."

"The devil fly away with him!" mused Chichikov. "However, I will add another half-rouble." And he did so.

"Indeed?" said Sobakevitch. "Well, my last word upon it is—fifty roubles in assignats. That will mean a sheer loss to me, for nowhere else in the world could you buy better souls than mine."

"The old skinflint!" muttered Chichikov. Then he added aloud, with irritation in his tone: "See here. This is a serious matter. Any one but you would be thankful to get rid of the souls. Only a fool would stick to them, and continue to pay the tax."

"Yes, but remember (and I say it wholly in a friendly way) that transactions of this kind are not generally allowed, and that any one would say that a man who engages in them must have some rather doubtful advantage in view."

"Have it your own away," said Chichikov, with assumed indifference. "As a matter of fact, I am not purchasing for profit, as you suppose, but to humour a certain whim of mine. Two and a half roubles is the most that I can offer."

"Bless your heart!" retorted the host. "At least give me thirty roubles in assignats, and take the lot."

"No, for I see that you are unwilling to sell. I must say good-day to you."

"Hold on, hold on!" exclaimed Sobakevitch, retaining his guest's hand, and at the same moment treading heavily upon his toes—so heavily, indeed, that Chichikov gasped and danced with the pain.

"I BEG your pardon!" said Sobakevitch hastily. "Evidently I have hurt you. Pray sit down again."

"No," retorted Chichikov. "I am merely wasting my time, and must be off."

"Oh, sit down just for a moment. I have something more agreeable to say." And, drawing closer to his guest, Sobakevitch whispered in his ear, as though communicating to him a secret: "How about twenty-five roubles?"

"No, no, no!" exclaimed Chichikov. "I won't give you even a QUARTER of that. I won't advance another kopeck."

For a while Sobakevitch remained silent, and Chichikov did the same. This lasted for a couple of minutes, and, meanwhile, the aquiline-nosed Bagration gazed from the wall as though much interested in the bargaining.

"What is your outside price?" at length said Sobakevitch.

"Two and a half roubles."

"Then you seem to rate a human soul at about the same value as a boiled turnip. At least give me THREE roubles."

"No, I cannot."

"Pardon me, but you are an impossible man to deal with. However, even though it will mean a dead loss to me, and you have not shown a very nice spirit about it, I cannot well refuse to please a friend. I suppose a purchase deed had better be made out in order to have everything in order?"

"Of course."

"Then for that purpose let us repair to the town."

The affair ended in their deciding to do this on the morrow, and to arrange for the signing of a deed of purchase. Next, Chichikov requested a list of the peasants; to which Sobakevitch readily agreed. Indeed, he went to his writing-desk then and there, and started to indite a list which gave not only the peasants' names, but also their late qualifications.

Meanwhile Chichikov, having nothing else to do, stood looking at the spacious form of his host; and as he gazed at his back as broad as that of a cart horse, and at the legs as massive as the iron standards which adorn a street, he could not help inwardly ejaculating:

"Truly God has endowed you with much! Though not adjusted with nicety, at least you are strongly built. I wonder whether you were born a bear or whether you have come to it through your rustic life, with its tilling of crops and its trading with peasants? Yet no; I believe that, even if you had received a fashionable education, and had mixed with society, and had lived in St. Petersburg, you would still have been just the kulak 26 that you are. The only difference is that circumstances, as they stand, permit of your polishing off a stuffed shoulder of mutton at a meal; whereas in St. Petersburg you would have been unable to do so. Also, as circumstances stand, you have under you a number of peasants, whom you treat well for the reason that they are your property; whereas, otherwise, you would have had under you tchinovniks 27: whom you would have bullied because they were NOT your property. Also, you would have robbed the Treasury, since a kulak always remains a money-grubber."

"The list is ready," said Sobakevitch, turning round.

"Indeed? Then please let me look at it." Chichikov ran his eye over the document, and could not but marvel at its neatness and accuracy. Not only were there set forth in it the trade, the age, and the pedigree of every serf, but on the margin of the sheet were jotted remarks concerning each serf's conduct and sobriety. Truly it was a pleasure to look at it.

"And do you mind handing me the earnest money?" said Sobakevitch.

"Yes, I do. Why need that be done? You can receive the money in a lump sum as soon as we visit the town."

"But it is always the custom, you know," asserted Sobakevitch.

"Then I cannot follow it, for I have no money with me. However, here are ten roubles."

"Ten roubles, indeed? You might as well hand me fifty while you are about it."

Once more Chichikov started to deny that he had any money upon him, but Sobakevitch insisted so strongly that this was not so that at length the guest pulled out another fifteen roubles, and added them to the ten already produced.

"Kindly give me a receipt for the money," he added.

"A receipt? Why should I give you a receipt?"

"Because it is better to do so, in order to guard against mistakes."

"Very well; but first hand me over the money."

"The money? I have it here. Do you write out the receipt, and then the money shall be yours."

"Pardon me, but how am I to write out the receipt before I have seen the cash?"

Chichikov placed the notes in Sobakevitch's hand; whereupon the host moved nearer to the table, and added to the list of serfs a note that he had received for the peasants, therewith sold, the sum of twenty-five roubles, as earnest money. This done, he counted the notes once more.

"This is a very OLD note," he remarked, holding one up to the light. "Also, it is a trifle torn. However, in a friendly transaction one must not be too particular."

"What a kulak!" thought Chichikov to himself. "And what a brute beast!"

"Then you do not want any WOMEN souls?" queried Sobakevitch.

"I thank you, no."

"I could let you have some cheap—say, as between friends, at a rouble a head?"

"No, I should have no use for them."

"Then, that being so, there is no more to be said. There is no accounting for tastes. 'One man loves the priest, and another the priest's wife,' says the proverb."

Chichikov rose to take his leave. "Once more I would request of you," he said, "that the bargain be left as it is."

"Of course, of course. What is done between friends holds good because of their mutual friendship. Good-bye, and thank you for your visit. In advance I would beg that, whenever you should have an hour or two to spare, you will come and lunch with us again. Perhaps we might be able to do one another further service?"

"Not if I know it!" reflected Chichikov as he mounted his britchka. "Not I, seeing that I have had two and a half roubles per soul squeezed out of me by a brute of a kulak!"

Altogether he felt dissatisfied with Sobakevitch's behaviour. In spite of the man being a friend of the Governor and the Chief of Police, he had acted like an outsider in taking money for what was worthless rubbish. As the britchka left the courtyard Chichikov glanced back and saw Sobakevitch still standing on the verandah—apparently for the purpose of watching to see which way the guest's carriage would turn.

"The old villain, to be still standing there!" muttered Chichikov through his teeth; after which he ordered Selifan to proceed so that the vehicle's progress should be invisible from the mansion—the truth being that he had a mind next to visit Plushkin (whose serfs, to quote Sobakevitch, had a habit of dying like flies), but not to let his late host learn of his intention. Accordingly, on reaching the further end of the village, he hailed the first peasant whom he saw—a man who was in the act of hoisting a ponderous beam on to his shoulder before setting off with it, ant-like, to his hut.

"Hi!" shouted Chichikov. "How can I reach landowner Plushkin's place without first going past the mansion here?"

The peasant seemed nonplussed by the question.

"Don't you know?" queried Chichikov.

"No, barin," replied the peasant.

"What? You don't know skinflint Plushkin who feeds his people so badly?"

"Of course I do!" exclaimed the fellow, and added thereto an uncomplimentary expression of a species not ordinarily employed in polite society. We may guess that it was a pretty apt expression, since long after the man had become lost to view Chichikov was still laughing in his britchka. And, indeed, the language of the Russian populace is always forcible in its phraseology.

CHAPTER VI

Chichikov's amusement at the peasant's outburst prevented him from noticing that he had reached the centre of a large and populous village; but, presently, a violent jolt aroused him to the fact that he was driving over wooden pavements of a kind compared with which the cobblestones of the town had been as nothing. Like the keys of a piano, the planks kept rising and falling, and unguarded passage over them entailed either a bump on the back of the neck or a bruise on the forehead or a bite on the tip of one's tongue. At the same time Chichikov noticed a look of decay about the buildings of the village. The beams of the huts had grown dark with age, many of their roofs were riddled with holes, others had but a tile of the roof remaining, and yet others were reduced to the rib-like framework of the same. It would seem as though the inhabitants themselves had removed the laths and traverses, on the very natural plea that the huts were no protection against the rain, and therefore, since the latter entered in bucketfuls, there was no particular object to be gained by sitting in such huts when all the time there was the tavern and the highroad and other places to resort to.

Suddenly a woman appeared from an outbuilding—apparently the housekeeper of the mansion, but so roughly and dirtily dressed as almost to seem indistinguishable from a man. Chichikov inquired for the master of the place.

"He is not at home," she replied, almost before her interlocutor had had time to finish. Then she added: "What do you want with him?"

"I have some business to do," said Chichikov.

"Then pray walk into the house," the woman advised. Then she turned upon him a back that was smeared with flour and had a long slit in the lower portion of its covering. Entering a large, dark hall which reeked like a tomb, he passed into an equally dark parlour that was lighted only by such rays as contrived to filter through a crack under the door. When Chichikov opened the door in question, the spectacle of the untidiness within struck him almost with amazement. It would seem that the floor was never washed, and that the room was used as a receptacle for every conceivable kind of furniture. On a table stood a ragged chair, with, beside it, a clock minus a pendulum and covered all over with cobwebs. Against a wall leant a cupboard, full of old silver, glassware, and china. On a writing table, inlaid with mother-of-pearl which, in places, had broken away and left behind it a number of yellow grooves (stuffed with putty), lay a pile of finely written manuscript, an overturned marble press (turning green), an ancient book in a leather cover with red edges, a lemon dried and shrunken to the dimensions of a hazelnut, the broken arm of a chair, a tumbler containing the dregs of some liquid and three flies (the whole covered over with a sheet of notepaper), a pile of rags, two ink-encrusted pens, and a yellow toothpick with which the master of the house had picked his teeth (apparently) at least before the coming of the French to Moscow. As for the walls, they were hung with a medley of pictures. Among the latter was a long engraving of a battle scene, wherein soldiers in three-cornered hats were brandishing huge drums and slender lances. It lacked a glass, and was set in a frame ornamented with bronze fretwork and bronze corner rings. Beside it hung a huge, grimy oil painting representative of some flowers and fruit, half a water melon, a boar's head, and the pendent form of a dead wild duck. Attached to the ceiling there was a chandelier in a holland covering—the covering so dusty as closely to resemble a huge cocoon enclosing a caterpillar. Lastly, in one corner of the room lay a pile of articles which had evidently been adjudged unworthy of a place on the table. Yet what the pile consisted of it would have been difficult to say, seeing that the dust on the same was so thick that any hand which touched it would have at once resembled a glove. Prominently protruding from the pile was the shaft of a wooden spade and the antiquated sole of a shoe. Never would one have supposed that a living creature had tenanted the room, were it not that the presence of such a creature was betrayed by the spectacle of an old nightcap resting on the table.

Whilst Chichikov was gazing at this extraordinary mess, a side door opened and there entered the housekeeper who had met him near the outbuildings. But now Chichikov perceived this person to be a man rather than a woman, since a female housekeeper would have had no beard to shave, whereas the chin of the newcomer, with the lower portion of his cheeks, strongly resembled the curry-comb which is used for grooming horses. Chichikov assumed a questioning air, and waited to hear what the housekeeper might have to say. The housekeeper did the same. At length, surprised at the misunderstanding, Chichikov decided to ask the first question.

"Is the master at home?" he inquired.

"Yes," replied the person addressed.

"Then where is he?" continued Chichikov.

"Are you blind, my good sir?" retorted the other. "*I* am the master."

Involuntarily our hero started and stared. During his travels it had befallen him to meet various types of men—some of them, it may be, types which you and I have never encountered; but even to Chichikov this particular species was new. In the old man's face there was nothing very special—it was much like the wizened face of many another dotard, save that the chin was so greatly projected that whenever he spoke he was forced to wipe it with a handkerchief to avoid dribbling, and that his small eyes were not yet grown dull, but twinkled under their overhanging brows like the eyes of mice when, with attentive ears and sensitive whiskers, they snuff the air and peer forth from their holes to see whether a cat or a boy may not be in the vicinity. No, the most noticeable feature about the man was his clothes. In no way could it have been guessed of what his coat was made, for both its sleeves and its skirts were so ragged and filthy as to defy description, while instead of two posterior tails, there dangled four of those appendages, with, projecting from them, a torn newspaper. Also, around his neck there was wrapped something which might have been a stocking, a garter, or a stomacher, but was certainly not a tie. In short, had Chichikov chanced to encounter him at a church door, he would have bestowed upon him a copper or two (for, to do our hero justice, he had a sympathetic heart and never refrained from presenting a beggar with alms), but in the present case there was standing before him, not a mendicant, but a landowner—and a landowner possessed of fully a thousand serfs, the superior of all his neighbours in wealth of flour and grain, and the owner of storehouses, and so forth, that were crammed with homespun cloth and linen, tanned and undressed sheepskins, dried fish, and every conceivable species of produce. Nevertheless, such a phenomenon is rare in Russia, where the tendency is rather to prodigality than to parsimony.

For several minutes Plushkin stood mute, while Chichikov remained so dazed with the appearance of the host and everything else in the room, that he too, could not begin a conversation, but stood wondering how best to find words in which to explain the object of his visit. For a while he thought of expressing himself to the effect that, having heard so much of his host's benevolence and other rare qualities of spirit, he had considered it his duty to come and pay a tribute of respect; but presently even HE came to the conclusion that this would be overdoing the thing, and, after another glance round the room, decided that the phrase "benevolence and other rare qualities of spirit" might to advantage give place to "economy and genius for method." Accordingly, the speech mentally composed, he said aloud that, having heard of Plushkin's talents for thrifty and systematic management, he had considered himself bound to make the acquaintance of his host, and to present him with his personal compliments (I need hardly say that Chichikov could easily have alleged a better reason, had any better one happened, at the moment, to have come into his head).

With toothless gums Plushkin murmured something in reply, but nothing is known as to its precise terms beyond that it included a statement that the devil was at liberty to fly away with Chichikov's sentiments. However, the laws of Russian hospitality do not permit even of a miser infringing their rules; wherefore Plushkin added to the foregoing a more civil invitation to be seated.

"It is long since I last received a visitor," he went on. "Also, I feel bound to say that I can see little good in their coming. Once introduce the abominable custom of folk paying calls, and forthwith there will ensue such ruin to the management of estates that landowners will be forced to feed their horses on hay. Not for a long, long time have I eaten a meal away from home—although my own kitchen is a poor one, and has its chimney in such a state that, were it to become overheated, it would instantly catch fire."

"What a brute!" thought Chichikov. "I am lucky to have got through so much pastry and stuffed shoulder of mutton at Sobakevitch's!"

"Also," went on Plushkin, "I am ashamed to say that hardly a wisp of fodder does the place contain. But how can I get fodder? My lands are small, and the peasantry lazy fellows who hate work and think of nothing but the tavern. In the end, therefore, I shall be forced to go and spend my old age in roaming about the world."

"But I have been told that you possess over a thousand serfs?" said Chichikov.

"Who told you that? No matter who it was, you would have been justified in giving him the lie. He must have been a jester who wanted to make a fool of you. A thousand souls, indeed! Why, just reckon the taxes on them, and see what there would be left! For these three years that accursed fever has been killing off my serfs wholesale."

"Wholesale, you say?" echoed Chichikov, greatly interested.

"Yes, wholesale," replied the old man.

"Then might I ask you the exact number?"

"Fully eighty."

"Surely not?"

"But it is so."

"Then might I also ask whether it is from the date of the last census revision that you are reckoning these souls?"

"Yes, damn it! And since that date I have been bled for taxes upon a hundred and twenty souls in all."

"Indeed? Upon a hundred and twenty souls in all!" And Chichikov's surprise and elation were such that, this said, he remained sitting open-mouthed.

"Yes, good sir," replied Plushkin. "I am too old to tell you lies, for I have passed my seventieth year."

Somehow he seemed to have taken offence at Chichikov's almost joyous exclamation; wherefore the guest hastened to heave a profound sigh, and to observe that he sympathised to the full with his host's misfortunes.

"But sympathy does not put anything into one's pocket," retorted Plushkin. "For instance, I have a kinsman who is constantly plaguing me. He is a captain in the army, damn him, and all day he does nothing but call me 'dear uncle,' and kiss my hand, and express sympathy until I am forced to stop my ears. You see, he has squandered all his money upon his brother-officers, as well as made a fool of himself with an actress; so now he spends his time in telling me that he has a sympathetic heart!"

Chichikov hastened to explain that HIS sympathy had nothing in common with the captain's, since he dealt, not in empty words alone, but in actual deeds; in proof of which he was ready then and there (for the purpose of cutting the matter short, and of dispensing with circumlocution) to transfer to himself the obligation of paying the taxes due upon such serfs as Plushkin's as had, in the unfortunate manner just described, departed this world. The proposal seemed to astonish Plushkin, for he sat staring open-eyed. At length he inquired:

"My dear sir, have you seen military service?"

"No," replied the other warily, "but I have been a member of the CIVIL Service."

"Oh! Of the CIVIL Service?" And Plushkin sat moving his lips as though he were chewing something. "Well, what of your proposal?" he added presently. "Are you prepared to lose by it?"

"Yes, certainly, if thereby I can please you."

"My dear sir! My good benefactor!" In his delight Plushkin lost sight of the fact that his nose was caked with snuff of the consistency of thick coffee, and that his coat had parted in front and was disclosing some very unseemly underclothing. "What comfort you have brought to an old man! Yes, as God is my witness!"

For the moment he could say no more. Yet barely a minute had elapsed before this instantaneously aroused emotion had, as instantaneously, disappeared from his wooden features. Once more they assumed a careworn expression, and he even wiped his face with his handkerchief, then rolled it into a ball, and rubbed it to and fro against his upper lip.

"If it will not annoy you again to state the proposal," he went on, "what you undertake to do is to pay the annual tax upon these souls, and to remit the money either to me or to the Treasury?"

"Yes, that is how it shall be done. We will draw up a deed of purchase as though the souls were still alive and you had sold them to myself."

"Quite so—a deed of purchase," echoed Plushkin, once more relapsing into thought and the chewing motion of the lips. "But a deed of such a kind will entail certain expenses, and lawyers are so devoid of conscience! In fact, so extortionate is their avarice that they will charge one half a rouble, and then a sack of flour, and then a whole waggon-load of meal. I wonder that no one has yet called attention to the system."

Upon that Chichikov intimated that, out of respect for his host, he himself would bear the cost of the transfer of souls. This led Plushkin to conclude that his guest must be the kind of unconscionable fool who, while pretending to have been a member of the Civil Service, has in reality served in the army and run after actresses; wherefore the old man no longer disguised his delight, but called down blessings alike upon Chichikov's head and upon those of his children (he had never even inquired whether Chichikov possessed a family). Next, he shuffled to the window, and, tapping one of its panes, shouted the name of "Proshka." Immediately some one ran quickly into the hall, and, after much stamping of feet, burst into the room. This was Proshka—a thirteen-year-old youngster who was shod with boots of such dimensions as almost to engulf his legs as he walked. The reason why he had entered thus shod was that Plushkin only kept one pair of boots for the whole of his domestic staff. This universal pair was stationed in the hall of the mansion, so that any servant who was summoned to the house might don the said boots after wading barefooted through the mud of the courtyard, and enter the parlour dry-shod—subsequently leaving the boots where he had found them, and departing in his former barefooted condition. Indeed, had any one, on a slushy winter's morning, glanced from a window into the said courtyard, he would have seen Plushkin's servitors performing saltatory feats worthy of the most vigorous of stage-dancers.

"Look at that boy's face!" said Plushkin to Chichikov as he pointed to Proshka. "It is stupid enough, yet, lay anything aside, and in a trice he will have stolen it. Well, my lad, what do you want?"

He paused a moment or two, but Proshka made no reply.

"Come, come!" went on the old man. "Set out the samovar, and then give Mavra the key of the store-room—here it is—and tell her to get out some loaf sugar for tea. Here! Wait another moment, fool! Is the devil in your legs that they itch so to be off? Listen to what more I have to tell you. Tell Mavra that the sugar on the outside of the loaf has gone bad, so that she must scrape it off with a knife, and NOT throw away the scrapings, but give them to the poultry. Also, see that you yourself don't go into the storeroom, or I will give you a birching that you won't care for. Your appetite is good enough already, but a better one won't hurt you. Don't even TRY to go into the storeroom, for I shall be watching you from this window."

"You see," the old man added to Chichikov, "one can never trust these fellows." Presently, when Proshka and the boots had departed, he fell to gazing at his guest with an equally distrustful air, since certain features in Chichikov's benevolence now struck him as a little open to question, and he had begin to think to himself: "After all, the devil only knows who he is— whether a braggart, like most of these spendthrifts, or a fellow who is lying merely in order to get some tea out of me." Finally, his circumspection, combined with a desire to test his guest, led him to remark that it might be well to complete the transaction IMMEDIATELY, since he had not overmuch confidence in humanity, seeing that a man might be alive to-day and dead to-morrow.

To this Chichikov assented readily enough—merely adding that he should like first of all to be furnished with a list of the dead souls. This reassured Plushkin as to his guest's intention of doing business, so he got out his keys, approached a cupboard, and, having pulled back the door, rummaged among the cups and glasses with which it was filled. At length he said:

"I cannot find it now, but I used to possess a splendid bottle of liquor. Probably the servants have drunk it all, for they are such thieves. Oh no: perhaps this is it!"

Looking up, Chichikov saw that Plushkin had extracted a decanter coated with dust.

"My late wife made the stuff," went on the old man, "but that rascal of a housekeeper went and threw away a lot of it, and never even replaced the stopper. Consequently bugs and other nasty creatures got into the decanter, but I cleaned it out, and now beg to offer you a glassful."

The idea of a drink from such a receptacle was too much for Chichikov, so he excused himself on the ground that he had just had luncheon.

"You have just had luncheon?" re-echoed Plushkin. "Now, THAT shows how invariably one can tell a man of good society, wheresoever one may be. A man of that kind never eats anything—he always says that he has had enough. Very different that from the ways of a rogue, whom one can never satisfy, however much one may give him. For instance, that captain of mine is constantly begging me to let him have a meal—though he is about as much my nephew as I am his grandfather. As it happens, there is never a bite of anything in the house, so he has to go away empty. But about the list of those good-for-nothing souls—I happen to possess such a list, since I have drawn one up in readiness for the next revision."

With that Plushkin donned his spectacles, and once more started to rummage in the cupboard, and to smother his guest with dust as he untied successive packages of papers—so much so that his victim burst out sneezing. Finally he extracted a much-scribbled document in which the names of the deceased peasants lay as close-packed as a cloud of midges, for there were a hundred and twenty of them in all. Chichikov grinned with joy at the sight of the multitude. Stuffing the list into his pocket, he remarked that, to complete the transaction, it would be necessary to return to the town.

"To the town?" repeated Plushkin. "But why? Moreover, how could I leave the house, seeing that every one of my servants is either a thief or a rogue? Day by day they pilfer things, until soon I shall have not a single coat to hang on my back."

"Then you possess acquaintances in the town?"

"Acquaintances? No. Every acquaintance whom I ever possessed has either left me or is dead. But stop a moment. I DO know the President of the Council. Even in my old age he has once or twice come to visit me, for he and I used to be schoolfellows, and to go climbing walls together. Yes, him I do know. Shall I write him a letter?"

"By all means."

"Yes, him I know well, for we were friends together at school."

Over Plushkin's wooden features there had gleamed a ray of warmth—a ray which expressed, if not feeling, at all events feeling's pale reflection. Just such a phenomenon may be witnessed when, for a brief moment, a drowning man makes a last re-appearance on the surface of a river, and there rises from the crowd lining the banks a cry of hope that even yet the exhausted hands may clutch the rope which has been thrown him—may clutch it before the surface of the unstable element shall have resumed for ever its calm, dread vacuity. But the hope is short-lived, and the hands disappear. Even so did Plushkin's face, after its momentary manifestation of feeling, become meaner and more insensible than ever.

"There used to be a sheet of clean writing paper lying on the table," he went on. "But where it is now I cannot think. That comes of my servants being such rascals."

With that he fell to looking also under the table, as well as to hurrying about with cries of "Mavra, Mavra!" At length the call was answered by a woman with a plateful of the sugar of which mention has been made; whereupon there ensued the following conversation.

"What have you done with my piece of writing paper, you pilferer?"

"I swear that I have seen no paper except the bit with which you covered the glass."

"Your very face tells me that you have made off with it."

"Why should I make off with it? 'Twould be of no use to me, for I can neither read nor write."

"You lie! You have taken it away for the sexton to scribble upon."

"Well, if the sexton wanted paper he could get some for himself. Neither he nor I have set eyes upon your piece."

"Ah! Wait a bit, for on the Judgment Day you will be roasted by devils on iron spits. Just see if you are not!"

"But why should I be roasted when I have never even TOUCHED the paper? You might accuse me of any other fault than theft."

"Nay, devils shall roast you, sure enough. They will say to you, 'Bad woman, we are doing this because you robbed your master,' and then stoke up the fire still hotter."

"Nevertheless *I* shall continue to say, 'You are roasting me for nothing, for I never stole anything at all.' Why, THERE it is, lying on the table! You have been accusing me for no reason whatever!"

And, sure enough, the sheet of paper was lying before Plushkin's very eyes. For a moment or two he chewed silently. Then he went on:

"Well, and what are you making such a noise about? If one says a single word to you, you answer back with ten. Go and fetch me a candle to seal a letter with. And mind you bring a TALLOW candle, for it will not cost so much as the other sort. And bring me a match too."

Mavra departed, and Plushkin, seating himself, and taking up a pen, sat turning the sheet of paper over and over, as though in doubt whether to tear from it yet another morsel. At length he came to the conclusion that it was impossible to do so, and therefore, dipping the pen into the mixture of mouldy fluid and dead flies which the ink bottle contained, started to indite the letter in characters as bold as the notes of a music score, while momentarily checking the speed of his hand, lest it should meander too much over the paper, and crawling from line to line as though he regretted that there was so little vacant space left on the sheet.

"And do you happen to know any one to whom a few runaway serfs would be of use?" he asked as subsequently he folded the letter.

"What? You have some runaways as well?" exclaimed Chichikov, again greatly interested.

"Certainly I have. My son-in-law has laid the necessary information against them, but says that their tracks have grown cold. However, he is only a military man—that is to say, good at clinking a pair of spurs, but of no use for laying a plea before a court."

"And how many runaways have you?"

"About seventy."

"Surely not?"

"Alas, yes. Never does a year pass without a certain number of them making off. Yet so gluttonous and idle are my serfs that they are simply bursting with food, whereas I scarcely get enough to eat. I will take any price for them that you may care to offer. Tell your friends about it, and, should they find even a score of the runaways, it will repay them handsomely, seeing that a living serf on the census list is at present worth five hundred roubles."

"Perhaps so, but I am not going to let any one but myself have a finger in this," thought Chichikov to himself; after which he explained to Plushkin that a friend of the kind mentioned would be impossible to discover, since the legal expenses of the enterprise would lead to the said friend having to cut the very tail from his coat before he would get clear of the lawyers.

"Nevertheless," added Chichikov, "seeing that you are so hard pressed for money, and that I am so interested in the matter, I feel moved to advance you—well, to advance you such a trifle as would scarcely be worth mentioning."

"But how much is it?" asked Plushkin eagerly, and with his hands trembling like quicksilver.

"Twenty-five kopecks per soul."

"What? In ready money?"

"Yes—in money down."

"Nevertheless, consider my poverty, dear friend, and make it FORTY kopecks per soul."

"Venerable sir, would that I could pay you not merely forty kopecks, but five hundred roubles. I should be only too delighted if that were possible, since I perceive that you, an aged and respected gentleman, are suffering for your own goodness of heart."

"By God, that is true, that is true." Plushkin hung his head, and wagged it feebly from side to side. "Yes, all that I have done I have done purely out of kindness."

"See how instantaneously I have divined your nature! By now it will have become clear to you why it is impossible for me to pay you five hundred roubles per runaway soul: for by now you will have gathered the fact that I am not sufficiently rich. Nevertheless, I am ready to add another five kopecks, and so to make it that each runaway serf shall cost me, in all, thirty kopecks."

"As you please, dear sir. Yet stretch another point, and throw in another two kopecks."

"Pardon me, but I cannot. How many runaway serfs did you say that you possess? Seventy?"

"No; seventy-eight."

"Seventy-eight souls at thirty kopecks each will amount to—to—" only for a moment did our hero halt, since he was strong in his arithmetic, "—will amount to twenty-four roubles, ninety-six kopecks." 28

With that he requested Plushkin to make out the receipt, and then handed him the money. Plushkin took it in both hands, bore it to a bureau with as much caution as though he were carrying a liquid which might at any moment splash him in the face, and, arrived at the bureau, and glancing round once more, carefully packed the cash in one of his money bags, where, doubtless, it was destined to lie buried until, to the intense joy of his daughters and his son-in-law (and, perhaps, of the captain who claimed kinship with him), he should himself receive burial at the hands of Fathers Carp and Polycarp, the two priests attached to his village. Lastly, the money concealed, Plushkin re-seated himself in the armchair, and seemed at a loss for further material for conversation.

"Are you thinking of starting?" at length he inquired, on seeing Chichikov making a trifling movement, though the movement was only to extract from his pocket a handkerchief. Nevertheless the question reminded Chichikov that there was no further excuse for lingering.

"Yes, I must be going," he said as he took his hat.

"Then what about the tea?"

"Thank you, I will have some on my next visit."

"What? Even though I have just ordered the samovar to be got ready? Well, well! I myself do not greatly care for tea, for I think it an expensive beverage. Moreover, the price of sugar has risen terribly."

"Proshka!" he then shouted. "The samovar will not be needed. Return the sugar to Mavra, and tell her to put it back again. But no. Bring the sugar here, and *I* will put it back."

"Good-bye, dear sir," finally he added to Chichikov. "May the Lord bless you! Hand that letter to the President of the Council, and let him read it. Yes, he is an old friend of mine. We knew one another as schoolfellows."

With that this strange phenomenon, this withered old man, escorted his guest to the gates of the courtyard, and, after the guest had departed, ordered the gates to be closed, made the round of the outbuildings for the purpose of ascertaining whether the numerous watchmen were at their posts, peered into the kitchen (where, under the pretence of seeing whether his servants were being properly fed, he made a light meal of cabbage soup and gruel), rated the said servants soundly for their thievishness and general bad behaviour, and then returned to his room. Meditating in solitude, he fell to thinking how best he could contrive to recompense his guest for the latter's measureless benevolence. "I will present him," he thought to himself, "with a watch. It is a good silver article—not one of those cheap metal affairs; and though it has suffered some damage, he can easily get that put right. A young man always needs to give a watch to his betrothed."

"No," he added after further thought. "I will leave him the watch in my will, as a keepsake."

Meanwhile our hero was bowling along in high spirit. Such an unexpected acquisition both of dead souls and of runaway serfs had come as a windfall. Even before reaching Plushkin's village he had had a presentiment that he would do successful business there, but not business of such pre-eminent profitableness as had actually resulted. As he proceeded he whistled, hummed with hand placed trumpetwise to his mouth, and ended by bursting into a burst of melody so striking that Selifan, after listening for a while, nodded his head and exclaimed, "My word, but the master CAN sing!"

By the time they reached the town darkness had fallen, and changed the character of the scene. The britchka bounded over the cobblestones, and at length turned into the hostelry's courtyard, where the travellers were met by Petrushka. With one hand holding back the tails of his coat (which he never liked to see fly apart), the valet assisted his master to alight. The waiter ran out with candle in hand and napkin on shoulder. Whether or not Petrushka was glad to see the barin return it is impossible to say, but at all events he exchanged a wink with Selifan, and his ordinarily morose exterior seemed momentarily to brighten.

"Then you have been travelling far, sir?" said the waiter, as he lit the way upstarts.

"Yes," said Chichikov. "What has happened here in the meanwhile?"

"Nothing, sir," replied the waiter, bowing, "except that last night there arrived a military lieutenant. He has got room number sixteen."

"A lieutenant?"

"Yes. He came from Riazan, driving three grey horses."

On entering his room, Chichikov clapped his hand to his nose, and asked his valet why he had never had the windows opened.

"But I did have them opened," replied Petrushka. Nevertheless this was a lie, as Chichikov well knew, though he was too tired to contest the point. After ordering and consuming a light supper of sucking pig, he undressed, plunged beneath the bedclothes, and sank into the profound slumber which comes only to such fortunate folk as are troubled neither with mosquitoes nor fleas nor excessive activity of brain.

CHAPTER VII

When Chichikov awoke he stretched himself and realised that he had slept well. For a moment or two he lay on his back, and then suddenly clapped his hands at the recollection that he was now owner of nearly four hundred souls. At once he leapt out of bed without so much as glancing at his face in the mirror, though, as a rule, he had much solicitude for his features, and especially for his chin, of which he would make the most when in company with friends, and more particularly should any one happen to enter while he was engaged in the process of shaving. "Look how round my chin is!" was his usual formula. On the present occasion, however, he looked neither at chin nor at any other feature, but at once donned his flower-embroidered slippers of morroco leather (the kind of slippers in which, thanks to the Russian love for a dressing-gowned existence, the town of Torzhok does such a huge trade), and, clad only in a meagre shirt, so far forgot his elderliness and dignity as to cut a couple of capers after the fashion of a Scottish highlander—

alighting neatly, each time, on the flat of his heels. Only when he had done that did he proceed to business. Planting himself before his dispatch-box, he rubbed his hands with a satisfaction worthy of an incorruptible rural magistrate when adjourning for luncheon; after which he extracted from the receptacle a bundle of papers. These he had decided not to deposit with a lawyer, for the reason that he would hasten matters, as well as save expense, by himself framing and fair-copying the necessary deeds of indenture; and since he was thoroughly acquainted with the necessary terminology, he proceeded to inscribe in large characters the date, and then in smaller ones, his name and rank. By two o'clock the whole was finished, and as he looked at the sheets of names representing bygone peasants who had ploughed, worked at handicrafts, cheated their masters, fetched, carried, and got drunk (though SOME of them may have behaved well), there came over him a strange, unaccountable sensation. To his eye each list of names seemed to possess a character of its own; and even individual peasants therein seemed to have taken on certain qualities peculiar to themselves. For instance, to the majority of Madame Korobotchka's serfs there were appended nicknames and other additions; Plushkin's list was distinguished by a conciseness of exposition which had led to certain of the items being represented merely by Christian name, patronymic, and a couple of dots; and Sobakevitch's list was remarkable for its amplitude and circumstantiality, in that not a single peasant had such of his peculiar characteristics omitted as that the deceased had been "excellent at joinery," or "sober and ready to pay attention to his work." Also, in Sobakevitch's list there was recorded who had been the father and the mother of each of the deceased, and how those parents had behaved themselves. Only against the name of a certain Thedotov was there inscribed: "Father unknown, Mother the maidservant Kapitolina, Morals and Honesty good." These details communicated to the document a certain air of freshness, they seemed to connote that the peasants in question had lived but yesterday. As Chichikov scanned the list he felt softened in spirit, and said with a sigh:

"My friends, what a concourse of you is here! How did you all pass your lives, my brethren? And how did you all come to depart hence?"

As he spoke his eyes halted at one name in particular—that of the same Peter Saveliev Neuvazhai Korito who had once been the property of the window Korobotchka. Once more he could not help exclaiming:

"What a series of titles! They occupy a whole line! Peter Saveliev, I wonder whether you were an artisan or a plain muzhik. Also, I wonder how you came to meet your end; whether in a tavern, or whether through going to sleep in the middle of the road and being run over by a train of waggons. Again, I see the name, 'Probka Stepan, carpenter, very sober.' That must be the hero of whom the Guards would have been so glad to get hold. How well I can imagine him tramping the country with an axe in his belt and his boots on his shoulder, and living on a few groats'-worth of bread and dried fish per day, and taking home a couple of half-rouble pieces in his purse, and sewing the notes into his breeches, or stuffing them into his boots! In what manner came you by your end, Probka Stepan? Did you, for good wages, mount a scaffold around the cupola of the village church, and, climbing thence to the cross above, miss your footing on a beam, and fall headlong with none at hand but Uncle Michai—the good uncle who, scratching the back of his neck, and muttering, 'Ah, Vania, for once you have been too clever!' straightway lashed himself to a rope, and took your place? 'Maksim Teliatnikov, shoemaker.' A shoemaker, indeed? 'As drunk as a shoemaker,' says the proverb. *I* know what you were like, my friend. If you wish, I will tell you your whole history. You were apprenticed to a German, who fed you and your fellows at a common table, thrashed you with a strap, kept you indoors whenever you had made a mistake, and spoke of you in uncomplimentary terms to his wife and friends. At length, when your apprenticeship was over, you said to yourself, 'I am going to set up on my own account, and not just to scrape together a kopeck here and a kopeck there, as the Germans do, but to grow rich quick.' Hence you took a shop at a high rent, bespoke a few orders, and set to work to buy up some rotten leather out of which you could make, on each pair of boots, a double profit. But those boots split within a fortnight, and brought down upon your head dire showers of maledictions; with the result that gradually your shop grew empty of customers, and you fell to roaming the streets and exclaiming, 'The world is a very poor place indeed! A Russian cannot make a living for German competition.' Well, well! 'Elizabeta Vorobei!' But that is a WOMAN'S name! How comes SHE to be on the list? That villain Sobakevitch must have sneaked her in without my knowing it."

"'Grigori Goiezhai-ne-Doiedesh,'" he went on. "What sort of a man were YOU, I wonder? Were you a carrier who, having set up a team of three horses and a tilt waggon, left your home, your native hovel, for ever, and departed to cart merchandise to market? Was it on the highway that you surrendered your soul to God, or did your friends first marry you to some fat, red-faced soldier's daughter; after which your harness and team of rough, but sturdy, horses caught a highwayman's fancy, and you, lying on your pallet, thought things over until, willy-nilly, you felt that you must get up and make for the tavern, thereafter blundering into an icehole? Ah, our peasant of Russia! Never do you welcome death when it comes!"

"And you, my friends?" continued Chichikov, turning to the sheet whereon were inscribed the names of Plushkin's absconded serfs. "Although you are still alive, what is the good of you? You are practically dead. Whither, I wonder, have your fugitive feet carried you? Did you fare hardly at Plushkin's, or was it that your natural inclinations led you to prefer roaming the wilds and plundering travellers? Are you, by this time, in gaol, or have you taken service with other masters for the tillage of their lands? 'Eremei Kariakin, Nikita Volokita and Anton Volokita (son of the foregoing).' To judge from your surnames, you would seem to have been born gadabouts 29. 'Popov, household serf.' Probably you are an educated man, good Popov, and go in for polite thieving, as distinguished from the more vulgar cut-throat sort. In my mind's eye I seem to see a Captain of Rural Police challenging you for being without a passport; whereupon you stake your all upon a single throw. 'To whom do you belong?' asks the Captain, probably adding to his question a forcible expletive. 'To such and such a landowner,' stoutly you reply. 'And what are you doing here?' continues the Captain. 'I have just received permission to go and earn my obrok,' is your fluent explanation. 'Then where is your passport?' 'At Miestchanin 30 Pimenov's.' 'Pimenov's? Then are you Pimenov himself?' 'Yes, I am Pimenov himself.' 'He has given you his passport?' 'No, he has not given me his passport.' 'Come, come!' shouts the Captain with another forcible expletive. 'You are lying!' 'No, I am not,' is your dogged reply. 'It is only that last night I could not return him his passport, because I came home late; so I handed it to Antip Prochorov, the bell-ringer, for him to take care of.' 'Bell-ringer, indeed! Then HE gave you a passport?' 'No; I did not receive a passport from him either.' 'What?'—and here the Captain shouts another expletive—'How dare you keep on lying? Where is YOUR OWN passport?' 'I had one all right,' you reply cunningly, 'but must have dropped it somewhere on the road as I came along.' 'And what about that soldier's coat?' asks the Captain with an impolite addition. 'Whence did you get it? And what of the priest's cashbox and copper money?' 'About them I know nothing,' you reply doggedly. 'Never at any time have I committed a theft.' 'Then how is it that the coat was found at your place?' 'I do not know. Probably some one else put it there.' 'You rascal, you rascal!' shouts the Captain, shaking his head, and closing in upon you. 'Put the leg-irons upon him, and off with him to prison!' 'With pleasure,' you reply as, taking a snuff-box from your pocket, you offer a pinch to each of the two gendarmes who are manacling you, while also inquiring how long they have been discharged from the army, and in what wars they may have served. And in prison you remain until your case comes on, when the justice orders you to be removed from Tsarev-Kokshaika to such and such another prison, and a second justice orders you to be transferred thence to Vesiegonsk or somewhere else, and you go flitting from gaol to gaol, and saying each time, as you eye your new habitation, 'The last place was a good deal cleaner than this one is, and one could play babki 31 there, and stretch one's legs, and see a little society.'"

"'Abakum Thirov,'" Chichikov went on after a pause. "What of YOU, brother? Where, and in what capacity, are YOU disporting yourself? Have you gone to the Volga country, and become bitten with the life of freedom, and joined the fishermen of the river?"

Here, breaking off, Chichikov relapsed into silent meditation. Of what was he thinking as he sat there? Was he thinking of the fortunes of Abakum Thirov, or was he meditating as meditates every Russian when his thoughts once turn to the joys of an emancipated existence?

"Ah, well!" he sighed, looking at his watch. "It has now gone twelve o'clock. Why have I so forgotten myself? There is still much to be done, yet I go shutting myself up and letting my thoughts wander! What a fool I am!"

So saying, he exchanged his Scottish costume (of a shirt and nothing else) for attire of a more European nature; after which he pulled tight the waistcoat over his ample stomach, sprinkled himself with eau-de-Cologne, tucked his papers under his arm, took his fur cap, and set out for the municipal offices, for the purpose of completing the transfer of souls. The fact that he hurried along was not due to a fear of being late (seeing that the President of the Local Council was an intimate acquaintance of his, as well as a functionary who could shorten or prolong an interview at will, even as

Homer's Zeus was able to shorten or to prolong a night or a day, whenever it became necessary to put an end to the fighting of his favourite heroes, or to enable them to join battle), but rather to a feeling that he would like to have the affair concluded as quickly as possible, seeing that, throughout, it had been an anxious and difficult business. Also, he could not get rid of the idea that his souls were unsubstantial things, and that therefore, under the circumstances, his shoulders had better be relieved of their load with the least possible delay. Pulling on his cinnamon-coloured, bear-lined overcoat as he went, he had just stepped thoughtfully into the street when he collided with a gentleman dressed in a similar coat and an ear-lappeted fur cap. Upon that the gentleman uttered an exclamation. Behold, it was Manilov! At once the friends became folded in a strenuous embrace, and remained so locked for fully five minutes. Indeed, the kisses exchanged were so vigorous that both suffered from toothache for the greater portion of the day. Also, Manilov's delight was such that only his nose and lips remained visible—the eyes completely disappeared. Afterwards he spent about a quarter of an hour in holding Chichikov's hand and chafing it vigorously. Lastly, he, in the most pleasant and exquisite terms possible, intimated to his friend that he had just been on his way to embrace Paul Ivanovitch; and upon this followed a compliment of the kind which would more fittingly have been addressed to a lady who was being asked to accord a partner the favour of a dance. Chichikov had opened his mouth to reply—though even HE felt at a loss how to acknowledge what had just been said—when Manilov cut him short by producing from under his coat a roll of paper tied with red riband.

"What have you there?" asked Chichikov.

"The list of my souls."

"Ah!" And as Chichikov unrolled the document and ran his eye over it he could not but marvel at the elegant neatness with which it had been inscribed.

"It is a beautiful piece of writing," he said. "In fact, there will be no need to make a copy of it. Also, it has a border around its edge! Who worked that exquisite border?"

"Do not ask me," said Manilov.

"Did YOU do it?"

"No; my wife."

"Dear, dear!" Chichikov cried. "To think that I should have put her to so much trouble!"

"NOTHING could be too much trouble where Paul Ivanovitch is concerned."

Chichikov bowed his acknowledgements. Next, on learning that he was on his way to the municipal offices for the purpose of completing the transfer, Manilov expressed his readiness to accompany him; wherefore the pair linked arm in arm and proceeded together. Whenever they encountered a slight rise in the ground—even the smallest unevenness or difference of level—Manilov supported Chichikov with such energy as almost to lift him off his feet, while accompanying the service with a smiling implication that not if HE could help it should Paul Ivanovitch slip or fall. Nevertheless this conduct appeared to embarrass Chichikov, either because he could not find any fitting words of gratitude or because he considered the proceeding tiresome; and it was with a sense of relief that he debouched upon the square where the municipal offices—a large, three-storied building of a chalky whiteness which probably symbolised the purity of the souls engaged within—were situated. No other building in the square could vie with them in size, seeing that the remaining edifices consisted only of a sentry-box, a shelter for two or three cabmen, and a long hoarding—the latter adorned with the usual bills, posters, and scrawls in chalk and charcoal. At intervals, from the windows of the second and third stories of the municipal offices, the incorruptible heads of certain of the attendant priests of Themis would peer quickly forth, and as quickly disappear again—probably for the reason that a superior official had just entered the room. Meanwhile the two friends ascended the staircase—nay, almost flew up it, since, longing to get rid of Manilov's ever-supporting arm, Chichikov hastened his steps, and Manilov kept darting forward to anticipate any possible failure on the part of his companion's legs. Consequently the pair were breathless when they reached the first corridor. In passing it may be remarked that neither corridors nor rooms evinced any of that cleanliness and purity which marked the exterior of the building, for such attributes were not troubled about within, and anything that was dirty remained so, and donned no meritricious, purely external, disguise. It was as though Themis received her visitors in neglige and a dressing-gown. The author would also give a description of the various offices through which our hero passed, were it not that he (the author) stands in awe of such legal haunts.

Approaching the first desk which he happened to encounter, Chichikov inquired of the two young officials who were seated at it whether they would kindly tell him where business relating to serf-indenture was transacted.

"Of what nature, precisely, IS your business?" countered one of the youthful officials as he turned himself round.

"I desire to make an application."

"In connection with a purchase?"

"Yes. But, as I say, I should like first to know where I can find the desk devoted to such business. Is it here or elsewhere?"

"You must state what it is you have bought, and for how much. THEN we shall be happy to give you the information."

Chichikov perceived that the officials' motive was merely one of curiosity, as often happens when young tchinovniks desire to cut a more important and imposing figure than is rightfully theirs.

"Look here, young sirs," he said. "I know for a fact that all serf business, no matter to what value, is transacted at one desk alone. Consequently I again request you to direct me to that desk. Of course, if you do not know your business I can easily ask some one else."

To this the tchinovniks made no reply beyond pointing towards a corner of the room where an elderly man appeared to be engaged in sorting some papers. Accordingly Chichikov and Manilov threaded their way in his direction through the desks; whereupon the elderly man became violently busy.

"Would you mind telling me," said Chichikov, bowing, "whether this is the desk for serf affairs?"

The elderly man raised his eyes, and said stiffly:

"This is NOT the desk for serf affairs."

"Where is it, then?"

"In the Serf Department."

"And where might the Serf Department be?"

"In charge of Ivan Antonovitch."

"And where is Ivan Antonovitch?"

The elderly man pointed to another corner of the room; whither Chichikov and Manilov next directed their steps. As they advanced, Ivan Antonovitch cast an eye backwards and viewed them askance. Then, with renewed ardour, he resumed his work of writing.

"Would you mind telling me," said Chichikov, bowing, "whether this is the desk for serf affairs?"

It appeared as though Ivan Antonovitch had not heard, so completely did he bury himself in his papers and return no reply. Instantly it became plain that HE at least was of an age of discretion, and not one of your jejune chatterboxes and harum-scarums; for, although his hair was still thick and black, he had long ago passed his fortieth year. His whole face tended towards the nose—it was what, in common parlance, is known as a "pitcher-mug."

"Would you mind telling me," repeated Chichikov, "whether this is the desk for serf affairs?"

"It is that," said Ivan Antonovitch, again lowering his jug-shaped jowl, and resuming his writing.

"Then I should like to transact the following business. From various landowners in this canton I have purchased a number of peasants for transfer. Here is the purchase list, and it needs but to be registered."

"Have you also the vendors here?"

"Some of them, and from the rest I have obtained powers of attorney."

"And have you your statement of application?"

"Yes. I desire—indeed, it is necessary for me so to do—to hasten matters a little. Could the affair, therefore, be carried through to-day?"

"To-day? Oh, dear no!" said Ivan Antonovitch. "Before that can be done you must furnish me with further proofs that no impediments exist."

"Then, to expedite matters, let me say that Ivan Grigorievitch, the President of the Council, is a very intimate friend of mine."

"Possibly," said Ivan Antonovitch without enthusiasm. "But Ivan Grigorievitch alone will not do—it is customary to have others as well."

"Yes, but the absence of others will not altogether invalidate the transaction. I too have been in the service, and know how things can be done."

"You had better go and see Ivan Grigorievitch," said Ivan Antonovitch more mildly. "Should he give you an order addressed to whom it may concern, we shall soon be able to settle the matter."

Upon that Chichikov pulled from his pocket a paper, and laid it before Ivan Antonovitch. At once the latter covered it with a book.

Chichikov again attempted to show it to him, but, with a movement of his head, Ivan Antonovitch signified that that was unnecessary.

"A clerk," he added, "will now conduct you to Ivan Grigorievitch's room."

Upon that one of the toilers in the service of Themis—a zealot who had offered her such heartfelt sacrifice that his coat had burst at the elbows and lacked a lining—escorted our friends (even as Virgil had once escorted Dante) to the apartment of the Presence. In this sanctum were some massive armchairs, a table laden with two or three fat books, and a large looking-glass. Lastly, in (apparently) sunlike isolation, there was seated at the table the President. On arriving at the door of the apartment, our modern Virgil seemed to have become so overwhelmed with awe that, without daring even to intrude a foot, he turned back, and, in so doing, once more exhibited a back as shiny as a mat, and having adhering to it, in one spot, a chicken's feather. As soon as the two friends had entered the hall of the Presence they perceived that the President was NOT alone, but, on the contrary, had seated by his side Sobakevitch, whose form had hitherto been concealed by the intervening mirror. The newcomers' entry evoked sundry exclamations and the pushing back of a pair of Government chairs as the voluminous-sleeved Sobakevitch rose into view from behind the looking-glass. Chichikov the President received with an embrace, and for a while the hall of the Presence resounded with osculatory salutations as mutually the pair inquired after one another's health. It seemed that both had lately had a touch of that pain under the waistband which comes of a sedentary life. Also, it seemed that the President had just been conversing with Sobakevitch on the subject of sales of souls, since he now proceeded to congratulate Chichikov on the same—a proceeding which rather embarrassed our hero, seeing that Manilov and Sobakevitch, two of the vendors, and persons with whom he had bargained in the strictest privacy, were now confronting one another direct. However, Chichikov duly thanked the President, and then, turning to Sobakevitch, inquired after HIS health.

"Thank God, I have nothing to complain of," replied Sobakevitch: which was true enough, seeing that a piece of iron would have caught cold and taken to sneezing sooner than would that uncouthly fashioned landowner.

"Ah, yes; you have always had good health, have you not?" put in the President. "Your late father was equally strong."

"Yes, he even went out bear hunting alone," replied Sobakevitch.

"I should think that you too could worst a bear if you were to try a tussle with him," rejoined the President.

"Oh no," said Sobakevitch. "My father was a stronger man than I am." Then with a sigh the speaker added: "But nowadays there are no such men as he. What is even a life like mine worth?"

"Then you do not have a comfortable time of it?" exclaimed the President.

"No; far from it," rejoined Sobakevitch, shaking his head. "Judge for yourself, Ivan Grigorievitch. I am fifty years old, yet never in my life had been ill, except for an occasional carbuncle or boil. That is not a good sign. Sooner or later I shall have to pay for it." And he relapsed into melancholy.

"Just listen to the fellow!" was Chichikov's and the President's joint inward comment. "What on earth has HE to complain of?"

"I have a letter for you, Ivan Grigorievitch," went on Chichikov aloud as he produced from his pocket Plushkin's epistle.

"From whom?" inquired the President. Having broken the seal, he exclaimed: "Why, it is from Plushkin! To think that HE is still alive! What a strange world it is! He used to be such a nice fellow, and now—"

"And now he is a cur," concluded Sobakevitch, "as well as a miser who starves his serfs to death."

"Allow me a moment," said the President. Then he read the letter through. When he had finished he added: "Yes, I am quite ready to act as Plushkin's attorney. When do you wish the purchase deeds to be registered, Monsieur Chichikov—now or later?"

"Now, if you please," replied Chichikov. "Indeed, I beg that, if possible, the affair may be concluded to-day, since to-morrow I wish to leave the town. I have brought with me both the forms of indenture and my statement of application."

"Very well. Nevertheless we cannot let you depart so soon. The indentures shall be completed to-day, but you must continue your sojourn in our midst. I will issue the necessary orders at once."

So saying, he opened the door into the general office, where the clerks looked like a swarm of bees around a honeycomb (if I may liken affairs of Government to such an article?).

"Is Ivan Antonovitch here?" asked the President.

"Yes," replied a voice from within.

"Then send him here."

Upon that the pitcher-faced Ivan Antonovitch made his appearance in the doorway, and bowed.

"Take these indentures, Ivan Antonovitch," said the President, "and see that they—"

"But first I would ask you to remember," put in Sobakevitch, "that witnesses ought to be in attendance—not less than two on behalf of either party. Let us, therefore, send for the Public Prosecutor, who has little to do, and has even that little done for him by his chief clerk, Zolotucha. The Inspector of the Medical Department is also a man of leisure, and likely to be at home—if he has not gone out to a card party. Others also there are—all men who cumber the ground for nothing."

"Quite so, quite so," agreed the President, and at once dispatched a clerk to fetch the persons named.

"Also," requested Chichikov, "I should be glad if you would send for the accredited representative of a certain lady landowner with whom I have done business. He is the son of a Father Cyril, and a clerk in your offices."

"Certainly we shall call him here," replied the President. "Everything shall be done to meet your convenience, and I forbid you to present any of our officials with a gratuity. That is a special request on my part. No friend of mine ever pays a copper."

With that he gave Ivan Antonovitch the necessary instructions; and though they scarcely seemed to meet with that functionary's approval, upon the President the purchase deeds had evidently produced an excellent impression, more especially since the moment when he had perceived the sum total to amount to nearly a hundred thousand roubles. For a moment or two he gazed into Chichikov's eyes with an expression of profound satisfaction. Then he said:

"Well done, Paul Ivanovitch! You have indeed made a nice haul!"

"That is so," replied Chichikov.

"Excellent business! Yes, excellent business!"

"I, too, conceive that I could not well have done better. The truth is that never until a man has driven home the piles of his life's structure upon a lasting bottom, instead of upon the wayward chimeras of youth, will his aims in life assume a definite end." And, that said, Chichikov went on to deliver himself of a very telling indictment of Liberalism and our modern young men. Yet in his words there seemed to lurk a certain lack of conviction. Somehow he seemed secretly to be saying to himself, "My good sir, you are talking the most absolute rubbish, and nothing but rubbish." Nor did he even throw a glance at Sobakevitch and Manilov. It was as though he were uncertain what he might not encounter in their expression. Yet he need not have been afraid. Never once did Sobakevitch's face move a muscle, and, as for Manilov, he was too much under the spell of Chichikov's eloquence to do aught beyond nod his approval at intervals, and strike the kind of attitude which is assumed by lovers of music when a lady singer has, in rivalry of an accompanying violin, produced a note whereof the shrillness would exceed even the capacity of a bird's throstle.

"But why not tell Ivan Grigorievitch precisely what you have bought?" inquired Sobakevitch of Chichikov. "And why, Ivan Grigorievitch, do YOU not ask Monsieur Chichikov precisely what his purchases have consisted of? What a splendid lot of serfs, to be sure! I myself have sold him my wheelwright, Michiev."

"What? You have sold him Michiev?" exclaimed the President. "I know the man well. He is a splendid craftsman, and, on one occasion, made me a drozhki 32. Only, only—well, lately didn't you tell me that he is dead?"

"That Michiev is dead?" re-echoed Sobakevitch, coming perilously near to laughing. "Oh dear no! That was his brother. Michiev himself is very much alive, and in even better health than he used to be. Any day he could knock you up a britchka such as you could not procure even in Moscow. However, he is now bound to work for only one master."

"Indeed a splendid craftsman!" repeated the President. "My only wonder is that you can have brought yourself to part with him."

"Then think you that Michiev is the ONLY serf with whom I have parted? Nay, for I have parted also with Probka Stepan, my carpenter, with Milushkin, my bricklayer, and with Teliatnikov, my bootmaker. Yes, the whole lot I have sold."

And to the President's inquiry why he had so acted, seeing that the serfs named were all skilled workers and indispensable to a household, Sobakevitch replied that a mere whim had led him to do so, and thus the sale had owed its origin to a piece of folly. Then he hung his head as though already repenting of his rash act, and added:

"Although a man of grey hairs, I have not yet learned wisdom."

"But," inquired the President further, "how comes it about, Paul Ivanovitch, that you have purchased peasants apart from land? Is it for transferment elsewhere that you need them?"

"Yes."

"Very well, then. That is quite another matter. To what province of the country?"

"To the province of Kherson."

"Indeed? That region contains some splendid land," said the President; whereupon he proceeded to expatiate on the fertility of the Kherson pastures.

"And have you MUCH land there?" he continued.

"Yes; quite sufficient to accommodate the serfs whom I have purchased."

"And is there a river on the estate or a lake?"

"Both."

After this reply Chichikov involuntarily threw a glance at Sobakevitch; and though that landowner's face was as motionless as every other, the other seemed to detect in it: "You liar! Don't tell ME that you own both a river and a lake, as well as the land which you say you do."

Whilst the foregoing conversation had been in progress, various witnesses had been arriving on the scene. They consisted of the constantly blinking Public Prosecutor, the Inspector of the Medical Department, and others—all, to quote Sobakevitch, "men who cumbered the ground for nothing." With some of them, however, Chichikov was altogether unacquainted, since certain substitutes and supernumeraries had to be pressed into the service from among the ranks of the subordinate staff. There also arrived, in answer to the summons, not only the son of Father Cyril before mentioned, but also Father Cyril himself. Each such witness appended to his signature a full list of his dignities and qualifications: one man in printed characters, another in a flowing hand, a third in topsy-turvy characters of a kind never before seen in the Russian alphabet, and so forth. Meanwhile our friend Ivan Antonovitch comported himself with not a little address; and after the indentures had been signed, docketed, and registered, Chichikov found himself called upon to pay only the merest trifle in the way of Government percentage and fees for publishing the transaction in the Official Gazette. The reason of this was that the President had given orders that only half the usual charges were to be exacted from the present purchaser—the remaining half being somehow debited to the account of another applicant for serf registration.

"And now," said Ivan Grigorievitch when all was completed, "we need only to wet the bargain."

"For that too I am ready," said Chichikov. "Do you but name the hour. If, in return for your most agreeable company, I were not to set a few champagne corks flying, I should be indeed in default."

"But we are not going to let you charge yourself with anything whatsoever. WE must provide the champagne, for you are our guest, and it is for us—it is our duty, it is our bounden obligation—to entertain you. Look here, gentlemen. Let us adjourn to the house of the Chief of Police. He is the magician who needs but to wink when passing a fishmonger's or a wine merchant's. Not only shall we fare well at his place, but also we shall get a game of whist."

To this proposal no one had any objection to offer, for the mere mention of the fish shop aroused the witnesses' appetite. Consequently, the ceremony being over, there was a general reaching for hats and caps. As the party were passing through the general office, Ivan Antonovitch whispered in Chichikov's ear, with a courteous inclination of his jug-shaped physiognomy:

"You have given a hundred thousand roubles for the serfs, but have paid ME only a trifle for my trouble."

"Yes," replied Chichikov with a similar whisper, "but what sort of serfs do you suppose them to be? They are a poor, useless lot, and not worth even half the purchase money."

This gave Ivan Antonovitch to understand that the visitor was a man of strong character—a man from whom nothing more was to be expected.

"Why have you gone and purchased souls from Plushkin?" whispered Sobakevitch in Chichikov's other ear.

"Why did YOU go and add the woman Vorobei to your list?" retorted Chichikov.

"Vorobei? Who is Vorobei?"

"The woman 'Elizabet' Vorobei—'Elizabet,' not 'Elizabeta?'"

"I added no such name," replied Sobakevitch, and straightway joined the other guests.

At length the party arrived at the residence of the Chief of Police. The latter proved indeed a man of spells, for no sooner had he learnt what was afoot than he summoned a brisk young constable, whispered in his ear, adding laconically, "You understand, do you not?" and brought it about that, during the time that the guests were cutting for partners at whist in an adjoining room, the dining-table became laden with sturgeon, caviare, salmon, herrings, cheese, smoked tongue, fresh roe, and a potted variety of the same—all procured from the local fish market, and reinforced with additions from the host's own kitchen. The fact was that the worthy Chief of Police filled the office of a sort of father and general benefactor to the town, and that he moved among the citizens as though they constituted part and parcel of his own family, and watched over their shops and markets as though those establishments were merely his own private larder. Indeed, it would be difficult to say—so thoroughly did he perform his duties in this respect—whether the post most fitted him, or he the post. Matters were also so arranged that though his income more than doubled that of his predecessors, he had never lost the affection of his fellow townsmen. In particular did the tradesmen love him, since he was never above standing godfather to their children or dining at their tables. True, he had differences of opinion with them, and serious differences at that; but always these were skilfully adjusted by his slapping the offended ones jovially on the shoulder, drinking a glass of tea with them, promising to call at their houses and play a game of chess, asking after their belongings, and, should he learn that a child of theirs was ill, prescribing the proper medicine. In short, he bore the reputation of being a very good fellow.

On perceiving the feast to be ready, the host proposed that his guests should finish their whist after luncheon; whereupon all proceeded to the room whence for some time past an agreeable odour had been tickling the nostrils of those present, and towards the door of which Sobakevitch in particular had been glancing since the moment when he had caught sight of a huge sturgeon reposing on the sideboard. After a glassful of warm, olive-coloured vodka apiece—vodka of the tint to be seen only in the species of Siberian stone whereof seals are cut—the company applied themselves to knife-and-fork work, and, in so doing, evinced their several characteristics and tastes. For instance, Sobakevitch, disdaining lesser trifles, tackled the large sturgeon, and, during the time that his fellow guests were eating minor comestibles, and drinking and talking, contrived to consume more than a quarter of the whole fish; so that, on the host remembering the creature, and, with fork in hand, leading the way in its direction and saying, "What, gentlemen, think you of this striking product of nature?" there ensued the discovery that of the said product of nature there remained little beyond the tail, while Sobakevitch, with an air as though at least HE had not eaten it, was engaged in plunging his fork into a much more diminutive piece of fish which happened to be resting on an adjacent platter. After his divorce from the sturgeon, Sobakevitch ate and drank no more, but sat frowning and blinking in an armchair.

Apparently the host was not a man who believed in sparing the wine, for the toasts drunk were innumerable. The first toast (as the reader may guess) was quaffed to the health of the new landowner of Kherson; the second to the prosperity of his peasants and their safe transferment; and the third to the beauty of his future wife—a compliment which brought to our hero's lips a flickering smile. Lastly, he received from the company a pressing, as well as an unanimous, invitation to extend his stay in town for at least another fortnight, and, in the meanwhile, to allow a wife to be found for him.

"Quite so," agreed the President. "Fight us tooth and nail though you may, we intend to have you married. You have happened upon us by chance, and you shall have no reason to repent of it. We are in earnest on this subject."

"But why should I fight you tooth and nail?" said Chichikov, smiling. "Marriage would not come amiss to me, were I but provided with a betrothed."

"Then a betrothed you shall have. Why not? We will do as you wish."

"Very well," assented Chichikov.

"Bravo, bravo!" the company shouted. "Long live Paul Ivanovitch! Hurrah! Hurrah!" And with that every one approached to clink glasses with him, and he readily accepted the compliment, and accepted it many times in succession. Indeed, as the hours passed on, the hilarity of the company increased yet further, and more than once the President (a man of great urbanity when thoroughly in his cups) embraced the chief guest of the day with the heartfelt words, "My dearest fellow! My own most precious of friends!" Nay, he even started to crack his fingers, to dance around

Chichikov's chair, and to sing snatches of a popular song. To the champagne succeeded Hungarian wine, which had the effect of still further heartening and enlivening the company. By this time every one had forgotten about whist, and given himself up to shouting and disputing. Every conceivable subject was discussed, including politics and military affairs; and in this connection guests voiced jejune opinions for the expression of which they would, at any other time, have soundly spanked their offspring. Chichikov, like the rest, had never before felt so gay, and, imagining himself really and truly to be a landowner of Kherson, spoke of various improvements in agriculture, of the three-field system of tillage 33, and of the beatific felicity of a union between two kindred souls. Also, he started to recite poetry to Sobakevitch, who blinked as he listened, for he greatly desired to go to sleep. At length the guest of the evening realised that matters had gone far enough, so begged to be given a lift home, and was accommodated with the Public Prosecutor's drozhki. Luckily the driver of the vehicle was a practised man at his work, for, while driving with one hand, he succeeded in leaning backwards and, with the other, holding Chichikov securely in his place. Arrived at the inn, our hero continued babbling awhile about a flaxen-haired damsel with rosy lips and a dimple in her right cheek, about villages of his in Kherson, and about the amount of his capital. Nay, he even issued seignorial instructions that Selifan should go and muster the peasants about to be transferred, and make a complete and detailed inventory of them. For a while Selifan listened in silence; then he left the room, and instructed Petrushka to help the barin to undress. As it happened, Chichikov's boots had no sooner been removed than he managed to perform the rest of his toilet without assistance, to roll on to the bed (which creaked terribly as he did so), and to sink into a sleep in every way worthy of a landowner of Kherson. Meanwhile Petrushka had taken his master's coat and trousers of bilberry-coloured check into the corridor; where, spreading them over a clothes' horse, he started to flick and to brush them, and to fill the whole corridor with dust. Just as he was about to replace them in his master's room he happened to glance over the railing of the gallery, and saw Selifan returning from the stable. Glances were exchanged, and in an instant the pair had arrived at an instinctive understanding—an understanding to the effect that the barin was sound asleep, and that therefore one might consider one's own pleasure a little. Accordingly Petrushka proceeded to restore the coat and trousers to their appointed places, and then descended the stairs; whereafter he and Selifan left the house together. Not a word passed between them as to the object of their expedition. On the contrary, they talked solely of extraneous subjects. Yet their walk did not take them far; it took them only to the other side of the street, and thence into an establishment which immediately confronted the inn. Entering a mean, dirty courtyard covered with glass, they passed thence into a cellar where a number of customers were seated around small wooden tables. What thereafter was done by Selifan and Petrushka God alone knows. At all events, within an hour's time they issued, arm in arm, and in profound silence, yet remaining markedly assiduous to one another, and ever ready to help one another around an awkward corner. Still linked together—never once releasing their mutual hold—they spent the next quarter of an hour in attempting to negotiate the stairs of the inn; but at length even that ascent had been mastered, and they proceeded further on their way. Halting before his mean little pallet, Petrushka stood awhile in thought. His difficulty was how best to assume a recumbent position. Eventually he lay down on his face, with his legs trailing over the floor; after which Selifan also stretched himself upon the pallet, with his head resting upon Petrushka's stomach, and his mind wholly oblivious of the fact that he ought not to have been sleeping there at all, but in the servant's quarters, or in the stable beside his horses. Scarcely a moment had passed before the pair were plunged in slumber and emitting the most raucous snores; to which their master (next door) responded with snores of a whistling and nasal order. Indeed, before long every one in the inn had followed their soothing example, and the hostelry lay plunged in complete restfulness. Only in the window of the room of the newly-arrived lieutenant from Riazan did a light remain burning. Evidently he was a devotee of boots, for he had purchased four pairs, and was now trying on a fifth. Several times he approached the bed with a view to taking off the boots and retiring to rest; but each time he failed, for the reason that the boots were so alluring in their make that he had no choice but to lift up first one foot, and then the other, for the purpose of scanning their elegant welts.

CHAPTER VIII

It was not long before Chichikov's purchases had become the talk of the town; and various were the opinions expressed as to whether or not it was expedient to procure peasants for transferment. Indeed such was the interest taken by certain citizens in the matter that they advised the purchaser to provide himself and his convoy with an escort, in order to ensure their safe arrival at the appointed destination; but though Chichikov thanked the donors of this advice for the same, and declared that he should be very glad, in case of need, to avail himself of it, he declared also that there was no real need for an escort, seeing that the peasants whom he had purchased were exceptionally peace-loving folk, and that, being themselves consenting parties to the transferment, they would undoubtedly prove in every way tractable.

One particularly good result of this advertisement of his scheme was that he came to rank as neither more nor less than a millionaire. Consequently, much as the inhabitants had liked our hero in the first instance (as seen in Chapter I.), they now liked him more than ever. As a matter of fact, they were citizens of an exceptionally quiet, good-natured, easy-going disposition; and some of them were even well-educated. For instance, the President of the Local Council could recite the whole of Zhukovski's LUDMILLA by heart, and give such an impressive rendering of the passage "The pine forest was asleep and the valley at rest" (as well as of the exclamation "Phew!") that one felt, as he did so, that the pine forest and the valley really WERE as he described them. The effect was also further heightened by the manner in which, at such moments, he assumed the most portentous frown. For his part, the Postmaster went in more for philosophy, and diligently perused such works as Young's Night Thoughts, and Eckharthausen's A Key to the Mysteries of Nature; of which latter work he would make copious extracts, though no one had the slightest notion what they referred to. For the rest, he was a witty, florid little individual, and much addicted to a practice of what he called "embellishing" whatsoever he had to say—a feat which he performed with the aid of such by-the-way phrases as "my dear sir," "my good So-and-So," "you know," "you understand," "you may imagine," "relatively speaking," "for instance," and "et cetera"; of which phrases he would add sackfuls to his speech. He could also "embellish" his words by the simple expedient of half-closing, half-winking one eye; which trick communicated to some of his satirical utterances quite a mordant effect. Nor were his colleagues a wit inferior to him in enlightenment. For instance, one of them made a regular practice of reading Karamzin, another of conning the Moscow Gazette, and a third of never looking at a book at all. Likewise, although they were the sort of men to whom, in their more intimate movements, their wives would very naturally address such nicknames as "Toby Jug," "Marmot," "Fatty," "Pot Belly," "Smutty," "Kiki," and "Buzz-Buzz," they were men also of good heart, and very ready to extend their hospitality and their friendship when once a guest had eaten of their bread and salt, or spent an evening in their company. Particularly, therefore, did Chichikov earn these good folk's approval with his taking methods and qualities—so much so that the expression of that approval bid fair to make it difficult for him to quit the town, seeing that, wherever he went, the one phrase dinned into his ears was "Stay another week with us, Paul Ivanovitch." In short, he ceased to be a free agent. But incomparably more striking was the impression (a matter for unbounded surprise!) which he produced upon the ladies. Properly to explain this phenomenon I should need to say a great deal about the ladies themselves, and to describe in the most vivid of colours their social intercourse and spiritual qualities. Yet this would be a difficult thing for me to do, since, on the one hand, I should be hampered by my boundless respect for the womenfolk of all Civil Service officials, and, on the other hand—well, simply by the innate arduousness of the task. The ladies of N. were— But no, I cannot do it; my heart has already failed me. Come, come! The ladies of N. were distinguished for—But it is of no use; somehow my pen seems to refuse to move over the paper—it seems to be weighted as with a plummet of lead. Very well. That being so, I will merely say a word or two concerning the most prominent tints on the feminine palette of N.— merely a word or two concerning the outward appearance of its ladies, and a word or two concerning their more superficial characteristics. The ladies of N. were pre-eminently what is known as "presentable." Indeed, in that respect they might have served as a model to the ladies of many another town. That is to say, in whatever pertained to "tone," etiquette, the intricacies of decorum, and strict observance of the prevailing mode, they surpassed even the ladies of Moscow and St. Petersburg, seeing that they dressed with taste, drove about in carriages in the latest fashions, and never went out without the escort of a footman in gold-laced livery. Again, they looked upon a visiting card—even upon a make-shift affair consisting of an ace of diamonds or a two of clubs—as a sacred thing; so sacred that on one occasion two closely related ladies who had also been closely attached friends were known to fall out with one another over the mere fact of an omission to return a social call! Yes, in spite of the best efforts of husbands and kinsfolk to reconcile the antagonists, it became clear that, though all else in the world might conceivably be possible, never could the hatchet be buried between ladies who had quarrelled over a neglected visit. Likewise strenuous scenes used to take place over questions of precedence—scenes of a kind which had the effect of inspiring husbands to great and knightly ideas on the subject of protecting the fair. True, never did a duel actually take place, since all the husbands were officials belonging to the Civil Service; but at least a given combatant would strive to heap contumely upon his rival, and, as we all know, that is a resource which may prove even more effectual than a duel. As regards morality, the ladies of N. were nothing if not censorious, and would at once be fired with virtuous indignation when they heard of a case of vice or seduction. Nay, even to mere frailty they would award the lash without mercy. On the other hand, should any instance of what they called "third personism" occur among THEIR OWN circle, it was always kept dark—not a hint of what was going on being allowed to transpire, and even the wronged husband holding himself ready, should he meet with, or hear of, the "third person," to quote, in a mild and rational manner, the proverb, "Whom concerns it that a friend should consort with friend?" In addition, I may say that, like most of the female world of St. Petersburg, the ladies of N. were pre-eminently careful and refined in their choice of words and phrases. Never did a lady say, "I blew my nose," or "I perspired," or "I spat." No, it had to be, "I relieved my nose through the expedient of wiping it with my handkerchief," and so forth. Again, to say, "This glass, or this plate, smells badly," was forbidden. No, not even a hint to such an effect was to be dropped. Rather, the proper phrase, in such a case, was "This glass, or this plate, is not behaving very well,"—or some such formula.

In fact, to refine the Russian tongue the more thoroughly, something like half the words in it were cut out: which circumstance necessitated very frequent recourse to the tongue of France, since the same words, if spoken in French, were another matter altogether, and one could use even blunter ones than the ones originally objected to.

So much for the ladies of N., provided that one confines one's observations to the surface; yet hardly need it be said that, should one penetrate deeper than that, a great deal more would come to light. At the same time, it is never a very safe proceeding to peer deeply into the hearts of ladies; wherefore, restricting ourselves to the foregoing superficialities, let us proceed further on our way.

Hitherto the ladies had paid Chichikov no particular attention, though giving him full credit for his gentlemanly and urbane demeanour; but from the moment that there arose rumours of his being a millionaire other qualities of his began to be canvassed. Nevertheless, not ALL the ladies were governed by interested motives, since it is due to the term "millionaire" rather than to the character of the person who bears it, that the mere sound of the word exercises upon rascals, upon decent folk, and upon folk who are neither the one nor the other, an undeniable influence. A millionaire suffers from the disadvantage of everywhere having to behold meanness, including the sort of meanness which, though not actually based upon calculations of self-interest, yet runs after the wealthy man with smiles, and doffs his hat, and begs for invitations to houses where the millionaire is known to be going to dine. That a similar inclination to meanness seized upon the ladies of N. goes without saying; with the result that many a drawing-room heard it whispered that, if Chichikov was not exactly a beauty, at least he was sufficiently good-looking to serve for a husband, though he could have borne to have been a little more rotund and stout. To that there would be added scornful references to lean husbands, and hints that they resembled tooth-brushes rather than men—with many other feminine additions. Also, such crowds of feminine shoppers began to repair to the Bazaar as almost to constitute a crush, and something like a procession of carriages ensued, so long grew the rank of vehicles. For their part, the tradesmen had the joy of seeing highly priced dress materials which they had bought at fairs, and then been unable to dispose of, now suddenly become tradeable, and go off with a rush. For instance, on one occasion a lady appeared at Mass in a bustle which filled the church to an extent which led the verger on duty to bid the commoner folk withdraw to the porch, lest the lady's toilet should be soiled in the crush. Even Chichikov could not help privately remarking the attention which he aroused. On one occasion, when he returned to the inn, he found on his table a note addressed to himself. Whence it had come, and who had delivered it, he failed to discover, for the waiter declared that the person who had brought it had omitted to leave the name of the writer. Beginning abruptly with the words "I MUST write to you," the letter went on to say that between a certain pair of souls there existed a bond of sympathy; and this verity the epistle further confirmed with rows of full stops to the extent of nearly half a page. Next there followed a few reflections of a correctitude so remarkable that I have no choice but to quote them. "What, I would ask, is this life of ours?" inquired the writer. "'Tis nought but a vale of woe. And what, I would ask, is the world? 'Tis nought but a mob of unthinking humanity." Thereafter, incidentally remarking that she had just dropped a tear to the memory of her dear mother, who had departed this life twenty-five years ago, the (presumably) lady writer invited Chichikov to come forth into the wilds, and to leave for ever the city where, penned in noisome haunts, folk could not even draw their breath. In conclusion, the writer gave way to unconcealed despair, and wound up with the following verses:

> "Two turtle doves to thee, one day,
> My dust will show, congealed in death;
> And, cooing wearily, they'll say:
> 'In grief and loneliness she drew her closing breath.'"

True, the last line did not scan, but that was a trifle, since the quatrain at least conformed to the mode then prevalent. Neither signature nor date were appended to the document, but only a postscript expressing a conjecture that Chichikov's own heart would tell him who the writer was, and stating, in addition, that the said writer would be present at the Governor's ball on the following night.

This greatly interested Chichikov. Indeed, there was so much that was alluring and provocative of curiosity in the anonymous missive that he read it through a second time, and then a third, and finally said to himself: "I SHOULD like to know who sent it!" In short, he took the thing seriously, and spent over an hour in considering the same. At length, muttering a comment upon the epistle's efflorescent style, he refolded the document, and committed it to his dispatch-box in company with a play-bill and an invitation to a wedding—the latter of which had for the last seven years reposed in the self-same receptacle and in the self-same position. Shortly afterwards there arrived a card of invitation to the Governor's ball already referred to. In passing, it may be said that such festivities are not infrequent phenomena in county towns, for the reason that where Governors exist there must take place balls if from the local gentry there is to be evoked that respectful affection which is every Governor's due.

Thenceforth all extraneous thoughts and considerations were laid aside in favour of preparing for the coming function. Indeed, this conjunction of exciting and provocative motives led to Chichikov devoting to his toilet an amount of time never witnessed since the creation of the world. Merely in the contemplation of his features in the mirror, as he tried to communicate to them a succession of varying expressions, was an hour spent. First of all he strove to make his features assume an air of dignity and importance, and then an air of humble, but faintly satirical, respect, and then an air of respect guiltless of any alloy whatsoever. Next, he practised performing a series of bows to his reflection, accompanied with certain murmurs intended to bear a resemblance to a French phrase (though Chichikov knew not a single word of the Gallic tongue). Lastly came the performing of a series of what I might call "agreeable surprises," in the shape of twitchings of the brow and lips and certain motions of the tongue. In short, he did all that a man is apt to do when he is not only alone, but also certain that he is handsome and that no one is regarding him through a chink. Finally he tapped himself lightly on the chin, and said, "Ah, good old face!" In the same way, when he started to dress himself for the ceremony, the level of his high spirits remained unimpaired throughout the process. That is to say, while adjusting his braces and tying his tie, he shuffled his feet in what was not exactly a dance, but might be called the entr'acte of a dance: which performance had the not very serious result of setting a wardrobe a-rattle, and causing a brush to slide from the table to the floor.

Later, his entry into the ballroom produced an extraordinary effect. Every one present came forward to meet him, some with cards in their hands, and one man even breaking off a conversation at the most interesting point—namely, the point that "the Inferior Land Court must be made responsible for everything." Yes, in spite of the responsibility of the Inferior Land Court, the speaker cast all thoughts of it to the winds as he hurried to greet our hero. From every side resounded acclamations of welcome, and Chichikov felt himself engulfed in a sea of embraces. Thus, scarcely had he extricated himself from the arms of the President of the Local Council when he found himself just as firmly clasped in the arms of the Chief of Police, who, in turn, surrendered him to the Inspector of the Medical Department, who, in turn, handed him over to the Commissioner of Taxes, who, again, committed him to the charge of the Town Architect. Even the Governor, who hitherto had been standing among his womenfolk with a box of sweets in one hand and a lap-dog in the other, now threw down both sweets and lap-dog (the lap-dog giving vent to a yelp as he did so) and added his greeting to those of the rest of the company. Indeed, not a face was there to be seen on which ecstatic delight—or, at all events, the reflection of other people's ecstatic delight—was not painted. The same expression may be discerned on the faces of subordinate officials when, the newly arrived Director having made his inspection, the said officials are beginning to get over their first sense of awe on perceiving that he has found much to commend, and that he can even go so far as to jest and utter a few words of smiling approval. Thereupon every tchinovnik responds with a smile of double strength, and those who (it may be) have not heard a single word of the Director's speech smile out of sympathy with the rest, and even the gendarme who is posted at the distant door—a man, perhaps, who has never before compassed a smile, but is more accustomed to dealing out blows to the populace—summons up a kind of grin, even though the grin resembles the grimace of a man who is about to sneeze after inadvertently taking an over-large pinch of snuff. To all and sundry Chichikov responded with a bow, and felt extraordinarily at his ease as he did so. To right and left did he incline his head in the sidelong, yet unconstrained, manner that was his wont and never failed to charm the beholder. As for the ladies, they clustered around him in a shining bevy that was redolent of every species of perfume—of roses, of spring violets, and of mignonette; so much so that instinctively Chichikov raised his nose to snuff the air. Likewise the ladies' dresses displayed an endless profusion of taste and variety; and though the majority of their wearers evinced a tendency to embonpoint, those wearers knew how to call upon art for the concealment of the fact. Confronting them, Chichikov thought to himself: "Which of these beauties is the writer of the letter?" Then again he snuffed the air. When the ladies had, to a certain extent, returned to their seats, he resumed his attempts to discern (from glances and expressions) which of them could possibly be the unknown authoress. Yet, though those glances and expressions were too subtle, too insufficiently open, the difficulty in no way diminished his high spirits. Easily and gracefully did he exchange agreeable bandinage with one lady, and then approach another one with the short, mincing steps usually affected by young-old dandies who are fluttering around the fair. As he turned, not without dexterity, to right and left, he kept one leg slightly dragging behind the other, like a short tail or comma. This trick the ladies particularly admired. In short, they not only discovered in him a host of recommendations and attractions, but also began to see in his face a sort of grand, Mars-like, military expression—a thing which, as we know, never fails to please the feminine eye. Certain of the ladies even took to bickering over him, and, on perceiving that he spent most of his time standing near the door, some of their number hastened to occupy chairs nearer to his post of vantage. In fact, when a certain dame chanced to have the good fortune to anticipate a hated rival in the race there very nearly ensued a most lamentable scene—which, to many of those who had been desirous of doing exactly the same thing, seemed a peculiarly horrible instance of brazen-faced audacity.

So deeply did Chichikov become plunged in conversation with his fair pursuers—or rather, so deeply did those fair pursuers enmesh him in the toils of small talk (which they accomplished through the expedient of asking him endless subtle riddles which brought the sweat to his brow in his attempts to guess them)—that he forgot the claims of courtesy which required him first of all to greet his hostess. In fact, he remembered those claims only on hearing the Governor's wife herself addressing him. She had been standing before him for several minutes, and now greeted him with suave expressement and the words, "So HERE you are, Paul Ivanovitch!" But what she said next I am not in a position to report, for she spoke in the ultra-refined tone and vein wherein ladies and gentlemen customarily express themselves in high-class novels which have been written by experts more qualified than I am to describe salons, and able to boast of some acquaintance with good society. In effect, what the Governor's wife said was that she hoped—she greatly hoped—that Monsieur Chichikov's heart still contained a corner—even the smallest possible corner—for those whom he had so cruelly forgotten. Upon that Chichikov turned to her, and was on the point of returning a reply at least no worse than that which would have been returned, under similar circumstances, by the hero of a fashionable novelette, when he stopped short, as though thunderstruck.

Before him there was standing not only Madame, but also a young girl whom she was holding by the hand. The golden hair, the fine-drawn, delicate contours, the face with its bewitching oval—a face which might have served as a model for the countenance of the Madonna, since it was of a type rarely to be met with in Russia, where nearly everything, from plains to human feet, is, rather, on the gigantic scale; these features, I say, were those of the identical maiden whom Chichikov had encountered on the road when he had been fleeing from Nozdrev's. His emotion was such that he could not formulate a single intelligible syllable; he could merely murmur the devil only knows what, though certainly nothing of the kind which would have risen to the lips of the hero of a fashionable novel.

"I think that you have not met my daughter before?" said Madame. "She is just fresh from school."

He replied that he HAD had the happiness of meeting Mademoiselle before, and under rather unexpected circumstances; but on his trying to say something further his tongue completely failed him. The Governor's wife added a word or two, and then carried off her daughter to speak to some of the other guests.

Chichikov stood rooted to the spot, like a man who, after issuing into the street for a pleasant walk, has suddenly come to a halt on remembering that something has been left behind him. In a moment, as he struggles to recall what that something is, the mien of careless expectancy disappears from his face, and he no longer sees a single person or a single object in his vicinity. In the same way did Chichikov suddenly become oblivious to the scene around him. Yet all the while the melodious tongues of ladies were plying him with multitudinous hints and questions—hints and questions inspired with a desire to captivate. "Might we poor cumberers of the ground make so bold as to ask you what you are thinking of?" "Pray tell us where lie the happy regions in which your thoughts are wandering?" "Might we be informed of the name of her who has plunged you into this sweet abandonment of meditation?"—such were the phrases thrown at him. But to everything he turned a dead ear, and the phrases in question might as well have been stones dropped into a pool. Indeed, his rudeness soon reached the pitch of his walking away altogether, in order that he might go and reconnoitre wither the Governor's wife and daughter had retreated. But the ladies were not going to let him off so easily. Every one of them had made up her mind to use upon him her every weapon, and to exhibit whatsoever might chance to constitute her best point. Yet the ladies' wiles proved useless, for Chichikov paid not the smallest attention to them, even when the dancing had begun, but kept raising himself on tiptoe to peer over people's heads and ascertain in which direction the bewitching maiden with the golden hair had gone. Also, when seated, he continued to peep between his neighbours' backs and shoulders, until at last he discovered her sitting beside her mother, who was wearing a sort of Oriental turban and feather. Upon that one would have thought that his purpose was to carry the position by storm; for, whether moved by the influence of spring, or whether moved by a push from behind, he pressed forward with such desperate resolution that his elbow caused the Commissioner of Taxes to stagger on his feet, and would have caused him to lose his balance altogether but for the supporting row of guests in the rear. Likewise the Postmaster was made to give ground; whereupon he turned and eyed Chichikov with mingled astonishment and subtle irony. But Chichikov never even noticed him; he saw in the distance only the golden-haired beauty. At that moment she was drawing on a long glove and, doubtless, pining to be flying over the dancing-floor, where, with clicking heels, four couples had now begun to thread the mazes of the mazurka. In particular was a military staff-captain working body and soul and arms and legs to compass such a series of steps as were never before performed, even in a dream. However, Chichikov slipped past the mazurka dancers, and, almost treading on their heels, made his way towards the spot where Madame and her daughter were seated. Yet he approached them with great diffidence and none of his late mincing and prancing. Nay, he even faltered as he walked; his every movement had about it an air of awkwardness.

It is difficult to say whether or not the feeling which had awakened in our hero's breast was the feeling of love; for it is problematical whether or not men who are neither stout nor thin are capable of any such sentiment. Nevertheless, something strange, something which he could not altogether explain, had come upon him. It seemed as though the ball, with its talk and its clatter, had suddenly become a thing remote—that the orchestra had withdrawn behind a hill, and the scene grown misty, like the carelessly painted-in background of a picture. And from that misty void there could be seen glimmering only the delicate outlines of the bewitching maiden. Somehow her exquisite shape reminded him of an ivory toy, in such fair, white, transparent relief did it stand out against the dull blur of the surrounding throng.

Herein we see a phenomenon not infrequently observed—the phenomenon of the Chichikovs of this world becoming temporarily poets. At all events, for a moment or two our Chichikov felt that he was a young man again, if not exactly a military officer. On perceiving an empty chair beside the mother and daughter, he hastened to occupy it, and though conversation at first hung fire, things gradually improved, and he acquired more confidence.

At this point I must reluctantly deviate to say that men of weight and high office are always a trifle ponderous when conversing with ladies. Young lieutenants—or, at all events, officers not above the rank of captain—are far more successful at the game. How they contrive to be so God only knows. Let them but make the most inane of remarks, and at once the maiden by their side will be rocking with laughter; whereas, should a State Councillor enter into conversation with a damsel, and remark that the Russian Empire is one of vast extent, or utter a compliment which he has elaborated not without a certain measure of intelligence (however strongly the said compliment may smack of a book), of a surety the thing will fall flat. Even a witticism from him will be laughed at far more by him himself than it will by the lady who may happen to be listening to his remarks.

These comments I have interposed for the purpose of explaining to the reader why, as our hero conversed, the maiden began to yawn. Blind to this, however, he continued to relate to her sundry adventures which had befallen him in different parts of the world. Meanwhile (as need hardly be said) the rest of the ladies had taken umbrage at his behaviour. One of them purposely stalked past him to intimate to him the fact, as well as to jostle the Governor's daughter, and let the flying end of a scarf flick her face; while from a lady seated behind the pair came both a whiff of violets and a very venomous and sarcastic remark. Nevertheless, either he did not hear the remark or he PRETENDED not to hear it. This was unwise of him, since it never does to disregard ladies' opinions. Later—but too late—he was destined to learn this to his cost.

In short, dissatisfaction began to display itself on every feminine face. No matter how high Chichikov might stand in society, and no matter how much he might be a millionaire and include in his expression of countenance an indefinable element of grandness and martial ardour, there are certain things which no lady will pardon, whosoever be the person concerned. We know that at Governor's balls it is customary for the onlookers to compose verses at the expense of the dancers; and in this case the verses were directed to Chichikov's address. Briefly, the prevailing dissatisfaction grew until a tacit edict of proscription had been issued against both him and the poor young maiden.

But an even more unpleasant surprise was in store for our hero; for whilst the young lady was still yawning as Chichikov recounted to her certain of his past adventures and also touched lightly upon the subject of Greek philosophy, there appeared from an adjoining room the figure of Nozdrev. Whether he had come from the buffet, or whether he had issued from a little green retreat where a game more strenuous than whist had been in progress, or whether he had left the latter resort unaided, or whether he had been expelled therefrom, is unknown; but at all events when he entered the ballroom, he was in an elevated condition, and leading by the arm the Public Prosecutor, whom he seemed to have been dragging about for a long while past, seeing that the poor man was glancing from side to side as though seeking a means of putting an end to this personally conducted tour. Certainly he must have found the situation almost unbearable, in view of the fact that, after deriving inspiration from two glasses of tea not wholly undiluted with rum, Nozdrev was engaged in lying unmercifully. On sighting him in the distance, Chichikov at once decided to sacrifice himself. That is to say, he decided to vacate his present enviable position and make off with all possible speed, since he could see that an encounter with the newcomer would do him no good. Unfortunately at that moment the Governor buttonholed him with a request that he would come and act as arbiter between him (the Governor) and two ladies—the subject of dispute being the question as to whether or not woman's love is lasting. Simultaneously Nozdrev descried our hero and bore down upon him.

"Ah, my fine landowner of Kherson!" he cried with a smile which set his fresh, spring-rose-pink cheeks a-quiver. "Have you been doing much trade in departed souls lately?" With that he turned to the Governor. "I suppose your Excellency knows that this man traffics in dead peasants?" he bawled. "Look here, Chichikov. I tell you in the most friendly way possible that every one here likes you—yes, including even the Governor. Nevertheless, had I my way, I would hang you! Yes, by God I would!"

Chichikov's discomfiture was complete.

"And, would you believe it, your Excellency," went on Nozdrev, "but this fellow actually said to me, 'Sell me your dead souls!' Why, I laughed till I nearly became as dead as the souls. And, behold, no sooner do I arrive here than I am told that he has bought three million roubles' worth of peasants for transferment! For transferment, indeed! And he wanted to bargain with me for my DEAD ones! Look here, Chichikov. You are a swine! Yes, by God, you are an utter swine! Is not that so, your Excellency? Is not that so, friend Prokurator 34?"

But both his Excellency, the Public Prosecutor, and Chichikov were too taken aback to reply. The half-tipsy Nozdrev, without noticing them, continued his harangue as before.

"Ah, my fine sir!" he cried. "THIS time I don't mean to let you go. No, not until I have learnt what all this purchasing of dead peasants means. Look here. You ought to be ashamed of yourself. Yes, *I* say that—*I* who am one of your best friends." Here he turned to the Governor again. "Your Excellency," he continued, "you would never believe what inseperables this man and I have been. Indeed, if you had stood there and said to me, 'Nozdrev, tell me on your honour which of the two you love best—your father or Chichikov?' I should have replied, 'Chichikov, by God!'" With that he tackled our hero again, "Come, come, my friend!" he urged. "Let me imprint upon your cheeks a baiser or two. You will excuse me if I kiss him, will you not, your Excellency? No, do not resist me, Chichikov, but allow me to imprint at least one baiser upon your lily-white cheek." And in his efforts to force upon Chichikov what he termed his "baisers" he came near to measuring his length upon the floor.

Every one now edged away, and turned a deaf ear to his further babblings; but his words on the subject of the purchase of dead souls had none the less been uttered at the top of his voice, and been accompanied with such uproarious laughter that the curiosity even of those who had happened to be sitting or standing in the remoter corners of the room had been aroused. So strange and novel seemed the idea that the company stood with faces expressive of nothing but a dumb, dull wonder. Only some of the ladies (as Chichikov did not fail to remark) exchanged meaning, ill-natured winks and a series of sarcastic smiles: which circumstance still further increased his confusion. That Nozdrev was a notorious liar every one, of course, knew, and that he should have given vent to an idiotic outburst of this sort had surprised no one; but a dead soul—well, what was one to make of Nozdrev's reference to such a commodity?

Naturally this unseemly contretemps had greatly upset our hero; for, however foolish be a madman's words, they may yet prove sufficient to sow doubt in the minds of saner individuals. He felt much as does a man who, shod with well-polished boots, has just stepped into a dirty, stinking puddle. He tried to put away from him the occurrence, and to expand, and to enjoy himself once more. Nay, he even took a hand at whist.

But all was of no avail—matters kept going as awry as a badly-bent hoop. Twice he blundered in his play, and the President of the Council was at a loss to understand how his friend, Paul Ivanovitch, lately so good and so circumspect a player, could perpetrate such a mauvais pas as to throw away a particular king of spades which the President has been "trusting" as (to quote his own expression) "he would have trusted God." At supper, too, matters felt uncomfortable, even though the society at Chichikov's table was exceedingly agreeable and Nozdrev had been removed, owing to the fact that the ladies had found his conduct too scandalous to be borne, now that the delinquent had taken to seating himself on the floor and plucking at the skirts of passing lady dancers. As I say, therefore, Chichikov found the situation not a little awkward, and eventually put an end to it by leaving the supper room before the meal was over, and long before the hour when usually he returned to the inn.

In his little room, with its door of communication blocked with a wardrobe, his frame of mind remained as uncomfortable as the chair in which he was seated. His heart ached with a dull, unpleasant sensation, with a sort of oppressive emptiness.

"The devil take those who first invented balls!" was his reflection. "Who derives any real pleasure from them? In this province there exist want and scarcity everywhere: yet folk go in for balls! How absurd, too, were those overdressed women! One of them must have had a thousand roubles on her back, and all acquired at the expense of the overtaxed peasant, or, worse still, at that of the conscience of her neighbour. Yes, we all know why bribes are accepted, and why men become crooked in soul. It is all done to provide wives—yes, may the pit swallow them up!—with fal-lals. And for what purpose? That some woman may not have to reproach her husband with the fact that, say, the Postmaster's wife is wearing a better dress than she is—a dress which has cost a thousand roubles! 'Balls and gaiety, balls and gaiety' is the constant cry. Yet what folly balls are! They do not consort with the Russian spirit and genius, and the devil only knows why we have them. A grown, middle-aged man—a man dressed in black, and looking as stiff as a poker—suddenly takes the floor and begins shuffling his feet about, while another man, even though conversing with a companion on important business, will, the while, keep capering to right and left like a billy-goat! Mimicry, sheer mimicry! The fact that the Frenchman is at forty precisely what he was at fifteen leads us to imagine that we too, forsooth, ought to be the same. No; a ball leaves one feeling that one has done a wrong thing—so much so that one does not care even to think of it. It also leaves one's head perfectly empty, even as does the exertion of talking to a man of the world. A man of that kind chatters away, and touches lightly upon every conceivable subject, and talks in smooth, fluent phrases which he has culled from books without grazing their substance; whereas go and have a chat with a tradesman who knows at least ONE thing thoroughly, and through the medium of experience, and see whether his conversation will not be worth more than the prattle of a thousand chatterboxes. For what good does one get out of balls? Suppose that a competent writer were to describe such a scene exactly as it stands? Why, even in a book it would seem senseless, even as it certainly is in life. Are, therefore, such functions right or wrong? One would answer that the devil alone knows, and then spit and close the book."

Such were the unfavourable comments which Chichikov passed upon balls in general. With it all, however, there went a second source of dissatisfaction. That is to say, his principal grudge was not so much against balls as against the fact that at this particular one he had been exposed, he had been made to disclose the circumstance that he had been playing a strange, an ambiguous part. Of course, when he reviewed the contretemps in the light of pure reason, he could not but see that it mattered nothing, and that a few rude words were of no account now that the chief point had been attained; yet man is an odd creature, and Chichikov actually felt pained by the cold-shouldering administered to him by persons for whom he had not an atom of respect, and whose vanity and love of display he had only that moment been censuring. Still more, on viewing the matter clearly, he felt vexed to think that he himself had been so largely the cause of the catastrophe.

Yet he was not angry with HIMSELF—of that you may be sure, seeing that all of us have a slight weakness for sparing our own faults, and always do our best to find some fellow-creature upon whom to vent our displeasure—whether that fellow-creature be a servant, a subordinate official, or a wife. In the same way Chichikov sought a scapegoat upon whose shoulders he could lay the blame for all that had annoyed him. He found one in Nozdrev, and you may be sure that the scapegoat in question received a good drubbing from every side, even as an experienced captain or chief of police will give a knavish starosta or postboy a rating not only in the terms become classical, but also in such terms as the said captain or chief of police may invent for himself. In short, Nozdrev's whole lineage was passed in review; and many of its members in the ascending line fared badly in the process.

Meanwhile, at the other end of the town there was in progress an event which was destined to augment still further the unpleasantness of our hero's position. That is to say, through the outlying streets and alleys of the town there was clattering a vehicle to which it would be difficult precisely to assign a name, seeing that, though it was of a species peculiar to itself, it most nearly resembled a large, rickety water melon on wheels. Eventually this monstrosity drew up at the gates of a house where the archpriest of one of the churches resided, and from its doors there leapt a damsel clad in a jerkin and wearing a scarf over her head. For a while she thumped the gates so vigorously as to set all the dogs barking; then the gates stiffly opened, and admitted this unwieldy phenomenon of the road. Lastly, the barinia herself alighted, and stood revealed as Madame Korobotchka, widow of a Collegiate Secretary! The reason of her sudden arrival was that she had felt so uneasy about the possible outcome of Chichikov's whim, that during the three nights following his departure she had been unable to sleep a wink; whereafter, in spite of the fact that her horses were not shod, she had set off for the town, in order to learn at first hand how the dead souls were faring, and whether (which might God forfend!) she had not sold them at something like a third of their true value. The consequences of her venture the reader will learn from a conversation between two ladies. We will reserve it for the ensuing chapter.

CHAPTER IX

Next morning, before the usual hour for paying calls, there tripped from the portals of an orange-coloured wooden house with an attic storey and a row of blue pillars a lady in an elegant plaid cloak. With her came a footman in a many-caped greatcoat and a polished top hat with a gold band. Hastily, but gracefully, the lady ascended the steps let down from a koliaska which was standing before the entrance, and as soon as she had done so the footman shut her in, put up the steps again, and, catching hold of the strap behind the vehicle, shouted to the coachman, "Right away!" The reason of all this was that the lady was the possessor of a piece of intelligence that she was burning to communicate to a fellow-creature. Every moment she kept looking out of the carriage window, and perceiving, with almost speechless vexation, that, as yet, she was but half-way on her journey. The fronts of the houses appeared to her longer than usual, and in particular did the front of the white stone hospital, with its rows of narrow windows, seem interminable to a degree which at length forced her to ejaculate: "Oh, the cursed building! Positively there is no end to it!" Also, she twice adjured the coachman with the words, "Go quicker, Andrusha! You are a horribly long time over the journey this morning." But at length the goal was reached, and the koliaska stopped before a one-storied wooden mansion, dark grey in colour, and having white carvings over the windows, a tall wooden fence and narrow garden in front of the latter, and a few meagre trees looming white with an incongruous coating of road dust. In the windows of the building were also a few flower pots and a parrot that kept alternately dancing on the floor of its cage and hanging on to the ring of the same with its beak. Also, in the sunshine before the door two pet dogs were sleeping. Here there lived the lady's bosom friend. As soon as the bosom friend in question learnt of the newcomer's arrival, she ran down into the hall, and the two ladies kissed and embraced one another. Then they adjourned to the drawing-room.

"How glad I am to see you!" said the bosom friend. "When I heard some one arriving I wondered who could possibly be calling so early. Parasha declared that it must be the Vice-Governor's wife, so, as I did not want to be bored with her, I gave orders that I was to be reported 'not at home.'"

For her part, the guest would have liked to have proceeded to business by communicating her tidings, but a sudden exclamation from the hostess imparted (temporarily) a new direction to the conversation.

"What a pretty chintz!" she cried, gazing at the other's gown.

"Yes, it IS pretty," agreed the visitor. "On the other hand, Praskovia Thedorovna thinks that—"

In other words, the ladies proceeded to indulge in a conversation on the subject of dress; and only after this had lasted for a considerable while did the visitor let fall a remark which led her entertainer to inquire:

"And how is the universal charmer?"

"My God!" replied the other. "There has been SUCH a business! In fact, do you know why I am here at all?" And the visitor's breathing became more hurried, and further words seemed to be hovering between her lips like hawks preparing to stoop upon their prey. Only a person of the unhumanity of a "true friend" would have had the heart to interrupt her; but the hostess was just such a friend, and at once interposed with:

"I wonder how any one can see anything in the man to praise or to admire. For my own part, I think—and I would say the same thing straight to his face—that he is a perfect rascal."

"Yes, but do listen to what I have got to tell you."

"Oh, I know that some people think him handsome," continued the hostess, unmoved; "but *I* say that he is nothing of the kind—that, in particular, his nose is perfectly odious."

"Yes, but let me finish what I was saying." The guest's tone was almost piteous in its appeal.

"What is it, then?"

"You cannot imagine my state of mind! You see, this morning I received a visit from Father Cyril's wife—the Archpriest's wife—you know her, don't you? Well, whom do you suppose that fine gentleman visitor of ours has turned out to be?"

"The man who has built the Archpriest a poultry-run?"

"Oh dear no! Had that been all, it would have been nothing. No. Listen to what Father Cyril's wife had to tell me. She said that, last night, a lady landowner named Madame Korobotchka arrived at the Archpriest's house—arrived all pale and trembling—and told her, oh, such things! They sound like a piece out of a book. That is to say, at dead of night, just when every one had retired to rest, there came the most dreadful knocking imaginable, and some one screamed out, 'Open the gates, or we will break them down!' Just think! After this, how any one can say that the man is charming I cannot imagine."

"Well, what of Madame Korobotchka? Is she a young woman or good looking?"

"Oh dear no! Quite an old woman."

"Splendid indeed! So he is actually engaged to a person like that? One may heartily commend the taste of our ladies for having fallen in love with him!"

"Nevertheless, it is not as you suppose. Think, now! Armed with weapons from head to foot, he called upon this old woman, and said: 'Sell me any souls of yours which have lately died.' Of course, Madame Korobotchka answered, reasonably enough: 'I cannot sell you those souls, seeing that they have departed this world;' but he replied: 'No, no! They are NOT dead. 'Tis I who tell you that—I who ought to know the truth of the matter. I swear that they are still alive.' In short, he made such a scene that the whole village came running to the house, and children screamed, and men shouted, and no one could tell what it was all about. The affair seemed to me so horrible, so utterly horrible, that I trembled beyond belief as I listened to the story. 'My dearest madam,' said my maid, Mashka, 'pray look at yourself in the mirror, and see how white you are.' 'But I have no time for that,' I replied, 'as I must be off to tell my friend, Anna Grigorievna, the news.' Nor did I lose a moment in ordering the koliaska. Yet when my coachman, Andrusha, asked me for directions I could not get a word out—I just stood staring at him like a fool, until I thought he must think me mad. Oh, Anna Grigorievna, if you but knew how upset I am!"

"What a strange affair!" commented the hostess. "What on earth can the man have meant by 'dead souls'? I confess that the words pass my understanding. Curiously enough, this is the second time I have heard speak of those souls. True, my husband avers that Nozdrev was lying; yet in his lies there seems to have been a grain of truth."

"Well, just think of my state when I heard all this! 'And now,' apparently said Korobotchka to the Archpriest's wife, 'I am altogether at a loss what to do, for, throwing me fifteen roubles, the man forced me to sign a worthless paper—yes, me, an inexperienced, defenceless widow who knows nothing of business.' That such things should happen! TRY and imagine my feelings!"

"In my opinion, there is in this more than the dead souls which meet the eye."

"I think so too," agreed the other. As a matter of fact, her friend's remark had struck her with complete surprise, as well as filled her with curiosity to know what the word "more" might possibly signify. In fact, she felt driven to inquire: "What do YOU suppose to be hidden beneath it all?"

"No; tell me what YOU suppose?"

"What *I* suppose? I am at a loss to conjecture."

"Yes, but tell me what is in your mind?"

Upon this the visitor had to confess herself nonplussed; for, though capable of growing hysterical, she was incapable of propounding any rational theory. Consequently she felt the more that she needed tender comfort and advice.

"Then THIS is what I think about the dead souls," said the hostess. Instantly the guest pricked up her ears (or, rather, they pricked themselves up) and straightened herself and became, somehow, more modish, and, despite her not inconsiderable weight, posed herself to look like a piece of thistledown floating on the breeze.

"The dead souls," began the hostess.

"Are what, are what?" inquired the guest in great excitement.

"Are, are—"

"Tell me, tell me, for heaven's sake!"

"They are an invention to conceal something else. The man's real object is, is—TO ABDUCT THE GOVERNOR'S DAUGHTER."

So startling and unexpected was this conclusion that the guest sat reduced to a state of pale, petrified, genuine amazement.

"My God!" she cried, clapping her hands, "I should NEVER have guessed it!"

"Well, to tell you the truth, I guessed it as soon as ever you opened your mouth."

"So much, then, for educating girls like the Governor's daughter at school! Just see what comes of it!"

"Yes, indeed! And they tell me that she says things which I hesitate even to repeat."

"Truly it wrings one's heart to see to what lengths immorality has come."

"Some of the men have quite lost their heads about her, but for my part I think her not worth noticing."

"Of course. And her manners are unbearable. But what puzzles me most is how a travelled man like Chichikov could come to let himself in for such an affair. Surely he must have accomplices?"

"Yes; and I should say that one of those accomplices is Nozdrev."

"Surely not?"

"CERTAINLY I should say so. Why, I have known him even try to sell his own father! At all events he staked him at cards."

"Indeed? You interest me. I should never had thought him capable of such things."

"I always guessed him to be so."

The two ladies were still discussing the matter with acumen and success when there walked into the room the Public Prosecutor—bushy eyebrows, motionless features, blinking eyes, and all. At once the ladies hastened to inform him of the events related, adducing therewith full details both as to the purchase of dead souls and as to the scheme to abduct the Governor's daughter; after which they departed in different directions, for the purpose of raising the rest of the town. For the execution of this undertaking not more than half an hour was required. So thoroughly did they succeed in throwing dust in the public's eyes that for a while every one—more especially the army of public officials—was placed in the position of a schoolboy who, while still asleep, has had a bag of pepper thrown in his face by a party of more early-rising comrades. The questions now to be debated resolved themselves into two—namely, the question of the dead souls and the question of the Governor's daughter. To this end two parties were formed—the men's party and the feminine section. The men's party—the more absolutely senseless of the two—devoted its attention to the dead souls: the women's party occupied itself exclusively with the alleged abduction of the Governor's daughter. And here it may be said (to the ladies' credit) that the women's party displayed far more method and caution than did its rival faction, probably because the function in life of its members had always been that of managing and administering a household. With the ladies, therefore, matters soon assumed vivid and definite shape; they became clearly and irrefutably materialised; they stood stripped of all doubt and other impedimenta. Said some of the ladies in question, Chichikov had long been in love with the maiden, and the pair had kept tryst by the light of the moon, while the Governor would have given his consent (seeing that Chichikov was as rich as a Jew) but for the obstacle that Chichikov had deserted a wife already (how the worthy dames came to know that he was married remains a mystery), and the said deserted wife, pining with love for her faithless husband, had sent the Governor a letter of the most touching kind, so that Chichikov, on perceiving that the father and mother would never give their consent, had decided to abduct the girl. In other circles the matter was stated in a different way. That is to say, this section averred that Chichikov did NOT possess a wife, but that, as a man of subtlety and experience, he had bethought him of obtaining the daughter's hand through the expedient of first tackling the mother and carrying on with her an ardent liaison, and that, thereafter, he had made an application for the desired hand, but that the mother, fearing to commit a sin against religion, and feeling in her heart certain gnawings of conscience, had returned a blank refusal to Chichikov's request; whereupon Chichikov had decided to carry out the abduction alleged. To the foregoing, of course, there became appended various additional proofs and items of evidence, in proportion as the sensation spread to more remote corners of the town. At length, with these perfectings, the affair reached the ears of the Governor's wife herself. Naturally, as the mother of a family, and as the first lady in the town, and as a matron who had never before been suspected of things of the kind, she was highly offended when she heard the stories, and very justly so: with the result that her poor young daughter, though innocent, had to endure about as unpleasant a tete-a-tete as ever befell a maiden of sixteen, while, for his part, the Swiss footman received orders never at any time to admit Chichikov to the house.

Having done their business with the Governor's wife, the ladies' party descended upon the male section, with a view to influencing it to their own side by asserting that the dead souls were an invention used solely for the purpose of diverting suspicion and successfully affecting the abduction. And, indeed, more than one man was converted, and joined the feminine camp, in spite of the fact that thereby such seceders incurred strong names from their late comrades—names such as "old women," "petticoats," and others of a nature peculiarly offensive to the male sex.

Also, however much they might arm themselves and take the field, the men could not compass such orderliness within their ranks as could the women. With the former everything was of the antiquated and rough-hewn and ill-fitting and unsuitable and badly-adapted and inferior kind; their heads were full of nothing but discord and triviality and confusion and slovenliness of thought. In brief, they displayed everywhere the male bent, the rude, ponderous nature which is incapable either of managing a household or of jumping to a conclusion, as well as remains always distrustful and lazy and full of constant doubt and everlasting timidity. For instance, the men's party declared that the whole story was rubbish—that the alleged abduction of the Governor's daughter was the work rather of a military than of a civilian culprit; that the ladies were lying when they accused Chichikov of the deed; that a woman was like a money-bag—whatsoever you put into her she thenceforth retained; that the subject which really demanded attention was the dead souls, of which the devil only knew the meaning, but in which there certainly lurked something that was contrary to good order and discipline. One reason why the men's party was so certain that the dead souls connoted something contrary to good order and discipline, was that there had just been appointed to the province a new Governor-General—an event which, of course, had thrown the whole army of provincial tchinovniks into a state of great excitement, seeing that they knew that before long there would ensue transferments and sentences of censure, as well as the series of official dinners with which a Governor-General is accustomed to entertain his subordinates. "Alas," thought the army of tchinovniks, "it is probable that, should he learn of the gross reports at present afloat in our town, he will make such a fuss that we shall never hear the last of them." In particular did the Director of the Medical Department turn pale at the thought that possibly the new Governor-General would surmise the term "dead folk" to connote patients in the local hospitals who, for want of proper preventative measures, had died of sporadic fever. Indeed, might it not be that Chichikov was neither more nor less than an emissary of the said Governor-General, sent to conduct a secret inquiry? Accordingly he (the Director of the Medical Department) communicated this last supposition to the President of the Council, who, though at first inclined to ejaculate "Rubbish!" suddenly turned pale on propounding to himself the theory. "What if the souls purchased by Chichikov should REALLY be dead ones?"—a terrible thought considering that he, the President, had permitted their transferment to be registered, and had himself acted as Plushkin's representative! What if these things should reach the Governor-General's ears? He mentioned the matter to one friend and another, and they, in their turn, went white to the lips, for panic spreads faster and is even more destructive, than the dreaded black death. Also, to add to the tchinovniks' troubles, it so befell that just at this juncture there came into the local Governor's hands two documents of great importance. The first of them contained advices that, according to received evidence and reports, there was operating in the province a forger of rouble-notes who had been passing under various aliases and must therefore be sought for with the utmost diligence; while the second document was a letter from the Governor of a neighbouring province with regard to a malefactor who had there evaded apprehension—a letter conveying also a warning that, if in the province of the town of N. there should appear any suspicious individual who could produce neither references nor passports, he was to be arrested forthwith. These two documents left every one thunderstruck, for they knocked on the head all previous conceptions and theories. Not for a moment could it be supposed that the former document referred to Chichikov; yet, as each man pondered the position from his own point of view, he remembered that no one REALLY knew who Chichikov was; as also that his vague references to himself had—yes!—included statements that his career in the service had suffered much to the cause of Truth, and that he possessed a number of enemies who were seeking his life. This gave the tchinovniks further food for thought. Perhaps his life really DID stand in danger? Perhaps he really WAS being sought for by some one? Perhaps he really HAD done something of the kind above referred to? As a matter of fact, who was he?—not that it could actually be supposed that he was a forger of notes, still less a brigand, seeing that his exterior was respectable in the highest degree. Yet who was he? At length the tchinovniks decided to make enquiries among those of whom he had purchased souls, in order that at least it might be learnt what the purchases had consisted of, and what exactly underlay them, and whether, in passing, he had explained to any one his real intentions, or revealed to any one his identity. In the first instance, therefore, resort was had to Korobotchka. Yet little was gleaned from that source—merely a statement that he had bought of her some souls for fifteen roubles apiece, and also a quantity of feathers, while promising also to buy some other commodities in the future, seeing that, in particular, he had entered into a contract with the Treasury for lard, a fact constituting fairly presumptive proof that the man was a rogue, seeing that just such another fellow had bought a quantity of feathers, yet had cheated folk all round, and, in particular, had done the Archpriest out of over a hundred roubles. Thus the net result of Madame's cross-examination was to convince the tchinovniks that she was a garrulous, silly old woman. With regard to Manilov, he replied that he would answer for Chichikov as he would for himself, and that he would gladly sacrifice his property in toto if thereby he could attain even a tithe of the qualities which Paul Ivanovitch possessed. Finally, he delivered on Chichikov, with acutely-knitted brows, a eulogy couched in the most charming of terms, and coupled with sundry sentiments on the subject of friendship and affection in general. True, these remarks sufficed to indicate the tender impulses of the speaker's heart, but also they did nothing to enlighten his examiners concerning the business that was actually at hand. As for Sobakevitch, that landowner replied that he considered Chichikov an excellent fellow, as well as that the souls whom he had sold to his visitor had been in the truest sense of the word alive, but that he could not answer for anything which might occur in the future, seeing that any difficulties which might arise in the course of the actual transferment of souls would not be HIS fault, in view of the fact that God was lord of all, and that fevers and other mortal complaints were so numerous in the world, and that instances of whole villages perishing through the same could be found on record.

Finally, our friends the tchinovniks found themselves compelled to resort to an expedient which, though not particularly savoury, is not infrequently employed—namely, the expedient of getting lacqueys quietly to approach the servants of the person concerning whom information is desired, and to ascertain from them (the servants) certain details with regard to their master's life and antecedents. Yet even from this source very little was obtained, since Petrushka provided his interrogators merely with a taste of the smell of his living-room, and Selifan confined his replies to a statement that the barin had "been in the employment of the State, and also had served in the Customs."

In short, the sum total of the results gathered by the tchinovniks was that they still stood in ignorance of Chichikov's identity, but that he MUST be some one; wherefore it was decided to hold a final debate on the subject on what ought to be done, and who Chichikov could possibly be, and whether or not he was a man who ought to be apprehended and detained as not respectable, or whether he was a man who might himself be able to apprehend and detain THEM as persons lacking in respectability. The debate in question, it was proposed, should be held at the residence of the Chief of Police, who is known to our readers as the father and the general benefactor of the town.

CHAPTER X

On assembling at the residence indicated, the tchinovniks had occasion to remark that, owing to all these cares and excitements, every one of their number had grown thinner. Yes, the appointment of a new Governor-General, coupled with the rumours described and the reception of the two serious documents above-mentioned, had left manifest traces upon the features of every one present. More than one frockcoat had come to look too large for its wearer, and more than one frame had fallen away, including the frames of the President of the Council, the Director of the Medical Department, and the Public Prosecutor. Even a certain Semen Ivanovitch, who, for some reason or another, was never alluded to by his family name, but who wore on his index finger a ring with which he was accustomed to dazzle his lady friends, had diminished in bulk. Yet, as always happens at such junctures, there were also present a score of brazen individuals who had succeeded in NOT losing their presence of mind, even though they constituted a mere sprinkling. Of them the Postmaster formed one, since he was a man of equable temperament who could always say: "WE know you, Governor-Generals! We have seen three or four of you come and go, whereas WE have been sitting on the same stools these thirty years." Nevertheless a prominent feature of the gathering was the total absence of what is vulgarly known as "common sense." In general, we Russians do not make a good show at representative assemblies, for the reason that, unless there be in authority a leading spirit to control the rest, the affair always develops into confusion. Why this should be so one could hardly say, but at all events a success is scored only by such gatherings as have for their object dining and festivity—to wit, gatherings at clubs or in German-run restaurants. However, on the present occasion, the meeting was NOT one of this kind; it was a meeting convoked of necessity, and likely in view of the threatened calamity to affect every tchinovnik in the place. Also, in addition to the great divergency of views expressed thereat, there was visible in all the speakers an invincible tendency to indecision which led them at one moment to make assertions, and at the next to contradict the same. But on at least one point all seemed to agree—namely, that Chichikov's appearance and conversation were too respectable for him to be a forger or a disguised brigand. That is to say, all SEEMED to agree on the point; until a sudden shout arose from the direction of the Postmaster, who for some time past had been sitting plunged in thought.

"*I* can tell you," he cried, "who Chichikov is!"

"Who, then?" replied the crowd in great excitement.

"He is none other than Captain Kopeikin."

"And who may Captain Kopeikin be?"

Taking a pinch of snuff (which he did with the lid of his snuff-box half-open, lest some extraneous person should contrive to insert a not over-clean finger into the stuff), the Postmaster related the following story 35.

"After fighting in the campaign of 1812, there was sent home, wounded, a certain Captain Kopeikin—a headstrong, lively blade who, whether on duty or under arrest, made things lively for everybody. Now, since at Krasni or at Leipzig (it matters not which) he had lost an arm and a leg, and in those days no provision was made for wounded soldiers, and he could not work with his left arm alone, he set out to see his father. Unfortunately his father could only just support himself, and was forced to tell his son so; wherefore the Captain decided to go and apply for help in St. Petersburg, seeing that he had risked his life for his country, and had lost much blood in its service. You can imagine him arriving in the capital on a baggage waggon—in the capital which is like no other city in the world! Before him there lay spread out the whole field of life, like a sort of Arabian Nights—a picture made up of the Nevski Prospect, Gorokhovaia Street, countless tapering spires, and a number of bridges apparently supported on nothing—in fact, a regular second Nineveh. Well, he made shift to hire a lodging, but found everything so wonderfully furnished with blinds and Persian carpets and so forth that he saw it would mean throwing away a lot of money. True, as one walks the streets of St. Petersburg one seems to smell money by the thousand roubles, but our friend Kopeikin's bank was limited to a few score coppers and a little silver—not enough to buy a village with! At length, at the price of a rouble a day, he obtained a lodging in the sort of tavern where the daily ration is a bowl of cabbage soup and a crust of bread; and as he felt that he could not manage to live very long on fare of that kind he asked folk what he had better do. 'What you had better do?' they said. 'Well the Government is not here—it is in Paris, and the troops have not yet returned from the war; but there is a TEMPORARY Commission sitting, and you had better go and see what IT can do for you.' 'All right!' he said. 'I will go and tell the Commission that I have shed my blood, and sacrificed my life, for my country.' And he got up early one morning, and shaved himself with his left hand (since the expense of a barber was not worth while), and set out, wooden leg and all, to see the President of the Commission. But first he asked where the President lived, and was told that his house was in Naberezhnaia Street. And you may be sure that it was no peasant's hut, with its glazed windows and great mirrors and statues and lacqueys and brass door handles! Rather, it was the sort of place which you would enter only after you had bought a cheap cake of soap and indulged in a two hours' wash. Also, at the entrance there was posted a grand Swiss footman with a baton and an embroidered collar—a fellow looking like a fat, over-fed pug dog. However, friend Kopeikin managed to get himself and his wooden leg into the reception room, and there squeezed himself away into a corner, for fear lest he should knock down the gilded china with his elbow. And he stood waiting in great satisfaction at having arrived before the President had so much as left his bed and been served with his silver wash-basin. Nevertheless, it was only when Kopeikin had been waiting four hours that a breakfast waiter entered to say, 'The President will soon be here.' By now the room was as full of people as a plate is of beans, and when the President left the breakfast-room he brought with him, oh, such dignity and refinement, and such an air of the metropolis! First he walked up to one person, and then up to another, saying: 'What do YOU want? And what do YOU want? What can I do for YOU? What is YOUR business?' And at length he stopped before Kopeikin, and Kopeikin said to him: 'I have shed my blood, and lost both an arm and a leg, for my country, and am unable to work. Might I therefore dare to ask you for a little help, if the regulations should permit of it, or for a gratuity, or for a pension, or something of the kind?' Then the President looked at him, and saw that one of his legs was indeed a wooden one, and that an empty right sleeve was pinned to his uniform. 'Very well,' he said. 'Come to me again in a few days' time.' Upon this friend Kopeikin felt delighted. 'NOW I have done my job!' he thought to himself; and you may imagine how gaily he trotted along the pavement, and how he dropped into a tavern for a glass of vodka, and how he ordered a cutlet and some caper sauce and some other things for luncheon, and how he called for a bottle of wine, and how he went to the theatre in the evening! In short, he did himself thoroughly well. Next, he saw in the street a young English lady, as graceful as a swan, and set off after her on his wooden leg. 'But no,' he thought to himself. 'To the devil with that sort of thing just now! I will wait until I have drawn my pension. For the present I have spent enough.' (And I may tell you that by now he had got through fully half his money.) Two or three days later he went to see the President of the Commission again. 'I should be glad to know,' he said, 'whether by now you can do anything for me in return for my having shed my blood and suffered sickness and wounds on military service.' 'First of all,' said the President, 'I must tell you that nothing can be decided in your case without the authority of the Supreme Government. Without that sanction we cannot move in the matter. Surely you see how things stand until the army shall have returned from the war? All that I can advise you to do is wait for the Minister to return, and, in the meanwhile, to have patience. Rest assured that then you will not be overlooked. And if for the moment you have nothing to live upon, this is the best that I can do for you.' With that he handed Kopeikin a trifle until his case should have been decided. However, that was not what Kopeikin wanted. He had supposed that he would be given a gratuity of a thousand roubles straight away; whereas, instead of 'Drink and be merry,' it was 'Wait, for the time is not yet.' Thus, though his head had been full of soup plates and cutlets and English girls, he now descended the steps with his ears and his tail down—looking, in fact, like a poodle over which the cook has poured a bucketful of water. You see, St. Petersburg life had changed him not a little since first he had got a taste of it, and, now that the devil only knew how he was going to live, it came all the harder to him that he should have no more sweets to look forward to. Remember that a man in the prime of years has an appetite like a wolf; and as he passed a restaurant he could see a round-faced, holland-shirted, snow-white aproned fellow of a French chef preparing a dish delicious enough to make it turn to and eat itself; while, again, as he passed a fruit shop he could see delicacies looking out of a window for fools to come and buy them at a hundred roubles apiece. Imagine, therefore, his position! On the one hand, so to speak, were salmon and water-melons, while on the other hand was the bitter fare which passed at a tavern for luncheon. 'Well,' he thought to himself, 'let them do what they like with me at the Commission, but I intend to go and raise the whole place, and to tell every blessed functionary there that I have a mind to do as I choose.' And in truth this bold impertinence of a man did have the hardihood to return to the Commission. 'What do you want?' said the President. 'Why are you here for the third time? You have had your orders given you.' 'I daresay I have,' he retorted, 'but I am not going to be put off with THEM. I want some cutlets to eat, and a bottle of French wine, and a chance to go and amuse myself at the theatre.' 'Pardon me,' said the President. 'What you really need (if I may venture to mention it) is a little patience. You have been given something for food until the Military Committee shall have met, and then, doubtless, you will receive your proper reward, seeing that it would not be seemly that a man who has served his country should be left destitute. On the other hand, if, in the meanwhile, you desire to indulge in cutlets and theatre-going, please understand that we cannot help you, but you must make your own resources, and try as best you can to help yourself.' You can imagine that this went in at one of Kopeikin's ears, and out at the other; that it was like shooting peas at a stone wall.

Accordingly he raised a turmoil which sent the staff flying. One by one, he gave the mob of secretaries and clerks a real good hammering. 'You, and you, and you,' he said, 'do not even know your duties. You are law-breakers.' Yes, he trod every man of them under foot. At length the General himself arrived from another office, and sounded the alarm. What was to be done with a fellow like Kopeikin? The President saw that strong measures were imperative. 'Very well,' he said. 'Since you decline to rest satisfied with what has been given you, and quietly to await the decision of your case in St. Petersburg, I must find you a lodging. Here, constable, remove the man to gaol.' Then a constable who had been called to the door—a constable three ells in height, and armed with a carbine—a man well fitted to guard a bank—placed our friend in a police waggon. 'Well,' reflected Kopeikin, 'at least I shan't have to pay my fare for THIS ride. That's one comfort.' Again, after he had ridden a little way, he said to himself: 'they told me at the Commission to go and make my own means of enjoying myself. Very good. I'll do so.' However, what became of Kopeikin, and whither he went, is known to no one. He sank, to use the poet's expression, into the waters of Lethe, and his doings now lie buried in oblivion. But allow me, gentlemen, to piece together the further threads of the story. Not two months later there appeared in the forests of Riazan a band of robbers: and of that band the chieftain was none other than—"

"Allow me," put in the Head of the Police Department. "You have said that Kopeikin had lost an arm and a leg; whereas Chichikov—"

To say anything more was unnecessary. The Postmaster clapped his hand to his forehead, and publicly called himself a fool, though, later, he tried to excuse his mistake by saying that in England the science of mechanics had reached such a pitch that wooden legs were manufactured which would enable the wearer, on touching a spring, to vanish instantaneously from sight.

Various other theories were then propounded, among them a theory that Chichikov was Napoleon, escaped from St. Helena and travelling about the world in disguise. And if it should be supposed that no such notion could possibly have been broached, let the reader remember that these events took place not many years after the French had been driven out of Russia, and that various prophets had since declared that Napoleon was Antichrist, and would one day escape from his island prison to exercise universal sway on earth. Nay, some good folk had even declared the letters of Napoleon's name to constitute the Apocalyptic cipher!

As a last resort, the tchinovniks decided to question Nozdrev, since not only had the latter been the first to mention the dead souls, but also he was supposed to stand on terms of intimacy with Chichikov. Accordingly the Chief of Police dispatched a note by the hand of a commissionaire. At the time Nozdrev was engaged on some very important business—so much so that he had not left his room for four days, and was receiving his meals through the window, and no visitors at all. The business referred to consisted of the marking of several dozen selected cards in such a way as to permit of his relying upon them as upon his bosom friend. Naturally he did not like having his retirement invaded, and at first consigned the commissionaire to the devil; but as soon as he learnt from the note that, since a novice at cards was to be the guest of the Chief of Police that evening, a call at the latter's house might prove not wholly unprofitable he relented, unlocked the door of his room, threw on the first garments that came to hand, and set forth. To every question put to him by the tchinovniks he answered firmly and with assurance. Chichikov, he averred, had indeed purchased dead souls, and to the tune of several thousand roubles. In fact, he (Nozdrev) had himself sold him some, and still saw no reason why he should not have done so. Next, to the question of whether or not he considered Chichikov to be a spy, he replied in the affirmative, and added that, as long ago as his and Chichikov's joint schooldays, the said Chichikov had been known as "The Informer," and repeatedly been thrashed by his companions on that account. Again, to the question of whether or not Chichikov was a forger of currency notes the deponent, as before, responded in the affirmative, and appended thereto an anecdote illustrative of Chichikov's extraordinary dexterity of hand—namely, an anecdote to that effect that, once upon a time, on learning that two million roubles worth of counterfeit notes were lying in Chichikov's house, the authorities had placed seals upon the building, and had surrounded it on every side with an armed guard; whereupon Chichikov had, during the night, changed each of these seals for a new one, and also so arranged matters that, when the house was searched, the forged notes were found to be genuine ones!

Again, to the question of whether or not Chichikov had schemed to abduct the Governor's daughter, and also whether it was true that he,

Nozdrev, had undertaken to aid and abet him in the act, the witness replied that, had he not undertaken to do so, the affair would never have come off. At this point the witness pulled himself up, on realising that he had told a lie which might get him into trouble; but his tongue was not to be denied—the details trembling on its tip were too alluring, and he even went on to cite the name of the village church where the pair had arranged to be married, that of the priest who had performed the ceremony, the amount of the fees paid for the same (seventy-five roubles), and statements (1) that the priest had refused to solemnise the wedding until Chichikov had frightened him by threatening to expose the fact that he (the priest) had married Mikhail, a local corn dealer, to his paramour, and (2) that Chichikov had ordered both a koliaska for the couple's conveyance and relays of horses from the post-houses on the road. Nay, the narrative, as detailed by Nozdrev, even reached the point of his mentioning certain of the postillions by name! Next, the tchinovniks sounded him on the question of Chichikov's possible identity with Napoleon; but before long they had reason to regret the step, for Nozdrev responded with a rambling rigmarole such as bore no resemblance to anything possibly conceivable. Finally, the majority of the audience left the room, and only the Chief of Police remained to listen (in the hope of gathering something more); but at last even he found himself forced to disclaim the speaker with a gesture which said: "The devil only knows what the fellow is talking about!" and so voiced the general opinion that it was no use trying to gather figs of thistles.

Meanwhile Chichikov knew nothing of these events; for, having contracted a slight chill, coupled with a sore throat, he had decided to keep his room for three days; during which time he gargled his throat with milk and fig juice, consumed the fruit from which the juice had been extracted, and wore around his neck a poultice of camomile and camphor. Also, to while away the hours, he made new and more detailed lists of the souls which he had bought, perused a work by the Duchesse de la Valliere 36, rummaged in his portmanteau, looked through various articles and papers which he discovered in his dispatch-box, and found every one of these occupations tedious. Nor could he understand why none of his official friends had come to see him and inquire after his health, seeing that, not long since, there had been standing in front of the inn the drozhkis both of the Postmaster, the Public Prosecutor, and the President of the Council. He wondered and wondered, and then, with a shrug of his shoulders, fell to pacing the room. At length he felt better, and his spirits rose at the prospect of once more going out into the fresh air; wherefore, having shaved a plentiful growth of hair from his face, he dressed with such alacrity as almost to cause a split in his trousers, sprinkled himself with eau-de-Cologne, and wrapping himself in warm clothes, and turning up the collar of his coat, sallied forth into the street. His first destination was intended to be the Governor's mansion, and, as he walked along, certain thoughts concerning the Governor's daughter would keep whirling through his head, so that almost he forgot where he was, and took to smiling and cracking jokes to himself.

Arrived at the Governor's entrance, he was about to divest himself of his scarf when a Swiss footman greeted him with the words, "I am forbidden to admit you."

"What?" he exclaimed. "You do not know me? Look at me again, and see if you do not recognise me."

"Of course I recognise you," the footman replied. "I have seen you before, but have been ordered to admit any one else rather than Monsieur Chichikov."

"Indeed? And why so?"

"Those are my orders, and they must be obeyed," said the footman, confronting Chichikov with none of that politeness with which, on former occasions, he had hastened to divest our hero of his wrappings. Evidently he was of opinion that, since the gentry declined to receive the visitor, the latter must certainly be a rogue.

"I cannot understand it," said Chichikov to himself. Then he departed, and made his way to the house of the President of the Council. But so put about was that official by Chichikov's entry that he could not utter two consecutive words—he could only murmur some rubbish which left both his visitor and himself out of countenance. Chichikov wondered, as he left the house, what the President's muttered words could have meant, but failed to make head or tail of them. Next, he visited, in turn, the Chief of Police, the Vice-Governor, the Postmaster, and others; but in each case he either failed to be accorded admittance or was received so strangely, and with such a measure of constraint and conversational awkwardness and absence of mind and embarrassment, that he began to fear for the sanity of his hosts. Again and again did he strive to divine the cause, but could not do so; so he went wandering aimlessly about the town, without succeeding in making up his mind whether he or the officials had gone crazy. At length, in a state bordering upon bewilderment, he returned to the inn—to the establishment whence, that every afternoon, he had set forth in such exuberance of spirits. Feeling the need of something to do, he ordered tea, and, still marvelling at the strangeness of his position, was about to pour out the beverage when the door opened and Nozdrev made his appearance.

"What says the proverb?" he began. "'To see a friend, seven versts is not too long a round to make.' I happened to be passing the house, saw a light in your window, and thought to myself: 'Now, suppose I were to run up and pay him a visit? It is unlikely that he will be asleep.' Ah, ha! I see tea on your table! Good! Then I will drink a cup with you, for I had wretched stuff for dinner, and it is beginning to lie heavy on my stomach. Also, tell your man to fill me a pipe. Where is your own pipe?"

"I never smoke," rejoined Chichikov drily.

"Rubbish! As if I did not know what a chimney-pot you are! What is your man's name? Hi, Vakhramei! Come here!"

"Petrushka is his name, not Vakhramei."

"Indeed? But you USED to have a man called Vakhramei, didn't you?"

"No, never."

"Oh, well. Then it must be Derebin's man I am thinking of. What a lucky fellow that Derebin is! An aunt of his has gone and quarrelled with her son for marrying a serf woman, and has left all her property to HIM, to Derebin. Would that *I* had an aunt of that kind to provide against future contingencies! But why have you been hiding yourself away? I suppose the reason has been that you go in for abstruse subjects and are fond of reading" (why Nozdrev should have drawn these conclusions no one could possibly have said—least of all Chichikov himself). "By the way, I can tell you of something that would have found you scope for your satirical vein" (the conclusion as to Chichikov's "satirical vein" was, as before, altogether unwarranted on Nozdrev's part). "That is to say, you would have seen merchant Likhachev losing a pile of money at play. My word, you would have laughed! A fellow with me named Perependev said: 'Would that Chichikov had been here! It would have been the very thing for him!'" (As a matter of fact, never since the day of his birth had Nozdrev met any one of the name of Perependev.) "However, my friend, you must admit that you treated me rather badly the day that we played that game of chess; but, as I won the game, I bear you no malice. A propos, I am just from the President's, and ought to tell you that the feeling against you in the town is very strong, for every one believes you to be a forger of currency notes. I myself was sent for and questioned about you, but I stuck up for you through thick and thin, and told the tchinovniks that I had been at school with you, and had known your father. In fact, I gave the fellows a knock or two for themselves."

"You say that I am believed to be a forger?" said Chichikov, starting from his seat.

"Yes," said Nozdrev. "Why have you gone and frightened everybody as you have done? Some of our folk are almost out of their minds about it, and declare you to be either a brigand in disguise or a spy. Yesterday the Public Prosecutor even died of it, and is to be buried to-morrow" (this was true in so far as that, on the previous day, the official in question had had a fatal stroke—probably induced by the excitement of the public meeting). "Of course, *I* don't suppose you to be anything of the kind, but, you see, these fellows are in a blue funk about the new Governor-General, for they think he will make trouble for them over your affair. A propos, he is believed to be a man who puts on airs, and turns up his nose at everything; and if so, he will get on badly with the dvoriane, seeing that fellows of that sort need to be humoured a bit. Yes, my word! Should the new Governor-General shut himself up in his study, and give no balls, there will be the very devil to pay! By the way, Chichikov, that is a risky scheme of yours."

"What scheme to you mean?" Chichikov asked uneasily.

"Why, that scheme of carrying off the Governor's daughter. However, to tell the truth, I was expecting something of the kind. No sooner did I see you and her together at the ball than I said to myself: 'Ah, ha! Chichikov is not here for nothing!' For my own part, I think you have made a poor choice, for I can see nothing in her at all. On the other hand, the niece of a friend of mine named Bikusov—she IS a girl, and no mistake! A regular what you might call 'miracle in muslin!'"

"What on earth are you talking about?" asked Chichikov with his eyes distended. "HOW could I carry off the Governor's daughter? What on earth do you mean?"

"Come, come! What a secretive fellow you are! My only object in having come to see you is to lend you a helping hand in the matter. Look here. On condition that you will lend me three thousand roubles, I will stand you the cost of the wedding, the koliaska, and the relays of horses. I must have the money even if I die for it."

Throughout Nozdrev's maunderings Chichikov had been rubbing his eyes to ascertain whether or not he was dreaming. What with the charge of being a forger, the accusation of having schemed an abduction, the death of the Public Prosecutor (whatever might have been its cause), and the advent of a new Governor-General, he felt utterly dismayed.

"Things having come to their present pass," he reflected, "I had better not linger here—I had better be off at once."

Getting rid of Nozdrev as soon as he could, he sent for Selifan, and ordered him to be up at daybreak, in order to clean the britchka and to have everything ready for a start at six o'clock. Yet, though Selifan replied, "Very well, Paul Ivanovitch," he hesitated awhile by the door. Next, Chichikov bid Petrushka get out the dusty portmanteau from under the bed, and then set to work to cram into it, pell-mell, socks, shirts, collars (both clean and dirty), boot trees, a calendar, and a variety of other articles. Everything went into the receptacle just as it came to hand, since his one object was to obviate any possible delay in the morning's departure. Meanwhile the reluctant Selifan slowly, very slowly, left the room, as slowly descended the staircase (on each separate step of which he left a muddy foot-print), and, finally, halted to scratch his head. What that scratching may have meant no one could say; for, with the Russian populace, such a scratching may mean any one of a hundred things.

CHAPTER XI

Nevertheless events did not turn out as Chichikov had intended they should. In the first place, he overslept himself. That was check number one. In the second place, on his rising and inquiring whether the britchka had been harnessed and everything got ready, he was informed that neither of those two things had been done. That was check number two. Beside himself with rage, he prepared to give Selifan the wigging of his life, and, meanwhile, waited impatiently to hear what the delinquent had got to say in his defence. It goes without saying that when Selifan made his appearance in the doorway he had only the usual excuses to offer—the sort of excuses usually offered by servants when a hasty departure has become imperatively necessary.

"Paul Ivanovitch," he said, "the horses require shoeing."

"Blockhead!" exclaimed Chichikov. "Why did you not tell me of that before, you damned fool? Was there not time enough for them to be shod?"

"Yes, I suppose there was," agreed Selifan. "Also one of the wheels is in want of a new tyre, for the roads are so rough that the old tyre is worn through. Also, the body of the britchka is so rickety that probably it will not last more than a couple of stages."

"Rascal!" shouted Chichikov, clenching his fists and approaching Selifan in such a manner that, fearing to receive a blow, the man backed and dodged aside. "Do you mean to ruin me, and to break all our bones on the road, you cursed idiot? For these three weeks past you have been doing nothing at all; yet now, at the last moment, you come here stammering and playing the fool! Do you think I keep you just to eat and to drive yourself about? You must have known of this before? Did you, or did you not, know it? Answer me at once."

"Yes, I did know it," replied Selifan, hanging his head.

"Then why didn't you tell me about it?"

Selifan had no reply immediately ready, so continued to hang his head while quietly saying to himself: "See how well I have managed things! I knew what was the matter, yet I did not say."

"And now," continued Chichikov, "go you at once and fetch a blacksmith. Tell him that everything must be put right within two hours at the most. Do you hear? If that should not be done, I, I—I will give you the best flogging that ever you had in your life." Truly Chichikov was almost beside himself with fury.

Turning towards the door, as though for the purpose of going and carrying out his orders, Selifan halted and added:

"That skewbald, barin—you might think it well to sell him, seeing that he is nothing but a rascal? A horse like that is more of a hindrance than a help."

"What? Do you expect me to go NOW to the market-place and sell him?"

"Well, Paul Ivanovitch, he is good for nothing but show, since by nature he is a most cunning beast. Never in my life have I seen such a horse."

"Fool! Whenever I may wish to sell him I SHALL sell him. Meanwhile, don't you trouble your head about what doesn't concern you, but go and fetch a blacksmith, and see that everything is put right within two hours. Otherwise I will take the very hair off your head, and beat you till you haven't a face left. Be off! Hurry!"

Selifan departed, and Chichikov, his ill-humour vented, threw down upon the floor the poignard which he always took with him as a means of instilling respect into whomsoever it might concern, and spent the next quarter of an hour in disputing with a couple of blacksmiths—men who, as usual, were rascals of the type which, on perceiving that something is wanted in a hurry, at once multiplies its terms for providing the same. Indeed, for all Chichikov's storming and raging as he dubbed the fellows robbers and extortioners and thieves, he could make no impression upon the pair, since, true to their character, they declined to abate their prices, and, even when they had begun their work, spent upon it, not two hours, but five and a half. Meanwhile he had the satisfaction of experiencing that delightful time with which all travellers are familiar—namely, the time during which one sits in a room where, except for a litter of string, waste paper, and so forth, everything else has been packed. But to all things there comes an end, and there arrived also the long-awaited moment when the britchka had received the luggage, the faulty wheel had been fitted with a new tyre, the horses had been re-shod, and the predatory blacksmiths had departed with their gains. "Thank God!" thought Chichikov as the britchka rolled out of the gates of the inn, and the vehicle began to jolt over the cobblestones. Yet a feeling which he could not altogether have defined filled his breast as he gazed upon the houses and the streets and the garden walls which he might never see again. Presently, on turning a corner, the britchka was brought to a halt through the fact that along the street there was filing a seemingly endless funeral procession. Leaning forward in his britchka, Chichikov asked Petrushka whose obsequies the procession represented, and was told that they represented those of the Public Prosecutor. Disagreeably shocked, our hero hastened to raise the hood of the vehicle, to draw the curtains across the windows, and to lean back into a corner. While the britchka remained thus halted Selifan and Petrushka, their caps doffed, sat watching the progress of the cortege, after they had received strict instructions not to greet any fellow-servant whom they might recognise. Behind the hearse walked the whole body of tchinovniks, bare-headed; and though, for a moment or two, Chichikov feared that some of their number might discern him in his britchka, he need not have disturbed himself, since their attention was otherwise engaged. In fact, they were not even exchanging the small talk customary among members of such processions, but thinking exclusively of their own affairs, of the advent of the new Governor-General, and of the probable manner in which he would take up the reins of administration. Next came a number of carriages, from the windows of which peered the ladies in mourning toilets. Yet the movements of their hands and lips made it evident that they were indulging in animated conversation—probably about the Governor-General, the balls which he might be expected to give, and their own eternal fripperies and gewgaws. Lastly came a few empty drozhkis. As soon as the latter had passed, our hero was able to continue on his way. Throwing back the hood of the britchka, he said to himself:

"Ah, good friend, you have lived your life, and now it is over! In the newspapers they will say of you that you died regretted not only by your subordinates, but also by humanity at large, as well as that, a respected citizen, a kind father, and a husband beyond reproach, you went to your grave amid the tears of your widow and orphans. Yet, should those journals be put to it to name any particular circumstance which justified this eulogy of you, they would be forced to fall back upon the fact that you grew a pair of exceptionally thick eyebrows!"

With that Chichikov bid Selifan quicken his pace, and concluded: "After all, it is as well that I encountered the procession, for they say that to meet a funeral is lucky."

Presently the britchka turned into some less frequented streets, lines of wooden fencing of the kind which mark the outskirts of a town began to file by, the cobblestones came to an end, the macadam of the highroad succeeded to them, and once more there began on either side of the turnpike a procession of verst stones, road menders, and grey villages; inns with samovars and peasant women and landlords who came running out of yards with seivefuls of oats; pedestrians in worn shoes which, it might be, had covered eight hundred versts; little towns, bright with booths for the sale of flour in barrels, boots, small loaves, and other trifles; heaps of slag; much repaired bridges; expanses of field to right and to left; stout landowners; a mounted soldier bearing a green, iron-clamped box inscribed: "The—th Battery of Artillery"; long strips of freshly-tilled earth which gleamed green, yellow, and black on the face of the countryside. With it mingled long-drawn singing, glimpses of elm-tops amid mist, the far-off notes of bells, endless clouds of rocks, and the illimitable line of the horizon.

Ah, Russia, Russia, from my beautiful home in a strange land I can still see you! In you everything is poor and disordered and unhomely; in you the eye is neither cheered nor dismayed by temerities of nature which a yet more temerarious art has conquered; in you one beholds no cities with lofty, many-windowed mansions, lofty as crags, no picturesque trees, no ivy-clad ruins, no waterfalls with their everlasting spray and roar, no beetling precipices which confuse the brain with their stony immensity, no vistas of vines and ivy and millions of wild roses and ageless lines of blue hills which look almost unreal against the clear, silvery background of the sky. In you everything is flat and open; your towns project like points or signals from smooth levels of plain, and nothing whatsoever enchants or deludes the eye. Yet what secret, what invincible force draws me to you? Why does there ceaselessly echo and re-echo in my ears the sad song which hovers throughout the length and the breadth of your borders? What is the burden of that song? Why does it wail and sob and catch at my heart? What say the notes which thus painfully caress and embrace my soul, and flit, uttering their lamentations, around me? What is it you seek of me, O Russia? What is the hidden bond which subsists between us? Why do you regard me as you do? Why does everything within you turn upon me eyes full of yearning? Even at this moment, as I stand dumbly, fixedly, perplexedly contemplating your vastness, a menacing cloud, charged with gathering rain, seems to overshadow my head. What is it that your boundless expanses presage? Do they not presage that one day there will arise in you ideas as boundless as yourself? Do they not presage that one day you too will know no limits? Do they not presage that one day, when again you shall have room for their exploits, there will spring to life the heroes of old? How the power of your immensity enfolds me, and reverberates through all my being with a wild, strange spell, and flashes in my eyes with an almost supernatural radiance! Yes, a strange, brilliant, unearthly vista indeed do you disclose, O Russia, country of mine!

"Stop, stop, you fool!" shouted Chichikov to Selifan; and even as he spoke a troika, bound on Government business, came chattering by, and disappeared in a cloud of dust. To Chichikov's curses at Selifan for not having drawn out of the way with more alacrity a rural constable with moustaches of the length of an arshin added his quota.

What a curious and attractive, yet also what an unreal, fascination the term "highway" connotes! And how interesting for its own sake is a highway! Should the day be a fine one (though chilly) in mellowing autumn, press closer your travelling cloak, and draw down your cap over your ears, and snuggle cosily, comfortably into a corner of the britchka before a last shiver shall course through your limbs, and the ensuing warmth shall put to flight the autumnal cold and damp. As the horses gallop on their way, how delightfully will drowsiness come stealing upon you, and make your eyelids droop! For a while, through your somnolence, you will continue to hear the hard breathing of the team and the rumbling of the wheels; but at length, sinking back into your corner, you will relapse into the stage of snoring. And when you awake—behold! you will find that five stages have slipped away, and that the moon is shining, and that you have reached a strange town of churches and old wooden cupolas and blackened spires and white, half-timbered houses! And as the moonlight glints hither and thither, almost you will believe that the walls and the streets and the pavements of the place are spread with sheets—sheets shot with coal-black shadows which make the wooden roofs look all the brighter under the slanting beams of the pale luminary. Nowhere is a soul to be seen, for every one is plunged in slumber. Yet no. In a solitary window a light is flickering where some good burgher is mending his boots, or a baker drawing a batch of dough. O night and powers of heaven, how perfect is the blackness of your infinite vault—how lofty, how remote its inaccessible depths where it lies spread in an intangible, yet audible, silence! Freshly does the lulling breath of night blow in your face, until once more you relapse into snoring oblivion, and your poor neighbour turns angrily in his corner as he begins to be conscious of your weight. Then again you awake, but this time to find yourself confronted with only fields and steppes. Everywhere in the ascendant is the desolation of space. But suddenly the ciphers on a verst stone leap to the eye! Morning is rising, and on the chill, gradually paling line of the horizon you can see gleaming a faint gold streak. The wind freshens and grows keener, and you snuggle closer in your cloak; yet how glorious is that freshness, and how marvellous the sleep in which once again you become enfolded! A jolt!—and for the last time you return to consciousness. By now the sun is high in the heavens, and you hear a voice cry "gently, gently!" as a farm waggon issues from a by-road. Below, enclosed within an ample dike, stretches a sheet of water which glistens like copper in the sunlight. Beyond, on the side of a slope, lie some scattered peasants' huts, a manor house, and, flanking the latter, a village church with its cross flashing like a star. There also comes wafted to your ear the sound of peasants' laughter, while in your inner man you are becoming conscious of an appetite which is not to be withstood.

Oh long-drawn highway, how excellent you are! How often have I in weariness and despondency set forth upon your length, and found in you salvation and rest! How often, as I followed your leading, have I been visited with wonderful thoughts and poetic dreams and curious, wild impressions!

At this moment our friend Chichikov also was experiencing visions of a not wholly prosaic nature. Let us peep into his soul and share them. At first he remained unconscious of anything whatsoever, for he was too much engaged in making sure that he was really clear of the town; but as soon as he saw that it had completely disappeared, with its mills and factories and other urban appurtenances, and that even the steeples of the white stone churches had sunk below the horizon, he turned his attention to the road, and the town of N. vanished from his thoughts as completely as though he had not seen it since childhood. Again, in its turn, the road ceased to interest him, and he began to close his eyes and to loll his head against the cushions. Of this let the author take advantage, in order to speak at length concerning his hero; since hitherto he (the author) has been prevented from so doing by Nozdrev and balls and ladies and local intrigues—by those thousand trifles which seem trifles only when they are introduced into a book, but which, in life, figure as affairs of importance. Let us lay them aside, and betake ourselves to business.

Whether the character whom I have selected for my hero has pleased my readers is, of course, exceedingly doubtful. At all events the ladies will have failed to approve him for the fair sex demands in a hero perfection, and, should there be the least mental or physical stain on him—well, woe betide! Yes, no matter how profoundly the author may probe that hero's soul, no matter how clearly he may portray his figure as in a mirror, he will be given no credit for the achievement. Indeed, Chichikov's very stoutness and plenitude of years may have militated against him, for never is a hero pardoned for the former, and the majority of ladies will, in such case, turn away, and mutter to themselves: "Phew! What a beast!" Yes, the author is well aware of this. Yet, though he could not, to save his life, take a person of virtue for his principal character, it may be that this story contains themes never before selected, and that in it there projects the whole boundless wealth of Russian psychology; that it portrays, as well as Chichikov, the peasant who is gifted with the virtues which God has sent him, and the marvellous maiden of Russia who has not her like in all the world for her beautiful feminine spirituality, the roots of which lie buried in noble aspirations and boundless self-denial. In fact, compared with these types, the virtuous of other races seem lifeless, as does an inanimate volume when compared with the living word. Yes, each time that there arises in Russia a movement of thought, it becomes clear that the movement sinks deep into the Slavonic nature where it would but have skimmed the surface of other nations.—But why am I talking like this? Whither am I tending? It is indeed shameful that an author who long ago reached man's estate, and was brought up to a course of severe introspection and sober, solitary self-enlightenment, should give way to such jejune wandering from the point. To everything its proper time and place and turn. As I was saying, it does not lie in me to take a virtuous character for my hero: and I will tell you why. It is because it is high time that a rest were given to the "poor, but virtuous" individual; it is because the phrase "a man of worth" has grown into a by-word; it is because the "man of worth" has become converted into a horse, and there is not a writer but rides him and flogs him, in and out of season; it is because the "man of worth" has been starved until he has not a shred of his virtue left, and all that remains of his body is but the ribs and the hide; it is because the "man of worth" is for ever being smuggled upon the scene; it is because the "man of worth" has at length forfeited every one's respect. For these reasons do I reaffirm that it is high time to yoke a rascal to the shafts. Let us yoke that rascal.

Our hero's beginnings were both modest and obscure. True, his parents were dvoriane, but he in no way resembled them. At all events, a short, squab female relative who was present at his birth exclaimed as she lifted up the baby: "He is altogether different from what I had expected him to be. He ought to have taken after his maternal grandmother, whereas he has been born, as the proverb has it, 'like not father nor mother, but like a chance passer-by.'" Thus from the first life regarded the little Chichikov with sour distaste, and as through a dim, frost-encrusted window. A tiny room with diminutive casements which were never opened, summer or winter; an invalid father in a dressing-gown lined with lambskin, and with an ailing foot swathed in bandages—a man who was continually drawing deep breaths, and walking up and down the room, and spitting into a sandbox; a period of perpetually sitting on a bench with pen in hand and ink on lips and fingers; a period of being eternally confronted with the copy-book maxim, "Never tell a lie, but obey your superiors, and cherish virtue in your heart;" an everlasting scraping and shuffling of slippers up and down the room; a period of continually hearing a well-known, strident voice exclaim: "So you have been playing the fool again!" at times when the child, weary of the mortal monotony of his task, had added a superfluous embellishment to his copy; a period of experiencing the ever-familiar, but ever-unpleasant, sensation which ensued upon those words as the boy's ear was painfully twisted between two long fingers bent backwards at the tips— such is the miserable picture of that youth of which, in later life, Chichikov preserved but the faintest of memories! But in this world everything is liable to swift and sudden change; and, one day in early spring, when the rivers had melted, the father set forth with his little son in a teliezshka 37 drawn by a sorrel steed of the kind known to horsy folk as a soroka, and having as coachman the diminutive hunchback who, father of the only serf family belonging to the elder Chichikov, served as general factotum in the Chichikov establishment. For a day and a half the soroka conveyed them on their way; during which time they spent the night at a roadside inn, crossed a river, dined off cold pie and roast mutton, and eventually arrived at the county town. To the lad the streets presented a spectacle of unwonted brilliancy, and he gaped with amazement. Turning into a side alley wherein the mire necessitated both the most strenuous exertions on the soroka's part and the most vigorous castigation on the part of the driver and the barin, the conveyance eventually reached the gates of a courtyard which, combined with a small fruit garden containing various bushes, a couple of apple-trees in blossom, and a mean, dirty little shed, constituted the premises attached to an antiquated-looking villa. Here there lived a relative of the Chichikovs, a wizened old lady who went to market in person and dried her stockings at the samovar. On seeing the boy, she patted his cheek and expressed satisfaction at his physique; whereupon the fact became disclosed that here he was to abide for a while, for the purpose of attending a local school. After a night's rest his father prepared to betake himself homeward again; but no tears marked the parting between him and his son, he merely gave the lad a copper or two and (a far more important thing) the following injunctions. "See here, my boy. Do your lessons well, do not idle or play the fool, and above all things, see that you please your teachers. So long as you observe these rules you will make progress, and surpass your fellows, even if God shall have denied you brains, and you should fail in your studies. Also, do not consort overmuch with your comrades, for they will do you no good; but, should you do so, then make friends with the richer of them, since one day they may be useful to you. Also, never entertain or treat any one, but see that every one entertains and treats YOU. Lastly, and above all else, keep and save your every kopeck. To save money is the most important thing in life. Always a friend or a comrade may fail you, and be the first to desert you in a time of adversity; but never will a KOPECK fail you, whatever may be your plight. Nothing in the world cannot be done, cannot be attained, with the aid of money." These injunctions given, the father embraced his son, and set forth on his return; and though the son never again beheld his parent, the latter's words and precepts sank deep into the little Chichikov's soul.

The next day young Pavlushka made his first attendance at school. But no special aptitude in any branch of learning did he display. Rather, his distinguishing characteristics were diligence and neatness. On the other hand, he developed great intelligence as regards the PRACTICAL aspect of life. In a trice he divined and comprehended how things ought to be worked, and, from that time forth, bore himself towards his school-fellows in such a way that, though they frequently gave him presents, he not only never returned the compliment, but even on occasions pocketed the gifts for the mere purpose of selling them again. Also, boy though he was, he acquired the art of self-denial. Of the trifle which his father had given him on parting he spent not a kopeck, but, the same year, actually added to his little store by fashioning a bullfinch of wax, painting it, and selling the same at a handsome profit. Next, as time went on, he engaged in other speculations—in particular, in the scheme of buying up eatables, taking his seat in class beside boys who had plenty of pocket-money, and, as soon as such opulent individuals showed signs of failing attention (and, therefore, of growing appetite), tendering them, from beneath the desk, a roll of pudding or a piece of gingerbread, and charging according to degree of appetite and size of portion. He also spent a couple of months in training a mouse, which he kept confined in a little wooden cage in his bedroom.

At length, when the training had reached the point that, at the several words of command, the mouse would stand upon its hind legs, lie down, and get up again, he sold the creature for a respectable sum. Thus, in time, his gains attained the amount of five roubles; whereupon he made himself a purse and then started to fill a second receptacle of the kind. Still more studied was his attitude towards the authorities. No one could sit more quietly in his place on the bench than he. In the same connection it may be remarked that his teacher was a man who, above all things, loved peace and good behaviour, and simply could not abide clever, witty boys, since he suspected them of laughing at him. Consequently any lad who had once attracted the master's attention with a manifestation of intelligence needed but to shuffle in his place, or unintentionally to twitch an eyebrow, for the said master at once to burst into a rage, to turn the supposed offender out of the room, and to visit him with unmerciful punishment. "Ah, my fine fellow," he would say, "I'LL cure you of your impudence and want of respect! I know you through and through far better than you know yourself, and will take good care that you have to go down upon your knees and curb your appetite." Whereupon the wretched lad would, for no cause of which he was aware, be forced to wear out his breeches on the floor and go hungry for days. "Talents and gifts," the schoolmaster would declare, "are so much rubbish. I respect only good behaviour, and shall award full marks to those who conduct themselves properly, even if they fail to learn a single letter of their alphabet: whereas to those in whom I may perceive a tendency to jocularity I shall award nothing, even though they should outdo Solon himself." For the same reason he had no great love of the author Krylov, in that the latter says in one of his Fables: "In my opinion, the more one sings, the better one works;" and often the pedagogue would relate how, in a former school of his, the silence had been such that a fly could be heard buzzing on the wing, and for the space of a whole year not a single pupil sneezed or coughed in class, and so complete was the absence of all sound that no one could have told that there was a soul in the place. Of this mentor young Chichikov speedily appraised the mentality; wherefore he fashioned his behaviour to correspond with it. Not an eyelid, not an eyebrow, would he stir during school hours, howsoever many pinches he might receive from behind; and only when the bell rang would he run to anticipate his fellows in handing the master the three-cornered cap which that dignitary customarily sported, and then to be the first to leave the class-room, and contrive to meet the master not less than two or three times as the latter walked homeward, in order that, on each occasion, he might doff his cap. And the scheme proved entirely successful. Throughout the period of his attendance at school he was held in high favour, and, on leaving the establishment, received full marks for every subject, as well as a diploma and a book inscribed (in gilt letters) "For Exemplary Diligence and the Perfection of Good Conduct." By this time he had grown into a fairly good-looking youth of the age when the chin first calls for a razor; and at about the same period his father died, leaving behind him, as his estate, four waistcoats completely worn out, two ancient frockcoats, and a small sum of money. Apparently he had been skilled only in RECOMMENDING the saving of kopecks—not in ACTUALLY PRACTISING the art. Upon that Chichikov sold the old house and its little parcel of land for a thousand roubles, and removed, with his one serf and the serf's family, to the capital, where he set about organising a new establishment and entering the Civil Service. Simultaneously with his doing so, his old schoolmaster lost (through stupidity or otherwise) the establishment over which he had hitherto presided, and in which he had set so much store by silence and good behaviour. Grief drove him to drink, and when nothing was left, even for that purpose, he retired—ill, helpless, and starving—into a broken-down, cheerless hovel. But certain of his former pupils—the same clever, witty lads whom he had once been wont to accuse of impertinence and evil conduct generally—heard of his pitiable plight, and collected for him what money they could, even to the point of selling their own necessaries. Only Chichikov, when appealed to, pleaded inability, and compromised with a contribution of a single piatak 38: which his old schoolfellows straightway returned him—full in the face, and accompanied with a shout of "Oh, you skinflint!" As for the poor schoolmaster, when he heard what his former pupils had done, he buried his face in his hands, and the tears gushed from his failing eyes as from those of a helpless infant. "God has brought you but to weep over my death-bed," he murmured feebly; and added with a profound sigh, on hearing of Chichikov's conduct: "Ah, Pavlushka, how a human being may become changed! Once you were a good lad, and gave me no trouble; but now you are become proud indeed!"

Yet let it not be inferred from this that our hero's character had grown so blase and hard, or his conscience so blunted, as to preclude his experiencing a particle of sympathy or compassion. As a matter of fact, he was capable both of the one and the other, and would have been glad to assist his old teacher had no great sum been required, or had he not been called upon to touch the fund which he had decided should remain intact. In other words, the father's injunction, "Guard and save every kopeck," had become a hard and fast rule of the son's. Yet the youth had no particular attachment to money for money's sake; he was not possessed with the true instinct for hoarding and niggardliness. Rather, before his eyes there floated ever a vision of life and its amenities and advantages—a vision of carriages and an elegantly furnished house and recherche dinners; and it was in the hope that some day he might attain these things that he saved every kopeck and, meanwhile, stinted both himself and others. Whenever a rich man passed him by in a splendid drozhki drawn by swift and handsomely-caparisoned horses, he would halt as though deep in thought, and say to himself, like a man awakening from a long sleep: "That gentleman must have been a financier, he has so little hair on his brow." In short, everything connected with wealth and plenty produced upon him an ineffaceable impression. Even when he left school he took no holiday, so strong in him was the desire to get to work and enter the Civil Service. Yet, for all the encomiums contained in his diploma, he had much ado to procure a nomination to a Government Department; and only after a long time was a minor post found for him, at a salary of thirty or forty roubles a year. Nevertheless, wretched though this appointment was, he determined, by strict attention to business, to overcome all obstacles, and to win success. And, indeed, the self-denial, the patience, and the economy which he displayed were remarkable. From early morn until late at night he would, with indefatigable zeal of body and mind, remain immersed in his sordid task of copying official documents— never going home, snatching what sleep he could on tables in the building, and dining with the watchman on duty. Yet all the while he contrived to remain clean and neat, to preserve a cheerful expression of countenance, and even to cultivate a certain elegance of movement. In passing, it may be remarked that his fellow tchinovniks were a peculiarly plain, unsightly lot, some of them having faces like badly baked bread, swollen cheeks, receding chins, and cracked and blistered upper lips. Indeed, not a man of them was handsome. Also, their tone of voice always contained a note of sullenness, as though they had a mind to knock some one on the head; and by their frequent sacrifices to Bacchus they showed that even yet there remains in the Slavonic nature a certain element of paganism. Nay, the Director's room itself they would invade while still licking their lips, and since their breath was not over-aromatic, the atmosphere of the room grew not over-pleasant. Naturally, among such an official staff a man like Chichikov could not fail to attract attention and remark, since in everything—in cheerfulness of demeanour, in suavity of voice, and in complete neglect of the use of strong potions—he was the absolute antithesis of his companions. Yet his path was not an easy one to tread, for over him he had the misfortune to have placed in authority a Chief Clerk who was a graven image of elderly insensibility and inertia. Always the same, always unapproachable, this functionary could never in his life have smiled or asked civilly after an acquaintance's health. Nor had any one ever seen him a whit different in the street or at his own home from what he was in the office, or showing the least interest in anything whatever, or getting drunk and relapsing into jollity in his cups, or indulging in that species of wild gaiety which, when intoxicated, even a burglar affects. No, not a particle of this was there in him. Nor, for that matter, was there in him a particle of anything at all, whether good or bad: which complete negativeness of character produced rather a strange effect. In the same way, his wizened, marble-like features reminded one of nothing in particular, so primly proportioned were they. Only the numerous pockmarks and dimples with which they were pitted placed him among the number of those over whose faces, to quote the popular saying, "The Devil has walked by night to grind peas." In short, it would seem that no human agency could have approached such a man and gained his goodwill. Yet Chichikov made the effort. As a first step, he took to consulting the other's convenience in all manner of insignificant trifles—to cleaning his pens carefully, and, when they had been prepared exactly to the Chief Clerk's liking, laying them ready at his elbow; to dusting and sweeping from his table all superfluous sand and tobacco ash; to procuring a new mat for his inkstand; to looking for his hat—the meanest-looking hat that ever the world beheld—and having it ready for him at the exact moment when business came to an end; to brushing his back if it happened to become smeared with whitewash from a wall. Yet all this passed as unnoticed as though it had never been done. Finally, Chichikov sniffed into his superior's family and domestic life, and learnt that he possessed a grown-up daughter on whose face also there had taken place a nocturnal, diabolical grinding of peas. HERE was a quarter whence a fresh attack might be delivered! After ascertaining what church the daughter attended on Sundays, our hero took to contriving to meet her in a neat suit and a well-starched dickey: and soon the scheme began to work. The surly Chief Clerk wavered for a while; then ended by inviting Chichikov to tea. Nor could any man in the office have told you how it came about that before long Chichikov had removed to the Chief Clerk's house, and become a person necessary—indeed indispensable—to the household, seeing that he bought the flour and the sugar, treated the daughter as his betrothed, called the Chief Clerk "Papenka," and occasionally kissed "Papenka's" hand. In fact, every one at the office supposed that, at the end of February (i.e. before the beginning of Lent) there would take place a wedding. Nay, the surly father even began to agitate with the authorities on Chichikov's behalf, and so enabled our hero, on a vacancy occurring, to attain the stool of a Chief Clerk. Apparently this marked the consummation of Chichikov's relations with his host, for he hastened stealthily to pack his trunk and, the next day, figured in a fresh lodging. Also, he ceased to call the Chief Clerk "Papenka," or to kiss his hand; and the matter of the wedding came to as abrupt a termination as though it had never been mooted. Yet also he never failed to press his late host's hand, whenever he met him, and to invite him to tea; while, on the other hand, for all his immobility and dry indifference, the Chief Clerk never failed to shake his head with a muttered, "Ah, my fine fellow, you have grown too proud, you have grown too proud."

The foregoing constituted the most difficult step that our hero had to negotiate. Thereafter things came with greater ease and swifter success. Everywhere he attracted notice, for he developed within himself everything necessary for this world—namely, charm of manner and bearing, and great diligence in business matters. Armed with these resources, he next obtained promotion to what is known as "a fat post," and used it to the best advantage; and even though, at that period, strict inquiry had begun to be made into the whole subject of bribes, such inquiry failed to alarm him—nay, he actually turned it to account and thereby manifested the Russian resourcefulness which never fails to attain its zenith where extortion is concerned. His method of working was the following. As soon as a petitioner or a suitor put his hand into his pocket, to extract thence the necessary letters of recommendation for signature, Chichikov would smilingly exclaim as he detained his interlocutor's hand: "No, no! Surely you do not think that I—? But no, no! It is our duty, it is our obligation, and we do not require rewards for doing our work properly. So far as YOUR matter is concerned, you may rest easy. Everything shall be carried through tomorrow. But may I have your address? There is no need to trouble yourself, seeing that the documents can easily be brought to you at your residence." Upon which the delighted suitor would return home in raptures, thinking: "Here, at long last, is the sort of man so badly needed. A man of that kind is a jewel beyond price." Yet for a day, for two days—nay, even for three— the suitor would wait in vain so far as any messengers with documents were concerned. Then he would repair to the office—to find that his business had not so much as been entered upon! Lastly, he would confront the "jewel beyond price." "Oh, pardon me, pardon me!" Chichikov would exclaim in the politest of tones as he seized and grasped the visitor's hands. "The truth is that we have SUCH a quantity of business on hand! But the matter shall be put through to-morrow, and in the meanwhile I am most sorry about it." And with this would go the most fascinating of gestures. Yet neither on the morrow, nor on the day following, nor on the third would documents arrive at the suitor's abode. Upon that he would take thought as to whether something more ought not to have been done; and, sure enough, on his making inquiry, he would be informed that "something will have to be given to the copyists." "Well, there can be no harm in that," he would reply. "As a matter of fact, I have ready a tchetvertak 39 or two." "Oh, no, no," the answer would come. "Not a tchetvertak per copyist, but a rouble, is the fee." "What? A rouble per copyist?" "Certainly. What is there to grumble at in that? Of the money the copyists will receive a tchetvertak apiece, and the rest will go to the Government." Upon that the disillusioned suitor would fly out upon the new order of things brought about by the inquiry into illicit fees, and curse both the tchinovniks and their uppish, insolent behaviour. "Once upon a time," would the suitor lament, "one DID know what to do. Once one had tipped the Director a bank-note, one's affair was, so to speak, in the hat. But now one has to pay a rouble per copyist after waiting a week because otherwise it was impossible to guess how the wind might set! The devil fly away with all 'disinterested' and 'trustworthy' tchinovniks!" And certainly the aggrieved suitor had reason to grumble, seeing that, now that bribe-takers had ceased to exist, and Directors had uniformly become men of honour and integrity, secretaries and clerks ought not with impunity to have continued their thievish ways. In time there opened out to Chichikov a still wider field, for a Commission was appointed to supervise the erection of a Government building, and, on his being nominated to that body, he proved himself one of its most active members. The Commission got to work without delay, but for a space of six years had some trouble with the building in question. Either the climate hindered operations or the materials used were of the kind which prevents official edifices from ever rising higher than the basement. But, meanwhile, OTHER quarters of the town saw arise, for each member of the Commission, a handsome house of the NON-official style of architecture. Clearly the foundation afforded by the soil of those parts was better than that where the Government building was still engaged in hanging fire! Likewise the members of the Commission began to look exceedingly prosperous, and to blossom out into family life; and, for the first time in his existence, even Chichikov also departed from the iron laws of his self-imposed restraint and inexorable self-denial, and so far mitigated his heretofore asceticism as to show himself a man not averse to those amenities which, during his youth, he had been capable of renouncing. That is to say, certain superfluities began to make their appearance in his establishment. He engaged a good cook, took to wearing linen shirts, bought for himself cloth of a pattern worn by no one else in the province, figured in checks shot with the brightest of reds and browns, fitted himself out with two splendid horses (which he drove with a single pair of reins, added to a ring attachment for the trace horse), developed a habit of washing with a sponge dipped in eau-de-Cologne, and invested in soaps of the most expensive quality, in order to communicate to his skin a more elegant polish.

But suddenly there appeared upon the scene a new Director—a military man, and a martinet as regarded his hostility to bribe-takers and anything which might be called irregular. On the very day after his arrival he struck fear into every breast by calling for accounts, discovering hosts of deficits and missing sums, and directing his attention to the aforesaid fine houses of civilian architecture. Upon that there ensued a complete reshuffling.

Tchinovniks were retired wholesale, and the houses were sequestrated to the Government, or else converted into various pious institutions and schools for soldiers' children. Thus the whole fabric, and especially Chichikov, came crashing to the ground. Particularly did our hero's agreeable face displease the new Director. Why that was so it is impossible to say, but frequently, in cases of the kind, no reason exists. However, the Director conceived a mortal dislike to him, and also extended that enmity to the whole of Chichikov's colleagues. But inasmuch as the said Director was a military man, he was not fully acquainted with the myriad subtleties of the civilian mind; wherefore it was not long before, by dint of maintaining a discreet exterior, added to a faculty for humouring all and sundry, a fresh gang of tchinovniks succeeded in restoring him to mildness, and the General found himself in the hands of greater thieves than before, but thieves whom he did not even suspect, seeing that he believed himself to have selected men fit and proper, and even ventured to boast of possessing a keen eye for talent. In a trice the tchinovniks concerned appraised his spirit and character; with the result that the entire sphere over which he ruled became an agency for the detection of irregularities. Everywhere, and in every case, were those irregularities pursued as a fisherman pursues a fat sturgeon with a gaff; and to such an extent did the sport prove successful that almost in no time each participant in the hunt was seen to be in possession of several thousand roubles of capital. Upon that a large number of the former band of tchinovniks also became converted to paths of rectitude, and were allowed to re-enter the Service; but not by hook or by crook could Chichikov worm his way back, even though, incited thereto by sundry items of paper currency, the General's first secretary and principal bear leader did all he could on our hero's behalf. It seemed that the General was the kind of man who, though easily led by the nose (provided it was done without his knowledge) no sooner got an idea into his head than it stuck there like a nail, and could not possibly be extracted; and all that the wily secretary succeeded in procuring was the tearing up of a certain dirty fragment of paper—even that being effected only by an appeal to the General's compassion, on the score of the unhappy fate which, otherwise, would befall Chichikov's wife and children (who, luckily, had no existence in fact).

"Well," said Chichikov to himself, "I have done my best, and now everything has failed. Lamenting my misfortune won't help me, but only action." And with that he decided to begin his career anew, and once more to arm himself with the weapons of patience and self-denial. The better to effect this, he had, of course to remove to another town. Yet somehow, for a while, things miscarried. More than once he found himself forced to exchange one post for another, and at the briefest of notice; and all of them were posts of the meanest, the most wretched, order. Yet, being a man of the utmost nicety of feeling, the fact that he found himself rubbing shoulders with anything but nice companions did not prevent him from preserving intact his innate love of what was decent and seemly, or from cherishing the instinct which led him to hanker after office fittings of lacquered wood, with neatness and orderliness everywhere. Nor did he at any time permit a foul word to creep into his speech, and would feel hurt even if in the speech of others there occurred a scornful reference to anything which pertained to rank and dignity. Also, the reader will be pleased to know that our hero changed his linen every other day, and in summer, when the weather was very hot, EVERY day, seeing that the very faintest suspicion of an unpleasant odour offended his fastidiousness. For the same reason it was his custom, before being valeted by Petrushka, always to plug his nostrils with a couple of cloves. In short, there were many occasions when his nerves suffered rackings as cruel as a young girl's, and so helped to increase his disgust at having once more to associate with men who set no store by the decencies of life. Yet, though he braced himself to the task, this period of adversity told upon his health, and he even grew a trifle shabby. More than once, on happening to catch sight of himself in the mirror, he could not forbear exclaiming: "Holy Mother of God, but what a nasty-looking brute I have become!" and for a long while afterwards could not with anything like sang-froid contemplate his reflection. Yet throughout he bore up stoutly and patiently—and ended by being transferred to the Customs Department. It may be said that the department had long constituted the secret goal of his ambition, for he had noted the foreign elegancies with which its officials always contrived to provide themselves, and had also observed that invariably they were able to send presents of china and cambric to their sisters and aunts—well, to their lady friends generally. Yes, more than once he had said to himself with a sigh: "THAT is the department to which I ought to belong, for, given a town near the frontier, and a sensible set of colleagues, I might be able to fit myself out with excellent linen shirts." Also, it may be said that most frequently of all had his thoughts turned towards a certain quality of French soap which imparted a peculiar whiteness to the skin and a peerless freshness to the cheeks. Its name is known to God alone, but at least it was to be procured only in the immediate neighbourhood of the frontier. So, as I say, Chichikov had long felt a leaning towards the Customs, but for a time had been restrained from applying for the same by the various current advantages of the Building Commission; since rightly he had adjudged the latter to constitute a bird in the hand, and the former to constitute only a bird in the bush. But now he decided that, come what might, into the Customs he must make his way. And that way he made, and then applied himself to his new duties with a zeal born of the fact that he realised that fortune had specially marked him out for a Customs officer. Indeed, such activity, perspicuity, and ubiquity as his had never been seen or thought of. Within four weeks at the most he had so thoroughly got his hand in that he was conversant with Customs procedure in every detail. Not only could he weigh and measure, but also he could divine from an invoice how many arshins of cloth or other material a given piece contained, and then, taking a roll of the latter in his hand, could specify at once the number of pounds at which it would tip the scale. As for searchings, well, even his colleagues had to admit that he possessed the nose of a veritable bloodhound, and that it was impossible not to marvel at the patience wherewith he would try every button of the suspected person, yet preserve, throughout, a deadly politeness and an icy sang-froid which surpass belief. And while the searched were raging, and foaming at the mouth, and feeling that they would give worlds to alter his smiling exterior with a good, resounding slap, he would move not a muscle of his face, nor abate by a jot the urbanity of his demeanour, as he murmured, "Do you mind so far incommoding yourself as to stand up?" or "Pray step into the next room, madam, where the wife of one of our staff will attend you," or "Pray allow me to slip this penknife of mine into the lining of your coat" (after which he would extract thence shawls and towels with as much nonchalance as he would have done from his own travelling-trunk). Even his superiors acknowledged him to be a devil at the job, rather than a human being, so perfect was his instinct for looking into cart-wheels, carriage-poles, horses' ears, and places whither an author ought not to penetrate even in thought—places whither only a

Customs official is permitted to go. The result was that the wretched traveller who had just crossed the frontier would, within a few minutes, become wholly at sea, and, wiping away the perspiration, and breaking out into body flushes, would be reduced to crossing himself and muttering, "Well, well, well!" In fact, such a traveller would feel in the position of a schoolboy who, having been summoned to the presence of the headmaster for the ostensible purpose of being given an order, has found that he receives, instead, a sound flogging. In short, for some time Chichikov made it impossible for smugglers to earn a living. In particular, he reduced Polish Jewry almost to despair, so invincible, so almost unnatural, was the rectitude, the incorruptibility which led him to refrain from converting himself into a small capitalist with the aid of confiscated goods and articles which, "to save excessive clerical labour," had failed to be handed over to the Government. Also, without saying it goes that such phenomenally zealous and disinterested service attracted general astonishment, and, eventually, the notice of the authorities; whereupon he received promotion, and followed that up by mooting a scheme for the infallible detection of contrabandists, provided that he could be furnished with the necessary authority for carrying out the same. At once such authority was accorded him, as also unlimited power to conduct every species of search and investigation. And that was all he wanted. It happened that previously there had been formed a well-found association for smuggling on regular, carefully prepared lines, and that this daring scheme seemed to promise profit to the extent of some millions of money: yet, though he had long had knowledge of it, Chichikov had said to the association's emissaries, when sent to buy him over, "The time is not yet." But now that he had got all the reins into his hands, he sent word of the fact to the gang, and with it the remark, "The time is NOW." Nor was he wrong in his calculations, for, within the space of a year, he had acquired what he could not have made during twenty years of non-fraudulent service. With similar sagacity he had, during his early days in the department, declined altogether to enter into relations with the association, for the reason that he had then been a mere cipher, and would have come in for nothing large in the way of takings; but now—well, now it was another matter altogether, and he could dictate what terms he liked. Moreover, that the affair might progress the more smoothly, he suborned a fellow tchinovnik of the type which, in spite of grey hairs, stands powerless against temptation; and, the contract concluded, the association duly proceeded to business. Certainly business began brilliantly. But probably most of my readers are familiar with the oft-repeated story of the passage of Spanish sheep across the frontier in double fleeces which carried between their outer layers and their inner enough lace of Brabant to sell to the tune of millions of roubles; wherefore I will not recount the story again beyond saying that those journeys took place just when Chichikov had become head of the Customs, and that, had he not a hand in the enterprise, not all the Jews in the world could have brought it to success. By the time that three or four of these ovine invasions had taken place, Chichikov and his accomplice had come to be the possessors of four hundred thousand roubles apiece; while some even aver that the former's gains totalled half a million, owing to the greater industry which he had displayed in the matter. Nor can any one but God say to what a figure the fortunes of the pair might not eventually have attained, had not an awkward contretemps cut right across their arrangements. That is to say, for some reason or another the devil so far deprived these tchinovnik-conspirators of sense as to make them come to words with one another, and then to engage in a quarrel. Beginning with a heated argument, this quarrel reached the point of Chichikov—who was, possibly, a trifle tipsy—calling his colleague a priest's son; and though that description of the person so addressed was perfectly accurate, he chose to take offence, and to answer Chichikov with the words (loudly and incisively uttered), "It is YOU who have a priest for your father," and to add to that (the more to incense his companion), "Yes, mark you! THAT is how it is." Yet, though he had thus turned the tables upon Chichikov with a tu quoque, and then capped that exploit with the words last quoted, the offended tchinovnik could not remain satisfied, but went on to send in an anonymous document to the authorities. On the other hand, some aver that it was over a woman that the pair fell out—over a woman who, to quote the phrase then current among the staff of the Customs Department, was "as fresh and as strong as the pulp of a turnip," and that night-birds were hired to assault our hero in a dark alley, and that the scheme miscarried, and that in any case both Chichikov and his friend had been deceived, seeing that the person to whom the lady had really accorded her favours was a certain staff-captain named Shamsharev. However, only God knows the truth of the matter. Let the inquisitive reader ferret it out for himself. The fact remains that a complete exposure of the dealings with the contrabandists followed, and that the two tchinovniks were put to the question, deprived of their property, and made to formulate in writing all that they had done. Against this thunderbolt of fortune the State Councillor could make no headway, and in some retired spot or another sank into oblivion; but Chichikov put a brave face upon the matter, for, in spite of the authorities' best efforts to smell out his gains, he had contrived to conceal a portion of them, and also resorted to every subtle trick of intellect which could possibly be employed by an experienced man of the world who has a wide knowledge of his fellows. Nothing which could be effected by pleasantness of demeanour, by moving oratory, by clouds of flattery, and by the occasional insertion of a coin into a palm did he leave undone; with the result that he was retired with less ignominy than was his companion, and escaped actual trial on a criminal charge. Yet he issued stripped of all his capital, stripped of his imported effects, stripped of everything. That is to say, all that remained to him consisted of ten thousand roubles which he had stored against a rainy day, two dozen linen shirts, a small britchka of the type used by bachelors, and two serving-men named Selifan and Petrushka. Yes, and an impulse of kindness moved the tchinovniks of the Customs also to set aside for him a few cakes of the soap which he had found so excellent for the freshness of the cheeks. Thus once more our hero found himself stranded. And what an accumulation of misfortunes had descended upon his head!—though, true, he termed them "suffering in the Service in the cause of Truth." Certainly one would have thought that, after these buffetings and trials and changes of fortune—after this taste of the sorrows of life—he and his precious ten thousand roubles would have withdrawn to some peaceful corner in a provincial town, where, clad in a stuff dressing-gown, he could have sat and listened to the peasants quarrelling on festival days, or (for the sake of a breath of fresh air) have gone in person to the poulterer's to finger chickens for soup, and so have spent a quiet, but not wholly useless, existence; but nothing of the kind took place, and therein we must do justice to the strength of his character. In other words, although he had undergone what, to the majority of men, would have meant ruin and discouragement and a shattering of ideals, he still preserved his energy. True, downcast and angry, and full of resentment against the world in general, he felt furious with the injustice of fate, and dissatisfied with the dealings of men; yet he could not forbear courting additional experiences. In short, the patience which he displayed was such as to make the wooden persistency of the German—a persistency merely due to the slow, lethargic circulation of the Teuton's blood—seem nothing at all, seeing that by nature Chichikov's blood flowed strongly, and that he had to employ much force of will to curb within himself those elements which longed to burst forth and revel in freedom. He thought things over, and, as he did so, a certain spice of reason appeared in his reflections.

"How have I come to be what I am?" he said to himself. "Why has misfortune overtaken me in this way? Never have I wronged a poor person, or robbed a widow, or turned any one out of doors: I have always been careful only to take advantage of those who possess more than their share. Moreover, I have never gleaned anywhere but where every one else was gleaning; and, had I not done so, others would have gleaned in my place. Why, then, should those others be prospering, and I be sunk as low as a worm? What am I? What am I good for? How can I, in future, hope to look any honest father of a family in the face? How shall I escape being tortured with the thought that I am cumbering the ground? What, in the years to come, will my children say, save that 'our father was a brute, for he left us nothing to live upon?'"

Here I may remark that we have seen how much thought Chichikov devoted to his future descendants. Indeed, had not there been constantly recurring to his mind the insistent question, "What will my children say?" he might not have plunged into the affair so deeply. Nevertheless, like a wary cat which glances hither and thither to see whether its mistress be not coming before it can make off with whatsoever first falls to its paw (butter, fat, lard, a duck, or anything else), so our future founder of a family continued, though weeping and bewailing his lot, to let not a single detail escape his eye. That is to say, he retained his wits ever in a state of activity, and kept his brain constantly working. All that he required was a plan. Once more he pulled himself together, once more he embarked upon a life of toil, once more he stinted himself in everything, once more he left clean and decent surroundings for a dirty, mean existence. In other words, until something better should turn up, he embraced the calling of an ordinary attorney—a calling which, not then possessed of a civic status, was jostled on very side, enjoyed little respect at the hands of the minor legal fry (or, indeed, at its own), and perforce met with universal slights and rudeness. But sheer necessity compelled Chichikov to face these things. Among commissions entrusted to him was that of placing in the hands of the Public Trustee several hundred peasants who belonged to a ruined estate. The estate had reached its parlous condition through cattle disease, through rascally bailiffs, through failures of the harvest, through such epidemic diseases that had killed off the best workmen, and, last, but not least, through the senseless conduct of the owner himself, who had furnished a house in Moscow in the latest style, and then squandered his every kopeck, so that nothing was left for his further maintenance, and it became necessary to mortgage the remains—including the peasants—of the estate. In those days mortgage to the Treasury was an innovation looked upon with reserve, and, as attorney in the matter, Chichikov had first of all to "entertain" every official concerned (we know that, unless that be previously done, unless a whole bottle of madeira first be emptied down each clerical throat, not the smallest legal affair can be carried through), and to explain, for the barring of future attachments, that half of the peasants were dead.

"And are they entered on the revision lists?" asked the secretary. "Yes," replied Chichikov. "Then what are you boggling at?" continued the Secretary. "Should one soul die, another will be born, and in time grow up to take the first one's place." Upon that there dawned on our hero one of the most inspired ideas which ever entered the human brain. "What a simpleton I am!" he thought to himself. "Here am I looking about for my mittens when all the time I have got them tucked into my belt. Why, were I myself to buy up a few souls which are dead—to buy them before a new revision list shall have been made, the Council of Public Trust might pay me two hundred roubles apiece for them, and I might find myself with, say, a capital of two hundred thousand roubles! The present moment is particularly propitious, since in various parts of the country there has been an epidemic, and, glory be to God, a large number of souls have died of it. Nowadays landowners have taken to card-playing and junketting and wasting their money, or to joining the Civil Service in St. Petersburg; consequently their estates are going to rack and ruin, and being managed in any sort of fashion, and succeeding in paying their dues with greater difficulty each year. That being so, not a man of the lot but would gladly surrender to me his dead souls rather than continue paying the poll-tax; and in this fashion I might make—well, not a few kopecks. Of course there are difficulties, and, to avoid creating a scandal, I should need to employ plenty of finesse; but man was given his brain to USE, not to neglect. One good point about the scheme is that it will seem so improbable that in case of an accident, no one in the world will believe in it. True, it is illegal to buy or mortgage peasants without land, but I can easily pretend to be buying them only for transferment elsewhere. Land is to be acquired in the provinces of Taurida and Kherson almost for nothing, provided that one undertakes subsequently to colonise it; so to Kherson I will 'transfer' them, and long may they live there! And the removal of my dead souls shall be carried out in the strictest legal form; and if the authorities should want confirmation by testimony, I shall produce a letter signed by my own superintendent of the Khersonian rural police—that is to say, by myself. Lastly, the supposed village in Kherson shall be called Chichikovoe—better still Pavlovskoe, according to my Christian name."

In this fashion there germinated in our hero's brain that strange scheme for which the reader may or may not be grateful, but for which the author certainly is so, seeing that, had it never occurred to Chichikov, this story would never have seen the light.

After crossing himself, according to the Russian custom, Chichikov set about carrying out his enterprise. On pretence of selecting a place wherein to settle, he started forth to inspect various corners of the Russian Empire, but more especially those which had suffered from such unfortunate accidents as failures of the harvest, a high rate of mortality, or whatsoever else might enable him to purchase souls at the lowest possible rate. But he did not tackle his landowners haphazard: he rather selected such of them as seemed more particularly suited to his taste, or with whom he might with the least possible trouble conclude identical agreements; though, in the first instance, he always tried, by getting on terms of acquaintanceship—better still, of friendship—with them, to acquire the souls for nothing, and so to avoid purchase at all. In passing, my readers must not blame me if the characters whom they have encountered in these pages have not been altogether to their liking. The fault is Chichikov's rather than mine, for he is the master, and where he leads we must follow. Also, should my readers gird at me for a certain dimness and want of clarity in my principal characters and actors, that will be tantamount to saying that never do the broad tendency and the general scope of a work become immediately apparent. Similarly does the entry to every town—the entry even to the Capital itself—convey to the traveller such an impression of vagueness that at first everything looks grey and monotonous, and the lines of smoky factories and workshops seem never to be coming to an end; but in time there will begin also to stand out the outlines of six-storied mansions, and of shops and balconies, and wide perspectives of streets, and a medley of steeples, columns, statues, and turrets—the whole framed in rattle and roar and the infinite wonders which the hand and the brain of men have conceived. Of the manner in which Chichikov's first purchases were made the reader is aware. Subsequently he will see also how the affair progressed, and with what success or failure our hero met, and how Chichikov was called upon to decide and to overcome even more difficult problems than the foregoing, and by what colossal forces the levers of his far-flung tale are moved, and how eventually the horizon will become extended until everything assumes a grandiose and a lyrical tendency. Yes, many a verst of road remains to be travelled by a party made up of an elderly gentleman, a britchka of the kind affected by bachelors, a valet named Petrushka, a coachman named Selifan, and three horses which, from the Assessor to the skewbald, are known to us individually by name. Again, although I have given a full description of our hero's exterior (such as it is), I may yet be asked for an inclusive definition also of his moral personality. That he is no hero compounded of virtues and perfections must be already clear. Then WHAT is he? A villain? Why should we call him a villain? Why should we be so hard upon a fellow man? In these days our villains have ceased to exist. Rather it would be fairer to call him an ACQUIRER. The love of acquisition, the love of gain, is a fault common to many, and gives rise to many and many a transaction of the kind generally known as "not strictly honourable." True, such a character contains an element of ugliness, and the same reader who, on his journey through life, would sit at the board of a character of this kind, and spend a most agreeable time with him, would be the first to look at him askance if he should appear in the guise of the hero of a novel or a play. But wise is the reader who, on meeting such a character, scans him carefully, and, instead of shrinking from him with distaste, probes him to the springs of his being. The human personality contains nothing which may not, in the twinkling of an eye, become altogether changed—nothing in which, before you can look round, there may not spring to birth some cankerous worm which is destined to suck thence the essential juice. Yes, it is a common thing to see not only an overmastering passion, but also a passion of the most petty order, arise in a man who was born to better things, and lead him both to forget his greatest and most sacred obligations, and to see only in the veriest trifles the Great and the Holy. For human passions are as numberless as is the sand of the seashore, and go on to become his most insistent of masters. Happy, therefore, the man who may choose from among the gamut of human passions one which is noble! Hour by hour will that instinct grow and multiply in its measureless beneficence; hour by hour will it sink deeper and deeper into the infinite paradise of his soul. But there are passions of which a man cannot rid himself, seeing that they are born with him at his birth, and he has no power to abjure them. Higher powers govern those passions, and in them is something which will call to him, and refuse to be silenced, to the end of his life. Yes, whether in a guise of darkness, or whether in a guise which will become converted into a light to lighten the world, they will and must attain their consummation on life's field: and in either case they have been evoked for man's good. In the same way may the passion which drew our Chichikov onwards have been one that was independent of himself; in the same way may there have lurked even in his cold essence something which will one day cause men to humble themselves in the dust before the infinite wisdom of God.

Yet that folk should be dissatisfied with my hero matters nothing. What matters is the fact that, under different circumstances, their approval could have been taken as a foregone conclusion. That is to say, had not the author pried over-deeply into Chichikov's soul, nor stirred up in its depths what shunned and lay hidden from the light, nor disclosed those of his hero's thoughts which that hero would have not have disclosed even to his most intimate friend; had the author, indeed, exhibited Chichikov just as he exhibited himself to the townsmen of N. and Manilov and the rest; well, then we may rest assured that every reader would have been delighted with him, and have voted him a most interesting person. For it is not nearly so necessary that Chichikov should figure before the reader as though his form and person were actually present to the eye as that, on concluding a perusal of this work, the reader should be able to return, unharrowed in soul, to that cult of the card-table which is the solace and delight of all good Russians. Yes, readers of this book, none of you really care to see humanity revealed in its nakedness. "Why should we do so?" you say. "What would be the use of it? Do we not know for ourselves that human life contains much that is gross and contemptible? Do we not with our own eyes have to look upon much that is anything but comforting? Far better would it be if you would put before us what is comely and attractive, so that we might forget ourselves a little." In the same fashion does a landowner say to his bailiff: "Why do you come and tell me that the affairs of my estate are in a bad way? I know that without YOUR help. Have you nothing else to tell me? Kindly allow me to forget the fact, or else to remain in ignorance of it, and I shall be much obliged to you." Whereafter the said landowner probably proceeds to spend on his diversion the money which ought to have gone towards the rehabilitation of his affairs.

Possibly the author may also incur censure at the hands of those so-called "patriots" who sit quietly in corners, and become capitalists through making fortunes at the expense of others. Yes, let but something which they conceive to be derogatory to their country occur—for instance, let there be published some book which voices the bitter truth—and out they will come from their hiding-places like a spider which perceives a fly to be caught in its web. "Is it well to proclaim this to the world, and to set folk talking about it?" they will cry. "What you have described touches US, is OUR affair. Is conduct of that kind right? What will foreigners say? Does any one care calmly to sit by and hear himself traduced? Why should you lead foreigners to suppose that all is not well with us, and that we are not patriotic?" Well, to these sage remarks no answer can really be returned, especially to such of the above as refer to foreign opinion. But see here. There once lived in a remote corner of Russia two natives of the region indicated. One of those natives was a good man named Kifa Mokievitch, and a man of kindly disposition; a man who went through life in a dressing-gown, and paid no heed to his household, for the reason that his whole being was centred upon the province of speculation, and that, in particular, he was preoccupied with a philosophical problem usually stated by him thus: "A beast," he would say, "is born naked. Now, why should that be? Why should not a beast be born as a bird is born—that is to say, through the process of being hatched from an egg? Nature is beyond the understanding, however much one may probe her." This was the substance of Kifa Mokievitch's reflections. But herein is not the chief point. The other of the pair was a fellow named Mofi Kifovitch, and son to the first named. He was what we Russians call a "hero," and while his father was pondering the parturition of beasts, his, the son's, lusty, twenty-year-old temperament was violently struggling for development. Yet that son could tackle nothing without some accident occurring. At one moment would he crack some one's fingers in half, and at another would he raise a bump on somebody's nose; so that both at home and abroad every one and everything—from the serving-maid to the yard-dog—fled on his approach, and even the bed in his bedroom became shattered to splinters. Such was Mofi Kifovitch; and with it all he had a kindly soul. But herein is not the chief point. "Good sir, good Kifa Mokievitch," servants and neighbours would come and say to the father, "what are you going to do about your Moki Kifovitch? We get no rest from him, he is so above himself." "That is only his play, that is only his play," the father would reply. "What else can you expect? It is too late now to start a quarrel with him, and, moreover, every one would accuse me of harshness. True, he is a little conceited; but, were I to reprove him in public, the whole thing would become common talk, and folk would begin giving him a dog's name. And if they did that, would not their opinion touch me also, seeing that I am his father? Also, I am busy with philosophy, and have no time for such things. Lastly, Moki Kifovitch is my son, and very dear to my heart." And, beating his breast, Kifa Mokievitch again asserted that, even though his son should elect to continue his pranks, it would not be for HIM, for the father, to proclaim the fact, or to fall out with his offspring. And, this expression of paternal feeling uttered, Kifa Mokievitch left Moki Kifovitch to his heroic exploits, and himself returned to his beloved subject of speculation, which now included also the problem, "Suppose elephants were to take to being hatched from eggs, would not the shell of such eggs be of a thickness proof against cannonballs, and necessitate the invention of some new type of firearm?" Thus at the end of this little story we have these two denizens of a peaceful corner of Russia looking thence, as from a window, in less terror of doing what was scandalous than of having it SAID of them that they were acting scandalously. Yes, the feeling animating our so-called "patriots" is not true patriotism at all. Something else lies beneath it. Who, if not an author, is to speak aloud the truth? Men like you, my pseudo-patriots, stand in dread of the eye which is able to discern, yet shrink from using your own, and prefer, rather, to glance at everything unheedingly. Yes, after laughing heartily over Chichikov's misadventures, and perhaps even commending the author for his dexterity of observation and pretty turn of wit, you will look at yourselves with redoubled pride and a self-satisfied smile, and add: "Well, we agree that in certain parts of the provinces there exists strange and ridiculous individuals, as well as unconscionable rascals."

Yet which of you, when quiet, and alone, and engaged in solitary self-communion, would not do well to probe YOUR OWN souls, and to put to YOURSELVES the solemn question, "Is there not in ME an element of Chichikov?" For how should there not be? Which of you is not liable at any moment to be passed in the street by an acquaintance who, nudging his neighbour, may say of you, with a barely suppressed sneer: "Look! there goes Chichikov! That is Chichikov who has just gone by!"

But here are we talking at the top of our voices whilst all the time our hero lies slumbering in his britchka! Indeed, his name has been repeated so often during the recital of his life's history that he must almost have heard us! And at any time he is an irritable, irascible fellow when spoken of with disrespect. True, to the reader Chichikov's displeasure cannot matter a jot; but for the author it would mean ruin to quarrel with his hero, seeing that, arm in arm, Chichikov and he have yet far to go.

"Tut, tut, tut!" came in a shout from Chichikov. "Hi, Selifan!"

"What is it?" came the reply, uttered with a drawl.

"What is it? Why, how dare you drive like that? Come! Bestir yourself a little!"

And indeed, Selifan had long been sitting with half-closed eyes, and hands which bestowed no encouragement upon his somnolent steeds save an occasional flicking of the reins against their flanks; whilst Petrushka had lost his cap, and was leaning backwards until his head had come to rest against Chichikov's knees—a position which necessitated his being awakened with a cuff. Selifan also roused himself, and apportioned to the skewbald a few cuts across the back of a kind which at least had the effect of inciting that animal to trot; and when, presently, the other two horses followed their companion's example, the light britchka moved forwards like a piece of thistledown. Selifan flourished his whip and shouted, "Hi, hi!" as the inequalities of the road jerked him vertically on his seat; and meanwhile, reclining against the leather cushions of the vehicle's interior, Chichikov smiled with gratification at the sensation of driving fast. For what Russian does not love to drive fast? Which of us does not at times yearn to give his horses their head, and to let them go, and to cry, "To the devil with the world!"? At such moments a great force seems to uplift one as on wings; and one flies, and everything else flies, but contrariwise—both the verst stones, and traders riding on the shafts of their waggons, and the forest with dark lines of spruce and fir amid which may be heard the axe of the woodcutter and the croaking of the raven. Yes, out of a dim, remote distance the road comes towards one, and while nothing save the sky and the light clouds through which the moon is cleaving her way seem halted, the brief glimpses wherein one can discern nothing clearly have in them a pervading touch of mystery. Ah, troika, troika, swift as a bird, who was it first invented you? Only among a hardy race of folk can you have come to birth—only in a land which, though poor and rough, lies spread over half the world, and spans versts the counting whereof would leave one with aching eyes. Nor are you a modishly-fashioned vehicle of the road—a thing of clamps and iron. Rather, you are a vehicle but shapen and fitted with the axe or chisel of some handy peasant of Yaroslav. Nor are you driven by a coachman clothed in German livery, but by a man bearded and mittened. See him as he mounts, and flourishes his whip, and breaks into a long-drawn song! Away like the wind go the horses, and the wheels, with their spokes, become transparent circles, and the road seems to quiver beneath them, and a pedestrian, with a cry of astonishment, halts to watch the vehicle as it flies, flies, flies on its way until it becomes lost on the ultimate horizon—a speck amid a cloud of dust!

 And you, Russia of mine—are not you also speeding like a troika which nought can overtake? Is not the road smoking beneath your wheels, and the bridges thundering as you cross them, and everything being left in the rear, and the spectators, struck with the portent, halting to wonder whether you be not a thunderbolt launched from heaven? What does that awe-inspiring progress of yours foretell? What is the unknown force which lies within your mysterious steeds? Surely the winds themselves must abide in their manes, and every vein in their bodies be an ear stretched to catch the celestial message which bids them, with iron-girded breasts, and hooves which barely touch the earth as they gallop, fly forward on a mission of God? Whither, then, are you speeding, O Russia of mine? Whither? Answer me! But no answer comes—only the weird sound of your collar-bells. Rent into a thousand shreds, the air roars past you, for you are overtaking the whole world, and shall one day force all nations, all empires to stand aside, to give you way!

1841.

PART TWO

CHAPTER I

Why do I so persistently paint the poverty, the imperfections of Russian life, and delve into the remotest depths, the most retired holes and corners, of our Empire for my subjects? The answer is that there is nothing else to be done when an author's idiosyncrasy happens to incline him that way. So again we find ourselves in a retired spot. But what a spot!

Imagine, if you can, a mountain range like a gigantic fortress, with embrasures and bastions which appear to soar a thousand versts towards the heights of heaven, and, towering grandly over a boundless expanse of plain, are broken up into precipitous, overhanging limestone cliffs. Here and there those cliffs are seamed with water-courses and gullies, while at other points they are rounded off into spurs of green—spurs now coated with fleece-like tufts of young undergrowth, now studded with the stumps of felled trees, now covered with timber which has, by some miracle, escaped the woodman's axe. Also, a river winds awhile between its banks, then leaves the meadow land, divides into runlets (all flashing in the sun like fire), plunges, re-united, into the midst of a thicket of elder, birch, and pine, and, lastly, speeds triumphantly past bridges and mills and weirs which seem to be lying in wait for it at every turn.

At one particular spot the steep flank of the mountain range is covered with billowy verdure of denser growth than the rest; and here the aid of skilful planting, added to the shelter afforded by a rugged ravine, has enabled the flora of north and south so to be brought together that, twined about with sinuous hop-tendrils, the oak, the spruce fir, the wild pear, the maple, the cherry, the thorn, and the mountain ash either assist or check one another's growth, and everywhere cover the declivity with their straggling profusion. Also, at the edge of the summit there can be seen mingling with the green of the trees the red roofs of a manorial homestead, while behind the upper stories of the mansion proper and its carved balcony and a great semi-circular window there gleam the tiles and gables of some peasants' huts. Lastly, over this combination of trees and roofs there rises—overtopping everything with its gilded, sparkling steeple—an old village church. On each of its pinnacles a cross of carved gilt is stayed with supports of similar gilding and design; with the result that from a distance the gilded portions have the effect of hanging without visible agency in the air. And the whole—the three successive tiers of woodland, roofs, and crosses whole—lies exquisitely mirrored in the river below, where hollow willows, grotesquely shaped (some of them rooted on the river's banks, and some in the water itself, and all drooping their branches until their leaves have formed a tangle with the water lilies which float on the surface), seem to be gazing at the marvellous reflection at their feet.

Thus the view from below is beautiful indeed. But the view from above is even better. No guest, no visitor, could stand on the balcony of the mansion and remain indifferent. So boundless is the panorama revealed that surprise would cause him to catch at his breath, and exclaim: "Lord of Heaven, but what a prospect!" Beyond meadows studded with spinneys and water-mills lie forests belted with green; while beyond, again, there can be seen showing through the slightly misty air strips of yellow heath, and, again, wide-rolling forests (as blue as the sea or a cloud), and more heath, paler than the first, but still yellow. Finally, on the far horizon a range of chalk-topped hills gleams white, even in dull weather, as though it were lightened with perpetual sunshine; and here and there on the dazzling whiteness of its lower slopes some plaster-like, nebulous patches represent far-off villages which lie too remote for the eye to discern their details. Indeed, only when the sunlight touches a steeple to gold does one realise that each such patch is a human settlement. Finally, all is wrapped in an immensity of silence which even the far, faint echoes of persons singing in the void of the plain cannot shatter.

Even after gazing at the spectacle for a couple of hours or so, the visitor would still find nothing to say, save: "Lord of Heaven, but what a prospect!" Then who is the dweller in, the proprietor of, this manor—a manor to which, as to an impregnable fortress, entrance cannot be gained from the side where we have been standing, but only from the other approach, where a few scattered oaks offer hospitable welcome to the visitor, and then, spreading above him their spacious branches (as in friendly embrace), accompany him to the facade of the mansion whose top we have been regarding from the reverse aspect, but which now stands frontwise on to us, and has, on one side of it, a row of peasants' huts with red tiles and carved gables, and, on the other, the village church, with those glittering golden crosses and gilded open-work charms which seem to hang suspended in the air? Yes, indeed!—to what fortunate individual does this corner of the world belong? It belongs to Andrei Ivanovitch Tientietnikov, landowner of the canton of Tremalakhan, and, withal, a bachelor of about thirty.

Should my lady readers ask of me what manner of man is Tientietnikov, and what are his attributes and peculiarities, I should refer them to his neighbours. Of these, a member of the almost extinct tribe of intelligent staff officers on the retired list once summed up Tientietnikov in the phrase, "He is an absolute blockhead;" while a General who resided ten versts away was heard to remark that "he is a young man who, though not exactly a fool, has at least too much crowded into his head. I myself might have been of use to him, for not only do I maintain certain connections with St. Petersburg, but also—" And the General left his sentence unfinished. Thirdly, a captain-superintendent of rural police happened to remark in the course of conversation: "To-morrow I must go and see Tientietnikov about his arrears." Lastly, a peasant of Tientietnikov's own village, when asked what his barin was like, returned no answer at all. All of which would appear to show that Tientietnikov was not exactly looked upon with favour.

To speak dispassionately, however, he was not a bad sort of fellow—merely a star-gazer; and since the world contains many watchers of the skies, why should Tientietnikov not have been one of them? However, let me describe in detail a specimen day of his existence—one that will closely resemble the rest, and then the reader will be enabled to judge of Tientietnikov's character, and how far his life corresponded to the beauties of nature with which he lived surrounded.

On the morning of the specimen day in question he awoke very late, and, raising himself to a sitting posture, rubbed his eyes. And since those eyes were small, the process of rubbing them occupied a very long time, and throughout its continuance there stood waiting by the door his valet, Mikhailo, armed with a towel and basin. For one hour, for two hours, did poor Mikhailo stand there: then he departed to the kitchen, and returned to find his master still rubbing his eyes as he sat on the bed. At length, however, Tientietnikov rose, washed himself, donned a dressing-gown, and moved into the drawing-room for morning tea, coffee, cocoa, and warm milk; of all of which he partook but sparingly, while munching a piece of bread, and scattering tobacco ash with complete insouciance. Two hours did he sit over this meal, then poured himself out another cup of the rapidly cooling tea, and walked to the window. This faced the courtyard, and outside it, as usual, there took place the following daily altercation between a serf named Grigory (who purported to act as butler) and the housekeeper, Perfilievna.

Grigory. Ah, you nuisance, you good-for-nothing, you had better hold your stupid tongue.

Perfilievna. Yes; and don't you wish that I would?

Grigory. What? You so thick with that bailiff of yours, you housekeeping jade!

Perfilievna. Nay, he is as big a thief as you are. Do you think the barin doesn't know you? And there he is! He must have heard everything!

Grigory. Where?

Perfilievna. There—sitting by the window, and looking at us!

Next, to complete the hubbub, a serf child which had been clouted by its mother broke out into a bawl, while a borzoi puppy which had happened to get splashed with boiling water by the cook fell to yelping vociferously. In short, the place soon became a babel of shouts and squeals, and, after watching and listening for a time, the barin found it so impossible to concentrate his mind upon anything that he sent out word that the noise would have to be abated.

The next item was that, a couple of hours before luncheon time, he withdrew to his study, to set about employing himself upon a weighty work which was to consider Russia from every point of view: from the political, from the philosophical, and from the religious, as well as to resolve various problems which had arisen to confront the Empire, and to define clearly the great future to which the country stood ordained. In short, it was to be the species of compilation in which the man of the day so much delights. Yet the colossal undertaking had progressed but little beyond the sphere of projection, since, after a pen had been gnawed awhile, and a few strokes had been committed to paper, the whole would be laid aside in favour of the reading of some book; and that reading would continue also during luncheon and be followed by the lighting of a pipe, the playing of a solitary game of chess, and the doing of more or less nothing for the rest of the day.

The foregoing will give the reader a pretty clear idea of the manner in which it was possible for this man of thirty-three to waste his time. Clad constantly in slippers and a dressing-gown, Tientietnikov never went out, never indulged in any form of dissipation, and never walked upstairs. Nothing did he care for fresh air, and would bestow not a passing glance upon all those beauties of the countryside which moved visitors to such ecstatic admiration. From this the reader will see that Andrei Ivanovitch Tientietnikov belonged to that band of sluggards whom we always have with us, and who, whatever be their present appellation, used to be known by the nicknames of "lollopers," "bed pressers," and "marmots." Whether the type is a type originating at birth, or a type resulting from untoward circumstances in later life, it is impossible to say. A better course than to attempt to answer that question would be to recount the story of Tientietnikov's boyhood and upbringing.

Everything connected with the latter seemed to promise success, for at twelve years of age the boy—keen-witted, but dreamy of temperament, and inclined to delicacy—was sent to an educational establishment presided over by an exceptional type of master. The idol of his pupils, and the admiration of his assistants, Alexander Petrovitch was gifted with an extraordinary measure of good sense. How thoroughly he knew the peculiarities of the

Russian of his day! How well he understood boys! How capable he was of drawing them out! Not a practical joker in the school but, after perpetrating a prank, would voluntarily approach his preceptor and make to him free confession. True, the preceptor would put a stern face upon the matter, yet the culprit would depart with head held higher, not lower, than before, since in Alexander Petrovitch there was something which heartened—something which seemed to say to a delinquent: "Forward you! Rise to your feet again, even though you have fallen!" Not lectures on good behaviour was it, therefore, that fell from his lips, but rather the injunction, "I want to see intelligence, and nothing else. The boy who devotes his attention to becoming clever will never play the fool, for under such circumstances, folly disappears of itself." And so folly did, for the boy who failed to strive in the desired direction incurred the contempt of all his comrades, and even dunces and fools of senior standing did not dare to raise a finger when saluted by their juniors with opprobrious epithets. Yet "This is too much," certain folk would say to Alexander. "The result will be that your students will turn out prigs." "But no," he would reply. "Not at all. You see, I make it my principle to keep the incapables for a single term only, since that is enough for them; but to the clever ones I allot a double course of instruction." And, true enough, any lad of brains was retained for this finishing course. Yet he did not repress all boyish playfulness, since he declared it to be as necessary as a rash to a doctor, inasmuch as it enabled him to diagnose what lay hidden within.

Consequently, how the boys loved him! Never was there such an attachment between master and pupils. And even later, during the foolish years, when foolish things attract, the measure of affection which Alexander Petrovitch retained was extraordinary. In fact, to the day of his death, every former pupil would celebrate the birthday of his late master by raising his glass in gratitude to the mentor dead and buried—then close his eyelids upon the tears which would come trickling through them. Even the slightest word of encouragement from Alexander Petrovitch could throw a lad into a transport of tremulous joy, and arouse in him an honourable emulation of his fellows. Boys of small capacity he did not long retain in his establishment; whereas those who possessed exceptional talent he put through an extra course of schooling. This senior class—a class composed of specially-selected pupils—was a very different affair from what usually obtains in other colleges. Only when a boy had attained its ranks did Alexander demand of him what other masters indiscreetly require of mere infants—namely the superior frame of mind which, while never indulging in mockery, can itself bear ridicule, and disregard the fool, and keep its temper, and repress itself, and eschew revenge, and calmly, proudly retain its tranquillity of soul. In short, whatever avails to form a boy into a man of assured character, that did Alexander Petrovitch employ during the pupil's youth, as well as constantly put him to the test. How well he understood the art of life!

Of assistant tutors he kept but few, since most of the necessary instruction he imparted in person, and, without pedantic terminology and inflated diction and views, could so transmit to his listeners the inmost spirit of a lesson that even the youngest present absorbed its essential elements. Also, of studies he selected none but those which may help a boy to become a good citizen; and therefore most of the lectures which he delivered consisted of discourses on what may be awaiting a youth, as well as of such demarcations of life's field that the pupil, though seated, as yet, only at the desk, could beforehand bear his part in that field both in thought and spirit. Nor did the master CONCEAL anything. That is to say, without mincing words, he invariably set before his hearers the sorrows and the difficulties which may confront a man, the trials and the temptations which may beset him. And this he did in terms as though, in every possible calling and capacity, he himself had experienced the same. Consequently, either the vigorous development of self-respect or the constant stimulus of the master's eye (which seemed to say to the pupil, "Forward!"—that word which has become so familiar to the contemporary Russian, that word which has worked such wonders upon his sensitive temperament); one or the other, I repeat, would from the first cause the pupil to tackle difficulties, and only difficulties, and to hunger for prowess only where the path was arduous, and obstacles were many, and it was necessary to display the utmost strength of mind. Indeed, few completed the course of which I have spoken without issuing therefrom reliable, seasoned fighters who could keep their heads in the most embarrassing of official positions, and at times when older and wiser men, distracted with the annoyances of life, had either abandoned everything or, grown slack and indifferent, had surrendered to the bribe-takers and the rascals. In short, no ex-pupil of Alexander Petrovitch ever wavered from the right road, but, familiar with life and with men, armed with the weapons of prudence, exerted a powerful influence upon wrongdoers.

For a long time past the ardent young Tientietnikov's excitable heart had also beat at the thought that one day he might attain the senior class described. And, indeed, what better teacher could he have had befall him than its preceptor? Yet just at the moment when he had been transferred thereto, just at the moment when he had reached the coveted position, did his instructor come suddenly by his death! This was indeed a blow for the boy—indeed a terrible initial loss! In his eyes everything connected with the school seemed to undergo a change—the chief reason being the fact that to the place of the deceased headmaster there succeeded a certain Thedor Ivanovitch, who at once began to insist upon certain external rules, and to demand of the boys what ought rightly to have been demanded only of adults. That is to say, since the lads' frank and open demeanour savoured to him only of lack of discipline, he announced (as though in deliberate spite of his predecessor) that he cared nothing for progress and intellect, but that heed was to be paid only to good behaviour. Yet, curiously enough, good behaviour was just what he never obtained, for every kind of secret prank became the rule; and while, by day, there reigned restraint and conspiracy, by night there began to take place chambering and wantonness.

Also, certain changes in the curriculum of studies came about, for there were engaged new teachers who held new views and opinions, and confused their hearers with a multitude of new terms and phrases, and displayed in their exposition of things both logical sequence and a zest for modern discovery and much warmth of individual bias. Yet their instruction, alas! contained no LIFE—in the mouths of those teachers a dead language savoured merely of carrion. Thus everything connected with the school underwent a radical alteration, and respect for authority and the authorities waned, and tutors and ushers came to be dubbed "Old Thedor," "Crusty," and the like. And sundry other things began to take place—things which necessitated many a penalty and expulsion; until, within a couple of years, no one who had known the school in former days would now have recognised it.

Nevertheless Tientietnikov, a youth of retiring disposition, experienced no leanings towards the nocturnal orgies of his companions, orgies during which the latter used to flirt with damsels before the very windows of the headmaster's rooms, nor yet towards their mockery of all that was sacred, simply because fate had cast in their way an injudicious priest. No, despite its dreaminess, his soul ever remembered its celestial origin, and could not be diverted from the path of virtue. Yet still he hung his head, for, while his ambition had come to life, it could find no sort of outlet. Truly 'twere well if it had NOT come to life, for throughout the time that he was listening to professors who gesticulated on their chairs he could not help remembering the old preceptor who, invariably cool and calm, had yet known how to make himself understood. To what subjects, to what lectures, did the boy not have to listen!—to lectures on medicine, and on philosophy, and on law, and on a version of general history so enlarged that even three years failed to enable the professor to do more than finish the introduction thereto, and also the account of the development of some self-governing towns in Germany. None of the stuff remained fixed in Tientietnikov's brain save as shapeless clots; for though his native intellect could not tell him how instruction ought to be imparted, it at least told him that THIS was not the way. And frequently, at such moments he would recall Alexander Petrovitch, and give way to such grief that scarcely did he know what he was doing.

But youth is fortunate in the fact that always before it there lies a future; and in proportion as the time for his leaving school drew nigh, Tientietnikov's heart began to beat higher and higher, and he said to himself: "This is not life, but only a preparation for life. True life is to be found in the Public Service. There at least will there be scope for activity." So, bestowing not a glance upon that beautiful corner of the world which never failed to strike the guest or chance visitor with amazement, and reverencing not a whit the dust of his ancestors, he followed the example of most ambitious men of his class by repairing to St. Petersburg (whither, as we know, the more spirited youth of Russia from every quarter gravitates—there to enter the Public Service, to shine, to obtain promotion, and, in a word, to scale the topmost peaks of that pale, cold, deceptive elevation which is known as society). But the real starting-point of Tientietnikov's ambition was the moment when his uncle (one State Councillor Onifri Ivanovitch) instilled into him the maxim that the only means to success in the Service lay in good handwriting, and that, without that accomplishment, no one could ever hope to become a Minister or Statesman. Thus, with great difficulty, and also with the help of his uncle's influence, young Tientietnikov at length succeeded in being posted to a Department. On the day that he was conducted into a splendid, shining hall—a hall fitted with inlaid floors and lacquered desks as fine as though this were actually the place where the great ones of the Empire met for discussion of the fortunes of the State; on the day that he saw legions of handsome gentlemen of the quill-driving profession making loud scratchings with pens, and cocking their heads to one side; lastly on the day that he saw himself also allotted a desk, and requested to copy a document which appeared purposely to be one of the pettiest possible order (as a matter of fact it related to a sum of three roubles, and had taken half a year to produce)—well, at that moment a curious, an unwonted sensation seized upon the inexperienced youth, for the gentlemen around him appeared so exactly like a lot of college students. And, the further to complete the resemblance, some of them were engaged in reading trashy translated novels, which they kept hurriedly thrusting between the sheets of their apportioned work whenever the Director appeared, as though to convey the impression that it was to that work alone that they were applying themselves. In short, the scene seemed to Tientietnikov strange, and his former pursuits more important than his present, and his preparation for the Service preferable to the Service itself. Yes, suddenly he felt a longing for his old school; and as suddenly, and with all the vividness of life, there appeared before his vision the figure of Alexander Petrovitch. He almost burst into tears as he beheld his old master, and the room seemed to swim before his eyes, and the tchinovniks and the desks to become a blur, and his sight to grow dim. Then he thought to himself with an effort: "No, no! I WILL apply myself to my work, however petty it be at first." And hardening his heart and recovering his spirit, he determined then and there to perform his duties in such a manner as should be an example to the rest.

But where are compensations to be found? Even in St. Petersburg, despite its grim and murky exterior, they exist. Yes, even though thirty degrees of keen, cracking frost may have bound the streets, and the family of the North Wind be wailing there, and the Snowstorm Witch have heaped high the pavements, and be blinding the eyes, and powdering beards and fur collars and the shaggy manes of horses—even THEN there will be shining hospitably through the swirling snowflakes a fourth-floor window where, in a cosy room, and by the light of modest candles, and to the hiss of the samovar, there will be in progress a discussion which warms the heart and soul, or else a reading aloud of a brilliant page of one of those inspired Russian poets with whom God has dowered us, while the breast of each member of the company is heaving with a rapture unknown under a noontide sky.

Gradually, therefore, Tientietnikov grew more at home in the Service. Yet never did it become, for him, the main pursuit, the main object in life, which he had expected. No, it remained but one of a secondary kind. That is to say, it served merely to divide up his time, and enable him the more to value his hours of leisure. Nevertheless, just when his uncle was beginning to flatter himself that his nephew was destined to succeed in the profession, the said nephew elected to ruin his every hope. Thus it befell. Tientietnikov's friends (he had many) included among their number a couple of fellows of the species known as "embittered." That is to say, though good-natured souls of that curiously restless type which cannot endure injustice, nor anything which it conceives to be such, they were thoroughly unbalanced of conduct themselves, and, while demanding general agreement with their views, treated those of others with the scantiest of ceremony. Nevertheless these two associates exercised upon Tientietnikov—both by the fire of their eloquence and by the form of their noble dissatisfaction with society—a very strong influence; with the result that, through arousing in him an innate tendency to nervous resentment, they led him also to notice trifles which before had escaped his attention. An instance of this is seen in the fact that he conceived against Thedor Thedorovitch Lienitsin, Director of one of the Departments which was quartered in the splendid range of offices before mentioned, a dislike which proved the cause of his discerning in the man a host of hitherto unmarked imperfections. Above all things did Tientietnikov take it into his head that, when conversing with his superiors, Lienitsin became, of the moment, a stick of luscious sweetmeat, but that, when conversing with his inferiors, he approximated more to a vinegar cruet. Certain it is that, like all petty-minded individuals, Lienitsin made a note of any one who failed to offer him a greeting on festival days, and that he revenged himself upon any one whose visiting-card had not been handed to his butler. Eventually the youth's aversion almost attained the point of hysteria; until he felt that, come what might, he MUST insult the fellow in some fashion. To that task he applied himself con amore; and so thoroughly that he met with complete success. That is to say, he seized on an occasion to address Lienitsin in such fashion that the delinquent received notice either to apologise or to leave the Service; and when of these alternatives he chose the latter his uncle came to him, and made a terrified appeal. "For God's sake remember what you are doing!" he cried. "To think that, after beginning your career so well, you should abandon it merely for the reason that you have not fallen in with the sort of Director whom you prefer! What do you mean by it, what do you mean by it? Were others to regard things in the same way, the Service would find itself without a single individual. Reconsider your conduct—forego your pride and conceit, and make Lienitsin amends."

"But, dear Uncle," the nephew replied, "that is not the point. The point is, not that I should find an apology difficult to offer, seeing that, since Lienitsin is my superior, and I ought not to have addressed him as I did, I am clearly in the wrong. Rather, the point is the following. To my charge there has been committed the performance of another kind of service. That is to say, I am the owner of three hundred peasant souls, a badly administered estate, and a fool of a bailiff. That being so, whereas the State will lose little by having to fill my stool with another copyist, it will lose very much by causing three hundred peasant souls to fail in the payment of their taxes. As I say (how am I to put it?), I am a landowner who has preferred to enter the Public Service. Now, should I employ myself henceforth in conserving, restoring, and improving the fortunes of the souls whom God has entrusted to my care, and thereby provide the State with three hundred law-abiding, sober, hard-working taxpayers, how will that service of mine rank as inferior to the service of a department-directing fool like Lienitsin?"

On hearing this speech, the State Councillor could only gape, for he had not expected Tientietnikov's torrent of words. He reflected a few moments, and then murmured:

"Yes, but, but—but how can a man like you retire to rustication in the country? What society will you get there? Here one meets at least a general or a prince sometimes; indeed, no matter whom you pass in the street, that person represents gas lamps and European civilisation; but in the country, no matter what part of it you are in, not a soul is to be encountered save muzhiks and their women. Why should you go and condemn yourself to a state of vegetation like that?"

Nevertheless the uncle's expostulations fell upon deaf ears, for already the nephew was beginning to think of his estate as a retreat of a type more likely to nourish the intellectual faculties and afford the only profitable field of activity. After unearthing one or two modern works on agriculture, therefore, he, two weeks later, found himself in the neighbourhood of the home where his boyhood had been spent, and approaching the spot which never failed to enthral the visitor or guest. And in the young man's breast there was beginning to palpitate a new feeling—in the young man's soul there were reawakening old, long-concealed impressions; with the result that many a spot which had long been faded from his memory now filled him with interest, and the beautiful views on the estate found him gazing at them like a newcomer, and with a beating heart. Yes, as the road wound through a narrow ravine, and became engulfed in a forest where, both above and below, he saw three-centuries-old oaks which three men could not have spanned, and where Siberian firs and elms overtopped even the poplars, and as he asked the peasants to tell him to whom the forest belonged, and they replied, "To Tientietnikov," and he issued from the forest, and proceeded on his way through meadows, and past spinneys of elder, and of old and young willows, and arrived in sight of the distant range of hills, and, crossing by two different bridges the winding river (which he left successively to right and to left of him as he did so), he again questioned some peasants concerning the ownership of the meadows and the flooded lands, and was again informed that they all belonged to Tientietnikov, and then, ascending a rise, reached a tableland where, on one side, lay ungarnered fields of wheat and rye and barley, and, on the other, the country already traversed (but which now showed in shortened perspective), and then plunged into the shade of some forked, umbrageous trees which stood scattered over turf and extended to the manor-house itself, and caught glimpses of the carved huts of the peasants, and of the red roofs of the stone manorial outbuildings, and of the glittering pinnacles of the church, and felt his heart beating, and knew, without being told by any one, whither he had at length arrived—well, then the feeling which had been growing within his soul burst forth, and he cried in ecstasy:

"Why have I been a fool so long? Why, seeing that fate has appointed me to be ruler of an earthly paradise, did I prefer to bind myself in servitude as a scribe of lifeless documents? To think that, after I had been nurtured and schooled and stored with all the knowledge necessary for the diffusion of good among those under me, and for the improvement of my domain, and for the fulfilment of the manifold duties of a landowner who is at once judge, administrator, and constable of his people, I should have entrusted my estate to an ignorant bailiff, and sought to maintain an absentee guardianship over the affairs of serfs whom I have never met, and of whose capabilities and characters I am yet ignorant! To think that I should have deemed true estate-management inferior to a documentary, fantastical management of provinces which lie a thousand versts away, and which my foot has never trod, and where I could never have effected aught but blunders and irregularities!"

Meanwhile another spectacle was being prepared for him. On learning that the barin was approaching the mansion, the muzhiks collected on the verandah in very variety of picturesque dress and tonsure; and when these good folk surrounded him, and there arose a resounding shout of "Here is our Foster Father! He has remembered us!" and, in spite of themselves, some of the older men and women began weeping as they recalled his grandfather and great-grandfather, he himself could not restrain his tears, but reflected: "How much affection! And in return for what? In return for my never having come to see them—in return for my never having taken the least interest in their affairs!" And then and there he registered a mental vow to share their every task and occupation.

So he applied himself to supervising and administering. He reduced the amount of the barstchina 40, he decreased the number of working-days for the owner, and he augmented the sum of the peasants' leisure-time. He also dismissed the fool of a bailiff, and took to bearing a personal hand in everything—to being present in the fields, at the threshing-floor, at the kilns, at the wharf, at the freighting of barges and rafts, and at their conveyance down the river: wherefore even the lazy hands began to look to themselves. But this did not last long. The peasant is an observant individual, and Tientietnikov's muzhiks soon scented the fact that, though energetic and desirous of doing much, the barin had no notion how to do it, nor even how to set about it—that, in short, he spoke by the book rather than out of his personal knowledge. Consequently things resulted, not in master and men failing to understand one another, but in their not singing together, in their not producing the very same note.

That is to say, it was not long before Tientietnikov noticed that on the manorial lands, nothing prospered to the extent that it did on the peasants'. The manorial crops were sown in good time, and came up well, and every one appeared to work his best, so much so that Tientietnikov, who supervised the whole, frequently ordered mugs of vodka to be served out as a reward for the excellence of the labour performed. Yet the rye on the peasants' land had formed into ear, and the oats had begun to shoot their grain, and the millet had filled before, on the manorial lands, the corn had so much as grown to stalk, or the ears had sprouted in embryo. In short, gradually the barin realised that, in spite of favours conferred, the peasants were playing the rogue with him. Next he resorted to remonstrance, but was met with the reply, "How could we not do our best for our barin? You yourself saw how well we laboured at the ploughing and the sowing, for you gave us mugs of vodka for our pains."

"Then why have things turned out so badly?" the barin persisted.

"Who can say? It must be that a grub has eaten the crop from below. Besides, what a summer has it been—never a drop of rain!"

Nevertheless, the barin noted that no grub had eaten the PEASANTS' crops, as well as that the rain had fallen in the most curious fashion—namely, in patches. It had obliged the muzhiks, but had shed a mere sprinkling for the barin.

Still more difficult did he find it to deal with the peasant women. Ever and anon they would beg to be excused from work, or start making complaints of the severity of the barstchina. Indeed, they were terrible folk! However, Tientietnikov abolished the majority of the tithes of linen, hedge fruit, mushrooms, and nuts, and also reduced by one-half other tasks proper to the women, in the hope that they would devote their spare time to their own domestic concerns—namely, to sewing and mending, and to making clothes for their husbands, and to increasing the area of their kitchen gardens. Yet no such result came about. On the contrary, such a pitch did the idleness, the quarrelsomeness, and the intriguing and caballing of the fair sex attain that their helpmeets were for ever coming to the barin with a request that he would rid one or another of his wife, since she had become a nuisance, and to live with her was impossible.

Next, hardening his heart, the barin attempted severity. But of what avail was severity? The peasant woman remained always the peasant woman, and would come and whine that she was sick and ailing, and keep pitifully hugging to herself the mean and filthy rags which she had donned for the occasion. And when poor Tientietnikov found himself unable to say more to her than just, "Get out of my sight, and may the Lord go with you!" the next item in the comedy would be that he would see her, even as she was leaving his gates, fall to contending with a neighbour for, say, the possession of a turnip, and dealing out slaps in the face such as even a strong, healthy man could scarcely have compassed!

Again, amongst other things, Tientietnikov conceived the idea of establishing a school for his people; but the scheme resulted in a farce which left him in sackcloth and ashes. In the same way he found that, when it came to a question of dispensing justice and of adjusting disputes, the host of juridical subtleties with which the professors had provided him proved absolutely useless. That is to say, the one party lied, and the other party lied, and only the devil could have decided between them. Consequently he himself perceived that a knowledge of mankind would have availed him more than all the legal refinements and philosophical maxims in the world could do. He lacked something; and though he could not divine what it was, the situation brought about was the common one of the barin failing to understand the peasant, and the peasant failing to understand the barin, and both becoming disaffected. In the end, these difficulties so chilled Tientietnikov's enthusiasm that he took to supervising the labours of the field with greatly diminished attention. That is to say, no matter whether the scythes were softly swishing through the grass, or ricks were being built, or rafts were being loaded, he would allow his eyes to wander from his men, and to fall to gazing at, say, a red-billed, red-legged heron which, after strutting along the bank of a stream, would have caught a fish in its beak, and be holding it awhile, as though in doubt whether to swallow it. Next he would glance towards the spot where a similar bird, but one not yet in possession of a fish, was engaged in watching the doings of its mate. Lastly, with eyebrows knitted, and face turned to scan the zenith, he would drink in the smell of the fields, and fall to listening to the winged population of the air as from earth and sky alike the manifold music of winged creatures combined in a single harmonious chorus. In the rye the quail would be calling, and, in the grass, the corncrake, and over them would be wheeling flocks of twittering linnets. Also, the jacksnipe would be uttering its croak, and the lark executing its roulades where it had become lost in the sunshine, and cranes sending forth their trumpet-like challenge as they deployed towards the zenith in triangle-shaped flocks. In fact, the neighbourhood would seem to have become converted into one great concert of melody. O Creator, how fair is Thy world where, in remote, rural seclusion, it lies apart from cities and from highways!

But soon even this began to pall upon Tientietnikov, and he ceased altogether to visit his fields, or to do aught but shut himself up in his rooms, where he refused to receive even the bailiff when that functionary called with his reports. Again, although, until now, he had to a certain extent associated with a retired colonel of hussars—a man saturated with tobacco smoke—and also with a student of pronounced, but immature, opinions who culled the bulk of his wisdom from contemporary newspapers and pamphlets, he found, as time went on, that these companions proved as tedious as the rest, and came to think their conversation superficial, and their European method of comporting themselves—that is to say, the method of conversing with much slapping of knees and a great deal of bowing and gesticulation—too direct and unadorned. So these and every one else he decided to "drop," and carried this resolution into effect with a certain amount of rudeness. On the next occasion that Varvar Nikolaievitch Vishnepokromov called to indulge in a free-and-easy symposium on politics, philosophy, literature, morals, and the state of financial affairs in England (he was, in all matters which admit of superficial discussion, the pleasantest fellow alive, seeing that he was a typical representative both of the retired fire-eater and of the school of thought which is now becoming the rage)—when, I say, this next happened, Tientietnikov merely sent out to say that he was not at home, and then carefully showed himself at the window. Host and guest exchanged glances, and, while the one muttered through his teeth "The cur!" the other relieved his feelings with a remark or two on swine. Thus the acquaintance came to an abrupt end, and from that time forth no visitor called at the mansion.

Tientietnikov in no way regretted this, for he could now devote himself wholly to the projection of a great work on Russia. Of the scale on which this composition was conceived the reader is already aware. The reader also knows how strange, how unsystematic, was the system employed in it. Yet to say that Tientietnikov never awoke from his lethargy would not be altogether true. On the contrary, when the post brought him newspapers and reviews, and he saw in their printed pages, perhaps, the well-known name of some former comrade who had succeeded in the great field of Public Service, or had conferred upon science and the world's work some notable contribution, he would succumb to secret and suppressed grief, and involuntarily there would burst from his soul an expression of aching, voiceless regret that he himself had done so little. And at these times his existence would seem to him odious and repellent; at these times there would uprise before him the memory of his school days, and the figure of Alexander Petrovitch, as vivid as in life. And, slowly welling, the tears would course over Tientietnikov's cheeks.

What meant these repinings? Was there not disclosed in them the secret of his galling spiritual pain—the fact that he had failed to order his life aright, to confirm the lofty aims with which he had started his course; the fact that, always poorly equipped with experience, he had failed to attain the better and the higher state, and there to strengthen himself for the overcoming of hindrances and obstacles; the fact that, dissolving like overheated metal, his bounteous store of superior instincts had failed to take the final tempering; the fact that the tutor of his boyhood, a man in a thousand, had prematurely died, and left to Tientietnikov no one who could restore to him the moral strength shattered by vacillation and the will power weakened by want of virility—no one, in short, who could cry hearteningly to his soul "Forward!"—the word for which the Russian of every degree, of every class, of every occupation, of every school of thought, is for ever hungering.

Indeed, WHERE is the man who can cry aloud for any of us, in the Russian tongue dear to our soul, the all-compelling command "Forward!"? Who is there who, knowing the strength and the nature and the inmost depths of the Russian genius, can by a single magic incantation divert our ideals to the higher life? Were there such a man, with what tears, with what affection, would not the grateful sons of Russia repay him! Yet age succeeds to age, and our callow youth still lies wrapped in shameful sloth, or strives and struggles to no purpose. God has not yet given us the man able to sound the call.

One circumstance which almost aroused Tientietnikov, which almost brought about a revolution in his character, was the fact that he came very near to falling in love. Yet even this resulted in nothing. Ten versts away there lived the general whom we have heard expressing himself in highly uncomplimentary terms concerning Tientietnikov. He maintained a General-like establishment, dispensed hospitality (that is to say, was glad when his neighbours came to pay him their respects, though he himself never went out), spoke always in a hoarse voice, read a certain number of books, and had a daughter—a curious, unfamiliar type, but full of life as life itself. This maiden's name was Ulinka, and she had been strangely brought up, for, losing her mother in early childhood, she had subsequently received instruction at the hands of an English governess who knew not a single word of Russian. Moreover her father, though excessively fond of her, treated her always as a toy; with the result that, as she grew to years of discretion, she became wholly wayward and spoilt. Indeed, had any one seen the sudden rage which would gather on her beautiful young forehead when she was engaged in a heated dispute with her father, he would have thought her one of the most capricious beings in the world. Yet that rage gathered only when she had heard of injustice or harsh treatment, and never because she desired to argue on her own behalf, or to attempt to justify her own conduct. Also, that anger would disappear as soon as ever she saw any one whom she had formerly disliked fall upon evil times, and, at his first request for alms would, without consideration or subsequent regret, hand him her purse and its whole contents. Yes, her every act was strenuous, and when she spoke her whole personality seemed to be following hot-foot upon her thought—both her expression of face and her diction and the movements of her hands. Nay, the very folds of her frock had a similar appearance of striving; until one would have thought that all her self were flying in pursuit of her words. Nor did she know reticence: before any one she would disclose her mind, and no force could compel her to maintain silence when she desired to speak. Also, her enchanting, peculiar gait—a gait which belonged to her alone—was so absolutely free and unfettered that every one involuntarily gave her way. Lastly, in her presence churls seemed to become confused and fall to silence, and even the roughest and most outspoken would lose their heads, and have not a word to say; whereas the shy man would find himself able to converse as never in his life before, and would feel, from the first, as though he had seen her and known her at some previous period—during the days of some unremembered childhood, when he was at home, and spending a merry evening among a crowd of romping children. And for long afterwards he would feel as though his man's intellect and estate were a burden.

This was what now befell Tientietnikov; and as it did so a new feeling entered into his soul, and his dreamy life lightened for a moment.

At first the General used to receive him with hospitable civility, but permanent concord between them proved impossible; their conversation always merged into dissension and soreness, seeing that, while the General could not bear to be contradicted or worsted in an argument, Tientietnikov was a man of extreme sensitiveness. True, for the daughter's sake, the father was for a while deferred to, and thus peace was maintained; but this lasted only until the time when there arrived, on a visit to the General, two kinswomen of his—the Countess Bordirev and the Princess Uziakin, retired Court dames, but ladies who still kept up a certain connection with Court circles, and therefore were much fawned upon by their host. No sooner had they appeared on the scene than (so it seemed to Tientietnikov) the General's attitude towards the young man became colder—either he ceased to notice him at all or he spoke to him familiarly, and as to a person having no standing in society. This offended Tientietnikov deeply, and though, when at length he spoke out on the subject, he retained sufficient presence of mind to compress his lips, and to preserve a gentle and courteous tone, his face flushed and his inner man was boiling.

"General," he said, "I thank you for your condescension. By addressing me in the second person singular, you have admitted me to the circle of your most intimate friends. Indeed, were it not that a difference of years forbids any familiarity on my part, I should answer you in similar fashion."

The General sat aghast. At length, rallying his tongue and his faculties, he replied that, though he had spoken with a lack of ceremony, he had used the term "thou" merely as an elderly man naturally employs it towards a junior (he made no reference to difference of rank).

Nevertheless, the acquaintance broke off here, and with it any possibility of love-making. The light which had shed a momentary gleam before Tientietnikov's eyes had become extinguished for ever, and upon it there followed a darkness denser than before. Henceforth everything conduced to evolve the regime which the reader has noted—that regime of sloth and inaction which converted Tientietnikov's residence into a place of dirt and neglect. For days at a time would a broom and a heap of dust be left lying in the middle of a room, and trousers tossing about the salon, and pairs of worn-out braces adorning the what-not near the sofa. In short, so mean and untidy did Tientietnikov's mode of life become, that not only his servants, but even his very poultry ceased to treat him with respect. Taking up a pen, he would spend hours in idly sketching houses, huts, waggons, troikas, and flourishes on a piece of paper; while at other times, when he had sunk into a reverie, the pen would, all unknowingly, sketch a small head which had delicate features, a pair of quick, penetrating eyes, and a raised coiffure. Then suddenly the dreamer would perceive, to his surprise, that the pen had executed the portrait of a maiden whose picture no artist could adequately have painted; and therewith his despondency would become greater than ever, and, believing that happiness did not exist on earth, he would relapse into increased ennui, increased neglect of his responsibilities.

But one morning he noticed, on moving to the window after breakfast, that not a word was proceeding either from the butler or the housekeeper, but that, on the contrary, the courtyard seemed to smack of a certain bustle and excitement. This was because through the entrance gates (which the kitchen maid and the scullion had run to open) there were appearing the noses of three horses—one to the right, one in the middle, and one to the left, after the fashion of triumphal groups of statuary. Above them, on the box seat, were seated a coachman and a valet, while behind, again, there could be discerned a gentleman in a scarf and a fur cap. Only when the equipage had entered the courtyard did it stand revealed as a light spring britchka. And as it came to a halt, there leapt on to the verandah of the mansion an individual of respectable exterior, and possessed of the art of moving with the neatness and alertness of a military man.

Upon this Tientietnikov's heart stood still. He was unused to receiving visitors, and for the moment conceived the new arrival to be a Government official, sent to question him concerning an abortive society to which he had formerly belonged. (Here the author may interpolate the fact that, in Tientietnikov's early days, the young man had become mixed up in a very absurd affair. That is to say, a couple of philosophers belonging to a regiment of hussars had, together with an aesthete who had not yet completed his student's course and a gambler who had squandered his all, formed a secret society of philanthropic aims under the presidency of a certain old rascal of a freemason and the ruined gambler aforesaid. The scope of the society's work was to be extensive: it was to bring lasting happiness to humanity at large, from the banks of the Thames to the shores of Kamtchatka. But for this much money was needed: wherefore from the noble-minded members of the society generous contributions were demanded, and then forwarded to a destination known only to the supreme authorities of the concern. As for Tientietnikov's adhesion, it was brought about by the two friends already alluded to as "embittered"—good-hearted souls whom the wear and tear of their efforts on behalf of science, civilisation, and the future emancipation of mankind had ended by converting into confirmed drunkards. Perhaps it need hardly be said that Tientietnikov soon discovered how things stood, and withdrew from the association; but, meanwhile, the latter had had the misfortune so to have engaged in dealings not wholly creditable to gentlemen of noble origin as likewise to have become entangled in dealings with the police. Consequently, it is not to be wondered at that, though Tientietnikov had long severed his connection with the society and its policy, he still remained uneasy in his mind as to what might even yet be the result.)

However, his fears vanished the instant that the guest saluted him with marked politeness and explained, with many deferential poises of the head, and in terms at once civil and concise, that for some time past he (the newcomer) had been touring the Russian Empire on business and in the pursuit of knowledge, that the Empire abounded in objects of interest—not to mention a plenitude of manufactures and a great diversity of soil, and that, in spite of the fact that he was greatly struck with the amenities of his host's domain, he would certainly not have presumed to intrude at such an inconvenient hour but for the circumstance that the inclement spring weather, added to the state of the roads, had necessitated sundry repairs to his carriage at the hands of wheelwrights and blacksmiths. Finally he declared that, even if this last had NOT happened, he would still have felt unable to deny himself the pleasure of offering to his host that meed of homage which was the latter's due.

This speech—a speech of fascinating bonhomie—delivered, the guest executed a sort of shuffle with a half-boot of patent leather studded with buttons of mother-of-pearl, and followed that up by (in spite of his pronounced rotundity of figure) stepping backwards with all the elan of an india-rubber ball.

From this the somewhat reassured Tientietnikov concluded that his visitor must be a literary, knowledge-seeking professor who was engaged in roaming the country in search of botanical specimens and fossils; wherefore he hastened to express both his readiness to further the visitor's objects (whatever they might be) and his personal willingness to provide him with the requisite wheelwrights and blacksmiths. Meanwhile he begged his guest to consider himself at home, and, after seating him in an armchair, made preparations to listen to the newcomer's discourse on natural history.

But the newcomer applied himself, rather, to phenomena of the internal world, saying that his life might be likened to a barque tossed on the crests of perfidious billows, that in his time he had been fated to play many parts, and that on more than one occasion his life had stood in danger at the hands of foes. At the same time, these tidings were communicated in a manner calculated to show that the speaker was also a man of PRACTICAL capabilities. In conclusion, the visitor took out a cambric pocket-handkerchief, and sneezed into it with a vehemence wholly new to Tientietnikov's experience. In fact, the sneeze rather resembled the note which, at times, the trombone of an orchestra appears to utter not so much from its proper place on the platform as from the immediate neighbourhood of the listener's ear. And as the echoes of the drowsy mansion resounded to the report of the explosion there followed upon the same a wave of perfume, skilfully wafted abroad with a flourish of the eau-de-Cologne-scented handkerchief.

By this time the reader will have guessed that the visitor was none other than our old and respected friend Paul Ivanovitch Chichikov. Naturally, time had not spared him his share of anxieties and alarms; wherefore his exterior had come to look a trifle more elderly, his frockcoat had taken on a suggestion of shabbiness, and britchka, coachman, valet, horses, and harness alike had about them a sort of second-hand, worse-for-wear effect. Evidently the Chichikovian finances were not in the most flourishing of conditions. Nevertheless, the old expression of face, the old air of breeding and refinement, remained unimpaired, and our hero had even improved in the art of walking and turning with grace, and of dexterously crossing one leg over the other when taking a seat. Also, his mildness of diction, his discreet moderation of word and phrase, survived in, if anything, increased measure, and he bore himself with a skill which caused his tactfulness to surpass itself in sureness of aplomb. And all these accomplishments had their effect further heightened by a snowy immaculateness of collar and dickey, and an absence of dust from his frockcoat, as complete as though he had just arrived to attend a nameday festival. Lastly, his cheeks and chin were of such neat clean-shavenness that no one but a blind man could have failed to admire their rounded contours.

From that moment onwards great changes took place in Tientietnikov's establishment, and certain of its rooms assumed an unwonted air of cleanliness and order. The rooms in question were those assigned to Chichikov, while one other apartment—a little front chamber opening into the hall—became permeated with Petrushka's own peculiar smell. But this lasted only for a little while, for presently Petrushka was transferred to the servants' quarters, a course which ought to have been adopted in the first instance.

During the initial days of Chichikov's sojourn, Tientietnikov feared rather to lose his independence, inasmuch as he thought that his guest might hamper his movements, and bring about alterations in the established routine of the place. But these fears proved groundless, for Paul Ivanovitch displayed an extraordinary aptitude for accommodating himself to his new position. To begin with, he encouraged his host in his philosophical inertia by saying that the latter would help Tientietnikov to become a centenarian. Next, in the matter of a life of isolation, he hit things off exactly by remarking that such a life bred in a man a capacity for high thinking. Lastly, as he inspected the library and dilated on books in general, he contrived an opportunity to observe that literature safeguarded a man from a tendency to waste his time. In short, the few words of which he delivered himself were brief, but invariably to the point. And this discretion of speech was outdone by his discretion of conduct. That is to say, whether entering or leaving the room, he never wearied his host with a question if Tientietnikov had the air of being disinclined to talk; and with equal satisfaction the guest could either play chess or hold his tongue. Consequently Tientietnikov said to himself:

"For the first time in my life I have met with a man with whom it is possible to live. In general, not many of the type exist in Russia, and, though clever, good-humoured, well-educated men abound, one would be hard put to it to find an individual of equable temperament with whom one could share a roof for centuries without a quarrel arising. Anyway, Chichikov is the first of his sort that I have met."

For his part, Chichikov was only too delighted to reside with a person so quiet and agreeable as his host. Of a wandering life he was temporarily weary, and to rest, even for a month, in such a beautiful spot, and in sight of green fields and the slow flowering of spring, was likely to benefit him also from the hygienic point of view. And, indeed, a more delightful retreat in which to recuperate could not possibly have been found. The spring, long retarded by previous cold, had now begun in all its comeliness, and life was rampant. Already, over the first emerald of the grass, the dandelion was showing yellow, and the red-pink anemone was hanging its tender head; while the surface of every pond was a swarm of dancing gnats and midges, and the water-spider was being joined in their pursuit by birds which gathered from every quarter to the vantage-ground of the dry reeds. Every species of creature also seemed to be assembling in concourse, and taking stock of one another. Suddenly the earth became populous, the forest had opened its eyes, and the meadows were lifting up their voice in song. In the same way had choral dances begun to be weaved in the village, and everywhere that the eye turned there was merriment. What brightness in the green of nature, what freshness in the air, what singing of birds in the gardens of the mansion, what general joy and rapture and exaltation! Particularly in the village might the shouting and singing have been in honour of a wedding!

Chichikov walked hither, thither, and everywhere—a pursuit for which there was ample choice and facility. At one time he would direct his steps along the edge of the flat tableland, and contemplate the depths below, where still there lay sheets of water left by the floods of winter, and where the island-like patches of forest showed leafless boughs; while at another time he would plunge into the thicket and ravine country, where nests of birds weighted branches almost to the ground, and the sky was darkened with the criss-cross flight of cawing rooks. Again, the drier portions of the meadows could be crossed to the river wharves, whence the first barges were just beginning to set forth with pea-meal and barley and wheat, while at the same time one's ear would be caught with the sound of some mill resuming its functions as once more the water turned the wheel. Chichikov would also walk afield to watch the early tillage operations of the season, and observe how the blackness of a new furrow would make its way across the expanse of green, and how the sower, rhythmically striking his hand against the pannier slung across his breast, would scatter his fistfuls of seed with equal distribution, apportioning not a grain too much to one side or to the other.

In fact, Chichikov went everywhere. He chatted and talked, now with the bailiff, now with a peasant, now with a miller, and inquired into the manner and nature of everything, and sought information as to how an estate was managed, and at what price corn was selling, and what species of grain was best for spring and autumn grinding, and what was the name of each peasant, and who were his kinsfolk, and where he had bought his cow, and what he fed his pigs on. Chichikov also made inquiry concerning the number of peasants who had lately died: but of these there appeared to be few. And suddenly his quick eye discerned that Tientietnikov's estate was not being worked as it might have been—that much neglect and listlessness and pilfering and drunkenness was abroad; and on perceiving this, he thought to himself: "What a fool is that Tientietnikov! To think of letting a property like this decay when he might be drawing from it an income of fifty thousand roubles a year!"

Also, more than once, while taking these walks, our hero pondered the idea of himself becoming a landowner—not now, of course, but later, when his chief aim should have been achieved, and he had got into his hands the necessary means for living the quiet life of the proprietor of an estate. Yes, and at these times there would include itself in his castle-building the figure of a young, fresh, fair-faced maiden of the mercantile or other rich grade of society, a woman who could both play and sing. He also dreamed of little descendants who should perpetuate the name of Chichikov; perhaps a frolicsome little boy and a fair young daughter, or possibly, two boys and quite two or three daughters; so that all should know that he had really lived and had his being, that he had not merely roamed the world like a spectre or a shadow; so that for him and his the country should never be put to shame. And from that he would go on to fancy that a title appended to his rank would not be a bad thing—the title of State Councillor, for instance, which was deserving of all honour and respect. Ah, it is a common thing for a man who is taking a solitary walk so to detach himself from the irksome realities of the present that he is able to stir and to excite and to provoke his imagination to the conception of things he knows can never really come to pass!

Chichikov's servants also found the mansion to their taste, and, like their master, speedily made themselves at home in it. In particular did Petrushka make friends with Grigory the butler, although at first the pair showed a tendency to outbrag one another—Petrushka beginning by throwing dust in Grigory's eyes on the score of his (Petrushka's) travels, and Grigory taking him down a peg or two by referring to St. Petersburg (a city which Petrushka had never visited), and Petrushka seeking to recover lost ground by dilating on towns which he HAD visited, and Grigory capping this by naming some town which is not to be found on any map in existence, and then estimating the journey thither as at least thirty thousand versts—a statement which would so completely flabbergast the henchman of Chichikov's suite that he would be left staring open-mouthed, amid the general laughter of the domestic staff. However, as I say, the pair ended by swearing eternal friendship with one another, and making a practice of resorting to the village tavern in company.

For Selifan, however, the place had a charm of a different kind. That is to say, each evening there would take place in the village a singing of songs and a weaving of country dances; and so shapely and buxom were the maidens—maidens of a type hard to find in our present-day villages on large estates—that he would stand for hours wondering which of them was the best. White-necked and white-bosomed, all had great roving eyes, the gait of peacocks, and hair reaching to the waist. And as, with his hands clasping theirs, he glided hither and thither in the dance, or retired backwards towards a wall with a row of other young fellows, and then, with them, returned to meet the damsels—all singing in chorus (and laughing as they sang it), "Boyars, show me my bridegroom!" and dusk was falling gently, and from the other side of the river there kept coming far, faint, plaintive echoes of the melody—well, then our Selifan hardly knew whether he were standing upon his head or his heels. Later, when sleeping and when waking, both at noon and at twilight, he would seem still to be holding a pair of white hands, and moving in the dance.

Chichikov's horses also found nothing of which to disapprove. Yes, both the bay, the Assessor, and the skewbald accounted residence at Tientietnikov's a most comfortable affair, and voted the oats excellent, and the arrangement of the stables beyond all cavil. True, on this occasion each horse had a stall to himself; yet, by looking over the intervening partition, it was possible always to see one's fellows, and, should a neighbour take it into his head to utter a neigh, to answer it at once.

As for the errand which had hitherto led Chichikov to travel about Russia, he had now decided to move very cautiously and secretly in the matter. In fact, on noticing that Tientietnikov went in absorbedly for reading and for talking philosophy, the visitor said to himself, "No—I had better begin at the other end," and proceeded first to feel his way among the servants of the establishment. From them he learnt several things, and, in particular, that the barin had been wont to go and call upon a certain General in the neighbourhood, and that the General possessed a daughter, and that she and Tientietnikov had had an affair of some sort, but that the pair had subsequently parted, and gone their several ways. For that matter, Chichikov himself had noticed that Tientietnikov was in the habit of drawing heads of which each representation exactly resembled the rest.

Once, as he sat tapping his silver snuff-box after luncheon, Chichikov remarked:

"One thing you lack, and only one, Andrei Ivanovitch."

"What is that?" asked his host.

"A female friend or two," replied Chichikov.

Tientietnikov made no rejoinder, and the conversation came temporarily to an end.

But Chichikov was not to be discouraged; wherefore, while waiting for supper and talking on different subjects, he seized an opportunity to interject:

"Do you know, it would do you no harm to marry."

As before, Tientietnikov did not reply, and the renewed mention of the subject seemed to have annoyed him.

For the third time—it was after supper—Chichikov returned to the charge by remarking:

"To-day, as I was walking round your property, I could not help thinking that marriage would do you a great deal of good. Otherwise you will develop into a hypochondriac."

Whether Chichikov's words now voiced sufficiently the note of persuasion, or whether Tientietnikov happened, at the moment, to be unusually disposed to frankness, at all events the young landowner sighed, and then responded as he expelled a puff of tobacco smoke:

"To attain anything, Paul Ivanovitch, one needs to have been born under a lucky star."

And he related to his guest the whole history of his acquaintanceship and subsequent rupture with the General.

As Chichikov listened to the recital, and gradually realised that the affair had arisen merely out of a chance word on the General's part, he was astounded beyond measure, and gazed at Tientietnikov without knowing what to make of him.

"Andrei Ivanovitch," he said at length, "what was there to take offence at?"

"Nothing, as regards the actual words spoken," replied the other. "The offence lay, rather, in the insult conveyed in the General's tone." Tientietnikov was a kindly and peaceable man, yet his eyes flashed as he said this, and his voice vibrated with wounded feeling.

"Yet, even then, need you have taken it so much amiss?"

"What? Could I have gone on visiting him as before?"

"Certainly. No great harm had been done?"

"I disagree with you. Had he been an old man in a humble station of life, instead of a proud and swaggering officer, I should not have minded so much. But, as it was, I could not, and would not, brook his words."

"A curious fellow, this Tientietnikov!" thought Chichikov to himself.

"A curious fellow, this Chichikov!" was Tientietnikov's inward reflection.

"I tell you what," resumed Chichikov. "To-morrow I myself will go and see the General."

"To what purpose?" asked Tientietnikov, with astonishment and distrust in his eyes.

"To offer him an assurance of my personal respect."

"A strange fellow, this Chichikov!" reflected Tientietnikov.

"A strange fellow, this Tientietnikov!" thought Chichikov, and then added aloud: "Yes, I will go and see him at ten o'clock to-morrow; but since my britchka is not yet altogether in travelling order, would you be so good as to lend me your koliaska for the purpose?"

CHAPTER II

Tientietnikov's good horses covered the ten versts to the General's house in a little over half an hour. Descending from the koliaska with features attuned to deference, Chichikov inquired for the master of the house, and was at once ushered into his presence. Bowing with head held respectfully on one side and hands extended like those of a waiter carrying a trayful of teacups, the visitor inclined his whole body forward, and said:

"I have deemed it my duty to present myself to your Excellency. I have deemed it my duty because in my heart I cherish a most profound respect for the valiant men who, on the field of battle, have proved the saviours of their country."

That this preliminary attack did not wholly displease the General was proved by the fact that, responding with a gracious inclination of the head, he replied:

"I am glad to make your acquaintance. Pray be so good as to take a seat. In what capacity or capacities have you yourself seen service?"

"Of my service," said Chichikov, depositing his form, not exactly in the centre of the chair, but rather on one side of it, and resting a hand upon one of its arms, "—of my service the scene was laid, in the first instance, in the Treasury; while its further course bore me successively into the employ of the Public Buildings Commission, of the Customs Board, and of other Government Offices. But, throughout, my life has resembled a barque tossed on the crests of perfidious billows. In suffering I have been swathed and wrapped until I have come to be, as it were, suffering personified; while of the extent to which my life has been sought by foes, no words, no colouring, no (if I may so express it?) painter's brush could ever convey to you an adequate idea. And now, at length, in my declining years, I am seeking a corner in which to eke out the remainder of my miserable existence, while at the present moment I am enjoying the hospitality of a neighbour of your acquaintance."

"And who is that?"

"Your neighbour Tientietnikov, your Excellency."

Upon that the General frowned.

"Led me add," put in Chichikov hastily, "that he greatly regrets that on a former occasion he should have failed to show a proper respect for—for—"

"For what?" asked the General.

"For the services to the public which your Excellency has rendered. Indeed, he cannot find words to express his sorrow, but keeps repeating to himself: 'Would that I had valued at their true worth the men who have saved our fatherland!'"

"And why should he say that?" asked the mollified General. "I bear him no grudge. In fact, I have never cherished aught but a sincere liking for him, a sincere esteem, and do not doubt but that, in time, he may become a useful member of society."

"In the words which you have been good enough to utter," said Chichikov with a bow, "there is embodied much justice. Yes, Tientietnikov is in very truth a man of worth. Not only does he possess the gift of eloquence, but also he is a master of the pen."

"Ah, yes; he DOES write rubbish of some sort, doesn't he? Verses, or something of the kind?"

"Not rubbish, your Excellency, but practical stuff. In short, he is inditing a history."

"A HISTORY? But a history of what?"

"A history of, of—" For a moment or two Chichikov hesitated. Then, whether because it was a General that was seated in front of him, or because he desired to impart greater importance to the subject which he was about to invent, he concluded: "A history of Generals, your Excellency."

"Of Generals? Of WHAT Generals?"

"Of Generals generally—of Generals at large. That is to say, and to be more precise, a history of the Generals of our fatherland."

By this time Chichikov was floundering badly. Mentally he spat upon himself and reflected: "Gracious heavens! What rubbish I am talking!"

"Pardon me," went on his interlocutor, "but I do not quite understand you. Is Tientietnikov producing a history of a given period, or only a history made up of a series of biographies? Also, is he including ALL our Generals, or only those who took part in the campaign of 1812?"

"The latter, your Excellency—only the Generals of 1812," replied Chichikov. Then he added beneath his breath: "Were I to be killed for it, I could not say what that may be supposed to mean."

"Then why should he not come and see me in person?" went on his host. "Possibly I might be able to furnish him with much interesting material?"

"He is afraid to come, your Excellency."

"Nonsense! Just because of a hasty word or two! I am not that sort of man at all. In fact, I should be very happy to call upon HIM."

"Never would he permit that, your Excellency. He would greatly prefer to be the first to make advances." And Chichikov added to himself: "What a stroke of luck those Generals were! Otherwise, the Lord knows where my tongue might have landed me!"

At this moment the door into the adjoining room opened, and there appeared in the doorway a girl as fair as a ray of the sun—so fair, indeed, that Chichikov stared at her in amazement. Apparently she had come to speak to her father for a moment, but had stopped short on perceiving that there was some one with him. The only fault to be found in her appearance was the fact that she was too thin and fragile-looking.

"May I introduce you to my little pet?" said the General to Chichikov. "To tell you the truth, I do not know your name."

"That you should be unacquainted with the name of one who has never distinguished himself in the manner of which you yourself can boast is scarcely to be wondered at." And Chichikov executed one of his sidelong, deferential bows.

"Well, I should be delighted to know it."

"It is Paul Ivanovitch Chichikov, your Excellency." With that went the easy bow of a military man and the agile backward movement of an india-rubber ball.

"Ulinka, this is Paul Ivanovitch," said the General, turning to his daughter. "He has just told me some interesting news—namely, that our neighbour Tientietnikov is not altogether the fool we had at first thought him. On the contrary, he is engaged upon a very important work—upon a history of the Russian Generals of 1812."

"But who ever supposed him to be a fool?" asked the girl quickly. "What happened was that you took Vishnepokromov's word—the word of a man who is himself both a fool and a good-for-nothing."

"Well, well," said the father after further good-natured dispute on the subject of Vishnepokromov. "Do you now run away, for I wish to dress for luncheon. And you, sir," he added to Chichikov, "will you not join us at table?"

Chichikov bowed so low and so long that, by the time that his eyes had ceased to see nothing but his own boots, the General's daughter had disappeared, and in her place was standing a bewhiskered butler, armed with a silver soap-dish and a hand-basin.

"Do you mind if I wash in your presence?" asked the host.

"By no means," replied Chichikov. "Pray do whatsoever you please in that respect."

Upon that the General fell to scrubbing himself—incidentally, to sending soapsuds flying in every direction. Meanwhile he seemed so favourably disposed that Chichikov decided to sound him then and there, more especially since the butler had left the room.

"May I put to you a problem?" he asked.

"Certainly," replied the General. "What is it?"

"It is this, your Excellency. I have a decrepit old uncle who owns three hundred souls and two thousand roubles-worth of other property. Also, except for myself, he possesses not a single heir. Now, although his infirm state of health will not permit of his managing his property in person, he will not allow me either to manage it. And the reason for his conduct—his very strange conduct—he states as follows: 'I do not know my nephew, and very likely he is a spendthrift. If he wishes to show me that he is good for anything, let him go and acquire as many souls as *I* have acquired; and when he has done that I will transfer to him my three hundred souls as well.'"

"The man must be an absolute fool," commented the General.

"Possibly. And were that all, things would not be as bad as they are. But, unfortunately, my uncle has gone and taken up with his housekeeper, and has had children by her. Consequently, everything will now pass to THEM."

"The old man must have taken leave of his senses," remarked the General. "Yet how *I* can help you I fail to see."

"Well, I have thought of a plan. If you will hand me over all the dead souls on your estate—hand them over to me exactly as though they were still alive, and were purchasable property—I will offer them to the old man, and then he will leave me his fortune."

At this point the General burst into a roar of laughter such as few can ever have heard. Half-dressed, he subsided into a chair, threw back his head, and guffawed until he came near to choking. In fact, the house shook with his merriment, so much so that the butler and his daughter came running into the room in alarm.

It was long before he could produce a single articulate word; and even when he did so (to reassure his daughter and the butler) he kept momentarily relapsing into spluttering chuckles which made the house ring and ring again.

Chichikov was greatly taken aback.

"Oh, that uncle!" bellowed the General in paroxysms of mirth. "Oh, that blessed uncle! WHAT a fool he'll look! Ha, ha, ha! Dead souls offered him instead of live ones! Oh, my goodness!"

"I suppose I've put my foot in it again," ruefully reflected Chichikov. "But, good Lord, what a man the fellow is to laugh! Heaven send that he doesn't burst of it!"

"Ha, ha, ha!" broke out the General afresh. "WHAT a donkey the old man must be! To think of his saying to you: 'You go and fit yourself out with three hundred souls, and I'll cap them with my own lot'! My word! What a jackass!"

"A jackass, your Excellency?"

"Yes, indeed! And to think of the jest of putting him off with dead souls! Ha, ha, ha! WHAT wouldn't I give to see you handing him the title deeds? Who is he? What is he like? Is he very old?"

"He is eighty, your Excellency."

"But still brisk and able to move about, eh? Surely he must be pretty strong to go on living with his housekeeper like that?"

"Yes. But what does such strength mean? Sand runs away, your Excellency."

"The old fool! But is he really such a fool?"

"Yes, your Excellency."

"And does he go out at all? Does he see company? Can he still hold himself upright?"

"Yes, but with great difficulty."

"And has he any teeth left?"

"No more than two at the most."

"The old jackass! Don't be angry with me, but I must say that, though your uncle, he is also a jackass."

"Quite so, your Excellency. And though it grieves ME to have to confess that he is my uncle, what am I to do with him?"

Yet this was not altogether the truth. What would have been a far harder thing for Chichikov to have confessed was the fact that he possessed no uncles at all.

"I beg of you, your Excellency," he went on, "to hand me over those, those—"

"Those dead souls, eh? Why, in return for the jest I will give you some land as well. Yes, you can take the whole graveyard if you like. Ha, ha, ha! The old man! Ha, ha, ha! WHAT a fool he'll look! Ha, ha, ha!"

And once more the General's guffaws went ringing through the house.

[At this point there is a long hiatus in the original.]

CHAPTER

III

"If Colonel Koshkarev should turn out to be as mad as the last one it is a bad look-out," said Chichikov to himself on opening his eyes amid fields and open country—everything else having disappeared save the vault of heaven and a couple of low-lying clouds.

"Selifan," he went on, "did you ask how to get to Colonel Koshkarev's?"

"Yes, Paul Ivanovitch. At least, there was such a clatter around the koliaska that I could not; but Petrushka asked the coachman."

"You fool! How often have I told you not to rely on Petrushka? Petrushka is a blockhead, an idiot. Besides, at the present moment I believe him to be drunk."

"No, you are wrong, barin," put in the person referred to, turning his head with a sidelong glance. "After we get down the next hill we shall need but to keep bending round it. That is all."

"Yes, and I suppose you'll tell me that sivnkha is the only thing that has passed your lips? Well, the view at least is beautiful. In fact, when one has seen this place one may say that one has seen one of the beauty spots of Europe." This said, Chichikov added to himself, smoothing his chin: "What a difference between the features of a civilised man of the world and those of a common lacquey!"

Meanwhile the koliaska quickened its pace, and Chichikov once more caught sight of Tientietnikov's aspen-studded meadows. Undulating gently on elastic springs, the vehicle cautiously descended the steep incline, and then proceeded past water-mills, rumbled over a bridge or two, and jolted easily along the rough-set road which traversed the flats. Not a molehill, not a mound jarred the spine. The vehicle was comfort itself.

Swiftly there flew by clumps of osiers, slender elder trees, and silver-leaved poplars, their branches brushing against Selifan and Petrushka, and at intervals depriving the valet of his cap. Each time that this happened, the sullen-faced servitor fell to cursing both the tree responsible for the occurrence and the landowner responsible for the tree being in existence; yet nothing would induce him thereafter either to tie on the cap or to steady it with his hand, so complete was his assurance that the accident would never be repeated. Soon to the foregoing trees there became added an occasional birch or spruce fir, while in the dense undergrowth around their roots could be seen the blue iris and the yellow wood-tulip. Gradually the forest grew darker, as though eventually the obscurity would become complete. Then through the trunks and the boughs there began to gleam points of light like glittering mirrors, and as the number of trees lessened, these points grew larger, until the travellers debouched upon the shore of a lake four versts or so in circumference, and having on its further margin the grey, scattered log huts of a peasant village. In the water a great commotion was in progress. In the first place, some twenty men, immersed to the knee, to the breast, or to the neck, were dragging a large fishing-net inshore, while, in the second place, there was entangled in the same, in addition to some fish, a stout man shaped precisely like a melon or a hogshead. Greatly excited, he was shouting at the top of his voice: "Let Kosma manage it, you lout of a Denis! Kosma, take the end of the rope from Denis! Don't bear so hard on it, Thoma Bolshoy 41! Go where Thoma Menshov 42 is! Damn it, bring the net to land, will you!" From this it became clear that it was not on his own account that the stout man was worrying. Indeed, he had no need to do so, since his fat would in any case have prevented him from sinking. Yes, even if he had turned head over heels in an effort to dive, the water would persistently have borne him up; and the same if, say, a couple of men had jumped on his back—the only result would have been that he would have become a trifle deeper submerged, and forced to draw breath by spouting bubbles through his nose. No, the cause of his agitation was lest the net should break, and the fish escape: wherefore he was urging some additional peasants who were standing on the bank to lay hold of and to pull at, an extra rope or two.

"That must be the barin—Colonel Koshkarev," said Selifan.

"Why?" asked Chichikov.

"Because, if you please, his skin is whiter than the rest, and he has the respectable paunch of a gentleman."

Meanwhile good progress was being made with the hauling in of the barin; until, feeling the ground with his feet, he rose to an upright position, and at the same moment caught sight of the koliaska, with Chichikov seated therein, descending the declivity.

"Have you dined yet?" shouted the barin as, still entangled in the net, he approached the shore with a huge fish on his back. With one hand shading his eyes from the sun, and the other thrown backwards, he looked, in point of pose, like the Medici Venus emerging from her bath.

"No," replied Chichikov, raising his cap, and executing a series of bows.

"Then thank God for that," rejoined the gentleman.

"Why?" asked Chichikov with no little curiosity, and still holding his cap over his head.

"Because of THIS. Cast off the net, Thoma Menshov, and pick up that sturgeon for the gentleman to see. Go and help him, Telepen Kuzma."

With that the peasants indicated picked up by the head what was a veritable monster of a fish.

"Isn't it a beauty—a sturgeon fresh run from the river?" exclaimed the stout barin. "And now let us be off home. Coachman, you can take the lower road through the kitchen garden. Run, you lout of a Thoma Bolshoy, and open the gate for him. He will guide you to the house, and I myself shall be along presently."

Thereupon the barelegged Thoma Bolshoy, clad in nothing but a shirt, ran ahead of the koliaska through the village, every hut of which had hanging in front of it a variety of nets, for the reason that every inhabitant of the place was a fisherman. Next, he opened a gate into a large vegetable enclosure, and thence the koliaska emerged into a square near a wooden church, with, showing beyond the latter, the roofs of the manorial homestead.

"A queer fellow, that Koshkarev!" said Chichikov to himself.

"Well, whatever I may be, at least I'm here," said a voice by his side. Chichikov looked round, and perceived that, in the meanwhile, the barin had dressed himself and overtaken the carriage. With a pair of yellow trousers he was wearing a grass-green jacket, and his neck was as guiltless of a collar as Cupid's. Also, as he sat sideways in his drozhki, his bulk was such that he completely filled the vehicle. Chichikov was about to make some remark or another when the stout gentleman disappeared; and presently his drozhki re-emerged into view at the spot where the fish had been drawn to land, and his voice could be heard reiterating exhortations to his serfs. Yet when Chichikov reached the verandah of the house he found, to his intense surprise, the stout gentleman waiting to welcome the visitor. How he had contrived to convey himself thither passed Chichikov's comprehension. Host and guest embraced three times, according to a bygone custom of Russia. Evidently the barin was one of the old school.

"I bring you," said Chichikov, "a greeting from his Excellency."

"From whom?"

"From your relative General Alexander Dmitrievitch."

"Who is Alexander Dmitrievitch?"

"What? You do not know General Alexander Dmitrievitch Betrishev?" exclaimed Chichikov with a touch of surprise.

"No, I do not," replied the gentleman.

Chichikov's surprise grew to absolute astonishment.

"How comes that about?" he ejaculated. "I hope that I have the honour of addressing Colonel Koshkarev?"

"Your hopes are vain. It is to my house, not to his, that you have come; and I am Peter Petrovitch Pietukh—yes, Peter Petrovitch Pietukh."

Chichikov, dumbfounded, turned to Selifan and Petrushka.

"What do you mean?" he exclaimed. "I told you to drive to the house of Colonel Koshkarev, whereas you have brought me to that of Peter Petrovitch Pietukh."

"All the same, your fellows have done quite right," put in the gentleman referred to. "Do you" (this to Selifan and Petrushka) "go to the kitchen, where they will give you a glassful of vodka apiece. Then put up the horses, and be off to the servants' quarters."

"I regret the mistake extremely," said Chichikov.

"But it is not a mistake. When you have tried the dinner which I have in store for you, just see whether you think IT a mistake. Enter, I beg of you." And, taking Chichikov by the arm, the host conducted him within, where they were met by a couple of youths.

"Let me introduce my two sons, home for their holidays from the Gymnasium 43," said Pietukh. "Nikolasha, come and entertain our good visitor, while you, Aleksasha, follow me." And with that the host disappeared.

Chichikov turned to Nikolasha, whom he found to be a budding man about town, since at first he opened a conversation by stating that, as no good was to be derived from studying at a provincial institution, he and his brother desired to remove, rather, to St. Petersburg, the provinces not being worth living in.

"I quite understand," Chichikov thought to himself. "The end of the chapter will be confectioners' assistants and the boulevards."

"Tell me," he added aloud, "how does your father's property at present stand?"

"It is all mortgaged," put in the father himself as he re-entered the room. "Yes, it is all mortgaged, every bit of it."

"What a pity!" thought Chichikov. "At this rate it will not be long before this man has no property at all left. I must hurry my departure." Aloud he said with an air of sympathy: "That you have mortgaged the estate seems to me a matter of regret."

"No, not at all," replied Pietukh. "In fact, they tell me that it is a good thing to do, and that every one else is doing it. Why should I act differently from my neighbours? Moreover, I have had enough of living here, and should like to try Moscow—more especially since my sons are always begging me to give them a metropolitan education."

"Oh, the fool, the fool!" reflected Chichikov. "He is for throwing up everything and making spendthrifts of his sons. Yet this is a nice property, and it is clear that the local peasants are doing well, and that the family, too, is comfortably off. On the other hand, as soon as ever these lads begin their education in restaurants and theatres, the devil will away with every stick of their substance. For my own part, I could desire nothing better than this quiet life in the country."

"Let me guess what is in your mind," said Pietukh.

"What, then?" asked Chichikov, rather taken aback.

"You are thinking to yourself: 'That fool of a Pietukh has asked me to dinner, yet not a bite of dinner do I see.' But wait a little. It will be ready presently, for it is being cooked as fast as a maiden who has had her hair cut off plaits herself a new set of tresses."

"Here comes Platon Mikhalitch, father!" exclaimed Aleksasha, who had been peeping out of the window.

"Yes, and on a grey horse," added his brother.

"Who is Platon Mikhalitch?" inquired Chichikov.

"A neighbour of ours, and an excellent fellow."

The next moment Platon Mikhalitch himself entered the room, accompanied by a sporting dog named Yarb. He was a tall, handsome man, with extremely red hair. As for his companion, it was of the keen-muzzled species used for shooting.

"Have you dined yet?" asked the host.

"Yes," replied Platon.

"Indeed? What do you mean by coming here to laugh at us all? Do I ever go to YOUR place after dinner?"

The newcomer smiled. "Well, if it can bring you any comfort," he said, "let me tell you that I ate nothing at the meal, for I had no appetite."

"But you should see what I have caught—what sort of a sturgeon fate has brought my way! Yes, and what crucians and carp!"

"Really it tires one to hear you. How come you always to be so cheerful?"

"And how come YOU always to be so gloomy?" retorted the host.

"How, you ask? Simply because I am so."

"The truth is you don't eat enough. Try the plan of making a good dinner. Weariness of everything is a modern invention. Once upon a time one never heard of it."

"Well, boast away, but have you yourself never been tired of things?"

"Never in my life. I do not so much as know whether I should find time to be tired. In the morning, when one awakes, the cook is waiting, and the dinner has to be ordered. Then one drinks one's morning tea, and then the bailiff arrives for HIS orders, and then there is fishing to be done, and then one's dinner has to be eaten. Next, before one has even had a chance to utter a snore, there enters once again the cook, and one has to order supper; and when she has departed, behold, back she comes with a request for the following day's dinner! What time does THAT leave one to be weary of things?"

Throughout this conversation, Chichikov had been taking stock of the newcomer, who astonished him with his good looks, his upright, picturesque figure, his appearance of fresh, unwasted youthfulness, and the boyish purity, innocence, and clarity of his features. Neither passion nor care nor aught of the nature of agitation or anxiety of mind had ventured to touch his unsullied face, or to lay a single wrinkle thereon. Yet the touch of life which those emotions might have imparted was wanting. The face was, as it were, dreaming, even though from time to time an ironical smile disturbed it.

"I, too, cannot understand," remarked Chichikov, "how a man of your appearance can find things wearisome. Of course, if a man is hard pressed for money, or if he has enemies who are lying in wait for his life (as have certain folk of whom I know), well, then—"

"Believe me when I say," interrupted the handsome guest, "that, for the sake of a diversion, I should be glad of ANY sort of an anxiety. Would that some enemy would conceive a grudge against me! But no one does so. Everything remains eternally dull."

"But perhaps you lack a sufficiency of land or souls?"

"Not at all. I and my brother own ten thousand desiatins 44 of land, and over a thousand souls."

"Curious! I do not understand it. But perhaps the harvest has failed, or you have sickness about, and many of your male peasants have died of it?"

"On the contrary, everything is in splendid order, for my brother is the best of managers."

"Then to find things wearisome!" exclaimed Chichikov. "It passes my comprehension." And he shrugged his shoulders.

"Well, we will soon put weariness to flight," interrupted the host. "Aleksasha, do you run helter-skelter to the kitchen, and there tell the cook to serve the fish pasties. Yes, and where have that gawk of an Emelian and that thief of an Antoshka got to? Why have they not handed round the zakuski?"

At this moment the door opened, and the "gawk" and the "thief" in question made their appearance with napkins and a tray—the latter bearing six decanters of variously-coloured beverages. These they placed upon the table, and then ringed them about with glasses and platefuls of every conceivable kind of appetiser. That done, the servants applied themselves to bringing in various comestibles under covers, through which could be heard the hissing of hot roast viands. In particular did the "gawk" and the "thief" work hard at their tasks. As a matter of fact, their appellations had been given them merely to spur them to greater activity, for, in general, the barin was no lover of abuse, but, rather, a kind-hearted man who, like most Russians, could not get on without a sharp word or two. That is to say, he needed them for his tongue as he need a glass of vodka for his digestion. What else could you expect? It was his nature to care for nothing mild.

To the zakuski succeeded the meal itself, and the host became a perfect glutton on his guests' behalf. Should he notice that a guest had taken but a single piece of a comestible, he added thereto another one, saying: "Without a mate, neither man nor bird can live in this world." Should any one take two pieces, he added thereto a third, saying: "What is the good of the number 2? God loves a trinity." Should any one take three pieces, he would say: "Where do you see a waggon with three wheels? Who builds a three-cornered hut?" Lastly, should any one take four pieces, he would cap them with a fifth, and add thereto the punning quip, "Na piat opiat 45". After devouring at least twelve steaks of sturgeon, Chichikov ventured to think to himself, "My host cannot possibly add to THEM," but found that he was mistaken, for, without a word, Pietukh heaped upon his plate an enormous portion of spit-roasted veal, and also some kidneys. And what veal it was!

"That calf was fed two years on milk," he explained. "I cared for it like my own son."

"Nevertheless I can eat no more," said Chichikov.

"Do you try the veal before you say that you can eat no more."

"But I could not get it down my throat. There is no room left."

"If there be no room in a church for a newcomer, the beadle is sent for, and room is very soon made—yes, even though before there was such a crush that an apple couldn't have been dropped between the people. Do you try the veal, I say. That piece is the titbit of all."

So Chichikov made the attempt; and in very truth the veal was beyond all praise, and room was found for it, even though one would have supposed the feat impossible.

"Fancy this good fellow removing to St. Petersburg or Moscow!" said the guest to himself. "Why, with a scale of living like this, he would be ruined in three years." For that matter, Pietukh might well have been ruined already, for hospitality can dissipate a fortune in three months as easily as it can in three years.

The host also dispensed the wine with a lavish hand, and what the guests did not drink he gave to his sons, who thus swallowed glass after glass. Indeed, even before coming to table, it was possible to discern to what department of human accomplishment their bent was turned. When the meal was over, however, the guests had no mind for further drinking. Indeed, it was all that they could do to drag themselves on to the balcony, and there to relapse into easy chairs. Indeed, the moment that the host subsided into his seat—it was large enough for four—he fell asleep, and his portly presence, converting itself into a sort of blacksmith's bellows, started to vent, through open mouth and distended nostrils, such sounds as can have greeted the reader's ear but seldom—sounds as of a drum being beaten in combination with the whistling of a flute and the strident howling of a dog.

"Listen to him!" said Platon.

Chichikov smiled.

"Naturally, on such dinners as that," continued the other, "our host does NOT find the time dull. And as soon as dinner is ended there can ensue sleep."

"Yes, but, pardon me, I still fail to understand why you should find life wearisome. There are so many resources against ennui!"

"As for instance?"

"For a young man, dancing, the playing of one or another musical instrument, and—well, yes, marriage."

"Marriage to whom?"

"To some maiden who is both charming and rich. Are there none in these parts?"

"No."

"Then, were I you, I should travel, and seek a maiden elsewhere." And a brilliant idea therewith entered Chichikov's head. "This last resource," he added, "is the best of all resources against ennui."

"What resource are you speaking of?"

"Of travel."

"But whither?"

"Well, should it so please you, you might join me as my companion." This said, the speaker added to himself as he eyed Platon: "Yes, that would suit me exactly, for then I should have half my expenses paid, and could charge him also with the cost of mending the koliaska."

"And whither should we go?"

"In that respect I am not wholly my own master, as I have business to do for others as well as for myself. For instance, General Betristchev—an intimate friend and, I might add, a generous benefactor of mine—has charged me with commissions to certain of his relatives. However, though relatives are relatives, I am travelling likewise on my own account, since I wish to see the world and the whirligig of humanity—which, in spite of what people may say, is as good as a living book or a second education." As a matter of fact, Chichikov was reflecting, "Yes, the plan is an excellent one. I might even contrive that he should have to bear the whole of our expenses, and that his horses should be used while my own should be put out to graze on his farm."

"Well, why should I not adopt the suggestion?" was Platon's thought. "There is nothing for me to do at home, since the management of the estate is in my brother's hands, and my going would cause him no inconvenience. Yes, why should I not do as Chichikov has suggested?"

Then he added aloud:

"Would you come and stay with my brother for a couple of days? Otherwise he might refuse me his consent."

"With great pleasure," said Chichikov. "Or even for three days."

"Then here is my hand on it. Let us be off at once." Platon seemed suddenly to have come to life again.

"Where are you off to?" put in their host unexpectedly as he roused himself and stared in astonishment at the pair. "No, no, my good sirs. I have had the wheels removed from your koliaska, Monsieur Chichikov, and have sent your horse, Platon Mikhalitch, to a grazing ground fifteen versts away. Consequently you must spend the night here, and depart to-morrow morning after breakfast."

What could be done with a man like Pietukh? There was no help for it but to remain. In return, the guests were rewarded with a beautiful spring evening, for, to spend the time, the host organised a boating expedition on the river, and a dozen rowers, with a dozen pairs of oars, conveyed the party (to the accompaniment of song) across the smooth surface of the lake and up a great river with towering banks. From time to time the boat would pass under ropes, stretched across for purposes of fishing, and at each turn of the rippling current new vistas unfolded themselves as tier upon tier of woodland delighted the eye with a diversity of timber and foliage. In unison did the rowers ply their sculls, yet it was though of itself that the skiff shot forward, bird-like, over the glassy surface of the water; while at intervals the broad-shouldered young oarsman who was seated third from the bow would raise, as from a nightingale's throat, the opening staves of a boat song, and then be joined by five or six more, until the melody had come to pour forth in a volume as free and boundless as Russia herself. And Pietukh, too, would give himself a shake, and help lustily to support the chorus; and even Chichikov felt acutely conscious of the fact that he was a Russian. Only Platon reflected: "What is there so splendid in these melancholy songs? They do but increase one's depression of spirits."

The journey homeward was made in the gathering dusk. Rhythmically the oars smote a surface which no longer reflected the sky, and darkness had fallen when they reached the shore, along which lights were twinkling where the fisherfolk were boiling live eels for soup. Everything had now wended its way homeward for the night; the cattle and poultry had been housed, and the herdsmen, standing at the gates of the village cattle-pens, amid the trailing dust lately raised by their charges, were awaiting the milk-pails and a summons to partake of the eel-broth. Through the dusk came the hum of humankind, and the barking of dogs in other and more distant villages; while, over all, the moon was rising, and the darkened countryside was beginning to glimmer to light again under her beams. What a glorious picture! Yet no one thought of admiring it. Instead of galloping over the countryside on frisky cobs, Nikolasha and Aleksasha were engaged in dreaming of Moscow, with its confectioners' shops and the theatres of which a cadet, newly arrived on a visit from the capital, had just been telling them; while their father had his mind full of how best to stuff his guests with yet more food, and Platon was given up to yawning. Only in Chichikov was a spice of animation visible. "Yes," he reflected, "some day I, too, will become lord of such a country place." And before his mind's eye there arose also a helpmeet and some little Chichikovs.

By the time that supper was finished the party had again over-eaten themselves, and when Chichikov entered the room allotted him for the night, he lay down upon the bed, and prodded his stomach. "It is as tight as a drum," he said to himself. "Not another titbit of veal could now get into it." Also, circumstances had so brought it about that next door to him there was situated his host's apartment; and since the intervening wall was thin, Chichikov could hear every word that was said there. At the present moment the master of the house was engaged in giving the cook orders for what, under the guise of an early breakfast, promised to constitute a veritable dinner. You should have heard Pietukh's behests! They would have excited the appetite of a corpse.

"Yes," he said, sucking his lips, and drawing a deep breath, "in the first place, make a pasty in four divisions. Into one of the divisions put the sturgeon's cheeks and some viaziga 46, and into another division some buckwheat porridge, young mushrooms and onions, sweet milk, calves' brains, and anything else that you may find suitable—anything else that you may have got handy. Also, bake the pastry to a nice brown on one side, and but lightly on the other. Yes, and, as to the under side, bake it so that it will be all juicy and flaky, so that it shall not crumble into bits, but melt in the mouth like the softest snow that ever you heard of." And as he said this Pietukh fairly smacked his lips.

"The devil take him!" muttered Chichikov, thrusting his head beneath the bedclothes to avoid hearing more. "The fellow won't give one a chance to sleep."

Nevertheless he heard through the blankets:

"And garnish the sturgeon with beetroot, smelts, peppered mushrooms, young radishes, carrots, beans, and anything else you like, so as to have plenty of trimmings. Yes, and put a lump of ice into the pig's bladder, so as to swell it up."

Many other dishes did Pietukh order, and nothing was to be heard but his talk of boiling, roasting, and stewing. Finally, just as mention was being made of a turkey cock, Chichikov fell asleep.

Next morning the guest's state of repletion had reached the point of Platon being unable to mount his horse; wherefore the latter was dispatched homeward with one of Pietukh's grooms, and the two guests entered Chichikov's koliaska. Even the dog trotted lazily in the rear; for he, too, had over-eaten himself.

"It has been rather too much of a good thing," remarked Chichikov as the vehicle issued from the courtyard.

"Yes, and it vexes me to see the fellow never tire of it," replied Platon.

"Ah," thought Chichikov to himself, "if *I* had an income of seventy thousand roubles, as you have, I'd very soon give tiredness one in the eye! Take Murazov, the tax-farmer—he, again, must be worth ten millions. What a fortune!"

"Do you mind where we drive?" asked Platon. "I should like first to go and take leave of my sister and my brother-in-law."

"With pleasure," said Chichikov.

"My brother-in-law is the leading landowner hereabouts. At the present moment he is drawing an income of two hundred thousand roubles from a property which, eight years ago, was producing a bare twenty thousand."

"Truly a man worthy of the utmost respect! I shall be most interested to make his acquaintance. To think of it! And what may his family name be?"

"Kostanzhoglo."

"And his Christian name and patronymic?"

"Constantine Thedorovitch."

"Constantine Thedorovitch Kostanzhoglo. Yes, it will be a most interesting event to make his acquaintance. To know such a man must be a whole education."

Here Platon set himself to give Selifan some directions as to the way, a necessary proceeding in view of the fact that Selifan could hardly maintain his seat on the box. Twice Petrushka, too, had fallen headlong, and this necessitated being tied to his perch with a piece of rope. "What a clown!" had been Chichikov's only comment.

"This is where my brother-in-law's land begins," said Platon.

"They give one a change of view."

And, indeed, from this point the countryside became planted with timber; the rows of trees running as straight as pistol-shots, and having beyond them, and on higher ground, a second expanse of forest, newly planted like the first; while beyond it, again, loomed a third plantation of older trees. Next there succeeded a flat piece of the same nature.

"All this timber," said Platon, "has grown up within eight or ten years at the most; whereas on another man's land it would have taken twenty to attain the same growth."

"And how has your brother-in-law effected this?"

"You must ask him yourself. He is so excellent a husbandman that nothing ever fails with him. You see, he knows the soil, and also knows what ought to be planted beside what, and what kinds of timber are the best neighbourhood for grain. Again, everything on his estate is made to perform at least three or four different functions. For instance, he makes his timber not only serve as timber, but also serve as a provider of moisture and shade to a given stretch of land, and then as a fertiliser with its fallen leaves. Consequently, when everywhere else there is drought, he still has water, and when everywhere else there has been a failure of the harvest, on his lands it will have proved a success. But it is a pity that I know so little about it all as to be unable to explain to you his many expedients. Folk call him a wizard, for he produces so much. Nevertheless, personally I find what he does uninteresting."

"Truly an astonishing fellow!" reflected Chichikov with a glance at his companion. "It is sad indeed to see a man so superficial as to be unable to explain matters of this kind."

At length the manor appeared in sight—an establishment looking almost like a town, so numerous were the huts where they stood arranged in three tiers, crowned with three churches, and surrounded with huge ricks and barns. "Yes," thought Chichikov to himself, "one can see what a jewel of a landowner lives here." The huts in question were stoutly built and the intervening alleys well laid-out; while, wherever a waggon was visible, it looked serviceable and more or less new. Also, the local peasants bore an intelligent look on their faces, the cattle were of the best possible breed, and even the peasants' pigs belonged to the porcine aristocracy. Clearly there dwelt here peasants who, to quote the song, were accustomed to "pick up silver by the shovelful." Nor were Englishified gardens and parterres and other conceits in evidence, but, on the contrary, there ran an open view from the manor house to the farm buildings and the workmen's cots, so that, after the old Russian fashion, the barin should be able to keep an eye upon all that was going on around him. For the same purpose, the mansion was topped with a tall lantern and a superstructure—a device designed, not for ornament, nor for a vantage-spot for the contemplation of the view, but for supervision of the labourers engaged in distant fields. Lastly, the brisk, active servants who received the visitors on the verandah were very different menials from the drunken Petrushka, even though they did not wear swallow-tailed coats, but only Cossack tchekmenu 47 of blue homespun cloth.

The lady of the house also issued on to the verandah. With her face of the freshness of "blood and milk" and the brightness of God's daylight, she as nearly resembled Platon as one pea resembles another, save that, whereas he was languid, she was cheerful and full of talk.

"Good day, brother!" she cried. "How glad I am to see you! Constantine is not at home, but will be back presently."

"Where is he?"

"Doing business in the village with a party of factors," replied the lady as she conducted her guests to the drawing-room.

With no little curiosity did Chichikov gaze at the interior of the mansion inhabited by the man who received an annual income of two hundred thousand roubles; for he thought to discern therefrom the nature of its proprietor, even as from a shell one may deduce the species of oyster or snail which has been its tenant, and has left therein its impression. But no such conclusions were to be drawn. The rooms were simple, and even bare. Not a fresco nor a picture nor a bronze nor a flower nor a china what-not nor a book was there to be seen. In short, everything appeared to show that the proprietor of this abode spent the greater part of his time, not between four walls, but in the field, and that he thought out his plans, not in sybaritic fashion by the fireside, nor in an easy chair beside the stove, but on the spot where work was actually in progress—that, in a word, where those plans were conceived, there they were put into execution. Nor in these rooms could Chichikov detect the least trace of a feminine hand, beyond the fact that certain tables and chairs bore drying-boards whereon were arranged some sprinklings of flower petals.

"What is all this rubbish for?" asked Platon.

"It is not rubbish," replied the lady of the house. "On the contrary, it is the best possible remedy for fever. Last year we cured every one of our sick peasants with it. Some of the petals I am going to make into an ointment, and some into an infusion. You may laugh as much as you like at my potting and preserving, yet you yourself will be glad of things of the kind when you set out on your travels."

Platon moved to the piano, and began to pick out a note or two.

"Good Lord, what an ancient instrument!" he exclaimed. "Are you not ashamed of it, sister?"

"Well, the truth is that I get no time to practice my music. You see," she added to Chichikov, "I have an eight-year-old daughter to educate; and to hand her over to a foreign governess in order that I may have leisure for my own piano-playing—well, that is a thing which I could never bring myself to do."

"You have become a wearisome sort of person," commented Platon, and walked away to the window. "Ah, here comes Constantine," presently he added.

Chichikov also glanced out of the window, and saw approaching the verandah a brisk, swarthy-complexioned man of about forty, a man clad in a rough cloth jacket and a velveteen cap. Evidently he was one of those who care little for the niceties of dress. With him, bareheaded, there came a couple of men of a somewhat lower station in life, and all three were engaged in an animated discussion. One of the barin's two companions was a plain peasant, and the other (clad in a blue Siberian smock) a travelling factor. The fact that the party halted awhile by the entrance steps made it possible to overhear a portion of their conversation from within.

"This is what you peasants had better do," the barin was saying. "Purchase your release from your present master. I will lend you the necessary money, and afterwards you can work for me."

"No, Constantine Thedorovitch," replied the peasant. "Why should we do that? Remove us just as we are. You will know how to arrange it, for a cleverer gentleman than you is nowhere to be found. The misfortune of us muzhiks is that we cannot protect ourselves properly. The tavern-keepers sell us such liquor that, before a man knows where he is, a glassful of it has eaten a hole through his stomach, and made him feel as though he could drink a pail of water. Yes, it knocks a man over before he can look around. Everywhere temptation lies in wait for the peasant, and he needs to be cunning if he is to get through the world at all. In fact, things seem to be contrived for nothing but to make us peasants lose our wits, even to the tobacco which they sell us. What are folk like ourselves to do, Constantine Thedorovitch? I tell you it is terribly difficult for a muzhik to look after himself."

"Listen to me. This is how things are done here. When I take on a serf, I fit him out with a cow and a horse. On the other hand, I demand of him thereafter more than is demanded of a peasant anywhere else. That is to say, first and foremost I make him work. Whether a peasant be working for himself or for me, never do I let him waste time. I myself toil like a bullock, and I force my peasants to do the same, for experience has taught me that that is the only way to get through life. All the mischief in the world comes through lack of employment. Now, do you go and consider the matter, and talk it over with your mir 48."

"We have done that already, Constantine Thedorovitch, and our elders' opinion is: 'There is no need for further talk. Every peasant belonging to Constantine Thedorovitch is well off, and hasn't to work for nothing. The priests of his village, too, are men of good heart, whereas ours have been taken away, and there is no one to bury us.'"

"Nevertheless, do you go and talk the matter over again."

"We will, barin."

Here the factor who had been walking on the barin's other side put in a word.

"Constantine Thedorovitch," he said, "I beg of you to do as I have requested."

"I have told you before," replied the barin, "that I do not care to play the huckster. I am not one of those landowners whom fellows of your sort visit on the very day that the interest on a mortgage is due. Ah, I know your fraternity thoroughly, and know that you keep lists of all who have mortgages to repay. But what is there so clever about that? Any man, if you pinch him sufficiently, will surrender you a mortgage at half-price,—any man, that is to say, except myself, who care nothing for your money. Were a loan of mine to remain out three years, I should never demand a kopeck of interest on it."

"Quite so, Constantine Thedorovitch," replied the factor. "But I am asking this of you more for the purpose of establishing us on a business footing than because I desire to win your favour. Prey, therefore, accept this earnest money of three thousand roubles." And the man drew from his breast pocket a dirty roll of bank-notes, which, carelessly receiving, Kostanzhoglo thrust, uncounted, into the back pocket of his overcoat.

"Hm!" thought Chichikov. "For all he cares, the notes might have been a handkerchief."

When Kostanzhoglo appeared at closer quarters—that is to say, in the doorway of the drawing-room—he struck Chichikov more than ever with the swarthiness of his complexion, the dishevelment of his black, slightly grizzled locks, the alertness of his eye, and the impression of fiery southern origin which his whole personality diffused. For he was not wholly a Russian, nor could he himself say precisely who his forefathers had been. Yet, inasmuch as he accounted genealogical research no part of the science of estate-management, but a mere superfluity, he looked upon himself as, to all intents and purposes, a native of Russia, and the more so since the Russian language was the only tongue he knew.

Platon presented Chichikov, and the pair exchanged greetings.

"To get rid of my depression, Constantine," continued Platon, "I am thinking of accompanying our guest on a tour through a few of the provinces."

"An excellent idea," said Kostanzhoglo. "But precisely whither?" he added, turning hospitably to Chichikov.

"To tell you the truth," replied that personage with an affable inclination of the head as he smoothed the arm of his chair with his hand, "I am travelling less on my own affairs than on the affairs of others. That is to say, General Betristchev, an intimate friend, and, I might add, a generous benefactor, of mine, has charged me with commissions to some of his relatives. Nevertheless, though relatives are relatives, I may say that I am travelling on my own account as well, in that, in addition to possible benefit to my health, I desire to see the world and the whirligig of humanity, which constitute, so to speak, a living book, a second course of education."

"Yes, there is no harm in looking at other corners of the world besides one's own."

"You speak truly. There IS no harm in such a proceeding. Thereby one may see things which one has not before encountered, one may meet men with whom one has not before come in contact. And with some men of that kind a conversation is as precious a benefit as has been conferred upon me by the present occasion. I come to you, most worthy Constantine Thedorovitch, for instruction, and again for instruction, and beg of you to assuage my thirst with an exposition of the truth as it is. I hunger for the favour of your words as for manna."

"But how so? What can *I* teach you?" exclaimed Kostanzhoglo in confusion. "I myself was given but the plainest of educations."

"Nay, most worthy sir, you possess wisdom, and again wisdom. Wisdom only can direct the management of a great estate, that can derive a sound income from the same, that can acquire wealth of a real, not a fictitious, order while also fulfilling the duties of a citizen and thereby earning the respect of the Russian public. All this I pray you to teach me."

"I tell you what," said Kostanzhoglo, looking meditatively at his guest. "You had better stay with me for a few days, and during that time I can show you how things are managed here, and explain to you everything. Then you will see for yourself that no great wisdom is required for the purpose."

"Yes, certainly you must stay here," put in the lady of the house. Then, turning to her brother, she added: "And you too must stay. Why should you be in such a hurry?"

"Very well," he replied. "But what say YOU, Paul Ivanovitch?"

"I say the same as you, and with much pleasure," replied Chichikov. "But also I ought to tell you this: that there is a relative of General Betristchev's, a certain Colonel Koshkarev—"

"Yes, we know him; but he is quite mad."

"As you say, he is mad, and I should not have been intending to visit him, were it not that General Betristchev is an intimate friend of mine, as well as, I might add, my most generous benefactor."

"Then," said Kostanzhoglo, "do you go and see Colonel Koshkarev NOW. He lives less than ten versts from here, and I have a gig already harnessed. Go to him at once, and return here for tea."

"An excellent idea!" cried Chichikov, and with that he seized his cap.

Half an hour's drive sufficed to bring him to the Colonel's establishment. The village attached to the manor was in a state of utter confusion, since in every direction building and repairing operations were in progress, and the alleys were choked with heaps of lime, bricks, and beams of wood. Also, some of the huts were arranged to resemble offices, and superscribed in gilt letters "Depot for Agricultural Implements," "Chief Office of Accounts," "Estate Works Committee," "Normal School for the Education of Colonists," and so forth.

Chichikov found the Colonel posted behind a desk and holding a pen between his teeth. Without an instant's delay the master of the establishment—who seemed a kindly, approachable man, and accorded to his visitor a very civil welcome—plunged into a recital of the labour which it had cost him to bring the property to its present condition of affluence. Then he went on to lament the fact that he could not make his peasantry understand the incentives to labour which the riches of science and art provide; for instance, he had failed to induce his female serfs to wear corsets, whereas in Germany, where he had resided for fourteen years, every humble miller's daughter could play the piano. None the less, he said, he meant to peg away until every peasant on the estate should, as he walked behind the plough, indulge in a regular course of reading Franklin's Notes on Electricity, Virgil's Georgics, or some work on the chemical properties of soil.

"Good gracious!" mentally exclaimed Chichikov. "Why, I myself have not had time to finish that book by the Duchesse de la Valliere!"

Much else the Colonel said. In particular did he aver that, provided the Russian peasant could be induced to array himself in German costume, science would progress, trade increase, and the Golden Age dawn in Russia.

For a while Chichikov listened with distended eyes. Then he felt constrained to intimate that with all that he had nothing to do, seeing that his business was merely to acquire a few souls, and thereafter to have their purchase confirmed.

"If I understand you aright," said the Colonel, "you wish to present a Statement of Plea?"

"Yes, that is so."

"Then kindly put it into writing, and it shall be forwarded to the Office for the Reception of Reports and Returns. Thereafter that Office will consider it, and return it to me, who will, in turn, dispatch it to the Estate Works Committee, who will, in turn, revise it, and present it to the Administrator, who, jointly with the Secretary, will—"

"Pardon me," expostulated Chichikov, "but that procedure will take up a great deal of time. Why need I put the matter into writing at all? It is simply this. I want a few souls which are—well, which are, so to speak, dead."

"Very good," commented the Colonel. "Do you write down in your Statement of Plea that the souls which you desire are, 'so to speak, dead.'"

"But what would be the use of my doing so? Though the souls are dead, my purpose requires that they should be represented as alive."

"Very good," again commented the Colonel. "Do you write down in your Statement that 'it is necessary' (or, should you prefer an alternative phrase, 'it is requested,' or 'it is desiderated,' or 'it is prayed,') 'that the souls be represented as alive.' At all events, WITHOUT documentary process of that kind, the matter cannot possibly be carried through. Also, I will appoint a Commissioner to guide you round the various Offices."

And he sounded a bell; whereupon there presented himself a man whom, addressing as "Secretary," the Colonel instructed to summon the "Commissioner." The latter, on appearing, was seen to have the air, half of a peasant, half of an official.

"This man," the Colonel said to Chichikov, "will act as your escort."

What could be done with a lunatic like Koshkarev? In the end, curiosity moved Chichikov to accompany the Commissioner. The Committee for the Reception of Reports and Returns was discovered to have put up its shutters, and to have locked its doors, for the reason that the Director of the Committee had been transferred to the newly-formed Committee of Estate Management, and his successor had been annexed by the same Committee. Next, Chichikov and his escort rapped at the doors of the Department of Estate Affairs; but that Department's quarters happened to be in a state of repair, and no one could be made to answer the summons save a drunken peasant from whom not a word of sense was to be extracted. At length the escort felt himself moved to remark:

"There is a deal of foolishness going on here. Fellows like that drunkard lead the barin by the nose, and everything is ruled by the Committee of Management, which takes men from their proper work, and sets them to do any other it likes. Indeed, only through the Committee does ANYTHING get done."

By this time Chichikov felt that he had seen enough; wherefore he returned to the Colonel, and informed him that the Office for the

Reception of Reports and Returns had ceased to exist. At once the Colonel flamed to noble rage. Pressing Chichikov's hand in token of gratitude for the information which the guest had furnished, he took paper and pen, and noted eight searching questions under three separate headings: (1) "Why has the Committee of Management presumed to issue orders to officials not under its jurisdiction?" (2) "Why has the Chief Manager permitted his predecessor, though still in retention of his post, to follow him to another Department?" and (3) "Why has the Committee of Estate Affairs suffered the Office for the Reception of Reports and Returns to lapse?"

"Now for a row!" thought Chichikov to himself, and turned to depart; but his host stopped him, saying:

"I cannot let you go, for, in addition to my honour having become involved, it behoves me to show my people how the regular, the organised, administration of an estate may be conducted. Herewith I will hand over the conduct of your affair to a man who is worth all the rest of the staff put together, and has had a university education. Also, the better to lose no time, may I humbly beg you to step into my library, where you will find notebooks, paper, pens, and everything else that you may require. Of these articles pray make full use, for you are a gentleman of letters, and it is your and my joint duty to bring enlightenment to all."

So saying, he ushered his guest into a large room lined from floor to ceiling with books and stuffed specimens. The books in question were divided into sections—a section on forestry, a section on cattle-breeding, a section on the raising of swine, and a section on horticulture, together with special journals of the type circulated merely for the purposes of reference, and not for general reading. Perceiving that these works were scarcely of a kind calculated to while away an idle hour, Chichikov turned to a second bookcase. But to do so was to fall out of the frying-pan into the fire, for the contents of the second bookcase proved to be works on philosophy, while, in particular, six huge volumes confronted him under a label inscribed "A Preparatory Course to the Province of Thought, with the Theory of Community of Effort, Co-operation, and Subsistence, in its Application to a Right Understanding of the Organic Principles of a Mutual Division of Social Productivity." Indeed, wheresoever Chichikov looked, every page presented to his vision some such words as "phenomenon," "development," "abstract," "contents," and "synopsis." "This is not the sort of thing for me," he murmured, and turned his attention to a third bookcase, which contained books on the Arts. Extracting a huge tome in which some by no means reticent mythological illustrations were contained, he set himself to examine these pictures. They were of the kind which pleases mostly middle-aged bachelors and old men who are accustomed to seek in the ballet and similar frivolities a further spur to their waning passions. Having concluded his examination, Chichikov had just extracted another volume of the same species when Colonel Koshkarev returned with a document of some sort and a radiant countenance.

"Everything has been carried through in due form!" he cried. "The man whom I mentioned is a genius indeed, and I intend not only to promote him over the rest, but also to create for him a special Department. Herewith shall you hear what a splendid intellect is his, and how in a few minutes he has put the whole affair in order."

"May the Lord be thanked for that!" thought Chichikov. Then he settled himself while the Colonel read aloud:

"'After giving full consideration to the Reference which your Excellency has entrusted to me, I have the honour to report as follows:

"'(1) In the Statement of Plea presented by one Paul Ivanovitch Chichikov, Gentleman, Chevalier, and Collegiate Councillor, there lurks an error, in that an oversight has led the Petitioner to apply to Revisional Souls the term "Dead." Now, from the context it would appear that by this term the Petitioner desires to signify Souls Approaching Death rather than Souls Actually Deceased: wherefore the term employed betrays such an empirical instruction in letters as must, beyond doubt, have been confined to the Village School, seeing that in truth the Soul is Deathless.'

"The rascal!" Koshkarev broke off to exclaim delightedly. "He has got you there, Monsieur Chichikov. And you will admit that he has a sufficiently incisive pen?

"'(2) On this Estate there exist no Unmortgaged Souls whatsoever, whether Approaching Death or Otherwise; for the reason that all Souls thereon have been pledged not only under a First Deed of Mortgage, but also (for the sum of One Hundred and Fifty Roubles per Soul) under a Second,—the village of Gurmailovka alone excepted, in that, in consequence of a Suit having been brought against Landowner Priadistchev, and of a caveat having been pronounced by the Land Court, and of such caveat having been published in No. 42 of the Gazette of Moscow, the said Village has come within the Jurisdiction of the Court Above-Mentioned."

"Why did you not tell me all this before?" cried Chichikov furiously. "Why you have kept me dancing about for nothing?"

"Because it was absolutely necessary that you should view the matter through forms of documentary process. This is no jest on my part. The inexperienced may see things subconsciously, yet it is imperative that he should also see them CONSCIOUSLY."

But to Chichikov's patience an end had come. Seizing his cap, and casting all ceremony to the winds, he fled from the house, and rushed through the courtyard. As it happened, the man who had driven him thither had, warned by experience, not troubled even to take out the horses, since he knew that such a proceeding would have entailed not only the presentation of a Statement of Plea for fodder, but also a delay of twenty-four hours until the Resolution granting the same should have been passed. Nevertheless the Colonel pursued his guest to the gates, and pressed his hand warmly as he thanked him for having enabled him (the Colonel) thus to exhibit in operation the proper management of an estate. Also, he begged to state that, under the circumstances, it was absolutely necessary to keep things moving and circulating, since, otherwise, slackness was apt to supervene, and the working of the machine to grow rusty and feeble; but that, in spite of all, the present occasion had inspired him with a happy idea—namely, the idea of instituting a Committee which should be entitled "The Committee of Supervision of the Committee of Management," and which should have for its function the detection of backsliders among the body first mentioned.

It was late when, tired and dissatisfied, Chichikov regained Kostanzhoglo's mansion. Indeed, the candles had long been lit.

"What has delayed you?" asked the master of the house as Chichikov entered the drawing-room.

"Yes, what has kept you and the Colonel so long in conversation together?" added Platon.

"This—the fact that never in my life have I come across such an imbecile," was Chichikov's reply.

"Never mind," said Kostanzhoglo. "Koshkarev is a most reassuring phenomenon. He is necessary in that in him we see expressed in caricature all the more crying follies of our intellectuals—of the intellectuals who, without first troubling to make themselves acquainted with their own country, borrow silliness from abroad. Yet that is how certain of our landowners are now carrying on. They have set up 'offices' and factories and schools and 'commissions,' and the devil knows what else besides. A fine lot of wiseacres! After the French War in 1812 they had to reconstruct their affairs: and see how they have done it! Yet so much worse have they done it than a Frenchman would have done that any fool of a Peter Petrovitch Pietukh now ranks as a good landowner!"

"But he has mortgaged the whole of his estate?" remarked Chichikov.

"Yes, nowadays everything is being mortgaged, or is going to be." This said, Kostanzhoglo's temper rose still further. "Out upon your factories of hats and candles!" he cried. "Out upon procuring candle-makers from London, and then turning landowners into hucksters! To think of a Russian pomiestchik 49, a member of the noblest of callings, conducting workshops and cotton mills! Why, it is for the wenches of towns to handle looms for muslin and lace."

"But you yourself maintain workshops?" remarked Platon.

"I do; but who established them? They established themselves. For instance, wool had accumulated, and since I had nowhere to store it, I began to weave it into cloth—but, mark you, only into good, plain cloth of which I can dispose at a cheap rate in the local markets, and which is needed by peasants, including my own. Again, for six years on end did the fish factories keep dumping their offal on my bank of the river; wherefore, at last, as there was nothing to be done with it, I took to boiling it into glue, and cleared forty thousand roubles by the process."

"The devil!" thought Chichikov to himself as he stared at his host. "What a fist this man has for making money!"

"Another reason why I started those factories," continued Kostanzhoglo, "is that they might give employment to many peasants who would otherwise have starved. You see, the year happened to have been a lean one—thanks to those same industry-mongering landowners, in that they had neglected to sow their crops; and now my factories keep growing at the rate of a factory a year, owing to the circumstance that such quantities of remnants and cuttings become so accumulated that, if a man looks carefully to his management, he will find every sort of rubbish to be capable of bringing in a return—yes, to the point of his having to reject money on the plea that he has no need of it. Yet I do not find that to do all this I require to build a mansion with facades and pillars!"

"Marvellous!" exclaimed Chichikov. "Beyond all things does it surprise me that refuse can be so utilised."

"Yes, and that is what can be done by SIMPLE methods. But nowadays every one is a mechanic, and wants to open that money chest with an instrument instead of simply. For that purpose he hies him to England. Yes, THAT is the thing to do. What folly!" Kostanzhoglo spat and added: "Yet when he returns from abroad he is a hundred times more ignorant than when he went."

"Ah, Constantine," put in his wife anxiously, "you know how bad for you it is to talk like this."

"Yes, but how am I to help losing my temper? The thing touches me too closely, it vexes me too deeply to think that the Russian character should be degenerating. For in that character there has dawned a sort of Quixotism which never used to be there. Yes, no sooner does a man get a little education into his head than he becomes a Don Quixote, and establishes schools on his estate such as even a madman would never have dreamed of. And from that school there issues a workman who is good for nothing, whether in the country or in the town—a fellow who drinks and is for ever standing on his dignity. Yet still our landowners keep taking to philanthropy, to converting themselves into philanthropic knights-errant, and spending millions upon senseless hospitals and institutions, and so ruining themselves and turning their families adrift. Yes, that is all that comes of philanthropy."

Chichikov's business had nothing to do with the spread of enlightenment, he was but seeking an opportunity to inquire further concerning the putting of refuse to lucrative uses; but Kostanzhoglo would not let him get a word in edgeways, so irresistibly did the flow of sarcastic comment pour from the speaker's lips.

"Yes," went on Kostanzhoglo, "folk are always scheming to educate the peasant. But first make him well-off and a good farmer. THEN he will educate himself fast enough. As things are now, the world has grown stupid to a degree that passes belief. Look at the stuff our present-day scribblers write! Let any sort of a book be published, and at once you will see every one making a rush for it. Similarly will you find folk saying: 'The peasant leads an over-simple life. He ought to be familiarised with luxuries, and so led to yearn for things above his station.' And the result of such luxuries will be that the peasant will become a rag rather than a man, and suffer from the devil only knows what diseases, until there will remain in the land not a boy of eighteen who will not have experienced the whole gamut of them, and found himself left with not a tooth in his jaws or a hair on his pate. Yes, that is what will come of infecting the peasant with such rubbish. But, thank God, there is still one healthy class left to us—a class which has never taken up with the 'advantages' of which I speak. For that we ought to be grateful. And since, even yet, the Russian agriculturist remains the most respect-worthy man in the land, why should he be touched? Would to God every one were an agriculturist!"

"Then you believe agriculture to be the most profitable of occupations?" said Chichikov.

"The best, at all events—if not the most profitable. 'In the sweat of thy brow shalt thou till the land.' To quote that requires no great wisdom, for the experience of ages has shown us that, in the agricultural calling, man has ever remained more moral, more pure, more noble than in any other. Of course I do not mean to imply that no other calling ought to be practised: simply that the calling in question lies at the root of all the rest. However much factories may be established privately or by the law, there will still lie ready to man's hand all that he needs—he will still require none of those amenities which are sapping the vitality of our present-day folk, nor any of those industrial establishments which make their profit, and keep themselves going, by causing foolish measures to be adopted which, in the end, are bound to deprave and corrupt our unfortunate masses. I myself am determined never to establish any manufacture, however profitable, which will give rise to a demand for 'higher things,' such as sugar and tobacco—no not if I lose a million by my refusing to do so. If corruption MUST overtake the MIR, it shall not be through my hands. And I think that God will justify me in my resolve. Twenty years have I lived among the common folk, and I know what will inevitably come of such things."

"But what surprises me most," persisted Chichikov, "is that from refuse it should be possible, with good management, to make such an immensity of profit."

"And as for political economy," continued Kostanzhoglo, without noticing him, and with his face charged with bilious sarcasm, "—as for political economy, it is a fine thing indeed. Just one fool sitting on another fool's back, and flogging him along, even though the rider can see no further than his own nose! Yet into the saddle will that fool climb—spectacles and all! Oh, the folly, the folly of such things!" And the speaker spat derisively.

"That may be true," said his wife. "Yet you must not get angry about it. Surely one can speak on such subjects without losing one's temper?"

"As I listen to you, most worthy Constantine Thedorovitch," Chichikov hastened to remark, "it becomes plain to me that you have penetrated into the meaning of life, and laid your finger upon the essential root of the matter. Yet supposing, for a moment, we leave the affairs of humanity in general, and turn our attention to a purely individual affair, might I ask you how, in the case of a man becoming a landowner, and having a mind to grow wealthy as quickly as possible (in order that he may fulfil his bounden obligations as a citizen), he can best set about it?"

"How he can best set about growing wealthy?" repeated Kostanzhoglo. "Why,—"

"Let us go to supper," interrupted the lady of the house, rising from her chair, and moving towards the centre of the room, where she wrapped her shivering young form in a shawl. Chichikov sprang up with the alacrity of a military man, offered her his arm, and escorted her, as on parade, to the dining-room, where awaiting them there was the soup-toureen. From it the lid had just been removed, and the room was redolent of the fragrant odour of early spring roots and herbs. The company took their seats, and at once the servants placed the remainder of the dishes (under covers) upon the table and withdrew, for Kostanzhoglo hated to have servants listening to their employers' conversation, and objected still more to their staring at him all the while that he was eating.

When the soup had been consumed, and glasses of an excellent vintage resembling Hungarian wine had been poured out, Chichikov said to his host:

"Most worthy sir, allow me once more to direct your attention to the subject of which we were speaking at the point when the conversation became interrupted. You will remember that I was asking you how best a man can set about, proceed in, the matter of growing . . ."

[Here from the original two pages are missing.]

... "A property for which, had he asked forty thousand, I should still have demanded a reduction."

"Hm!" thought Chichikov; then added aloud: "But why do you not purchase it yourself?"

"Because to everything there must be assigned a limit. Already my property keeps me sufficiently employed. Moreover, I should cause our local dvoriane to begin crying out in chorus that I am exploiting their extremities, their ruined position, for the purpose of acquiring land for under its value. Of that I am weary."

"How readily folk speak evil!" exclaimed Chichikov.

"Yes, and the amount of evil-speaking in our province surpasses belief. Never will you hear my name mentioned without my being called also a miser and a usurer of the worst possible sort; whereas my accusers justify themselves in everything, and say that, 'though we have wasted our money, we have started a demand for the higher amenities of life, and therefore encouraged industry with our wastefulness, a far better way of doing things than that practised by Kostanzhoglo, who lives like a pig.'"

"Would *I* could live in your 'piggish' fashion!" ejaculated Chichikov.

"And so forth, and so forth. Yet what are the 'higher amenities of life'? What good can they do to any one? Even if a landowner of the day sets up a library, he never looks at a single book in it, but soon relapses into card-playing—the usual pursuit. Yet folk call me names simply because I do not waste my means upon the giving of dinners! One reason why I do not give such dinners is that they weary me; and another reason is that I am not used to them. But come you to my house for the purpose of taking pot luck, and I shall be delighted to see you. Also, folk foolishly say that I lend money on interest; whereas the truth is that if you should come to me when you are really in need, and should explain to me openly how you propose to employ my money, and I should perceive that you are purposing to use that money wisely, and that you are really likely to profit thereby—well, in that case you would find me ready to lend you all that you might ask without interest at all."

"That is a thing which it is well to know," reflected Chichikov.

"Yes," repeated Kostanzhoglo, "under those circumstances I should never refuse you my assistance. But I do object to throwing my money to the winds. Pardon me for expressing myself so plainly. To think of lending money to a man who is merely devising a dinner for his mistress, or planning to furnish his house like a lunatic, or thinking of taking his paramour to a masked ball or a jubilee in honour of some one who had better never have been born!"

And, spitting, he came near to venting some expression which would scarcely have been becoming in the presence of his wife. Over his face the dark shadow of hypochondria had cast a cloud, and furrows had formed on his brow and temples, and his every gesture bespoke the influence of a hot, nervous rancour.

"But allow me once more to direct your attention to the subject of our recently interrupted conversation," persisted Chichikov as he sipped a glass of excellent raspberry wine. "That is to say, supposing I were to acquire the property which you have been good enough to bring to my notice, how long would it take me to grow rich?"

"That would depend on yourself," replied Kostanzhoglo with grim abruptness and evident ill-humour. "You might either grow rich quickly or you might never grow rich at all. If you made up your mind to grow rich, sooner or later you would find yourself a wealthy man."

"Indeed?" ejaculated Chichikov.

"Yes," replied Kostanzhoglo, as sharply as though he were angry with Chichikov. "You would merely need to be fond of work: otherwise you would effect nothing. The main thing is to like looking after your property. Believe me, you would never grow weary of doing so. People would have it that life in the country is dull; whereas, if I were to spend a single day as it is spent by some folk, with their stupid clubs and their restaurants and their theatres, I should die of ennui. The fools, the idiots, the generations of blind dullards! But a landowner never finds the days wearisome—he has not the time. In his life not a moment remains unoccupied; it is full to the brim. And with it all goes an endless variety of occupations. And what occupations! Occupations which genuinely uplift the soul, seeing that the landowner walks with nature and the seasons of the year, and takes part in, and is intimate with, everything which is evolved by creation. For let us look at the round of the year's labours. Even before spring has arrived there will have begun a general watching and a waiting for it, and a preparing for sowing, and an apportioning of crops, and a measuring of seed grain by byres, and drying of seed, and a dividing of the workers into teams.

For everything needs to be examined beforehand, and calculations must be made at the very start. And as soon as ever the ice shall have melted, and the rivers be flowing, and the land have dried sufficiently to be workable, the spade will begin its task in kitchen and flower garden, and the plough and the harrow their tasks in the field; until everywhere there will be tilling and sowing and planting. And do you understand what the sum of that labour will mean? It will mean that the harvest is being sown, that the welfare of the world is being sown, that the food of millions is being put into the earth. And thereafter will come summer, the season of reaping, endless reaping; for suddenly the crops will have ripened, and rye-sheaf will be lying heaped upon rye-sheaf, with, elsewhere, stocks of barley, and of oats, and of wheat. And everything will be teeming with life, and not a moment will there need to be lost, seeing that, had you even twenty eyes, you would have need for them all. And after the harvest festivities there will be grain to be carted to byre or stacked in ricks, and stores to be prepared for the winter, and storehouses and kilns and cattle-sheds to be cleaned for the same purpose, and the women to be assigned their tasks, and the totals of everything to be calculated, so that one may see the value of what has been done. And lastly will come winter, when in every threshing-floor the flail will be working, and the grain, when threshed, will need to be carried from barn to binn, and the mills require to be seen to, and the estate factories to be inspected, and the workmen's huts to be visited for the purpose of ascertaining how the muzhik is faring (for, given a carpenter who is clever with his tools, I, for one, am only too glad to spend an hour or two in his company, so cheering to me is labour). And if, in addition, one discerns the end to which everything is moving, and the manner in which the things of earth are everywhere multiplying and multiplying, and bringing forth more and more fruit to one's profiting, I cannot adequately express what takes place in a man's soul. And that, not because of the growth in his wealth—money is money and no more—but because he will feel that everything is the work of his own hands, and that he has been the cause of everything, and its creator, and that from him, as from a magician, there has flowed bounty and goodness for all. In what other calling will you find such delights in prospect?" As he spoke, Kostanzhoglo raised his face, and it became clear that the wrinkles had fled from it, and that, like the Tsar on the solemn day of his crowning, Kostanzhoglo's whole form was diffusing light, and his features had in them a gentle radiance. "In all the world," he repeated, "you will find no joys like these, for herein man imitates the God who projected creation as the supreme happiness, and now demands of man that he, too, should act as the creator of prosperity. Yet there are folk who call such functions tedious!"

Kostanzhoglo's mellifluous periods fell upon Chichikov's ear like the notes of a bird of paradise. From time to time he gulped, and his softened eyes expressed the pleasure which it gave him to listen.

"Constantine, it is time to leave the table," said the lady of the house, rising from her seat. Every one followed her example, and Chichikov once again acted as his hostess's escort—although with less dexterity of deportment than before, owing to the fact that this time his thoughts were occupied with more essential matters of procedure.

"In spite of what you say," remarked Platon as he walked behind the pair, "I, for my part, find these things wearisome."

But the master of the house paid no attention to his remark, for he was reflecting that his guest was no fool, but a man of serious thought and speech who did not take things lightly. And, with the thought, Kostanzhoglo grew lighter in soul, as though he had warmed himself with his own words, and were exulting in the fact that he had found some one capable of listening to good advice.

When they had settled themselves in the cosy, candle-lighted drawing-room, with its balcony and the glass door opening out into the garden—a door through which the stars could be seen glittering amid the slumbering tops of the trees—Chichikov felt more comfortable than he had done for many a day past. It was as though, after long journeying, his own roof-tree had received him once more—had received him when his quest had been accomplished, when all that he wished for had been gained, when his travelling-staff had been laid aside with the words "It is finished." And of this seductive frame of mind the true source had been the eloquent discourse of his hospitable host. Yes, for every man there exist certain things which, instantly that they are said, seem to touch him more closely, more intimately, than anything has done before. Nor is it an uncommon occurrence that in the most unexpected fashion, and in the most retired of retreats, one will suddenly come face to face with a man whose burning periods will lead one to forget oneself and the tracklessness of the route and the discomfort of one's nightly halting-places, and the futility of crazes and the falseness of tricks by which one human being deceives another. And at once there will become engraven upon one's memory—vividly, and for all time—the evening thus spent. And of that evening one's remembrance will hold true, both as to who was present, and where each such person sat, and what he or she was wearing, and what the walls and the stove and other trifling features of the room looked like.

In the same way did Chichikov note each detail that evening—both the appointments of the agreeable, but not luxuriously furnished, room, and the good-humoured expression which reigned on the face of the thoughtful host, and the design of the curtains, and the amber-mounted pipe smoked by Platon, and the way in which he kept puffing smoke into the fat jowl of the dog Yarb, and the sneeze which, on each such occasion, Yarb vented, and the laughter of the pleasant-faced hostess (though always followed by the words "Pray do not tease him any more") and the cheerful candle-light, and the cricket chirping in a corner, and the glass door, and the spring night which, laying its elbows upon the tree-tops, and spangled with stars, and vocal with the nightingales which were pouring forth warbled ditties from the recesses of the foliage, kept glancing through the door, and regarding the company within.

"How it delights me to hear your words, good Constantine Thedorovitch!" said Chichikov. "Indeed, nowhere in Russia have I met with a man of equal intellect."

Kostanzhoglo smiled, while realising that the compliment was scarcely deserved.

"If you want a man of GENUINE intellect," he said, "I can tell you of one. He is a man whose boot soles are worth more than my whole body."

"Who may he be?" asked Chichikov in astonishment.

"Murazov, our local Commissioner of Taxes."

"Ah! I have heard of him before," remarked Chichikov.

"He is a man who, were he not the director of an estate, might well be a director of the Empire. And were the Empire under my direction, I should at once appoint him my Minister of Finance."

"I have heard tales beyond belief concerning him—for instance, that he has acquired ten million roubles."

"Ten? More than forty. Soon half Russia will be in his hands."

"You don't say so?" cried Chichikov in amazement.

"Yes, certainly. The man who has only a hundred thousand roubles to work with grows rich but slowly, whereas he who has millions at his disposal can operate over a greater radius, and so back whatsoever he undertakes with twice or thrice the money which can be brought against him. Consequently his field becomes so spacious that he ends by having no rivals. Yes, no one can compete with him, and, whatsoever price he may fix for a given commodity, at that price it will have to remain, nor will any man be able to outbid it."

"My God!" muttered Chichikov, crossing himself, and staring at Kostanzhoglo with his breath catching in his throat. "The mind cannot grasp it—it petrifies one's thoughts with awe. You see folk marvelling at what Science has achieved in the matter of investigating the habits of cowbugs, but to me it is a far more marvellous thing that in the hands of a single mortal there can become accumulated such gigantic sums of money. But may I ask whether the great fortune of which you speak has been acquired through honest means?"

"Yes; through means of the most irreproachable kind—through the most honourable of methods."

"Yet so improbable does it seem that I can scarcely believe it. Thousands I could understand, but millions—!"

"On the contrary, to make thousands honestly is a far more difficult matter than to make millions. Millions are easily come by, for a millionaire has no need to resort to crooked ways; the way lies straight before him, and he needs but to annex whatsoever he comes across. No rival will spring up to oppose him, for no rival will be sufficiently strong, and since the millionaire can operate over an extensive radius, he can bring (as I have said) two or three roubles to bear upon any one else's one. Consequently, what interest will he derive from a thousand roubles? Why, ten or twenty per cent. at the least."

"And it is beyond measure marvellous that the whole should have started from a single kopeck."

"Had it started otherwise, the thing could never have been done at all. Such is the normal course. He who is born with thousands, and is brought up to thousands, will never acquire a single kopeck more, for he will have been set up with the amenities of life in advance, and so never come to stand in need of anything. It is necessary to begin from the beginning rather than from the middle; from a kopeck rather than from a rouble; from the bottom rather than from the top. For only thus will a man get to know the men and conditions among which his career will have to be carved. That is to say, through encountering the rough and the tumble of life, and through learning that every kopeck has to be beaten out with a three-kopeck nail, and through worsting knave after knave, he will acquire such a degree of perspicuity and wariness that he will err in nothing which he may tackle, and never come to ruin. Believe me, it is so. The beginning, and not the middle, is the right starting point. No one who comes to me and says, 'Give me a hundred thousand roubles, and I will grow rich in no time,' do I believe, for he is likely to meet with failure rather than with the success of which he is so assured. 'Tis with a kopeck, and with a kopeck only, that a man must begin."

"If that is so, *I* shall grow rich," said Chichikov, involuntarily remembering the dead souls. "For of a surety *I* began with nothing."

"Constantine, pray allow Paul Ivanovitch to retire to rest," put in the lady of the house. "It is high time, and I am sure you have talked enough."

"Yes, beyond a doubt you will grow rich," continued Kostanzhoglo, without heeding his wife. "For towards you there will run rivers and rivers of gold, until you will not know what to do with all your gains."

As though spellbound, Chichikov sat in an aureate world of ever-growing dreams and fantasies. All his thoughts were in a whirl, and on a carpet of future wealth his tumultuous imagination was weaving golden patterns, while ever in his ears were ringing the words, "towards you there will run rivers and rivers of gold."

"Really, Constantine, DO allow Paul Ivanovitch to go to bed."

"What on earth is the matter?" retorted the master of the household testily. "Pray go yourself if you wish to." Then he stopped short, for the snoring of Platon was filling the whole room, and also—outrivalling it—that of the dog Yarb. This caused Kostanzhoglo to realise that bedtime really had arrived; wherefore, after he had shaken Platon out of his slumbers, and bidden Chichikov good night, all dispersed to their several chambers, and became plunged in sleep.

All, that is to say, except Chichikov, whose thoughts remained wakeful, and who kept wondering and wondering how best he could become the owner, not of a fictitious, but of a real, estate. The conversation with his host had made everything clear, had made the possibility of his acquiring riches manifest, had made the difficult art of estate management at once easy and understandable; until it would seem as though particularly was his nature adapted for mastering the art in question. All that he would need to do would be to mortgage the dead souls, and then to set up a genuine establishment. Already he saw himself acting and administering as Kostanzhoglo had advised him—energetically, and through personal oversight, and undertaking nothing new until the old had been thoroughly learned, and viewing everything with his own eyes, and making himself familiar with each member of his peasantry, and abjuring all superfluities, and giving himself up to hard work and husbandry. Yes, already could he taste the pleasure which would be his when he had built up a complete industrial organisation, and the springs of the industrial machine were in vigorous working order, and each had become able to reinforce the other. Labour should be kept in active operation, and, even as, in a mill, flour comes flowing from grain, so should cash, and yet more cash, come flowing from every atom of refuse and remnant. And all the while he could see before him the landowner who was one of the leading men in Russia, and for whom he had conceived such an unbounded respect. Hitherto only for rank or for opulence had Chichikov respected a man—never for mere intellectual power; but now he made a first exception in favour of Kostanzhoglo, seeing that he felt that nothing undertaken by his host could possibly come to naught. And another project which was occupying Chichikov's mind was the project of purchasing the estate of a certain landowner named Khlobuev. Already Chichikov had at his disposal ten thousand roubles, and a further fifteen thousand he would try and borrow of Kostanzhoglo (seeing that the latter had himself said that he was prepared to help any one who really desired to grow rich); while, as for the remainder, he would either raise the sum by mortgaging the estate or force Khlobuev to wait for it—just to tell him to resort to the courts if such might be his pleasure.

Long did our hero ponder the scheme; until at length the slumber which had, these four hours past, been holding the rest of the household in its embraces enfolded also Chichikov, and he sank into oblivion.

CHAPTER IV

Next day, with Platon and Constantine, Chichikov set forth to interview Khlobuev, the owner whose estate Constantine had consented to help Chichikov to purchase with a non-interest-bearing, uncovenanted loan of ten thousand roubles. Naturally, our hero was in the highest of spirits. For the first fifteen versts or so the road led through forest land and tillage belonging to Platon and his brother-in-law; but directly the limit of these domains was reached, forest land began to be replaced with swamp, and tillage with waste. Also, the village in Khlobuev's estate had about it a deserted air, and as for the proprietor himself, he was discovered in a state of drowsy dishevelment, having not long left his bed. A man of about forty, he had his cravat crooked, his frockcoat adorned with a large stain, and one of his boots worn through. Nevertheless he seemed delighted to see his visitors.

"What?" he exclaimed. "Constantine Thedorovitch and Platon Mikhalitch? Really I must rub my eyes! Never again in this world did I look to see callers arriving. As a rule, folk avoid me like the devil, for they cannot disabuse their minds of the idea that I am going to ask them for a loan. Yes, it is my own fault, I know, but what would you? To the end will swine cheat swine. Pray excuse my costume. You will observe that my boots are in holes. But how can I afford to get them mended?"

"Never mind," said Constantine. "We have come on business only. May I present to you a possible purchaser of your estate, in the person of Paul Ivanovitch Chichikov?"

"I am indeed glad to meet you!" was Khlobuev's response. "Pray shake hands with me, Paul Ivanovitch."

Chichikov offered one hand, but not both.

"I can show you a property worth your attention," went on the master of the estate. "May I ask if you have yet dined?"

"Yes, we have," put in Constantine, desirous of escaping as soon as possible. "To save you further trouble, let us go and view the estate at once."

"Very well," replied Khlobuev. "Pray come and inspect my irregularities and futilities. You have done well to dine beforehand, for not so much as a fowl is left in the place, so dire are the extremities to which you see me reduced."

Sighing deeply, he took Platon by the arm (it was clear that he did not look for any sympathy from Constantine) and walked ahead, while Constantine and Chichikov followed.

"Things are going hard with me, Platon Mikhalitch," continued Khlobuev. "How hard you cannot imagine. No money have I, no food, no boots. Were I still young and a bachelor, it would have come easy to me to live on bread and cheese; but when a man is growing old, and has got a wife and five children, such trials press heavily upon him, and, in spite of himself, his spirits sink."

"But, should you succeed in selling the estate, that would help to put you right, would it not?" said Platon.

"How could it do so?" replied Khlobuev with a despairing gesture. "What I might get for the property would have to go towards discharging my debts, and I should find myself left with less than a thousand roubles besides."

"Then what do you intend to do?"

"God knows."

"But is there NOTHING to which you could set your hand in order to clear yourself of your difficulties?"

"How could there be?"

"Well, you might accept a Government post."

"Become a provincial secretary, you mean? How could I obtain such a post? They would not offer me one of the meanest possible kind. Even supposing that they did, how could I live on a salary of five hundred roubles—I who have a wife and five children?"

"Then try and obtain a bailiff's post."

"Who would entrust their property to a man who has squandered his own estate?"

"Nevertheless, when death and destitution threaten, a man must either do something or starve. Shall I ask my brother to use his influence to procure you a post?"

"No, no, Platon Mikhalitch," sighed Khlobuev, gripping the other's hand. "I am no longer serviceable—I am grown old before my time, and find that liver and rheumatism are paying me for the sins of my youth. Why should the Government be put to a loss on my account?—not to speak of the fact that for every salaried post there are countless numbers of applicants. God forbid that, in order to provide me with a livelihood further burdens should be imposed upon an impoverished public!"

"Such are the results of improvident management!" thought Platon to himself. "The disease is even worse than my slothfulness."

Meanwhile Kostanzhoglo, walking by Chichikov's side, was almost taking leave of his senses.

"Look at it!" he cried with a wave of his hand. "See to what wretchedness the peasant has become reduced! Should cattle disease come, Khlobuev will have nothing to fall back upon, but will be forced to sell his all—to leave the peasant without a horse, and therefore without the means to labour, even though the loss of a single day's work may take years of labour to rectify. Meanwhile it is plain that the local peasant has become a mere dissolute, lazy drunkard. Give a muzhik enough to live upon for twelve months without working, and you will corrupt him for ever, so inured to rags and vagrancy will he grow. And what is the good of that piece of pasture there—of that piece on the further side of those huts? It is a mere flooded tract. Were it mine, I should put it under flax, and clear five thousand roubles, or else sow it with turnips, and clear, perhaps, four thousand. And see how the rye is drooping, and nearly laid. As for wheat, I am pretty sure that he has not sown any. Look, too, at those ravines! Were they mine, they would be standing under timber which even a rook could not top. To think of wasting such quantities of land! Where land wouldn't bear corn, I should dig it up, and plant it with vegetables. What ought to be done is that Khlobuev ought to take a spade into his own hands, and to set his wife and children and servants to do the same; and even if they died of the exertion, they would at least die doing their duty, and not through guzzling at the dinner table."

This said, Kostanzhoglo spat, and his brow flushed with grim indignation.

Presently they reached an elevation whence the distant flashing of a river, with its flood waters and subsidiary streams, caught the eye, while, further off, a portion of General Betristchev's homestead could be discerned among the trees, and, over it, a blue, densely wooded hill which Chichikov guessed to be the spot where Tientietnikov's mansion was situated.

"This is where I should plant timber," said Chichikov. "And, regarded as a site for a manor house, the situation could scarcely be beaten for beauty of view."

"You seem to get great store upon views and beauty," remarked Kostanzhoglo with reproof in his tone. "Should you pay too much attention to those things, you might find yourself without crops or view. Utility should be placed first, not beauty. Beauty will come of itself. Take, for example, towns. The fairest and most beautiful towns are those which have built themselves—those in which each man has built to suit his own exclusive circumstances and needs; whereas towns which men have constructed on regular, string-taut lines are no better than collections of barracks. Put beauty aside, and look only to what is NECESSARY."

"Yes, but to me it would always be irksome to have to wait. All the time that I was doing so I should be hungering to see in front of me the sort of prospect which I prefer."

"Come, come! Are you a man of twenty-five—you who have served as a tchinovnik in St. Petersburg? Have patience, have patience. For six years work, and work hard. Plant, sow, and dig the earth without taking a moment's rest. It will be difficult, I know—yes, difficult indeed; but at the end of that time, if you have thoroughly stirred the soil, the land will begin to help you as nothing else can do. That is to say, over and above your seventy or so pairs of hands, there will begin to assist in the work seven hundred pairs of hands which you cannot see. Thus everything will be multiplied tenfold. I myself have ceased even to have to lift a finger, for whatsoever needs to be done gets done of itself. Nature loves patience: always remember that. It is a law given her of God Himself, who has blessed all those who are strong to endure."

"To hear your words is to be both encouraged and strengthened," said Chichikov. To this Kostanzhoglo made no reply, but presently went on:

"And see how that piece of land has been ploughed! To stay here longer is more than I can do. For me, to have to look upon such want of orderliness and foresight is death. Finish your business with Khlobuev without me, and whatsoever you do, get this treasure out of that fool's hands as quickly as possible, for he is dishonouring God's gifts."

And Kostanzhoglo, his face dark with the rage that was seething in his excitable soul, left Chichikov, and caught up the owner of the establishment.

"What, Constantine Thedorovitch?" cried Khlobuev in astonishment. "Just arrived, you are going already?"

"Yes; I cannot help it; urgent business requires me at home." And entering his gig, Kostanzhoglo drove rapidly away. Somehow Khlobuev seemed to divine the cause of his sudden departure.

"It was too much for him," he remarked. "An agriculturist of that kind does not like to have to look upon the results of such feckless management as mine. Would you believe it, Paul Ivanovitch, but this year I have been unable to sow any wheat! Am I not a fine husbandman? There was no seed for the purpose, nor yet anything with which to prepare the ground. No, I am not like Constantine Thedorovitch, who, I hear, is a perfect Napoleon in his particular line. Again and again the thought occurs to me, 'Why has so much intellect been put into that head, and only a drop or two into my own dull pate?' Take care of that puddle, gentlemen. I have told my peasants to lay down planks for the spring, but they have not done so. Nevertheless my heart aches for the poor fellows, for they need a good example, and what sort of an example am I? How am *I* to give them orders? Pray take them under your charge, Paul Ivanovitch, for I cannot teach them orderliness and method when I myself lack both. As a matter of fact, I should have given them their freedom long ago, had there been any use in my doing so; for even I can see that peasants must first be afforded the means of earning a livelihood before they can live. What they need is a stern, yet just, master who shall live with them, day in, day out, and set them an example of tireless energy. The present-day Russian—I know of it myself—is helpless without a driver. Without one he falls asleep, and the mould grows over him."

"Yet I cannot understand WHY he should fall asleep and grow mouldy in that fashion," said Platon. "Why should he need continual surveillance to keep him from degenerating into a drunkard and a good-for-nothing?"

"The cause is lack of enlightenment," said Chichikov.

"Possibly—only God knows. Yet enlightenment has reached us right enough. Do we not attend university lectures and everything else that is befitting? Take my own education. I learnt not only the usual things, but also the art of spending money upon the latest refinement, the latest amenity—the art of familiarising oneself with whatsoever money can buy. How, then, can it be said that I was educated foolishly? And my comrades' education was the same. A few of them succeeded in annexing the cream of things, for the reason that they had the wit to do so, and the rest spent their time in doing their best to ruin their health and squander their money. Often I think there is no hope for the present-day Russian. While desiring to do everything, he accomplishes nothing. One day he will scheme to begin a new mode of existence, a new dietary; yet before evening he will have so over-eaten himself as to be unable to speak or do aught but sit staring like an owl. The same with every one."

"Quite so," agreed Chichikov with a smile. "'Tis everywhere the same story."

"To tell the truth, we are not born to common sense. I doubt whether Russia has ever produced a really sensible man. For my own part, if I see my neighbour living a regular life, and making money, and saving it, I begin to distrust him, and to feel certain that in old age, if not before, he too will be led astray by the devil—led astray in a moment. Yes, whether or not we be educated, there is something we lack. But what that something is passes my understanding."

On the return journey the prospect was the same as before. Everywhere the same slovenliness, the same disorder, was displaying itself unadorned:

the only difference being that a fresh puddle had formed in the middle of the village street. This want and neglect was noticeable in the peasants' quarters equally with the quarters of the barin. In the village a furious woman in greasy sackcloth was beating a poor young wench within an ace of her life, and at the same time devoting some third person to the care of all the devils in hell; further away a couple of peasants were stoically contemplating the virago—one scratching his rump as he did so, and the other yawning. The same yawn was discernible in the buildings, for not a roof was there but had a gaping hole in it. As he gazed at the scene Platon himself yawned. Patch was superimposed upon patch, and, in place of a roof, one hut had a piece of wooden fencing, while its crumbling window-frames were stayed with sticks purloined from the barin's barn. Evidently the system of upkeep in vogue was the system employed in the case of Trishkin's coat—the system of cutting up the cuffs and the collar into mendings for the elbows.

"No, I do not admire your way of doing things," was Chichikov's unspoken comment when the inspection had been concluded and the party had re-entered the house. Everywhere in the latter the visitors were struck with the way in which poverty went with glittering, fashionable profusion. On a writing-table lay a volume of Shakespeare, and, on an occasional table, a carved ivory back-scratcher. The hostess, too, was elegantly and fashionably attired, and devoted her whole conversation to the town and the local theatre. Lastly, the children—bright, merry little things—were well-dressed both as regards boys and girls. Yet far better would it have been for them if they had been clad in plain striped smocks, and running about the courtyard like peasant children. Presently a visitor arrived in the shape of a chattering, gossiping woman; whereupon the hostess carried her off to her own portion of the house, and, the children following them, the men found themselves alone.

"How much do you want for the property?" asked Chichikov of Khlobuev. "I am afraid I must request you to name the lowest possible sum, since I find the estate in a far worse condition than I had expected to do."

"Yes, it IS in a terrible state," agreed Khlobuev. "Nor is that the whole of the story. That is to say, I will not conceal from you the fact that, out of a hundred souls registered at the last revision, only fifty survive, so terrible have been the ravages of cholera. And of these, again, some have absconded; wherefore they too must be reckoned as dead, seeing that, were one to enter process against them, the costs would end in the property having to pass en bloc to the legal authorities. For these reasons I am asking only thirty-five thousand roubles for the estate."

Chichikov (it need hardly be said) started to haggle.

"Thirty-five thousand?" he cried. "Come, come! Surely you will accept TWENTY-five thousand?"

This was too much for Platon's conscience.

"Now, now, Paul Ivanovitch!" he exclaimed. "Take the property at the price named, and have done with it. The estate is worth at least that amount—so much so that, should you not be willing to give it, my brother-in-law and I will club together to effect the purchase."

"That being so," said Chichikov, taken aback, "I beg to agree to the price in question. At the same time, I must ask you to allow me to defer payment of one-half of the purchase money until a year from now."

"No, no, Paul Ivanovitch. Under no circumstances could I do that. Pay me half now, and the rest in . . . 50 You see, I need the money for the redemption of the mortgage."

"That places me in a difficulty," remarked Chichikov. "Ten thousand roubles is all that at the moment I have available." As a matter of fact, this was not true, seeing that, counting also the money which he had borrowed of Kostanzhoglo, he had at his disposal TWENTY thousand. His real reason for hesitating was that he disliked the idea of making so large a payment in a lump sum.

"I must repeat my request, Paul Ivanovitch," said Khlobuev, "—namely, that you pay me at least fifteen thousand immediately."

"The odd five thousand *I* will lend you," put in Platon to Chichikov.

"Indeed?" exclaimed Chichikov as he reflected: "So he also lends money!"

In the end Chichikov's dispatch-box was brought from the koliaska, and Khlobuev received thence ten thousand roubles, together with a promise that the remaining five thousand should be forthcoming on the morrow; though the promise was given only after Chichikov had first proposed that THREE thousand should be brought on the day named, and the rest be left over for two or three days longer, if not for a still more protracted period. The truth was that Paul Ivanovitch hated parting with money. No matter how urgent a situation might have been, he would still have preferred to pay a sum to-morrow rather than to-day. In other words, he acted as we all do, for we all like keeping a petitioner waiting. "Let him rub his back in the hall for a while," we say. "Surely he can bide his time a little?" Yet of the fact that every hour may be precious to the poor wretch, and that his business may suffer from the delay, we take no account. "Good sir," we say, "pray come again to-morrow. To-day I have no time to spare you."

"Where do you intend henceforth to live?" inquired Platon. "Have you any other property to which you can retire?"

"No," replied Khlobuev. "I shall remove to the town, where I possess a small villa. That would have been necessary, in any case, for the children's sake. You see, they must have instruction in God's word, and also lessons in music and dancing; and not for love or money can these things be procured in the country."

"Nothing to eat, yet dancing lessons for his children!" reflected Chichikov.

"An extraordinary man!" was Platon's unspoken comment.

"However, we must contrive to wet our bargain somehow," continued Khlobuev. "Hi, Kirushka! Bring that bottle of champagne."

"Nothing to eat, yet champagne to drink!" reflected Chichikov. As for Platon, he did not know WHAT to think.

In Khlobuev's eyes it was de rigueur that he should provide a guest with champagne; but, though he had sent to the town for some, he had been met with a blank refusal to forward even a bottle of kvass on credit. Only the discovery of a French dealer who had recently transferred his business from St. Petersburg, and opened a connection on a system of general credit, saved the situation by placing Khlobuev under the obligation of patronising him.

The company drank three glassfuls apiece, and so grew more cheerful. In particular did Khlobuev expand, and wax full of civility and friendliness, and scatter witticisms and anecdotes to right and left. What knowledge of men and the world did his utterances display! How well and accurately could he divine things! With what appositeness did he sketch the neighbouring landowners! How clearly he exposed their faults and failings! How thoroughly he knew the story of certain ruined gentry—the story of how, why, and through what cause they had fallen upon evil days! With what comic originality could he describe their little habits and customs!

In short, his guests found themselves charmed with his discourse, and felt inclined to vote him a man of first-rate intellect.

"What most surprises me," said Chichikov, "is how, in view of your ability, you come to be so destitute of means or resources."

"But I have plenty of both," said Khlobuev, and with that went on to deliver himself of a perfect avalanche of projects. Yet those projects proved to be so uncouth, so clumsy, so little the outcome of a knowledge of men and things, that his hearers could only shrug their shoulders and mentally exclaim: "Good Lord! What a difference between worldly wisdom and the capacity to use it!" In every case the projects in question were based upon the imperative necessity of at once procuring from somewhere two hundred—or at least one hundred—thousand roubles. That done (so Khlobuev averred), everything would fall into its proper place, the holes in his pockets would become stopped, his income would be quadrupled, and he would find himself in a position to liquidate his debts in full. Nevertheless he ended by saying: "What would you advise me to do? I fear that the philanthropist who would lend me two hundred thousand roubles or even a hundred thousand, does not exist. It is not God's will that he should."

"Good gracious!" inwardly ejaculated Chichikov. "To suppose that God would send such a fool two hundred thousand roubles!"

"However," went on Khlobuev, "I possess an aunt worth three millions—a pious old woman who gives freely to churches and monasteries, but finds a difficulty in helping her neighbour. At the same time, she is a lady of the old school, and worth having a peep at. Her canaries alone number four hundred, and, in addition, there is an army of pug-dogs, hangers-on, and servants. Even the youngest of the servants is sixty, but she calls them all 'young fellows,' and if a guest happens to offend her during dinner, she orders them to leave him out when handing out the dishes. THERE'S a woman for you!"

Platon laughed.

"And what may her family name be?" asked Chichikov. "And where does she live?"

"She lives in the county town, and her name is Alexandra Ivanovna Khanasarov."

"Then why do you not apply to her?" asked Platon earnestly. "It seems to me that, once she realised the position of your family, she could not possibly refuse you."

"Alas! nothing is to be looked for from that quarter," replied Khlobuev. "My aunt is of a very stubborn disposition—a perfect stone of a woman. Moreover, she has around her a sufficient band of favourites already. In particular is there a fellow who is aiming for a Governorship, and to that end has managed to insinuate himself into the circle of her kinsfolk. By the way," the speaker added, turning to Platon, "would you do me a favour? Next week I am giving a dinner to the associated guilds of the town."

Platon stared. He had been unaware that both in our capitals and in our provincial towns there exists a class of men whose lives are an enigma—men who, though they will seem to have exhausted their substance, and to have become enmeshed in debt, will suddenly be reported as in funds, and on the point of giving a dinner! And though, at this dinner, the guests will declare that the festival is bound to be their host's last fling, and that for a certainty he will be haled to prison on the morrow, ten years or more will elapse, and the rascal will still be at liberty, even though, in the meanwhile, his debts will have increased!

In the same way did the conduct of Khlobuev's menage afford a curious phenomenon, for one day the house would be the scene of a solemn Te Deum, performed by a priest in vestments, and the next of a stage play performed by a troupe of French actors in theatrical costume. Again, one day would see not a morsel of bread in the house, and the next day a banquet and generous largesse given to a party of artists and sculptors. During these seasons of scarcity (sufficiently severe to have led any one but Khlobuev to seek suicide by hanging or shooting), the master of the house would be preserved from rash action by his strongly religious disposition, which, contriving in some curious way to conform with his irregular mode of life, enabled him to fall back upon reading the lives of saints, ascetics, and others of the type which has risen superior to its misfortunes. And at such times his spirit would become softened, his thoughts full of gentleness, and his eyes wet with tears; he would fall to saying his prayers, and invariably some strange coincidence would bring an answer thereto in the shape of an unexpected measure of assistance. That is to say, some former friend of his would remember him, and send him a trifle in the way of money; or else some female visitor would be moved by his story to let her impulsive, generous heart proffer him a handsome gift; or else a suit whereof tidings had never even reached his ears would end by being decided in his favour.

And when that happened he would reverently acknowledge the immensity of the mercy of Providence, gratefully tender thanksgiving for the same, and betake himself again to his irregular mode of existence.

"Somehow I feel sorry for the man," said Platon when he and Chichikov had taken leave of their host, and left the house.

"Perhaps so, but he is a hopeless prodigal," replied the other. "Personally I find it impossible to compassionate such fellows."

And with that the pair ceased to devote another thought to Khlobuev. In the case of Platon, this was because he contemplated the fortunes of his fellows with the lethargic, half-somnolent eye which he turned upon all the rest of the world; for though the sight of distress of others would cause his heart to contract and feel full of sympathy, the impression thus produced never sank into the depths of his being. Accordingly, before many minutes were over he had ceased to bestow a single thought upon his late host. With Chichikov, however, things were different. Whereas Platon had ceased to think of Khlobuev no more than he had ceased to think of himself, Chichikov's mind had strayed elsewhere, for the reason that it had become taken up with grave meditation on the subject of the purchase just made. Suddenly finding himself no longer a fictitious proprietor, but the owner of a real, an actually existing, estate, he became contemplative, and his plans and ideas assumed such a serious vein as imparted to his features an unconsciously important air.

"Patience and hard work!" he muttered to himself. "The thing will not be difficult, for with those two requisites I have been familiar from the days of my swaddling clothes. Yes, no novelty will they be to me. Yet, in middle age, shall I be able to compass the patience whereof I was capable in my youth?"

However, no matter how he regarded the future, and no matter from what point of view he considered his recent acquisition, he could see nothing but advantage likely to accrue from the bargain. For one thing, he might be able to proceed so that, first the whole of the estate should be mortgaged, and then the better portions of land sold outright. Or he might so contrive matters as to manage the property for a while (and thus become a landowner like Kostanzhoglo, whose advice, as his neighbour and his benefactor, he intended always to follow), and then to dispose of the property by private treaty (provided he did not wish to continue his ownership), and still to retain in his hands the dead and abandoned souls. And another possible coup occurred to his mind. That is to say, he might contrive to withdraw from the district without having repaid Kostanzhoglo at all! Truly a splendid idea! Yet it is only fair to say that the idea was not one of Chichikov's own conception. Rather, it had presented itself—mocking, laughing, and winking—unbidden. Yet the impudent, the wanton thing! Who is the procreator of suddenly born ideas of the kind? The thought that he was now a real, an actual, proprietor instead of a fictitious—that he was now a proprietor of real land, real rights of timber and pasture, and real serfs who existed not only in the imagination, but also in veritable actuality—greatly elated our hero. So he took to dancing up and down in his seat, to rubbing his hands together, to winking at himself, to holding his fist, trumpet-wise, to his mouth (while making believe to execute a march), and even to uttering aloud such encouraging nicknames and phrases as "bulldog" and "little fat capon." Then suddenly recollecting that he was not alone, he hastened to moderate his behaviour and endeavoured to stifle the endless flow of his good spirits; with the result that when Platon, mistaking certain sounds for utterances addressed to himself, inquired what his companion had said, the latter retained the presence of mind to reply "Nothing."

Presently, as Chichikov gazed about him, he saw that for some time past the koliaska had been skirting a beautiful wood, and that on either side the road was bordered with an edging of birch trees, the tenderly-green, recently-opened leaves of which caused their tall, slender trunks to show up with the whiteness of a snowdrift. Likewise nightingales were warbling from the recesses of the foliage, and some wood tulips were glowing yellow in the grass. Next (and almost before Chichikov had realised how he came to be in such a beautiful spot when, but a moment before, there had been visible only open fields) there glimmered among the trees the stony whiteness of a church, with, on the further side of it, the intermittent, foliage-buried line of a fence; while from the upper end of a village street there was advancing to meet the vehicle a gentleman with a cap on his head, a knotted cudgel in his hands, and a slender-limbed English dog by his side.

"This is my brother," said Platon. "Stop, coachman." And he descended from the koliaska, while Chichikov followed his example. Yarb and the strange dog saluted one another, and then the active, thin-legged, slender-tongued Azor relinquished his licking of Yarb's blunt jowl, licked Platon's hands instead, and, leaping upon Chichikov, slobbered right into his ear.

The two brothers embraced.

"Really, Platon," said the gentleman (whose name was Vassili), "what do you mean by treating me like this?"

"How so?" said Platon indifferently.

"What? For three days past I have seen and heard nothing of you! A groom from Pietukh's brought your cob home, and told me you had departed on an expedition with some barin. At least you might have sent me word as to your destination and the probable length of your absence. What made you act so? God knows what I have not been wondering!"

"Does it matter?" rejoined Platon. "I forgot to send you word, and we have been no further than Constantine's (who, with our sister, sends you his greeting). By the way, may I introduce Paul Ivanovitch Chichikov?"

The pair shook hands with one another. Then, doffing their caps, they embraced.

"What sort of man is this Chichikov?" thought Vassili. "As a rule my brother Platon is not over-nice in his choice of acquaintances." And, eyeing our hero as narrowly as civility permitted, he saw that his appearance was that of a perfectly respectable individual.

Chichikov returned Vassili's scrutiny with a similar observance of the dictates of civility, and perceived that he was shorter than Platon, that his hair was of a darker shade, and that his features, though less handsome, contained far more life, animation, and kindliness than did his brother's. Clearly he indulged in less dreaming, though that was an aspect which Chichikov little regarded.

"I have made up my mind to go touring our Holy Russia with Paul Ivanovitch," said Platon. "Perhaps it will rid me of my melancholy."

"What has made you come to such a sudden decision?" asked the perplexed Vassili (very nearly he added: "Fancy going travelling with a man whose acquaintance you have just made, and who may turn out to be a rascal or the devil knows what!" But, in spite of his distrust, he contented himself with another covert scrutiny of Chichikov, and this time came to the conclusion that there was no fault to be found with his exterior).

The party turned to the right, and entered the gates of an ancient courtyard attached to an old-fashioned house of a type no longer built—

the type which has huge gables supporting a high-pitched roof. In the centre of the courtyard two great lime trees covered half the surrounding space with shade, while beneath them were ranged a number of wooden benches, and the whole was encircled with a ring of blossoming lilacs and cherry trees which, like a beaded necklace, reinforced the wooden fence, and almost buried it beneath their clusters of leaves and flowers. The house, too, stood almost concealed by this greenery, except that the front door and the windows peered pleasantly through the foliage, and that here and there between the stems of the trees there could be caught glimpses of the kitchen regions, the storehouses, and the cellar. Lastly, around the whole stood a grove, from the recesses of which came the echoing songs of nightingales.

Involuntarily the place communicated to the soul a sort of quiet, restful feeling, so eloquently did it speak of that care-free period when every one lived on good terms with his neighbour, and all was simple and unsophisticated. Vassili invited Chichikov to seat himself, and the party approached, for that purpose, the benches under the lime trees; after which a youth of about seventeen, and clad in a red shirt, brought decanters containing various kinds of kvass (some of them as thick as syrup, and others hissing like aerated lemonade), deposited the same upon the table, and, taking up a spade which he had left leaning against a tree, moved away towards the garden. The reason of this was that in the brothers' household, as in that of Kostanzhoglo, no servants were kept, since the whole staff were rated as gardeners, and performed that duty in rotation—Vassili holding that domestic service was not a specialised calling, but one to which any one might contribute a hand, and therefore one which did not require special menials to be kept for the purpose. Moreover, he held that the average Russian peasant remains active and willing (rather than lazy) only so long as he wears a shirt and a peasant's smock; but that as soon as ever he finds himself put into a German tailcoat, he becomes awkward, sluggish, indolent, disinclined to change his vest or take a bath, fond of sleeping in his clothes, and certain to breed fleas and bugs under the German apparel. And it may be that Vassili was right. At all events, the brothers' peasantry were exceedingly well clad—the women, in particular, having their head-dresses spangled with gold, and the sleeves of their blouses embroidered after the fashion of a Turkish shawl.

"You see here the species of kvass for which our house has long been famous," said Vassili to Chichikov. The latter poured himself out a glassful from the first decanter which he lighted upon, and found the contents to be linden honey of a kind never tasted by him even in Poland, seeing that it had a sparkle like that of champagne, and also an effervescence which sent a pleasant spray from the mouth into the nose.

"Nectar!" he proclaimed. Then he took some from a second decanter. It proved to be even better than the first. "A beverage of beverages!" he exclaimed. "At your respected brother-in-law's I tasted the finest syrup which has ever come my way, but here I have tasted the very finest kvass."

"Yet the recipe for the syrup also came from here," said Vassili, "seeing that my sister took it with her. By the way, to what part of the country, and to what places, are you thinking of travelling?"

"To tell the truth," replied Chichikov, rocking himself to and fro on the bench, and smoothing his knee with his hand, and gently inclining his head, "I am travelling less on my own affairs than on the affairs of others. That is to say, General Betristchev, an intimate friend, and, I might add, a generous benefactor of mine, has charged me with commissions to some of his relatives. Nevertheless, though relatives are relatives, I may say that I am travelling on my own account as well, in that, in addition to possible benefit to my health, I desire to see the world and the whirligig of humanity, which constitute, to so speak, a living book, a second course of education."

Vassili took thought. "The man speaks floridly," he reflected, "yet his words contain a certain element of truth." After a moment's silence he added to Platon: "I am beginning to think that the tour might help you to bestir yourself. At present you are in a condition of mental slumber. You have fallen asleep, not so much from weariness or satiety, as through a lack of vivid perceptions and impressions. For myself, I am your complete antithesis. I should be only too glad if I could feel less acutely, if I could take things less to heart."

"Emotion has become a disease with you," said Platon. "You seek your own troubles, and make your own anxieties."

"How can you say that when ready-made anxieties greet one at every step?" exclaimed Vassili. "For example, have you heard of the trick which Lienitsin has just played us—of his seizing the piece of vacant land whither our peasants resort for their sports? That piece I would not sell for all the money in the world. It has long been our peasants' play-ground, and all the traditions of our village are bound up with it. Moreover, for me, old custom is a sacred thing for which I would gladly sacrifice everything else."

"Lienitsin cannot have known of this, or he would not have seized the land," said Platon. "He is a newcomer, just arrived from St. Petersburg. A few words of explanation ought to meet the case."

"But he DOES know of what I have stated; he DOES know of it. Purposely I sent him word to that affect, yet he has returned me the rudest of answers."

"Then go yourself and explain matters to him."

"No, I will not do that; he has tried to carry off things with too high a hand. But YOU can go if you like."

"I would certainly go were it not that I scarcely like to interfere. Also, I am a man whom he could easily hoodwink and outwit."

"Would it help you if *I* were to go?" put in Chichikov. "Pray enlighten me as to the matter."

Vassili glanced at the speaker, and thought to himself: "What a passion the man has for travelling!"

"Yes, pray give me an idea of the kind of fellow," repeated Chichikov, "and also outline to me the affair."

"I should be ashamed to trouble you with such an unpleasant commission," replied Vassili. "He is a man whom I take to be an utter rascal. Originally a member of a family of plain dvoriane in this province, he entered the Civil Service in St. Petersburg, then married some one's natural daughter in that city, and has returned to lord it with a high hand. I cannot bear the tone he adopts. Our folk are by no means fools. They do not look upon the current fashion as the Tsar's ukaz any more than they look upon St. Petersburg as the Church."

"Naturally," said Chichikov. "But tell me more of the particulars of the quarrel."

"They are these. He needs additional land and, had he not acted as he has done, I would have given him some land elsewhere for nothing; but, as it is, the pestilent fellow has taken it into his head to—"

"I think I had better go and have a talk with him. That might settle the affair. Several times have people charged me with similar commissions, and never have they repented of it. General Betristchev is an example."

"Nevertheless I am ashamed that you should be put to the annoyance of having to converse with such a fellow."

[At this point there occurs a long hiatus.]

"And above all things, such a transaction would need to be carried through in secret," said Chichikov. "True, the law does not forbid such things, but there is always the risk of a scandal."

"Quite so, quite so," said Lienitsin with head bent down.

"Then we agree!" exclaimed Chichikov. "How charming! As I say, my business is both legal and illegal. Though needing to effect a mortgage, I desire to put no one to the risk of having to pay the two roubles on each living soul; wherefore I have conceived the idea of relieving landowners of that distasteful obligation by acquiring dead and absconded souls who have failed to disappear from the revision list. This enables me at once to perform an act of Christian charity and to remove from the shoulders of our more impoverished proprietors the burden of tax-payment upon souls of the kind specified. Should you yourself care to do business with me, we will draw up a formal purchase agreement as though the souls in question were still alive."

"But it would be such a curious arrangement," muttered Lienitsin, moving his chair and himself a little further away. "It would be an arrangement which, er—er—"

"Would involve you in no scandal whatever, seeing that the affair would be carried through in secret. Moreover, between friends who are well-disposed towards one another—"

"Nevertheless—"

Chichikov adopted a firmer and more decided tone. "I repeat that there would be no scandal," he said. "The transaction would take place as between good friends, and as between friends of mature age, and as between friends of good status, and as between friends who know how to keep their own counsel." And, so saying, he looked his interlocutor frankly and generously in the eyes.

Nevertheless Lienitsin's resourcefulness and acumen in business matters failed to relieve his mind of a certain perplexity—and the less so since he had contrived to become caught in his own net. Yet, in general, he possessed neither a love for nor a talent for underhand dealings, and, had not fate and circumstances favoured Chichikov by causing Lienitsin's wife to enter the room at that moment, things might have turned out very differently from what they did. Madame was a pale, thin, insignificant-looking young lady, but none the less a lady who wore her clothes a la St. Petersburg, and cultivated the society of persons who were unimpeachably comme il faut. Behind her, borne in a nurse's arms, came the first fruits of the love of husband and wife. Adopting his most telling method of approach (the method accompanied with a sidelong inclination of the head and a sort of hop), Chichikov hastened to greet the lady from the metropolis, and then the baby. At first the latter started to bellow disapproval, but the words "Agoo, agoo, my pet!" added to a little cracking of the fingers and a sight of a beautiful seal on a watch chain, enabled Chichikov to weedle the infant into his arms; after which he fell to swinging it up and down until he had contrived to raise a smile on its face—a circumstance which greatly delighted the parents, and finally inclined the father in his visitor's favour. Suddenly, however—whether from pleasure or from some other cause—the infant misbehaved itself!

"My God!" cried Madame. "He has gone and spoilt your frockcoat!"

True enough, on glancing downwards, Chichikov saw that the sleeve of his brand-new garment had indeed suffered a hurt. "If I could catch you alone, you little devil," he muttered to himself, "I'd shoot you!"

Host, hostess and nurse all ran for eau-de-Cologne, and from three sides set themselves to rub the spot affected.

"Never mind, never mind; it is nothing," said Chichikov as he strove to communicate to his features as cheerful an expression as possible. "What does it matter what a child may spoil during the golden age of its infancy?"

To himself he remarked: "The little brute! Would it could be devoured by wolves. It has made only too good a shot, the cussed young ragamuffin!"

How, after this—after the guest had shown such innocent affection for the little one, and magnanimously paid for his so doing with a brand-new suit—could the father remain obdurate? Nevertheless, to avoid setting a bad example to the countryside, he and Chichikov agreed to carry through the transaction PRIVATELY, lest, otherwise, a scandal should arise.

"In return," said Chichikov, "would you mind doing me the following favour? I desire to mediate in the matter of your difference with the Brothers Platonov. I believe that you wish to acquire some additional land? Is not that so?"

[Here there occurs a hiatus in the original.]

Everything in life fulfils its function, and Chichikov's tour in search of a fortune was carried out so successfully that not a little money passed into his pockets. The system employed was a good one: he did not steal, he merely used. And every one of us at times does the same: one man with regard to Government timber, and another with regard to a sum belonging to his employer, while a third defrauds his children for the sake of an actress, and a fourth robs his peasantry for the sake of smart furniture or a carriage. What can one do when one is surrounded on every side with roguery, and everywhere there are insanely expensive restaurants, masked balls, and dances to the music of gipsy bands? To abstain when every one else is indulging in these things, and fashion commands, is difficult indeed!

Chichikov was for setting forth again, but the roads had now got into a bad state, and, in addition, there was in preparation a second fair—one for the dvoriane only. The former fair had been held for the sale of horses, cattle, cheese, and other peasant produce, and the buyers had been merely cattle-jobbers and kulaks; but this time the function was to be one for the sale of manorial produce which had been bought up by wholesale dealers at Nizhni Novgorod, and then transferred hither. To the fair, of course, came those ravishers of the Russian purse who, in the shape of Frenchmen with pomades and Frenchwomen with hats, make away with money earned by blood and hard work, and, like the locusts of Egypt (to use Kostanzhoglo's term) not only devour their prey, but also dig holes in the ground and leave behind their eggs.

Although, unfortunately, the occurrence of a bad harvest retained many landowners at their country houses, the local tchinovniks (whom the failure of the harvest did NOT touch) proceeded to let themselves go—as also, to their undoing, did their wives. The reading of books of the type diffused, in these modern days, for the inoculation of humanity with a craving for new and superior amenities of life had caused every one to conceive a passion for experimenting with the latest luxury; and to meet this want the French wine merchant opened a new establishment in the shape of a restaurant as had never before been heard of in the province—a restaurant where supper could be procured on credit as regarded one-half, and for an unprecedentedly low sum as regarded the other. This exactly suited both heads of boards and clerks who were living in hope of being able some day to resume their bribes-taking from suitors. There also developed a tendency to compete in the matter of horses and liveried flunkeys; with the result that despite the damp and snowy weather exceedingly elegant turnouts took to parading backwards and forwards. Whence these equipages had come God only knows, but at least they would not have disgraced St. Petersburg. From within them merchants and attorneys doffed their caps to ladies, and inquired after their health, and likewise it became a rare sight to see a bearded man in a rough fur cap, since every one now went about clean-shaven and with dirty teeth, after the European fashion.

"Sir, I beg of you to inspect my goods," said a tradesman as Chichikov was passing his establishment. "Within my doors you will find a large variety of clothing."

"Have you a cloth of bilberry-coloured check?" inquired the person addressed.

"I have cloths of the finest kind," replied the tradesman, raising his cap with one hand, and pointing to his shop with the other. Chichikov entered, and in a trice the proprietor had dived beneath the counter, and appeared on the other side of it, with his back to his wares and his face towards the customer. Leaning forward on the tips of his fingers, and indicating his merchandise with just the suspicion of a nod, he requested the gentleman to specify exactly the species of cloth which he required.

"A cloth with an olive-coloured or a bottle-tinted spot in its pattern—anything in the nature of bilberry," explained Chichikov.

"That being so, sir, I may say that I am about to show you clothes of a quality which even our illustrious capitals could not surpass. Hi, boy! Reach down that roll up there—number 34. No, NOT that one, fool! Such fellows as you are always too good for your job. There—hand it to me. This is indeed a nice pattern!"

Unfolding the garment, the tradesman thrust it close to Chichikov's nose in order that he might not only handle, but also smell it.

"Excellent, but not what I want," pronounced Chichikov. "Formerly I was in the Custom's Department, and therefore wear none but cloth of the latest make. What I want is of a ruddier pattern than this—not exactly a bottle-tinted pattern, but something approaching bilberry."

"I understand, sir. Of course you require only the very newest thing. A cloth of that kind I DO possess, sir, and though excessive in price, it is of a quality to match."

Carrying the roll of stuff to the light—even stepping into the street for the purpose—the shopman unfolded his prize with the words, "A truly beautiful shade! A cloth of smoked grey, shot with flame colour!"

The material met with the customer's approval, a price was agreed upon, and with incredible celerity the vendor made up the purchase into a brown-paper parcel, and stowed it away in Chichikov's koliaska.

At this moment a voice asked to be shown a black frockcoat.

"The devil take me if it isn't Khlobuev!" muttered our hero, turning his back upon the newcomer. Unfortunately the other had seen him.

"Come, come, Paul Ivanovitch!" he expostulated. "Surely you do not intend to overlook me? I have been searching for you everywhere, for I have something important to say to you."

"My dear sir, my very dear sir," said Chichikov as he pressed Khlobuev's hand, "I can assure you that, had I the necessary leisure, I should at all times be charmed to converse with you." And mentally he added: "Would that the Evil One would fly away with you!"

Almost at the same time Murazov, the great landowner, entered the shop. As he did so our hero hastened to exclaim: "Why, it is Athanasi Vassilievitch! How ARE you, my very dear sir?"

"Well enough," replied Murazov, removing his cap (Khlobuev and the shopman had already done the same). "How, may I ask, are YOU?"

"But poorly," replied Chichikov, "for of late I have been troubled with indigestion, and my sleep is bad. I do not get sufficient exercise."

However, instead of probing deeper into the subject of Chichikov's ailments, Murazov turned to Khlobuev.

"I saw you enter the shop," he said, "and therefore followed you, for I have something important for your ear. Could you spare me a minute or two?"

"Certainly, certainly," said Khlobuev, and the pair left the shop together.

"I wonder what is afoot between them," said Chichikov to himself.

"A wise and noble gentleman, Athanasi Vassilievitch!" remarked the tradesman. Chichikov made no reply save a gesture.

"Paul Ivanovitch, I have been looking for you everywhere," Lienitsin's voice said from behind him, while again the tradesman hastened to remove his cap. "Pray come home with me, for I have something to say to you."

Chichikov scanned the speaker's face, but could make nothing of it. Paying the tradesman for the cloth, he left the shop.

Meanwhile Murazov had conveyed Khlobuev to his rooms.

"Tell me," he said to his guest, "exactly how your affairs stand. I take it that, after all, your aunt left you something?"

"It would be difficult to say whether or not my affairs are improved," replied Khlobuev. "True, fifty souls and thirty thousand roubles came to me from Madame Khanasarova, but I had to pay them away to satisfy my debts. Consequently I am once more destitute. But the important point is that there was trickery connected with the legacy, and shameful trickery at that. Yes, though it may surprise you, it is a fact that that fellow Chichikov—"

"Yes, Semen Semenovitch, but, before you go on to speak of Chichikov, pray tell me something about yourself, and how much, in your opinion, would be sufficient to clear you of your difficulties?"

"My difficulties are grievous," replied Khlobuev. "To rid myself of them, and also to have enough to go on with, I should need to acquire at least a hundred thousand roubles, if not more. In short, things are becoming impossible for me."

"And, had you the money, what should you do with it?"

"I should rent a tenement, and devote myself to the education of my children. Not a thought should I give to myself, for my career is over, seeing that it is impossible for me to re-enter the Civil Service and I am good for nothing else."

"Nevertheless, when a man is leading an idle life he is apt to incur temptations which shun his better-employed brother."

"Yes, but beyond question I am good for nothing, so broken is my health, and such a martyr I am to dyspepsia."

"But how do you propose to live without working? How can a man like you exist without a post or a position of any kind? Look around you at the works of God. Everything has its proper function, and pursues its proper course. Even a stone can be used for one purpose or another. How, then, can it be right for a man who is a thinking being to remain a drone?"

"But I should not be a drone, for I should employ myself with the education of my children."

"No, Semen Semenovitch—no: THAT you would find the hardest task of all. For how can a man educate his children who has never even educated himself? Instruction can be imparted to children only through the medium of example; and would a life like yours furnish them with a profitable example—a life which has been spent in idleness and the playing of cards? No, Semen Semenovitch. You had far better hand your children over to me. Otherwise they will be ruined. Do not think that I am jesting. Idleness has wrecked your life, and you must flee from it. Can a man live with nothing to keep him in place? Even a journeyman labourer who earns the barest pittance may take an interest in his occupation."

"Athanasi Vassilievitch, I have tried to overcome myself, but what further resource lies open to me? Can I who am old and incapable re-enter the Civil Service and spend year after year at a desk with youths who are just starting their careers? Moreover, I have lost the trick of taking bribes; I should only hinder both myself and others; while, as you know, it is a department which has an established caste of its own. Therefore, though I have considered, and even attempted to obtain, every conceivable post, I find myself incompetent for them all. Only in a monastery should I—"

"Nay, nay. Monasteries, again, are only for those who have worked. To those who have spent their youth in dissipation such havens say what the ant said to the dragonfly—namely, 'Go you away, and return to your dancing.' Yes, even in a monastery do folk toil and toil—they do not sit playing whist." Murazov looked at Khlobuev, and added: "Semen Semenovitch, you are deceiving both yourself and me."

Poor Khlobuev could not utter a word in reply, and Murazov began to feel sorry for him.

"Listen, Semen Semenovitch," he went on. "I know that you say your prayers, and that you go to church, and that you observe both Matins and Vespers, and that, though averse to early rising, you leave your bed at four o'clock in the morning before the household fires have been lit."

"Ah, Athanasi Vassilievitch," said Khlobuev, "that is another matter altogether. That I do, not for man's sake, but for the sake of Him who has ordered all things here on earth. Yes, I believe that He at least can feel compassion for me, that He at least, though I be foul and lowly, will pardon me and receive me when all men have cast me out, and my best friend has betrayed me and boasted that he has done it for a good end."

Khlobuev's face was glowing with emotion, and from the older man's eyes also a tear had started.

"You will do well to hearken unto Him who is merciful," he said. "But remember also that, in the eyes of the All-Merciful, honest toil is of equal merit with a prayer. Therefore take unto yourself whatsoever task you may, and do it as though you were doing it, not unto man, but unto God. Even though to your lot there should fall but the cleaning of a floor, clean that floor as though it were being cleaned for Him alone. And thence at least this good you will reap: that there will remain to you no time for what is evil—for card playing, for feasting, for all the life of this gay world. Are you acquainted with Ivan Potapitch?"

"Yes, not only am I acquainted with him, but I also greatly respect him."

"Time was when Ivan Potapitch was a merchant worth half a million roubles. In everything did he look but for gain, and his affairs prospered exceedingly, so much so that he was able to send his son to be educated in France, and to marry his daughter to a General. And whether in his office or at the Exchange, he would stop any friend whom he encountered and carry him off to a tavern to drink, and spend whole days thus employed. But at last he became bankrupt, and God sent him other misfortunes also. His son! Ah, well! Ivan Potapitch is now my steward, for he had to begin life over again. Yet once more his affairs are in order, and, had it been his wish, he could have restarted in business with a capital of half a million roubles. 'But no,' he said. 'A steward am I, and a steward will I remain to the end; for, from being full-stomached and heavy with dropsy, I have become strong and well.' Not a drop of liquor passes his lips, but only cabbage soup and gruel. And he prays as none of the rest of us pray, and he helps the poor as none of the rest of us help them; and to this he would add yet further charity if his means permitted him to do so."

Poor Khlobuev remained silent, as before.

The elder man took his two hands in his.

"Semen Semenovitch," he said, "you cannot think how much I pity you, or how much I have had you in my thoughts. Listen to me. In the monastery there is a recluse who never looks upon a human face. Of all men whom I know he has the broadest mind, and he breaks not his silence save to give advice. To him I went and said that I had a friend (though I did not actually mention your name) who was in great trouble of soul. Suddenly the recluse interrupted me with the words: 'God's work first, and our own last. There is need for a church to be built, but no money wherewith to build it. Money must be collected to that end.' Then he shut to the wicket. I wondered to myself what this could mean, and concluded that the recluse had been unwilling to accord me his counsel. Next I repaired to the Archimandrite, and had scarce reached his door when he inquired of me whether I could commend to him a man meet to be entrusted with the collection of alms for a church—a man who should belong to the dvoriane or to the more lettered merchants, but who would guard the trust as he would guard the salvation of his soul. On the instant thought I to myself: 'Why should not the Holy Father appoint my friend Semen Semenovitch? For the way of suffering would benefit him greatly; and as he passed with his ledger from landowner to peasant, and from peasant to townsman, he would learn where folk dwell, and who stands in need of aught, and thus would become better acquainted with the countryside than folk who dwell in cities. And, thus become, he would find that his services were always in demand.' Only of late did the Governor-General say to me that, could he but be furnished with the name of a secretary who should know his work not only by the book but also by experience, he would give him a great sum, since nothing is to be learned by the former means, and, through it, much confusion arises."

"You confound me, you overwhelm me!" said Khlobuev, staring at his companion in open-eyed astonishment. "I can scarcely believe that your words are true, seeing that for such a trust an active, indefatigable man would be necessary. Moreover, how could I leave my wife and children unprovided for?"

"Have no fear," said Murazov, "I myself will take them under my care, as well as procure for the children a tutor. Far better and nobler were it for you to be travelling with a wallet, and asking alms on behalf of God, then to be remaining here and asking alms for yourself alone. Likewise, I will furnish you with a tilt-waggon, so that you may be saved some of the hardships of the journey, and thus be preserved in good health. Also, I will give you some money for the journey, in order that, as you pass on your way, you may give to those who stand in greater need than their fellows. Thus, if, before giving, you assure yourself that the recipient of the alms is worthy of the same, you will do much good; and as you travel you will become acquainted with all men and sundry, and they will treat you, not as a tchinovnik to be feared, but as one to whom, as a petitioner on behalf of the Church, they may unloose their tongues without peril."

"I feel that the scheme is a splendid one, and would gladly bear my part in it were it not likely to exceed my strength."

"What is there that does NOT exceed your strength?" said Murazov. "Nothing is wholly proportionate to it—everything surpasses it. Help from above is necessary: otherwise we are all powerless. Strength comes of prayer, and of prayer alone. When a man crosses himself, and cries, 'Lord, have mercy upon me!' he soon stems the current and wins to the shore. Nor need you take any prolonged thought concerning this matter. All that you need do is to accept it as a commission sent of God. The tilt-waggon can be prepared for you immediately; and then, as soon as you have been to the Archimandrite for your book of accounts and his blessing, you will be free to start on your journey."

"I submit myself to you, and accept the commission as a divine trust."

And even as Khlobuev spoke he felt renewed vigour and confidence arise in his soul, and his mind begin to awake to a sense of hopefulness of eventually being able to put to flight his troubles. And even as it was, the world seemed to be growing dim to his eyes. . . .

Meanwhile, plea after plea had been presented to the legal authorities, and daily were relatives whom no one had before heard of putting in an appearance. Yes, like vultures to a corpse did these good folk come flocking to the immense property which Madam Khanasarov had left behind her. Everywhere were heard rumours against Chichikov, rumours with regard to the validity of the second will, rumours with regard to will number one, and rumours of larceny and concealment of funds. Also, there came to hand information with regard both to Chichikov's purchase of dead souls and to his conniving at contraband goods during his service in the Customs Department. In short, every possible item of evidence was exhumed, and the whole of his previous history investigated. How the authorities had come to suspect and to ascertain all this God only knows, but the fact remains that there had fallen into the hands of those authorities information concerning matters of which Chichikov had believed only himself and the four walls to be aware. True, for a time these matters remained within the cognisance of none but the functionaries concerned, and failed to reach Chichikov's ears; but at length a letter from a confidential friend gave him reason to think that the fat was about to fall into the fire. Said the letter briefly: "Dear sir, I beg to advise you that possibly legal trouble is pending, but that you have no cause for uneasiness, seeing that everything will be attended to by yours very truly." Yet, in spite of its tenor, the epistle reassured its recipient. "What a genius the fellow is!" thought Chichikov to himself. Next, to complete his satisfaction, his tailor arrived with the new suit which he had ordered. Not without a certain sense of pride did our hero inspect the frockcoat of smoked grey shot with flame colour and look at it from every point of view, and then try on the breeches—the latter fitting him like a picture, and quite concealing any deficiencies in the matter of his thighs and calves (though, when buckled behind, they left his stomach projecting like a drum). True, the customer remarked that there appeared to be a slight tightness under the right armpit, but the smiling tailor only rejoined that that would cause the waist to fit all the better. "Sir," he said triumphantly, "you may rest assured that the work has been executed exactly as it ought to have been executed. No one, except in St. Petersburg, could have done it better." As a matter of fact, the tailor himself hailed from St. Petersburg, but called himself on his signboard "Foreign Costumier from London and Paris"—the truth being that by the use of a double-barrelled flourish of cities superior to mere "Karlsruhe" and "Copenhagen" he designed to acquire business and cut out his local rivals.

Chichikov graciously settled the man's account, and, as soon as he had gone, paraded at leisure, and con amore, and after the manner of an artist of aesthetic taste, before the mirror. Somehow he seemed to look better than ever in the suit, for his cheeks had now taken on a still more interesting air, and his chin an added seductiveness, while his white collar lent tone to his neck, the blue satin tie heightened the effect of the collar, the fashionable dickey set off the tie, the rich satin waistcoat emphasised the dickey, and the smoked-grey-shot-with-flame-colour frockcoat, shining like silk, splendidly rounded off the whole. When he turned to the right he looked well: when he turned to the left he looked even better. In short, it was a costume worthy of a Lord Chamberlain or the species of dandy who shrinks from swearing in the Russian language, but amply relieves his feelings in the language of France. Next, inclining his head slightly to one side, our hero endeavoured to pose as though he were addressing a middle-aged lady of exquisite refinement; and the result of these efforts was a picture which any artist might have yearned to portray. Next, his delight led him gracefully to execute a hop in ballet fashion, so that the wardrobe trembled and a bottle of eau-de-Cologne came crashing to the floor. Yet even this contretemps did not upset him; he merely called the offending bottle a fool, and then debated whom first he should visit in his attractive guise.

Suddenly there resounded through the hall a clatter of spurred heels, and then the voice of a gendarme saying: "You are commanded to present yourself before the Governor-General!" Turning round, Chichikov stared in horror at the spectacle presented; for in the doorway there was standing an apparition wearing a huge moustache, a helmet surmounted with a horsehair plume, a pair of crossed shoulder-belts, and a gigantic sword! A whole army might have been combined into a single individual! And when Chichikov opened his mouth to speak the apparition repeated, "You are commanded to present yourself before the Governor-General," and at the same moment our hero caught sight both of a second apparition outside the door and of a coach waiting beneath the window. What was to be done? Nothing whatever was possible. Just as he stood—in his smoked-grey-shot-with-flame-colour suit—he had then and there to enter the vehicle, and, shaking in every limb, and with a gendarme seated by his side, to start for the residence of the Governor-General.

And even in the hall of that establishment no time was given him to pull himself together, for at once an aide-de-camp said: "Go inside immediately, for the Prince is awaiting you." And as in a dream did our hero see a vestibule where couriers were being handed dispatches, and then a salon which he crossed with the thought, "I suppose I am not to be allowed a trial, but shall be sent straight to Siberia!" And at the thought his heart started beating in a manner which the most jealous of lovers could not have rivalled. At length there opened a door, and before him he saw a study full of portfolios, ledgers, and dispatch-boxes, with, standing behind them, the gravely menacing figure of the Prince.

"There stands my executioner," thought Chichikov to himself. "He is about to tear me to pieces as a wolf tears a lamb."

Indeed, the Prince's lips were simply quivering with rage.

"Once before did I spare you," he said, "and allow you to remain in the town when you ought to have been in prison: yet your only return for my clemency has been to revert to a career of fraud—and of fraud as dishonourable as ever a man engaged in."

"To what dishonourable fraud do you refer, your Highness?" asked Chichikov, trembling from head to foot.

The Prince approached, and looked him straight in the eyes.

"Let me tell you," he said, "that the woman whom you induced to witness a certain will has been arrested, and that you will be confronted with her."

The world seemed suddenly to grow dim before Chichikov's sight.

"Your Highness," he gasped, "I will tell you the whole truth, and nothing but the truth. I am guilty—yes, I am guilty; but I am not so guilty as you think, for I was led away by rascals."

"That any one can have led you away is impossible," retorted the Prince. "Recorded against your name there stand more felonies than even the most hardened liar could have invented. I believe that never in your life have you done a deed not innately dishonourable—that not a kopeck have you ever obtained by aught but shameful methods of trickery and theft, the penalty for which is Siberia and the knut. But enough of this! From this room you will be conveyed to prison, where, with other rogues and thieves, you will be confined until your trial may come on. And this is lenient treatment on my part, for you are worse, far worse, than the felons who will be your companions. THEY are but poor men in smocks and sheepskins, whereas YOU—" Without concluding his words, the Prince shot a glance at Chichikov's smoked-grey-shot-with-flame-colour apparel.

Then he touched a bell.

"Your Highness," cried Chichikov, "have mercy upon me! You are the father of a family! Spare me for the sake of my aged mother!"

"Rubbish!" exclaimed the Prince. "Even as before you besought me for the sake of a wife and children whom you did not even possess, so now you would speak to me of an aged mother!"

"Your Highness," protested Chichikov, "though I am a wretch and the lowest of rascals, and though it is true that I lied when I told you that I possessed a wife and children, I swear that, as God is my witness, it has always been my DESIRE to possess a wife, and to fulfil all the duties of a man and a citizen, and to earn the respect of my fellows and the authorities. But what could be done against the force of circumstances? By hook or by crook I have ever been forced to win a living, though confronted at every step by wiles and temptations and traitorous enemies and despoilers. So much has this been so that my life has, throughout, resembled a barque tossed by tempestuous waves, a barque driven at the mercy of the winds. Ah, I am only a man, your Highness!"

And in a moment the tears had gushed in torrents from his eyes, and he had fallen forward at the Prince's feet—fallen forward just as he was, in his smoked-grey-shot-with-flame-colour frockcoat, his velvet waistcoat, his satin tie, and his exquisitely fitting breeches, while from his neatly brushed pate, as again and again he struck his hand against his forehead, there came an odorous whiff of best-quality eau-de-Cologne.

"Away with him!" exclaimed the Prince to the gendarme who had just entered. "Summon the escort to remove him."

"Your Highness!" Chichikov cried again as he clasped the Prince's knees; but, shuddering all over, and struggling to free himself, the Prince repeated his order for the prisoner's removal.

"Your Highness, I say that I will not leave this room until you have accorded me mercy!" cried Chichikov as he clung to the Prince's leg with such tenacity that, frockcoat and all, he began to be dragged along the floor.

"Away with him, I say!" once more the Prince exclaimed with the sort of indefinable aversion which one feels at the sight of a repulsive insect which he cannot summon up the courage to crush with his boot. So convulsively did the Prince shudder that Chichikov, clinging to his leg, received a kick on the nose. Yet still the prisoner retained his hold; until at length a couple of burly gendarmes tore him away and, grasping his arms, hurried him—pale, dishevelled, and in that strange, half-conscious condition into which a man sinks when he sees before him only the dark, terrible figure of death, the phantom which is so abhorrent to all our natures—from the building. But on the threshold the party came face to face with Murazov, and in Chichikov's heart the circumstance revived a ray of hope. Wresting himself with almost supernatural strength from the grasp of the escorting gendarmes, he threw himself at the feet of the horror-stricken old man.

"Paul Ivanovitch," Murazov exclaimed, "what has happened to you?"

"Save me!" gasped Chichikov. "They are taking me away to prison and death!"

Yet almost as he spoke the gendarmes seized him again, and hurried him away so swiftly that Murazov's reply escaped his ears.

A damp, mouldy cell which reeked of soldiers' boots and leggings, an unvarnished table, two sorry chairs, a window closed with a grating, a crazy stove which, while letting the smoke emerge through its cracks, gave out no heat—such was the den to which the man who had just begun to taste the sweets of life, and to attract the attention of his fellows with his new suit of smoked-grey-shot-with-flame-colour, now found himself consigned. Not even necessaries had he been allowed to bring away with him, nor his dispatch-box which contained all his booty. No, with the indenture deeds of the dead souls, it was lodged in the hands of a tchinovnik; and as he thought of these things Chichikov rolled about the floor, and felt the cankerous worm of remorse seize upon and gnaw at his heart, and bite its way ever further and further into that heart so defenceless against its ravages, until he made up his mind that, should he have to suffer another twenty-four hours of this misery, there would no longer be a Chichikov in the world. Yet over him, as over every one, there hung poised the All-Saving Hand; and, an hour after his arrival at the prison, the doors of the gaol opened to admit Murazov.

Compared with poor Chichikov's sense of relief when the old man entered his cell, even the pleasure experienced by a thirsty, dusty traveller when he is given a drink of clear spring water to cool his dry, parched throat fades into insignificance.

"Ah, my deliverer!" he cried as he rose from the floor, where he had been grovelling in heartrending paroxysms of grief. Seizing the old man's hand, he kissed it and pressed it to his bosom. Then, bursting into tears, he added: "God Himself will reward you for having come to visit an unfortunate wretch!"

Murazov looked at him sorrowfully, and said no more than "Ah, Paul Ivanovitch, Paul Ivanovitch! What has happened?"

"What has happened?" cried Chichikov. "I have been ruined by an accursed woman. That was because I could not do things in moderation—I was powerless to stop myself in time, Satan tempted me, and drove me from my senses, and bereft me of human prudence. Yes, truly I have sinned, I have sinned! Yet how came I so to sin? To think that a dvorianin—yes, a dvorianin—should be thrown into prison without process or trial! I repeat, a dvorianin! Why was I not given time to go home and collect my effects? Whereas now they are left with no one to look after them! My dispatch-box, my dispatch-box! It contained my whole property, all that my heart's blood and years of toil and want have been needed to acquire. And now everything will be stolen, Athanasi Vassilievitch—everything will be taken from me! My God!"

And, unable to stand against the torrent of grief which came rushing over his heart once more, he sobbed aloud in tones which penetrated even the thickness of the prison walls, and made dull echoes awake behind them. Then, tearing off his satin tie, and seizing by the collar, the smoked-grey-shot-with-flame-colour frockcoat, he stripped the latter from his shoulders.

"Ah, Paul Ivanovitch," said the old man, "how even now the property which you have acquired is blinding your eyes, and causing you to fail to realise your terrible position!"

"Yes, my good friend and benefactor," wailed poor Chichikov despairingly, and clasping Murazov by the knees. "Yet save me if you can! The Prince is fond of you, and would do anything for your sake."

"No, Paul Ivanovitch; however much I might wish to save you, and however much I might try to do so, I could not help you as you desire; for it is to the power of an inexorable law, and not to the authority of any one man, that you have rendered yourself subject."

"Satan tempted me, and has ended by making of me an outcast from the human race!" Chichikov beat his head against the wall and struck the table with his fist until the blood spurted from his hand. Yet neither his head nor his hand seemed to be conscious of the least pain.

"Calm yourself, Paul Ivanovitch," said Murazov. "Calm yourself, and consider how best you can make your peace with God. Think of your miserable soul, and not of the judgment of man."

"I will, Athanasi Vassilievitch, I will. But what a fate is mine! Did ever such a fate befall a man? To think of all the patience with which I have gathered my kopecks, of all the toil and trouble which I have endured! Yet what I have done has not been done with the intention of robbing any one, nor of cheating the Treasury. Why, then, did I gather those kopecks? I gathered them to the end that one day I might be able to live in plenty, and also to have something to leave to the wife and children whom, for the benefit and welfare of my country, I hoped eventually to win and maintain. That was why I gathered those kopecks. True, I worked by devious methods—that I fully admit; but what else could I do? And even devious methods I employed only when I saw that the straight road would not serve my purpose so well as a crooked. Moreover, as I toiled, the appetite for those methods grew upon me. Yet what I took I took only from the rich; whereas villains exist who, while drawing thousands a year from the Treasury, despoil the poor, and take from the man with nothing even that which he has. Is it not the cruelty of fate, therefore, that, just when I was beginning to reap the harvest of my toil—to touch it, so to speak, with the tip of one finger—there should have arisen a sudden storm which has sent my barque to pieces on a rock? My capital had nearly reached the sum of three hundred thousand roubles, and a three-storied house was as good as mine, and twice over I could have bought a country estate. Why, then, should such a tempest have burst upon me? Why should I have sustained such a blow? Was not my life already like a barque tossed to and fro by the billows? Where is Heaven's justice—where is the reward for all my patience, for my boundless perseverance? Three times did I have to begin life afresh, and each time that I lost my all I began with a single kopeck at a moment when other men would have given themselves up to despair and drink. How much did I not have to overcome. How much did I not have to bear! Every kopeck which I gained I had to make with my whole strength; for though, to others, wealth may come easily, every coin of mine had to be 'forged with a nail worth three kopecks' as the proverb has it. With such a nail—with the nail of an iron, unwearying perseverance—did *I* forge my kopecks."

Convulsively sobbing with a grief which he could not repress, Chichikov sank upon a chair, tore from his shoulders the last ragged, trailing remnants of his frockcoat, and hurled them from him. Then, thrusting his fingers into the hair which he had once been so careful to preserve, he pulled it out by handfuls at a time, as though he hoped through physical pain to deaden the mental agony which he was suffering.

Meanwhile Murazov sat gazing in silence at the unwonted spectacle of a man who had lately been mincing with the gait of a worldling or a military fop now writhing in dishevelment and despair as he poured out upon the hostile forces by which human ingenuity so often finds itself outwitted a flood of invective.

"Paul Ivanovitch, Paul Ivanovitch," at length said Murazov, "what could not each of us rise to be did we but devote to good ends the same measure of energy and of patience which we bestow upon unworthy objects! How much good would not you yourself have effected! Yet I do not grieve so much for the fact that you have sinned against your fellow as I grieve for the fact that you have sinned against yourself and the rich store of gifts and opportunities which has been committed to your care. Though originally destined to rise, you have wandered from the path and fallen."

"Ah, Athanasi Vassilievitch," cried poor Chichikov, clasping his friend's hands, "I swear to you that, if you would but restore me my freedom, and recover for me my lost property, I would lead a different life from this time forth. Save me, you who alone can work my deliverance! Save me!"

"How can I do that? So to do I should need to procure the setting aside of a law. Again, even if I were to make the attempt, the Prince is a strict administrator, and would refuse on any consideration to release you."

"Yes, but for you all things are possible. It is not the law that troubles me: with that I could find a means to deal. It is the fact that for no offence at all I have been cast into prison, and treated like a dog, and deprived of my papers and dispatch-box and all my property. Save me if you can."

Again clasping the old man's knees, he bedewed them with his tears.

"Paul Ivanovitch," said Murazov, shaking his head, "how that property of yours still seals your eyes and ears, so that you cannot so much as listen to the promptings of your own soul!"

"Ah, I will think of my soul, too, if only you will save me."

"Paul Ivanovitch," the old man began again, and then stopped. For a little while there was a pause.

"Paul Ivanovitch," at length he went on, "to save you does not lie within my power. Surely you yourself see that? But, so far as I can, I will endeavour to, at all events, lighten your lot and procure your eventual release. Whether or not I shall succeed I do not know; but I will make the attempt. And should I, contrary to my expectations, prove successful, I beg of you, in return for these my efforts, to renounce all thought of benefit from the property which you have acquired. Sincerely do I assure you that, were I myself to be deprived of my property (and my property greatly exceeds yours in magnitude), I should not shed a single tear. It is not the property of which men can deprive us that matters, but the property of which no one on earth can deprive or despoil us. You are a man who has seen something of life—to use your own words, you have been a barque tossed hither and thither by tempestuous waves: yet still will there be left to you a remnant of substance on which to live, and therefore I beseech you to settle down in some quiet nook where there is a church, and where none but plain, good-hearted folk abide. Or, should you feel a yearning to leave behind you posterity, take in marriage a good woman who shall bring you, not money, but an aptitude for simple, modest domestic life. But this life—the life of turmoil, with its longings and its temptations—forget, and let it forget YOU; for there is no peace in it. See for yourself how, at every step, it brings one but hatred and treachery and deceit."

"Indeed, yes!" agreed the repentant Chichikov. "Gladly will I do as you wish, since for many a day past have I been longing to amend my life, and to engage in husbandry, and to reorder my affairs. A demon, the tempter Satan himself, has beguiled me and led me from the right path."

Suddenly there had recurred to Chichikov long-unknown, long-unfamiliar feelings. Something seemed to be striving to come to life again in him—something dim and remote, something which had been crushed out of his boyhood by the dreary, deadening education of his youthful days, by his desolate home, by his subsequent lack of family ties, by the poverty and niggardliness of his early impressions, by the grim eye of fate—an eye which had always seemed to be regarding him as through a misty, mournful, frost-encrusted window-pane, and to be mocking at his struggles for freedom. And as these feelings came back to the penitent a groan burst from his lips, and, covering his face with his hands, he moaned: "It is all true, it is all true!"

"Of little avail are knowledge of the world and experience of men unless based upon a secure foundation," observed Murazov. "Though you have fallen, Paul Ivanovitch, awake to better things, for as yet there is time."

"No, no!" groaned Chichikov in a voice which made Murazov's heart bleed. "It is too late, too late. More and more is the conviction gaining upon me that I am powerless, that I have strayed too far ever to be able to do as you bid me. The fact that I have become what I am is due to my early schooling; for, though my father taught me moral lessons, and beat me, and set me to copy maxims into a book, he himself stole land from his neighbours, and forced me to help him. I have even known him to bring an unjust suit, and defraud the orphan whose guardian he was! Consequently I know and feel that, though my life has been different from his, I do not hate roguery as I ought to hate it, and that my nature is coarse, and that in me there is no real love for what is good, no real spark of that beautiful instinct for well-doing which becomes a second nature, a settled habit. Also, never do I yearn to strive for what is right as I yearn to acquire property. This is no more than the truth. What else could I do but confess it?"

The old man sighed.

"Paul Ivanovitch," he said, "I know that you possess will-power, and that you possess also perseverance. A medicine may be bitter, yet the patient will gladly take it when assured that only by its means can he recover. Therefore, if it really be that you have no genuine love for doing good, do good by FORCING yourself to do so. Thus you will benefit yourself even more than you will benefit him for whose sake the act is performed. Only force yourself to do good just once and again, and, behold, you will suddenly conceive the TRUE love for well-doing. That is so, believe me. 'A kingdom is to be won only by striving,' says the proverb. That is to say, things are to be attained only by putting forth one's whole strength, since nothing short of one's whole strength will bring one to the desired goal. Paul Ivanovitch, within you there is a source of strength denied to many another man. I refer to the strength of an iron perseverance. Cannot THAT help you to overcome? Most men are weak and lack will-power, whereas I believe that you possess the power to act a hero's part."

Sinking deep into Chichikov's heart, these words would seem to have aroused in it a faint stirring of ambition, so much so that, if it was not fortitude which shone in his eyes, at all events it was something virile, and of much the same nature.

"Athanasi Vassilievitch," he said firmly, "if you will but petition for my release, as well as for permission for me to leave here with a portion of my property, I swear to you on my word of honour that I will begin a new life, and buy a country estate, and become the head of a household, and save money, not for myself, but for others, and do good everywhere, and to the best of my ability, and forget alike myself and the feasting and debauchery of town life, and lead, instead, a plain, sober existence."

"In that resolve may God strengthen you!" cried the old man with unbounded joy. "And I, for my part, will do my utmost to procure your release. And though God alone knows whether my efforts will be successful, at all events I hope to bring about a mitigation of your sentence. Come, let me embrace you! How you have filled my heart with gladness! With God's help, I will now go to the Prince."

And the next moment Chichikov found himself alone. His whole nature felt shaken and softened, even as, when the bellows have fanned the furnace to a sufficient heat, a plate compounded even of the hardest and most fire-resisting metal dissolves, glows, and turns to the liquefied state.

"I myself can feel but little," he reflected, "but I intend to use my every faculty to help others to feel. I myself am but bad and worthless, but I intend to do my utmost to set others on the right road. I myself am but an indifferent Christian, but I intend to strive never to yield to temptation, but to work hard, and to till my land with the sweat of my brow, and to engage only in honourable pursuits, and to influence my fellows in the same direction. For, after all, am I so very useless? At least I could maintain a household, for I am frugal and active and intelligent and steadfast. The only thing is to make up my mind to it."

Thus Chichikov pondered; and as he did so his half-awakened energies of soul touched upon something. That is to say, dimly his instinct divined that every man has a duty to perform, and that that duty may be performed here, there, and everywhere, and no matter what the circumstances and the emotions and the difficulties which compass a man about. And with such clearness did Chichikov mentally picture to himself the life of grateful toil which lies removed from the bustle of towns and the temptations which man, forgetful of the obligation of labour, has invented to beguile an hour of idleness that almost our hero forgot his unpleasant position, and even felt ready to thank Providence for the calamity which had befallen him, provided that it should end in his being released, and in his receiving back a portion of his property.

Presently the massive door of the cell opened to admit a tchinovnik named Samosvitov, a robust, sensual individual who was reputed by his comrades to be something of a rake. Had he served in the army, he would have done wonders, for he would have stormed any point, however dangerous and inaccessible, and captured cannon under the very noses of the foe; but, as it was, the lack of a more warlike field for his energies caused him to devote the latter principally to dissipation. Nevertheless he enjoyed great popularity, for he was loyal to the point that, once his word had been given, nothing would ever make him break it. At the same time, some reason or another led him to regard his superiors in the light of a hostile battery which, come what might, he must breach at any weak or unguarded spot or gap which might be capable of being utilised for the purpose.

"We have all heard of your plight," he began as soon as the door had been safely closed behind him. "Yes, every one has heard of it. But never mind. Things will yet come right. We will do our very best for you, and act as your humble servants in everything. Thirty thousand roubles is our price—no more."

"Indeed?" said Chichikov. "And, for that, shall I be completely exonerated?"

"Yes, completely, and also given some compensation for your loss of time."

"And how much am I to pay in return, you say?"

"Thirty thousand roubles, to be divided among ourselves, the Governor-General's staff, and the Governor-General's secretary."

"But how is even that to be managed, for all my effects, including my dispatch-box, will have been sealed up and taken away for examination?"

"In an hour's time they will be within your hands again," said Samosvitov. "Shall we shake hands over the bargain?"

Chichikov did so with a beating heart, for he could scarcely believe his ears.

"For the present, then, farewell," concluded Samosvitov. "I have instructed a certain mutual friend that the important points are silence and presence of mind."

"Hm!" thought Chichikov. "It is to my lawyer that he is referring."

Even when Samosvitov had departed the prisoner found it difficult to credit all that had been said. Yet not an hour had elapsed before a messenger arrived with his dispatch-box and the papers and money therein practically undisturbed and intact! Later it came out that Samosvitov had assumed complete authority in the matter. First, he had rebuked the gendarmes guarding Chichikov's effects for lack of vigilance, and then sent word to the Superintendent that additional men were required for the purpose; after which he had taken the dispatch-box into his own charge, removed from it every paper which could possibly compromise Chichikov, sealed up the rest in a packet, and ordered a gendarme to convey the whole to their owner on the pretence of forwarding him sundry garments necessary for the night. In the result Chichikov received not only his papers, but also some warm clothing for his hypersensitive limbs. Such a swift recovery of his treasures delighted him beyond expression, and, gathering new hope, he began once more to dream of such allurements as theatre-going and the ballet girl after whom he had for some time past been dangling. Gradually did the country estate and the simple life begin to recede into the distance: gradually did the town house and the life of gaiety begin to loom larger and larger in the foreground. Oh, life, life!

Meanwhile in Government offices and chancellories there had been set on foot a boundless volume of work. Clerical pens slaved, and brains skilled in legal casus toiled; for each official had the artist's liking for the curved line in preference to the straight. And all the while, like a hidden magician, Chichikov's lawyer imparted driving power to that machine which caught up a man into its mechanism before he could even look round. And the complexity of it increased and increased, for Samosvitov surpassed himself in importance and daring. On learning of the place of confinement of the woman who had been arrested, he presented himself at the doors, and passed so well for a smart young officer of gendarmery that the sentry saluted and sprang to attention.

"Have you been on duty long?" asked Samosvitov.

"Since this morning, your Excellency."

"And shall you soon be relieved?"

"In three hours from now, your Excellency."

"Presently I shall want you, so I will instruct your officer to have you relieved at once."

"Very good, your Excellency."

Hastening home, thereafter, at top speed, and donning the uniform of a gendarme, with a false moustache and a pair of false whiskers—an ensemble in which the devil himself would not have known him, Samosvitov then made for the gaol where Chichikov was confined, and, en route, impressed into the service the first street woman whom he encountered, and handed her over to the care of two young fellows of like sort with himself. The next step was to hurry back to the prison where the original woman had been interned, and there to intimate to the sentry that he, Samosvitov (with whiskers and rifle complete), had been sent to relieve the said sentry at his post—a proceeding which, of course, enabled the newly-arrived relief to ensure, while performing his self-assumed turn of duty, that for the woman lying under arrest there should be substituted the woman recently recruited to the plot, and that the former should then be conveyed to a place of concealment where she was highly unlikely to be discovered.

Meanwhile, Samosvitov's feats in the military sphere were being rivalled by the wonders worked by Chichikov's lawyer in the civilian field of action. As a first step, the lawyer caused it to be intimated to the local Governor that the Public Prosecutor was engaged in drawing up a report to his, the local Governor's, detriment; whereafter the lawyer caused it to be intimated also to the Chief of Gendarmery that a certain confidential official was engaged in doing the same by HIM; whereafter, again, the lawyer confided to the confidential official in question that, owing to the documentary exertions of an official of a still more confidential nature than the first, he (the confidential official first-mentioned) was in a fair way to find himself in the same boat as both the local Governor and the Chief of Gendarmery: with the result that the whole trio were reduced to a frame of mind in which they were only too glad to turn to him (Samosvitov) for advice. The ultimate and farcical upshot was that report came crowding upon report, and that such alleged doings were brought to light as the sun had never before beheld. In fact, the documents in question employed anything and everything as material, even to announcing that such and such an individual had an illegitimate son, that such and such another kept a paid mistress, and that such and such a third was troubled with a gadabout wife; whereby there became interwoven with and welded into Chichikov's past history and the story of the dead souls such a crop of scandals and innuendoes that by no manner of means could any mortal decide to which of these rubbishy romances to award the palm, since all of them presented an equal claim to that honour. Naturally, when, at length, the dossier reached the Governor-General himself it simply flabbergasted the poor man; and even the exceptionally clever and energetic secretary to whom he deputed the making of an abstract of the same very nearly lost his reason with the strain of attempting to lay hold of the tangled end of the skein. It happened that just at that time the Prince had several other important affairs on hand, and affairs of a very unpleasant nature. That is to say, famine had made its appearance in one portion of the province, and the tchinovniks sent to distribute food to the people had done their work badly; in another portion of the province certain Raskolniki 51 were in a state of ferment, owing to the spreading of a report than an Antichrist had arisen who would not even let the dead rest, but was purchasing them wholesale—wherefore the said Raskolniki were summoning folk to prayer and repentance, and, under cover of capturing the Antichrist in question, were bludgeoning non-Antichrists in batches; lastly, the peasants of a third portion of the province had risen against the local landowners and superintendents of police, for the reason that certain rascals had started a rumour that the time was come when the peasants themselves were to become landowners, and to wear frockcoats, while the landowners in being were about to revert to the peasant state, and to take their own wares to market; wherefore one of the local volosts52, oblivious of the fact that an order of things of that kind would lead to a superfluity alike of landowners and of superintendents of police, had refused to pay its taxes, and necessitated recourse to forcible measures. Hence it was in a mood of the greatest possible despondency that the poor Prince was sitting plunged when word was brought to him that the old man who had gone bail for Chichikov was waiting to see him.

"Show him in," said the Prince; and the old man entered.

"A fine fellow your Chichikov!" began the Prince angrily. "You defended him, and went bail for him, even though he had been up to business which even the lowest thief would not have touched!"

"Pardon me, your Highness; I do not understand to what you are referring."

"I am referring to the matter of the fraudulent will. The fellow ought to have been given a public flogging for it."

"Although to exculpate Chichikov is not my intention, might I ask you whether you do not think the case is non-proven? At all events, sufficient evidence against him is still lacking."

"What? We have as chief witness the woman who personated the deceased, and I will have her interrogated in your presence."

Touching a bell, the Prince ordered her to be sent for.

"It is a most disgraceful affair," he went on; "and, ashamed though I am to have to say it, some of our leading tchinovniks, including the local Governor himself, have become implicated in the matter. Yet you tell me that this Chichikov ought not to be confined among thieves and rascals!" Clearly the Governor-General's wrath was very great indeed.

"Your Highness," said Murazov, "the Governor of the town is one of the heirs under the will: wherefore he has a certain right to intervene. Also, the fact that extraneous persons have meddled in the matter is only what is to be expected from human nature. A rich woman dies, and no exact, regular disposition of her property is made. Hence there comes flocking from every side a cloud of fortune hunters. What else could one expect? Such is human nature."

"Yes, but why should such persons go and commit fraud?" asked the Prince irritably. "I feel as though not a single honest tchinovnik were available—as though every one of them were a rogue."

"Your Highness, which of us is altogether beyond reproach? The tchinovniks of our town are human beings, and no more. Some of them are men of worth, and nearly all of them men skilled in business—though also, unfortunately, largely inter-related."

"Now, tell me this, Athanasi Vassilievitch," said the Prince, "for you are about the only honest man of my acquaintance. What has inspired in you such a penchant for defending rascals?"

"This," replied Murazov. "Take any man you like of the persons whom you thus term rascals. That man none the less remains a human being. That being so, how can one refuse to defend him when all the time one knows that half his errors have been committed through ignorance and stupidity? Each of us commits faults with every step that we take; each of us entails unhappiness upon others with every breath that we draw—and that although we may have no evil intention whatever in our minds. Your Highness himself has, before now, committed an injustice of the gravest nature."

"*I* have?" cried the Prince, taken aback by this unexpected turn given to the conversation.

Murazov remained silent for a moment, as though he were debating something in his thoughts. Then he said:

"Nevertheless it is as I say. You committed the injustice in the case of the lad Dierpiennikov."

"What, Athanasi Vassilievitch? The fellow had infringed one of the Fundamental Laws! He had been found guilty of treason!"

"I am not seeking to justify him; I am only asking you whether you think it right that an inexperienced youth who had been tempted and led away by others should have received the same sentence as the man who had taken the chief part in the affair. That is to say, although Dierpiennikov and the man Voron-Drianni received an equal measure of punishment, their CRIMINALITY was not equal."

"If," exclaimed the Prince excitedly, "you know anything further concerning the case, for God's sake tell it me at once. Only the other day did I forward a recommendation that St. Petersburg should remit a portion of the sentence."

"Your Highness," replied Murazov, "I do not mean that I know of anything which does not lie also within your own cognisance, though one circumstance there was which might have told in the lad's favour had he not refused to admit it, lest another should suffer injury. All that I have in my mind is this. On that occasion were you not a little over-hasty in coming to a conclusion? You will understand, of course, that I am judging only according to my own poor lights, and for the reason that on more than one occasion you have urged me to be frank. In the days when I myself acted as a chief of gendarmery I came in contact with a great number of accused—some of them bad, some of them good; and in each case I found it well also to consider a man's past career, for the reason that, unless one views things calmly, instead of at once decrying a man, he is apt to take alarm, and to make it impossible thereafter to get any real confession from him. If, on the other hand, you question a man as friend might question friend, the result will be that straightway he will tell you everything, nor ask for mitigation of his penalty, nor bear you the least malice, in that he will understand that it is not you who have punished him, but the law."

The Prince relapsed into thought; until presently there entered a young tchinovnik. Portfolio in hand, this official stood waiting respectfully. Care and hard work had already imprinted their insignia upon his fresh young face; for evidently he had not been in the Service for nothing. As a matter of fact, his greatest joy was to labour at a tangled case, and successfully to unravel it.

[At this point a long hiatus occurs in the original.]

"I will send corn to the localities where famine is worst," said Murazov, "for I understand that sort of work better than do the tchinovniks, and will personally see to the needs of each person. Also, if you will allow me, your Highness, I will go and have a talk with the Raskolniki. They are more likely to listen to a plain man than to an official. God knows whether I shall succeed in calming them, but at least no tchinovnik could do so, for officials of the kind merely draw up reports and lose their way among their own documents—with the result that nothing comes of it. Nor will I accept from you any money for these purposes, since I am ashamed to devote as much as a thought to my own pocket at a time when men are dying of hunger. I have a large stock of grain lying in my granaries; in addition to which, I have sent orders to Siberia that a new consignment shall be forwarded me before the coming summer."

"Of a surety will God reward you for your services, Athanasi Vassilievitch! Not another word will I say to you on the subject, for you yourself feel that any words from me would be inadequate. Yet tell me one thing: I refer to the case of which you know. Have I the right to pass over the case? Also, would it be just and honourable on my part to let the offending tchinovniks go unpunished?"

"Your Highness, it is impossible to return a definite answer to those two questions: and the more so because many rascals are at heart men of rectitude. Human problems are difficult things to solve. Sometimes a man may be drawn into a vicious circle, so that, having once entered it, he ceases to be himself."

"But what would the tchinovniks say if I allowed the case to be passed over? Would not some of them turn up their noses at me, and declare that they have effected my intimidation? Surely they would be the last persons in the world to respect me for my action?"

"Your Highness, I think this: that your best course would be to call them together, and to inform them that you know everything, and to explain to them your personal attitude (exactly as you have explained it to me), and to end by at once requesting their advice and asking them what each of them would have done had he been placed in similar circumstances."

"What? You think that those tchinovniks would be so accessible to lofty motives that they would cease thereafter to be venal and meticulous? I should be laughed at for my pains."

"I think not, your Highness. Even the baser section of humanity possesses a certain sense of equity. Your wisest plan, your Highness, would be to conceal nothing and to speak to them as you have just spoken to me. If, at present, they imagine you to be ambitious and proud and unapproachable and self-assured, your action would afford them an opportunity of seeing how the case really stands. Why should you hesitate? You would but be exercising your undoubted right. Speak to them as though delivering not a message of your own, but a message from God."

"I will think it over," the Prince said musingly, "and meanwhile I thank you from my heart for your good advice."

"Also, I should order Chichikov to leave the town," suggested Murazov.

"Yes, I will do so. Tell him from me that he is to depart hence as quickly as possible, and that the further he should remove himself, the better it will be for him. Also, tell him that it is only owing to your efforts that he has received a pardon at my hands."

Murazov bowed, and proceeded from the Prince's presence to that of Chichikov. He found the prisoner cheerfully enjoying a hearty dinner which, under hot covers, had been brought him from an exceedingly excellent kitchen. But almost the first words which he uttered showed Murazov that the prisoner had been having dealings with the army of bribe-takers; as also that in those transactions his lawyer had played the principal part.

"Listen, Paul Ivanovitch," the old man said. "I bring you your freedom, but only on this condition—that you depart out of the town forthwith. Therefore gather together your effects, and waste not a moment, lest worse befall you. Also, of all that a certain person has contrived to do on your behalf I am aware; wherefore let me tell you, as between ourselves, that should the conspiracy come to light, nothing on earth can save him, and in his fall he will involve others rather then be left unaccompanied in the lurch, and not see the guilt shared. How is it that when I left you recently you were in a better frame of mind than you are now? I beg of you not to trifle with the matter. Ah me! what boots that wealth for which men dispute and cut one another's throats? Do they think that it is possible to prosper in this world without thinking of the world to come? Believe me when I say that, until a man shall have renounced all that leads humanity to contend without giving a thought to the ordering of spiritual wealth, he will never set his temporal goods either upon a satisfactory foundation. Yes, even as times of want and scarcity may come upon nations, so may they come upon individuals. No matter what may be said to the contrary, the body can never dispense with the soul. Why, then, will you not try to walk in the right way, and, by thinking no longer of dead souls, but only of your only living one, regain, with God's help, the better road? I too am leaving the town to-morrow. Hasten, therefore, lest, bereft of my assistance, you meet with some dire misfortune."

And the old man departed, leaving Chichikov plunged in thought. Once more had the gravity of life begun to loom large before him.

"Yes, Murazov was right," he said to himself. "It is time that I were moving."

Leaving the prison—a warder carrying his effects in his wake—he found Selifan and Petrushka overjoyed at seeing their master once more at liberty.

"Well, good fellows?" he said kindly. "And now we must pack and be off."

"True, true, Paul Ivanovitch," agreed Selifan. "And by this time the roads will have become firmer, for much snow has fallen. Yes, high time is it that we were clear of the town. So weary of it am I that the sight of it hurts my eyes."

"Go to the coachbuilder's," commanded Chichikov, "and have sledge-runners fitted to the koliaska."

Chichikov then made his way into the town—though not with the object of paying farewell visits (in view of recent events, that might have given rise to some awkwardness), but for the purpose of paying an unobtrusive call at the shop where he had obtained the cloth for his latest suit. There he now purchased four more arshins of the same smoked-grey-shot-with-flame-colour material as he had had before, with the intention of having it made up by the tailor who had fashioned the previous costume; and by promising double remuneration he induced the tailor in question so to hasten the cutting out of the garments that, through sitting up all night over the work, the man might have the whole ready by break of day. True, the goods were delivered a trifle after the appointed hour, yet the following morning saw the coat and breeches completed; and while the horses were being put to, Chichikov tried on the clothes, and found them equal to the previous creation, even though during the process he caught sight of a bald patch on his head, and was led mournfully to reflect: "Alas! Why did I give way to such despair? Surely I need not have torn my hair out so freely?"

Then, when the tailor had been paid, our hero left the town. But no longer was he the old Chichikov—he was only a ruin of what he had been, and his frame of mind might have been compared to a building recently pulled down to make room for a new one, while the new one had not yet been erected owing to the non-receipt of the plans from the architect. Murazov, too, had departed, but at an earlier hour, and in a tilt-waggon with Ivan Potapitch.

An hour later the Governor-General issued to all and sundry officials a notice that, on the occasion of his departure for St. Petersburg, he would be glad to see the corps of tchinovniks at a private meeting. Accordingly all ranks and grades of officialdom repaired to his residence, and there awaited—not without a certain measure of trepidation and of searching of heart—the Governor-General's entry. When that took place he looked neither clear nor dull. Yet his bearing was proud, and his step assured. The tchinovniks bowed—some of them to the waist, and he answered their salutations with a slight inclination of the head. Then he spoke as follows:

"Since I am about to pay a visit to St. Petersburg, I have thought it right to meet you, and to explain to you privately my reasons for doing so. An affair of a most scandalous character has taken place in our midst. To what affair I am referring I think most of those present will guess. Now, an automatic process has led to that affair bringing about the discovery of other matters. Those matters are no less dishonourable than the primary one; and to that I regret to have to add that there stand involved in them certain persons whom I had hitherto believed to be honourable. Of the object aimed at by those who have complicated matters to the point of making their resolution almost impossible by ordinary methods I am aware; as also I am aware of the identity of the ringleader, despite the skill with which he has sought to conceal his share in the scandal. But the principal point is, that I propose to decide these matters, not by formal documentary process, but by the more summary process of court-martial, and that I hope, when the circumstances have been laid before his Imperial Majesty, to receive from him authority to adopt the course which I have mentioned. For I conceive that when it has become impossible to resolve a case by civil means, and some of the necessary documents have been burnt, and attempts have been made (both through the adduction of an excess of false and extraneous evidence and through the framing of fictitious reports) to cloud an already sufficiently obscure investigation with an added measure of complexity,—when all these circumstances have arisen, I conceive that the only possible tribunal to deal with them is a military tribunal. But on that point I should like your opinion."

The Prince paused for a moment or two, as though awaiting a reply; but none came, seeing that every man had his eyes bent upon the floor, and many of the audience had turned white in the face.

"Then," he went on, "I may say that I am aware also of a matter which those who have carried it through believe to lie only within the cognisance of themselves. The particulars of that matter will not be set forth in documentary form, but only through process of myself acting as plaintiff and petitioner, and producing none but ocular evidence."

Among the throng of tchinovniks some one gave a start, and thereby caused others of the more apprehensive sort to fall to trembling in their shoes.

"Without saying does it go that the prime conspirators ought to undergo deprivation of rank and property, and that the remainder ought to be dismissed from their posts; for though that course would cause a certain proportion of the innocent to suffer with the guilty, there would seem to be no other course available, seeing that the affair is one of the most disgraceful nature, and calls aloud for justice. Therefore, although I know that to some my action will fail to serve as a lesson, since it will lead to their succeeding to the posts of dismissed officials, as well as that others hitherto considered honourable will lose their reputation, and others entrusted with new responsibilities will continue to cheat and betray their trust,—although all this is known to me, I still have no choice but to satisfy the claims of justice by proceeding to take stern measures. I am also aware that I shall be accused of undue severity; but, lastly, I am aware that it is my duty to put aside all personal feeling, and to act as the unconscious instrument of that retribution which justice demands."

Over ever face there passed a shudder. Yet the Prince had spoken calmly, and not a trace of anger or any other kind of emotion had been visible on his features.

"Nevertheless," he went on, "the very man in whose hands the fate of so many now lies, the very man whom no prayer for mercy could ever have influenced, himself desires to make a request of you. Should you grant that request, all will be forgotten and blotted out and pardoned, for I myself will intercede with the Throne on your behalf. That request is this. I know that by no manner of means, by no preventive measures, and by no penalties will dishonesty ever be completely extirpated from our midst, for the reason that its roots have struck too deep, and that the dishonourable traffic in bribes has become a necessity to, even the mainstay of, some whose nature is not innately venal. Also, I know that, to many men, it is an impossibility to swim against the stream. Yet now, at this solemn and critical juncture, when the country is calling aloud for saviours, and it is the duty of every citizen to contribute and to sacrifice his all, I feel that I cannot but issue an appeal to every man in whom a Russian heart and a spark of what we understand by the word 'nobility' exist. For, after all, which of us is more guilty than his fellow? It may be to ME the greatest culpability should be assigned, in that at first I may have adopted towards you too reserved an attitude, that I may have been over-hasty in repelling those who desired but to serve me, even though of their services I did not actually stand in need. Yet, had they really loved justice and the good of their country, I think that they would have been less prone to take offence at the coldness of my attitude, but would have sacrificed their feelings and their personality to their superior convictions. For hardly can it be that I failed to note their overtures and the loftiness of their motives, or that I would not have accepted any wise and useful advice proffered. At the same time, it is for a subordinate to adapt himself to the tone of his superior, rather than for a superior to adapt himself to the tone of his subordinate. Such a course is at once more regular and more smooth of working, since a corps of subordinates has but one director, whereas a director may have a hundred subordinates. But let us put aside the question of comparative culpability. The important point is, that before us all lies the duty of rescuing our fatherland. Our fatherland is suffering, not from the incursion of a score of alien tongues, but from our own acts, in that, in addition to the lawful administration, there has grown up a second administration possessed of infinitely greater powers than the system established by law. And that second administration has established its conditions, fixed its tariff of prices, and published that tariff abroad; nor could any ruler, even though the wisest of legislators and administrators, do more to correct the evil than limit it in the conduct of his more venal tchinovniks by setting over them, as their supervisors, men of superior rectitude. No, until each of us shall come to feel that, just as arms were taken up during the period of the upheaval of nations, so now each of us must make a stand against dishonesty, all remedies will end in failure. As a Russian, therefore—as one bound to you by consanguinity and identity of blood—I make to you my appeal. I make it to those of you who understand wherein lies nobility of thought. I invite those men to remember the duty which confronts us, whatsoever our respective stations; I invite them to observe more closely their duty, and to keep more constantly in mind their obligations of holding true to their country, in that before us the future looms dark, and that we can scarcely. . . ."

[Here the manuscript of the original comes abruptly to an end.]

PLAY

Translated by Thomas Seltzer

THE INSPECTOR-GENERAL

A comedy in five acts

Introduction

The Inspector-General is a national institution. To place a purely literary valuation upon it and call it the greatest of Russian comedies would not convey the significance of its position either in Russian literature or in Russian life itself. There is no other single work in the modern literature of any language that carries with it the wealth of associations which the Inspector-General does to the educated Russian. The Germans have their Faust; but Faust is a tragedy with a cosmic philosophic theme. In England it takes nearly all that is implied in the comprehensive name of Shakespeare to give the same sense of bigness that a Russian gets from the mention of the Revizor.

That is not to say that the Russian is so defective in the critical faculty as to balance the combined creative output of the greatest English dramatist against Gogol's one comedy, or even to attribute to it the literary value of any of Shakespeare's better plays. What the Russian's appreciation indicates is the pregnant role that literature plays in the life of intellectual Russia. Here literature is not a luxury, not a diversion. It is bone of the bone, flesh of the flesh, not only of the intelligentsia, but also of a growing number of the common people, intimately woven into their everyday existence, part and parcel of their thoughts, their aspirations, their social, political and economic life. It expresses their collective wrongs and sorrows, their collective hopes and strivings. Not only does it serve to lead the movements of the masses, but it is an integral component element of those movements. In a word, Russian literature is completely bound up with the life of Russian society, and its vitality is but the measure of the spiritual vitality of that society.

This unique character of Russian literature may be said to have had its beginning with the Inspector-General. Before Gogol most Russian writers, with few exceptions, were but weak imitators of foreign models. The drama fashioned itself chiefly upon French patterns. The Inspector-General and later Gogol's novel, Dead Souls, established that tradition in Russian letters which was followed by all the great writers from Dostoyevsky down to Gorky.

As with one blow, Gogol shattered the notions of the theatre-going public of his day of what a comedy should be. The ordinary idea of a play at that time in Russia seems to have been a little like our own tired business man's. And the shock the Revizor gave those early nineteenth-century Russian audiences is not unlike the shocks we ourselves get when once in a while a theatrical manager is courageous enough to produce a bold modern European play. Only the intensity of the shock was much greater. For Gogol dared not only bid defiance to the accepted method; he dared to introduce a subject-matter that under the guise of humor audaciously attacked the very foundation of the state, namely, the officialdom of the Russian bureaucracy. That is why the Revizor marks such a revolution in the world of Russian letters. In form it was realistic, in substance it was vital. It showed up the rottenness and corruption of the instruments through which the Russian government functioned. It held up to ridicule, directly, all the officials of a typical Russian municipality, and, indirectly, pointed to the same system of graft and corruption among the very highest servants of the crown.

What wonder that the Inspector-General became a sort of comedy-epic in the land of the Czars, the land where each petty town-governor is almost an absolute despot, regulating his persecutions and extortions according to the sage saying of the town-governor in the play, "That's the way God made the world, and the Voltairean free-thinkers can talk against it all they like, it won't do any good." Every subordinate in the town administration, all the way down the line to the policemen, follow—not always so scrupulously—the law laid down by the same authority, "Graft no higher than your rank." As in city and town, so in village and hamlet. It is the tragedy of Russian life, which has its roots in that more comprehensive tragedy, Russian despotism, the despotism that gives the sharp edge to official corruption. For there is no possible redress from it except in violent revolutions.

That is the prime reason why the Inspector-General, a mere comedy, has such a hold on the Russian people and occupies so important a place in Russian literature. And that is why a Russian critic says, "Russia possesses only one comedy, the Inspector-General."

The second reason is the brilliancy and originality with which this national theme was executed. Gogol was above all else the artist. He was not a radical, nor even a liberal. He was strictly conservative. While hating the bureaucracy, yet he never found fault with the system itself or with the autocracy. Like most born artists, he was strongly individualistic in temperament, and his satire and ridicule were aimed not at causes, but at effects. Let but the individuals act morally, and the system, which Gogol never questioned, would work beautifully. This conception caused Gogol to concentrate his best efforts upon delineation of character. It was the characters that were to be revealed, their actions to be held up to scorn and ridicule, not the conditions which created the characters and made them act as they did. If any lesson at all was to be drawn from the play it was not a sociological lesson, but a moral one. The individual who sees himself mirrored in it may be moved to self-purgation; society has nothing to learn from it.

Yet the play lives because of the social message it carries. The creation proved greater than the creator. The author of the Revizor was a poor critic of his own work. The Russian people rejected his estimate and put their own upon it. They knew their officials and they entertained no illusions concerning their regeneration so long as the system that bred them continued to live. Nevertheless, as a keen satire and a striking exposition of the workings of the hated system itself, they hailed the Revizor with delight. And as such it has remained graven in Russia's conscience to this day.

It must be said that "Gogol himself grew with the writing of the Revizor." Always a careful craftsman, scarcely ever satisfied with the first version of a story or a play, continually changing and rewriting, he seems to have bestowed special attention on perfecting this comedy. The subject, like that of Dead Souls, was suggested to him by the poet Pushkin, and was based on a true incident. Pushkin at once recognized Gogol's genius and looked upon the young author as the rising star of Russian literature. Their acquaintance soon ripened into intimate friendship, and Pushkin missed no opportunity to encourage and stimulate him in his writings and help him with all the power of his great influence. Gogol began to work on the play at the close of 1834, when he was twenty-five years old. It was first produced in St. Petersburg, in 1836. Despite the many elaborations it had undergone before Gogol permitted it to be put on the stage, he still did not feel satisfied, and he began to work on it again in 1838. It was not brought down to its present final form until 1842.

Thus the Revizor occupied the mind of the author over a period of eight years, and resulted in a product which from the point of view of characterization and dramatic technique is almost flawless. Yet far more important is the fact that the play marked an epoch in Gogol's own literary development. When he began on it, his ambitions did not rise above making it a comedy of pure fun, but, gradually, in the course of his working on it, the possibilities of the subject unfolded themselves and influenced his entire subsequent career. His art broadened and deepened and grew more serious. If Pushkin's remark, that "behind his laughter you feel the sad tears," is true of some of Gogol's former productions, it is still truer of the Revizor and his later works.

A new life had begun for him, he tells us himself, when he was no longer "moved by childish notions, but by lofty ideas full of truth." "It was Pushkin," he writes, "who made me look at the thing seriously. I saw that in my writings I laughed vainly, for nothing, myself not knowing why. If I was to laugh, then I had better laugh over things that are really to be laughed at. In the Inspector-General I resolved to gather together all the bad in Russia I then knew into one heap, all the injustice that was practised in those places and in those human relations in which more than in anything justice is demanded of men, and to have one big laugh over it all. But that, as is well known, produced an outburst of excitement. Through my laughter, which never before came to me with such force, the reader sensed profound sorrow. I myself felt that my laughter was no longer the same as it had been, that in my writings I could no longer be the same as in the past, and that the need to divert myself with innocent, careless scenes had ended along with my young years."

With the strict censorship that existed in the reign of Czar Nicholas I, it required powerful influence to obtain permission for the production of the comedy. This Gogol received through the instrumentality of his friend, Zhukovsky, who succeeded in gaining the Czar's personal intercession. Nicholas himself was present at the first production in April, 1836, and laughed and applauded, and is said to have remarked, "Everybody gets it, and I most of all."

Naturally official Russia did not relish this innovation in dramatic art, and indignation ran high among them and their supporters. Bulgarin led the attack. Everything that is usually said against a new departure in literature or art was said against the Revizor. It was not original. It was improbable, impossible, coarse, vulgar; lacked plot. It turned on a stale anecdote that everybody knew. It was a rank farce. The characters were mere caricatures. "What sort of a town was it that did not hold a single honest soul?"

Gogol's sensitive nature shrank before the tempest that burst upon him, and he fled from his enemies all the way out of Russia. "Do what you please about presenting the play in Moscow," he writes to Shchepkin four days after its first production in St. Petersburg. "I am not going to bother about it. I am sick of the play and all the fussing over it. It produced a great noisy effect. All are against me . . . they abuse me and go to see it. No tickets can be obtained for the fourth performance."

But the best literary talent of Russia, with Pushkin and Bielinsky, the greatest critic Russia has produced, at the head, ranged itself on his side.

Nicolay Vasilyevich Gogol was born in Sorochintzy, government of Poltava, in 1809. His father was a Little Russian, or Ukrainian, landowner, who exhibited considerable talent as a playwright and actor. Gogol was educated at home until the age of ten, then went to Niezhin, where he entered the gymnasium in 1821. Here he edited a students' manuscript magazine called the Star, and later founded a students' theatre, for which he was both manager and actor. It achieved such success that it was patronized by the general public.

In 1829 Gogol went to St. Petersburg, where he thought of becoming an actor, but he finally gave up the idea and took a position as a subordinate government clerk. His real literary career began in 1830 with the publication of a series of stories of Little Russian country life called Nights on a Farm near Dikanka. In 1831 he became acquainted with Pushkin and Zhukovsky, who introduced the "shy Khokhol" (nickname for "Little Russian"), as he was called, to the house of Madame O. A. Smirnov, the centre of "an intimate circle of literary men and the flower of intellectual society." The same year he obtained a position as instructor of history at the Patriotic Institute, and in 1834 was made professor of history at the University of St. Petersburg. Though his lectures were marked by originality and vivid presentation, he seems on the whole not to have been successful as a professor, and he resigned in 1835.

During this period he kept up his literary activity uninterruptedly, and in 1835 published his collection of stories, Mirgorod, containing How Ivan Ivanovich Quarreled with Ivan Nikiforovich, Taras Bulba, and others. This collection firmly established his position as a leading author. At the same time he was at work on several plays. The Vladimir Cross, which was to deal with the higher St. Petersburg functionaries in the same way as the Revizor with the lesser town officials, was never concluded, as Gogol realized the impossibility of placing them on the Russian stage. A few strong scenes were published. The comedy Marriage, finished in 1835, still finds a place in the Russian theatrical repertoire. The Gamblers, his only other complete comedy, belongs to a later period.

After a stay abroad, chiefly in Italy, lasting with some interruptions for seven years (1836-1841), he returned to his native country, bringing with him the first part of his greatest work, Dead Souls. The novel, published the following year, produced a profound impression and made Gogol's literary reputation supreme. Pushkin, who did not live to see its publication, on hearing the first chapters read, exclaimed, "God, how sad our Russia is!" And Alexander Hertzen characterized it as "a wonderful book, a bitter, but not hopeless rebuke of contemporary Russia." Aksakov went so far as to call it the Russian national epic, and Gogol the Russian Homer.

Unfortunately the novel remained incomplete. Gogol began to suffer from a nervous illness which induced extreme hypochondria. He became excessively religious, fell under the influence of pietists and a fanatical priest, sank more and more into mysticism, and went on a pilgrimage to

Jerusalem to worship at the Holy Sepulchre. In this state of mind he came to consider all literature, including his own, as pernicious and sinful.

After burning the manuscript of the second part of Dead Souls, he began to rewrite it, had it completed and ready for the press by 1851, but kept the copy and burned it again a few days before his death (1852), so that it is extant only in parts.

THOMAS SELTZER.

Characters of the Play

ANTON ANTONOVICH SKVOZNIK-DMUKHANOVSKY, the Governor.
ANNA ANDREYEVNA, his wife.
MARYA ANTONOVNA, his daughter.
LUKA LUKICH KHLOPOV, the Inspector of Schools.
His Wife.
AMMOS FIODOROVICH LIAPKIN-TIAPKIN, the Judge.
ARTEMY FILIPPOVICH ZEMLIANIKA, the Superintendent of Charities.
IVAN KUZMICH SHPEKIN, the Postmaster.
PIOTR IVANOVICH DOBCHINSKY. } Country Squires.
PIOTR IVANOVICH BOBCHINSKY. }
IVAN ALEKSANDROVICH KHLESTAKOV, an official from St. Petersburg.
OSIP, his servant.
CHRISTIAN IVANOVICH HÜBNER, the district Doctor.

FIODR ANDREYEVICH LULIUKOV. \} ex-officials, esteemed
IVAN LAZAREVICH RASTAKOVSKY. \} personages
STEPAN IVANOVICH KOROBKIN. \} of the town.
STEPAN ILYICH UKHOVERTOV, the Police Captain.
SVISTUNOV.
PUGOVITZYN. \} Police Sergeants.
DERZHIMORDA.
ABDULIN, a Merchant.
FEVRONYA PETROVA POSHLIOPKINA, the Locksmith's wife.
The Widow of a non-commissioned Officer.
MISHKA, the Governor's Servant.
Servant at the Inn.
Guests, Merchants, Citizens, and Petitioners.

Characters and Costumes

DIRECTIONS FOR ACTORS

THE GOVERNOR.—A man grown old in the service, by no means a fool in his own way. Though he takes bribes, he carries himself with dignity. He is of a rather serious turn and even given somewhat to ratiocination. He speaks in a voice neither too loud nor too low and says neither too much nor too little. Every word of his counts. He has the typical hard stern features of the official who has worked his way up from the lowest rank in the arduous government service. Coarse in his inclinations, he passes rapidly from fear to joy, from servility to arrogance. He is dressed in uniform with frogs and wears Hessian boots with spurs. His hair with a sprinkling of gray is close-cropped.

ANNA ANDREYEVNA.—A provincial coquette, still this side of middle age, educated on novels and albums and on fussing with household affairs and servants. She is highly inquisitive and has streaks of vanity. Sometimes she gets the upper hand over her husband, and he gives in simply because at the moment he cannot find the right thing to say. Her ascendency, however, is confined to mere trifles and takes the form of lecturing and twitting. She changes her dress four times in the course of the play.

KHLESTAKOV.—A skinny young man of about twenty-three, rather stupid, being, as they say, "without a czar in his head," one of those persons called an "empty vessel" in the government offices. He speaks and acts without stopping to think and utterly lacks the power of concentration. The words burst from his mouth unexpectedly. The more naiveté and ingenousness the actor puts into the character the better will he sustain the role. Khlestakov is dressed in the latest fashion.

OSIP.—A typical middle-aged servant, grave in his address, with eyes always a bit lowered. He is argumentative and loves to read sermons directed at his master. His voice is usually monotonous. To his master his tone is blunt and sharp, with even a touch of rudeness. He is the cleverer of the two and grasps a situation more quickly. But he does not like to talk. He is a silent, uncommunicative rascal. He wears a shabby gray or blue coat.

BOBCHINSKY AND DOBCHINSKY.—Short little fellows, strikingly like each other. Both have small paunches, and talk rapidly, with emphatic gestures of their hands, features and bodies. Dobchinsky is slightly the taller and more subdued in manner. Bobchinsky is freer, easier and livelier. They are both exceedingly inquisitive.

LIAPKIN-TIAPKIN.—He has read four or five books and so is a bit of a freethinker. He is always seeing a hidden meaning in things and therefore puts weight into every word he utters. The actor should preserve an expression of importance throughout. He speaks in a bass voice, with a prolonged rattle and wheeze in his throat, like an old-fashioned clock, which buzzes before it strikes.

ZEMLIANIKA.—Very fat, slow and awkward; but for all that a sly, cunning scoundrel. He is very obliging and officious.

SHPEKIN.—Guileless to the point of simplemindedness. The other characters require no special explanation, as their originals can be met almost anywhere.

The actors should pay especial attention to the last scene. The last word uttered must strike all at once, suddenly, like an electric shock. The whole group should change its position at the same instant. The ladies must all burst into a simultaneous cry of astonishment, as if with one throat. The neglect of these directions may ruin the whole effect.

ACT I

A Room in the Governor's House.

SCENE I

Anton Antonovich, the Governor, Artemy Filippovich, the Superintendent of Charities, Luka Lukich, the Inspector of Schools, Ammos Fiodorovich, the Judge, Stepan Ilyich, Christian Ivanovich, the Doctor, and two Police Sergeants.

GOVERNOR.
   I have called you together, gentlemen, to tell you an unpleasant piece of news. An Inspector-General is coming.
AMMOS FIOD.
   What, an Inspector-General?
ARTEMY FIL.
   What, an Inspector-General?

GOVERNOR.

Yes, an Inspector from St. Petersburg, incognito. And with secret instructions, too.

AMMOS.

A pretty how-do-you-do!

ARTEMY.

As if we hadn't enough trouble without an Inspector!

LUKA LUKICH.

Good Lord! With secret instructions!

GOVERNOR.

I had a sort of presentiment of it. Last night I kept dreaming of two rats—regular monsters! Upon my word, I never saw the likes of them—black and supernaturally big. They came in, sniffed, and then went away.—Here's a letter I'll read to you—from Andrey Ivanovich. You know him, Artemy Filippovich. Listen to what he writes: "My dear friend, godfather and benefactor—[He mumbles, glancing rapidly down the page.]—and to let you know"—Ah, that's it—"I hasten to let you know, among other things, that an official has arrived here with instructions to inspect the whole government, and your district especially. [Raises his finger significantly.] I have learned of his being here from highly trustworthy sources, though he pretends to be a private person. So, as you have your little peccadilloes, you know, like everybody else—you are a sensible man, and you don't let the good things that come your way slip by—" [Stopping] H'm, that's his junk—"I advise you to take precautions, as he may arrive any hour, if he hasn't already, and is not staying somewhere incognito.—Yesterday—" The rest are family matters. "Sister Anna Krillovna is here visiting us with her husband. Ivan Krillovich has grown very fat and is always playing the fiddle"—et cetera, et cetera. So there you have the situation we are confronted with, gentlemen.

AMMOS.

An extraordinary situation, most extraordinary! Something behind it, I am sure.

LUKA.

But why, Anton Antonovich? What for? Why should we have an Inspector?

GOVERNOR.

It's fate, I suppose. [Sighs.] Till now, thank goodness, they have been nosing about in other towns. Now our turn has come.

AMMOS.

My opinion is, Anton Antonovich, that the cause is a deep one and rather political in character. It means this, that Russia—yes—that Russia intends to go to war, and the Government has secretly commissioned an official to find out if there is any treasonable activity anywhere.

GOVERNOR.

The wise man has hit on the very thing. Treason in this little country town! As if it were on the frontier! Why, you might gallop three years away from here and reach nowhere.

AMMOS.

No, you don't catch on—you don't—The Government is shrewd. It makes no difference that our town is so remote. The Government is on the look-out all the same—

GOVERNOR [cutting him short].

On the look-out, or not on the look-out, anyhow, gentlemen, I have given you warning. I have made some arrangements for myself, and I advise you to do the same. You especially, Artemy Filippovich. This official, no doubt, will want first of all to inspect your department. So you had better see to it that everything is in order, that the night-caps are clean, and the patients don't go about as they usually do, looking as grimy as blacksmiths.

ARTEMY.

Oh, that's a small matter. We can get night-caps easily enough.

GOVERNOR.

And over each bed you might hang up a placard stating in Latin or some other language—that's your end of it, Christian Ivanovich—the name of the disease, when the patient fell ill, the day of the week and the month. And I don't like your invalids to be smoking such strong tobacco. It makes you sneeze when you come in. It would be better, too, if there weren't so many of them. If there are a large number, it will instantly be ascribed to bad supervision or incompetent medical treatment.

ARTEMY.

    Oh, as to treatment, Christian Ivanovich and I have worked out our own system. Our rule is: the nearer to nature the better. We use no expensive medicines. A man is a simple affair. If he dies, he'd die anyway. If he gets well, he'd get well anyway. Besides, the doctor would have a hard time making the patients understand him. He doesn't know a word of Russian.

    The Doctor gives forth a sound intermediate between M and A.

GOVERNOR.

    And you, Ammos Fiodorovich, had better look to the courthouse. The attendants have turned the entrance hall where the petitioners usually wait into a poultry yard, and the geese and goslings go poking their beaks between people's legs. Of course, setting up housekeeping is commendable, and there is no reason why a porter shouldn't do it. Only, you see, the courthouse is not exactly the place for it. I had meant to tell you so before, but somehow it escaped my memory.

AMMOS.

    Well, I'll have them all taken into the kitchen to-day. Will you come and dine with me?

GOVERNOR.

    Then, too, it isn't right to have the courtroom littered up with all sorts of rubbish—to have a hunting-crop lying right among the papers on your desk. You're fond of sport, I know, still it's better to have the crop removed for the present. When the Inspector is gone, you may put it back again. As for your assessor, he's an educated man, to be sure, but he reeks of spirits, as if he had just emerged from a distillery. That's not right either. I had meant to tell you so long ago, but something or other drove the thing out of my mind. If his odor is really a congenital defect, as he says, then there are ways of remedying it. You might advise him to eat onion or garlic, or something of the sort. Christian Ivanovich can help him out with some of his nostrums.

    The Doctor makes the same sound as before.

AMMOS.

    No, there's no cure for it. He says his nurse struck him when he was a child, and ever since he has smelt of vodka.

GOVERNOR.

Well, I just wanted to call your attention to it. As regards the internal administration and what Andrey Ivanovich in his letter calls "little peccadilloes," I have nothing to say. Why, of course, there isn't a man living who hasn't some sins to answer for. That's the way God made the world, and the Voltairean freethinkers can talk against it all they like, it won't do any good.

AMMOS.

What do you mean by sins? Anton Antonovich? There are sins and sins. I tell everyone plainly that I take bribes. I make no bones about it. But what kind of bribes? White greyhound puppies. That's quite a different matter.

GOVERNOR.

H'm. Bribes are bribes, whether puppies or anything else.

AMMOS.

Oh, no, Anton Antonovich. But if one has a fur overcoat worth five hundred rubles, and one's wife a shawl—

GOVERNOR.

[testily]. And supposing greyhound puppies are the only bribes you take? You're an atheist, you never go to church, while I at least am a firm believer and go to church every Sunday. You—oh, I know you. When you begin to talk about the Creation it makes my flesh creep.

AMMOS.

Well, it's a conclusion I've reasoned out with my own brain.

GOVERNOR.

Too much brain is sometimes worse than none at all.—However, I merely mentioned the courthouse. I dare say nobody will ever look at it. It's an enviable place. God Almighty Himself seems to watch over it. But you, Luka Lukich, as inspector of schools, ought to have an eye on the teachers. They are very learned gentlemen, no doubt, with a college education, but they have funny habits—inseparable from the profession, I know. One of them, for instance, the man with the fat face—I forget his name—is sure, the moment he takes his chair, to screw up his face like this. [Imitates him.] And then he has a trick of sticking his hand under his necktie and smoothing down his beard. It doesn't matter, of course, if he makes a face at the pupils; perhaps it's even necessary. I'm no judge of that. But you yourself will admit that if he does it to a visitor, it may turn out very badly. The Inspector, or anyone else, might take it as meant for himself, and then the deuce knows what might come of it.

LUKA.

But what can I do? I have told him about it time and again. Only the other day when the marshal of the nobility came into the class-room, he made such a face at him as I had never in my life seen before. I dare say it was with the best intentions; But I get reprimanded for permitting radical ideas to be instilled in the minds of the young.

GOVERNOR.

And then I must call your attention to the history teacher. He has a lot of learning in his head and a store of facts. That's evident. But he lectures with such ardor that he quite forgets himself. Once I listened to him. As long as he was talking about the Assyrians and Babylonians, it was not so bad. But when he reached Alexander of Macedon, I can't describe what came over him. Upon my word, I thought a fire had broken out. He jumped down from the platform, picked up a chair and dashed it to the floor. Alexander of Macedon was a hero, it is true. But that's no reason for breaking chairs. The state must bear the cost.

LUKA.

Yes, he is a hot one. I have spoken to him about it several times. He only says: "As you please, but in the cause of learning I will even sacrifice my life."

GOVERNOR.

Yes, it's a mysterious law of fate. Your clever man is either a drunkard, or he makes such grimaces that you feel like running away.

LUKA.

Ah, Heaven save us from being in the educational department! One's afraid of everything. Everybody meddles and wants to show that he is as clever as you.

GOVERNOR.

Oh, that's nothing. But this cursed incognito! All of a sudden he'll look in: "Ah, so you're here, my dear fellows! And who's the judge here?" says he. "Liapkin-Tiapkin." "Bring Liapkin-Tiapkin here.—And who is the Superintendent of Charities?" "Zemlianika."—"Bring Zemlianika here!"—That's what's bad.

SCENE II

Enter Ivan Kuzmich, the Postmaster.

POSTMASTER.
Tell me, gentlemen, who's coming? What chinovnik?
GOVERNOR.
What, haven't you heard?
POSTMASTER.
Bobchinsky told me. He was at the postoffice just now.
GOVERNOR.
Well, what do you think of it?
POSTMASTER.
What do I think of it? Why, there'll be a war with the Turks.
AMMOS.
Exactly. Just what I thought.
GOVERNOR [sarcastically].
Yes, you've both hit in the air precisely.
POSTMASTER.
It's war with the Turks for sure, all fomented by the French.
GOVERNOR.
Nonsense! War with the Turks indeed. It's we who are going to get it, not the Turks. You may count on that. Here's a letter to prove it.
POSTMASTER.
In that case, then, we won't go to war with the Turks.
GOVERNOR.
Well, how do you feel about it, Ivan Kuzmich?
POSTMASTER.
How do I feel? How do YOU feel about it, Anton Antonovich?
GOVERNOR.
I? Well, I'm not afraid, but I just feel a little—you know—The merchants and townspeople bother me. I seem to be unpopular with them. But the Lord knows if I've taken from some I've done it without a trace of ill-feeling. I even suspect—[Takes him by the arm and walks aside with him.]—I even suspect that I may have been denounced. Or why would they send an Inspector to us? Look here, Ivan Kuzmich, don't you think you could—ahem!—just open a little every letter that passes

through your office and read it—for the common benefit of us all, you know—to see if it contains any kind of information against me, or is only ordinary correspondence. If it is all right, you can seal it up again, or simply deliver the letter opened.

POSTMASTER.

Oh, I know. You needn't teach me that. I do it not so much as a precaution as out of curiosity. I just itch to know what's doing in the world. And it's very interesting reading, I tell you. Some letters are fascinating—parts of them written grand—more edifying than the Moscow Gazette.

GOVERNOR.

Tell me, then, have you read anything about any official from St. Petersburg?

POSTMASTER.

No, nothing about a St. Petersburg official, but plenty about Kostroma and Saratov ones. A pity you don't read the letters. There are some very fine passages in them. For instance, not long ago a lieutenant writes to a friend describing a ball very wittily.—Splendid! "Dear friend," he says, "I live in the regions of the Empyrean, lots of girls, bands playing, flags flying." He's put a lot of feeling into his description, a whole lot. I've kept the letter on purpose. Would you like to read it?

GOVERNOR.

No, this is no time for such things. But please, Ivan Kuzmich, do me the favor, if ever you chance upon a complaint or denunciation, don't hesitate a moment, hold it back.

POSTMASTER.

I will, with the greatest pleasure.

AMMOS.

You had better be careful. You may get yourself into trouble.

POSTMASTER.

Goodness me!

GOVERNOR.

Never mind, never mind. Of course, it would be different if you published it broadcast. But it's a private affair, just between us.

AMMOS.

Yes, it's a bad business—I really came here to make you a present of a puppy, sister to the dog you know about. I suppose you have heard that Cheptovich and Varkhovinsky have started a suit. So now I live in clover. I hunt hares first on the one's estate, then on the other's.

GOVERNOR.

I don't care about your hares now, my good friend. That cursed incognito is on my brain. Any moment the door may open and in walk—

SCENE III

Enter Bobchinsky and Dobchinsky, out of breath.

BOBCHINSKY.

What an extraordinary occurrence!

DOBCHINSKY.

An unexpected piece of news!

ALL.

What is it? What is it?

DOBCHINSKY.

Something quite unforeseen. We were about to enter the inn—

BOBCHINSKY [interrupting].

Yes, Piotr Ivanovich and I were entering the inn—

DOBCHINSKY [interrupting].

Please, Piotr Ivanovich, let me tell.

BOBCHINSKY.

No, please, let me—let me. You can't. You haven't got the style for it.

DOBCHINSKY.

Oh, but you'll get mixed up and won't remember everything.

BOBCHINSKY.

Yes, I will, upon my word, I will. PLEASE don't interrupt! Do let me tell the news—don't interrupt! Pray, oblige me, gentlemen, and tell Dobchinsky not to interrupt.

GOVERNOR.

Speak, for Heaven's sake! What is it? My heart is in my mouth! Sit down, gentlemen, take seats. Piotr Ivanovich, here's a chair for you. [All seat themselves around Bobchinsky and Dobchinsky.] Well, now, what is it? What is it?

BOBCHINSKY.

Permit me, permit me. I'll tell it all just as it happened. As soon as I had the pleasure of taking leave of you after you were good enough to be bothered with the letter which you had received, sir, I ran out—now, please don't keep interrupting, Dobchinsky. I know all about it, all, I tell you.—So I ran out to see Korobkin. But not finding Korobkin at home, I went off to Rastakovsky, and not seeing him, I went to Ivan Kuzmich to tell him of the news you'd got. Going on from there I met Dobchinsky—

DOBCHINSKY [interjecting].

At the stall where they sell pies—

BOBCHINSKY.

At the stall where they sell pies. Well, I met Dobchinsky and I said to him: "Have you heard the news that came to Anton Antonovich in a letter which is absolutely reliable?" But Piotr Ivanovich had already heard of it from your housekeeper, Avdotya, who, I don't know why, had been sent to Filipp Antonovich Pachechuyev—

DOBCHINSKY [interrupting].

To get a little keg for French brandy.

BOBCHINSKY.

Yes, to get a little keg for French brandy. So then I went with Dobchinsky to Pachechuyev's.—Will you stop, Piotr Ivanovich? Please don't interrupt.—So off we went to Pachechuyev's, and on the way Dobchinsky said: "Let's go to the inn," he said. "I haven't eaten a thing since morning. My stomach is growling." Yes, sir, his stomach was growling. "They've just got in a supply of fresh salmon at the inn," he said. "Let's take a bite." We had hardly entered the inn when we saw a young man—

DOBCHINSKY [Interrupting].

Of rather good appearance and dressed in ordinary citizen's clothes.

BOBCHINSKY.

Yes, of rather good appearance and dressed in citizen's clothes—walking up and down the room. There was something out of the usual about his face, you know, something deep—and a manner about him—and here [raises his hand to his forehead and turns it around several times] full, full of everything. I had a sort of feeling, and I said to Dobchinsky,

"Something's up. This is no ordinary matter." Yes, and Dobchinsky beckoned to the landlord, Vlas, the innkeeper, you know,—three weeks ago his wife presented him with a baby—a bouncer—he'll grow up just like his father and keep a tavern.—Well, we beckoned to Vlas, and Dobchinsky asked him on the quiet, "Who," he asked, "is that young man?" "That young man," Vlas replied, "that young man"—Oh, don't interrupt, Piotr Ivanovich, please don't interrupt. You can't tell the story. Upon my word, you can't. You lisp and one tooth in your mouth makes you whistle. I know what I'm saying. "That young man," he said, "is an official."—Yes, sir.—"On his way from St. Petersburg. And his name," he said, "is Ivan Aleksandrovich Khlestakov, and he's going," he said "to the government of Saratov," he said. "And he acts so queerly. It's the second week he's been here and he's never left the house; and he won't pay a penny, takes everything on account." When Vlas told me that, a light dawned on me from above, and I said to Piotr Ivanovich, "Hey!"—

DOBCHINSKY.

No, Piotr Ivanovich, I said "HEY!"

BOBCHINSKY.

Well first YOU said it, then I did. "Hey!" said both of us, "And why does he stick here if he's going to Saratov?"—Yes, sir, that's he, the official.

GOVERNOR.

Who? What official?

BOBCHINSKY.

Why, the official who you were notified was coming, the Inspector.

GOVERNOR [terrified].

Great God! What's that you're saying. It can't be he.

DOBCHINSKY.

It is, though. Why, he doesn't pay his bills and he doesn't leave. Who else can it be? And his postchaise is ordered for Saratov.

BOBCHINSKY.

It's he, it's he, it's he—why, he's so alert, he scrutinized everything. He saw that Dobchinsky and I were eating salmon—chiefly on account of Dobchinsky's stomach—and he looked at our plates so hard that I was frightened to death.

GOVERNOR.

The Lord have mercy on us sinners! In what room is he staying?

DOBCHINSKY.

Room number 5 near the stairway.

BOBCHINSKY.

In the same room that the officers quarreled in when they passed through here last year.

GOVERNOR.

How long has he been here?

DOBCHINSKY.

Two weeks. He came on St. Vasili's day.

GOVERNOR.

Two weeks! [Aside.] Holy Fathers and saints preserve me! In those two weeks I have flogged the wife of a non-commissioned officer, the prisoners were not given their rations, the streets are dirty as a pothouse—a scandal, a disgrace! [Clutches his head with both hands.]

ARTEMY.

What do you think, Anton Antonovich, hadn't we better go in state to the inn?

AMMOS.

No, no. First send the chief magistrate, then the clergy, then the merchants. That's what it says in the book. The Acts of John the Freemason.

GOVERNOR.

No, no, leave it to me. I have been in difficult situations before now. They have passed off all right, and I was even rewarded with thanks. Maybe the Lord will help us out this time, too. [Turns to Bobchinsky.] You say he's a young man?

BOBCHINSKY.

Yes, about twenty-three or four at the most.

GOVERNOR.

So much the better. It's easier to pump things out of a young man. It's tough if you've got a hardened old devil to deal with. But a young man is all on the surface. You, gentlemen, had better see to your end of things while I go unofficially, by myself, or with Dobchinsky here, as though for a walk, to see that the visitors that come to town are properly accommodated. Here, Svistunov. [To one of the Sergeants.]

SVISTUNOV.

Sir.

GOVERNOR.

Go instantly to the Police Captain—or, no, I'll want you. Tell somebody to send him here as quickly as possibly and then come back.

Svistunov hurries off.

ARTEMY.

Let's go, let's go, Ammos Fiodorovich. We may really get into trouble.

AMMOS.

What have you got to be afraid of? Put clean nightcaps on the patients and the thing's done.

ARTEMY.

Nightcaps! Nonsense! The patients were ordered to have oatmeal soup. Instead of that there's such a smell of cabbage in all the corridors that you've got to hold your nose.

AMMOS.

Well, my mind's at ease. Who's going to visit the court? Supposing he does look at the papers, he'll wish he had left them alone. I have been on the bench fifteen years, and when I take a look into a report, I despair. King Solomon in all his wisdom could not tell what is true and what is not true in it.

The Judge, the Superintendent of Charities, the School Inspector, and Postmaster go out and bump up against the Sergeant in the doorway as the latter returns.

SCENE IV

The Governor, Bobchinsky, Dobchinsky, and Sergeant Svistunov.

GOVERNOR.

Well, is the cab ready?

SVISTUNOV.

Yes, sir.

GOVERNOR.

Go out on the street—or, no, stop—go and bring—why, where are the others? Why are you alone? Didn't I give orders for Prokhorov to be here? Where is Prokhorov?

SVISTUNOV.

Prokhorov is in somebody's house and can't go on duty just now.

GOVERNOR.

Why so?

SVISTUNOV.

Well, they brought him back this morning dead drunk. They poured two buckets of water over him, but he hasn't sobered up yet.

GOVERNOR [clutching his head with both hands].

For Heaven's sake! Go out on duty quick—or, no, run up to my room, do you hear? And fetch my sword and my new hat. Now, Piotr Ivanovich, [to Dobchinsky] come.

BOBCHINSKY.

And me—me, too. Let me come, too, Anton Antonovich.

GOVERNOR.

No, no, Bobchinsky, it won't do. Besides there is not enough room in the cab.

BOBCHINSKY.

Oh, that doesn't matter. I'll follow the cab on foot—on foot. I just want to peep through a crack—so—to see that manner of his—how he acts.

GOVERNOR [turning to the Sergeant and taking his sword].

Be off and get the policemen together. Let them each take a—there, see how scratched my sword is. It's that dog of a merchant, Abdulin. He sees the Governor's sword is old and doesn't provide a new one. Oh, the sharpers! I'll bet they've got their petitions against me ready in their coat-tail pockets.—Let each take a street in his hand—I don't mean a street—a broom—and sweep the street leading to the inn, and sweep it clean, and—do you hear? And see here, I know you, I know your tricks. You insinuate yourselves into the inn and walk off with silver spoons in your boots. Just you look out. I keep my ears pricked. What have you been up to with the merchant, Chorniayev, eh? He gave you two yards of cloth for your uniform and you stole the whole piece. Take care. You're only a Sergeant. Don't graft higher than your rank. Off with you.

SCENE V

Enter the Police Captain.

GOVERNOR.

Hello, Stepan Ilyich, where the dickens have you been keeping yourself? What do you mean by acting that way?

CAPTAIN.

Why, I was just outside the gate.

GOVERNOR.

Well, listen, Stepan Ilyich. An official has come from St. Petersburg. What have you done about it?

CAPTAIN.

What you told me to. I sent Sergeant Pugovichyn with policemen to clean the street.

GOVERNOR.

Where is Derzhimorda?

CAPTAIN.

He has gone off on the fire engine.

GOVERNOR.

And Prokhorov is drunk?

CAPTAIN.

Yes.

GOVERNOR.

How could you allow him to get drunk?

CAPTAIN.

God knows. Yesterday there was a fight outside the town. He went to restore order and was brought back drunk.

GOVERNOR.

Well, then, this is what you are to do.—Sergeant Pugovichyn—he is tall. So he is to stand on duty on the bridge for appearance' sake. Then the old fence near the bootmaker's must be pulled down at once and a post stuck up with a whisp of straw so as to look like grading. The more debris there is the more it will show the governor's activity.— Good God, though, I forgot that about forty cart-loads of rubbish have been dumped against that fence. What a vile, filthy town this is! A monument, or even only a fence, is erected, and instantly they bring a lot of dirt together, from the devil knows where, and dump it there. [Heaves a sigh.] And if the functionary that has come here asks any of the officials whether they are satisfied, they are to say, "Perfectly satisfied, your Honor"; and if anybody is not satisfied, I'll give him something to be dissatisfied about afterwards.—Ah, I'm a sinner, a terrible sinner. [Takes the hat-box, instead of his hat.] Heaven only grant that I may soon get this matter over and done with; then I'll donate a candle such as has never been offered before. I'll levy a hundred pounds of wax from every damned merchant. Oh my, oh my! Come, let's go, Piotr Ivanovich. [Tries to put the hat-box on his head instead of his hat.]

CAPTAIN.

Anton Antonovich, that's the hat-box, not your hat.

GOVERNOR [throwing the box down].

If it's the hat-box, it's the hat-box, the deuce take it!—And if he asks why the church at the hospital for which the money was appropriated five years ago has not been built, don't let them forget to say that the building was begun but was destroyed by fire. I sent in a report about it, you know. Some blamed fool might forget and let out that the building was never even begun. And tell Derzhimorda not to be so free with his fists. Guilty or innocent, he makes them all see stars in the cause of public order.—Come on, come on, Dobchinsky. [Goes out and returns.] And don't let the soldiers appear on the streets with nothing on. That rotten garrison wear their coats directly over their undershirts. All go out.

SCENE VI

Anna Andreyevna and Marya Antonovna rush in on the stage.

ANNA.

Where are they? Where are they? Oh, my God! [opening the door.] Husband! Antosha! Anton! [hurriedly, to Marya.] It's all your fault. Dawdling! Dawdling!—"I want a pin—I want a scarf." [Runs to the window and calls.] Anton, where are you going? Where are you going? What! He has come? The Inspector? He has a moustache? What kind of a moustache?

GOVERNOR [from without].

Wait, dear. Later.

ANNA.

Wait? I don't want to wait. The idea, wait! I only want one word. Is he a colonel or what? Eh? [Disgusted.] There, he's gone! You'll pay for it! It's all your fault—you, with your "Mamma, dear, wait a moment, I'll just pin my scarf. I'll come directly." Yes, directly! Now we have missed the news. It's all your confounded coquettishness. You heard the Postmaster was here and so you must prink and prim yourself in front of the mirror—look on this side and that side and all around. You imagine he's smitten with you. But I can tell you he makes a face at you the moment you turn your back.

MARYA.

It can't be helped, mamma. We'll know everything in a couple of hours anyway.

ANNA.

In a couple of hours! Thank you! A nice answer. Why don't you say, in a month. We'll know still more in a month. [She leans out of the window.] Here, Avdotya! I say! Have you heard whether anybody has come, Avdotya?—No, you goose, you didn't—He waved his hands? Well, what of it? Let him wave his hands. But you should have asked him anyhow. You couldn't find out, of course, with your head full of nonsense and lovers. Eh, what? They left in a hurry? Well, you should have run after the carriage. Off with you, off with you at once, do you hear? Run and ask everybody where they are. Be sure and find out who the newcomer is and what he is like, do you hear? Peep through a crack and find everything out—what sort of eyes he has, whether they are black or blue, and be back here instantly, this minute, do you hear? Quick, quick, quick!

She keeps on calling and they both stand at the window until the curtain drops.

ACT II

A small room in the inn, bed, table, travelling bag, empty bottle, boots, clothes brush, etc.

SCENE I

OSIP [lying on his master's bed].

The devil take it! I'm so hungry. There's a racket in my belly, as if a whole regiment were blowing trumpets. We'll never reach home. I'd like to know what we are going to do. Two months already since we left St. Pete. He's gone through all his cash, the precious buck, so now he sticks here with his tail between his legs and takes it easy. We'd have had enough and more than enough to pay for the fare, but no he must exhibit himself in every town. [Imitates him.] "Osip, get me the best room to be had and order the best dinner they serve. I can't stand bad food. I must have the best." It would be all right for a somebody, but for a common copying clerk! Goes and gets acquainted with the other travellers, plays cards, and plays himself out of his last penny. Oh, I'm sick of this life. It's better in our village, really. There isn't so much going on, but then there is less to bother about. You get yourself a wife and lie on the stove all the time and eat pie. Of course, if you wanted to tell the truth, there's no denying it that there's nothing like living in St. Pete. All you want is money. And then you can live smart and classy—theeadres, dogs to dance for you, everything, and everybody talks so genteel, pretty near like in high society. If you go to the Schukin bazaar, the shopkeepers cry, "Gentlemen," at you. You sit with the officials in the ferry boat. If you want company, you go into a shop. A sport there will tell you about life in the barracks and explain the meaning of every star in the sky, so that you see them all as if you held them in your hand. Then an old officer's wife will gossip, or a pretty chambermaid will dart a look at you—ta, ta, ta! [Smirks and wags his head.] And what deucedly civil manners they have, too. You never hear no impolite language. They always say "Mister" to you. If you are tired of walking, why you take a cab and sit in it like a lord. And if you don't feel like paying, then you don't. Every house has an open-work gate and you can slip through and the devil himself won't catch you. There's one bad thing, though; sometimes you get first class eats and sometimes you're so starved you nearly drop—like now. It's all his fault. What can you do with him? His dad sends him money to keep him going, but the devil a lot it does. He goes off on a spree, rides in cabs, gets me to buy a theeadre ticket for him every day, and in a week look at him—sends me to the old clo'es man to sell his new dress coat. Sometimes he gets rid of everything down to his last shirt and is left with nothing except his coat and overcoat. Upon my word, it's the truth. And such fine cloth, too. English, you know. One dress coat costs him a hundred and fifty rubles and he sells it to the old clo'es man for twenty. No use saying nothing about his pants. They go for a song. And why? Because he doesn't tend to his business. Instead of sticking to his job, he gads about on the Prospect and plays cards. Ah, if the old gentleman only knew it! He wouldn't care that you are an official. He'd lift up your little shirtie and would lay it on so that you'd go about rubbing yourself for a week. If you have a job, stick to it. Here's the innkeeper says he won't let you have anything to eat unless you pay your back bills. Well, and suppose we don't pay. [Sighing.] Oh, good God! If only I could get cabbage soup. I think I could eat up the whole world now. There's a knock at the door. I suppose it's him. [Rises from the bed hastily.]

SCENE II

Osip and Khlestakov.

KHLESTAKOV.

Here! [Hands him his cap and cane.] What, been warming the bed again!

OSIP.

Why should I have been warming the bed? Have I never seen a bed before?

KHLESTAKOV.

You're lying. The bed's all tumbled up.

OSIP.

What do I want a bed for? Don't I know what a bed is like? I have legs and can use them to stand on. I don't need your bed.

KHLESTAKOV [walking up and down the room].

Go see if there isn't some tobacco in the pouch.

OSIP.

What tobacco? You emptied it out four days ago.

KHLESTAKOV [pacing the room and twisting his lips. Finally he says in a loud resolute voice].

Listen—a—Osip.

OSIP.

Yes, sir?

KHLESTAKOV [In a voice just as loud, but not quite so resolute].

Go down there.

OSIP.

Where?

KHLESTAKOV [in a voice not at all resolute, nor loud, but almost in entreaty].

Down to the restaurant—tell them—to send up dinner.

OSIP.
> No, I won't.

KHLESTAKOV.
> How dare you, you fool!

OSIP.
> It won't do any good, anyhow. The landlord said he won't let you have anything more to eat.

KHLESTAKOV.
> How dare he! What nonsense is this?

OSIP.
> He'll go to the Governor, too, he says. It's two weeks now since you've paid him, he says. You and your master are cheats, he says, and your master is a blackleg besides, he says. We know the breed. We've seen swindlers like him before.

KHLESTAKOV.
> And you're delighted, I suppose, to repeat all this to me, you donkey.

OSIP.
> "Every Tom, Dick and Harry comes and lives here," he says, "and runs up debts so that you can't even put him out. I'm not going to fool about it," he says, "I'm going straight to the Governor and have him arrested and put in jail."

KHLESTAKOV.
> That'll do now, you fool. Go down at once and tell him to have dinner sent up. The coarse brute! The idea!

OSIP.
> Hadn't I better call the landlord here?

KHLESTAKOV.
> What do I want the landlord for? Go and tell him yourself.

OSIP.
> But really, master—

KHLESTAKOV.
> Well, go, the deuce take you. Call the landlord.
> Osip goes out.

SCENE III

KHLESTAKOV [alone].

I am so ravenously hungry. I took a little stroll thinking I could walk off my appetite. But, hang it, it clings. If I hadn't dissipated so in Penza I'd have had enough money to get home with. The infantry captain did me up all right. Wonderful the way the scoundrel cut the cards! It didn't take more than a quarter of an hour for him to clean me out of my last penny. And yet I would give anything to have another set-to with him. Only I never will have the chance.—What a rotten town this is! You can't get anything on credit in the grocery shops here. It's deucedly mean, it is. [He whistles, first an air from Robert le Diable, then a popular song, then a blend of the two.] No one's coming.

SCENE IV

Khlestakov, Osip, and a Servant.

SERVANT.

The landlord sent me up to ask what you want.

KHLESTAKOV.

Ah, how do you do, brother! How are you? How are you?

SERVANT.

All right, thank you.

KHLESTAKOV.

And how are you getting on in the inn? Is business good?

SERVANT.

Yes, business is all right, thank you.

KHLESTAKOV.

Many guests?

SERVANT.

Plenty.

KHLESTAKOV.

See here, good friend. They haven't sent me dinner yet. Please hurry them up! See that I get it as soon as possible. I have some business to attend to immediately after dinner.

SERVANT.

The landlord said he won't let you have anything any more. He was all for going to the Governor to-day and making a complaint against you.

KHLESTAKOV.

What's there to complain about? Judge for yourself, friend. Why, I've got to eat. If I go on like this I'll turn into a skeleton. I'm hungry, I'm not joking.

SERVANT.

Yes, sir, that's what he said. "I won't let him have no dinner," he said, "till he pays for what he has already had." That was his answer.

KHLESTAKOV.

Try to persuade him.

SERVANT.

But what shall I tell him?

KHLESTAKOV.

Explain that it's a serious matter, I've got to eat. As for the money, of course—He thinks that because a muzhik like him can go without food a whole day others can too. The idea!

SERVANT.

Well, all right. I'll tell him.

The Servant and Osip go out.

SCENE V

Khlestakov alone.

KHLESTAKOV.

A bad business if he refuses to let me have anything. I'm so hungry. I've never been so hungry in my life. Shall I try to raise something on my clothes? Shall I sell my trousers? No, I'd rather starve than come home without a St. Petersburg suit. It's a shame Joachim wouldn't let me have a carriage on hire. It would have been great to ride home in a carriage, drive up under the porte-cochere of one of the neighbors with lamps lighted and Osip behind in livery. Imagine the stir it would have created. "Who is it? What's that?" Then my footman walks in [draws himself up and imitates] and an-nounces: "Ivan Aleksandrovich

Khlestakov of St. Petersburg. Will you receive him?" Those country lubbers don't even know what it means to "receive." If any lout of a country squire pays them a visit, he stalks straight into the drawing-room like a bear. Then you step up to one of their pretty girls and say: "Dee-lighted, madam." [Rubs his hands and bows.] Phew! [Spits.] I feel positively sick, I'm so hungry.

SCENE VI

Khlestakov, Osip, and later the Servant.

KHLESTAKOV.
Well?
OSIP.
They're bringing dinner.
KHLESTAKOV [claps his hands and wriggles in his chair].
Dinner, dinner, dinner!
SERVANT [with plates and napkin].
This is the last time the landlord will let you have dinner.
KHLESTAKOV.
The landlord, the landlord! I spit on your landlord. What have you got there?
SERVANT.
Soup and roast beef.
KHLESTAKOV.
What! Only two courses?
SERVANT.
That's all.
KHLESTAKOV.
Nonsense! I won't take it. What does he mean by that? Ask him. It's not enough.
SERVANT.
The landlord says it's too much.
KHLESTAKOV.
Why is there no sauce?
SERVANT.
There is none.

KHLESTAKOV.

Why not? I saw them preparing a whole lot when I passed through the kitchen. And in the dining-room this morning two short little men were eating salmon and lots of other things.

SERVANT.

Well, you see, there is some and there isn't.

KHLESTAKOV.

Why "isn't"?

SERVANT.

Because there isn't any.

KHLESTAKOV.

What, no salmon, no fish, no cutlets?

SERVANT.

Only for the better kind of folk.

KHLESTAKOV.

You're a fool.

SERVANT.

Yes, sir.

KHLESTAKOV.

You measly suckling pig. Why can they eat and I not? Why the devil can't I eat, too? Am I not a guest the same as they?

SERVANT.

No, not the same. That's plain.

KHLESTAKOV.

How so?

SERVANT.

That's easy. THEY pay, that's it.

KHLESTAKOV.

I'm not going to argue with you, simpleton! [Ladles out the soup and begins to eat.] What, you call that soup? Simply hot water poured into a cup. No taste to it at all. It only stinks. I don't want it. Bring me some other soup.

SERVANT.

All right. I'll take it away. The boss said if you didn't want it, you needn't take it.

KHLESTAKOV [putting his hand over the dishes].

Well, well, leave it alone, you fool. You may be used to treat other people this way, but I'm not that sort. I advise you not to try it on me. My God! What soup! [Goes on eating.] I don't think anybody in the world tasted such soup. Feathers floating on the top instead of butter. [Cuts the piece of chicken in the soup.] Oh, oh, oh! What a bird!—Give me the roast beef. There's a little soup left, Osip. Take it. [Cuts the meat.] What sort of roast beef is this? This isn't roast beef.

SERVANT.
What else is it?

KHLESTAKOV.
The devil knows, but it isn't roast beef. It's roast iron, not roast beef. [Eats.] Scoundrels! Crooks! The stuff they give you to eat! It makes your jaws ache to chew one piece of it. [Picks his teeth with his fingers.] Villains! It's as tough as the bark of a tree. I can't pull it out no matter how hard I try. Such meat is enough to ruin one's teeth. Crooks! [Wipes his mouth with the napkin.] Is there nothing else?

SERVANT.
No.

KHLESTAKOV.
Scoundrels! Blackguards! They might have given some decent pastry, or something, the lazy good-for-nothings! Fleecing their guests! That's all they're good for.

[The Servant takes the dishes and carries them out accompanied by Osip.]

SCENE VII

Khlestakov alone.

KHLESTAKOV.
It's just as if I had eaten nothing at all, upon my word. It has only whetted my appetite. If I only had some change to send to the market and buy some bread.

OSIP [entering].
The Governor has come, I don't know what for. He's inquiring about you.

KHLESTAKOV [in alarm].
There now! That inn-keeper has gone and made a complaint against me. Suppose he really claps me into jail? Well! If he does it in a gentlemanly way, I may—No, no, I won't. The officers and the people are all out on

the street and I set the fashion for them and the merchant's daughter and I flirted. No, I won't. And pray, who is he? How dare he, actually? What does he take me for? A tradesman? I'll tell him straight out, "How dare you? How—"

[The door knob turns and Khlestakov goes pale and shrinks back.]

SCENE VIII

Khlestakov, the Governor, and Dobchinsky.
The Governor advances a few steps and stops. They stare at each other a few moments wide-eyed and frightened.

GOVERNOR [recovering himself a little and saluting military fashion].

I have come to present my compliments, sir.

KHLESTAKOV [bows].

How do you do, sir?

GOVERNOR.

Excuse my intruding.

KHLESTAKOV.

Pray don't mention it.

GOVERNOR.

It's my duty as chief magistrate of this town to see that visitors and persons of rank should suffer no inconveniences.

KHLESTAKOV [a little halting at first, but toward the end in a loud, firm voice].

Well—what was—to be—done? It's not—my fault. I'm—really going to pay. They will send me money from home. [Bobchinsky peeps in at the door.] He's most to blame. He gives me beef as hard as a board and the soup—the devil knows what he put into it. I ought to have pitched it out of the window. He starves me the whole day. His tea is so peculiar—it smells of fish, not tea. So why should I—The idea!

GOVERNOR [scared].

Excuse me! I assure you, it's not my fault. I always have good beef in the market here. The Kholmogory merchants bring it, and they are sober, well-behaved people. I'm sure I don't know where he gets his bad meat from. But if anything is wrong, may I suggest that you allow me to take you to another place?

KHLESTAKOV.

No, I thank you. I don't care to leave. I know what the other place is—the jail. What right have you, I should like to know—how dare you?—Why, I'm in the government service at St. Petersburg. [Puts on a bold front.] I—I—I—

GOVERNOR [aside].

My God, how angry he is. He has found out everything. Those damned merchants have told him everything.

KHLESTAKOV [with bravado].

I won't go even if you come here with your whole force. I'll go straight to the minister. [Bangs his fist on the table.] What do you mean? What do you mean?

GOVERNOR [drawing himself up stiffly and shaking all over].

Have pity on me. Don't ruin me. I have a wife and little children. Don't bring misfortune on a man.

KHLESTAKOV.

No, I won't go. What's that got to do with me? Must I go to jail because you have a wife and little children? Great! [Bobchinsky looks in at the door and disappears in terror.] No, much obliged to you. I will not go.

GOVERNOR [trembling].

It was my inexperience. I swear to you, it was nothing but my inexperience and insufficient means. Judge for yourself. The salary I get is not enough for tea and sugar. And if I have taken bribes, they were mere trifles—something for the table, or a coat or two. As for the officer's widow to whom they say I gave a beating, she's in business now, and it's a slander, it's a slander that I beat her. Those scoundrels here invented the lie. They are ready to murder me. That's the kind of people they are.

KHLESTAKOV.

Well. I've nothing to do with them. [Reflecting.] I don't see, though, why you should talk to me about your scoundrels or officer's widow. An officer's widow is quite a different matter.—But don't you dare to beat me. You can't do it to me—no, sir, you can't. The idea! Look at him! I'll pay, I'll pay the money. Just now I'm out of cash. That's why I stay here—because I haven't a single kopek.

GOVERNOR [aside].

Oh, he's a shrewd one. So that's what he's aiming at? He's raised such a cloud of dust you can't tell what direction he's going. Who can guess what he wants? One doesn't know where to begin. But I will try. Come what may, I'll try—hit or miss. [Aloud.] H'm, if you really are in want of money, I'm ready to serve you. It is my duty to assist strangers in town.

KHLESTAKOV.

Lend me some, lend me some. Then I'll settle up immediately with the landlord. I only want two hundred rubles. Even less would do.

GOVERNOR.

There's just two hundred rubles. [Giving him the money.] Don't bother to count it.

KHLESTAKOV [taking it].

Very much obliged to you. I'll send it back to you as soon as I get home. I just suddenly found myself without—H'm—I see you are a gentleman. Now it's all different.

GOVERNOR [aside].

Well, thank the Lord, he's taken the money. Now I suppose things will move along smoothly. I slipped four hundred instead of two into his hand.

KHLESTAKOV.

Ho, Osip! [Osip enters.] Tell the servant to come. [To the Governor and Dobchinsky.] Please be seated. [To Dobchinsky.] Please take a seat, I beg of you.

GOVERNOR.

Don't trouble. We can stand.

KHLESTAKOV.

But, please, please be seated. I now see perfectly how open-hearted and generous you are. I confess I thought you had come to put me in—[To Dobchinsky.] Do take a chair.

The Governor and Dobchinsky sit down. Bobchinsky looks in at the door and listens.

GOVERNOR [aside].

I must be bolder. He wants us to pretend he is incognito. Very well, we will talk nonsense, too. We'll pretend we haven't the least idea who he is. [Aloud.] I was going about in the performance of my duty with Piotr Ivanovich Dobchinsky here—he's a landed proprietor here—and we came to the inn to see whether the guests are properly accommodated—because I'm not like other governors, who don't care about anything. No, apart from my duty, out of pure Christian philanthropy, I wish every mortal to be decently treated. And as if to reward me for my pains, chance has afforded me this pleasant acquaintance.

KHLESTAKOV.

I, too, am delighted. Without your aid, I confess, I should have had to stay here a long time. I didn't know how in the world to pay my bill.

GOVERNOR [aside].

Oh, yes, fib on.—Didn't know how to pay his bill! May I ask where your Honor is going?

KHLESTAKOV.

I'm going to my own village in the Government of Saratov.

GOVERNOR [aside, with an ironical expression on his face].

The Government of Saratov! H'm, h'm! And doesn't even blush! One must be on the qui vive with this fellow. [Aloud.] You have undertaken a great task. They say travelling is disagreeable because of the delay in getting horses but, on the other hand, it is a diversion. You are travelling for your own amusement, I suppose?

KHLESTAKOV.

No, my father wants me. He's angry because so far I haven't made headway in the St. Petersburg service. He thinks they stick the Vladimir in your buttonhole the minute you get there. I'd like him to knock about in the government offices for a while.

GOVERNOR [aside].

How he fabricates! Dragging in his old father, too. [Aloud.] And may I ask whether you are going there to stay for long?

KHLESTAKOV.

I really don't know. You see, my father is stubborn and stupid—an old dotard as hard as a block of wood. I'll tell him straight out, "Do what you will, I can't live away from St. Petersburg." Really, why should I waste my life among peasants? Our times make different demands on us. My soul craves enlightenment.

GOVERNOR [aside].

He can spin yarns all right. Lie after lie and never trips. And such an ugly insignificant-looking creature, too. Why, it seems to me I could crush him with my finger nails. But wait, I'll make you talk. I'll make you tell me things. [Aloud.] You were quite right in your observation, that one can do nothing in a dreary out-of-the-way place. Take this town, for instance. You lie awake nights, you work hard for your country, you don't spare yourself, and the reward? You don't know when it's coming. [He looks round the room.] This room seems rather damp.

KHLESTAKOV.

Yes, it's a dirty room. And the bugs! I've never experienced anything like them. They bite like dogs.

GOVERNOR.

You don't say! An illustrious guest like you to be subjected to such annoyance at the hands of—whom? Of vile bugs which should never have been born. And I dare say, it's dark here, too.

KHLESTAKOV.

Yes, very gloomy. The landlord has introduced the custom of not providing candles. Sometimes I want to do something—read a bit, or, if the fancy strikes me, write something.—I can't. It's a dark room, yes, very dark.

GOVERNOR.

I wonder if I might be bold enough to ask you—but, no, I'm unworthy.

KHLESTAKOV.

What is it?

GOVERNOR.

No, no, I'm unworthy. I'm unworthy.

KHLESTAKOV.

But what is it?

GOVERNOR.

If I might be bold enough—I have a fine room for you at home, light and cosy. But no, I feel it is too great an honor. Don't be offended. Upon my word, I made the offer out of the simplicity of my heart.

KHLESTAKOV.

On the contrary, I accept your invitation with pleasure. I should feel much more comfortable in a private house than in this disreputable tavern.

GOVERNOR.

I'm only too delighted. How glad my wife will be. It's my character, you know. I've always been hospitable from my very childhood, especially when my guest is a distinguished person. Don't think I say this out of flattery. No, I haven't that vice. I only speak from the fullness of my heart.

KHLESTAKOV.

I'm greatly obliged to you. I myself hate double-faced people. I like your candor and kind-heartedness exceedingly. And I am free to say, I ask for nothing else than devotion and esteem—esteem and devotion.

SCENE IX

The above and the Servant, accompanied by Osip. Bobchinsky peeps in at the door.

SERVANT.

Did your Honor wish anything?

KHLESTAKOV.

Yes, let me have the bill.

SERVANT.

I gave you the second one a little while ago.

KHLESTAKOV.

Oh, I can't remember your stupid accounts. Tell me what the whole comes to.

SERVANT.

You were pleased to order dinner the first day. The second day you only took salmon. And then you took everything on credit.

KHLESTAKOV.

Fool! [Starts to count it all up now.] How much is it altogether?

GOVERNOR.

Please don't trouble yourself. He can wait. [To the Servant.] Get out of here. The money will be sent to you.

KHLESTAKOV.

Yes, that's so, of course. [He puts the money in his pocket.]

The Servant goes out. Bobchinsky peeps in at the door.

SCENE X

The Governor, Khlestakov and Dobchinsky.

GOVERNOR.
Would you care to inspect a few institutions in our town now—the philanthropic institutions, for instance, and others?

KHLESTAKOV.
But what is there to see?

GOVERNOR.
Well, you'll see how they're run—the order in which we keep them.

KHLESTAKOV.
Oh, with the greatest pleasure. I'm ready.

Bobchinsky puts his head in at the door.

GOVERNOR.
And then, if you wish, we can go from there and inspect the district school and see our method of education.

KHLESTAKOV.
Yes, yes, if you please.

GOVERNOR.
Afterwards, if you should like to visit our town jails and prisons, you will see how our criminals are kept.

KHLESTAKOV.
Yes, yes, but why go to prison? We had better go to see the philanthropic institutions.

GOVERNOR.
As you please. Do you wish to ride in your own carriage, or with me in the cab?

KHLESTAKOV.
I'd rather take the cab with you.

GOVERNOR [to Dobchinsky].
Now there'll be no room for you, Piotr Ivanovich.

DOBCHINSKY.
It doesn't matter. I'll walk.

GOVERNOR [aside, to Dobchinsky].
Listen. Run as fast as you can and take two notes, one to Zemlianika at the hospital, the other to my wife. [To Khlestakov.] May I take the

liberty of asking you to permit me to write a line to my wife to tell her to make ready to receive our honored guest?

KHLESTAKOV.

Why go to so much trouble? However, there is the ink. I don't know whether there is any paper. Would the bill do?

GOVERNOR.

Yes, that'll do. [Writes, talking to himself at the same time.] We'll see how things will go after lunch and several stout-bellied bottles. We have some Russian Madeira, not much to look at, but it will knock an elephant off its legs. If I only knew what he is and how much I have to be [on] my guard.

He finishes writing and gives the notes to Dobchinsky. As the latter walks across the stage, the door suddenly falls in, and Bobchinsky tumbles in with it to the floor. All exclaim in surprise. Bobchinsky rises.

KHLESTAKOV.

Have you hurt yourself?

BOBCHINSKY.

Oh, it's nothing—nothing at all—only a little bruise on my nose. I'll run in to Dr. Hübner's. He has a sort of plaster. It'll soon pass away.

GOVERNOR [making an angry gesture at Bobchinsky. To Khlestakov].

Oh, it's nothing. Now, if you please, sir, we'll go. I'll tell your servant to carry your luggage over. [Calls Osip.] Here, my good fellow, take all your master's things to my house, the Governor's. Anyone will tell you where it is. By your leave, sir. [Makes way for Khlestakov and follows him; then turns and says reprovingly to Bobchinsky.] Couldn't you find some other place to fall in? Sprawling out here like a lobster!

Goes out. After him Bobchinsky.

Curtain falls.

ACT III

SCENE: The same as in Act I.

SCENE I

Anna Andreyevna and Marya Antonovna standing at the window in the same positions as at the end of Act I.

ANNA.
There now! We've been waiting a whole hour. All on account of your silly prinking. You were completely dressed, but no, you have to keep on dawdling.— Provoking! Not a soul to be seen, as though on purpose, as though the whole world were dead.

MARYA.
Now really, mamma, we shall know all about it in a minute or two. Avdotya must come back soon. [Looks out of the

window and exclaims.] Oh, mamma, someone is coming—there down the street!

ANNA.

Where? Just your imagination again!—Why, yes, someone is coming. I wonder who it is. A short man in a frock coat. Who can it be? Eh? The suspense is awful! Who can it be, I wonder.

MARYA.

Dobchinsky, mamma.

ANNA.

Dobchinsky! Your imagination again! It's not Dobchinsky at all. [Waves her handkerchief.] Ho, you! Come here! Quick!

MARYA.

It is Dobchinsky, mamma.

ANNA.

Of course, you've got to contradict. I tell you, it's not Dobchinsky.

MARYA.

Well, well, mamma? Isn't it Dobchinsky?

ANNA.

Yes, it is, I see now. Why do you argue about it? [Calls through the window.] Hurry up, quick! You're so slow. Well, where are they? What? Speak from where you are. It's all the same. What? He is very strict? Eh? And how about my husband? [Moves away a little from the window, exasperated.] He is so stupid. He won't say a word until he is in the room.

SCENE II

Enter Dobchinsky.

ANNA.

Now tell me, aren't you ashamed? You were the only one I relied on to act decently. They all ran away and you after them, and till now I haven't been able to find out a thing. Aren't you ashamed? I stood godmother to your Vanichka and Lizanko, and this is the way you treat me.

DOBCHINSKY.

Godmother, upon my word, I ran so fast to pay my respects to you that I'm all out of breath. How do you do, Marya Antonovna?

MARYA.

Good afternoon, Piotr Ivanovich.

ANNA.

Well, tell me all about it. What is happening at the inn?

DOBCHINSKY.

I have a note for you from Anton Antonovich.

ANNA.

But who is he? A general?

DOBCHINSKY.

No, not a general, but every bit as good as a general, I tell you. Such culture! Such dignified manners!

ANNA.

Ah! So he is the same as the one my husband got a letter about.

DOBCHINSKY.

Exactly. It was Piotr Ivanovich and I who first discovered him.

ANNA.

Tell me, tell me all about it.

DOBCHINSKY.

It's all right now, thank the Lord. At first he received Anton Antonovich rather roughly. He was angry and said the inn was not run properly, and he wouldn't come to the Governor's house and he didn't want to go to jail on account of him. But then when he found out that Anton Antonovich was not to blame and they got to talking more intimately, he changed right away, and, thank Heaven, everything went well. They've gone now to inspect the philanthropic institutions. I confess that Anton Antonovich had already begun to suspect that a secret denunciation had been lodged against him. I myself was trembling a little, too.

ANNA.

What have you to be afraid of? You're not an official.

DOBCHINSKY.

Well, you see, when a Grand Mogul speaks, you feel afraid.

ANNA.

That's all rubbish. Tell me, what is he like personally? Is he young or old?

DOBCHINSKY.

Young—a young man of about twenty-three. But he talks as if he were older. "If you will allow me," he says, "I will go there and there." [Waves his hands.] He does it all with such distinction. "I like," he says, "to read and write, but I am prevented because my room is rather dark."

ANNA.

And what sort of a looking man is he, dark or fair?

DOBCHINSKY.

Neither. I should say rather chestnut. And his eyes dart about like little animals. They make you nervous.

ANNA.

Let me see what my husband writes. [Reads.] "I hasten to let you know, dear, that my position was extremely uncomfortable, but relying on the mercy of God, two pickles extra and a half portion of caviar, one ruble and twenty-five kopeks." [Stops.] I don't understand. What have pickles and caviar got to do with it?

DOBCHINSKY.

Oh, Anton Antonovich hurriedly wrote on a piece of scrap paper. There's a kind of bill on it.

ANNA.

Oh, yes, I see. [Goes on reading.] "But relying on the mercy of God, I believe all will turn out well in the end. Get a room ready quickly for the distinguished guest—the one with the gold wall paper. Don't bother to get any extras for dinner because we'll have something at the hospital with Artemy Filippovich. Order a little more wine, and tell Abdulin to send the best, or I'll wreck his whole cellar. I kiss your hand, my dearest, and remain yours, Anton Skvoznik-Dmukhanovsky." Oh my! I must hurry. Hello, who's there? Mishka?

DOBCHINSKY [Runs to the door and calls.] Mishka! Mishka! Mishka! [Mishka enters.]

ANNA.

Listen! Run over to Abdulin—wait, I'll give you a note. [She sits down at the table and writes, talking all the while.] Give this to Sidor, the coachman, and tell him to take it to Abdulin and bring back the wine. And get to work at once and make the gold room ready for a guest. Do it nicely. Put a bed in it, a wash basin and pitcher and everything else.

DOBCHINSKY.

Well, I'm going now, Anna Andreyevna, to see how he does the inspecting.

ANNA.

Go on, I'm not keeping you.

SCENE III

Anna Andreyevna and Marya Antonovna.

ANNA.

Now, Mashenka, we must attend to our toilet. He's a metropolitan swell and God forbid that he should make fun of us. You put on your blue dress with the little flounces. It's the most becoming.

MARYA.

The idea, mamma! The blue dress! I can't bear it. Liapkin-Tiapkin's wife wears blue and so does Zemlianika's daughter. I'd rather wear my flowered dress.

ANNA.

Your flowered dress! Of course, just to be contrary. You'll look lots better in blue because I'm going to wear my dun-colored dress. I love dun-color.

MARYA.

Oh, mamma, it isn't a bit becoming to you.

ANNA.

What, dun-color isn't becoming to me?

MARYA.

No, not a bit. I'm positive it isn't. One's eyes must be quite dark to go with dun-color.

ANNA.

That's nice! And aren't my eyes dark? They are as dark as can be. What nonsense you talk! How can they be anything but dark when I always draw the queen of clubs.

MARYA.

Why, mamma, you are more like the queen of hearts.

ANNA.

Nonsense! Perfect nonsense! I never was a queen of hearts. [She goes out hurriedly with Marya and speaks behind the scenes.] The ideas she gets into her head! Queen of hearts! Heavens! What do you think of that? As they go out, a door opens through which Mishka sweeps dirt on to the stage. Osip enters from another door with a valise on his head.

SCENE IV

Mishka and Osip.

OSIP.

Where is this to go?

MISHKA.

In here, in here.

OSIP.

Wait, let me fetch breath first. Lord! What a wretched life! On an empty stomach any load seems heavy.

MISHKA.

Say, uncle, will the general be here soon?

OSIP.

What general?

MISHKA.

Your master.

OSIP.

My master? What sort of a general is he?

MISHKA.

Isn't he a general?

OSIP.

Yes, he's a general, only the other way round.

MISHKA.

Is that higher or lower than a real general?

OSIP.

Higher.

MISHKA.

Gee whiz! That's why they are raising such a racket about him here.

OSIP.

Look here, young man, I see you're a smart fellow. Get me something to eat, won't you?

MISHKA.

There isn't anything ready yet for the likes of you. You won't eat plain food. When your master takes his meal, they'll let you have the same as he gets.

OSIP.

But have you got any plain stuff?

MISHKA.

We have cabbage soup, porridge and pie.

OSIP.

That's all right. We'll eat cabbage soup, porridge and pie, we'll eat everything. Come, help me with the valise. Is there another way to go out there?

MISHKA.

Yes.

They both carry the valise into the next room.

SCENE V

The Sergeants open both folding doors. Khlestakov enters followed by the Governor, then the Superintendent of Charities, the Inspector of Schools, Dobchinsky and Bobchinsky with a plaster on his nose. The Governor points to a piece of paper lying on the floor, and the Sergeants rush to pick it up, pushing each other in their haste.

KHLESTAKOV.

Excellent institutions. I like the way you show strangers everything in your town. In other towns they didn't show me a thing.

GOVERNOR.

In other towns, I venture to observe, the authorities and officials look out for themselves more. Here, I may say, we have no other thought than to win the Government's esteem through good order, vigilance, and efficiency.

KHLESTAKOV.

The lunch was excellent. I've positively overeaten. Do you set such a fine table every day?

GOVERNOR.

In honor of so agreeable a guest we do.

KHLESTAKOV.

I like to eat well. That's what a man lives for—to pluck the flowers of pleasure. What was that fish called?

ARTEMY [running up to him].

Labardan.

KHLESTAKOV.

It was delicious. Where was it we had our lunch? In the hospital, wasn't it?

ARTEMY.

Precisely, in the hospital.

KHLESTAKOV.

Yes, yes, I remember. There were beds there. The patients must have gotten well. There don't seem to have been many of them.

ARTEMY.

About ten are left. The rest recovered. The place is so well run, there is such perfect order. It may seem incredible to you, but ever since I've taken over the management, they all recover like flies. No sooner does a patient enter the hospital than he feels better. And we obtain this result not so much by medicaments as by honesty and orderliness.

GOVERNOR.

In this connection may I venture to call your attention to what a brain-racking job the office of Governor is. There are so many matters he has to give his mind to just in connection with keeping the town clean and repairs and alterations. In a word, it is enough to upset the most competent person. But, thank God, all goes well. Another governor, of course, would look out for his own advantage. But believe me, even nights in bed I keep thinking: "Oh, God, how could I manage things in such a way that the government would observe my devotion to duty and be satisfied?" Whether the government will reward me or not, that of course, lies with them. At least I'll have a clear conscience. When the whole town is in order, the streets swept clean, the prisoners well kept, and few drunkards—what more do I want? Upon my word, I don't even crave honors. Honors, of course, are alluring; but as against the happiness which comes from doing one's duty, they are nothing but dross and vanity.

ARTEMY [aside].

Oh, the do-nothing, the scoundrel! How he holds forth! I wish the Lord had blessed me with such a gift!

KHLESTAKOV.

That's so. I admit I sometimes like to philosophize, too. Sometimes it's prose, and sometimes it comes out poetry.

BOBCHINSKY [to Dobchinsky].

How true, how true it all is, Piotr Ivanovich. His remarks are great. It's evident that he is an educated man.

KHLESTAKOV.

Would you tell me, please, if you have any amusements here, any circles where one could have a game of cards?

GOVERNOR [aside].

Ahem! I know what you are aiming at, my boy. [Aloud.] God forbid! Why, no one here has even heard of such a thing as card-playing circles. I myself have never touched a card. I don't know how to play. I can never look at cards with indifference, and if I happen to see a king of diamonds or some such thing, I am so disgusted I have to spit out. Once I made a house of cards for the children, and then I dreamt of those confounded things the whole night. Heavens! How can people waste their precious time over cards!

LUKA LUKICH [aside].

But he faroed me out of a hundred rubles yesterday, the rascal.

GOVERNOR.

I'd rather employ my time for the benefit of the state.

KHLESTAKOV.

Oh, well, that's rather going too far. It all depends upon the point of view. If, for instance, you pass when you have to treble stakes, then of course—No, don't say that a game of cards isn't very tempting sometimes.

SCENE VI

The above, Anna Andreyevna and Marya Antonovna.

GOVERNOR.

Permit me to introduce my family, my wife and daughter.

KHLESTAKOV [bowing].

I am happy, madam, to have the pleasure of meeting you.

ANNA.

Our pleasure in meeting so distinguished a person is still greater.

KHLESTAKOV [showing off].

Excuse me, madam, on the contrary, my pleasure is the greater.

ANNA.

Impossible. You condescend to say it to compliment me. Won't you please sit down?

KHLESTAKOV.

Just to stand near you is bliss. But if you insist, I will sit down. I am so, so happy to be at your side at last.

ANNA.

I beg your pardon, but I dare not take all the nice things you say to myself. I suppose you must have found travelling very unpleasant after living in the capital.

KHLESTAKOV.

Extremely unpleasant. I am accustomed, comprenez-vous, to life in the fashionable world, and suddenly to find myself on the road, in dirty inns with dark rooms and rude people—I confess that if it were not for this chance which—[giving Anna a look and showing off] compensated me for everything—

ANNA.

It must really have been extremely unpleasant for you.

KHLESTAKOV.

At this moment, however, I find it exceedingly pleasant, madam.

ANNA.

Oh, I cannot believe it. You do me much honor. I don't deserve it.

KHLESTAKOV.

Why don't you deserve it? You do deserve it, madam.

ANNA.

I live in a village.

KHLESTAKOV.

Well, after all, a village too has something. It has its hills and brooks. Of course it's not to be compared with St. Petersburg. Ah, St. Petersburg! What a life, to be sure! Maybe you think I am only a copying clerk. No,

I am on a friendly footing with the chief of our department. He slaps me on the back. "Come, brother," he says, "and have dinner with me." I just drop in the office for a couple of minutes to say this is to be done so, and that is to be done that way. There's a rat of a clerk there for copying letters who does nothing but scribble all the time—tr, tr— They even wanted to make me a college assessor, but I think to myself, "What do I want it for?" And the doorkeeper flies after me on the stairs with the shoe brush. "Allow me to shine your boots for you, Ivan Aleksandrovich," he says. [To the Governor.] Why are you standing, gentleman? Please sit down.

{GOVERNOR. Our rank is such that we can very
Together { well stand. {ARTEMY. We don't mind standing.
{LUKA. Please don't trouble.

KHLESTAKOV.

Please sit down without the rank. [The Governor and the rest sit down.] I don't like ceremony. On the contrary, I always like to slip by unobserved. But it's impossible to conceal oneself, impossible. I no sooner show myself in a place than they say, "There goes Ivan Aleksandrovich!" Once I was even taken for the commander-in-chief. The soldiers rushed out of the guard-house and saluted. Afterwards an officer, an intimate acquaintance of mine, said to me: "Why, old chap, we completely mistook you for the commander-in-chief."

ANNA.

Well, I declare!

KHLESTAKOV.

I know pretty actresses. I've written a number of vaudevilles, you know. I frequently meet literary men. I am on an intimate footing with Pushkin. I often say to him: "Well, Pushkin, old boy, how goes it?" "So, so, partner," he'd reply, "as usual." He's a great original.

ANNA.

So you write too? How thrilling it must be to be an author! You write for the papers also, I suppose?

KHLESTAKOV.

Yes, for the papers, too. I am the author of a lot of works—The Marriage of Figaro, Robert le Diable, Norma. I don't even remember all the names. I did it just by chance. I hadn't meant to write, but a theatrical manager said, "Won't you please write something for me?" I thought to myself: "All right, why not?" So I did it all in one evening, surprised everybody. I am extraordinarily light of thought. All that has appeared under the name of Baron Brambeus was written by me, and the The Frigate of Hope and The Moscow Telegraph.

ANNA.

What! So you are Brambeus?

KHLESTAKOV.

Why, yes. And I revise and whip all their articles into shape. Smirdin gives me forty thousand for it.

ANNA.

I suppose, then, that Yury Miroslavsky is yours too.

KHLESTAKOV.

Yes, it's mine.

ANNA.

I guessed at once.

MARYA.

But, mamma, it says that it's by Zagoskin.

ANNA.

There! I knew you'd be contradicting even here.

KHLESTAKOV.

Oh, yes, it's so. That was by Zagoskin. But there is another Yury Miroslavsky which was written by me.

ANNA.

That's right. I read yours. It's charming.

KHLESTAKOV.

I admit I live by literature. I have the first house in St. Petersburg. It is well known as the house of Ivan Aleksandrovich. [Addressing the company in general.] If any of you should come to St. Petersburg, do please call to see me. I give balls, too, you know.

ANNA.

I can guess the taste and magnificence of those balls.

KHLESTAKOV.

Immense! For instance, watermelon will be served costing seven hundred rubles. The soup comes in the tureen straight from Paris by steamer. When the lid is raised, the aroma of the steam is like nothing

The Inspector-General

else in the world. And we have formed a circle for playing whist—the Minister of Foreign Affairs, the French, the English and the German Ambassadors and myself. We play so hard we kill ourselves over the cards. There's nothing like it. After it's over I'm so tired I run home up the stairs to the fourth floor and tell the cook, "Here, Marushka, take my coat"—What am I talking about?—I forgot that I live on the first floor. One flight up costs me—My foyer before I rise in the morning is an interesting spectacle indeed—counts and princes jostling each other and humming like bees. All you hear is buzz, buzz, buzz. Sometimes the Minister—[The Governor and the rest rise in awe from their chairs.] Even my mail comes addressed "Your Excellency." And once I even had charge of a department. A strange thing happened. The head of the department went off, disappeared, no one knew where. Of course there was a lot of talk about how the place would be filled, who would fill it, and all that sort of thing. There were ever so many generals hungry for the position, and they tried, but they couldn't cope with it. It's too hard. Just on the surface it looks easy enough; but when you come to examine it closely, it's the devil of a job. When they saw they couldn't manage, they came to me. In an instant the streets were packed full with couriers, nothing but couriers and couriers—thirty-five thousand of them, imagine! Pray, picture the situation to yourself! "Ivan Aleksandrovich, do come and take the directorship of the department." I admit I was a little embarrassed. I came out in my dressing-gown. I wanted to decline, but I thought it might reach the Czar's ears, and, besides, my official record—"Very well, gentlemen," I said, "I'll accept the position, I'll accept. So be it. But mind," I said, "na-na-na, LOOK SHARP is the word with me, LOOK SHARP!" And so it was. When I went through the offices of my department, it was a regular earthquake, Everyone trembled and shook like a leaf. [The Governor and the rest tremble with fright. Khlestakov works himself up more and more as he speaks.] Oh, I don't like to joke. I got all of them thoroughly scared, I tell you. Even the Imperial Council is afraid of me. And really, that's the sort I am. I don't spare anybody. I tell them all, "I know myself, I know myself." I am everywhere, everywhere. I go to Court daily. Tomorrow they are going to make me a field-marsh— He slips and almost falls, but is respectfully held up by the officials.

GOVERNOR [walks up to him trembling from top to toe and speaking with a great effort].

Your Ex-ex-ex- KHLESTAKOV [curtly]. What is it?
GOVERNOR.

Your Ex-ex-ex- KHLESTAKOV [as before]. I can't make out a thing, it's all nonsense.
GOVERNOR.

Your Ex-ex—Your 'lency—Your Excellency, wouldn't you like to rest a bit? Here's a room and everything you may need.
KHLESTAKOV.

Nonsense—rest! However, I'm ready for a rest. Your lunch was fine, gentlemen. I am satisfied, I am satisfied. [Declaiming.] Labardan! Labardan!

He goes into the next room followed by the Governor.

SCENE VII

The same without Khlestakov and the Governor.
BOBCHINSKY [to Dobchinsky].

There's a man for you, Piotr Ivanovich. That's what I call a man. I've never in my life been in the presence of so important a personage. I almost died of fright. What do you think is his rank, Piotr Ivanovich?
DOBCHINSKY.

I think he's almost a general.
BOBCHINSKY.

And I think a general isn't worth the sole of his boots. But if he is a general, then he must be the generalissimo himself. Did you hear how he bullies the Imperial Council? Come, let's hurry off to Ammos Fiodorovich and Korobkin and tell them about it. Good-by, Anna Andreyevna.
DOBCHINSKY.

Good afternoon, godmother.

Both go out.
ARTEMY.

It makes your heart sink and you don't know why. We haven't even our uniforms on. Suppose after he wakes up from his nap he goes and sends a report about us to St. Petersburg. [He goes out sunk in thought, with the School Inspector, both saying.] Good-by, madam.

SCENE VIII

Anna Andreyevna and Marya Antonovna.

ANNA.

Oh, how charming he is!

MARYA.

A perfect dear!

ANNA.

Such refined manners. You can recognize the big city article at once. How he carries himself, and all that sort of thing! Exquisite! I'm just crazy for young men like him. I am in ecstasies—beside myself. He liked me very much though. I noticed he kept looking at me all the time.

MARYA.

Oh, mamma, he looked at me.

ANNA.

No more nonsense please. It's out of place now.

MARYA.

But really, mamma, he did look at me.

ANNA.

There you go! For God's sake, don't argue. You mustn't. That's enough. What would he be looking at you for? Please tell me, why would he be looking at you?

MARYA.

It's true, mamma. He kept looking at me. He looked at me when he began to speak about literature and he looked at me afterwards, when he told about how he played whist with the ambassadors.

ANNA.

Well, maybe he looked at you once or twice and might have said to himself, "Oh, well, I'll give her a look."

SCENE IX

The same and the Governor.

GOVERNOR.
Sh-sh!

ANNA.
What is it?

GOVERNOR.
I wish I hadn't given him so much to drink. Suppose even half of what he said is true? [Sunk in thought.] How can it not be true? A man in his cups is always on the surface. What's in his heart is on his tongue. Of course he fibbed a little. No talking is possible without some lying. He plays cards with the ministers and he visits the Court. Upon my word the more you think the less you know what's going on in your head. I'm as dizzy as if I were standing in a belfry, or if I were going to be hanged, the devil take it!

ANNA.
And I didn't feel the least bit afraid. I simply saw a high-toned, cultured man of the world, and his rank and titles didn't make me feel a bit queer.

GOVERNOR.
Oh, well, you women. To say women and enough's said. Everything is froth and bubble to you. All of a sudden you blab out words that don't make the least sense. The worst you'd get would be a flogging; but it means ruination to the husband.—Say, my dear, you are as familiar with him as if he were another Bobchinsky.

ANNA.
Leave that to us. Don't bother about that. [Glancing at Marya.] We know a thing or two in that line.

GOVERNOR [to himself].
Oh, what's the good of talking to you! Confound it all! I can't get over my fright yet. [Opens the door and calls.] Mishka, tell the sergeants, Svistunov and Derzhimorda, to come here. They are near the gate. [After a pause of silence.] The world has turned into a queer place. If at least the people were visible so you could see them; but they are such a skinny, thin race. How in the world could you tell what he is? After

all you can tell a military man; but when he wears a frock-coat, it's like a fly with clipped wings. He kept it up a long time in the inn, got off a lot of allegories and ambiguities so that you couldn't make out head or tail. Now he's shown himself up at last.—Spouted even more than necessary. It's evident that he's a young man.

SCENE X

The same and Osip. All rush to meet Osip, beckoning to him.

ANNA.
Come here, my good man.
GOVERNOR.
Hush! Tell me, tell me, is he asleep?
OSIP.
No, not yet. He's stretching himself a little.
ANNA.
What's your name?
OSIP.
Osip, madam.
GOVERNOR [to his wife and daughter].
That'll do, that'll do. [To Osip.] Well, friend, did they give you a good meal?
OSIP.
Yes, sir, very good. Thank you kindly.
ANNA.
Your master has lots of counts and princes visiting him, hasn't he?
OSIP [aside].
What shall I say? Seeing as they've given me such good feed now, I s'pose they'll do even better later. [Aloud.] Yes, counts do visit him.
MARYA.
Osip, darling, isn't your master just grand?
ANNA.
Osip, please tell me, how is he—
GOVERNOR.
Do stop now. You just interfere with your silly talk. Well, friend, how—

ANNA.

What is your master's rank?

OSIP.

The usual rank.

GOVERNOR.

For God's sake, your stupid questions keep a person from getting down to business. Tell me, friend, what sort of a man is your master? Is he strict? Does he rag and bully a fellow—you know what I mean—does he or doesn't he?

OSIP.

Yes, he likes things to be just so. He insists on things being just so.

GOVERNOR.

I like your face. You must be a fine man, friend. What—?

ANNA.

Listen, Osip, does your master wear uniform in St. Petersburg?

GOVERNOR.

Enough of your tattle now, really. This is a serious matter, a matter of life and death. (To Osip.) Yes, friend, I like you very much. It's rather chilly now and when a man's travelling an extra glass of tea or so is rather welcome. So here's a couple of rubles for some tea.

OSIP [taking the money.] Thank you, much obliged to you, sir. God grant you health and long life. You've helped a poor man.

GOVERNOR.

That's all right. I'm glad to do it. Now, friend—

ANNA.

Listen, Osip, what kind of eyes does your master like most?

MARYA.

Osip, darling, what a dear nose your master has!

GOVERNOR.

Stop now, let me speak. [To Osip.] Tell me, what does your master care for most? I mean, when he travels what does he like?

OSIP.

As for sights, he likes whatever happens to come along. But what he likes most of all is to be received well and entertained well.

GOVERNOR.

Entertained well?

OSIP.
> Yes, for instance, I'm nothing but a serf and yet he sees to it that I should be treated well, too. S'help me God! Say we'd stop at some place and he'd ask, "Well, Osip, have they treated you well?" "No, badly, your Excellency." "Ah," he'd say, "Osip, he's not a good host. Remind me when we get home." "Oh, well," thinks I to myself [with a wave of his hand]. "I am a simple person. God be with them."

GOVERNOR.
> Very good. You talk sense. I've given you something for tea. Here's something for buns, too.

OSIP.
> You are too kind, your Excellency. [Puts the money in his pocket.] I'll sure drink your health, sir.

ANNA.
> Come to me, Osip, and I'll give you some, too.

MARYA.
> Osip, darling, kiss your master for me.

Khlestakov is heard to give a short cough in the next room.

GOVERNOR.
> Hush! [Rises on tip-toe. The rest of the conversation in the scene is carried on in an undertone.] Don't make a noise, for heaven's sake! Go, it's enough.

ANNA.
> Come, Mashenka, I'll tell you something I noticed about our guest that I can't tell you unless we are alone together. [They go out.]

GOVERNOR.
> Let them talk away. If you went and listened to them, you'd want to stop up your ears. [To Osip.] Well, friend—

SCENE XI

The same, Derzhimorda and Svistunov.

GOVERNOR.
> Sh—sh! Bandy-legged bears—thumping their boots on the floor! Bump, bump as if a thousand pounds were being unloaded from a wagon. Where in the devil have you been knocking about?

DERZHIMORDA.

I had your order—

GOVERNOR.

Hush! [Puts his hand over Derzhimorda's mouth.] Like a bull bellowing. [Mocking him.] "I had your order—" Makes a noise like an empty barrel. [To Osip.] Go, friend, and get everything ready for your master. And you two, you stand on the steps and don't you dare budge from the spot. And don't let any strangers enter the house, especially the merchants. If you let a single one in, I'll—The instant you see anybody with a petition, or even without a petition and he looks as if he wanted to present a petition against me, take him by the scruff of the neck, give him a good kick, [shows with his foot] and throw him out. Do you hear? Hush—hush!

He goes out on tiptoe, preceded by the Sergeants.

Curtain falls

ACT IV

SCENE: *Same as in Act III.*

SCENE I

Enter cautiously, almost on tiptoe, Ammos Fiodorovich, Artemy Filippovich, the Postmaster, Luka Lukich, Dobchinsky and Bobchinsky in full dress-uniform.

AMMOS.
> For God's sake, gentlemen, quick, form your line, and let's have more order. Why, man alive, he goes to Court and rages at the Imperial Council. Draw up in military line, strictly in military line. You, Piotr Ivanovich, take your place there, and you, Piotr Ivanovich, stand here. [Both the Piotr Ivanoviches run on tiptoe to the places indicated.]

ARTEMY.

Do as you please, Ammos Fiodorovich, I think we ought to try.

AMMOS.

Try what?

ARTEMY.

It's clear what.

AMMOS.

Grease?

ARTEMY.

Exactly, grease.

AMMOS.

It's risky, the deuce take it. He'll fly into a rage at us. He's a government official, you know. Perhaps it should be given to him in the form of a gift from the nobility for some sort of memorial?

POSTMASTER.

Or, perhaps, tell him some money has been sent here by post and we don't know for whom?

ARTEMY.

You had better look out that he doesn't send you by post a good long ways off. Look here, things of such a nature are not done this way in a well-ordered state. What's the use of a whole regiment here? We must present ourselves to him one at a time, and do—what ought to be done, you know—so that eyes do not see and ears do not hear. That's the way things are done in a well-ordered society. You begin it, Ammos Fiodorovich, you be the first.

AMMOS.

You had better go first. The distinguished guest has eaten in your institution.

ARTEMY.

Then Luka Lukich, as the enlightener of youth, should go first.

LUKA.

I can't, I can't, gentlemen. I confess I am so educated that the moment an official a single degree higher than myself speaks to me, my heart stands still and I get as tongue-tied as though my tongue were caught in the mud. No, gentlemen, excuse me. Please let me off.

ARTEMY.
> It's you who have got to do it, Ammos Fiodorovich. There's no one else. Why, every word you utter seems to be issuing from Cicero's mouth.

AMMOS.
> What are you talking about! Cicero! The idea! Just because a man sometimes waxes enthusiastic over house dogs or hunting hounds.

ALL [pressing him].
> No, not over dogs, but the Tower of Babel, too. Don't forsake us, Ammos Fiodorovich, help us. Be our Saviour!

AMMOS.
> Let go of me, gentlemen.
>
> Footsteps and coughing are heard in Khlestakov's room. All hurry to the door, crowding and jostling in their struggle to get out. Some are uncomfortably squeezed, and half-suppressed cries are heard.

BOBCHINSKY'S VOICE.
> Oh, Piotr Ivanovich, you stepped on my foot.

ARTEMY.
> Look out, gentlemen, look out. Give me a chance to atone for my sins. You are squeezing me to death.
>
> Exclamations of "Oh! Oh!" Finally they all push through the door, and the stage is left empty.

SCENE II

Enter Khlestakov, looking sleepy.

KHLESTAKOV [alone].
> I seem to have had a fine snooze. Where did they get those mattresses and feather beds from? I even perspired. After the meal yesterday they must have slipped something into me that knocked me out. I still feel a pounding in my head. I see I can have a good time here. I like hospitality, and I must say I like it all the more if people entertain me out of a pure heart and not from interested motives. The Governor's daughter is not a bad one at all, and the mother is also a woman you can still—I don't know, but I do like this sort of life.

SCENE III

Khlestakov and the Judge.

JUDGE [comes in and stops. Talking to himself].

Oh, God, bring me safely out of this! How my knees are knocking together! [Drawing himself up and holding the sword in his hand. Aloud.] I have the honor to present myself—Judge of the District Court here, College Assessor Liapkin-Tiapkin.

KHLESTAKOV.

Please be seated. So you are the Judge here?

JUDGE.

I was elected by the nobility in 1816 and I have served ever since.

KHLESTAKOV.

Does it pay to be a judge?

JUDGE.

After serving three terms I was decorated with the Vladimir of the third class with the approval of the government. [Aside.] I have the money in my hand and my hand is on fire.

KHLESTAKOV.

I like the Vladimir. Anna of the third class is not so nice.

JUDGE [slightly extending his balled fist. Aside].

Good God! I don't know where I'm sitting. I feel as though I were on burning coals.

KHLESTAKOV.

What have you got in your hand there?

AMMOS [getting all mixed up and dropping the bills on the floor].

Nothing.

KHLESTAKOV.

How so, nothing? I see money has dropped out of it.

AMMOS [shaking all over].

Oh no, oh no, not at all! [Aside.] Oh, Lord! Now I'm under arrest and they've brought a wagon to take me.

KHLESTAKOV.

Yes, it IS money. [Picking it up.]

AMMOS [aside].

It's all over with me. I'm lost! I'm lost!

KHLESTAKOV.

I tell you what—lend it to me.

AMMOS [eagerly].

Why, of course, of course—with the greatest pleasure. [Aside.] Bolder! Bolder! Holy Virgin, stand by me!

KHLESTAKOV.

I've run out of cash on the road, what with one thing and another, you know. I'll let you have it back as soon as I get to the village.

AMMOS.

Please don't mention it! It is a great honor to have you take it. I'll try to deserve it—by putting forth the best of my feeble powers, by my zeal and ardor for the government. [Rises from the chair and draws himself up straight with his hands hanging at his sides.] I will not venture to disturb you longer with my presence. You don't care to give any orders?

KHLESTAKOV.

What orders?

JUDGE.

I mean, would you like to give orders for the district court here?

KHLESTAKOV.

What for? I have nothing to do with the court now. No, nothing. Thank you very much.

AMMOS [bowing and leaving. Aside.].

Now the town is ours.

KHLESTAKOV.

The Judge is a fine fellow.

SCENE IV

Khlestakov and the Postmaster.

POSTMASTER [in uniform, sword in hand. Drawing himself up].

I have the honor to present myself—Postmaster, Court Councilor Shpekin.

KHLESTAKOV.

I'm glad to meet you. I like pleasant company very much. Take a seat. Do you live here all the time?

POSTMASTER.

    Yes, sir. Quite so.

KHLESTAKOV.

    I like this little town. Of course, there aren't many people. It's not very lively. But what of it? It isn't the capital. Isn't that so—it isn't the capital?

POSTMASTER.

    Quite so, quite so.

KHLESTAKOV.

    It's only in the capital that you find bon-ton and not a lot of provincial lubbers. What is your opinion? Isn't that so?

POSTMASTER.

    Quite so. [Aside.] He isn't a bit proud. He inquires about everything.

KHLESTAKOV.

    And yet you'll admit that one can live happily in a little town.

POSTMASTER.

    Quite so.

KHLESTAKOV.

    In my opinion what you want is this—you want people to respect you and to love you sincerely. Isn't that so?

POSTMASTER.

    Exactly.

KHLESTAKOV.

    I'm glad you agree with me. Of course, they call me queer. But that's the kind of character I am. [Looking him in the face and talking to himself.] I think I'll ask this postmaster for a loan. [Aloud.] A strange accident happened to me and I ran out of cash on the road. Can you lend me three hundred rubles?

POSTMASTER.

    Of course. I shall esteem it a piece of great good fortune. I am ready to serve you with all my heart.

KHLESTAKOV.

    Thank you very much. I must say, I hate like the devil to deny myself on the road. And why should I? Isn't that so?

POSTMASTER.

Quite so. [Rises, draws himself up, with his sword in his hand.] I'll not venture to disturb you any more. Would you care to make any remarks about the post office administration?

KHLESTAKOV.

No, nothing.

The Postmaster bows and goes out.

KHLESTAKOV [lighting a cigar].

It seems to me the Postmaster is a fine fellow, too. He's certainly obliging. I like people like that.

SCENE V

Khlestakov and Luka Lukich, who is practically pushed in on the stage. A voice behind him is heard saying nearly aloud, "Don't be chickenhearted."

LUKA [drawing himself up, trembling, with his hand on his sword].

I have the honor to present myself—School Inspector, Titular Councilor Khlopov.

KHLESTAKOV.

I'm glad to see you. Take a seat, take a seat. Will you have a cigar? [Offers him a cigar.]

LUKA [to himself, hesitating].

There now! That's something I hadn't anticipated. To take or not to take?

KHLESTAKOV.

Take it, take it. It's a pretty good cigar. Of course not what you get in St. Petersburg. There I used to smoke twenty-five cent cigars. You feel like kissing yourself after having smoked one of them. Here, light it. [Hands him a candle.]

Luka Lukich tries to light the cigar shaking all over.

KHLESTAKOV.

Not that end, the other.

LUKA [drops the cigar from fright, spits and shakes his hands. Aside].

Confound it! My damned timidity has ruined me!

KHLESTAKOV.

I see you are not a lover of cigars. I confess smoking is my weakness—smoking and the fair sex. Not for the life of me can I remain indifferent to the fair sex. How about you? Which do you like more, brunettes or blondes?

Luka Lukich remains silent, at a complete loss what to say.

KHLESTAKOV.

Tell me frankly, brunettes or blondes?

LUKA.

I don't dare to know.

KHLESTAKOV.

No, no, don't evade. I'm bound to know your taste.

LUKA.

I venture to report to you—[Aside.] I don't know what I'm saying.

KHLESTAKOV.

Ah, you don't want to say. I suppose some little brunette or other has cast a spell over you. Confess, she has, hasn't she?

Luka Lukich remains silent.

KHLESTAKOV.

Ah, you're blushing. You see. Why don't you speak?

LUKA.

I'm scared, your Hon—High—Ex—[Aside.] Done for! My confounded tongue has undone me!

KHLESTAKOV.

You're scared? There IS something awe-inspiring in my eyes, isn't there? At least I know not a single woman can resist them. Isn't that so?

LUKA.

Exactly.

KHLESTAKOV.

A strange thing happened to me on the road. I ran entirely out of cash. Can you lend me three hundred rubles?

LUKA [clutching his pockets. Aside].

A fine business if I haven't got the money! I have! I have! [Takes out the bills and gives them to him, trembling.]

KHLESTAKOV.

Thank you very much.

LUKA [drawing himself up, with his hand on his sword].

I will not venture to disturb you with my presence any longer.

KHLESTAKOV.

Good-by.

LUKA [dashes out almost at a run, saying aside.] Well, thank the Lord! Maybe he won't inspect the schools.

SCENE VI

Khlestakov and Artemy Filippovich.

ARTEMY [enters and draws himself up, his hand on his sword].

I have the honor to present myself—Superintendent of Charities, Court Councilor Zemlianika.

KHLESTAKOV.

Howdeedo? Please sit down.

ARTEMY.

I had the honor of receiving you and personally conducting you through the philanthropic institutions committed to my care.

KHLESTAKOV.

Oh, yes, I remember. You treated me to a dandy lunch.

ARTEMY.

I am glad to do all I can in behalf of my country.

KHLESTAKOV.

I admit, my weakness is a good cuisine.—Tell me, please, won't you—it seems to me you were a little shorter yesterday, weren't you?

ARTEMY.

Quite possible. [After a pause.] I may say I spare myself no pains and perform the duties of my office with the utmost zeal. [Draws his chair closer and speaks in a lowered tone.] There's the postmaster, for example, he does absolutely nothing. Everything is in a fearful state of neglect. The mail is held up. Investigate for yourself, if you please, and you will see. The Judge, too, the man who was here just now, does nothing but hunt hares, and he keeps his dogs in the court rooms, and his conduct, if I must confess—and for the benefit of the fatherland, I must confess, though he is my relative and friend—his conduct is in the highest degree reprehensible. There is a squire here by the name of Dobchinsky, whom you were pleased to see. Well, the moment Dobchinsky leaves the house, the Judge is there with Dobchinsky's wife. I can swear to it. You just take a look at the children. Not one of them resembles Dobchinsky. All of them, even the little girl, are the very image of the Judge.

KHLESTAKOV.

You don't say so. I never imagined it.

ARTEMY.

Then take the School Inspector here. I don't know how the government could have entrusted him with such an office. He's worse than a Jacobin freethinker, and he instils such pernicious ideas into the minds of the young that I can hardly describe it. Hadn't I better put it all down on paper, if you so order?

KHLESTAKOV.

Very well, why not? I should like it very much. I like to kill the weary hours reading something amusing, you know. What is your name? I keep forgetting.

ARTEMY.

Zemlianika.

KHLESTAKOV.

Oh, yes, Zemlianika. Tell me, Mr. Zemlianika, have you any children?

ARTEMY.

Of course. Five. Two are already grown up.

KHLESTAKOV.

You don't say! Grown up! And how are they—how are they—a—a?

ARTEMY.

You mean that you deign to ask what their names are?

KHLESTAKOV.

Yes, yes, what are their names?

ARTEMY.

Nikolay, Ivan, Yelizaveta, Marya and Perepetuya.

KHLESTAKOV.

Good.

ARTEMY.

I don't venture to disturb you any longer with my presence and rob you of your time dedicated to the performance of your sacred duties— [Bows and makes to go.]

KHLESTAKOV [escorting him].

Not at all. What you told me is all very funny. Call again, please. I like that sort of thing very much. [Turns back and reopens the door, calling.] I say, there! What is your——I keep forgetting. What is your first name and your patronymic?

ARTEMY.

Artemy Filippovich.

KHLESTAKOV.

Do me a favor, Artemy Filippovich. A curious accident happened to me on the road. I've run entirely out of cash. Have you four hundred rubles to lend me?

ARTEMY.

I have.

KHLESTAKOV.

That comes in pat. Thank you very much.

SCENE VII

Khlestakov, Bobchinsky, and Dobchinsky.

BOBCHINSKY.

I have the honor to present myself—a resident of this town, Piotr, son of Ivan Bobchinsky.

DOBCHINSKY.

I am Piotr, son of Ivan Dobchinsky, a squire.

KHLESTAKOV.

Oh, yes, I've met you before. I believe you fell? How's your nose?

BOBCHINSKY.

It's all right. Please don't trouble. It's dried up, dried up completely.

KHLESTAKOV.

That's nice. I'm glad it's dried up. [Suddenly and abruptly.] Have you any money?

DOBCHINSKY.

Money? How's that—money?

KHLESTAKOV.

A thousand rubles to lend me.

BOBCHINSKY.

Not so much as that, honest to God I haven't. Have you, Piotr Ivanovich?

DOBCHINSKY.

I haven't got it with me, because my money—I beg to inform you—is deposited in the State Savings Bank.

KHLESTAKOV.

Well, if you haven't a thousand, then a hundred.

BOBCHINSKY [fumbling in his pockets].

Have you a hundred rubles, Piotr Ivanovich? All I have is forty.

DOBCHINSKY [examining his pocket-book].

I have only twenty-five.

BOBCHINSKY.

Look harder, Piotr Ivanovich. I know you have a hole in your pocket, and the money must have dropped down into it somehow.

DOBCHINSKY.

No, honestly, there isn't any in the hole either.

KHLESTAKOV.

Well, never mind. I merely mentioned the matter. Sixty-five will do. [Takes the money.]

DOBCHINSKY.

May I venture to ask a favor of you concerning a very delicate matter?

KHLESTAKOV.

What is it?

DOBCHINSKY.

It's a matter of an extremely delicate nature. My oldest son—I beg to inform you—was born before I was married.

KHLESTAKOV.

Indeed?

DOBCHINSKY.

That is, only in a sort of way. He is really my son, just as if he had been born in wedlock. I made up everything afterwards, set everything right, as it should be, with the bonds of matrimony, you know. Now, I venture to inform you, I should like to have him altogether—that is, I should like him to be altogether my legitimate son and be called Dobchinsky the same as I.

KHLESTAKOV.

That's all right. Let him be called Dobchinsky. That's possible.

DOBCHINSKY.

I shouldn't have troubled you; but it's a pity, he is such a talented youngster. He gives the greatest promise. He can recite different poems by heart; and whenever he gets hold of a penknife, he makes little carriages as skilfully as a conjurer. Here's Piotr Ivanovich. He knows. Am I not right?

BOBCHINSKY.

Yes, the lad is very talented.

KHLESTAKOV.

All right, all right. I'll try to do it for you. I'll speak to—I hope—it'll be done, it'll all be done. Yes, yes. [Turning to Bobchinsky.] Have you anything you'd like to say to me?

BOBCHINSKY.

Why, of course. I have a most humble request to make.

KHLESTAKOV.

What is it?

BOBCHINSKY.

I beg your Highness or your Excellency most worshipfully, when you get back to St. Petersburg, please tell all the high personages there, the senators and the admirals, that Piotr Ivanovich Bobchinsky lives in this town. Say this: "Piotr Ivanovich lives there."

KHLESTAKOV.

Very well.

BOBCHINSKY.

And if you should happen to speak to the Czar, then tell him, too: "Your Majesty," tell him, "Your Majesty, Piotr Ivanovich Bobchinsky lives in this town."

KHLESTAKOV.

Very well.

BOBCHINSKY.

Pardon me for having troubled you with my presence.

KHLESTAKOV.

Not at all, not at all. It was my pleasure. [Sees them to the door.]

SCENE VIII

KHLESTAKOV [alone].

My, there are a lot of officials here. They seem to be taking me for a government functionary. To be sure, I threw dust in their eyes yesterday. What a bunch of fools! I'll write all about it to Triapichkin in St. Petersburg. He'll write them up in the papers. Let him give them a nice walloping.—Ho, Osip, give me paper and ink.

OSIP [looking in at the door].

D'rectly.

KHLESTAKOV.

Anybody gets caught in Triapichkin's tongue had better look out. For the sake of a witticism he wouldn't spare his own father. They are good people though, these officials. It's a nice trait of theirs to lend me money. I'll just see how much it all mounts up to. Here's three hundred from the Judge and three hundred from the Postmaster—six hundred, seven hundred, eight hundred—What a greasy bill!—Eight hundred, nine hundred.—Oho! Rolls up to more than a thousand! Now, if I get you, captain, now! We'll see who'll do whom!

SCENE IX

Khlestakov and Osip entering with paper and ink.

KHLESTAKOV.

Now, you simpleton, you see how they receive and treat me. [Begins to write.]

OSIP.

Yes, thank God! But do you know what, Ivan Aleksandrovich?

KHLESTAKOV.

What?

OSIP.

Leave this place. Upon my word, it's time.

KHLESTAKOV [writing].

What nonsense! Why?

OSIP.

Just so. God be with them. You've had a good time here for two days. It's enough. What's the use of having anything more to do with them? Spit on them. You don't know what may happen. Somebody else may turn up. Upon my word, Ivan Aleksandrovich. And the horses here are fine. We'll gallop away like a breeze.

KHLESTAKOV [writing].

No, I'd like to stay a little longer. Let's go tomorrow.

OSIP.

Why tomorrow? Let's go now, Ivan Aleksandrovich, now, 'pon my word. To be sure, it's a great honor and all that. But really we'd better go as quick as we can. You see, they've taken you for somebody else, honest. And your dad will be angry because you dilly-dallied so long. We'd gallop off so smartly. They'd give us first-class horses here.

KHLESTAKOV [writing].

All right. But first take this letter to the postoffice, and, if you like, order post horses at the same time. Tell the postilions that they should drive like couriers and sing songs, and I'll give them a ruble each. [Continues to write.] I wager Triapichkin will die laughing.

OSIP.

I'll send the letter off by the man here. I'd rather be packing in the meanwhile so as to lose no time.

KHLESTAKOV.

All right. Bring me a candle.

OSIP [outside the door, where he is heard speaking].

Say, partner, go to the post office and mail a letter, and tell the postmaster to frank it. And have a coach sent round at once, the very best courier coach; and tell them the master doesn't pay fare. He travels at the expense of the government. And make them hurry, or else the master will be angry. Wait, the letter isn't ready yet.

KHLESTAKOV.

I wonder where he lives now, on Pochtamtskaya or Grokhovaya Street. He likes to move often, too, to get out of paying rent. I'll make a guess and send it to Pochtamtskaya Street. [Folds the letter and addresses it.]

Osip brings the candle. Khlestakov seals the letter with sealing wax. At that moment Derzhimorda's voice is heard saying: "Where are you going, whiskers? You've been told that nobody is allowed to come in."

KHLESTAKOV [giving the letter to Osip].

There, have it mailed.

MERCHANT'S VOICE.

Let us in, brother. You have no right to keep us out. We have come on business.

DERZHIMORDA'S VOICE.

Get out of here, get out of here! He doesn't receive anybody. He's asleep.

The disturbance outside grows louder.

KHLESTAKOV.

What's the matter there, Osip? See what the noise is about.

OSIP [looking through the window].

There are some merchants there who want to come in, and the sergeant won't let them. They are waving papers. I suppose they want to see you.

KHLESTAKOV [going to the window].

What is it, friends?

MERCHANT'S VOICE.

We appeal for your protection. Give orders, your Lordship, that our petitions be received.

KHLESTAKOV.

Let them in, let them in. Osip, tell them to come in.

Osip goes out.

KHLESTAKOV [takes the petitions through the window, unfolds one of them and reads].

"To his most honorable, illustrious financial Excellency, from the merchant Abdulin. . . ." The devil knows what this is! There's no such title.

SCENE X

Khlestakov and Merchants, with a basket of wine and sugar loaves.

KHLESTAKOV.

What is it, friends?

MERCHANTS.

We beseech your favor.

KHLESTAKOV.

What do you want?

MERCHANTS.

Don't ruin us, your Worship. We suffer insult and wrong wholly without cause.

KHLESTAKOV.

From whom?

A MERCHANT.

Why, from our governor here. Such a governor there never was yet in the world, your Worship. No words can describe the injuries he inflicts upon us. He has taken the bread out of our mouths by quartering soldiers on us, so that you might as well put your neck in a noose. He doesn't treat you as you deserve. He catches hold of your beard and says, "Oh, you Tartar!" Upon my word, if we had shown him any disrespect, but we obey all the laws and regulations. We don't mind giving him what his wife and daughter need for their clothes, but no, that's not enough. So help me God! He comes to our shop and takes whatever his eyes fall on. He sees a piece of cloth and says, "Oh, my friends, that's a fine piece of goods. Take it to my house." So we take it to his house. It will be almost forty yards.

KHLESTAKOV.

Is it possible? My, what a swindler!

MERCHANTS.

So help us God! No one remembers a governor like him. When you see him coming you hide everything in the shop. It isn't only that he wants a few delicacies and fineries. He takes every bit of trash, too—prunes that have been in the barrel seven years and that even the boy in my shop would not eat, and he grabs a fist full. His name day is St. Anthony's, and you'd think there's nothing else left in the world to bring him and that he doesn't want any more. But no, you must give him more. He says St. Onufry's is also his name day. What's to be done? You have to take things to him on St. Onufry's day, too.

KHLESTAKOV.

Why, he's a plain robber.

MERCHANTS.

Yes, indeed! And try to contradict him, and he'll fill your house with a whole regiment of soldiers. And if you say anything, he orders the doors closed. "I won't inflict corporal punishment on you," he says, "or put you in the rack. That's forbidden by law," he says. "But I'll make you swallow salt herring, my good man."

KHLESTAKOV.

What a swindler! For such things a man can be sent to Siberia.

MERCHANTS.

It doesn't matter where you are pleased to send him. Only the farthest away from here the better. Father, don't scorn to accept our bread and salt. We pay our respects to you with sugar and a basket of wine.

KHLESTAKOV.

No, no. Don't think of it. I don't take bribes. Oh, if, for example, you would offer me a loan of three hundred rubles, that's quite different. I am willing to take a loan.

MERCHANTS.

If you please, father. [They take out money.] But what is three hundred? Better take five hundred. Only help us.

KHLESTAKOV.

Very well. About a loan I won't say a word. I'll take it.

MERCHANTS [proffering him the money on a silver tray].

Do please take the tray, too.

KHLESTAKOV.

Very well. I can take the tray, too.

MERCHANTS [bowing].

Then take the sugar at the same time.

KHLESTAKOV.

Oh, no. I take no bribes.

OSIP.

Why don't you take the sugar, your Highness? Take it. Everything will come in handy on the road. Give here the sugar and that case. Give them here. It'll all be of use. What have you got there—a string? Give it here. A string will be handy on the road, too, if the coach or something else should break—for tying it up.

MERCHANTS.

Do us this great favor, your illustrious Highness. Why, if you don't help us in our appeal to you, then we simply don't know how we are to exist. We might as well put our necks in a noose.

KHLESTAKOV.

Positively, positively. I shall exert my efforts in your behalf.

[The Merchants leave. A woman's voice is heard saying:]

"Don't you dare not to let me in. I'll make a complaint against you to him himself. Don't push me that way. It hurts."

KHLESTAKOV.

Who is there? [Goes to the window.] What is it, mother?

[Two women's voices are heard:] "We beseech your grace, father. Give orders, your Lordship, for us to be heard."

KHLESTAKOV.

Let her in.

SCENE XI

Khlestakov, the Locksmith's Wife, and the non-commissioned Officer's Widow.

LOCK.'S WIFE [kneeling].

I beseech your grace.

WIDOW.

I beseech your grace.

KHLESTAKOV.

Who are you?

WIDOW.

Ivanova, widow of a non-commissioned officer.

LOCK.'S WIFE.

Fevronya Petrova Poshliopkina, the wife of a locksmith, a burgess of this town. My father—

KHLESTAKOV.

Stop! One at a time. What do you want?

LOCK.'S WIFE.

I beg for your grace. I beseech your aid against the governor. May God send all evil upon him. May neither he nor his children nor his uncles nor his aunts ever prosper in any of their undertakings.

KHLESTAKOV.

What's the matter?

LOCK.'S WIFE.

He ordered my husband to shave his forehead as a soldier, and our turn hadn't come, and it is against the law, my husband being a married man.

KHLESTAKOV.

How could he do it, then?

LOCK.'S WIFE.

He did it, he did it, the blackguard! May God smite him both in this world and the next. If he has an aunt, may all harm descend upon her. And if his father is living, may the rascal perish, may he choke to death. Such a cheat! The son of the tailor should have been levied. And he is a drunkard, too. But his parents gave the governor a rich present, so he fastened on the son of the tradeswoman, Panteleyeva. And Panteleyeva also sent his wife three pieces of linen. So then he comes to me. "What do you want your husband for?" he says. "He isn't any good to you any more." It's for me to know whether he is any good or not. That's my business. The old cheat! "He's a thief," he says. "Although he hasn't stolen anything, that doesn't matter. He is going to steal. And he'll be recruited next year anyway." How can I do without a husband? I am not a strong woman. The skunk! May none of his kith and kin ever see the light of God. And if he has a mother-in-law, may she, too,—

KHLESTAKOV.

All right, all right. Well, and you?

[Addressing the Widow and leading the Locksmith's Wife to the door.]

LOCK.'S WIFE [leaving].

Don't forget, father. Be kind and gracious to me.

WIDOW.

I have come to complain against the Governor, father.

KHLESTAKOV.

What is it? What for? Be brief.

WIDOW.

He flogged me, father.

KHLESTAKOV.

How so?

WIDOW.

By mistake, my father. Our women got into a squabble in the market, and when the police came, it was all over, and they took me and reported me—I couldn't sit down for two days.

KHLESTAKOV.

But what's to be done now?

WIDOW.

There's nothing to be done, of course. But if you please, order him to pay a fine for the mistake. I can't undo my luck. But the money would be very useful to me now.

KHLESTAKOV.

All right, all right. Go now, go. I'll see to it. [Hands with petitions are thrust through the window.] Who else is out there? [Goes to the window.] No, no. I don't want to, I don't want to. [Leaves the window.] I'm sick of it, the devil take it! Don't let them in, Osip.

OSIP [calling through the window].

Go away, go away! He has no time. Come tomorrow.

The door opens and a figure appears in a shag cloak, with unshaven beard, swollen lip, and a bandage over his cheek. Behind him appear a whole line of others.

OSIP.

Go away, go away! What are you crowding in here for?

He puts his hands against the stomach of the first one, and goes out through the door, pushing him and banging the door behind.

SCENE XII

Khlestakov and Marya Antonovna.

MARYA.

Oh!

KHLESTAKOV.

What frightened you so, mademoiselle?

MARYA.
>I wasn't frightened.

KHLESTAKOV [showing off].
>Please, miss. It's a great pleasure to me that you took me for a man who—May I venture to ask you where you were going?

MARYA.
>I really wasn't going anywhere.

KHLESTAKOV.
>But why weren't you going anywhere?

MARYA.
>I was wondering whether mamma was here.

KHLESTAKOV.
>No. I'd like to know why you weren't going anywhere.

MARYA.
>I should have been in your way. You were occupied with important matters.

KHLESTAKOV [showing off].
>Your eyes are better than important matters. You cannot possibly disturb me. No, indeed, by no means. On the contrary, you afford me great pleasure.

MARYA.
>You speak like a man from the capital.

KHLESTAKOV.
>For such a beautiful lady as you. May I give myself the pleasure of offering you a chair? But no, you should have, not a chair, but a throne.

MARYA.
>I really don't know—I really must go [She sits down.]

KHLESTAKOV.
>What a beautiful scarf that is.

MARYA.
>You are making fun of me. You're only ridiculing the provincials.

KHLESTAKOV.
>Oh, mademoiselle, how I long to be your scarf, so that I might embrace your lily neck.

MARYA.

I haven't the least idea what you are talking about—scarf!—Peculiar weather today, isn't it?

KHLESTAKOV.

Your lips, mademoiselle, are better than any weather.

MARYA.

You are just saying that—I should like to ask you—I'd rather you would write some verses in my album for a souvenir. You must know very many.

KHLESTAKOV.

Anything you desire, mademoiselle. Ask! What verses will you have?

MARYA.

Any at all. Pretty, new verses.

KHLESTAKOV.

Oh, what are verses! I know a lot of them.

MARYA.

Well, tell me. What verses will you write for me?

KHLESTAKOV.

What's the use? I know them anyway.

MARYA.

I love them so.

KHLESTAKOV.

I have lots of them—of every sort. If you like, for example, I'll give you this: "Oh, thou, mortal man, who in thy anguish murmurest against God—" and others. I can't remember them now. Besides, it's all bosh. I'd rather offer you my love instead, which ever since your first glance—[Moves his chair nearer.]

MARYA.

Love? I don't understand love. I never knew what love is. [Moves her chair away.]

KHLESTAKOV.

Why do you move your chair away? It is better for us to sit near each other.

MARYA [moving away].

Why near? It's all the same if it's far away.

KHLESTAKOV [moving nearer].

Why far? It's all the same if it's near.

MARYA [moving away].

But what for?

KHLESTAKOV [moving nearer].

It only seems near to you. Imagine it's far. How happy I would be, mademoiselle, if I could clasp you in my embrace.

MARYA [looking through the window].

What is that? It looked as if something had flown by. Was it a magpie or some other bird?

KHLESTAKOV [kisses her shoulder and looks through the window].

It's a magpie.

MARYA [rises indignantly].

No, that's too much—Such rudeness, such impertinence.

KHLESTAKOV [holding her back].

Forgive me, mademoiselle. I did it only out of love—only out of love, nothing else.

MARYA.

You take me for a silly provincial wench. [Struggles to go away.]

KHLESTAKOV [still holding her back].

It's out of love, really—out of love. It was just a little fun. Marya Antonovna, don't be angry. I'm ready to beg your forgiveness on my knees. [Falls on his knees.] Forgive me, do forgive me! You see, I am on my knees.

SCENE XIII

The same and Anna Andreyevna.

ANNA [seeing Khlestakov on his knees].

Oh, what a situation!

KHLESTAKOV [rising].

Oh, the devil!

ANNA [to Marya].

What does this mean? What does this behavior mean?

MARYA.

I, mother—

ANNA.

Go away from here. Do you hear? And don't you dare to show your face to me. [Marya goes out in tears.] Excuse me. I must say I'm greatly astonished.

KHLESTAKOV [aside].

She's very appetizing, too. She's not bad-looking, either. [Flings himself on his knees.] Madam, you see I am burning with love.

ANNA.

What! You on your knees? Please get up, please get up. This floor isn't very clean.

KHLESTAKOV.

No, I must be on my knees before you. I must. Pronounce the verdict. Is it life or death?

ANNA.

But please—I don't quite understand the significance of your words. If I am not mistaken, you are making a proposal for my daughter.

KHLESTAKOV.

No, I am in love with you. My life hangs by a thread. If you don't crown my steadfast love, then I am not fit to exist in this world. With a burning flame in my bosom, I pray for your hand.

ANNA.

But please remember I am in a certain way—married.

KHLESTAKOV.

That's nothing. Love knows no distinction. It was Karamzin who said: "The laws condemn." We will fly in the shadow of a brook. Your hand! I pray for your hand!

SCENE XIV

The same and Marya Antonovna.

MARYA [running in suddenly].

Mamma, papa says you should—[seeing Khlestakov on his knees, exclaims:] Oh, what a situation!

ANNA.

Well, what do you want? Why did you come in here? What for? What sort of flightiness is this? Breaks in like a cat leaping out of smoke.

Well, what have you found so wonderful? What's gotten into your head again? Really, she behaves like a child of three. She doesn't act a bit like a girl of eighteen, not a bit. I don't know when you'll get more sense into your head, when you'll behave like a decent, well-bred girl, when you'll know what good manners are and a proper demeanor.

MARYA [through her tears].

Mamma, I really didn't know—

ANNA.

There's always a breeze blowing through your head. You act like Liapkin-Tiapkin's daughter. Why should you imitate them? You shouldn't imitate them. You have other examples to follow. You have your mother before you. She's the example to follow.

KHLESTAKOV [seizing Marya's hand].

Anna Andreyevna, don't oppose our happiness. Give your blessing to our constant love.

ANNA [in surprise].

So it's in her you are—

KHLESTAKOV.

Decide—life or death?

ANNA.

Well, there, you fool, you see? Our guest is pleased to go down on his knees for such trash as you. You, running in suddenly as if you were out of your mind. Really, it would be just what you deserve, if I refused. You are not worthy of such happiness.

MARYA.

I won't do it again, mamma, really I won't.

SCENE XV

The same and the Governor in precipitate haste.

GOVERNOR.

Your Excellency, don't ruin me, don't ruin me.

KHLESTAKOV.

What's the matter?

GOVERNOR.

The merchants have complained to your Excellency. I assure you on my honor that not one half of what they said is so. They themselves are cheats. They give short measure and short weight. The officer's widow lied to you when she said I flogged her. She lied, upon my word, she lied. She flogged herself.

KHLESTAKOV.

The devil take the officer's widow. What do I care about the officer's widow.

GOVERNOR.

Don't believe them, don't believe them. They are rank liars; a mere child wouldn't believe them. They are known all over town as liars. And as for cheating, I venture to inform you that there are no swindlers like them in the whole of creation.

ANNA.

Do you know what honor Ivan Aleksandrovich is bestowing upon us? He is asking for our daughter's hand.

GOVERNOR.

What are you talking about? Mother has lost her wits. Please do not be angry, your Excellency. She has a touch of insanity. Her mother was like that, too.

KHLESTAKOV.

Yes, I am really asking for your daughter's hand. I am in love with her.

GOVERNOR.

I cannot believe it, your Excellency.

ANNA.

But when you are told!

KHLESTAKOV.

I am not joking. I could go crazy, I am so in love.

GOVERNOR.

I daren't believe it. I am unworthy of such an honor.

KHLESTAKOV.

If you don't consent to give me your daughter Marya Antonovna's hand, then I am ready to do the devil knows what.

GOVERNOR.

I cannot believe it. You deign to joke, your Excellency.

ANNA.

My, what a blockhead! Really! When you are told over and over again!

GOVERNOR.

I can't believe it.

KHLESTAKOV.

Give her to me, give her to me! I am a desperate man and I may do anything. If I shoot myself, you will have a law-suit on your hands.

GOVERNOR.

Oh, my God! I am not guilty either in thought or in action. Please do not be angry. Be pleased to act as your mercy wills. Really, my head is in such a state I don't know what is happening. I have turned into a worse fool than I've ever been in my life.

ANNA.

Well, give your blessing.

Khlestakov goes up to Marya Antonovna.

GOVERNOR.

May God bless you, but I am not guilty. [Khlestakov kisses Marya. The Governor looks at them.] What the devil! It's really so. [Rubs his eyes.] They are kissing. Oh, heavens! They are kissing. Actually to be our son-in-law! [Cries out, jumping with glee.] Ho, Anton! Ho, Anton! Ho, Governor! So that's the turn events have taken!

SCENE XVI

The same and Osip.

OSIP.

The horses are ready.

KHLESTAKOV.

Oh! All right. I'll come presently.

GOVERNOR.

What's that? Are you leaving?

KHLESTAKOV.

Yes, I'm going.

GOVERNOR.

Then when—that is—I thought you were pleased to hint at a wedding.

KHLESTAKOV.

Oh—for one minute only—for one day—to my uncle, a rich old man. I'll be back tomorrow.

GOVERNOR.

We would not venture, of course, to hold you back, and we hope for your safe return.

KHLESTAKOV.

Of course, of course, I'll come back at once. Good-by, my dear—no, I simply can't express my feelings. Good-by, my heart. [Kisses Marya's hand.]

GOVERNOR.

Don't you need something for the road? It seems to me you were pleased to be short of cash.

KHLESTAKOV, Oh, no, what for? [After a little thought.] However, if you like.

GOVERNOR.

How much will you have?

KHLESTAKOV.

You gave me two hundred then, that is, not two hundred, but four hundred—I don't want to take advantage of your mistake—you might let me have the same now so that it should be an even eight hundred.

GOVERNOR.

Very well. [Takes the money out of his pocket-book.] The notes happen to be brand-new, too, as though on purpose.

KHLESTAKOV.

Oh, yes. [Takes the bills and looks at them.] That's good. They say new money means good luck.

GOVERNOR.

Quite right.

KHLESTAKOV.

Good-by, Anton Antonovich. I am very much obliged to you for your hospitality. I admit with all my heart that I have never got such a good reception anywhere. Good-by, Anna Andreyevna. Good-by, my sweetheart, Marya Antonovna.

All go out.

Behind the Scenes.

KHLESTAKOV.

Good-by, angel of my soul, Marya Antonovna.

GOVERNOR.

What's that? You are going in a plain mail-coach?

KHLESTAKOV.

Yes, I'm used to it. I get a headache from a carriage with springs.

POSTILION.

Ho!

GOVERNOR.

Take a rug for the seat at least. If you say so, I'll tell them to bring a rug.

KHLESTAKOV.

No, what for? It's not necessary. However, let them bring a rug if you please.

GOVERNOR.

Ho, Avdotya. Go to the store-room and bring the very best rug from there, the Persian rug with the blue ground. Quick!

POSTILION.

Ho!

GOVERNOR.

When do you say we are to expect you back?

KHLESTAKOV.

Tomorrow, or the day after.

OSIP.

Is this the rug? Give it here. Put it there. Now put some hay on this side.

POSTILION.

Ho!

OSIP.

Here, on this side. More. All right. That will be fine. [Beats the rug down with his hand.] Now take the seat, your Excellency.

KHLESTAKOV.

Good-by, Anton Antonovich.

GOVERNOR.

Good-by, your Excellency.

ANNA } MARYA} Good-by, Ivan Aleksandrovich.

KHLESTAKOV.

Good-by, mother.

POSTILION.

Get up, my boys!

The bell rings and the curtain drops.

ACT V

SCENE: *Same as in Act IV.*

SCENE I

Governor, Anna Andreyevna, and Marya Antonovna.

GOVERNOR.
Well, Anna Andreyevna, eh? Did you ever imagine such a thing? Such a rich prize? I'll be—. Well, confess frankly, it never occurred to you even in your dreams, did it? From just a simple governor's wife suddenly—whew!—I'll be hanged!—to marry into the family of such a big gun.

ANNA.
Not at all. I knew it long ago. It seems wonderful to you because you are so plain. You never saw decent people.

GOVERNOR.

I'm a decent person myself, mother. But, really, think, Anna Andreyevna, what gay birds we have turned into now, you and I. Eh, Anna Andreyevna? High fliers, by Jove! Wait now, I'll give those fellows who were so eager to present their petitions and denunciations a peppering. Ho, who's there? [Enter a Sergeant.] Is it you, Ivan Karpovich? Call those merchants here, brother, won't you? I'll give it to them, the scoundrels! To make such complaints against me! The damned pack of Jews! Wait, my dear fellows. I used to dose you down to your ears. Now I'll dose you down to your beards. Make a list of all who came to protest against me, especially the mean petty scribblers who cooked the petitions up for them, and announce to all that they should know what honor the Heavens have bestowed upon the Governor, namely this: that he is marrying his daughter, not to a plain ordinary man, but to one the like of whom has never yet been in the world, who can do everything, everything, everything, everything! Proclaim it to all so that everybody should know. Shout it aloud to the whole world. Ring the bell, the devil take it! It is a triumph, and we will make it a triumph. [The Sergeant goes out.] So that's the way, Anna Andreyevna, eh? What shall we do now? Where shall we live? Here or in St. Pete?

ANNA.

In St. Petersburg, of course. How could we remain here?

GOVERNOR.

Well, if St. Pete, then St. Pete. But it would be good here, too. I suppose the governorship could then go to the devil, eh, Anna Andreyevna?

ANNA.

Of course. What's a governorship?

GOVERNOR.

Don't you think, Anna Andreyevna, I can rise to a high rank now, he being hand in glove with all the ministers, and visiting the court? In time I can be promoted to a generalship. What do you think, Anna Andreyevna? Can I become a general?

ANNA.

I should say so. Of course you can.

GOVERNOR.

Ah, the devil take it, it's nice to be a general. They hang a ribbon across your shoulders. What ribbon is better, the red St. Anne or the blue St. Andrew?

ANNA.

The blue St. Andrew, of course.

GOVERNOR.

What! My, you're aiming high. The red one is good, too. Why does one want to be a general? Because when you go travelling, there are always couriers and aides on ahead with "Horses"! And at the stations they refuse to give the horses to others. They all wait, all those councilors, captains, governors, and you don't take the slightest notice of them. You dine somewhere with the governor-general. And the town-governor—I'll keep him waiting at the door. Ha, ha, ha! [He bursts into a roar of laughter, shaking all over.] That's what's so alluring, confound it!

ANNA.

You always like such coarse things. You must remember that our life will have to be completely changed, that your acquaintances will not be a dog-lover of a judge, with whom you go hunting hares, or a Zemlianika. On the contrary, your acquaintances will be people of the most refined type, counts, and society aristocrats. Only really I am afraid of you. You sometimes use words that one never hears in good society.

GOVERNOR.

What of it? A word doesn't hurt.

ANNA.

It's all right when you are a town-governor, but there the life is entirely different.

GOVERNOR.

Yes, they say there are two kinds of fish there, the sea-eel and the smelt, and before you start to eat them, the saliva flows in your mouth.

ANNA.

That's all he thinks about—fish. I shall insist upon our house being the first in the capital and my room having so much amber in it that when you come in you have to shut your eyes. [She shuts her eyes and sniffs.] Oh, how good!

SCENE II

The same and the Merchants.

GOVERNOR.

Ah, how do you do, my fine fellows?

MERCHANTS [bowing].

We wish you health, father.

GOVERNOR.

Well, my dearly beloved friends, how are you? How are your goods selling? So you complained against me, did you, you tea tanks, you scurvy hucksters? Complain, against me? You crooks, you pirates, you. Did you gain a lot by it, eh? Aha, you thought you'd land me in prison? May seven devils and one she-devil take you! Do you know that—

ANNA.

Good heavens, Antosha, what words you use!

GOVERNOR [irritated].

Oh, it isn't a matter of words now. Do you know that the very official to whom you complained is going to marry my daughter? Well, what do you say to that? Now I'll make you smart. You cheat the people, you make a contract with the government, and you do the government out of a hundred thousand, supplying it with rotten cloth; and when you give fifteen yards away gratis, you expect a reward besides. If they knew, they would send you to—And you strut about sticking out your paunches with a great air of importance: "I'm a merchant, don't touch me." "We," you say, "are as good as the nobility." Yes, the nobility, you monkey-faces. The nobleman is educated. If he gets flogged in school, it is for a purpose, to learn something useful. And you—start out in life learning trickery. Your master beats you for not being able to cheat. When you are still little boys and don't know the Lord's Prayer, you already give short measure and short weight. And when your bellies swell and your pockets fill up, then you assume an air of importance. Whew! What marvels! Because you guzzle sixteen samovars full a day, that's why you put on an air of importance. I spit on your heads and on your importance.

MERCHANTS [bowing].

We are guilty, Anton Antonovich.

GOVERNOR.

Complaining, eh? And who helped you with that grafting when you built a bridge and charged twenty thousand for wood when there wasn't even a hundred rubles' worth used? I did. You goat beards. Have you forgotten? If I had informed on you, I could have despatched you to Siberia. What do you say to that?

A MERCHANT.

I'm guilty before God, Anton Antonovich. The evil spirit tempted me. We will never complain against you again. Ask whatever satisfaction you want, only don't be angry.

GOVERNOR.

Don't be angry! Now you are crawling at my feet. Why? Because I am on top now. But if the balance dipped the least bit your way, then you would trample me in the very dirt—you scoundrels! And you would crush me under a beam besides.

MERCHANTS [prostrating themselves].

Don't ruin us, Anton Antonovich.

GOVERNOR.

Don't ruin us! Now you say, don't ruin us! And what did you say before? I could give you—[shrugging his shoulders and throwing up his hands.] Well, God forgive you. Enough. I don't harbor malice for long. Only look out now. Be on your guard. My daughter is going to marry, not an ordinary nobleman. Let your congratulations be—you understand? Don't try to get away with a dried sturgeon or a loaf of sugar. Well, leave now, in God's name.

Merchants leave.

SCENE III

The same, Ammos Fiodorovich, Artemy Filippovich, then Rastakovsky.

AMMOS [in the doorway].

Are we to believe the report, Anton Antonovich? A most extraordinary piece of good fortune has befallen you, hasn't it?

ARTEMY.

I have the honor to congratulate you on your unusual good fortune. I was glad from the bottom of my heart when I heard it. [Kisses Anna's hand.] Anna Andreyevna! [Kissing Marya's hand.] Marya Antonovna! Rastakovsky enters.

RASTAKOVSKY.

I congratulate you, Anton Antonovich. May God give you and the new couple long life and may He grant you numerous progeny—grandchildren and great-grand-children. Anna Andreyevna! [Kissing her hand.] Marya Antonovna! [Kissing her hand.]

SCENE IV

The same, Korobkin and his Wife, Liuliukov.

KOROBKIN.

I have the honor to congratulate you, Anton Antonovich, and you, Anna Andreyevna [kissing her hand] and you Marya Antonovna [kissing her hand].

KOROBKIN'S WIFE.

I congratulate you from the bottom of my heart, Anna Andreyevna, on your new stroke of good fortune.

LIULIUKOV.

I have the honor to congratulate you, Anna Andreyevna. [Kisses her hand and turns to the audience, smacks his lips, putting on a bold front.] Marya Antonovna, I have the honor to congratulate you. [Kisses her hand and turns to the audience in the same way.]

SCENE V

A number of Guests enter. They kiss Anna's hand saying: "Anna Andreyevna," then Marya's hand, saying "Marya Antonovna."

Bobchinsky and Dobchinsky enter jostling each other.

BOBCHINSKY.

I have the honor to congratulate you.

DOBCHINSKY.

Anton Antonovich, I have the honor to congratulate you.

BOBCHINSKY.

On the happy event.

DOBCHINSKY.
   Anna Andreyevna!
BOBCHINSKY.
   Anna Andreyevna!
   They bend over her hand at the same time and bump foreheads.
DOBCHINSKY.
   Marya Antonovna! [Kisses her hand.] I have the honor to congratulate you. You will enjoy the greatest happiness. You will wear garments of gold and eat the most delicate soups, and you will pass your time most entertainingly.
BOBCHINSKY [breaking in].
   God give you all sorts of riches and of money and a wee tiny little son, like this. [Shows the size with his hands.] So that he can sit on the palm of your hand. The little fellow will be crying all the time, "Wow, wow, wow."

SCENE VI

More Guests enter and kiss the ladies' hands, among them Luka Lukich and his wife.
LUKA LUKICH.
   I have the honor.
LUKA'S WIFE [running ahead].
   Congratulate you, Anna Andreyevna. [They kiss.] Really, I was so glad to hear of it. They tell me, "Anna Andreyevna has betrothed her daughter." "Oh, my God," I think to myself. It made me so glad that I said to my husband, "Listen, Lukanchik, that's a great piece of fortune for Anna Andreyevna." "Well," think I to myself, "thank God!" And I say to him, "I'm so delighted that I'm consumed with impatience to tell it to Anna Andreyevna herself." "Oh, my God," think I to myself, "it's just as Anna Andreyevna expected. She always did expect a good match for her daughter. And now what luck! It happened just exactly as she wanted it to happen." Really, it made me so glad that I couldn't say a word. I cried and cried. I simply screamed, so that Luka Lukich said to me, "What are you crying so for, Nastenka?" "Lukanchik," I said, "I don't know myself. The tears just keep flowing like a stream."

GOVERNOR.

Please sit down, ladies and gentlemen. Ho, Mishka, bring some more chairs in.

The Guests seat themselves.

SCENE VII

The same, the Police Captain and Sergeants.

CAPTAIN.

I have the honor to congratulate you, your Honor, and to wish you long years of prosperity.

GOVERNOR.

Thank you, thank you! Please sit down, gentlemen.

The Guests seat themselves.

AMMOS.

But please tell us, Anton Antonovich, how did it all come about, and how did it all—ahem!—go?

GOVERNOR.

It went in a most extraordinary way. He condescended to make the proposal in his own person.

ANNA.

In the most respectful and most delicate manner. He spoke beautifully. He said: "Anna Andreyevna, I have only a feeling of respect for your worth." And such a handsome, cultured man! His manners so genteel! "Believe me, Anna Andreyevna," he says, "life is not worth a penny to me. It is only because I respect your rare qualities."

MARYA.

Oh, mamma, it was to me he said that.

ANNA.

Shut up! You don't know anything. And don't meddle in other people's affairs. "Anna Andreyevna," he says, "I am enraptured." That was the flattering way he poured out his soul. And when I was going to say, "We cannot possibly hope for such an honor," he suddenly went down on his knees, and so aristocratically! "Anna Andreyevna," he says, "don't make me the most miserable of men. Consent to respond to my feelings, or else I'll put an end to my life."

MARYA.

Really, mamma, it was to me he said that.

ANNA.

Yes, of course—to you, too. I don't deny it.

GOVERNOR.

He even frightened us. He said he would put a bullet through his brains. "I'll shoot myself, I'll shoot myself," he said.

MANY GUESTS.

Well, for the Lord's sake!

AMMOS.

How remarkable!

LUKA.

It must have been fate that so ordained.

ARTEMY.

Not fate, my dear friend. Fate is a turkey-hen. It was the Governor's services that brought him this piece of fortune. [Aside.] Good luck always does crawl into the mouths of swine like him.

AMMOS.

If you like, Anton Antonovich, I'll sell you the dog we were bargaining about.

GOVERNOR.

I don't care about dogs now.

AMMOS.

Well, if you don't want it, then we'll agree on some other dog.

KOROBKIN'S WIFE.

Oh, Anna Andreyevna, how happy I am over your good fortune. You can't imagine how happy I am.

KOROBKIN.

But where, may I ask, is the distinguished guest now? I heard he had gone away for some reason or other.

GOVERNOR.

Yes, he's gone off for a day on a highly important matter.

ANNA.

To his uncle—to ask his blessing.

GOVERNOR.

To ask his blessing. But tomorrow—[He sneezes, and all burst into one exclamation of well-wishes.] Thank you very much. But tomorrow he'll be back. [He sneezes, and is congratulated again. Above the other voices are heard those of the following.]

{CAPTAIN. I wish you health, your Honor.

{BOBCHINSKY. A hundred years and a sack of ducats.

{DOBCHINSKY. May God increase it to a thousand.

{ARTEMY. May you go to hell!

{KOROBKIN'S WIFE. The devil take you!

GOVERNOR.

I'm very much obliged to you. I wish you the same.

ANNA.

We intend to live in St. Petersburg now. I must say, the atmosphere here is too village-like. I must say, it's extremely unpleasant. My husband, too—he'll be made a general there.

GOVERNOR.

Yes, confound it, gentlemen, I admit I should very much like to be a general.

LUKA.

May God grant that you get a generalship.

RASTAKOVSKY.

From man it is impossible, but from God everything is possible.

AMMOS.

High merits, high honors.

ARTEMY.

Reward according to service.

AMMOS [aside].

The things he'll do when he becomes a general. A generalship suits him as a saddle suits a cow. It's a far cry to his generalship. There are better men than you, and they haven't been made generals yet.

ARTEMY [aside].

The devil take it—he's aiming for a generalship. Well, maybe he will become a general after all. He's got the air of importance, the devil take him! [Addressing the Governor.] Don't forget us then, Anton Antonovich.

AMMOS.

And if anything happens—for instance, some difficulty in our affairs—don't refuse us your protection.

KOROBKIN.

Next year I am going to take my son to the capital to put him in government service. So do me the kindness to give me your protection. Be a father to the orphan.

GOVERNOR.

I am ready for my part—ready to exert my efforts on your behalf.

ANNA.

Antosha, you are always ready with your promises. In the first place, you won't have time to think of such things. And how can you—how is it possible for you, to burden yourself with such promises?

GOVERNOR.

Why not, my dear? It's possible occasionally.

ANNA.

Of course it's possible. But you can't give protection to every small potato.

KOROBKIN'S WIFE.

Do you hear the way she speaks of us?

GUEST.

She's always been that way. I know her. Seat her at table and she'll put her feet on it.

SCENE VIII

The same and the Postmaster, who rushes in with an unsealed letter in his hand.

POSTMASTER.

A most astonishing thing, ladies and gentlemen! The official whom we took to be an inspector-general is not an inspector-general.

ALL.

How so? Not an inspector-general?

POSTMASTER.

No, not a bit of it. I found it out from the letter.

GOVERNOR.

What are you talking about? What are you talking about? What letter?

POSTMASTER.

His own letter. They bring a letter to the postoffice, I glance at the address and I see Pochtamtskaya Street. I was struck dumb. "Well," I think to myself, "I suppose he found something wrong in the postoffice department and is informing the government." So I unsealed it.

GOVERNOR.

How could you?

POSTMASTER.

I don't know myself. A supernatural power moved me. I had already summoned a courier to send it off by express; but I was overcome by a greater curiosity than I have ever felt in my life. "I can't, I can't," I hear a voice telling me. "I can't." But it pulled me and pulled me. In one ear I heard, "Don't open the letter. You will die like a chicken," and in the other it was just as if the devil were whispering, "Open it, open it." And when I cracked the sealing wax, I felt as if I were on fire; and when I opened the letter, I froze, upon my word, I froze. And my hands trembled, and everything whirled around me.

GOVERNOR.

But how did you dare to open it? The letter of so powerful a personage?

POSTMASTER.

But that's just the point—he's neither powerful nor a personage.

GOVERNOR.

Then what is he in your opinion?

POSTMASTER.

He's neither one thing nor another. The devil knows what he is.

GOVERNOR [furiously].

How neither one thing nor another? How do you dare to call him neither one thing nor another? And the devil knows what besides? I'll put you under arrest.

POSTMASTER.

Who—you?

GOVERNOR.

Yes, I.

POSTMASTER.

You haven't the power.

GOVERNOR.

Do you know that he's going to marry my daughter? That I myself am going to be a high official and will have the power to exile to Siberia?

POSTMASTER.

Oh, Anton Antonovich, Siberia! Siberia is far away. I'd rather read the letter to you. Ladies and gentlemen, permit me to read the letter.

ALL.

Do read it.

POSTMASTER [reads].

"I hasten to inform you, my dear friend, what wonderful things have happened to me. On the way here an infantry captain did me out of my last penny, so that the innkeeper here wanted to send me to jail, when suddenly, thanks to my St. Petersburg appearance and dress, the whole town took me for a governor-general. Now I am staying at the governor's home. I am having a grand time and I am flirting desperately with his wife and daughter. I only haven't decided whom to begin with. I think with the mother first, because she seems ready to accept all terms. You remember how hard up we were taking our meals wherever we could without paying for them, and how once the pastry cook grabbed me by the collar for having charged pies that I ate to the king of England? Now it is quite different. They lend me all the money I want. They are an awful lot of originals. You would split your sides laughing at them. I know you write for the papers. Put them in your literature. In the first place the Governor is as stupid as an old horse—"

GOVERNOR.

Impossible! That can't be in the letter.

POSTMASTER [showing the letter].

Read for yourself.

GOVERNOR [reads].

"As an old horse." Impossible! You put it in yourself.

POSTMASTER.

How could I?

ARTEMY.

Go on reading.

LUKA.

Go on reading.

POSTMASTER [continuing to read].

"The Governor is as stupid as an old horse—"

GOVERNOR.

Oh, the devil! He's got to read it again. As if it weren't there anyway.

POSTMASTER [continuing to read].

H'm, h'm—"an old horse. The Postmaster is a good man, too." [Stops reading.] Well, here he's saying something improper about me, too.

GOVERNOR.

Go on—read the rest.

POSTMASTER.

What for?

GOVERNOR.

The deuce take it! Once we have begun to read it, we must read it all.

ARTEMY.

If you will allow me, I will read it. [Puts on his eye-glasses and reads.] "The Postmaster is just like the porter Mikheyev in our office, and the scoundrel must drink just as hard."

POSTMASTER [to the audience].

A bad boy! He ought to be given a licking. That's all.

ARTEMY [continues to read].

"The Superintendent of Char-i-i—" [Stammers.]

KOROBKIN.

Why did you stop?

ARTEMY.

The handwriting isn't clear. Besides, it's evident that he's a blackguard.

KOROBKIN.

Give it to me. I believe my eyesight is better.

ARTEMY [refusing to give up the letter].

No. This part can be omitted. After that it's legible.

KOROBKIN.

Let me have it please. I'll see for myself.

ARTEMY.

I can read it myself. I tell you that after this part it's all legible.

POSTMASTER.

No, read it all. Everything so far could be read.

ALL.

Give him the letter, Artemy Filippovich, give it to him. [To Korobkin.] You read it.

ARTEMY.

Very well. [Gives up the letter.] Here it is. [Covers a part of it with his finger.] Read from here on. [All press him.]

POSTMASTER.

Read it all, nonsense, read it all.

KOROBKIN [reading].

"The Superintendent of Charities, Zemlianika, is a regular pig in a cap."

ARTEMY [to the audience].

Not a bit witty. A pig in a cap! Have you ever seen a pig wear a cap?

KOROBKIN [continues reading].

"The School Inspector reeks of onions."

LUKA [to the audience].

Upon my word, I never put an onion to my mouth.

AMMOS [aside].

Thank God, there's nothing about me in it.

KOROBKIN [continues reading].

"The Judge—"

AMMOS.

There! [Aloud.] Ladies and gentlemen, I think the letter is far too long. To the devil with it! Why should we go on reading such trash?

LUKA.

No.

POSTMASTER.

No, go on.

ARTEMY.

Go on reading.

KOROBKIN.

"The Judge, Liapkin-Tiapkin, is extremely mauvais ton." [He stops.] That must be a French word.

AMMOS.

The devil knows what it means. It wouldn't be so bad if all it means is "cheat." But it may mean something worse.

KOROBKIN [continues reading].

"However, the people are hospitable and kindhearted. Farewell, my dear Triapichkin. I want to follow your example and take up literature. It's tiresome to live this way, old boy. One wants food for the mind, after all. I see I must engage in something lofty. Address me: Village of Podkatilovka in the Government of Saratov." [Turns the letter and reads the address.] "Mr. Ivan Vasilyevich Triapichkin, St. Petersburg, Pochtamtskaya Street, House Number 97, Courtyard, third floor, right."

A LADY.

What an unexpected rebuke!

GOVERNOR.

He has cut my throat and cut it for good. I'm done for, completely done for. I see nothing. All I see are pigs' snouts instead of faces, and nothing more. Catch him, catch him! [Waves his hand.]

POSTMASTER.

Catch him! How? As if on purpose, I told the overseer to give him the best coach and three. The devil prompted me to give the order.

KOROBKIN'S WIFE.

Here's a pretty mess.

AMMOS.

Confound it, he borrowed three hundred rubles from me.

ARTEMY.

He borrowed three hundred from me, too.

POSTMASTER [sighing].

And from me, too.

BOBCHINSKY.

And sixty-five from me and Piotr Ivanovich.

AMMOS [throwing up his hands in perplexity].

How's that, gentlemen? Really, how could we have been so off our guard?

GOVERNOR [beating his forehead].

How could I, how could I, old fool? I've grown childish, stupid mule. I have been in the service thirty years. Not one merchant, not one contractor has been able to impose on me. I have over-reached one swindler after another. I have caught crooks and sharpers that were ready to rob the whole world. I have fooled three governor-generals. As for governor-generals, [with a wave of his hand] it is not even worth talking about them.

ANNA.

But how is it possible, Antosha? He's engaged to Mashenka.

GOVERNOR [in a rage].

Engaged! Rats! Fiddlesticks! So much for your engagement! Thrusts her engagement at me now! [In a frenzy.] Here, look at me! Look at me, the whole world, the whole of Christendom. See what a fool the governor was made of. Out upon him, the fool, the old scoundrel! [Shakes his fist at himself.] Oh, you fat-nose! To take an icicle, a rag for a personage of rank! Now his coach bells are jingling all along the road. He is publishing the story to the whole world. Not only will you be made a laughing-stock of, but some scribbler, some ink-splasher will put you into a comedy. There's the horrid sting. He won't spare either rank or station. And everybody will grin and clap his hands. What are you laughing at? You are laughing at yourself, oh you! [Stamps his feet.] I would give it to all those ink-splashers! You scribblers, damned liberals, devil's brood! I would tie you all up in a bundle, I would grind you into meal, and give it to the devil. [Shakes his fist and stamps his heel on the floor. After a brief silence.] I can't come to myself. It's really true, whom the gods want to punish they first make mad. In what did that nincompoop resemble an inspector-general? In nothing, not even half the little finger of an inspector-general. And all of a sudden everybody is going about saying, "Inspector-general, inspector-general." Who was the first to say it? Tell me.

ARTEMY [throwing up his hands].

I couldn't tell how it happened if I had to die for it. It is just as if a mist had clouded our brains. The devil has confounded us.

AMMOS.

Who was the first to say it? These two here, this noble pair. [Pointing to Dobchinsky and Bobchinsky.]

BOBCHINSKY.

So help me God, not I. I didn't even think of it.

DOBCHINSKY.

I didn't say a thing, not a thing.

ARTEMY.

Of course you did.

LUKA.

Certainly. You came running here from the inn like madmen. "He's come, he's come. He doesn't pay." Found a rare bird!

GOVERNOR.

Of course it was you. Town gossips, damned liars!

ARTEMY.

The devil take you with your inspector-general and your tattle.

GOVERNOR.

You run about the city, bother everybody, confounded chatterboxes. You spread gossip, you short-tailed magpies, you!

AMMOS.

Damned bunglers!

LUKA.

Simpletons.

ARTEMY.

Pot-bellied mushrooms!

All crowd around them.

BOBCHINSKY.

Upon my word, it wasn't I. It was Piotr Ivanovich.

DOBCHINSKY.

No, Piotr Ivanovich, you were the first.

BOBCHINSKY.

No, no. You were the first.

LAST SCENE

The same and a Gendarme.

GENDARME.

An official from St. Petersburg sent by imperial order has arrived, and wants to see you all at once. He is stopping at the inn.

All are struck as by a thunderbolt. A cry of amazement bursts from the ladies simultaneously. The whole group suddenly shifts positions and remains standing as if petrified.

SILENT SCENE

The Governor stands in the center rigid as a post, with outstretched hands and head thrown backward. On his right are his wife and daughter straining toward him. Back of them the Postmaster, turned toward the audience, metamorphosed into a question mark. Next to him, at the edge of the group, three lady guests leaning on each other, with a most satirical expression on their faces directed straight at the Governor's family. To the left of the Governor is Zemlianika, his head to one side as if listening. Behind him is the Judge with outspread hands almost crouching on the ground and pursing his lips as if to whistle or say: "A nice pickle we're in!" Next to him is Korobkin, turned toward the audience, with eyes screwed up and making a venomous gesture at the Governor. Next to him, at the edge of the group, are Dobchinsky and Bobchinsky, gesticulating at each other, open-mouthed and wide-eyed. The other guests remain standing stiff. The whole group retain the same position of rigidity for almost a minute and a half.

The curtain falls.

THE END

SHORT STORIES

1

The Overcoat

Translated by Thomas Seltzer

In the department of—but it is better not to mention the department. There is nothing more irritable than departments, regiments, courts of justice, and, in a word, every branch of public service. Each individual attached to them nowadays thinks all society insulted in his person. Quite recently a complaint was received from a justice of the peace, in which he plainly demonstrated that all the imperial institutions were going to the dogs, and that the Czar's sacred name was being taken in vain; and in proof he appended to the complaint a romance in which the justice of the peace is made to appear about once every ten lines, and sometimes in a drunken condition. Therefore, in order to avoid all unpleasantness, it will be better to describe the department in question only as a certain department.

So, in a certain department there was a certain official—not a very high one, it must be allowed—short of stature, somewhat pock-marked, red-haired, and short-sighted, with a bald forehead, wrinkled cheeks, and a complexion of the kind known as sanguine. The St. Petersburg climate was responsible for this. As for his official status, he was what is called a perpetual titular councillor, over which, as is well known, some writers make merry, and crack their jokes, obeying the praiseworthy custom of attacking those who cannot bite back.

His family name was Bashmatchkin. This name is evidently derived from "bashmak" (shoe); but when, at what time, and in what manner, is not known. His father and grandfather, and all the Bashmatchkins, always wore boots, which only had new heels two or three times a year. His name was Akakiy Akakievitch. It may strike the reader as rather singular and far-fetched, but he may rest assured that it was by no means far-fetched, and that the circumstances were such that it would have been impossible to give him any other.

This is how it came about.

Akakiy Akakievitch was born, if my memory fails me not, in the evening of the 23rd of March. His mother, the wife of a Government official and a very fine woman, made all due arrangements for having the child baptised. She was lying on the bed opposite the door; on her right stood the godfather, Ivan Ivanovitch Eroshkin, a most estimable man, who served as presiding officer of the senate, while the godmother, Anna Semenovna Byelobrushkova, the wife of an officer of the quarter, and a woman of rare virtues. They offered the mother her choice of three names, Mokiya, Sossiya, or that the child should be called after the martyr Khozdazat. "No," said the good woman, "all those names are poor." In order to please her they opened the calendar to another place; three more names appeared, Triphiliy, Dula, and Varakhasiy. "This is a judgment," said the old woman. "What names! I truly never heard the like. Varada or Varukh might have been borne, but not Triphiliy and Varakhasiy!" They turned to another page and found Pavsikakhiy and Vakhtisiy. "Now I see," said the old woman, "that it is plainly fate. And since such is the case, it will be better to name him after his father. His father's name was Akakiy, so let his son's be Akakiy too." In this manner he became Akakiy Akakievitch. They christened the child, whereat he wept and made a grimace, as though he foresaw that he was to be a titular councillor.

In this manner did it all come about. We have mentioned it in order that the reader might see for himself that it was a case of necessity, and that it was utterly impossible to give him any other name. When and how he entered the department, and who appointed him, no one could remember. However much the directors and chiefs of all kinds were changed, he was always to be seen in the same place, the same attitude, the same occupation; so that it was afterwards affirmed that he had been born in undress uniform with a bald head. No respect was shown him in the department. The porter not only did not rise from his seat when he passed, but never even glanced at him, any more than if a fly had flown through the reception-room. His superiors treated him in coolly despotic fashion. Some sub-chief would thrust a paper under his nose without so much as saying, "Copy," or "Here's a nice interesting affair," or anything else agreeable, as is customary amongst well-bred officials. And he took it, looking only at the paper and not observing who handed it to him, or whether he had the right to do so; simply took it, and set about copying it.

The young officials laughed at and made fun of him, so far as their official wit permitted; told in his presence various stories concocted about him, and about his landlady, an old woman of seventy; declared that she beat him; asked when the wedding was to be; and strewed bits of paper over his head, calling them snow. But Akakiy Akakievitch answered not a word, any more than if there had been no one there besides himself. It even had no effect upon his work: amid all these annoyances he never made a single mistake in a letter. But if the joking became wholly unbearable, as when they jogged his hand and prevented his attending to his work, he would exclaim, "Leave me alone! Why do you insult me?" And there was something strange in the words and the voice in which they were uttered. There was in it something which moved to pity; so much that one young man, a new-comer, who, taking pattern by the others, had permitted himself to make sport of Akakiy, suddenly stopped short, as though all about him had undergone a transformation, and presented itself in a different aspect. Some unseen force repelled him from the comrades whose acquaintance he had made, on the supposition that they were well-bred and polite men. Long afterwards, in his gayest moments, there recurred to his mind the little official with the bald forehead, with his heart-rending words, "Leave me alone! Why do you insult me?" In these moving words, other words resounded—"I am thy brother." And the young man covered his face with his hand; and many a time afterwards, in the course of his life, shuddered at seeing how much inhumanity there is in man, how much savage coarseness is concealed beneath delicate, refined worldliness, and even, O God! in that man whom the world acknowledges as honourable and noble.

It would be difficult to find another man who lived so entirely for his duties. It is not enough to say that Akakiy laboured with zeal: no, he laboured with love. In his copying, he found a varied and agreeable employment. Enjoyment was written on his face: some letters were even favourites with him; and when he encountered these, he smiled, winked, and worked with his lips, till it seemed as though each letter might be read in his face, as his pen traced it. If his pay had been in proportion to his zeal, he would, perhaps, to his great surprise, have been made even a councillor of state. But he worked, as his companions, the wits, put it, like a horse in a mill.

Moreover, it is impossible to say that no attention was paid to him. One director being a kindly man, and desirous of rewarding him for his long service, ordered him to be given something more important than mere copying. So he was ordered to make a report of an already concluded affair to another department: the duty consisting simply in changing the heading and altering a few words from the first to the third person. This caused him so much toil that he broke into a perspiration, rubbed his forehead, and finally said, "No, give me rather something to copy." After that they let him copy on forever.

Outside this copying, it appeared that nothing existed for him. He gave no thought to his clothes: his undress uniform was not green, but a sort of rusty-meal colour. The collar was low, so that his neck, in spite of the fact that it was not long, seemed inordinately so as it emerged from it, like the necks of those plaster cats which wag their heads, and are carried about upon the heads of scores of image sellers. And something was always sticking to his uniform, either a bit of hay or some trifle. Moreover, he had a peculiar knack, as he walked along the street, of arriving beneath a window just as all sorts of rubbish were being flung out of it: hence he always bore about on his hat scraps of melon rinds and other such articles. Never once in his life did he give heed to what was going on every day in the street; while it is well known that his young brother officials train the range of their glances till they can see when any one's trouser straps come undone upon the opposite sidewalk, which always brings a malicious smile to their faces. But Akakiy Akakievitch saw in all things the clean, even strokes of his written lines; and only when a horse thrust his nose, from some unknown quarter, over his shoulder, and sent a whole gust of wind down his neck from his nostrils, did he observe that he was not in the middle of a page, but in the middle of the street.

On reaching home, he sat down at once at the table, supped his cabbage soup up quickly, and swallowed a bit of beef with onions, never noticing their taste, and gulping down everything with flies and anything else which the Lord happened to send at the moment. His stomach filled, he rose from the table, and copied papers which he had brought home. If there happened to be none, he took copies for himself, for his own gratification, especially if the document was noteworthy, not on account of its style, but of its being addressed to some distinguished person.

Even at the hour when the grey St. Petersburg sky had quite dispersed, and all the official world had eaten or dined, each as he could, in accordance with the salary he received and his own fancy; when all were resting from the departmental jar of pens, running to and fro from their own and other people's indispensable occupations, and from all the work that an uneasy man makes willingly for himself, rather than what is necessary; when officials hasten to dedicate to pleasure the time which is left to them, one bolder than the rest going to the theatre; another, into the street looking under all the bonnets; another wasting his evening in compliments to some pretty girl, the star of a small official circle; another—and this is the common case of all—visiting his comrades on the fourth or third floor, in two small rooms with an ante-room or kitchen, and some pretensions to fashion, such as a lamp or some other trifle which has cost many a sacrifice of dinner or pleasure trip; in a word, at the hour when all officials disperse among the contracted quarters of their friends, to play whist, as they sip their tea from glasses with a kopek's worth of sugar, smoke long pipes, relate at times some bits of gossip which a Russian man can never, under any circumstances, refrain from, and, when there is nothing else to talk of, repeat eternal anecdotes about the commandant to whom they had sent word that the tails of the horses on the Falconet Monument had been cut off, when all strive to divert themselves, Akakiy Akakievitch indulged in no kind of diversion. No one could ever say that he had seen him at any kind of evening party. Having written to his heart's content, he lay down to sleep, smiling at the thought of the coming day—of what God might send him to copy on the morrow.

Thus flowed on the peaceful life of the man, who, with a salary of four hundred rubles, understood how to be content with his lot; and thus it would have continued to flow on, perhaps, to extreme old age, were it not that there are various ills strewn along the path of life for titular councillors as well as for private, actual, court, and every other species of councillor, even for those who never give any advice or take any themselves.

There exists in St. Petersburg a powerful foe of all who receive a salary of four hundred rubles a year, or thereabouts. This foe is no other than the Northern cold, although it is said to be very healthy. At nine o'clock in the morning, at the very hour when the streets are filled with men bound for the various official departments, it begins to bestow such powerful and piercing nips on all noses impartially that the poor officials really do not know what to do with them. At an hour when the foreheads of even those who occupy exalted positions ache with the cold, and tears start to their eyes, the poor titular councillors are sometimes quite unprotected. Their only salvation lies in traversing as quickly as possible, in their thin little cloaks, five or six streets, and then warming their feet in the porter's room, and so thawing all their talents and qualifications for official service, which had become frozen on the way.

Akakiy Akakievitch had felt for some time that his back and shoulders suffered with peculiar poignancy, in spite of the fact that he tried to traverse the distance with all possible speed. He began finally to wonder whether the fault did not lie in his cloak. He examined it thoroughly at home, and discovered that in two places, namely, on the back and shoulders, it had become thin as gauze: the cloth was worn to such a degree that he could see through it, and the lining had fallen into pieces. You must know that Akakiy Akakievitch's cloak served as an object of ridicule to the officials: they even refused it the noble name of cloak, and called it a cape. In fact, it was of singular make: its collar diminishing year by year, but serving to patch its other parts. The patching did not exhibit great skill on the part of the tailor, and was, in fact, baggy and ugly. Seeing how the matter stood, Akakiy Akakievitch decided that it would be necessary to take the cloak to Petrovitch, the tailor, who lived somewhere on the fourth floor up a dark stair-case, and who, in spite of his having but one eye, and pock-marks all over his face, busied himself with considerable success in repairing the trousers and coats of officials and others; that is to say, when he was sober and not nursing some other scheme in his head.

It is not necessary to say much about this tailor; but, as it is the custom to have the character of each personage in a novel clearly defined, there is no help for it, so here is Petrovitch the tailor. At first he was called only Grigoriy, and was some gentleman's serf; he commenced calling himself Petrovitch from the time when he received his free papers, and further began to drink heavily on all holidays, at first on the great ones, and then on all church festivities without discrimination, wherever a cross stood in the calendar. On this point he was faithful to ancestral custom; and when quarrelling with his wife, he called her a low female and a German. As we have mentioned his wife, it will be necessary to say a word or two about her. Unfortunately, little is known of her beyond the fact that Petrovitch has a wife, who wears a cap and a dress; but cannot lay claim to beauty, at least, no one but the soldiers of the guard even looked under her cap when they met her.

Ascending the staircase which led to Petrovitch's room—which staircase was all soaked with dish-water, and reeked with the smell of spirits which affects the eyes, and is an inevitable adjunct to all dark stairways in St. Petersburg houses—ascending the stairs, Akakiy Akakievitch pondered how much Petrovitch would ask, and mentally resolved not to give more than two rubles. The door was open; for the mistress, in cooking some fish, had raised such a smoke in the kitchen that not even the beetles were visible. Akakiy Akakievitch passed through the kitchen unperceived, even by the housewife, and at length reached a room where he beheld Petrovitch seated on a large unpainted table, with his legs tucked under him like a Turkish pasha. His feet were bare, after the fashion of tailors who sit at work; and the first thing which caught the eye was his thumb, with a deformed nail thick and strong as a turtle's shell. About Petrovitch's neck hung a skein of silk and thread, and upon his knees lay some old garment. He had been trying unsuccessfully for three minutes to thread his needle, and was enraged at the darkness and even at the thread, growling in a low voice, "It won't go through, the barbarian! you pricked me, you rascal!"

Akakiy Akakievitch was vexed at arriving at the precise moment when Petrovitch was angry; he liked to order something of Petrovitch when the latter was a little downhearted, or, as his wife expressed it, "when he had settled himself with brandy, the one-eyed devil!" Under such circumstances, Petrovitch generally came down in his price very readily, and even bowed and returned thanks. Afterwards, to be sure, his wife would come, complaining that her husband was drunk, and so had fixed the price too low; but, if only a ten-kopek piece were added, then the matter was settled. But now it appeared that Petrovitch was in a sober condition, and therefore rough, taciturn, and inclined to demand, Satan only knows what price. Akakiy Akakievitch felt this, and would gladly have beat a retreat; but he was in for it. Petrovitch screwed up his one eye very intently at him, and Akakiy Akakievitch involuntarily said: "How do you do, Petrovitch?"

"I wish you a good morning, sir," said Petrovitch, squinting at Akakiy Akakievitch's hands, to see what sort of booty he had brought.

"Ah! I—to you, Petrovitch, this—" It must be known that Akakiy Akakievitch expressed himself chiefly by prepositions, adverbs, and scraps of phrases which had no meaning whatever. If the matter was a very difficult one, he had a habit of never completing his sentences; so that frequently, having begun a phrase with the words, "This, in fact, is quite—" he forgot to go on, thinking that he had already finished it.

"What is it?" asked Petrovitch, and with his one eye scanned Akakievitch's whole uniform from the collar down to the cuffs, the back, the tails and the button-holes, all of which were well known to him, since they were his own handiwork. Such is the habit of tailors; it is the first thing they do on meeting one.

"But I, here, this—Petrovitch—a cloak, cloth—here you see, everywhere, in different places, it is quite strong—it is a little dusty, and looks old, but it is new, only here in one place it is a little—on the back, and here on one of the shoulders, it is a little worn, yes, here on this shoulder it is a little—do you see? that is all. And a little work—"

Petrovitch took the cloak, spread it out, to begin with, on the table, looked hard at it, shook his head, reached out his hand to the window-sill for his snuff-box, adorned with the portrait of some general, though what general is unknown, for the place where the face should have been had been rubbed through by the finger, and a square bit of paper had been pasted over it. Having taken a pinch of snuff, Petrovitch held up the cloak, and inspected it against the light, and again shook his head once more. After which he again lifted the general-adorned lid with its bit of pasted paper, and having stuffed his nose with snuff, closed and put away the snuff-box, and said finally, "No, it is impossible to mend it; it's a wretched garment!"

Akakiy Akakievitch's heart sank at these words.

"Why is it impossible, Petrovitch?" he said, almost in the pleading voice of a child; "all that ails it is, that it is worn on the shoulders. You must have some pieces—"

"Yes, patches could be found, patches are easily found," said Petrovitch, "but there's nothing to sew them to. The thing is completely rotten; if you put a needle to it—see, it will give way."

"Let it give way, and you can put on another patch at once."

"But there is nothing to put the patches on to; there's no use in strengthening it; it is too far gone. It's lucky that it's cloth; for, if the wind were to blow, it would fly away."

"Well, strengthen it again. How will this, in fact—"

"No," said Petrovitch decisively, "there is nothing to be done with it. It's a thoroughly bad job. You'd better, when the cold winter weather comes on, make yourself some gaiters out of it, because stockings are not warm. The Germans invented them in order to make more money." Petrovitch loved, on all occasions, to have a fling at the Germans. "But it is plain you must have a new cloak."

At the word "new," all grew dark before Akakiy Akakievitch's eyes, and everything in the room began to whirl round. The only thing he saw clearly was the general with the paper face on the lid of Petrovitch's snuff-box. "A new one?" said he, as if still in a dream: "why, I have no money for that."

"Yes, a new one," said Petrovitch, with barbarous composure.

"Well, if it came to a new one, how would it—?"

"You mean how much would it cost?"

"Yes."

"Well, you would have to lay out a hundred and fifty or more," said Petrovitch, and pursed up his lips significantly. He liked to produce powerful effects, liked to stun utterly and suddenly, and then to glance sideways to see what face the stunned person would put on the matter.

"A hundred and fifty rubles for a cloak!" shrieked poor Akakiy Akakievitch, perhaps for the first time in his life, for his voice had always been distinguished for softness.

"Yes, sir," said Petrovitch, "for any kind of cloak. If you have a marten fur on the collar, or a silk-lined hood, it will mount up to two hundred."

"Petrovitch, please," said Akakiy Akakievitch in a beseeching tone, not hearing, and not trying to hear, Petrovitch's words, and disregarding all his "effects," "some repairs, in order that it may wear yet a little longer."

"No, it would only be a waste of time and money," said Petrovitch; and Akakiy Akakievitch went away after these words, utterly discouraged. But Petrovitch stood for some time after his departure, with significantly compressed lips, and without betaking himself to his work, satisfied that he would not be dropped, and an artistic tailor employed.

Akakiy Akakievitch went out into the street as if in a dream. "Such an affair!" he said to himself: "I did not think it had come to—" and then after a pause, he added, "Well, so it is! see what it has come to at last! and I never imagined that it was so!" Then followed a long silence, after which he exclaimed, "Well, so it is! see what already—nothing unexpected that—it would be nothing—what a strange circumstance!" So saying, instead of going home, he went in exactly the opposite direction without himself suspecting it. On the way, a chimney-sweep bumped up against him, and blackened his shoulder, and a whole hatful of rubbish landed on him from the top of a house which was building. He did not notice it; and only when he ran against a watchman, who, having planted his halberd beside him, was shaking some snuff from his box into his horny hand, did he recover himself a little, and that because the watchman said, "Why are you poking yourself into a man's very face? Haven't you the pavement?" This caused him to look about him, and turn towards home.

There only, he finally began to collect his thoughts, and to survey his position in its clear and actual light, and to argue with himself, sensibly and frankly, as with a reasonable friend with whom one can discuss private and personal matters. "No," said Akakiy Akakievitch, "it is impossible to reason with Petrovitch now; he is that—evidently his wife has been beating him. I'd better go to him on Sunday morning; after Saturday night he will be a little cross-eyed and sleepy, for he will want to get drunk, and his wife won't give him any money; and at such a time, a ten-kopek piece in his hand will—he will become more fit to reason with, and then the cloak, and that—" Thus argued Akakiy Akakievitch with himself, regained his courage, and waited until the first Sunday, when, seeing from afar that Petrovitch's wife had left the house, he went straight to him.

Petrovitch's eye was, indeed, very much askew after Saturday: his head drooped, and he was very sleepy; but for all that, as soon as he knew what it was a question of, it seemed as though Satan jogged his memory. "Impossible," said he: "please to order a new one." Thereupon Akakiy Akakievitch handed over the ten-kopek piece. "Thank you, sir; I will drink your good health," said Petrovitch: "but as for the cloak, don't trouble yourself about it; it is good for nothing. I will make you a capital new one, so let us settle about it now."

Akakiy Akakievitch was still for mending it; but Petrovitch would not hear of it, and said, "I shall certainly have to make you a new one, and you may depend upon it that I shall do my best. It may even be, as the fashion goes, that the collar can be fastened by silver hooks under a flap."

Then Akakiy Akakievitch saw that it was impossible to get along without a new cloak, and his spirit sank utterly. How, in fact, was it to be done? Where was the money to come from? He might, to be sure, depend, in part, upon his present at Christmas; but that money had long been allotted beforehand. He must have some new trousers, and pay a debt of long standing to the shoemaker for putting new tops to his old boots, and he must order three shirts from the seamstress, and a couple of pieces of linen. In short, all his money must be spent; and even if the director should be so kind as to order him to receive forty-five rubles instead of forty, or even fifty, it would be a mere nothing, a mere drop in the ocean towards the funds necessary for a cloak: although he knew that Petrovitch was often wrong-headed enough to blurt out some outrageous price, so that even his own wife could not refrain from exclaiming, "Have you lost your senses, you fool?" At one time he would not work at any price, and now it was quite likely that he had named a higher sum than the cloak would cost.

But although he knew that Petrovitch would undertake to make a cloak for eighty rubles, still, where was he to get the eighty rubles from? He might possibly manage half, yes, half might be procured, but where was the other half to come from? But the reader must first be told where the first half came from. Akakiy Akakievitch had a habit of putting, for every ruble he spent, a groschen into a small box, fastened with a lock and key, and with a slit in the top for the reception of money. At the end of every half-year he counted over the heap of coppers, and changed it for silver. This he had done for a long time, and in the course of years, the sum had mounted up to over forty rubles. Thus he had one half on hand; but where was he to find the other half? where was he to get another forty rubles from? Akakiy Akakievitch thought and thought, and decided that it would be necessary to curtail his ordinary expenses, for the space of one year at least, to dispense with tea in the evening; to burn no candles, and, if there was anything which he must do, to go into his landlady's room, and work by her light. When he went into the street, he must walk as lightly as he could, and as cautiously, upon the stones, almost upon tiptoe, in order not to wear his heels down in too short a time; he must give the laundress as little to wash as possible; and, in order not to wear out his clothes, he must take them off, as soon as he got home, and wear only his cotton dressing-gown, which had been long and carefully saved.

To tell the truth, it was a little hard for him at first to accustom himself to these deprivations; but he got used to them at length, after a fashion, and all went smoothly. He even got used to being hungry in the evening, but he made up for it by treating himself, so to say, in spirit, by bearing ever in mind the idea of his future cloak. From that time forth his existence seemed to become, in some way, fuller, as if he were married, or as if some other man lived in him, as if, in fact, he were not alone, and some pleasant friend had consented to travel along life's path with him, the friend being no other than the cloak, with thick wadding and a strong lining incapable of wearing out. He became more lively, and even his character grew firmer, like that of a man who has made up his mind, and set himself a goal. From his face and gait, doubt and indecision, all hesitating and wavering traits disappeared of themselves. Fire gleamed in his eyes, and occasionally the boldest and most daring ideas flitted through his mind; why not, for instance, have marten fur on the collar? The thought of this almost made him absent-minded. Once, in copying a letter, he nearly made a mistake, so that he exclaimed almost aloud, "Ugh!" and crossed himself. Once, in the course of every month, he had a conference with Petrovitch on the subject of the cloak, where it would be better to buy the cloth, and the colour, and the price. He always returned home satisfied, though troubled, reflecting that the time would come at last when it could all be bought, and then the cloak made.

The affair progressed more briskly than he had expected. Far beyond all his hopes, the director awarded neither forty nor forty-five rubles for Akakiy Akakievitch's share, but sixty. Whether he suspected that Akakiy Akakievitch needed a cloak, or whether it was merely chance, at all events, twenty extra rubles were by this means provided. This circumstance hastened matters. Two or three months more of hunger and Akakiy Akakievitch had accumulated about eighty rubles. His heart, generally so quiet, began to throb. On the first possible day, he went shopping in company with Petrovitch. They bought some very good cloth, and at a reasonable rate too, for they had been considering the matter for six months, and rarely let a month pass without their visiting the shops to inquire prices. Petrovitch himself said that no better cloth could be had. For lining, they selected a cotton stuff, but so firm and thick that Petrovitch declared it to be better than silk, and even prettier and more glossy. They did not buy the marten fur, because it was, in fact, dear, but in its stead, they picked out the very best of cat-skin which could be found in the shop, and which might, indeed, be taken for marten at a distance.

Petrovitch worked at the cloak two whole weeks, for there was a great deal of quilting: otherwise it would have been finished sooner. He charged twelve rubles for the job, it could not possibly have been done for less. It was all sewed with silk, in small, double seams; and Petrovitch went over each seam afterwards with his own teeth, stamping in various patterns.

It was—it is difficult to say precisely on what day, but probably the most glorious one in Akakiy Akakievitch's life, when Petrovitch at length brought home the cloak. He brought it in the morning, before the hour when it was necessary to start for the department. Never did a cloak arrive so exactly in the nick of time; for the severe cold had set in, and it seemed to threaten to increase. Petrovitch brought the cloak himself as befits a good tailor. On his countenance was a significant expression, such as Akakiy Akakievitch had never beheld there. He seemed fully sensible that he had done no small deed, and crossed a gulf separating tailors who only put in linings, and execute repairs, from those who make new things. He took the cloak out of the pocket handkerchief in which he had brought it. The handkerchief was fresh from the laundress, and he put it in his pocket for use. Taking out the cloak, he gazed proudly at it, held it up with both hands, and flung it skilfully over the shoulders of Akakiy Akakievitch. Then he pulled it and fitted it down behind with his hand, and he draped it around Akakiy Akakievitch without buttoning it. Akakiy Akakievitch, like an experienced man, wished to try the sleeves. Petrovitch helped him on with them, and it turned out that the sleeves were satisfactory also. In short, the cloak appeared to be perfect, and most seasonable. Petrovitch did not neglect to observe that it was only because he lived in a narrow street, and had no signboard, and had known Akakiy Akakievitch so long, that he had made it so cheaply; but that if he had been in business on the Nevsky Prospect, he would have charged seventy-five rubles for the making alone. Akakiy Akakievitch did not care to argue this point with Petrovitch. He paid him, thanked him, and set out at once in his new cloak for the department. Petrovitch followed him, and, pausing in the street, gazed long at the cloak in the distance, after which he went to one side expressly to run through a crooked alley, and emerge again into the street beyond to gaze once more upon the cloak from another point, namely, directly in front.

Meantime Akakiy Akakievitch went on in holiday mood. He was conscious every second of the time that he had a new cloak on his shoulders; and several times he laughed with internal satisfaction. In fact, there were two advantages, one was its warmth, the other its beauty. He saw nothing of the road, but suddenly found himself at the department. He took off his cloak in the ante-room, looked it over carefully, and confided it to the especial care of the attendant. It is impossible to say precisely how it was that every one in the department knew at once that Akakiy Akakievitch had a new cloak, and that the "cape" no longer existed. All rushed at the same moment into the ante-room to inspect it. They congratulated him and said pleasant things to him, so that he began at first to smile and then to grow ashamed. When all surrounded him, and said that the new cloak must be "christened," and that he must give a whole evening at least to this, Akakiy Akakievitch lost his head completely, and did not know where he stood, what to answer, or how to get out of it. He stood blushing all over for several minutes, and was on the point of assuring them with great simplicity that it was not a new cloak, that it was so and so, that it was in fact the old "cape."

At length one of the officials, a sub-chief probably, in order to show that he was not at all proud, and on good terms with his inferiors, said, "So be it, only I will give the party instead of Akakiy Akakievitch; I invite you all to tea with me to-night; it happens quite a propos, as it is my name-day." The officials naturally at once offered the sub-chief their congratulations and accepted the invitations with pleasure. Akakiy Akakievitch would have declined, but all declared that it was discourteous, that it was simply a sin and a shame, and that he could not possibly refuse. Besides, the notion became pleasant to him when he recollected that he should thereby have a chance of wearing his new cloak in the evening also.

That whole day was truly a most triumphant festival day for Akakiy Akakievitch. He returned home in the most happy frame of mind, took off his cloak, and hung it carefully on the wall, admiring afresh the cloth and the lining. Then he brought out his old, worn-out cloak, for comparison. He looked at it and laughed, so vast was the difference. And long after dinner he laughed again when the condition of the "cape" recurred to his mind. He dined cheerfully, and after dinner wrote nothing, but took his ease for a while on the bed, until it got dark. Then he dressed himself leisurely, put on his cloak, and stepped out into the street. Where the host lived, unfortunately we cannot say: our memory begins to fail us badly; and the houses and streets in St. Petersburg have become so mixed up in our head that it is very difficult to get anything out of it again in proper form. This much is certain, that the official lived in the best part of the city; and therefore it must have been anything but near to Akakiy Akakievitch's residence. Akakiy Akakievitch was first obliged to traverse a kind of wilderness of deserted, dimly-lighted streets; but in proportion as he approached the official's quarter of the city, the streets became more lively, more populous, and more brilliantly illuminated. Pedestrians began to appear; handsomely dressed ladies were more frequently encountered; the men had otter skin collars to their coats; peasant waggoners, with their grate-like sledges stuck over with brass-headed nails, became rarer; whilst on the other hand, more and more drivers in red velvet caps, lacquered sledges and bear-skin coats began to appear, and carriages with rich hammer-cloths flew swiftly through the streets, their wheels scrunching the snow. Akakiy Akakievitch gazed upon all this as upon a novel sight. He had not been in the streets during the evening for years. He halted out of curiosity before a shop-window to look at a picture representing a handsome woman, who had thrown off her shoe, thereby baring her whole foot in a very pretty way; whilst behind her the head of a man with whiskers and a handsome moustache peeped through the doorway of another room. Akakiy Akakievitch shook his head and laughed, and then went on his way. Why did he laugh? Either because he had met with a thing utterly unknown, but for which every one cherishes, nevertheless, some sort of feeling; or else he thought, like many officials, as follows: "Well, those French! What is to be said? If they do go in anything of that sort, why—" But possibly he did not think at all.

Akakiy Akakievitch at length reached the house in which the sub-chief lodged. The sub-chief lived in fine style: the staircase was lit by a lamp; his apartment being on the second floor. On entering the vestibule, Akakiy Akakievitch beheld a whole row of goloshes on the floor. Among them, in the centre of the room, stood a samovar or tea-urn, humming and emitting clouds of steam. On the walls hung all sorts of coats and cloaks, among which there were even some with beaver collars or velvet facings. Beyond, the buzz of conversation was audible, and became clear and loud when the servant came out with a trayful of empty glasses, cream-jugs, and sugar-bowls. It was evident that the officials had arrived long before, and had already finished their first glass of tea.

Akakiy Akakievitch, having hung up his own cloak, entered the inner room. Before him all at once appeared lights, officials, pipes, and card-tables; and he was bewildered by the sound of rapid conversation rising from all the tables, and the noise of moving chairs. He halted very awkwardly in the middle of the room, wondering what he ought to do. But they had seen him. They received him with a shout, and all thronged at once into the ante-room, and there took another look at his cloak. Akakiy Akakievitch, although somewhat confused, was frank-hearted, and could not refrain from rejoicing when he saw how they praised his cloak. Then, of course, they all dropped him and his cloak, and returned, as was proper, to the tables set out for whist.

All this, the noise, the talk, and the throng of people was rather overwhelming to Akakiy Akakievitch. He simply did not know where he stood, or where to put his hands, his feet, and his whole body. Finally he sat down by the players, looked at the cards, gazed at the face of one and another, and after a while began to gape, and to feel that it was wearisome, the more so as the hour was already long past when he usually went to bed. He wanted to take leave of the host; but they would not let him go, saying that he must not fail to drink a glass of champagne in honour of his new garment. In the course of an hour, supper, consisting of vegetable salad, cold veal, pastry, confectioner's pies, and champagne, was served. They made Akakiy Akakievitch drink two glasses of champagne, after which he felt things grow livelier.

Still, he could not forget that it was twelve o'clock, and that he should have been at home long ago. In order that the host might not think of some excuse for detaining him, he stole out of the room quickly, sought out, in the ante-room, his cloak, which, to his sorrow, he found lying on the floor, brushed it, picked off every speck upon it, put it on his shoulders, and descended the stairs to the street.

In the street all was still bright. Some petty shops, those permanent clubs of servants and all sorts of folk, were open. Others were shut, but, nevertheless, showed a streak of light the whole length of the door-crack, indicating that they were not yet free of company, and that probably some domestics, male and female, were finishing their stories and conversations whilst leaving their masters in complete ignorance as to their whereabouts. Akakiy Akakievitch went on in a happy frame of mind: he even started to run, without knowing why, after some lady, who flew past like a flash of lightning. But he stopped short, and went on very quietly as before, wondering why he had quickened his pace. Soon there spread before him those deserted streets, which are not cheerful in the daytime, to say nothing of the evening. Now they were even more dim and lonely: the lanterns began to grow rarer, oil, evidently, had been less liberally supplied. Then came wooden houses and fences: not a soul anywhere; only the snow sparkled in the streets, and mournfully veiled the low-roofed cabins with their closed shutters. He approached the spot where the street crossed a vast square with houses barely visible on its farther side, a square which seemed a fearful desert.

Afar, a tiny spark glimmered from some watchman's box, which seemed to stand on the edge of the world. Akakiy Akakievitch's cheerfulness diminished at this point in a marked degree. He entered the square, not without an involuntary sensation of fear, as though his heart warned him of some evil. He glanced back and on both sides, it was like a sea about him. "No, it is better not to look," he thought, and went on, closing his eyes. When he opened them, to see whether he was near the end of the square, he suddenly beheld, standing just before his very nose, some bearded individuals of precisely what sort he could not make out. All grew dark before his eyes, and his heart throbbed.

"But, of course, the cloak is mine!" said one of them in a loud voice, seizing hold of his collar. Akakiy Akakievitch was about to shout "watch," when the second man thrust a fist, about the size of a man's head, into his mouth, muttering, "Now scream!"

Akakiy Akakievitch felt them strip off his cloak and give him a push with a knee: he fell headlong upon the snow, and felt no more. In a few minutes he recovered consciousness and rose to his feet; but no one was there. He felt that it was cold in the square, and that his cloak was gone; he began to shout, but his voice did not appear to reach to the outskirts of the square. In despair, but without ceasing to shout, he started at a run across the square, straight towards the watchbox, beside which stood the watchman, leaning on his halberd, and apparently curious to know what kind of a customer was running towards him and shouting. Akakiy Akakievitch ran up to him, and began in a sobbing voice to shout that he was asleep, and attended to nothing, and did not see when a man was robbed. The watchman replied that he had seen two men stop him in the middle of the square, but supposed that they were friends of his; and that, instead of scolding vainly, he had better go to the police on the morrow, so that they might make a search for whoever had stolen the cloak.

Akakiy Akakievitch ran home in complete disorder; his hair, which grew very thinly upon his temples and the back of his head, wholly disordered; his body, arms, and legs covered with snow. The old woman, who was mistress of his lodgings, on hearing a terrible knocking, sprang hastily from her bed, and, with only one shoe on, ran to open the door, pressing the sleeve of her chemise to her bosom out of modesty; but when she had opened it, she fell back on beholding Akakiy Akakievitch in such a state. When he told her about the affair, she clasped her hands, and said that he must go straight to the district chief of police, for his subordinate would turn up his nose, promise well, and drop the matter there. The very best thing to do, therefore, would be to go to the district chief, whom she knew, because Finnish Anna, her former cook, was now nurse at his house. She often saw him passing the house; and he was at church every Sunday, praying, but at the same time gazing cheerfully at everybody; so that he must be a good man, judging from all appearances. Having listened to this opinion, Akakiy Akakievitch betook himself sadly to his room; and how he spent the night there any one who can put himself in another's place may readily imagine.

Early in the morning, he presented himself at the district chief's; but was told that this official was asleep. He went again at ten and was again informed that he was asleep; at eleven, and they said: "The superintendent is not at home;" at dinner time, and the clerks in the ante-room would not admit him on any terms, and insisted upon knowing his business. So that at last, for once in his life, Akakiy Akakievitch felt an inclination to show some spirit, and said curtly that he must see the chief in person; that they ought not to presume to refuse him entrance; that he came from the department of justice, and that when he complained of them, they would see.

The clerks dared make no reply to this, and one of them went to call the chief, who listened to the strange story of the theft of the coat. Instead of directing his attention to the principal points of the matter, he began to question Akakiy Akakievitch: Why was he going home so late? Was he in the habit of doing so, or had he been to some disorderly house? So that Akakiy Akakievitch got thoroughly confused, and left him without knowing whether the affair of his cloak was in proper train or not.

All that day, for the first time in his life, he never went near the department. The next day he made his appearance, very pale, and in his old cape, which had become even more shabby. The news of the robbery of the cloak touched many; although there were some officials present who never lost an opportunity, even such a one as the present, of ridiculing Akakiy Akakievitch. They decided to make a collection for him on the spot, but the officials had already spent a great deal in subscribing for the director's portrait, and for some book, at the suggestion of the head of that division, who was a friend of the author; and so the sum was trifling.

One of them, moved by pity, resolved to help Akakiy Akakievitch with some good advice at least, and told him that he ought not to go to the police, for although it might happen that a police-officer, wishing to win the approval of his superiors, might hunt up the cloak by some means, still his cloak would remain in the possession of the police if he did not offer legal proof that it belonged to him. The best thing for him, therefore, would be to apply to a certain prominent personage; since this prominent personage, by entering into relations with the proper persons, could greatly expedite the matter.

As there was nothing else to be done, Akakiy Akakievitch decided to go to the prominent personage. What was the exact official position of the prominent personage remains unknown to this day. The reader must know that the prominent personage had but recently become a prominent personage, having up to that time been only an insignificant person. Moreover, his present position was not considered prominent in comparison with others still more so. But there is always a circle of people to whom what is insignificant in the eyes of others, is important enough. Moreover, he strove to increase his importance by sundry devices; for instance, he managed to have the inferior officials meet him on the staircase when he entered upon his service; no one was to presume to come directly to him, but the strictest etiquette must be observed; the collegiate recorder must make a report to the government secretary, the government secretary to the titular councillor, or whatever other man was proper, and all business must come before him in this manner. In Holy Russia all is thus contaminated with the love of imitation; every man imitates and copies his superior. They even say that a certain titular councillor, when promoted to the head of some small separate room, immediately partitioned off a private room for himself, called it the audience chamber, and posted at the door a lackey with red collar and braid, who grasped the handle of the door and opened to all comers; though the audience chamber could hardly hold an ordinary writing-table.

The manners and customs of the prominent personage were grand and imposing, but rather exaggerated. The main foundation of his system was strictness. "Strictness, strictness, and always strictness!" he generally said; and at the last word he looked significantly into the face of the person to whom he spoke. But there was no necessity for this, for the half-score of subordinates who formed the entire force of the office were properly afraid; on catching sight of him afar off they left their work and waited, drawn up in line, until he had passed through the room. His ordinary converse with his inferiors smacked of sternness, and consisted chiefly of three phrases: "How dare you?" "Do you know whom you are speaking to?" "Do you realise who stands before you?"

Otherwise he was a very kind-hearted man, good to his comrades, and ready to oblige; but the rank of general threw him completely off his balance. On receiving any one of that rank, he became confused, lost his way, as it were, and never knew what to do. If he chanced to be amongst his equals he was still a very nice kind of man, a very good fellow in many respects, and not stupid; but the very moment that he found himself in the society of people but one rank lower than himself he became silent; and his situation aroused sympathy, the more so as he felt himself that he might have been making an incomparably better use of his time. In his eyes there was sometimes visible a desire to join some interesting conversation or group; but he was kept back by the thought, "Would it not be a very great condescension on his part? Would it not be familiar? and would he not thereby lose his importance?" And in consequence of such reflections he always remained in the same dumb state, uttering from time to time a few monosyllabic sounds, and thereby earning the name of the most wearisome of men.

To this prominent personage Akakiy Akakievitch presented himself, and this at the most unfavourable time for himself though opportune for the prominent personage. The prominent personage was in his cabinet conversing gaily with an old acquaintance and companion of his childhood whom he had not seen for several years and who had just arrived when it was announced to him that a person named Bashmatchkin had come. He asked abruptly, "Who is he?"—"Some official," he was informed. "Ah, he can wait! this is no time for him to call," said the important man.

It must be remarked here that the important man lied outrageously: he had said all he had to say to his friend long before; and the conversation had been interspersed for some time with very long pauses, during which they merely slapped each other on the leg, and said, "You think so, Ivan Abramovitch!" "Just so, Stepan Varlamitch!" Nevertheless, he ordered that the official should be kept waiting, in order to show his friend, a man who had not been in the service for a long time, but had lived at home in the country, how long officials had to wait in his ante-room.

At length, having talked himself completely out, and more than that, having had his fill of pauses, and smoked a cigar in a very comfortable arm-chair with reclining back, he suddenly seemed to recollect, and said to the secretary, who stood by the door with papers of reports, "So it seems that there is a tchinovnik waiting to see me. Tell him that he may come in." On perceiving Akakiy Akakievitch's modest mien and his worn undress uniform, he turned abruptly to him and said, "What do you want?" in a curt hard voice, which he had practised in his room in private, and before the looking-glass, for a whole week before being raised to his present rank.

Akakiy Akakievitch, who was already imbued with a due amount of fear, became somewhat confused: and as well as his tongue would permit, explained, with a rather more frequent addition than usual of the word "that," that his cloak was quite new, and had been stolen in the most inhuman manner; that he had applied to him in order that he might, in some way, by his intermediation—that he might enter into correspondence with the chief of police, and find the cloak.

For some inexplicable reason this conduct seemed familiar to the prominent personage. "What, my dear sir!" he said abruptly, "are you not acquainted with etiquette? Where have you come from? Don't you know how such matters are managed? You should first have entered a complaint about this at the court below: it would have gone to the head of the department, then to the chief of the division, then it would have been handed over to the secretary, and the secretary would have given it to me."

"But, your excellency," said Akakiy Akakievitch, trying to collect his small handful of wits, and conscious at the same time that he was perspiring terribly, "I, your excellency, presumed to trouble you because secretaries—are an untrustworthy race."

"What, what, what!" said the important personage. "Where did you get such courage? Where did you get such ideas? What impudence towards their chiefs and superiors has spread among the young generation!" The prominent personage apparently had not observed that Akakiy Akakievitch was already in the neighbourhood of fifty. If he could be called a young man, it must have been in comparison with some one who was twenty. "Do you know to whom you speak? Do you realise who stands before you? Do you realise it? do you realise it? I ask you!" Then he stamped his foot and raised his voice to such a pitch that it would have frightened even a different man from Akakiy Akakievitch.

Akakiy Akakievitch's senses failed him; he staggered, trembled in every limb, and, if the porters had not run to support him, would have fallen to the floor. They carried him out insensible. But the prominent personage, gratified that the effect should have surpassed his expectations, and quite intoxicated with the thought that his word could even deprive a man of his senses, glanced sideways at his friend in order to see how he looked upon this, and perceived, not without satisfaction, that his friend was in a most uneasy frame of mind, and even beginning, on his part, to feel a trifle frightened.

Akakiy Akakievitch could not remember how he descended the stairs and got into the street. He felt neither his hands nor feet. Never in his life had he been so rated by any high official, let alone a strange one. He went staggering on through the snow-storm, which was blowing in the streets, with his mouth wide open; the wind, in St. Petersburg fashion, darted upon him from all quarters, and down every cross-street. In a twinkling it had blown a quinsy into his throat, and he reached home unable to utter a word. His throat was swollen, and he lay down on his bed. So powerful is sometimes a good scolding!

The next day a violent fever showed itself. Thanks to the generous assistance of the St. Petersburg climate, the malady progressed more rapidly than could have been expected: and when the doctor arrived, he found, on feeling the sick man's pulse, that there was nothing to be done, except to prescribe a fomentation, so that the patient might not be left entirely without the beneficent aid of medicine; but at the same time, he predicted his end in thirty-six hours. After this he turned to the landlady, and said, "And as for you, don't waste your time on him: order his pine coffin now, for an oak one will be too expensive for him." Did Akakiy Akakievitch hear these fatal words? and if he heard them, did they produce any overwhelming effect upon him? Did he lament the bitterness of his life?—We know not, for he continued in a delirious condition. Visions incessantly appeared to him, each stranger than the other. Now he saw Petrovitch, and ordered him to make a cloak, with some traps for robbers, who seemed to him to be always under the bed; and cried every moment to the landlady to pull one of them from under his coverlet. Then he inquired why his old mantle hung before him when he had a new cloak. Next he fancied that he was standing before the prominent person, listening to a thorough setting-down, and saying, "Forgive me, your excellency!" but at last he began to curse, uttering the most horrible words, so that his aged landlady crossed herself, never in her life having heard anything of the kind from him, the more so as those words followed directly after the words "your excellency." Later on he talked utter nonsense, of which nothing could be made: all that was evident being, that his incoherent words and thoughts hovered ever about one thing, his cloak.

At length poor Akakiy Akakievitch breathed his last. They sealed up neither his room nor his effects, because, in the first place, there were no heirs, and, in the second, there was very little to inherit beyond a bundle of goose-quills, a quire of white official paper, three pairs of socks, two or three buttons which had burst off his trousers, and the mantle already known to the reader. To whom all this fell, God knows. I confess that the person who told me this tale took no interest in the matter. They carried Akakiy Akakievitch out and buried him.

And St. Petersburg was left without Akakiy Akakievitch, as though he had never lived there. A being disappeared who was protected by none, dear to none, interesting to none, and who never even attracted to himself the attention of those students of human nature who omit no opportunity of thrusting a pin through a common fly, and examining it under the microscope. A being who bore meekly the jibes of the department, and went to his grave without having done one unusual deed, but to whom, nevertheless, at the close of his life appeared a bright visitant in the form of a cloak, which momentarily cheered his poor life, and upon whom, thereafter, an intolerable misfortune descended, just as it descends upon the mighty of this world!

Several days after his death, the porter was sent from the department to his lodgings, with an order for him to present himself there immediately; the chief commanding it. But the porter had to return unsuccessful, with the answer that he could not come; and to the question, "Why?" replied, "Well, because he is dead! he was buried four days ago." In this manner did they hear of Akakiy Akakievitch's death at the department, and the next day a new official sat in his place, with a handwriting by no means so upright, but more inclined and slanting.

But who could have imagined that this was not really the end of Akakiy Akakievitch, that he was destined to raise a commotion after death, as if in compensation for his utterly insignificant life? But so it happened, and our poor story unexpectedly gains a fantastic ending.

A rumour suddenly spread through St. Petersburg that a dead man had taken to appearing on the Kalinkin Bridge and its vicinity at night in the form of a tchinovnik seeking a stolen cloak, and that, under the pretext of its being the stolen cloak, he dragged, without regard to rank or calling, every one's cloak from his shoulders, be it cat-skin, beaver, fox, bear, sable; in a word, every sort of fur and skin which men adopted for their covering. One of the department officials saw the dead man with his own eyes and immediately recognised in him Akakiy Akakievitch. This, however, inspired him with such terror that he ran off with all his might, and therefore did not scan the dead man closely, but only saw how the latter threatened him from afar with his finger. Constant complaints poured in from all quarters that the backs and shoulders, not only of titular but even of court councillors, were exposed to the danger of a cold on account of the frequent dragging off of their cloaks.

Arrangements were made by the police to catch the corpse, alive or dead, at any cost, and punish him as an example to others in the most severe manner. In this they nearly succeeded; for a watchman, on guard in Kirushkin Alley, caught the corpse by the collar on the very scene of his evil deeds, when attempting to pull off the frieze coat of a retired musician. Having seized him by the collar, he summoned, with a shout, two of his comrades, whom he enjoined to hold him fast while he himself felt for a moment in his boot, in order to draw out his snuff-box and refresh his frozen nose. But the snuff was of a sort which even a corpse could not endure. The watchman having closed his right nostril with his finger, had no sooner succeeded in holding half a handful up to the left than the corpse sneezed so violently that he completely filled the eyes of all three. While they raised their hands to wipe them, the dead man vanished completely, so that they positively did not know whether they had actually had him in their grip at all. Thereafter the watchmen conceived such a terror of dead men that they were afraid even to seize the living, and only screamed from a distance, "Hey, there! go your way!" So the dead tchinovnik began to appear even beyond the Kalinkin Bridge, causing no little terror to all timid people.

But we have totally neglected that certain prominent personage who may really be considered as the cause of the fantastic turn taken by this true history. First of all, justice compels us to say that after the departure of poor, annihilated Akakiy Akakievitch he felt something like remorse. Suffering was unpleasant to him, for his heart was accessible to many good impulses, in spite of the fact that his rank often prevented his showing his true self. As soon as his friend had left his cabinet, he began to think about poor

Akakiy Akakievitch. And from that day forth, poor Akakiy Akakievitch, who could not bear up under an official reprimand, recurred to his mind almost every day. The thought troubled him to such an extent that a week later he even resolved to send an official to him, to learn whether he really could assist him; and when it was reported to him that Akakiy Akakievitch had died suddenly of fever, he was startled, hearkened to the reproaches of his conscience, and was out of sorts for the whole day.

Wishing to divert his mind in some way, and drive away the disagreeable impression, he set out that evening for one of his friends' houses, where he found quite a large party assembled. What was better, nearly every one was of the same rank as himself, so that he need not feel in the least constrained. This had a marvellous effect upon his mental state. He grew expansive, made himself agreeable in conversation, in short, he passed a delightful evening. After supper he drank a couple of glasses of champagne—not a bad recipe for cheerfulness, as every one knows. The champagne inclined him to various adventures; and he determined not to return home, but to go and see a certain well-known lady of German extraction, Karolina Ivanovna, a lady, it appears, with whom he was on a very friendly footing.

It must be mentioned that the prominent personage was no longer a young man, but a good husband and respected father of a family. Two sons, one of whom was already in the service, and a good-looking, sixteen-year-old daughter, with a rather retrousse but pretty little nose, came every morning to kiss his hand and say, "Bonjour, papa." His wife, a still fresh and good-looking woman, first gave him her hand to kiss, and then, reversing the procedure, kissed his. But the prominent personage, though perfectly satisfied in his domestic relations, considered it stylish to have a friend in another quarter of the city. This friend was scarcely prettier or younger than his wife; but there are such puzzles in the world, and it is not our place to judge them. So the important personage descended the stairs, stepped into his sledge, said to the coachman, "To Karolina Ivanovna's," and, wrapping himself luxuriously in his warm cloak, found himself in that delightful frame of mind than which a Russian can conceive no better, namely, when you think of nothing yourself, yet when the thoughts creep into your mind of their own accord, each more agreeable than the other, giving you no trouble either to drive them away or seek them. Fully satisfied, he recalled all the gay features of the evening just passed, and all the mots which had made the little circle laugh. Many of them he repeated in a low voice, and found them quite as funny as before; so it is not surprising that he should laugh heartily at them. Occasionally, however, he was interrupted by gusts of wind, which, coming suddenly, God knows whence or why, cut his face, drove masses of snow into it, filled out his cloak-collar like a sail, or suddenly blew it over his head with supernatural force, and thus caused him constant trouble to disentangle himself.

Suddenly the important personage felt some one clutch him firmly by the collar. Turning round, he perceived a man of short stature, in an old, worn uniform, and recognised, not without terror, Akakiy Akakievitch. The official's face was white as snow, and looked just like a corpse's. But the horror of the important personage transcended all bounds when he saw the dead man's mouth open, and, with a terrible odour of the grave, gave vent to the following remarks: "Ah, here you are at last! I have you, that—by the collar! I need your cloak; you took no trouble about mine, but reprimanded me; so now give up your own."

The pallid prominent personage almost died of fright. Brave as he was in the office and in the presence of inferiors generally, and although, at the sight of his manly form and appearance, every one said, "Ugh! how much character he had!" at this crisis, he, like many possessed of an heroic exterior, experienced such terror, that, not without cause, he began to fear an attack of illness. He flung his cloak hastily from his shoulders and shouted to his coachman in an unnatural voice, "Home at full speed!" The coachman, hearing the tone which is generally employed at critical moments and even accompanied by something much more tangible, drew his head down between his shoulders in case of an emergency, flourished his whip, and flew on like an arrow. In a little more than six minutes the prominent personage was at the entrance of his own house. Pale, thoroughly scared, and cloakless, he went home instead of to Karolina Ivanovna's, reached his room somehow or other, and passed the night in the direst distress; so that the next morning over their tea his daughter said, "You are very pale to-day, papa." But papa remained silent, and said not a word to any one of what had happened to him, where he had been, or where he had intended to go.

This occurrence made a deep impression upon him. He even began to say: "How dare you? do you realise who stands before you?" less frequently to the under-officials, and if he did utter the words, it was only after having first learned the bearings of the matter. But the most noteworthy point was, that from that day forward the apparition of the dead tchinovnik ceased to be seen. Evidently the prominent personage's cloak just fitted his shoulders; at all events, no more instances of his dragging cloaks from people's shoulders were heard of. But many active and apprehensive persons could by no means reassure themselves, and asserted that the dead tchinovnik still showed himself in distant parts of the city.

In fact, one watchman in Kolomna saw with his own eyes the apparition come from behind a house. But being rather weak of body, he dared not arrest him, but followed him in the dark, until, at length, the apparition looked round, paused, and inquired, "What do you want?" at the same time showing a fist such as is never seen on living men. The watchman said, "It's of no consequence," and turned back instantly. But the apparition was much too tall, wore huge moustaches, and, directing its steps apparently towards the Obukhoff bridge, disappeared in the darkness of the night.

2

The Nose

Translated by Claud Field

I

On the 25th March, 18—, a very strange occurrence took place in St Petersburg. On the Ascension Avenue there lived a barber of the name of Ivan Jakovlevitch. He had lost his family name, and on his signboard, on which was depicted the head of a gentleman with one cheek soaped, the only inscription to be read was, "Bloodletting done here."

On this particular morning he awoke pretty early. Becoming aware of the smell of fresh-baked bread, he sat up a little in bed, and saw his wife, who had a special partiality for coffee, in the act of taking some fresh-baked bread out of the oven.

"To-day, Prasskovna Ossipovna," he said, "I do not want any coffee; I should like a fresh loaf with onions."

"The blockhead may eat bread only as far as I am concerned," said his wife to herself; "then I shall have a chance of getting some coffee." And she threw a loaf on the table.

For the sake of propriety, Ivan Jakovlevitch drew a coat over his shirt, sat down at the table, shook out some salt for himself, prepared two onions, assumed a serious expression, and began to cut the bread. After he had cut the loaf in two halves, he looked, and to his great astonishment saw something whitish sticking in it. He carefully poked round it with his knife, and felt it with his finger.

"Quite firmly fixed!" he murmured in his beard. "What can it be?"

He put in his finger, and drew out—a nose!

Ivan Jakovlevitch at first let his hands fall from sheer astonishment; then he rubbed his eyes and began to feel it. A nose, an actual nose; and, moreover, it seemed to be the nose of an acquaintance! Alarm and terror were depicted in Ivan's face; but these feelings were slight in comparison with the disgust which took possession of his wife.

"Whose nose have you cut off, you monster?" she screamed, her face red with anger. "You scoundrel! You tippler! I myself will report you to the police! Such a rascal! Many customers have told me that while you were shaving them, you held them so tight by the nose that they could hardly sit still."

But Ivan Jakovlevitch was more dead than alive; he saw at once that this nose could belong to no other than to Kovaloff, a member of the Municipal Committee whom he shaved every Sunday and Wednesday.

"Stop, Prasskovna Ossipovna! I will wrap it in a piece of cloth and place it in the corner. There it may remain for the present; later on I will take it away."

"No, not there! Shall I endure an amputated nose in my room? You understand nothing except how to strop a razor. You know nothing of the duties and obligations of a respectable man. You vagabond! You good-for-nothing! Am I to undertake all responsibility for you at the police-office? Ah, you soap-smearer! You blockhead! Take it away where you like, but don't let it stay under my eyes!"

Ivan Jakovlevitch stood there flabbergasted. He thought and thought, and knew not what he thought.

"The devil knows how that happened!" he said at last, scratching his head behind his ear. "Whether I came home drunk last night or not, I really don't know; but in all probability this is a quite extraordinary occurrence, for a loaf is something baked and a nose is something different. I don't understand the matter at all." And Ivan Jakovlevitch was silent. The thought that the police might find him in unlawful possession of a nose and arrest him, robbed him of all presence of mind. Already he began

to have visions of a red collar with silver braid and of a sword—and he trembled all over.

At last he finished dressing himself, and to the accompaniment of the emphatic exhortations of his spouse, he wrapped up the nose in a cloth and issued into the street.

He intended to lose it somewhere—either at somebody's door, or in a public square, or in a narrow alley; but just then, in order to complete his bad luck, he was met by an acquaintance, who showered inquiries upon him. "Hullo, Ivan Jakovlevitch! Whom are you going to shave so early in the morning?" etc., so that he could find no suitable opportunity to do what he wanted. Later on he did let the nose drop, but a sentry bore down upon him with his halberd, and said, "Look out! You have let something drop!" and Ivan Jakovlevitch was obliged to pick it up and put it in his pocket.

A feeling of despair began to take possession of him; all the more as the streets became more thronged and the merchants began to open their shops. At last he resolved to go to the Isaac Bridge, where perhaps he might succeed in throwing it into the Neva.

But my conscience is a little uneasy that I have not yet given any detailed information about Ivan Jakovlevitch, an estimable man in many ways.

Like every honest Russian tradesman, Ivan Jakovlevitch was a terrible drunkard, and although he shaved other people's faces every day, his own was always unshaved. His coat (he never wore an overcoat) was quite mottled, i.e. it had been black, but become brownish-yellow; the collar was quite shiny, and instead of the three buttons, only the threads by which they had been fastened were to be seen.

Ivan Jakovlevitch was a great cynic, and when Kovaloff, the member of the Municipal Committee, said to him, as was his custom while being shaved, "Your hands always smell, Ivan Jakovlevitch!" the latter answered, "What do they smell of?" "I don't know, my friend, but they smell very strong." Ivan Jakovlevitch after taking a pinch of snuff would then, by way of reprisals, set to work to soap him on the cheek, the upper lip, behind the ears, on the chin, and everywhere.

This worthy man now stood on the Isaac Bridge. At first he looked round him, then he leant on the railings of the bridge, as though he wished to look down and see how many fish were swimming past, and secretly threw the nose, wrapped in a little piece of cloth, into the water. He felt as though a ton weight had been lifted off him, and laughed cheerfully. Instead, however, of going to shave any officials, he turned his steps to a building, the sign-board of which bore the legend "Teas served here," in order to have a glass of punch, when suddenly he perceived at the other end of the bridge a police inspector of imposing exterior, with long whiskers, three-cornered hat, and sword hanging at his side. He nearly fainted; but the police inspector beckoned to him with his hand and said, "Come here, my dear sir."

Ivan Jakovlevitch, knowing how a gentleman should behave, took his hat off quickly, went towards the police inspector and said, "I hope you are in the best of health."

"Never mind my health. Tell me, my friend, why you were standing on the bridge."

"By heaven, gracious sir, I was on the way to my customers, and only looked down to see if the river was flowing quickly."

"That is a lie! You won't get out of it like that. Confess the truth."

"I am willing to shave Your Grace two or even three times a week gratis," answered Ivan Jakovlevitch.

"No, my friend, don't put yourself out! Three barbers are busy with me already, and reckon it a high honour that I let them show me their skill. Now then, out with it! What were you doing there?"

Ivan Jakovlevitch grew pale. But here the strange episode vanishes in mist, and what further happened is not known.

II

Kovaloff, the member of the Municipal Committee, awoke fairly early that morning, and made a droning noise—"Brr! Brr!"—through his lips, as he always did, though he could not say why. He stretched himself, and told his valet to give him a little mirror which was on the table. He wished to look at the heat-boil which had appeared on his nose the previous evening; but to his great astonishment, he saw that instead of his nose he had a perfectly smooth vacancy in his face. Thoroughly alarmed, he ordered some water to be brought, and rubbed his eyes with a towel. Sure enough, he had no longer a nose! Then he sprang out of bed, and shook himself violently! No, no nose any more! He dressed himself and went at once to the police superintendent.

But before proceeding further, we must certainly give the reader some information about Kovaloff, so that he may know what sort of a man this member of the Municipal Committee really was. These committee-men, who obtain that title by means of certificates of learning, must not be compared with the committee-men appointed for the Caucasus district, who are of quite a different kind. The learned committee-man—but Russia is such a wonderful country that when one committee-man is spoken of all the others from Riga to Kamschatka refer it to themselves. The same is also true of all other titled officials. Kovaloff had been a Caucasian committee-man two years previously, and could not forget that he had occupied that position; but in order to enhance his own importance, he never called himself "committee-man" but "Major."

"Listen, my dear," he used to say when he met an old woman in the street who sold shirt-fronts; "go to my house in Sadovaia Street and ask 'Does Major Kovaloff live here?' Any child can tell you where it is."

Accordingly we will call him for the future Major Kovaloff. It was his custom to take a daily walk on the Neffsky Avenue. The collar of his shirt was always remarkably clean and stiff. He wore the same style of whiskers as those that are worn by governors of districts, architects, and regimental doctors; in short, all those who have full red cheeks and play a good game of whist. These whiskers grow straight across the cheek towards the nose.

Major Kovaloff wore a number of seals, on some of which were engraved armorial bearings, and others the names of the days of the week. He had come to St Petersburg with the view of obtaining some position corresponding to his rank, if possible that of vice-governor of a province; but he was prepared to be content with that of a bailiff in some department or other. He was, moreover, not disinclined to marry, but only such a lady who could bring with her a dowry of two hundred thousand roubles. Accordingly, the reader can judge for himself what his sensations were when he found in his face, instead of a fairly symmetrical nose, a broad, flat vacancy.

To increase his misfortune, not a single droshky was to be seen in the street, and so he was obliged to proceed on foot. He wrapped himself up in his cloak, and held his handkerchief to his face as though his nose bled. "But perhaps it is all only my imagination; it is impossible that a nose should drop off in such a silly way," he thought, and stepped into a confectioner's shop in order to look into the mirror.

Fortunately no customer was in the shop; only small shop-boys were cleaning it out, and putting chairs and tables straight. Others with sleepy faces were carrying fresh cakes on trays, and yesterday's newspapers stained with coffee were still lying about. "Thank God no one is here!" he said to himself. "Now I can look at myself leisurely."

He stepped gingerly up to a mirror and looked.

"What an infernal face!" he exclaimed, and spat with disgust. "If there were only something there instead of the nose, but there is absolutely nothing."

He bit his lips with vexation, left the confectioner's, and resolved, quite contrary to his habit, neither to look nor smile at anyone on the street. Suddenly he halted as if rooted to the spot before a door, where something extraordinary happened. A carriage drew up at the entrance; the carriage door was opened, and a gentleman in uniform came out and hurried up the steps. How great was Kovaloff's terror and astonishment when he saw that it was his own nose!

At this extraordinary sight, everything seemed to turn round with him. He felt as though he could hardly keep upright on his legs; but, though trembling all over as though with fever, he resolved to wait till the nose should return to the carriage. After about two minutes the nose actually came out again. It wore a gold-embroidered uniform with a stiff, high collar, trousers of chamois leather, and a sword hung at its side. The hat, adorned with a plume, showed that it held the rank of a state-councillor. It was obvious that it was paying "duty-calls." It looked round on both sides, called to the coachman "Drive on," and got into the carriage, which drove away.

Poor Kovaloff nearly lost his reason. He did not know what to think of this extraordinary procedure. And indeed how was it possible that the nose, which only yesterday he had on his face, and which could neither walk nor drive, should wear a uniform. He ran after the carriage, which fortunately had stopped a short way off before the Grand Bazar of Moscow. He hurried towards it and pressed through a crowd of beggar-women with their faces bound up, leaving only two openings for the eyes, over whom he had formerly so often made merry.

There were only a few people in front of the Bazar. Kovaloff was so agitated that he could decide on nothing, and looked for the nose everywhere. At last he saw it standing before a shop. It seemed half buried in its stiff collar, and was attentively inspecting the wares displayed.

"How can I get at it?" thought Kovaloff. "Everything—the uniform, the hat, and so on—show that it is a state-councillor. How the deuce has that happened?"

He began to cough discreetly near it, but the nose paid him not the least attention.

"Honourable sir," said Kovaloff at last, plucking up courage, "honourable sir."

"What do you want?" asked the nose, and turned round.

"It seems to me strange, most respected sir—you should know where you belong—and I find you all of a sudden—where? Judge yourself."

"Pardon me, I do not understand what you are talking about. Explain yourself more distinctly."

"How shall I make my meaning plainer to him?" Then plucking up fresh courage, he continued, "Naturally—besides I am a Major. You must admit it is not befitting that I should go about without a nose. An old apple-woman on the Ascension Bridge may carry on her business without one, but since I am on the look out for a post; besides in many houses I am acquainted with ladies of high position—Madame Tchektyriev, wife of a state-councillor, and many others. So you see—I do not know, honourable sir, what you——" (here the Major shrugged his shoulders). "Pardon me; if one regards the matter from the point of view of duty and honour—you will yourself understand——"

"I understand nothing," answered the nose. "I repeat, please explain yourself more distinctly."

"Honourable sir," said Kovaloff with dignity, "I do not know how I am to understand your words. It seems to me the matter is as clear as possible. Or do you wish—but you are after all my own nose!"

The nose looked at the Major and wrinkled its forehead. "There you are wrong, respected sir; I am myself. Besides, there can be no close relations between us. To judge by the buttons of your uniform, you must be in quite a different department to mine." So saying, the nose turned away.

Kovaloff was completely puzzled; he did not know what to do, and still less what to think. At this moment he heard the pleasant rustling of a lady's dress, and there approached an elderly lady wearing a quantity of lace, and by her side her graceful daughter in a white dress which set off her slender figure to advantage, and wearing a light straw hat. Behind the ladies marched a tall lackey with long whiskers.

Kovaloff advanced a few steps, adjusted his cambric collar, arranged his seals which hung by a little gold chain, and with smiling face fixed his eyes on the graceful lady, who bowed lightly like a spring flower, and raised to her brow her little white hand with transparent fingers. He smiled still more when he spied under the brim of her hat her little round chin, and part of her cheek faintly tinted with rose-colour. But suddenly he sprang back as though he had been scorched. He remembered that he had nothing but an absolute blank in place of a nose, and tears started to his eyes. He turned round in order to tell the gentleman in uniform that he was only a state-councillor in appearance, but really a scoundrel and a rascal, and nothing else but his own nose; but the nose was no longer there. He had had time to go, doubtless in order to continue his visits.

His disappearance plunged Kovaloff into despair. He went back and stood for a moment under a colonnade, looking round him on all sides in hope of perceiving the nose somewhere. He remembered very well that it wore a hat with a plume in it and a gold-embroidered uniform; but he had not noticed the shape of the cloak, nor the colour of the carriages and the horses, nor even whether a lackey stood behind it, and, if so, what sort of livery he wore. Moreover, so many carriages were passing that it would have been difficult to recognise one, and even if he had done so, there would have been no means of stopping it.

The day was fine and sunny. An immense crowd was passing to and fro in the Neffsky Avenue; a variegated stream of ladies flowed along the pavement. There was his acquaintance, the Privy Councillor, whom he was accustomed to style "General," especially when strangers were present. There was Iarygin, his intimate friend who always lost in the evenings at whist; and there another Major, who had obtained the rank of committee-man in the Caucasus, beckoned to him.

"Go to the deuce!" said Kovaloff *sotto voce*. "Hi! coachman, drive me straight to the superintendent of police." So saying, he got into a droshky and continued to shout all the time to the coachman "Drive hard!"

"Is the police superintendent at home?" he asked on entering the front hall.

"No, sir," answered the porter, "he has just gone out."

"Ah, just as I thought!"

"Yes," continued the porter, "he has only just gone out; if you had been a moment earlier you would perhaps have caught him."

Kovaloff, still holding his handkerchief to his face, re-entered the droshky and cried in a despairing voice "Drive on!"

"Where?" asked the coachman.

"Straight on!"

"But how? There are cross-roads here. Shall I go to the right or the left?"

This question made Kovaloff reflect. In his situation it was necessary to have recourse to the police; not because the affair had anything to do with them directly but because they acted more promptly than other authorities. As for demanding any explanation from the department to which the nose claimed to belong, it would, he felt, be useless, for the answers of that gentleman showed that he regarded nothing as sacred, and he might just as likely have lied in this matter as in saying that he had never seen Kovaloff.

But just as he was about to order the coachman to drive to the police-station, the idea occurred to him that this rascally scoundrel who, at their first meeting, had behaved so disloyally towards him, might, profiting by the delay, quit the city secretly; and then all his searching would be in vain, or might last over a whole month. Finally, as though visited with a heavenly inspiration, he resolved to go directly to an advertisement office, and to advertise the loss of his nose, giving all its distinctive characteristics in detail, so that anyone who found it might bring it at once to him, or at any rate inform him where it lived. Having decided on this course, he ordered the coachman to drive to the advertisement office, and all the way he continued to punch him in the back—"Quick, scoundrel! quick!"

"Yes, sir!" answered the coachman, lashing his shaggy horse with the reins.

At last they arrived, and Kovaloff, out of breath, rushed into a little room where a grey-haired official, in an old coat and with spectacles on his nose, sat at a table holding his pen between his teeth, counting a heap of copper coins.

"Who takes in the advertisements here?" exclaimed Kovaloff.

"At your service, sir," answered the grey-haired functionary, looking up and then fastening his eyes again on the heap of coins before him.

"I wish to place an advertisement in your paper——"

"Have the kindness to wait a minute," answered the official, putting down figures on paper with one hand, and with the other moving two balls on his calculating-frame.

A lackey, whose silver-laced coat showed that he served in one of the houses of the nobility, was standing by the table with a note in his hand, and speaking in a lively tone, by way of showing himself sociable. "Would you believe it, sir, this little dog is really not worth twenty-four kopecks, and for my own part I would not give a farthing for it; but the countess is quite gone upon it, and offers a hundred roubles' reward to anyone who finds it. To tell you the truth, the tastes of these people are very different from ours; they don't mind giving five hundred or a thousand roubles for a poodle or a pointer, provided it be a good one."

The official listened with a serious air while counting the number of letters contained in the note. At either side of the table stood a number of housekeepers, clerks and porters, carrying notes. The writer of one wished to sell a barouche, which had been brought from Paris in 1814 and had been very little used; others wanted to dispose of a strong droshky which wanted one spring, a spirited horse seventeen years old, and so on. The room where these people were collected was very small, and the air was very close; but Kovaloff was not affected by it, for he had covered his face with a handkerchief, and because his nose itself was heaven knew where.

"Sir, allow me to ask you—I am in a great hurry," he said at last impatiently.

"In a moment! In a moment! Two roubles, twenty-four kopecks—one minute! One rouble, sixty-four kopecks!" said the grey-haired official, throwing their notes back to the housekeepers and porters. "What do you wish?" he said, turning to Kovaloff.

"I wish—" answered the latter, "I have just been swindled and cheated, and I cannot get hold of the perpetrator. I only want you to insert an advertisement to say that whoever brings this scoundrel to me will be well rewarded."

"What is your name, please?"

"Why do you want my name? I have many lady friends—Madame Tchektyriev, wife of a state-councillor, Madame Podtotchina, wife of a Colonel. Heaven forbid that they should get to hear of it. You can simply write 'committee-man,' or, better, 'Major.'"

"And the man who has run away is your serf."

"Serf! If he was, it would not be such a great swindle! It is the nose which has absconded."

"H'm! What a strange name. And this Mr Nose has stolen from you a considerable sum?"

"Mr Nose! Ah, you don't understand me! It is my own nose which has gone, I don't know where. The devil has played a trick on me."

"How has it disappeared? I don't understand."

"I can't tell you how, but the important point is that now it walks about the city itself a state-councillor. That is why I want you to advertise that whoever gets hold of it should bring it as soon as possible to me. Consider; how can I live without such a prominent part of my body? It is not as if it were merely a little toe; I would only have to put my foot in my boot and no one would notice its absence. Every Thursday I call on the wife of M. Tchektyriev, the state-councillor; Madame Podtotchina, a Colonel's wife who has a very pretty daughter, is one of my acquaintances; and what am I to do now? I cannot appear before them like this."

The official compressed his lips and reflected. "No, I cannot insert an advertisement like that," he said after a long pause.

"What! Why not?"

"Because it might compromise the paper. Suppose everyone could advertise that his nose was lost. People already say that all sorts of nonsense and lies are inserted."

"But this is not nonsense! There is nothing of that sort in my case."

"You think so? Listen a minute. Last week there was a case very like it. An official came, just as you have done, bringing an advertisement for the insertion of which he paid two roubles, sixty-three kopecks; and this advertisement simply announced the loss of a black-haired poodle. There did not seem to be anything out of the way in it, but it was really a satire; by the poodle was meant the cashier of some establishment or other."

"But I am not talking of a poodle, but my own nose; i.e. almost myself."

"No, I cannot insert your advertisement."

"But my nose really has disappeared!"

"That is a matter for a doctor. There are said to be people who can provide you with any kind of nose you like. But I see that you are a witty man, and like to have your little joke."

"But I swear to you on my word of honour. Look at my face yourself."

"Why put yourself out?" continued the official, taking a pinch of snuff. "All the same, if you don't mind," he added with a touch of curiosity, "I should like to have a look at it."

The committee-man removed the handkerchief from before his face.

"It certainly does look odd," said the official. "It is perfectly flat like a freshly fried pancake. It is hardly credible."

"Very well. Are you going to hesitate any more? You see it is impossible to refuse to advertise my loss. I shall be particularly obliged to you, and I shall be glad that this incident has procured me the pleasure of making your acquaintance." The Major, we see, did not even shrink from a slight humiliation.

"It certainly is not difficult to advertise it," replied the official; "but I don't see what good it would do you. However, if you lay so much stress on it, you should apply to someone who has a skilful pen, so that he may describe it as a curious, natural freak, and publish the article in the *Northern Bee*" (here he took another pinch) "for the benefit of youthful readers" (he wiped his nose), "or simply as a matter worthy of arousing public curiosity."

The committee-man felt completely discouraged. He let his eyes fall absent-mindedly on a daily paper in which theatrical performances were advertised. Reading there the name of an actress whom he knew to be pretty, he involuntarily smiled, and his hand sought his pocket to see if he had a blue ticket—for in Kovaloff's opinion superior officers like himself should not take a lesser-priced seat; but the thought of his lost nose suddenly spoilt everything.

The official himself seemed touched at his difficult position. Desiring to console him, he tried to express his sympathy by a few polite words. "I much regret," he said, "your extraordinary mishap. Will you not try a pinch of snuff? It clears the head, banishes depression, and is a good preventive against hæmorrhoids."

So saying, he reached his snuff-box out to Kovaloff, skilfully concealing at the same time the cover, which was adorned with the portrait of some lady or other.

This act, quite innocent in itself, exasperated Kovaloff. "I don't understand what you find to joke about in the matter," he exclaimed angrily. "Don't you see that I lack precisely the essential feature for taking snuff? The devil take your snuff-box. I don't want to look at snuff now, not even the best, certainly not your vile stuff!"

So saying, he left the advertisement office in a state of profound irritation, and went to the commissary of police. He arrived just as this dignitary was reclining on his couch, and saying to himself with a sigh of satisfaction, "Yes, I shall make a nice little sum out of that."

It might be expected, therefore, that the committee-man's visit would be quite inopportune.

This police commissary was a great patron of all the arts and industries; but what he liked above everything else was a cheque. "It is a thing," he used to say, "to which it is not easy to find an equivalent; it requires no food, it does not take up much room, it stays in one's pocket, and if it falls, it is not broken."

The commissary accorded Kovaloff a fairly frigid reception, saying that the afternoon was not the best time to come with a case, that nature required one to rest a little after eating (this showed the committee-man that the commissary was acquainted with the aphorisms of the ancient sages), and that respectable people did not have their noses stolen.

The last allusion was too direct. We must remember that Kovaloff was a very sensitive man. He did not mind anything said against him as an individual, but he could not endure any reflection on his rank or social position. He even believed that in comedies one might allow attacks on junior officers, but never on their seniors.

The commissary's reception of him hurt his feelings so much that he raised his head proudly, and said with dignity, "After such insulting expressions on your part, I have nothing more to say." And he left the place.

He reached his house quite wearied out. It was already growing dark. After all his fruitless search, his room seemed to him melancholy and even ugly. In the vestibule he saw his valet Ivan stretched on the leather couch and amusing himself by spitting at the ceiling, which he did very cleverly, hitting every time the same spot. His servant's equanimity enraged him; he struck him on the forehead with his hat, and said, "You good-for-nothing, you are always playing the fool!"

Ivan rose quickly and hastened to take off his master's cloak.

Once in his room, the Major, tired and depressed, threw himself in an armchair and, after sighing a while, began to soliloquise:

"In heaven's name, why should such a misfortune befall me? If I had lost an arm or a leg, it would be less insupportable; but a man without a nose! Devil take it!—what is he good for? He is only fit to be thrown out of the window. If it had been taken from me in war or in a duel, or if I had lost it by my own fault! But it has disappeared inexplicably. But no! it is impossible," he continued after reflecting a few moments, "it is incredible that a nose can disappear like that—quite incredible. I must be dreaming, or suffering from some hallucination; perhaps I swallowed, by mistake instead of water, the brandy with which I rub my chin after being shaved. That fool of an Ivan must have forgotten to take it away, and I must have swallowed it."

In order to find out whether he were really drunk, the Major pinched himself so hard that he unvoluntarily uttered a cry. The pain convinced him that he was quite wide awake. He walked slowly to the looking-glass and at first closed his eyes, hoping to see his nose suddenly in its proper place; but on opening them, he started back. "What a hideous sight!" he exclaimed.

It was really incomprehensible. One might easily lose a button, a silver spoon, a watch, or something similar; but a loss like this, and in one's own dwelling!

After considering all the circumstances, Major Kovaloff felt inclined to suppose that the cause of all his trouble should be laid at the door of Madame Podtotchina, the Colonel's wife, who wished him to marry her daughter. He himself paid her court readily, but always avoided coming to the point. And when the lady one day told him point-blank that she wished him to marry her daughter, he gently drew back, declaring that he was still too young, and that he had to serve five years more before he would be forty-two. This must be the reason why the lady, in revenge, had resolved to bring him into disgrace, and had hired two sorceresses for that object.

The Nose

One thing was certain—his nose had not been cut off; no one had entered his room, and as for Ivan Jakovlevitch—he had been shaved by him on Wednesday, and during that day and the whole of Thursday his nose had been there, as he knew and well remembered. Moreover, if his nose had been cut off he would naturally have felt pain, and doubtless the wound would not have healed so quickly, nor would the surface have been as flat as a pancake.

All kinds of plans passed through his head: should he bring a legal action against the wife of a superior officer, or should he go to her and charge her openly with her treachery?

His reflections were interrupted by a sudden light, which shone through all the chinks of the door, showing that Ivan had lit the wax-candles in the vestibule. Soon Ivan himself came in with the lights. Kovaloff quickly seized a handkerchief and covered the place where his nose had been the evening before, so that his blockhead of a servant might not gape with his mouth wide open when he saw his master's extraordinary appearance.

Scarcely had Ivan returned to the vestibule than a stranger's voice was heard there.

"Does Major Kovaloff live here?" it asked.

"Come in!" said the Major, rising rapidly and opening the door.

He saw a police official of pleasant appearance, with grey whiskers and fairly full cheeks—the same who at the commencement of this story was standing at the end of the Isaac Bridge. "You have lost your nose?" he asked.

"Exactly so."

"It has just been found."

"What—do you say?" stammered Major Kovaloff.

Joy had suddenly paralysed his tongue. He stared at the police commissary on whose cheeks and full lips fell the flickering light of the candle.

"How was it?" he asked at last.

"By a very singular chance. It has been arrested just as it was getting into a carriage for Riga. Its passport had been made out some time ago in the name of an official; and what is still more strange, I myself took it at first for a gentleman. Fortunately I had my glasses with me, and then I saw at once that it was a nose. I am shortsighted, you know, and as you stand before me I cannot distinguish your nose, your beard, or anything else. My mother-in-law can hardly see at all."

Kovaloff was beside himself with excitement. "Where is it? Where? I will hasten there at once."

"Don't put yourself out. Knowing that you need it, I have brought it with me. Another singular thing is that the principal culprit in the matter is a scoundrel of a barber living in the Ascension Avenue, who is now safely locked up. I had long suspected him of drunkenness and theft; only the day before yesterday he stole some buttons in a shop. Your nose is quite uninjured." So saying, the police commissary put his hand in his pocket and brought out the nose wrapped up in paper.

"Yes, yes, that is it!" exclaimed Kovaloff. "Will you not stay and drink a cup of tea with me?"

"I should like to very much, but I cannot. I must go at once to the House of Correction. The cost of living is very high nowadays. My mother-in-law lives with me, and there are several children; the eldest is very hopeful and intelligent, but I have no means for their education."

After the commissary's departure, Kovaloff remained for some time plunged in a kind of vague reverie, and did not recover full consciousness for several moments, so great was the effect of this unexpected good news. He placed the recovered nose carefully in the palm of his hand, and examined it again with the greatest attention.

"Yes, this is it!" he said to himself. "Here is the heat-boil on the left side, which came out yesterday." And he nearly laughed aloud with delight.

But nothing is permanent in this world. Joy in the second moment of its arrival is already less keen than in the first, is still fainter in the third, and finishes by coalescing with our normal mental state, just as the circles which the fall of a pebble forms on the surface of water, gradually die away. Kovaloff began to meditate, and saw that his difficulties were not yet over; his nose had been recovered, but it had to be joined on again in its proper place.

And suppose it could not? As he put this question to himself, Kovaloff grew pale. With a feeling of indescribable dread, he rushed towards his dressing-table, and stood before the mirror in order that he might not place his nose crookedly. His hands trembled.

Very carefully he placed it where it had been before. Horror! It did not remain there. He held it to his mouth and warmed it a little with his breath, and then placed it there again; but it would not hold.

"Hold on, you stupid!" he said.

But the nose seemed to be made of wood, and fell back on the table with a strange noise, as though it had been a cork. The Major's face began to twitch feverishly. "Is it possible that it won't stick?" he asked himself, full of alarm. But however often he tried, all his efforts were in vain.

He called Ivan, and sent him to fetch the doctor who occupied the finest flat in the mansion. This doctor was a man of imposing appearance, who had magnificent black whiskers and a healthy wife. He ate fresh apples every morning, and cleaned his teeth with extreme care, using five different tooth-brushes for three-quarters of an hour daily.

The doctor came immediately. After having asked the Major when this misfortune had happened, he raised his chin and gave him a fillip with his finger just where the nose had been, in such a way that the Major suddenly threw back his head and struck the wall with it. The doctor said that did not matter; then, making him turn his face to the right, he felt the vacant place and said "H'm!" then he made him turn it to the left and did the same; finally he again gave him a fillip with his finger, so that the Major started like a horse whose teeth are being examined. After this experiment, the doctor shook his head and said, "No, it cannot be done. Rather remain as you are, lest something worse happen. Certainly one could replace it at once, but I assure you the remedy would be worse than the disease."

"All very fine, but how am I to go on without a nose?" answered Kovaloff. "There is nothing worse than that. How can I show myself with such a villainous appearance? I go into good society, and this evening I am invited to two parties. I know several ladies, Madame Tchektyriev, the wife of a state-councillor, Madame Podtotchina—although after what she has done, I don't want to have anything to do with her except through the agency of the police. I beg you," continued Kovaloff in a supplicating tone, "find some way or other of replacing it; even if it is not quite firm, as long as it holds at all; I can keep it in place sometimes with my hand, whenever there is any risk. Besides, I do not even dance, so that it is not likely to be injured by any sudden movement. As to your fee, be in no anxiety about that; I can well afford it."

"Believe me," answered the doctor in a voice which was neither too high nor too low, but soft and almost magnetic, "I do not treat patients from love of gain. That would be contrary to my principles and to my art. It is true that I accept fees, but that is only not to hurt my patients' feelings by refusing them. I could certainly replace your nose, but I assure you on my word of honour, it would only make matters worse. Rather let Nature do her own work. Wash the place often with cold water, and I assure you that even without a nose, you will be just as well as if you had one. As to the nose itself, I advise you to have it preserved in a bottle of spirits, or, still better, of warm vinegar mixed with two spoonfuls of brandy, and then you can sell it at a good price. I would be willing to take it myself, provided you do not ask too much."

"No, no, I shall not sell it at any price. I would rather it were lost again."

"Excuse me," said the doctor, taking his leave. "I hoped to be useful to you, but I can do nothing more; you are at any rate convinced of my goodwill." So saying, the doctor left the room with a dignified air.

Kovaloff did not even notice his departure. Absorbed in a profound reverie, he only saw the edge of his snow-white cuffs emerging from the sleeves of his black coat.

The next day he resolved, before bringing a formal action, to write to the Colonel's wife and see whether she would not return to him, without further dispute, that of which she had deprived him.

The letter ran as follows:

"To Madame Alexandra Podtotchina,

"I hardly understand your method of action. Be sure that by adopting such a course you will gain nothing, and will certainly not succeed in making me marry your daughter. Believe me, the story of my nose has become well known; it is you and no one else who have taken the principal part in it. Its unexpected separation from the place which it occupied, its flight and its appearances sometimes in the disguise of an official, sometimes in proper person, are nothing but the consequence of unholy spells employed by you or by persons who, like you, are addicted to such honourable pursuits. On my part, I wish to inform you, that if the above-mentioned nose is not restored to-day to its proper place, I shall be obliged to have recourse to legal procedure.

"For the rest, with all respect, I have the honour to be your humble servant,

"Platon Kovaloff."

The reply was not long in coming, and was as follows:

"Major Platon Kovaloff,—

"Your letter has profoundly astonished me. I must confess that I had not expected such unjust reproaches on your part. I assure you that the official of whom you speak has not been at my house, either disguised or in his proper person. It is true that Philippe Ivanovitch Potantchikoff has paid visits at my house, and though he has actually asked for my daughter's hand, and was a man of good breeding, respectable and intelligent, I never gave him any hope.

"Again, you say something about a nose. If you intend to imply by that that I wished to snub you, i.e. to meet you with a refusal, I am very astonished because, as you well know, I was quite of the opposite mind. If after this you wish to ask for my daughter's hand, I should be glad to gratify you, for such has also been the object of my most fervent desire, in the hope of the accomplishment of which, I remain, yours most sincerely,

"Alexandra Podtotchina."

"No," said Kovaloff, after having reperused the letter, "she is certainly not guilty. It is impossible. Such a letter could not be written by a criminal." The committee-man was experienced in such matters, for he had been often officially deputed to conduct criminal investigations while in the Caucasus. "But then how and by what trick of fate has the thing happened?" he said to himself with a gesture of discouragement. "The devil must be at the bottom of it."

Meanwhile the rumour of this extraordinary event had spread all over the city, and, as is generally the case, not without numerous additions. At that period there was a general disposition to believe in the miraculous; the public had recently been impressed by experiments in magnetism. The story of the floating chairs in Koniouchennaia Street was still quite recent, and there was nothing astonishing in hearing soon afterwards that Major Kovaloff's nose was to be seen walking every day at three o'clock on the Neffsky Avenue. The crowd of curious spectators which gathered there daily was enormous. On one occasion someone spread a report that the nose was in Junker's stores and immediately the place was besieged by such a crowd that the police had to interfere and establish order. A certain speculator with a grave, whiskered face, who sold cakes at a theatre door, had some strong wooden benches made which he placed before the window of the stores, and obligingly invited the public to stand on them and look in, at the modest charge of twenty-four kopecks. A veteran colonel, leaving his house earlier than usual expressly for the purpose, had the greatest difficulty in elbowing his way through the crowd, but to his great indignation he saw nothing in the store window but an ordinary flannel waistcoat and a coloured lithograph representing a young girl darning a stocking, while an elegant youth in a waistcoat with large lappels watched her from behind a tree. The picture had hung in the same place for more than ten years. The colonel went off, growling savagely to himself, "How can the fools let themselves be excited by such idiotic stories?"

Then another rumour got abroad, to the effect that the nose of Major Kovaloff was in the habit of walking not on the Neffsky Avenue but in the Tauris Gardens. Some students of the Academy of Surgery went there on purpose to see it. A high-born lady wrote to the keeper of the gardens asking him to show her children this rare phenomenon, and to give them some suitable instruction on the occasion.

All these incidents were eagerly collected by the town wits, who just then were very short of anecdotes adapted to amuse ladies. On the other hand, the minority of solid, sober people were very much displeased. One gentleman asserted with great indignation that he could not understand how in our enlightened age such absurdities could spread abroad, and he was astonished that the Government did not direct their attention to the matter. This gentleman evidently belonged to the category of those people who wish the Government to interfere in everything, even in their daily quarrels with their wives.

But here the course of events is again obscured by a veil.

III

Strange events happen in this world, events which are sometimes entirely improbable. The same nose which had masqueraded as a state-councillor, and caused so much sensation in the town, was found one morning in its proper place, i.e. between the cheeks of Major Kovaloff, as if nothing had happened.

The Nose

This occurred on 7th April. On awaking, the Major looked by chance into a mirror and perceived a nose. He quickly put his hand to it; it was there beyond a doubt!

"Oh!" exclaimed Kovaloff. For sheer joy he was on the point of performing a dance barefooted across his room, but the entrance of Ivan prevented him. He told him to bring water, and after washing himself, he looked again in the glass. The nose was there! Then he dried his face with a towel and looked again. Yes, there was no mistake about it!

"Look here, Ivan, it seems to me that I have a heat-boil on my nose," he said to his valet.

And he thought to himself at the same time, "That will be a nice business if Ivan says to me 'No, sir, not only is there no boil, but your nose itself is not there!'"

But Ivan answered, "There is nothing, sir; I can see no boil on your nose."

"Good! Good!" exclaimed the Major, and snapped his fingers with delight.

At this moment the barber, Ivan Jakovlevitch, put his head in at the door, but as timidly as a cat which has just been beaten for stealing lard.

"Tell me first, are your hands clean?" asked Kovaloff when he saw him.

"Yes, sir."

"You lie."

"I swear they are perfectly clean, sir."

"Very well; then come here."

Kovaloff seated himself. Jakovlevitch tied a napkin under his chin, and in the twinkling of an eye covered his beard and part of his cheeks with a copious creamy lather.

"There it is!" said the barber to himself, as he glanced at the nose. Then he bent his head a little and examined it from one side. "Yes, it actually is the nose—really, when one thinks——" he continued, pursuing his mental soliloquy and still looking at it. Then quite gently, with infinite precaution, he raised two fingers in the air in order to take hold of it by the extremity, as he was accustomed to do.

"Now then, take care!" Kovaloff exclaimed.

Ivan Jakovlevitch let his arm fall and felt more embarrassed than he had ever done in his life. At last he began to pass the razor very lightly over the Major's chin, and although it was very difficult to shave him without using the olfactory organ as a point of support, he succeeded, however, by placing his wrinkled thumb against the Major's lower jaw and cheek, thus overcoming all obstacles and bringing his task to a safe conclusion.

When the barber had finished, Kovaloff hastened to dress himself, took a droshky, and drove straight to the confectioner's. As he entered it, he ordered a cup of chocolate. He then stepped straight to the mirror; the nose was there!

He returned joyfully, and regarded with a satirical expression two officers who were in the shop, one of whom possessed a nose not much larger than a waistcoat button.

After that he went to the office of the department
where he had applied for the post of vice-governor of a province or Government bailiff. As he passed through the hall of reception, he cast a glance at the mirror; the nose was there! Then he went to pay a visit to another committee-man, a very sarcastic personage, to whom he was accustomed to say in answer to his raillery, "Yes, I know, you are the funniest fellow in St Petersburg."

On the way he said to himself, "If the Major does not burst into laughter at the sight of me, that is a most certain sign that everything is in its accustomed place."

But the Major said nothing. "Very good!" thought Kovaloff.

As he returned, he met Madame Podtotchina with her daughter. He accosted them, and they responded very graciously. The conversation lasted a long time, during which he took more than one pinch of snuff, saying to himself, "No, you haven't caught me yet, coquettes that you are! And as to the daughter, I shan't marry her at all."

After that, the Major resumed his walks on the Neffsky Avenue and his visits to the theatre as if nothing had happened. His nose also remained in its place as if it had never quitted it. From that time he was always to be seen smiling, in a good humour, and paying attentions to pretty girls.

IV

Such was the occurrence which took place in the northern capital of our vast empire. On considering the account carefully we see that there is a good deal which looks improbable about it. Not to speak of the strange disappearance of the nose, and its appearance in different places under the disguise of a councillor of state, how was it that Kovaloff did not understand that one cannot decently advertise for a lost nose? I do not mean to say that he would have had to pay too much for the advertisement—that is a mere trifle, and I am not one of those who attach too much importance to money; but to advertise in such a case is not proper nor befitting.

Another difficulty is—how was the nose found in the baked loaf, and how did Ivan Jakovlevitch himself—no, I don't understand it at all!

But the most incomprehensible thing of all is, how authors can choose such subjects for their stories. That really surpasses my understanding. In the first place, no advantage results from it for the country; and in the second place, no harm results either.

All the same, when one reflects well, there really is something in the matter. Whatever may be said to the contrary, such cases do occur—rarely, it is true, but now and then actually.

3

Memoirs of a Madman

Translated by Claud Field

October 3rd.—A strange occurrence has taken place to-day. I got up fairly late, and when Mawra brought me my clean boots, I asked her how late it was. When I heard it had long struck ten, I dressed as quickly as possible.

To tell the truth, I would rather not have gone to the office at all to-day, for I know beforehand that our department-chief will look as sour as vinegar. For some time past he has been in the habit of saying to me, "Look here, my friend; there is something wrong with your head. You often rush about as though you were possessed. Then you make such confused abstracts of the documents that the devil himself cannot make them out; you write the title without any capital letters, and add neither the date nor the docket-number." The long-legged scoundrel! He is certainly envious of me, because I sit in the director's work-room, and mend His Excellency's pens. In a word, I should not have gone to the office if I had not hoped to meet the accountant, and perhaps squeeze a little advance out of this skinflint.

A terrible man, this accountant! As for his advancing one's salary once in a way—you might sooner expect the skies to fall. You may beg and beseech him, and be on the very verge of ruin—this grey devil won't budge an inch. At the same time, his own cook at home, as all the world knows, boxes his ears.

I really don't see what good one gets by serving in our department. There are no plums there. In the fiscal and judicial offices it is quite different. There some ungainly fellow sits in a corner and writes and writes; he has such a shabby coat and such an ugly mug that one would like to spit on both of them. But you should see what a splendid country-house he has rented. He would not condescend to accept a gilt porcelain cup as a present. "You can give that to your family doctor," he would say. Nothing less than a pair of chestnut horses, a fine carriage, or a beaver-fur coat worth three hundred roubles would be good enough for him. And yet he seems so mild and quiet, and asks so amiably, "Please lend me your penknife; I wish to mend my pen." Nevertheless, he knows how to scarify a petitioner till he has hardly a whole stitch left on his body.

In our office it must be admitted everything is done in a proper and gentlemanly way; there is more cleanness and elegance than one will ever find in Government offices. The tables are mahogany, and everyone is addressed as "sir." And truly, were it not for this official propriety, I should long ago have sent in my resignation.

I put on my old cloak, and took my umbrella, as a light rain was falling. No one was to be seen on the streets except some women, who had flung their skirts over their heads. Here and there one saw a cabman or a shopman with his umbrella up. Of the higher classes one only saw an official here and there. One I saw at the street-crossing, and thought to myself, "Ah! my friend, you are not going to the office, but after that young lady who walks in front of you. You are just like the officers who run after every petticoat they see."

As I was thus following the train of my thoughts, I saw a carriage stop before a shop just as I was passing it. I recognised it at once; it was our director's carriage. "He has nothing to do in the shop," I said to myself; "it must be his daughter."

I pressed myself close against the wall. A lackey opened the carriage door, and, as I had expected, she fluttered like a bird out of it. How proudly she looked right and left; how she drew her eyebrows together, and shot lightnings from her eyes—good heavens! I am lost, hopelessly lost!

But why must she come out in such abominable weather? And yet they say women are so mad on their finery!

She did not recognise me. I had wrapped myself as closely as possible in my cloak. It was dirty and old-fashioned, and I would not have liked to have been seen by her wearing it. Now they wear cloaks with long collars, but mine has only a short double collar, and the cloth is of inferior quality.

Her little dog could not get into the shop, and remained outside. I know this dog; its name is "Meggy."

Before I had been standing there a minute, I heard a voice call, "Good day, Meggy!"

Who the deuce was that? I looked round and saw two ladies hurrying by under an umbrella—one old, the other fairly young. They had already passed me when I heard the same voice say again, "For shame, Meggy!"

What was that? I saw Meggy sniffing at a dog which ran behind the ladies. The deuce! I thought to myself, "I am not drunk? That happens pretty seldom."

"No, Fidel, you are wrong," I heard Meggy say quite distinctly. "I was—bow—wow!—I was—bow! wow! wow!—very ill."

What an extraordinary dog! I was, to tell the truth, quite amazed to hear it talk human language. But when I considered the matter well, I ceased to be astonished. In fact, such things have already happened in the world. It is said that in England a fish put its head out of water and said a word or two in such an extraordinary language that learned men have been puzzling over them for three years, and have not succeeded in interpreting them yet. I also read in the paper of two cows who entered a shop and asked for a pound of tea.

Meanwhile what Meggy went on to say seemed to me still more remarkable. She added, "I wrote to you lately, Fidel; perhaps Polkan did not bring you the letter."

Now I am willing to forfeit a whole month's salary if I ever heard of dogs writing before. This has certainly astonished me. For some little time past I hear and see things which no other man has heard and seen.

"I will," I thought, "follow that dog in order to get to the bottom of the matter. Accordingly, I opened my umbrella and went after the two ladies. They went down Bean Street, turned through Citizen Street and Carpenter Street, and finally halted on the Cuckoo Bridge before a large house. I know this house; it is Sverkoff's. What a monster he is! What sort of people live there! How many cooks, how many bagmen! There are brother officials of mine also there packed on each other like herrings. And I have a friend there, a fine player on the cornet."

The ladies mounted to the fifth story. "Very good," thought I; "I will make a note of the number, in order to follow up the matter at the first opportunity."

October 4th.—To-day is Wednesday, and I was as usual in the office. I came early on purpose, sat down, and mended all the pens.

Our director must be a very clever man. The whole room is full of bookcases. I read the titles of some of the books; they were very learned, beyond the comprehension of people of my class, and all in French and German. I look at his face; see! how much dignity there is in his eyes. I never hear a single superfluous word from his mouth, except that when he hands over the documents, he asks "What sort of weather is it?"

No, he is not a man of our class; he is a real statesman. I have already noticed that I am a special favourite of his. If now his daughter also—ah! what folly—let me say no more about it!

I have read the *Northern Bee*. What foolish people the French are! By heavens! I should like to tackle them all, and give them a thrashing. I have also read a fine description of a ball given by a landowner of Kursk. The landowners of Kursk write a fine style.

Then I noticed that it was already half-past twelve, and the director had not yet left his bedroom. But about half-past one something happened which no pen can describe.

The door opened. I thought it was the director; I jumped up with my documents from the seat, and—then—she—herself—came into the room. Ye saints! how beautifully she was dressed. Her garments were whiter than a swan's plumage—oh how splendid! A sun, indeed, a real sun!

She greeted me and asked, "Has not my father come yet?"

Ah! what a voice. A canary bird! A real canary bird!

"Your Excellency," I wanted to exclaim, "don't have me executed, but if it must be done, then kill me rather with your own angelic hand." But, God knows why, I could not bring it out, so I only said, "No, he has not come yet."

She glanced at me, looked at the books, and let her handkerchief fall. Instantly I started up, but slipped on the infernal polished floor, and nearly broke my nose. Still I succeeded in picking up the handkerchief. Ye heavenly choirs, what a handkerchief! So tender and soft, of the finest cambric. It had the scent of a general's rank!

She thanked me, and smiled so amiably that her sugar lips nearly melted. Then she left the room.

After I had sat there about an hour, a flunkey came in and said, "You can go home, Mr Ivanovitch; the director has already gone out!"

I cannot stand these lackeys! They hang about the vestibules, and scarcely vouchsafe to greet one with a nod. Yes, sometimes it is even worse; once one of these rascals offered me his snuff-box without even getting up from his chair. "Don't you know then, you country-bumpkin, that I am an official and of aristocratic birth?"

This time, however, I took my hat and overcoat quietly; these people naturally never think of helping one on with it. I went home, lay a good while on the bed, and wrote some verses in my note:

> "'Tis an hour since I saw thee,
> And it seems a whole long year;
> If I loathe my own existence,
> How can I live on, my dear?"
> I think they are by Pushkin.

In the evening I wrapped myself in my cloak, hastened to the director's house, and waited there a long time to see if she would come out and get into the carriage. I only wanted to see her once, but she did not come.

November 6th.—Our chief clerk has gone mad. When I came to the office to-day he called me to his room and began as follows: "Look here, my friend, what wild ideas have got into your head?"

"How! What? None at all," I answered.

"Consider well. You are already past forty; it is quite time to be reasonable. What do you imagine? Do you think I don't know all your tricks? Are you trying to pay court to the director's daughter? Look at yourself and realise what you are! A nonentity, nothing else. I would not give a kopeck for you. Look well in the glass. How can you have such thoughts with such a caricature of a face?"

May the devil take him! Because his own face has a certain resemblance to a medicine-bottle, because he has a curly bush of hair on his head, and sometimes combs it upwards, and sometimes plasters it down in all kinds of queer ways, he thinks that he can do everything. I know well, I know why he is angry with me. He is envious; perhaps he has noticed the tokens of favour which have been graciously shown me. But why should I bother about him? A councillor! What sort of important animal is that? He wears a gold chain with his watch, buys himself boots at thirty roubles a pair; may the deuce take him! Am I a tailor's son or some other obscure cabbage? I am a nobleman! I can also work my way up. I am just forty-two—an age when a man's real career generally begins. Wait a bit, my friend! I too may get to a superior's rank; or perhaps, if God is gracious, even to a higher one. I shall make a name which will far outstrip yours. You think there are no able men except yourself? I only need to order a fashionable coat and wear a tie like yours, and you would be quite eclipsed.

But I have no money—that is the worst part of it!

November 8th.—I was at the theatre. "The Russian House-Fool" was performed. I laughed heartily. There was also a kind of musical comedy which contained amusing hits at barristers. The language was very broad; I wonder the censor passed it. In the comedy lines occur which accuse the merchants of cheating; their sons are said to lead immoral lives, and to behave very disrespectfully towards the nobility.

The critics also are criticised; they are said only to be able to find fault, so that authors have to beg the public for protection.

Our modern dramatists certainly write amusing things. I am very fond of the theatre. If I have only a kopeck in my pocket, I always go there. Most of my fellow-officials are uneducated boors, and never enter a theatre unless one throws free tickets at their head.

One actress sang divinely. I thought also of—but silence!

November 9th.—About eight o'clock I went to the office. The chief clerk pretended not to notice my arrival. I for my part also behaved as though he were not in existence. I read through and collated documents. About four o'clock I left. I passed by the director's house, but no one was to be seen. After dinner I lay for a good while on the bed.

November 11th.—To-day I sat in the director's room, mended twenty-three pens for him, and for Her—for Her Excellence, his daughter, four more.

The director likes to see many pens lying on his table. What a head he must have! He continually wraps himself in silence, but I don't think the smallest trifle escapes his eye. I should like to know what he is generally thinking of, what is really going on in this brain; I should like to get acquainted with the whole manner of life of these gentlemen, and get a closer view of their cunning courtiers' arts, and all the activities of these circles. I have often thought of asking His Excellence about them; but—the deuce knows why!—every time my tongue failed me and I could get nothing out but my meteorological report.

I wish I could get a look into the spare-room whose door I so often see open. And a second small room behind the spare-room excites my curiosity. How splendidly it is fitted up; what a quantity of mirrors and choice china it contains! I should also like to cast a glance into those regions where Her Excellency, the daughter, wields the sceptre. I should like to see how all the scent-bottles and boxes are arranged in her boudoir, and the flowers which exhale so delicious a scent that one is half afraid to breathe. And her clothes lying about which are too ethereal to be called clothes—but silence!

To-day there came to me what seemed a heavenly inspiration. I remembered the conversation between the two dogs which I had overheard on the Nevski Prospect. "Very good," I thought; "now I see my way clear. I must get hold of the correspondence which these two silly dogs have carried on with each other. In it I shall probably find many things explained."

I had already once called Meggy to me and said to her, "Listen, Meggy! Now we are alone together; if you like, I will also shut the door so that no one can see us. Tell me now all that you know about your mistress. I swear to you that I will tell no one."

But the cunning dog drew in its tail, ruffled up its hair, and went quite quietly out of the door, as though it had heard nothing.

I had long been of the opinion that dogs are much cleverer than men. I also believed that they could talk, and that only a certain obstinacy kept them from doing so. They are especially watchful animals, and nothing escapes their observation. Now, cost what it may, I will go to-morrow to Sverkoff's house in order to ask after Fidel, and if I have luck, to get hold of all the letters which Meggy has written to her.

November 12th.—To-day about two o'clock in the afternoon I started in order, by some means or other, to see Fidel and question her.

I cannot stand this smell of Sauerkraut which assails one's olfactory nerves from all the shops in Citizen Street. There also exhales such an odour from under each house door, that one must hold one's nose and pass by quickly. There ascends also so much smoke and soot from the artisans' shops that it is almost impossible to get through it.

When I had climbed up to the sixth story, and had rung the bell, a rather pretty girl with a freckled face came out. I recognised her as the companion of the old lady. She blushed a little and asked "What do you want?"

"I want to have a little conversation with your dog."

She was a simple-minded girl, as I saw at once. The dog came running and barking loudly. I wanted to take hold of it, but the abominable beast nearly caught hold of my nose with its teeth. But in a corner of the room I saw its sleeping-basket. Ah! that was what I wanted. I went to it, rummaged in the straw, and to my great satisfaction drew out a little packet of small pieces of paper. When the hideous little dog saw this, it first bit me in the calf of the leg, and then, as soon as it had become aware of my theft, it began to whimper and to fawn on me; but I said, "No, you little beast; good-bye!" and hastened away.

I believe the girl thought me mad; at any rate she was thoroughly alarmed.

When I reached my room I wished to get to work at once, and read through the letters by daylight, since I do not see well by candle-light; but the wretched Mawra had got the idea of sweeping the floor. These blockheads of Finnish women are always clean where there is no need to be.

I then went for a little walk and began to think over what had happened. Now at last I could get to the bottom of all facts, ideas and motives! These letters would explain everything. Dogs are clever fellows; they know all about politics, and I will certainly find in the letters all I want, especially the character of the director and all his relationships. And through these letters I will get information about her who—but silence!

Towards evening I came home and lay for a good while on the bed.

November 13th.—Now let us see! The letter is fairly legible but the handwriting is somewhat doggish.

"Dear Fidel!—I cannot get accustomed to your ordinary name, as if they could not have found a better one for you! Fidel! How tasteless! How ordinary! But this is not the time to discuss it. I am very glad that we thought of corresponding with each other."

(The letter is quite correctly written. The punctuation and spelling are perfectly right. Even our head clerk does not write so simply and clearly, though he declares he has been at the University. Let us go on.)

"I think that it is one of the most refined joys of this world to interchange thoughts, feelings, and impressions."

(H'm! This idea comes from some book which has been translated from German. I can't remember the title.)

"I speak from experience, although I have not gone farther into the world than just before our front door. Does not my life pass happily and comfortably? My mistress, whom her father calls Sophie, is quite in love with me."

(Ah! Ah!—but better be silent!)

"Her father also often strokes me. I drink tea and coffee with cream. Yes, my dear, I must confess to you that I find no satisfaction in those large, gnawed-at bones which Polkan devours in the kitchen. Only the bones of wild fowl are good, and that only when the marrow has not been sucked out of them. They taste very nice with a little sauce, but there should be no green stuff in it. But I know nothing worse than the habit of giving dogs balls of bread kneaded up. Someone sits at table, kneads a bread-ball with dirty fingers, calls you and sticks it in your mouth. Good manners forbid your refusing it, and you eat it—with disgust it is true, but you eat it."

(The deuce! What is this? What rubbish! As if she could find nothing more suitable to write about! I will see if there is anything more reasonable on the second page.)

"I am quite willing to inform you of everything that goes on here. I have already mentioned the most important person in the house, whom Sophie calls 'Papa.' He is a very strange man."

(Ah! Here we are at last! Yes, I knew it; they have a politician's penetrating eye for all things. Let us see what she says about "Papa.")

"... a strange man. Generally he is silent; he only speaks seldom, but about a week ago he kept on repeating to himself, 'Shall I get it or not?' In one hand he took a sheet of paper; the other he stretched out as though to receive something, and repeated, 'Shall I get it or not?' Once he turned to me with the question, 'What do you think, Meggy?' I did not understand in the least what he meant, sniffed at his boots, and went away. A week later he came home with his face beaming. That morning he was visited by several officers in uniform who congratulated him. At the dinner-table he was in a better humour than I have ever seen him before."

(Ah! he is ambitious then! I must make a note of that.)

"Pardon, my dear, I hasten to conclude, etc., etc. To-morrow I will finish the letter."

. . . . . .

"Now, good morning; here I am again at your service. To-day my mistress Sophie . . ."

(Ah! we will see what she says about Sophie. Let us go on!)

"... was in an unusually excited state. She went to a ball, and I was glad that I could write to you in her absence. She likes going to balls, although she gets dreadfully irritated while dressing. I cannot understand, my dear, what is the pleasure in going to a ball. She comes home from the ball at six o'clock in the early morning, and to judge by her pale and emaciated face, she has had nothing to eat. I could, frankly speaking, not endure such an existence. If I could not get partridge with sauce, or the wing of a roast chicken, I don't know what I should do. Porridge with sauce is also tolerable, but I can get up no enthusiasm for carrots, turnips, and artichokes."

The style is very unequal! One sees at once that it has not been written by a man. The beginning is quite intelligent, but at the end the canine nature breaks out. I will read another letter; it is rather long and there is no date.

"Ah, my dear, how delightful is the arrival of spring! My heart beats as though it expected something. There is a perpetual ringing in my ears, so that I often stand with my foot raised, for several minutes at a time, and listen towards the door. In confidence I will tell you that I have many admirers. I often sit on the window-sill and let them pass in review. Ah! if you knew what miscreations there are among them; one, a clumsy house-dog, with stupidity written on his face, walks the street with an important air and imagines that he is an extremely important person, and that the eyes of all the world are fastened on him. I don't pay him the least attention, and pretend not to see him at all.

"And what a hideous bulldog has taken up his post opposite my window! If he stood on his hind-legs, as the monster probably cannot, he would be taller by a head than my mistress's papa, who himself has a stately figure. This lout seems, moreover, to be very impudent. I growl at him, but he does not seem to mind that at all. If he at least would only wrinkle his forehead! Instead of that, he stretches out his tongue, droops his big ears, and stares in at the window—this rustic boor! But do you think, my dear, that my heart remains proof against all temptations? Alas no! If you had only seen that gentlemanly dog who crept through the fence of the neighbouring house. 'Treasure' is his name. Ah, my dear, what a delightful snout he has!"

(To the deuce with the stuff! What rubbish it is! How can one blacken paper with such absurdities. Give me a man. I want to see a man! I need some food to nourish and refresh my mind, and get this silliness instead. I will turn the page to see if there is anything better on the other side.)

"Sophie sat at the table and sewed something. I looked out of the window and amused myself by watching the passers-by. Suddenly a flunkey entered and announced a visitor—'Mr Teploff.'

"'Show him in!' said Sophie, and began to embrace me. 'Ah! Meggy, Meggy, do you know who that is? He is dark, and belongs to the Royal Household; and what eyes he has! Dark and brilliant as fire.'

"Sophie hastened into her room. A minute later a young gentleman with black whiskers entered. He went to the mirror, smoothed his hair, and looked round the room. I turned away and sat down in my place.

"Sophie entered and returned his bow in a friendly manner.

"I pretended to observe nothing, and continued to look out of the window. But I leant my head a little on one side to hear what they were talking about. Ah, my dear! what silly things they discussed—how a lady executed the wrong figure in dancing; how a certain Boboff, with his expansive shirt-frill, had looked like a stork and nearly fallen down; how a certain Lidina imagined she had blue eyes when they were really green, etc.

"I do not know, my dear, what special charm she finds in her Mr Teploff, and why she is so delighted with him."

(It seems to me myself that there is something wrong here. It is impossible that this Teploff should bewitch her. We will see further.)

"If this gentleman of the Household pleases her, then she must also be pleased, according to my view, with that official who sits in her papa's writing-room. Ah, my dear, if you know what a figure he is! A regular tortoise!"

(What official does she mean?)

"He has an extraordinary name. He always sits there and mends the pens. His hair looks like a truss of hay. Her papa always employs him instead of a servant."

(I believe this abominable little beast is referring to me. But what has my hair got to do with hay?)

"Sophie can never keep from laughing when she sees him."

You lie, cursed dog! What a scandalous tongue! As if I did not know that it is envy which prompts you, and that here there is treachery at work—yes, the treachery of the chief clerk. This man hates me implacably; he has plotted against me, he is always seeking to injure me. I'll look through one more letter; perhaps it will make the matter clearer.

"Fidel, my dear, pardon me that I have not written for so long. I was floating in a dream of delight. In truth, some author remarks, 'Love is a second life.' Besides, great changes are going on in the house. The young chamberlain is always here. Sophie is wildly in love with him. Her papa is quite contented. I heard from Gregor, who sweeps the floor, and is in the habit of talking to himself, that the marriage will soon be celebrated. Her papa will at any rate get his daughter married to a general, a colonel, or a chamberlain."

Deuce take it! I can read no more. It is all about chamberlains and generals. I should like myself to be a general—not in order to sue for her hand and all that—no, not at all; I should like to be a general merely in order to see people wriggling, squirming, and hatching plots before me.

And then I should like to tell them that they are both of them not worth spitting on. But it is vexatious! I tear the foolish dog's letters up in a thousand pieces.

December 3rd.—It is not possible that the marriage should take place; it is only idle gossip. What does it signify if he is a chamberlain! That is only a dignity, not a substantial thing which one can see or handle. His chamberlain's office will not procure him a third eye in his forehead. Neither is his nose made of gold; it is just like mine or anyone else's nose. He does not eat and cough, but smells and sneezes with it. I should like to get to the bottom of the mystery—whence do all these distinctions come? Why am I only a titular councillor?

Perhaps I am really a count or a general, and only appear to be a titular councillor. Perhaps I don't even know who and what I am. How many cases there are in history of a simple gentleman, or even a burgher or peasant, suddenly turning out to be a great lord or baron? Well, suppose that I appear suddenly in a general's uniform, on the right shoulder an epaulette, on the left an epaulette, and a blue sash across my breast, what sort of a tune would my beloved sing then? What would her papa, our director, say? Oh, he is ambitious! He is a freemason, certainly a freemason; however much he may conceal it, I have found it out. When he gives anyone his hand, he only reaches out two fingers. Well, could not I this minute be nominated a general or a superintendent? I should like to know why I am a titular councillor—why just that, and nothing more?

December 5th.—To-day I have been reading papers the whole morning. Very strange things are happening in Spain. I have not understood them all. It is said that the throne is vacant, the representatives of the people are in difficulties about finding an occupant, and riots are taking place.

All this appears to me very strange. How can the throne be vacant? It is said that it will be occupied by a woman. A woman cannot sit on a throne. That is impossible. Only a king can sit on a throne. They say that there is no king there, but that is not possible. There cannot be a kingdom without a king. There must be a king, but he is hidden away somewhere. Perhaps he is actually on the spot, and only some domestic complications, or fears of the neighbouring Powers, France and other countries, compel him to remain in concealment; there might also be other reasons.

December 8th.—I was nearly going to the office, but various considerations kept me from doing so. I keep on thinking about these Spanish affairs. How is it possible that a woman should reign? It would not be allowed, especially by England. In the rest of Europe the political situation is also critical; the Emperor of Austria——

These events, to tell the truth, have so shaken and shattered me, that I could really do nothing all day. Mawra told me that I was very absent-minded at table. In fact, in my absent-mindedness I threw two plates on the ground so that they broke in pieces.

After dinner I felt weak, and did not feel up to making abstracts of reports. I lay most of the time on my bed, and thought of the Spanish affairs.

The year 2000: April 43rd.—To-day is a day of splendid triumph. Spain has a king; he has been found, and I am he. I discovered it to-day; all of a sudden it came upon me like a flash of lightning.

I do not understand how I could imagine that I am a titular councillor. How could such a foolish idea enter my head? It was fortunate that it occurred to no one to shut me up in an asylum. Now it is all clear, and as plain as a pikestaff. Formerly—I don't know why—everything seemed veiled in a kind of mist. That is, I believe, because people think that the human brain is in the head. Nothing of the sort; it is carried by the wind from the Caspian Sea.

For the first time I told Mawra who I am. When she learned that the king of Spain stood before her, she struck her hands together over her head, and nearly died of alarm. The stupid thing had never seen the king of Spain before!

I comforted her, however, at once by assuring her that I was not angry with her for having hitherto cleaned my boots badly. Women are stupid things; one cannot interest them in lofty subjects. She was frightened because she thought all kings of Spain were like Philip II. But I explained to her that there was a great difference between me and him. I did not go to the office.

Why the deuce should I? No, my dear friends, you won't get me there again! I am not going to worry myself with your infernal documents any more.

Marchember 86. Between day and night.—To-day the office-messenger came and summoned me, as I had not been there for three weeks. I went just for the fun of the thing. The chief clerk thought I would bow humbly before him, and make excuses; but I looked at him quite indifferently, neither angrily nor mildly, and sat down quietly at my place as though I noticed no one. I looked at all this rabble of scribblers, and thought, "If you only knew who is sitting among you! Good heavens! what a to-do you would make. Even the chief clerk would bow himself to the earth before me as he does now before the director."

A pile of reports was laid before me, of which to make abstracts, but I did not touch them with one finger.

After a little time there was a commotion in the office, and there a report went round that the director was coming. Many of the clerks vied with each other to attract his notice; but I did not stir. As he came through our room, each one hastily buttoned up his coat; but I had no idea of doing anything of the sort. What is the director to me? Should I stand up before him? Never. What sort of a director is he? He is a bottle-stopper, and no director. A quite ordinary, simple bottle-stopper—nothing more. I felt quite amused as they gave me a document to sign.

They thought I would simply put down my name—"So-and-so, Clerk." Why not? But at the top of the sheet, where the director generally writes his name, I inscribed "Ferdinand VIII." in bold characters. You should have seen what a reverential silence ensued. But I made a gesture with my hand, and said, "Gentlemen, no ceremony please!" Then I went out, and took my way straight to the director's house.

He was not at home. The flunkey wanted not to let me in, but I talked to him in such a way that he soon dropped his arms.

I went straight to Sophie's dressing-room. She sat before the mirror. When she saw me, she sprang up and took a step backwards; but I did not tell her that I was the king of Spain.

But I told her that a happiness awaited her, beyond her power to imagine; and that in spite of all our enemies' devices we should be united. That was all which I wished to say to her, and I went out. Oh, what cunning creatures these women are! Now I have found out what woman really is. Hitherto no one knew whom a woman really loves; I am the first to discover it—she loves the devil. Yes, joking apart, learned men write nonsense when they pronounce that she is this and that; she loves the devil—that is all. You see a woman looking through her lorgnette from a box in the front row. One thinks she is watching that stout gentleman who wears an order. Not a bit of it! She is watching the devil who stands behind his back. He has hidden himself there, and beckons to her with his finger. And she marries him—actually—she marries him!

That is all ambition, and the reason is that there is under the tongue a little blister in which there is a little worm of the size of a pin's head. And this is constructed by a barber in Bean Street; I don't remember his name at the moment, but so much is certain that, in conjunction with a midwife, he wants to spread Mohammedanism all over the world, and that in consequence of this a large number of people in France have already adopted the faith of Islam.

No date. The day had no date.—I went for a walk incognito on the Nevski Prospect. I avoided every appearance of being the king of Spain. I felt it below my dignity to let myself be recognised by the whole world, since I must first present myself at court. And I was also restrained by the fact that I have at present no Spanish national costume. If I could only get a cloak! I tried to have a consultation with a tailor, but these people are real asses! Moreover, they neglect their business, dabble in speculation, and have become loafers. I will have a cloak made out of my new official uniform which I have only worn twice. But to prevent this botcher of a tailor spoiling it, I will make it myself with closed doors, so that no one sees me. Since the cut must be altogether altered, I have used the scissors myself.

I don't remember the date. The devil knows what month it was. The cloak is quite ready. Mawra exclaimed aloud when I put it on. I will, however, not present myself at court yet; the Spanish deputation has not yet arrived. It would not be befitting if I appeared without them. My appearance would be less imposing. From hour to hour I expect them.

The 1st.—The extraordinary long delay of the deputies in coming astonishes me. What can possibly keep them? Perhaps France has a hand in the matter;

it is certainly hostilely inclined. I went to the post office to inquire whether the Spanish deputation had come. The postmaster is an extraordinary blockhead who knows nothing. "No," he said to me, "there is no Spanish deputation here; but if you want to send them a letter, we will forward it at the fixed rate." The deuce! What do I want with a letter? Letters are nonsense. Letters are written by apothecaries. . . .

Madrid, February 30th.—So I am in Spain after all! It has happened so quickly that I could hardly take it in. The Spanish deputies came early this morning, and I got with them into the carriage. This unexpected promptness seemed to me strange. We drove so quickly that in half an hour we were at the Spanish frontier. Over all Europe now there are cast-iron roads, and the steamers go very fast. A wonderful country, this Spain!

As we entered the first room, I saw numerous persons with shorn heads. I guessed at once that they must be either grandees or soldiers, at least to judge by their shorn heads.

The Chancellor of the State, who led me by the hand, seemed to me to behave in a very strange way; he pushed me into a little room and said, "Stay here, and if you call yourself 'King Ferdinand' again, I will drive the wish to do so out of you."

I knew, however, that that was only a test, and I reasserted my conviction; on which the Chancellor gave me two such severe blows with a stick on the back, that I could have cried out with the pain. But I restrained myself, remembering that this was a usual ceremony of old-time chivalry when one was inducted into a high position, and in Spain the laws of chivalry prevail up to the present day. When I was alone, I determined to study State affairs; I discovered that Spain and China are one and the same country, and it is only through ignorance that people regard them as separate kingdoms. I advise everyone urgently to write down the word "Spain" on a sheet of paper; he will see that it is quite the same as China.

But I feel much annoyed by an event which is about to take place tomorrow; at seven o'clock the earth is going to sit on the moon. This is foretold by the famous English chemist, Wellington. To tell the truth, I often felt uneasy when I thought of the excessive brittleness and fragility of the moon. The moon is generally repaired in Hamburg, and very imperfectly. It is done by a lame cooper, an obvious blockhead who has no idea how to do it. He took waxed thread and olive-oil—hence that pungent smell over all the earth which compels people to hold their noses. And this makes the moon so fragile that no men can live on it, but only noses. Therefore we cannot see our noses, because they are on the moon.

When I now pictured to myself how the earth, that massive body, would crush our noses to dust, if it sat on the moon, I became so uneasy, that I immediately put on my shoes and stockings and hastened into the council-hall to give the police orders to prevent the earth sitting on the moon.

The grandees with the shorn heads, whom I met in great numbers in the hall, were very intelligent people, and when I exclaimed, "Gentlemen! let us save the moon, for the earth is going to sit on it," they all set to work to fulfil my imperial wish, and many of them clambered up the wall in order to take the moon down. At that moment the Imperial Chancellor came in. As soon as he appeared, they all scattered, but I alone, as king, remained. To my astonishment, however, the Chancellor beat me with the stick and drove me to my room. So powerful are ancient customs in Spain!

January in the same year, following after

February.—I can never understand what kind of a country this Spain really is. The popular customs and rules of court etiquette are quite extraordinary. I do not understand them at all, at all. To-day my head was shorn, although I exclaimed as loudly as I could, that I did not want to be a monk. What happened afterwards, when they began to let cold water trickle on my head, I do not know. I have never experienced such hellish torments. I nearly went mad, and they had difficulty in holding me. The significance of this strange custom is entirely hidden from me. It is a very foolish and unreasonable one.

Nor can I understand the stupidity of the kings who have not done away with it before now. Judging by all the circumstances, it seems to me as though I had fallen into the hands of the Inquisition, and as though the man whom I took to be the Chancellor was the Grand Inquisitor. But yet I cannot understand how the king could fall into the hands of the Inquisition. The affair may have been arranged by France—especially Polignac—he is a hound, that Polignac! He has sworn to compass my death, and now he is hunting me down. But I know, my friend, that you are only a tool of the English. They are clever fellows, and have a finger in every pie. All the world knows that France sneezes when England takes a pinch of snuff.

The 25th.—To-day the Grand Inquisitor came into my room; when I heard his steps in the distance, I hid myself under a chair. When he did not see me, he began to call. At first he called "Poprishchin!" I made no answer. Then he called "Axanti Ivanovitch! Titular Councillor! Nobleman!" I still kept silence. "Ferdinand the Eighth, King of Spain!" I was on the point of putting out my head, but I thought, "No, brother, you shall not deceive me! You shall not pour water on my head again!"

But he had already seen me and drove me from under the chair with his stick. The cursed stick really hurts one. But the following discovery compensated me for all the pain, i.e. that every cock has his Spain under his feathers. The Grand Inquisitor went angrily away, and threatened me with some punishment or other. I felt only contempt for his powerless spite, for I know that he only works like a machine, like a tool of the English.

34 March. February, 349.—No, I have no longer power to endure. O God! what are they going to do with me? They pour cold water on my head. They take no notice of me, and seem neither to see nor hear. Why do they torture me? What do they want from one so wretched as myself? What can I give them? I possess nothing. I cannot bear all their tortures; my head aches as though everything were turning round in a circle. Save me! Carry me away! Give me three steeds swift as the wind! Mount your seat, coachman, ring bells, gallop horses, and carry me straight out of this world. Farther, ever farther, till nothing more is to be seen!

Ah! the heaven bends over me already; a star glimmers in the distance; the forest with its dark trees in the moonlight rushes past; a bluish mist floats under my feet; music sounds in the cloud; on the one side is the sea, on the other, Italy; beyond I also see Russian peasants' houses. Is not my parents' house there in the distance? Does not my mother sit by the window? O mother, mother, save your unhappy son! Let a tear fall on his aching head! See how they torture him! Press the poor orphan to your bosom! He has no rest in this world; they hunt him from place to place.

Mother, mother, have pity on your sick child! And do you know that the Bey of Algiers has a wart under his nose?